Yale Language Series

Biblical
TEXT AND WORKBOOK
Hebrew

SECOND EDITION

FULLY REVISED BY

VICTORIA HOFFER

BONNIE PEDROTTI KITTEL,

VICTORIA HOFFER, AND

REBECCA ABTS WRIGHT

YALE UNIVERSITY

YALE UNIVERSITY PRESS / NEW HAVEN AND LONDON

Publisher: Mary Jane Peluso
Production Controller: Aldo Cupo
Editorial Assistant: Gretchen Rings
Designed by Mary Valencia.
Set in Meridien type by Integrated Publishing Solutions, Grand Rapids, MI.

Printed in the United States of America.

Library of Congress Cataloging-in-Publication Data

Kittel, Bonnie Pedrotti.
    Biblical Hebrew : text and workbook / Bonnie Pedrotti Kittel, Victoria Hoffer,
and Rebecca Abts Wright. — 2nd ed.
        p.   cm. — (Yale language series)
    English and Hebrew.
    Includes bibliographical references and index.
    ISBN 978-0-300-09862-4 (cloth : alk. paper)
        1. Hebrew language—Grammar—Textbooks.   2. Hebrew language—Readers—Bible.
    I. Hoffer, Victoria, 1943–   II. Wright, Rebecca Abts, 1948–   III. Title.   IV. Series.
    PJ4567.3.K5   2004
    492.4′82421—dc22   2004040723

A catalogue record for this book is available from the Library of Congress and the British Library.

The paper in this book meets the guidelines for permanence and durability of the Committee on Production Guidelines for Book Longevity of the Council on Library Resources.

10 9 8 7 6 5 4 3

For my students

Your efforts, insights, engagement, and talent infuse every aspect of this project

מַרְבֶּה תּוֹרָה מַרְבֶּה חַיִּים
מַרְבֶּה יְשִׁיבָה מַרְבֶּה חָכְמָה
מַרְבֶּה עֵצָה מַרְבֶּה תְבוּנָה
מַרְבֶּה צְדָקָה מַרְבֶּה שָׁלוֹם

Pirqei Avot 2:8

CONTENTS

———◆———

LESSON 7
וַיִּתֵּן אַבְרָהָם אֶת־כָּל־אֲשֶׁר־לוֹ לְיִצְחָק:

REVIEW AND DRILL 2

LESSON 8
וַיֵּדְעוּ כִּי־שְׁמִי יהוה

LESSON 9
וְהֵם לֹא יָדְעוּ כִּי שֹׁמֵעַ יוֹסֵף

LESSON 10
וַיָּבֹא אֶל־אָבִיו וַיֹּאמֶר אָבִי וַיֹּאמֶר הִנֶּנִּי

CONTENTS

CONTENTS

CONTENTS

ACKNOWLEDGMENTS

This project was transformed from an idea into a reality several years ago when Mary Jane Peluso came to Yale University Press as foreign languages publisher. From the very beginning, she has been helpful, encouraging, and always there. Most important, Mary Jane has had the knack of countering my anxieties by making everything seem possible. Her interest, high standards, and expertise have buoyed me all along the way. I am equally indebted to Nancy Moore, manuscript editor, who helped me through the final processes with infinite, gentle patience, attending to every detail with interest and concern. Finally, no author could have had the help of a more competent, patient, and conscientious proofreader than Suzanne Estelle-Holmer. What a pity that despite her help I still have to accept responsibility for all errors missed or introduced at a stage too late to correct them.

One thing a textbook always needs is the input of those who do not let errors, big or small, slip by. My youngest daughter, Alex, spent hours during the summer of her pre-freshman year of college editing, pointing out vague language—which I had hoped no one would notice—assembling and typing the bibliography, and tending to computer crises with calm and competence. James Alexander—friend and former student—gave of himself unstintingly. Not only did he edit and check every biblical citation down to the maqqefs and metegs, he verified every cross reference, every jot and tittle of the textbook and most of the Supplement. He was available to render opinions, which I sought with frequency, and to make suggestions, and he showed boundless enthusiasm at all times. In addition to all that, he supported the project financially so that the students—who were the musicians—could get some tangible reward for their work. My gratitude to Jim is without measure.

Two contributors offering specialized skills to the overall endeavor are Brian McDonald and Geraldine Dickel. Brian proofread some of the Supplement, sang one of the songs, and is applying his expert language and computer skills in preparing the Answer Key. How wonderful it is to trust someone's work so completely that one can thank him in advance with complete confidence! Geraldine Dickel wrote the block and script alphabets with care and precision, offering students a fine hand on which to model their own writing.

To the musicians I owe more than thanks. You made the CDs far surpass my expectations. And the one, in many ways, most responsible for this success is Mary Jane Donohue. During an intensive summer Hebrew course, she started bringing grammar songs to class. From the first פָּקַד פָּקְדָה I knew that the musical component of this project was headed in a new direction. The songs kept coming. The students kept singing. Janie's creativity and talent are boundless. Joining her in singing a number of the songs are classmates Ingrid Lilly, Christine Luckritz, Michael Peppard, Kristin Dunn, and her husband, Michael Sullivan, who, though he did not take the course, willingly lent his voice and exuberant personality. These performers composed, rehearsed, sang, played instruments, and suffered in a hot, stuffy recording studio. After being exiled by a flood one evening, they returned to finish the job even though exams were fast upon them. Of these singers, Michael Peppard deserves special mention because not only did he lend his beautiful voice to this group, he joined "the boys"—Chandler Poling, Michael Hirsch, and Ian Doescher—as the needed fourth to the barbershop style of וַיִּפְרֹק and the Nif`al song. In addition, he led rehearsals of both groups with uncommon tact, thus getting the best out of everybody. When we had problems near the end of production, there was Michael willing to sing yet again.

Michael Hirsch not only sang, he played the guitar for both student groups and for Rabbi Wainhaus. How he came up with all those nuanced accompaniments, I will never know. He adjusted to everyone's style, he put in a huge number of hours rehearsing, he never settled for anything less than perfect. His talent permeates this project. Ian Doescher—what does one say about Ian? He writes, he arranges, he sings, he directs, he is a one-man band par excellence. His creativity and cleverness are, in a word, astonishing. He can even make vocabulary lists come to life. Then there is Dorothy Goldberg, now on her way to becoming a cantor. Her magnificent harmonies, some of which she came up with on the spot, and her feel for the material give us some magnificent renderings of Psalms. Ashley Grant wrote an affecting, easy-to-learn melody to Psalm 121, and Charissa Wilson set Psalm 23 to the tune of a favorite hymn and sang it exquisitely. Aside from this bevy of talented students (plus one spouse), there is Rabbi Wainhaus—Alvin—who took hours out of a hectic and demanding schedule to sing for this project. His magnificent voice and his genuine engagement with and love of this music are clearly evident in song after moving song. And, with little notice, Alvin's daughter, Maya, stepped in to sing, too. The beautiful male voice cantillating Exodus 3:1–17 and 1 Kings 19:1–12 belongs to Daniel Lovins, who offered his time and talent out of an interest in and a conviction of the importance of this endeavor. Ultimately, the success of the recordings is due to Matthew Croasmun, a skilled musician and engineer, who handled not only equipment with expertise but egos as well! Aside from taking care of all the technical aspects, he composed, accompanied, directed, and performed. He spent countless, tiring hours editing. His is the talent that brought the CDs to life.

To all of you I owe a great deal.

INTRODUCTION TO THE SECOND EDITION

The purpose of the second edition of *Biblical Hebrew* is the same as the first, which is to get students reading Biblical Hebrew prose, and even a bit of poetry, as soon as possible. Ideally, the changes to the textbook and the addition of the CDs and Supplement will make it easier and more enjoyable for students to acquire those skills.

Superficially, the second edition is not strikingly different: the overall concept has not been altered, and its organization and lesson sentences remain the same. But there have been some major modifications and rewriting. The most significant of these is to the design of the vocabulary section. It is more closely keyed to Brown-Driver-Briggs to train students in the use of an academic dictionary; it has been reorganized to better interface with the readings; it is cross referenced to the lessons where such referencing is relevant; it lists derivatives and homonyms together to facilitate association and memorization; it is fuller to help students see at a glance different forms of nouns and verbs; and most important, perhaps, is that it is easier to use since what needs to be memorized for each entry is set in boldface. Word assignments have also been changed. Students are not responsible for learning a block of words over a certain number of lessons. Instead a specific number of words is assigned per lesson: more words per lesson before the reading of extended passages; less after. This pace allows for more opportunity to review and thus absorb. Most pedagogically significant, two new study aids have been added: the recording of words in sets of ten on ☉ אֵלֶּא הַדְּבָרִים and vocabulary review exercises at the end of the Supplement.

In addition, glosses to the readings have been refined and shortened, and explanations are more precise. Lessons and excurses have been clarified either by rephrasing, abbreviating, or in some cases, rounding out explanations. Exercises have been pruned, and a few sentences after the lessons have been removed because their meanings suffer too much out of context. Verb charts have been more completely filled in and more charts added: the strong verb and 3rd ה with suffixes, for example. There is also a chart of prepositions with suffixes. One small but significant change is to the reading exercise on page 5 of the first edition. In keeping with the second edition's emphasis on oral fluency, that half-page exercise of words, which a beginner could not understand, has become a full-page Proper Names and Places Reading Exercise, so that one should know immediately, and without external feedback, if he or she is pronouncing the words at least close to correctly. The short writing exercise in the first edition has been expanded into two full writing exercises—one for block, one for script—to familiarize students with both styles. The result of these changes is a tighter, yet more comprehensive textbook.

The most exciting modification to the first edition is that the audiotape, an optional accompaniment to that volume, has been replaced by three compact disks that are integrated into every phase of the course. ☉ ב א has a program of reading exercises to help with pronunciation, four of the readings cantillated to Masoretic notation, and some seventeen songs for learning paradigms and grammar concepts. Biblical Hebrew was never like this! Grammatically clear expositions set to catchy tunes make students want to study those hollows and Hifʿils. The cantillations allow the phrasing of passages and verbal sounds and interplay to become apparent. ☉ אֵלֶּה הַדְּבָרִים records all the vocabulary words, in groups of ten, from English to Hebrew. Relieving the tedium of listening to simple translations are clips of songs and mnemonic devices sprinkled throughout. The resulting combination of seriousness and entertainment should make studying simple and fun, and the medium allows one to review any batch of words with the push of a button! ☉ שַׁבְּחִי consists of over thirty songs, most of which have been taken from Psalms. The melodies to these verses span a range of genres, which represent a variety of both Jewish and Christian ways of hearing the text. One may ask, why songs with a textbook? Aside from the obvious reason that they are aesthetic, pleasurable, and often moving, they help with pronunciation, vocabulary, and grammar. They make the assertion that the Bible is a text that is meant to be heard and not just silently read and parsed. And one need not wait long for this enjoyment, for as soon as one can read, one is ready to sing. The first two songs recommended are for following along—in one's Hebrew Bible, of course—then slow, short songs are assigned to be learned. As a student's skills increase, he or she can go back to songs sung early on in the course and translate more and more of their components. There is no doubt that to thoroughly enjoy and appreciate Biblical Hebrew, one must become comfortable with its sounds, rhythms, and verbal and compositional devices. To that end, CD assignments—designated by a ☉—are given at the end of every lesson. May there be many hours of pleasure and reward from this experience.

The third component to the learning program is the *Supplement to Biblical Hebrew*. Keyed to the lessons in the textbook, the Supplement has two functions: one is to provide reinforcement or additional explanation for concepts learned; the other is to give deeper explanations that interest some students but can be ignored by those who are not ready or interested. The two kinds of topics are distinguished by their preformative designators. The details that should be of interest or use to everyone have an **S** before their coordinant number; the more advanced have a 𝕊. The Supplement is peppered with a variety of mini-quizzes and some true or false questions. (Answers are given in notes at the bottom of each page.) They add variety to the exercises in the main textbook to keep review interesting

Finally, an Answer Key to the textbook is available on-line at **www.yalebooks.com/biblicalhebrew**, in PDF, and thus downloadable to be printed out as needed.

No one can eliminate the hard work necessary to learning any language, but one can try to make the effort gratifying. I hope that the changes and additions to the second edition of *Biblical Hebrew* help do just that.

INTRODUCTION TO THE FIRST EDITION

The purpose of this book is to get students reading Biblical Hebrew prose, and even a bit of poetry, as soon as possible. To effect this we take an uncommon approach by teaching (in descending order of frequency) the most common constructions, the most common verbs, the most common grammar, and syntax. Because all Hebrew in the book—whether for teaching, illustration, or drill—is Biblical, from the very first students experience the joy of working with genuine material.

In each lesson, a verse or segment generates the concepts to be learned and the workbook style of this grammar demands constant participation. To help students decipher words, explanations focus on recurring, key features rather than on historical and exceptional formations, as the latter tend to spark interest and have value at a more advanced level of learning. Of course, verb paradigms and other didactic necessities are not neglected. Conscientious study of this mixture equips students to approach passages with some analytic skill as early as Lesson 13 when extended Biblical passages are first assigned for reading.

A major section of the book is devoted to annotations to the readings, but only very rarely do the comments translate; rather they identify potential difficulties, and guide the students through a reasoning process which consistently allows them to figure out such critical components as the root of the word, the part of speech, and the syntactical setting. At all times interpretive comments focus on the Hebrew idiom, alerting students to the fact that we are reading this text in a time and culture far removed from its origins, and that we are working with a language which is built quite differently from English. If we can transmit an appreciation for the structure and beauty of the Hebrew text, then we will have succeeded in our task.

The only way we have to explain Biblical Hebrew grammar and syntax is to use English nomenclature. Common structures in English such as adjective, adverb, phrase, and sentence do not always function the same way in a Semitic language such as Hebrew. It is because of this disparity that we decided to develop the Glossary. Its entries focus on points of grammar as well as a vocabulary of terminology, which are valuable in understanding the Biblical text.

A decision we made early on was to omit transliteration although there are many systems around. Some are highly phonetic; these make use of so many diacritical symbols, and require such a sophisticated knowledge of phonics in order to be comprehensible that it is almost like learning a third language to be able to read this Anglicized Hebrew. Other more literal methods are not standardized, and the easiest ones assume that Hebrew sounds are familiar to the English reader, which, of course, they may not be. Practicing reading the lesson sentences and later the more lengthy passages, even if labored at first, should help the students develop skill in reading Hebrew in Hebrew. For those who might find it useful, a tape for reading practice is available.

A necessary but regrettable omission is of accent marks in most places, most particularly in verb charts. Because of the design of the Hebrew font, the inclusion of the accent often obscured the visibility of a vowel. So the accent marks had to go.

The reader will surely notice that punctuation is missing in Hebrew-English segments of the text. We agonized over this decision. But where does one insert the punctuation when Hebrew is read in this direction: ⟵ and then one has to proceed in this direction: ⟶ There simply is no graceful way out of such a predicament, and so we had to assume that readers would be flexible enough to adjust to compensatory measures. When switching from Hebrew to English, we left extra space to create a visual pause, and, of course, a capital letter will signal the start of a new English sentence.

This book is an outgrowth of the elementary Biblical Hebrew course taught by Professor Bonnie Kittel during her tenure at the Yale Divinity School. Along with being an inspiring scholar, Bonnie was an exceptionally gifted and talented teacher. She transmitted her love and enthusiasm for Biblical Hebrew to her students. Not insignificantly, Bonnie was always sensitive to traditions not her own. Bonnie's untimely death was tragic, creating a great personal and professional loss. We hope that her creative style and ability to excite all of those who learned from her are reflected in this volume.

Deuteronomy 30:14 כִּי־קָרוֹב אֵלֶיךָ הַדָּבָר מְאֹד בְּפִיךָ וּבִלְבָבְךָ לַעֲשֹׂתוֹ

ABBREVIATIONS AND SYMBOLS

abs.   absolute

alt.   alternate

art.   article

attrib.   attributive

BDB   *The New Brown-Driver-Briggs-Gesenius Hebrew and English Lexicon*

BH   *Biblical Hebrew* (the textbook)

cog.   cognate

const.   construct

def.   definite

du.   dual

E.K.   *A Comprehensive Etymological Dictionary of the Hebrew Language for Readers of English,* by Ernst Klein

f.   feminine

ḥ   a throaty H sound

Hi.   Hifʿil

Ho.   Hofʿal

Ht.   Hitpaʿel

imp.   imperative

infin.   infinitve

K-H   *The Hebrew and Aramaic Lexicon of the Old Testament,* by Koehler and Baumgartner

m.   masculine

MT   Masoretic Text

mt.   mountain

Ni.   Nifʿal

obj.   object

Pi.   Piʿel

part.   participle

pass.   passive

pl.   plural

Po.   Polʿel

prep.   preposition

prob.   probably

Pu.   Puʿal

Q.	Qal
rel.	related
S	Supplement
𝕊	Supplement, advanced discussions
sg.	singular
subj.	subject
sugg.	suggested
v.	verse
vb.	verb
?	maybe, not certain
√	root
ⓘ	irregular
💿	CD
→	symbol is used to indicate change, usually from a concrete to abstract expression
אַבֵן	caret (here over the א) is a generic accent sign
⌷	root letter
⌷̇	root letter with dagesh
⊡	letter with dagesh
____	letter(s) but not necessarily root letters
⟷	what is on one side of the arrow is equivalent to what is on the other
✡	appears beside some exercise sentences to identify those which may be more difficult than the others.
★	in the Glossary, to identify a term which may be specific to this book

READING AND WRITING

HEBREW ALPHABET

A.

Name	Sound	Letter	Name	Sound	Letter
lamed	l	ל	alef	silent	א
mem	m	ם מ	bet	b	ב
nun	n	ן נ	(vet)	v	ב
sameḥ	s	ס	gimel	g	ג
ayin	silent	ע	dalet	d	ד
peh	p	פ	heh	h	ה
(feh)	f	ף פ	vav	v	ו
tsadeh	ts	ץ צ	zayin	z	ז
qof	q	ק	ḥet	ḥ	ח
resh	r	ר	tet	t	ט
shin	sh	שׁ	yod	y	י
(sin)	s	שׂ	khof	k	ך כ
tav	t	ת	(ḥof)	ḥ	ך כ

Modern Hebrew equivalents are shown for the consonants. This will be true for the vowels as well. This is by far the simplest system for Hebrew pronunciation. Note the following:

א and ע once throat sounds, are treated as silent letters by most modern speakers.

ג and ג have the sound of "g" as in "gum."

ו now pronounced with a "v" sound, was originally pronounced as a "w" (the letter name is often written as "waw").

ח and כ are both a throaty "h" sound—like the "ch" in the Scottish word Loch. This sound will be designated by "ḥ."

ט ת and ת are all simple "t" sounds.

ס and שׂ are both "s" sounds.

צ is most closely approximated in English by the sound of "ts" as in hits.

ק has a hard "q" sound close to "k," never the sound of our "qu."

שׂ שׁ In some Biblical Hebrew dictionaries שׁ is listed before שׂ but in concordances (and in modern Hebrew) the two are often treated as the same letter or else שׂ precedes שׁ

3

Hebrew is read from right to left; books (such as the Bible) begin at the "back." Note that some letters have two forms. The second is called the **final form**, as it is used only at the end of a word. The first form is used at the beginning and middle of a word. Locate both forms of each letter in the examples below:

khof	mem	nun	peh	tsadeh
כל	מה	נפל	פנים	צדק
מלך	שם	בן	כסף	ארץ

VOWEL POINTS

Full Vowels

B.	Name	Sign	Sound	Class
	qamats	◌ָ	a (father)	A
	pataḥ	◌ַ	a (father)	A
	segol	◌ֶ	eh (set)	I/A
	tsere (plene)	◌ֵי	ei (sleigh)	I
	tsere (defectiva)	◌ֵ	ei/eh (sleigh or set)	I
	ḥireq (plene)	◌ִי	i (machine)	I
	ḥireq (defectiva)	◌ִ	i/ih (machine or hit)	I
	shureq	וּ	u (flute)	U
	qibbuts	◌ֻ	u (flute)	U
	ḥolem (plene)	וֹ	o (hope)	U
	ḥolem (defectiva)	◌ֹ	o (hope)	U
	qamats ḥatuf	◌ָ	o (hold)	U

Shewa and Composite Shewas

	Name	Sign	Sound	Class
	simple shewa	◌ְ	no sound	silent
	simple shewa	◌ְ	slight sound (McCoy)	vocal
	composite pataḥ	◌ֲ	a (around)	A
	composite segol	◌ֱ	eh (effect)	I/A
	composite qamats	◌ֳ	o (olfactory)	U

Note the following:

More than one vowel may have the same sound, e.g.: shureq וּ and qibbuts ◌ֻ are both heard as "u" in flute.

Qamats and qamats ḥatuf are represented by the same symbol but are pronounced differently. Their distinguishing characteristics are discussed in Lesson 6.

Two common marks that affect pronunciation are **maqqef** כָּל־ which means that the word(s) before it are not accented, and **meteg** ◌ֽ which indicates an open syllable. The following words show the Hebrew pointing (vowel) system.

meteg ↓ יְ֒ is open syllable   maqqef ↓ כָּל־ is unaccented

יֵרְדָה	יִשְׂרָאֵל	אָב	כָּל־	אֲשֶׁר
נְאֻם	חֳלִי אֱלֹהִים	בְּנִי	הוֹלֵךְ	וַיִּשְׁמְעוּ

VOCALIZATION

C. The Hebrew alphabet is the oldest in the world still in use today; our own alphabet is a descendant of it by a circuitous route. The text of the Hebrew Bible we use today reflects several periods of development. Originally only the consonants were used. By the time of the Israelite kingdoms, some consonants י ו ה were used to indicate certain vowels:

ה ah   י i/ei   ו oo/oh

These letters, called *matres lectionis* (mothers of reading) or vowel letters, continued to be used as consonants as well. Much later, in the Middle Ages, a system of dots and dashes was devised to indicate every vowel. This was done by scholars we call Masoretes. By that time, the text was so sacred that the vowel letters י ו ה could not be removed, so the dot-dash system was used <u>in addition</u> to the vowel letters. For example:

ei (as in sl**eigh**) can be represented by either ..ְי or ..

i (as in mach**i**ne) can be represented by .ִי or .ִ

o (as in h**o**pe) can be represented by either וֹ or .ֹ

u as in (fl**u**te) can be represented by וּ or ..ֻ

The spellings <u>with</u> the vowel letters are considered to be long or longer than those without the vowel letters. Spelling rules during the period in which the texts were written varied a good deal, and the vagaries were usually preserved by the Masoretes. That is why you may see the same word spelled different ways in the text. For example: יֵשֵׁב and יוֹשֵׁב To distinguish the spellings there are two terms: יֵשֵׁב is **defectiva** spelling, and יוֹשֵׁב is **plene** (or full) spelling. If a word is usually written with a vowel letter, however, it means that the vowel is long and that it is basically unchangeable, whatever else is added to a word.

The proper way to sound out a word is to sound the first consonant, then the vowel with it, then the next consonant and vowel combination, and so on. The last consonant most often has no vowel sound and rounds off (closes) the syllable.

דָּ|בָ|ר   מֶּ|לֶ|ךְ   אֱ|לֹ|הִים ⟵ no sound for א

↑ pronounce the vowel

Usually, the final syllable in a word is accented or stressed. In most cases, printed texts mark the accented syllables. In this book a generic accent sign ˋ is used in most places when the word is not accented on the final syllable.

D. Where no vowel sound was heard, the shewa ְ was used. Either it has no sound (**silent shewa**) or a very slight sound (**vocal shewa**) to link the consonants together.

A shewa is heard as a slight "uh" sound (vocal shewa) when:

1. It is under the first consonant in a word — דְ|בָ|רִים (↑ vocal shewa)

2. It is the second shewa in a row — יִ|שְׁ|מְ|עוּ (vocal shewa ↑ ↑ silent shewa)

3. It follows a long vowel — וּ|לְ|אָ|דָם (vocal shewa ↑ ↑ long vowel)

4. It is under a letter that is followed by the same letter — יְבָרֶכְךָ *he will bless you*; ך כ ↑ vocal shewa

5. It is under a letter with dagesh forte[1] — מְיַלְּדוֹת *midwives* (dagesh forte ↑ vocal shewa)

6. Composite shewas ֲ ֱ ֳ are, by definition, vocal. They are used under gutturals and sometimes ר when a vocal shewa is needed. (See items 1–5 above.)

E. Aside from the vowel signs, another mark was used to indicate more precisely how certain consonants were pronounced. This mark, called a **dagesh**, is simply a dot in the center of a letter. The dagesh was also used in certain grammatical constructions you will learn, and so can be found in most letters. In some letters it always indicates different pronunciation as well:

With Dagesh			**Without Dagesh**		
b		בּ	v		ב
p		פּ	f	ף	פ
k	ךּ	כּ	ḥ	ך	כ

Three other letters תּ דּ גּ were distinguished by different pronunciation when a dagesh appeared in them, but these distinctions are no longer made in modern Hebrew pronunciation, in which

1. Dagesh forte is addressed in Lesson 1. If a shewa makes a dagesh forte disappear (addressed in Lesson 2), is the shewa still vocal? This is a matter about which grammarians argue.

these letters have only one sound each. We will follow this practice in pronunciation, but the dagesh will still be written in these three letters. These six consonants ת פ כ ד ג ב are known as the **BeGaDKePHaT** letters.

Some letters do not take dagesh. These are the **gutturals** ע ח ה א and the letter ר

F. Some letters become **quiescent**; that is, they drop out of pronunciation altogether. This happens if a silent letter would have a simple shewa ְ under it. In these cases, the consonant is written (remember, it is part of the sacred text), but the shewa is not:

$$ וַיֹּאמֶר $$

consonant, no shewa ↑

Assignments

A. Using the textbook and ⊛ ב א tracks 2–3, memorize the alphabet and learn to recognize and pronounce the vowels.

B. Practice reading out loud using the Proper Names and Places Reading Exercise (Reading and Writing G).

C. Learn to write either block or script as your teacher wishes. Both styles are demonstrated in the Writing Exercises (Reading and Writing H).

D. Throughout the course, use the Supplement to review, reinforce, and test what you have learned. References to sections in the Supplement will be designated by an **S** followed by the corresponding lesson reference in the textbook. Some discussions in the Supplement—those designated by a 𝕊— deal with material that may be more advanced or go into more detail than appeals to many beginners. Those sections may be skipped and returned to at a later stage of study.

G. PROPER NAMES AND PLACES READING EXERCISE

	D	C	B	A	
	דָּן	רוּת	שָׂרָה	אָדָם	1
	דִּינָה	גָּד	מֹשֶׁה	לוֹט	2
	יוֹסֵף	לֵאָה	רָחֵל	יִצְחָק	3
	יְהוּדָה	יִשְׂרָאֵל	אָשֵׁר	לֵוִי	4
	רְאוּבֵן	רִבְקָה	עֵשָׂו	יַעֲקֹב	5
	בִּנְיָמִין	אַהֲרֹן	אֶפְרַיִם	זְבֻלוּן	6
	גִּדְעוֹן	דָּנִיֵּאל	יִשְׁמָעֵאל	הָגָר	7
	שְׁמוּאֵל	הֶבֶל	קַיִן	דָּוִד	8
	צִיּוֹן	מִרְיָם	שָׁאוּל	עֵדֶן	9
	אֵלִיָּהוּ	יוֹנָה	דְּבֹרָה	חַנָּה	10
	כַּרְמֶל	בֹּעַז	לְבָנוֹן	בָּבֶל	11
	עָמוֹס	כְּנַעַן	סִינַי	יְרִיחוֹ	12
	יְהוֹנָתָן	יְהוֹשֻׁעַ	מְנַשֶּׁה	בֵּית לֶחֶם	13
	שִׁמְשׁוֹן	דְּלִילָה	מַלְכִּי־צֶדֶק	נִינְוֵה	14
	זְכַרְיָהוּ	חֲבַקּוּק	גָּלְיָת	בִּלְעָם	15
	מִצְרַיִם Egypt	אַבְשָׁלֹם	אִיזֶבֶל	אֲבִיגַיִל	16
	נְחֶמְיָה	עֶזְרָא	מָרְדְּחַי	אֶסְתֵּר	17

11

H. BLOCK AND SCRIPT WRITING EXERCISE

Block Writing

אַ   א

בּ   ב

ג   ג

ד   ד

ה   ה

ו   ו

ז   ז

ח   ח

ט   ט

י   י

כ   ך   כּ   כ

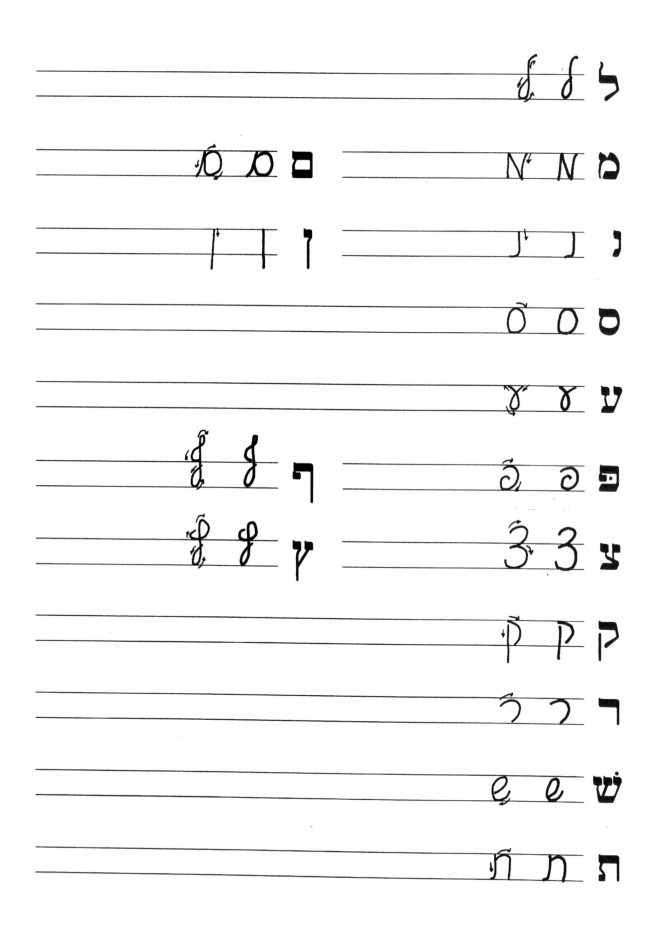

א אֵC Cִ

ב בֹ בֹ

ג גֹ גֹ

ד דֹ דֹ

ה הֹ הֹ

ו ו ו

ז זֹ זֹ

ח חֹ חֹ

ט טֹ טֹ

י י י

ך כֹ כֹ ך כֹ כֹ

LESSONS

LESSON 1

וַיֹּאמֶר יהוה

Genesis 3:13

1.1a Read

Referring to the alphabet and vowel listings, pronounce the two words of the lesson sentence, reading from right to left: consonant, vowel, consonant, etc. Most Hebrew words have the stress on the final syllable. When a word in the lesson sentence has the accent elsewhere, as in וַיֹּאמֶר an accent mark will be used.

1.1b The vowels of the second word יהוה have been omitted intentionally. In the Bible it is written with two different sets of vowels: יְהֹוָה and יֱהֹוִה. The first, some people think, approximates the original sound of the divine name, and thus they pronounce it "Yahweh." Those who do not like to say "Yahweh" use "Adonai," or Lord in English. Outside of liturgical settings, some Jews substitute הַשֵּׁם "The Name," for "Adonai."[1] (You will hear this substitution in some of the songs on ☉שַׁבְּחִי) The second set of vowel markings are those of another divine name, אֱלֹהִים When these vowels are used, the word is to be pronounced "Eloheem."

1.2 Count the Consonants וַיֹּאמֶר

In most aspects Hebrew is a very simple language. Almost every word contains a root of three consonants. The first step in finding the root is to count the consonants in a word. So, ו = 1 consonant. Notice the dot in the yod י A dot in a consonant is called a **dagesh**.

> If there is a full vowel immediately preceding the letter containing the dagesh, the dagesh is a **dagesh forte** (or strong dagesh). It has the effect of doubling the letter in which it appears and is, almost always, grammatically significant.

Here the י is preceded by a full vowel (pataḥ ַ under the ו is the preceding vowel), so the dagesh is a dagesh forte י = יּ Thus, ו = 1 consonant, י = 2 consonants, א = 1 consonant, מ = 1 consonant, and ר = 1 consonant, for a total of 6 consonants.

---

1. For a more detailed explanation, see Fox, pp. xxix–xxx.

1.3 **Find the Root**

You must separate three consonants from the word in order to identify the root. Since the root consonants will generally appear together, you can expect to find the non-root consonants at either the beginning (right) or the end (left) of the word.

1.3a A ו at the beginning of a word means *and* regardless of the vowel that appears with it. It cannot stand by itself as a word in Hebrew.

1.3b When such a ו is followed by a patah ◌ַ and a dagesh appears in the next letter ◌ וַ the construction is called **vav conversive**.

1.3c A vav conversive indicates:

---

1. The word is a **verb**.

2. The subject of the verb, a pronoun, is indicated by the consonant following the vav, which here is י When such a subject pronoun precedes the root, this pronoun is called a prefix, and we say that the verb has **prefix form**.

3. The verb should be translated in the **past tense**.

1.3d Having accounted for וַי you are left with three letters אמר which you can assume are the root.

1.4 Verb Analysis

You now have   ◌ וַ   = vav conversive

י   = prefix pronoun (subject)

אמר   = root (meaning *say*)

As an aid to translation, we make a chart for verbs:

Root	Stem	Form	Person/Gender/Number			Special Features
אמר	Qal	prefix	3	m.	sg.	vav conversive

1.4a **Stem** indicates whether there has been some change in the basic meaning of the root. Variations from the basic meaning are indicated by additions to the root. When there are no additional letters or other indicators, as is the case here, the stem is the **Qal**, the most basic and common stem. One writes "Qal" or "Q" in the Stem column.

1.4b **Form** In this column we write "prefix," indicating prefix form.

1.4c **Person, Gender, Number** We said that יְ is the prefix, the pronoun subject.

יְ as a prefix indicates the third person masculine subject of the verb. In this case, the number of the subject is singular, "he" (for the plural, a special ending is added to the word). So "3 m. sg." (third masculine singular) is written in this column. "Vav conversive " is written in the Special Features column.

1.5 Translation
Reading the analysis chart from right to left, you can translate:

vav conversive	= *and* (followed by past tense translation)
3 m. sg. prefix	= *he*
Qal	= basic meaning of root
אמר	= *say*

Translation: *and-he-said*

1.6 יהוה This is the sacred four-letter name for God. (1.1b) וַיֹּאמֶר יהוה is literally *and-he-said-Lord*. In Biblical Hebrew, the normal word order is verb-subject. So the "he" contained in the verb refers to the subject, יהוה and you can properly translate *and the Lord said*. (You now know about 4% of the Hebrew Bible's vocabulary.)

You might wonder whether וַיֹּאמֶר יהוה could also be translated *and he said, "Lord."* The answer is yes.

Assignments

A. It will be assumed that you are responsible for learning the contents of each lesson as part of every assignment.

B. Vocabulary: the particles plus words 1–10.

Note: What you need to memorize for each entry is set in **boldface.**

Vocabulary words are recorded—from English to Hebrew—in blocks of ten on אֵלֶּה הַדְּבָרִים⊙ and there are vocabulary exercises—also in blocks of ten—at the back of the Supplement.

C. Review alphabet and vowels, using ⊙ א ב tracks 2–3, as necessary.

D. Practice reading using the Proper Names and Places Reading Exercise (Reading and Writing G), and in the Supplement, do **S1.1a**.

E. ⊙שַׁבְּחִי track 2: following along in your Bible, listen to the song שַׁבְּחִי Psalm 147:12. Note that הַשֵּׁם the substitute term for יהוה (1.1b) is used in this recording.

LESSON 2

———

וַיְדַבֵּר אֱלֹהִים אֶל־מֹשֶׁה וַיֹּאמֶר אֵלָיו אֲנִי יהוה

Exodus 6:2

2.1 Pronounce the words in the above verse. This is assumed to be the first step in all subsequent lessons.

2.2 Count the Consonants וַיְדַבֵּר

$$ו = 1$$

$$י = 2 \qquad \text{What kind of dagesh is in the } י \text{ _____ (1.2)}$$

$$ד = 1$$

$$ב = \text{\_\_\_\_} \qquad \text{What kind of dagesh is this? _____ (1.2)}$$

$$ר = 1$$

7 total

2.3 Verb Analysis

2.3a What is the initial ☐ וַ _____ (1.3b)

2.3b What is the י _____ (1.3c) Form? _____ (1.3c)

Person, Gender, Number? _____ (1.3c, 1.4c)

2.3c This leaves four consonants דבבר from which you must extract the root.

> The doubling of the middle letter of a root by a dagesh forte indicates a change or augment to the root and thus a change in stem. We call this stem the **Pìel.**

דבר is thus the root of three consonants. In general the Pìel yields an intensive meaning of the root, although that doesn't show in this verb, and there are other functions of the Pìel. דִּבֵּר is one of the many Pìels thought to be denominative, that is, built from an original noun. The Pìel of the root דבר means *speak*. (This verb is used almost exclusively in the Pìel. Examples of verbs used in both Qal and Pìel stems will be studied later.)

2.3d   You have accounted for all seven letters of the word, so you can fill in the analysis:

Root	Stem	Form	Person/Gender/Number	Special Features

2.3e   Translation

Using the analysis chart, you can translate:

vav conversive = *and* (plus past tense translation) (1.3c)

3 m. sg. prefix = *he* (1.5)

Pi`el = denominative meaning

דבר = *speak*

Translation: *and he spoke*

2.4   אֱלֹהִים means *Elohim* or *God*. What is the relationship of *God* to the verb? _____ _____ (1.6) Note that this appears to be the longest word in the verse. Nouns, like verbs, are built primarily on three-letter roots. Here the root has a masculine plural ending; יִם (י is the plural indicator; ם ends the word.) אֱלֹהִים can, and does, mean *gods*. But most often in the Bible it is used for *God*, with 3 m. sg. verbs. So *God* is the subject referred to by the 3 m. sg. prefix pronoun.

Translation: *and God spoke*

2.5   אֶל־ is a preposition meaning _____ The dash, called a **maqqef**, merely indicates that this word is closely related to, and pronounced with, the next word without a separate accent.

2.6   מֹשֶׁה pronounced "Mo-shéh," is the name *Moses; and God spoke to Moses*

2.7   וַיֹּאמֶר Referring, if necessary, to 1.2–1.4, fill in the chart:

Root	Stem	Form	Person/Gender/Number	Special Features

2.8   Using the chart and reading from right to left, translate: _____ (1.5)

2.9   אֵלָיו

2.9a   Notice the syllable אֶל in this word. Here it means the same thing as אֶל in 2.5.

> A ו or וֹ at the end of a word is the third person masculine singular pronoun suffix,
> ***him*** or ***his***; ***it*** or ***its***.

2.9b   Suffixes are either objective (*him/it*) or possessive (*his/its*). A suffix attached to a preposition is the object of that preposition, and therefore objective. There is a י after אֶל because some prepositions, אֶל being one, take י before a suffix is added.

Translation: *to him*

 אֲנִי יְהוָה

2.10a   אֲנִי means *I*. יְהוָה means _____ (1.1b)

2.10b
> In Hebrew two nouns (or a noun and a pronoun or predicate adjective) can be linked by writing them together. In English we usually link nouns by writing some form of the verb *to be* between them. Such a Hebrew construction (in which *to be* is understood) is called a **noun sentence**.

Translation: *I am (the) Lord*

2.11   Translation of verse: *And God spoke to Moses and he said to him, "I am (the) Lord."*

2.12   Special Note

In the Masoretic Text the first word of our verse is spelled וַיְדַבֵּר (without the dagesh in the י) rather than וַיְּדַבֵּר (with dagesh in the י as one would want). Dagesh forte is frequently omitted when the vowel under the consonant is shewa. From now on, we will follow the Masoretic spelling וַיְדַבֵּר

Assignments

A.   Vocabulary: words 1–20. Exercises for Lessons 2–5 may draw on words 1–50.

B.   ✆ א ב tracks 2–3: review alphabet and vowels.

   ✆ א ב track 4: read aloud lesson sentences 1–5 (follow using Table of Contents)

   ✆ שַׁבְּחִי track 3: listen to שִׁמְעָה **Psalm 97:8**. How many vav conversive constructions are in the song?

24

C. Translate:

1   וַיֹּאמֶר יהוה אֵלָיו   *Hosea 1:4*

2   וַיְדַבֵּר יהוה אֶל־מֹשֶׁה וְאֶל אַהֲרֹן   *Exodus 6:13*

3   וַיֹּאמֶר מֹשֶׁה אֶל־אַהֲרֹן   *Exodus 32:21*

4   יהוה אֶחָד   *Deuteronomy 6:4*

LESSON 3

וַיֵּלֶךְ דָּוִד מִשָּׁם

1 Samuel 22:1

3.1   Count the Consonants וַיֵּלֶךְ

There is a total of five consonants. As you now know, ☐ וַ is a _____
_____ (1.3b), and יֵ is a _____ (1.3c, 1.4c). You are thus left with
only two consonants לֶךְ Since you need three for the root, one consonant is missing. You can
determine where the letter is missing (beginning, middle, or end) and which letter is missing by
the vowel underneath the prefix pronoun: וַיֵּלֶךְ

↑

> When a root letter is missing from a prefix form of the verb, the position of the missing
>
> letter and also which letter is missing is indicated by the vowel under the prefix conso-
>
> nant. If this vowel is tsere ֵ then the root letter is missing from the beginning of the
>
> root and will usually be a יֵ

In one exceptional case לֶךְ the missing letter is ה So the root is הלך meaning *go, walk*.

3.1a   ךְ is the one consonant that never appears without a vowel of its own. If it has no vowel, a
shewa is inserted: ךְ

3.2   Verb Analysis

Based on the above information, you should be able now to fill in the verb chart:

Root	Stem	Form	Person/Gender/Number	Special Features

The stem should be no problem, for no letters have been added to the root, and missing letters
do not affect the stem determination. So the stem is Qal (basic meaning).

3.2a Translation

Reading the analysis chart from right to left, you can translate:

vav conversive = _____

3 m. sg. prefix = _____

Qal = basic meaning

הָלַךְ = *go*

Translation: *and he went*

3.3 דָּוִד is *David*, in case you had not guessed. Notice the dagesh in the first ד Since it is not immediately preceded by a full vowel, it is not a dagesh forte. We call this dagesh a **dagesh lene** (weak dagesh). A dagesh lene may affect pronunciation but has no grammatical significance. (Review Vocalization E for information on pronunciation changes with dagesh.)

> A dagesh in a consonant that is not immediately preceded by a full vowel is a **dagesh lene.** It has no grammatical significance.

The normal order of the Hebrew sentence is _____ (1.6). So the first two words of this lesson sentence are translated: _____

3.3a

	Dagesh Forte	**Dagesh Lene**
In what letters	All except	Most usually in[1]
	א ה ח ע ר	ב ג ד כ פ ת
Preceded by full vowel?[2]	Yes	No

3.4 מִשָּׁם

3.4a What kind of dagesh is in the שׁ _____ (1.2)

3.4b In Hebrew a number of small words are always or frequently fused to the following word. The most frequent of these particles, or short words, is ו which you have already seen. (1.3a) Another is the preposition מִן However, this preposition undergoes a change when it is attached to a word. The ן drops out and a dagesh forte takes its place in the following letter. In grammatical

---

1. Other consonants can have dagesh lene in the first letter of a word in particular accentual environments. See **S 17.3b**.
2. Shewa and the composite shewas are not considered **full** vowels.

terms, we say that the ן has been assimilated to (has come to sound like) the following letter, causing a doubling of that letter to take place.

> ⬛ מְ attached to the beginning of a word is the preposition מִן which means *from, away from*.

3.4c שָׁם means *there*. So מִשָּׁם means *from there*.

3.4d This assimilation of letters, or the dropping out of one and the doubling of its neighbor, can be seen in many places in English.

in + mobile	→	immobile
in + logical	→	illogical
in + reverent	→	irreverent

3.5 Translation of verse: _____

Assignments

A. Vocabulary: words 1–30.

B. Using the Table of Contents and ☺ א ב track 5, read lesson sentences 6–10.

C. ☺ שַׁבְּחִי track 4: listen to and learn אֵלִי אַתָּה **Psalm 118:28**.

D. Translate:

1 וַיֵּלֶךְ אַבְרָהָם *Genesis 22:13*

2 וַיְדַבֵּר אֱלֹהִים אֶל־נֹחַ [נֹחַ famous "arkitect"] *Genesis 8:15*

3 וַיֵּלֶךְ אֵלָיו *1 Samuel 15:32*

4 וַיֵּלֶךְ מִשָּׁם יִצְחָק *Genesis 26:17*

5 וַיֹּאמֶר שְׁלֹמֹה *2 Chronicles 1:8*

LESSON 4

וְלֹא־שָׁמַע הַמֶּלֶךְ אֶל־הָעָם

1 Kings 12:15

4.1 וְלֹא־שָׁמַע הַמֶּלֶךְ

4.1a וְלֹא What does וְ at the beginning of a word mean? _____ (1.3a)

לֹא means *not.*

4.2 Verb Analysis שָׁמַע

4.2a Since there are only three letters, you can assume that שׁמע is the root.

Root	Stem	Form	Person/Gender/Number	Special Features

Is there any indication of a change in the basic meaning of the root? _____

What do you call this stem? _____ (1.4a) Previous verb forms examined were prefix, in which the subject pronoun was attached to the front of the verb. (1.3c) There is a second form of the verb in which the pronoun is placed after the root.

> The form of the verb with the subject pronoun indicated at the end is called **affix form**; this subject pronoun is called the affix.[1]

Notice the vowel under the שׁ in שָׁמַע

> A qamats ָ under the first <u>root</u> letter of a verb is the regular vowel of both the Qal stem and the affix form.

Write "affix" in the Form column.

---

1. Don't confuse the term "affix" with "suffix" (see Glossary).

29

וְלֹא־שָׁמַע הַמֶּלֶךְ אֶל־הָעָם

In the affix form, the subject pronoun comes at the end of the word, after the root:

שׁמע
root

affix pronoun goes here ↑

4.2b For one person, gender, and number (PGN), the 3 m. sg., the pronoun is lacking. In this case you can identify the stem and form of the verb by the vowels under the root letters, but that it is 3 m. sg. can be ascertained only by the fact that there is no added pronoun ending. All other affix PGNs have a pronoun following the root. Write 3 m. sg. in the PGN column. Look carefully at this form, for it is very common.

Qal Affix

3 m. sg.	2 m. sg.
שָׁמַע	שָׁמַעְתָּ
root	**root**
	pronoun ↑

4.2c Translation

An affix form of a verb is normally translated in the past tense, so you may translate, using the analysis chart: *he listened, did listen, has listened,* or *had listened,* depending on context.

4.2d A negative statement is formed by putting לֹא in front of the verb, as we have here. The whole phrase then becomes: *and he did not listen*

4.3 הַמֶּלֶךְ

How many letters? _____ What kind of dagesh is in the מ _____ (1.2)

The combination ◻ הַ at the beginning of a word means *the.*

מֶלֶךְ means _____ What is the relationship of this word to the verb? _____ (1.6) Translation: _____

4.4 Pronunciation

4.4a The sound of כ is quite different from that of כּ and is notoriously difficult for English speakers. The sound of כּ is close to English "k." כ is a harsh "ḫ," close to the sound for the letter ח Thus, מֶלֶךְ is pronounced "meh-leḫ."

Although the ךְ in מֶלֶךְ has dots in it, they are a shewa and **not** dagesh plus ḥireq. In a few exceptional cases a final ךְ will have both a dagesh and a shewa, but they will be written separately:

Genesis 50:1 וַיֵּבְךְּ

and he wept

30

וְלֹא־שָׁמַע הַמֶּ֫לֶךְ אֶל־הָעָם

4.4b One group of nouns is pronounced with the accent on the first, rather than the last, syllable. Since many of these nouns have two segols ֶ ֶ for their vowels, they are called **segolates**. מֶלֶךְ is a segolate noun, so it is accented מֶ֫לֶךְ

4.5 אֶל־הָעָם

4.5a אֶל־ means ________ (2.5)

4.5b הָעָם

What does הָ mean? It sounds like הַ◻ּ in 4.3, but you will notice a difference between this ה and the one in 4.3. The change in vowel takes place because ע cannot accept a dagesh, (3.3a) so the vowel with the definite article was lengthened in compensation. הָ before some gutturals is the same as הַ◻ּ in meaning. (For more detail on vocalization of the definite article, see **S 4.5b** and **S 21.3a**.) עָם is a noun meaning *people.*

4.6 Write the translation for the entire sentence: ________________________________

____

4.7 Extra Grammar

You have been introduced to the 3 m. sg. Qal affix, which is vocalized אָמַר

The 3 m. sg. Piʿel affix looks like this: דִּבֵּר

Piʿel		Qal
ר ב ד	root	ר מ א
⌴ ⌴ּ ⌴	stem indicator	no augment
⌴ ⌴ּ ⌴ִ	regular vowel	⌴ ⌴ ⌴ָ
ר בֵּ דִּ	affix	ר מַ אָ

Fill in the prefix + vav conversive for the 3 m. sg. in the chart below:

Piʿel		Qal
ר ב ד	root	ר מ א
⌴ ⌴ּ ⌴	stem indicator	no augment
⌴ ⌴ּ ⌴ ___ְ	regular vowel	not regular
⌴ ⌴ ⌴ ____	prefix + vav conversive	⌴ ⌴ ⌴ ____

וְלֹא־שָׁמַע הַמֶּלֶךְ אֶל־הָעָם

Assignments

A. Vocabulary: words 1–40.

B. Put each of the following verbs into the two columns according to form and stem. You do not need to know what the root means in order to make these determinations.

Form	Stem	
Prefix/vav Conversive or Affix	Qal or Pi`el	
_____	_____	וַיֹּאמֶר
_____	_____	נִסָּה
_____	_____	אָהַב
_____	_____	וַיַּחְבֹּשׁ
_____	_____	וַיִּבְקַע
_____	_____	וַיֵּלֶךְ
_____	_____	וַיַּעֲרֹךְ
_____	_____	וַיְדַבֵּר
_____	_____	וַיִּשְׁלַח
_____	_____	וַיְשַׁלַּח
_____	_____	יָדַע
_____	_____	חָשַׁךְ

C. 🔊 א ב tracks 4–5: review—reading out loud—lesson sentences 1–10.

🔊 שַׁבְּחִי track 4: review אֵלִי אַתָּה **Psalm 118:28** and listen to הוֹדוּ *Give Thanks!* (track 5).

D. Translate:

1 וְלֹא שָׁמַע אֵלָיו *Jeremiah 37:14*

2 הָלַךְ דָּוִד *1 Kings 9:4*

3 לֹא־דִבֶּר יהוה *1 Kings 22:28*

4 דִּבֶּר יהוה אֶל־הָעָם *Jeremiah 36:7*

5 עַם יָצָא *Numbers 22:5*

REVIEW AND DRILL 1

I. Vocabulary

Vocabulary in these exercises may draw on words 1–50.

II. Translate Hebrew to English

Note that many of the verses include proper names. If you don't know the traditional English spellings, transliteration is fine.

Verb forms:

הָלַךְ   וַיִּשְׁמַע   שָׁמַע   וַיֹּאמֶר   דִּבֶּר   אָמַר   וַיֵּלֶךְ   וַיְדַבֵּר

Verses:

1   הַמֶּלֶךְ לֹא רָאָה *2 Samuel 14:24*

2   דִּבֶּר הָאִישׁ *Genesis 42:30 (review 4.5 if necessary)*

3   וַיִּשְׁמַע הַמֶּלֶךְ־יְהוֹיָקִים *Jeremiah 26:21*

4   וַיהוה לֹא דִבֶּר *Ezekiel 22:28*

5   וַיִּשְׁלַח...אֶל־הַמֶּלֶךְ חִזְקִיָּהוּ *2 Kings 18:17*

6   וַיֵּלֶךְ אַבְרָם כַּאֲשֶׁר דִּבֶּר אֵלָיו יהוה [*as* כַּאֲשֶׁר] *Genesis 12:4*

7   וַיֹּאמֶר הַמֶּלֶךְ אֲחַשְׁוֵרוֹשׁ *Esther 8:7*

8   נָתַן הַמֶּלֶךְ אַרְתַּחְשַׁסְתְּא לְעֶזְרָא *Ezra 7:11*

9   כִּי־שָׁמַע הָעָם *2 Samuel 19:3*

10   וַיִּקְרָא יהוה לְמֹשֶׁה [*call* קרא] *Exodus 19:20*

11   וַיִּשְׁמַע אַבְרָהָם אֶל־עֶפְרוֹן *Genesis 23:16*

12   וַיִּקְרָא שָׁם אַבְרָם *Genesis 13:4*

III. Translate English to Hebrew:

Verb forms: Use vav conversive forms where "and" appears; use affix forms for verbs without "and." (The verbs above can serve as models.)

> he spoke   and he said   and he heard   he went   he said   and he walked

Sentences:

1. The king did not go from there.

2. The people did not listen to God.

33

3. And God heard.

4. And God spoke to Abraham.

5. And David said to the people, "I am David." (2:10b)

6. And Moses listened to the people.

7. The Lord said.

8. The king spoke to him.

LESSON 5

דְּבַר־יהוה אֲשֶׁר הָיָה אֶל־הוֹשֵׁעַ

Hosea 1:1

5.1   דְּבַר־יהוה

5.1a   What kind of dagesh is in the דּ _____ (3.3a)

5.1b   דְּבַר

דְּבַר is related to the root דבר which you encountered in Lesson 2. The verb root means

_____ (2.3c) In this case, you have a noun rather than a verb. What might a noun

from this same root mean? If you guessed *word,* you are catching on to the way Hebrew is built.

דָּבָר means *word, thing, event.*

יהוה means _____

Notice the maqqef (2.5) linking דְּבַר and יהוה The Masoretes used the maqqef in their accentual system to indicate that the word or words before it did not receive a separate stress. It
can be a great help to beginning students, since such accent combinations can occur only where
grammatical relationships are close. In the particular case of דְּבַר־יהוה the relationship is
called a **construct chain**.

We can diagram it like this:

יהוה   דְּבָר
the two nouns are separate links

By putting the links together in Hebrew, one after the other, we get a chain:

דְּבַר־יהוה

To render this chain in English, we link the individual words most usually with *of:*

word-of-the-Lord

35

5.1c In some cases, the vowel(s) of the word in the construct are shortened or reduced, as is the case with the first word in the lesson sentence: דָּבָר becomes דְּבַר when it is in construct relationship to another word. (ַ is shorter than ָ and ְ is the shortest sound. See **S 5.1c–5.1c.3.**)

5.1d Translation: *word of the Lord*

5.2 There is another aspect of construct chains that is important. To use our phrase as an example, we can label the words:

יהוה   דְּבַר

(last link) absolute   **construct (first link)**

In Hebrew, the definite article (*the* ◌ַ הַ), which you saw in 4.3, can be attached only to the absolute, never to the construct. The construct can never carry components that make a noun definite, but the absolute may carry these components.

5.2a

> A noun can be definite (specific) in several ways:
> 1. If it has the definite article
> 2. If it is a proper noun (a name)
> 3. If it has a possessive pronoun (*my, his,* etc.)

Of our two nouns, which is definite? _____

Why? _____

> In a construct chain, if the absolute is definite, the whole chain is definite—in translating, you can place the definite article ***the*** in front of the whole chain.

Translation of our chain: ***the*** *word of the Lord* or ***the*** *word of Adonai*

5.3 אֲשֶׁר הָיָה

5.3a אֲשֶׁר means *which, who, whom*. It is the all-purpose **relative pronoun** in Hebrew and does not decline.

5.3b הָיָה is a new verb, but you studied its form in Lesson 4. The landmark vowel is the ָ under the first root letter.

Root	Stem	Form	Person/Gender/Number	Special Features

Is הָיָה a prefix form? _____ (1.3c) Is it an affix form? _____ (4.2a) What is the stem? _____ (4.2a)

Translation of the phrase: *which (it) happened*

5.3c Hebrew does not have a neuter gender, but you can supply a neuter pronoun in English when that makes an appropriate translation. Notice that in good English you do not have to say the pronoun *he* or *it* in this phrase—*which* takes its place.

5.3d In Hebrew, the word *happens* to people; in English, you can preserve that sense or use more colloquial terminology: *came to*

5.4 אֶל־הוֹשֵׁעַ

אֶל means _____ (2.5) הוֹשֵׁעַ is a name. In fact, it is the name of the prophetic book from which this sentence is taken. Notice the pataḥ ַ which is written slightly to the right of the ע It is to be pronounced <u>before</u> the final consonant of the word and occurs only in words ending in ע or ח It is called **furtive pataḥ** because it sneaks in before the final consonant to make pronunciation easier.

5.5 Write your translation of the lesson sentence: _____

_____

5.6 Identify each of the following words and phrases as definite or indefinite. You do not need to be able to translate them in order to determine this; you simply need to know the "rules" in 5.2a. For those that are definite, you should be able to explain how you know they are definite. The proper names are not difficult ones.

הַדְּבָרִים	הָעִיר (4.5b)	וּבֶּגֶד (1.3a)
אַבְרָהָם	רַגְלָיו	מַלְכּוֹ (2.9a)
הַמָּקוֹם	צֹאן	מַצֵּבָה
עֵינָיו	שְׁנֵי וְעָרָיו	וְהַנַּעַר
שֵׁם	הַמַּאֲכֶלֶת	הַר
הַשָּׂדֶה	מָקוֹם	הַיּוֹם
סֻלָּם	שֵׁם־הַמָּקוֹם	הַשֶּׁמֶשׁ
בֵּית אֱלֹהִים	הָאָרֶץ	שַׁעַר הַשָּׁמַיִם

דְּבַר־יהוה אֲשֶׁר הָיָה אֶל־הוֹשֵׁעַ

Assignments

A. Vocabulary: words 1–50. Use ⊙ אֵלֶּה הַדְּבָרִים tracks 2–7 to test yourself.

B. ⊙ א ב track 6: read lesson sentences 11–15.

⊙ שַׁבְּחִי track 6: learn אָנָּה יהוה **Psalm 118:25**. Both the word הוֹשֵׁעַ in the song and the name of the prophet הוֹשֵׁעַ are from the root ישׁע meaning *save*.

C. Translate:

1	הַדָּבָר אֲשֶׁר הָיָה אֶל־יִרְמְיָהוּ *Jeremiah 11:1*
2	וְלֹא־שָׁמַע יהוה *Deuteronomy 1:45*
3	דְּבַר־יהוה אֵלָיו *Genesis 15:4*
4	וְלֹא־הָלַךְ *Numbers 24:1*
5	הָיָה דְבַר־יהוה אֶל־אַבְרָם *Genesis 15:1*
6	וְלֹא שָׁמַע מֶלֶךְ *Judges 11:17*
7	אֲשֶׁר לֹא הָלַךְ *Psalms 1:1*
8	לֹא־שָׁמַע הַמֶּלֶךְ *2 Chronicles 10:16*
9	הַדָּבָר יָצָא מִפִּי הַמֶּלֶךְ [פִּי is the construct form of פֶּה *mouth*] *Esther 7:8*
10	שָׁמַע אֱלֹהִים *Genesis 21:17*

LESSON 6

וַיָּבֹאוּ עַד־הַיַּרְדֵּן הוּא וְכָל־בְּנֵי יִשְׂרָאֵל

Joshua 3:1

6.1 Verb Analysis וַיָּבֹאוּ

Root	Stem	Form	Person/Gender/Number	Special Features

By now you should be able to recognize almost immediately the way in which this verb begins, and you can fill in the Form column and the Special Features column on the chart.

The prefix pronoun יְ is what person and gender? _____ (1.4c) Notice the וּ___ at the end of the verb. When this is added to a prefix form and the prefix יְ is used, the verb is no longer 3 masculine singular but 3 masculine plural:

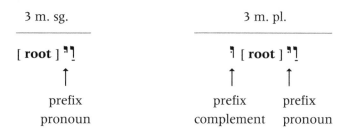

3 m. sg.	3 m. pl.
וַיְ [root]	וַיְ [root] וּ
↑	↑ ↑
prefix pronoun	prefix complement · prefix pronoun

> The letter(s) indicating PGN that occur after the root in prefix form verbs are called the **prefix complement**.

Fill in the PGN column. How many letters are left now? _____ Where do you look for the indication of the missing letter in such a case? _____ _____ (3.1)

6.1a

> When the vowel under the prefix pronoun is qamats ָ the missing root letter will be in the middle of the root and will be וּ or וֹ or יְ___ This type of verb is called a **hollow verb**.

39

In this case, neither **בִּיא** nor **בּוֹא** exists, so **בּוֹא** is the root. Is there any indication of a stem change? _____ So the stem will be _____ (1.4a)

Translation of verb: _____

6.2 עַד־הַיַּרְדֵּן

הַיַּרְדֵּן | ◌ הַ is the _____ meaning _____ (4.3)

יַרְדֵּן is the major river in Israel: _____ What kind of dagesh is

in the י _____ What kind of dagesh is in the ד _____ (3.3a)

6.3 הוּא וְכָל־בְּנֵי יִשְׂרָאֵל

הוּא means _____

וְכָל | וְ means _____ (1.3a). כָּל or כּוֹל means *all, every.*

6.3a Pronunciation

כָּל | כּוֹל is the second most frequent word in the Hebrew Bible and is common in all four possible forms: construct and absolute, both with and without dagesh lene.

	Absolute		Construct
With dagesh	כּוֹל	כָּל	כָּל־
Without dagesh	כוֹל	כָל	כָל־

Refer back to 4.4a for a discussion of the pronunciation of כ The following section discusses the pronunciation of the vowel.

6.3b Qamats ḥatuf

How can you tell the qamats ḥatuf from the qamats? They look exactly the same, but a qamats ḥatuf is really a short ḥolem. When the ambiguous vowel ◌ָ is in a closed, unaccented syllable, it is a qamats ḥatuf and pronounced close to the "o" in "h**o**ld;" otherwise (and by far the most often), it is qamats and pronounced as the "a" in "f**a**ther."

	Accented	Unaccented
Open	הָאָרֶץ	שָׁמַע
Closed	מִשָּׁם	וְכָל־בְּנֵי

↑ qamats ḥatuf

40

וַיָּבֹאוּ עַד־הַיַּרְדֵּן הוּא וְכָל־בְּנֵי יִשְׂרָאֵל

The form of כֹּל with ָ is a construct form, so וְכָל begins a _____

_____ (5.1b) The dagesh in בְּנֵי is a _____ (3.3a)

6.3c Notice the יִ__ on the end of this word.

> The occurrence of יִ__ at the end of a word is the sign of a masculine plural noun that is in construct relationship with the noun that follows.

As in the singular, a plural noun in construct can cause a change in vowels (shortening or reduction) of other vowels in the word, as is the case with בְּנֵי (**S 5.1c-3c**)

6.3d יִשְׂרָאֵל means _____ The final noun of a construct chain is called the

_____ (5.2) How are the words of the chain linked in English?

_____ (5.1b) Is the absolute definite? _____ (5.2a) So

the whole chain is _____ Translation of the whole chain

(3 members): _____

6.3e How does this entire phrase הוּא וְכָל־בְּנֵי יִשְׂרָאֵל relate to the verb? _____

_____ (1.6) Note that הוּא וְכָל־בְּנֵי יִשְׂרָאֵל is treated as a

compound subject, and thus requires a plural verb. Also note that the prepositional phrase

עַד־הַיַּרְדֵּן is inserted between the verb and its subject. This construction is frequently found

in Hebrew.

6.4 Translation of verse: _____

_____

•

6.5 Construct and Absolute

6.5a בֵּן is a masculine singular noun. This form, written in bold in the vocabulary list—and the

form in which nouns are always listed in the lexicon—is the absolute form. In this lesson, you

have learned the masculine plural construct form בְּנֵי There are two other forms of בֵּן which

you have not yet studied: the singular construct and the plural absolute.

Here are the four possible forms for בֵּן

	Absolute	Construct
Singular	בֵּן	בֶּן
Plural	בָּנִים	בְּנֵי

For the singular construct, no special ending is added, but vowels may shorten or reduce. Compare the two singular forms of דָּבָר in the box below. In the masculine plural noun, you can tell the difference between construct and absolute by the ending. (There are vowel changes as well.) The plural absolute ending is ____ Consulting the forms of בֵּן above, fill in the endings for the plural forms of דָּבָר in the box.

	Absolute	Construct
Singular	דָּבָר	דְּבַר
Plural	דְּבָ____	דִּבְ____

You have already learned one noun that is almost always used in the masculine plural, though its meaning may be singular: אֱלֹהִים Circle the plural ending. (Don't forget that the ḥireq ◌ִ is part of the ending.) The construct form will be _____ (In this case there are no vowel changes except in the ending itself.)

6.5b Noun endings give information about **N**umber and **G**ender. As a mnemonic device, we will refer to them as endiNGs.

6.6 Extra Grammar

הוּא the third masculine singular independent subject pronoun has other important functions:

1. הוּא can be one of the elements in a noun sentence. As such, depending on the context, it may be translated *that*, *that one*, *he* or *it*.

Genesis 24:65 וַיֹּאמֶר הָעֶבֶד הוּא אֲדֹנִי

and the servant said, "He (or that one) is my master"

2. הוּא may emphasize the subject pronoun of the verb.

Exodus 4:16 וְדִבֶּר־הוּא לָךְ

and he will speak to you

42

3. Sometimes הוּא appears between two nouns that form a noun sentence; it is called a copula in this case and provides the same linking function as the verb *to be* in addition to its emphatic function, as in item 2.

Deuteronomy 4:35 יהוה הוּא הָאֱלֹהִים

the Lord *he* is God

Assignments

A. Vocabulary: words 1–60.

B. ⊙ **א ב** track 7: read lesson sentences 16–20.

⊙ שַׁבְּחִי review your songs and listen to מִי הָאִישׁ **Psalm 34:13–14** (track 7). מִי means *who*.
What does מִי הָאִישׁ mean?

C. Translate:

וַיָּבֹא עַד־חֶבְרוֹן	*Numbers 13:22* 1
וַיָּבֹאוּ עַד־חָרָן	*Genesis 11:31* 2
וַיְדַבְּרוּ בְּנֵי יוֹסֵף	*Joshua 17:14* 3
וְלֹא הָלַךְ בְּדֶרֶךְ יהוה	*2 Kings 21:22* 4
וַיֵּלְכוּ וַיָּבֹאוּ אֶל־מֹשֶׁה	*Numbers 13:26* 5
דְּבַר־יהוה אֲשֶׁר הָיָה אֶל־מִיכָה	*Micah 1:1* 6
וַיֹּאמֶר אֵלָיו מֶלֶךְ־יִשְׂרָאֵל	*1 Kings 20:40* 7
אָמַר יהוה אֱלֹהֵי יִשְׂרָאֵל	*Exodus 5:1* 8
דִּבְרֵי יִרְמְיָהוּ בֶּן־חִלְקִיָּהוּ	*Jeremiah 1:1* 9
וַיִּשְׁמְעוּ אֵלָיו בְּנֵי־יִשְׂרָאֵל	*Deuteronomy 34:9* 10
וַיֹּאמְרוּ אֶל־מֹשֶׁה	*Exodus 20:19* 11

D. Analyze in chart form:

וַיֵּלְכוּ	וַיָּבֹא	וַיְדַבְּרוּ	הָלַךְ	וַיָּבֹאוּ
	הָיָה	וַיִּשְׁמְעוּ	אָמַר	וַיֹּאמְרוּ

43

LESSON 7

$$\text{וַיִּתֵּן אַבְרָהָם אֶת־כָּל־אֲשֶׁר־לוֹ לְיִצְחָק:}$$

Genesis 25:5

7.1 Verb Analysis וַיִּתֵּן

7.1a What kind of dagesh is in the י _____ (1.2) What kind of dagesh is in the ת _____
_____ (1.2)

Root	Stem	Form	Person/Gender/Number	Special Features

You should be able to determine immediately the form (1.3b and 1.3c) and the PGN. (1.4c)
In so doing you have accounted for וַיּ How many letters are left? _____ What are they?
_____ (Be sure you take account of the dagesh forte in the ת) This is the
proper number for a Hebrew root, but no Hebrew root ever begins with two identical letters. So
the root cannot be תתן

> Whenever a root appears to begin with two identical letters, due to the use of a dagesh
> forte, the first root letter is actually a נ which has been assimilated to (has come to sound
> like) the second root letter.

The real root here is therefore נתן
What is the stem? _____ (Remember, you have accounted for the dagesh forte by
the assimilated נ rule, so this cannot be a Pi'el.)

> A dagesh never does "double duty"; it never stands for more than one consonant at
> a time.

7.1b Translation of phrase וַיִּתֵּן אַבְרָהָם

What is the relation of these two words? _____ (1.6)

Translate the phrase: _____

7.2 אֶת־כָּל־אֲשֶׁר־לוֹ

אֶת is the sign of the **definite direct object** (DDO). It is not translated; it merely indicates that the word or words that follow:

1. are the object of the verb action and

2. are definite.

7.2a When not joined by a maqqef to the following word, the vowel is ֵ rather than ֶ

אֶת־כָּל־   אֵת כָּל־

7.2b כָּל means _____ (6.3) אֲשֶׁר means _____ (5.3a)

7.2c לוֹ short as it is, is made up of two parts: וֹ and לְ

לְ means *to, for*; like וְ *and*, it must always be connected with some other element. וֹ = וֹ at the end of a word, and thus means _____ (2.9a) So לוֹ means *to him*. Aside from this function as an indirect object marker, לְ is also often used to indicate possession, so that לוֹ could mean *his*.

Do not confuse this לוֹ with לֹא or לוֹא meaning *not*.

Notice that this whole phrase is tied together by maqqefs. This indicates close relationship of the words. In this case the whole phrase is the direct object of the verb. (Usually the direct object is only one noun.) This object is also <u>definite</u>.

Review what makes a noun definite. (5.2a) These rules apply in determining definiteness for the verb object too. So this accounts for the use of אֶת In order to make proper English of this phrase, you must treat it as a noun sentence and add a form of the verb *to be*.

Translation: _____

7.3 לְיִצְחָק

לְ at the beginning of a word can mean _____ (7.2c)

Translation: _____

7.4 Translation of verse: _____

7.5 Extra Grammar

לְ is used with great frequency. It can be synonymous with אֶל and the two are often (but not always) interchangeable in grammatical constructions.

Two uses of לְ are seen in the verse just studied:

1. It is regularly used to indicate possession and is the equivalent of the English verb *have*, in the sense of *possess*. בֵּן לוֹ *he has a son*, etc.

2. It often indicates the indirect object of the verb, the one who receives the action of the direct object. Our lesson sentence consists of:

indirect object (noun + prep.)	←— direct object (noun or noun clause)	←— subject (noun)	←— verb
לְיִצְחָק	אֶת־כָּל־אֲשֶׁר־לוֹ	אַבְרָהָם	וַיִּתֵּן

While in English the preposition before an indirect object is sometimes left out, it is invariably present in Hebrew. So you can also describe לְיִצְחָק as a prepositional phrase, and יִצְחָק as the object of the preposition.

7.6 Sort the following masculine nouns into the appropriate categories. It is not necessary to be able to translate them. At this point you are not equipped to recognize construct singular nouns out of context. If the nouns below have no special endiNGs, you may assume they are absolute singular.

Absolute Singular	Absolute Plural	Construct Plural	
_____	_____	_____	דְּבָרִים
_____	_____	_____	בֵּן
_____	_____	_____	הָרִים
_____	_____	_____	שְׁנֵי
_____	_____	_____	הַמָּקוֹם
_____	_____	_____	וְהָעֵצִים
_____	_____	_____	עֲצֵי
_____	_____	_____	בְּנֵי

וַיִּתֵּן אַבְרָהָם אֶת־כָּל־אֲשֶׁר־לוֹ לְיִצְחָק:

Absolute Singular	Absolute Plural	Construct Plural	
_____	_____	_____	יָד
_____	_____	_____	מֶלֶךְ
_____	_____	_____	אִישׁ
_____	_____	_____	אֱלֹהֵי
_____	_____	_____	מְלָכִים
_____	_____	_____	דִּבְרֵי

Assignments

A. Vocabulary: words 1–70.

B. 🄰 🄱 📀 tracks 6–7: review—reading aloud—lesson sentences 11–20. שַׁבְּחִי 📀 track 8: learn מַה־טֹּבוּ Numbers 24:5.

C. Translate:

1   וַיַּעֲקֹב נָתַן לְעֵשָׂו לֶחֶם [_bread, food_ לֶחֶם] *Genesis 25:34*

2   אֲשֶׁר־נָתַן אֱלֹהִים לְאַבְרָהָם *Genesis 28:4*

3   וַיִּשְׁמְעוּ כָל־יִשְׂרָאֵל *1 Kings 3:28*

4   וַיִּתֶּן־לוֹ אֶת־רָחֵל *Genesis 29:28*

5   וַיִּשְׁמְעוּ . . . אֵת הַדְּבָרִים *Jeremiah 26:10*

6   וַיֹּאמְרוּ לוֹ *Judges 15:13*

7   וַיִּשְׁמְעוּ אֶת־דְּבַר יהוה *1 Kings 12:24*

REVIEW AND DRILL 2

Remember:

וֹ‏____ at the end of a word can be either a possessive or an objective pronoun. When attached to a noun, it is possessive; attached to a verb or preposition, it is objective.

דִּבְּרוֹ *he spoke <u>it</u>*   דְּבָרוֹ *<u>his</u> word*

(As is often the case, vowel changes occur when the suffix is added.)

I. Chart and Translate:

וַיִּשְׁמְעוּ	וַיֵּלְכוּ	וַיִּתֵּן
הָלַךְ	וַיִּתְּנוּ	וַיְדַבְּרוּ
וַיָּבֹאוּ	וַיֹּאמְרוּ	הָיָה

II. Translate:

דֶּרֶךְ דָּוִד	כָּל־בְּנֵי יִשְׂרָאֵל
בֶּן־מֶלֶךְ	אֱלֹהֵי יִשְׂרָאֵל
דַּרְכֵי הַבֵּן	בְּנֵי אַבְרָהָם
יַד יהוה	כָּל־מַלְכֵי־יִשְׂרָאֵל
עַם־הָאָרֶץ	דִּבְרֵי מֹשֶׁה

1.   *2 Kings 21:21* [*his father* אָבִיו] וַיֵּלֶךְ בְּכָל־הַדֶּרֶךְ אֲשֶׁר־הָלַךְ אָבִיו

2.   *2 Kings 22:2* וַיֵּלֶךְ בְּכָל־דֶּרֶךְ דָּוִד אָבִיו

(In sentences 1 and 2, note the different ways of making the construct chain definite.)

3.   *2 Chronicles 11:4* וַיִּשְׁמְעוּ אֶת־דִּבְרֵי יהוה

4.   *Genesis 19:5* וַיִּקְרְאוּ אֶל־לוֹט וַיֹּאמְרוּ לוֹ

5.   *Genesis 20:8* וַיְדַבֵּר אֵת כָּל־הַדְּבָרִים

6.   *Genesis 31:1* וַיִּשְׁמַע אֶת־דִּבְרֵי בְנֵי־לָבָן

7.   *1 Samuel 12:6* יהוה אֲשֶׁר עָשָׂה אֶת־מֹשֶׁה וְאֶת־אַהֲרֹן

8.   *Genesis 11:31* וַיָּבֹאוּ עַד־חָרָן וַיֵּשְׁבוּ שָׁם

9.   *2 Chronicles 28:2* וַיֵּלֶךְ בְּדַרְכֵי מַלְכֵי יִשְׂרָאֵל

10.   *Numbers 11:10* וַיִּשְׁמַע מֹשֶׁה אֶת־הָעָם

48

11   וַיְדַבֵּר אֱלֹהִים אֵת כָּל־הַדְּבָרִים   *Exodus 20:1*

12   וַיִּשְׁמַע שְׁמוּאֵל אֵת כָּל־דִּבְרֵי הָעָם   *1 Samuel 8:21*

13   רָאָה יַעֲקֹב אֶת־רָחֵל   *Genesis 29:10*

14   אַבְרָם יָשַׁב בְּאֶרֶץ־כְּנָעַן   *Genesis 13:12*

15   וַיִּשְׁמְעוּ אֵלָיו בְּנֵי־יִשְׂרָאֵל   *Deuteronomy 34:9*

16   לֹא־לָקַח יִשְׂרָאֵל אֶת־אֶרֶץ מוֹאָב   *Judges 11:15*

17   אֲשֶׁר לָקַח מִיַּד יְהוֹאָחָז   *2 Kings 13:25*

18   וַיְדַבְּרוּ אֵלָיו אֵת כָּל־דִּבְרֵי יוֹסֵף אֲשֶׁר דִּבֶּר   *Genesis 45:27*

19   וַיִּשְׁמַע פַּרְעֹה אֶת־הַדָּבָר   *Exodus 2:15*

III.   Translate English to Hebrew:

the kings of Israel   in the way of Israel   all the words of Moses

the son of the king   God of Abraham   the ways of God

to the people of Israel

1.   I am the king of Israel.

2.   And Moses spoke to the people all which God said to him.

3.   The Lord did not listen to the sons of David.

4.   And all Israel came to the Jordan.

5.   God gave a king to the people.

6.   And he went to the king who was in Israel.

LESSON 8

◆

וְיָדְעוּ כִּי־שְׁמִי יהוה

Jeremiah 16:21

8.1 Verb Analysis וְיָדְעוּ

8.1a What does an initial וְ mean? _____ (1.3a) Is this a vav conversive? _____ (1.3b)

8.1b You need to locate the root, and you have some help:

> וּ____ is a plural verb ending, and וּ____ rarely ends anything except a verb form.

8.1c Since this is not a vav conversive form, the chance that וּ is part of the root, rather than the prefix pronoun, is greatly increased. What consonants are thus the probable root? _____

Root	Stem	Form	Person/Gender/Number	Special Features

What is the stem? _____ (4.2a) What is the form? _____ (4.2a)

You will remember that the third person masculine singular affix has no pronoun element at the end but that the other subject pronouns will be written at the end of the affix forms. In this case, the simple ending וּ____ gives us the third person plural, both masculine and feminine. Compare this third person common plural affix form (3 c. pl.) with the 3 m. pl. prefix form:

Affix Form	Prefix Form
וּ יָדְע	יִ שְׁמְע וּ

Affix Form:
וּ = affix pronoun
יָדְע = root

Prefix Form:
יִ = prefix pronoun
שְׁמְע = root
וּ = prefix complement

8.1d An affix form is normally translated in the past tense in English. (4.2c)

50

> An initial וֹ used with an affix form verb forms a construction often best rendered by the English future tense. For convenient reference, we will call this construction the **vav reversive**.

On the chart, indicate this with "vav rev." in the Special Features column.

יָדַע means _____ Translation of the verb: _____

8.1e   Note the small vertical line to the left of the vowel under the וֹ It is called a **meteg** and indicates a slight hesitation in pronunciation between the vowel and the following consonant. The meteg keeps the syllable open (thus the qamats cannot be a qamats ḥatuf [6.3b]) and shows that the following shewa is a vocal shewa.

8.2   כִּי means _____

8.3   שְׁמִי יהוה

> יָ__ at the end of a singular noun is normally the first person singular suffix.

Suffixes are possessive or object pronouns. (2.9b)   שֵׁם is a noun meaning _____

> A suffix attached to a noun is a possessive pronoun.

שְׁמִי means *my name*. Notice that the vowels of the noun can change when a possessive suffix is added.

8.3a   יהוה means _____ The two-word phrase means _____ (2.10b) _____

8.4   Translation of verse: _____

8.5   Synopsis of Shortening
You have seen that shortening or reduction of vowels at the front of a word can occur under the following circumstances:

1. a masculine singular noun is in construct (5.1c)   בֶּן ← בֵּן
2. a masculine plural noun is in construct (6.3c)   בְּנֵי ← בָּנִים
3. a maqqef ties a word to another word (7.2a)   אֶת־ ← אֵת
4. a suffix is added to a word (8.3)   שְׁמִי ← שֵׁם

51

———

The topic of vowel changes is covered in greater detail in **S 5.1c–5.1c.3**

8.6 For each **ו** in the words below, tell whether the **ו** is a plain conjunction, vav conversive, vav reversive, possessive suffix, object suffix, prefix complement, affix pronoun, part of the root of the word, or plene spelling.

בְּנוֹ		וְהָאֱלֹהִים	
אֵלָיו		חֲמֹרוֹ	
וַיַּחְבֹּשׁ		יוֹם	
הוּא		לוֹ	
וַיֵּדְעוּ		וְכָל	
יוֹסֵף		וַיֹּאמְרוּ	
שָׁמְעוּ		נְעָרָיו	

Assignments

A. Vocabulary: words 1–80.

B. Read aloud lesson sentences 1–20; use 💿 **ב א** tracks 4–7 as necessary.

C. 💿 שַׁבְּחִי track 9: listen to דוֹדִי לִי **Song of Songs 2:16** and **3:6**. דוֹד means *beloved*. What, then, does דוֹדִי לִי mean?

D. Translate the following. From now on, a few sentences will be marked with a ✡ These have elements that are more "challenging." (In other words, they're hard.) Do try to figure them out before looking them up.

1 דָּוִד לֹא יָדַע *1 Kings 1:11*

2 לֹא יָדְעוּ אֶת־יהוה *1 Samuel 2:12*

3 וַיָּבֹאוּ כָל־עַם הָאָרֶץ *2 Kings 11:18*

4 הוּא אֱלֹהֵי הָאֱלֹהִים *Deuteronomy 10:17*

✡5 וְהָיָה יהוה לִי לֵאלֹהִים *Genesis 28:21*

✡6 אֲנִי יהוה הוּא שְׁמִי *Isaiah 42:8*

✡7 כִּי־לֹא־מֶלֶךְ יִשְׂרָאֵל הוּא *1 Kings 22:33*

8 וַיֵּדְעוּ כָל־הָעָם וְכָל־יִשְׂרָאֵל *2 Samuel 3:37*

9 וְאָמְרוּ אֶל־כָּל־אִישׁ יִשְׂרָאֵל *Deuteronomy 27:14*

10 וַיִּתֵּן יהוה לְיִשְׂרָאֵל אֶת־כָּל־הָאָרֶץ *Joshua 21:43*

LESSON 9

———◆———

וְהֵם לֹא יָדְעוּ כִּי שֹׁמֵעַ יוֹסֵף

Genesis 42:23

9.1   וְהֵם Initial וְ means _____ הֵם means *they.*

> הֵם is the 3 m. pl. independent subject pronoun.

9.2a   לֹא יָדְעוּ | לֹא means _____ (4.1a)

9.2b   Verb Analysis יָדְעוּ

Root	Stem	Form	Person/Gender/Number	Special Features

What tense will you use in translation? _____ (4.2c)

Translation of the first phrase: _____

9.3   כִּי שֹׁמֵעַ יוֹסֵף

כִּי means _____

שֹׁמֵעַ has an "extra" vowel at the end to facilitate pronunciation; it is called

_____ (5.4)

9.3a   Verb Analysis שֹׁמֵעַ

Root	Stem	Form	Person/Gender/Number	Special Features

שׁמע means _____ What is the stem? _____ (1.4a)

Is the form prefix? _____ Is the form affix? _____ (It is useful when determining form to ask these two questions first.)

> In the Qal stem, ḥolem וֹ or ֵ after the first root letter indicates the **participle** form.

Write "participle" in the Form column. Participles function as nouns and adjectives (thus they can take the definite article and prepositions) as well as verbs. Participles have noun endiNGs. Where there is no extra endiNG, the participle is masculine singular, as it is here. Participles have no person (no pronouns for first, second, or third person), but they modify nouns and pronouns. In the PGN column write "m. sg."

9.3b   Many students mistakenly believe that all participles in English end in "-ing" and conversely that all words ending in "-ing" are participles. Neither statement is true. Because participles may be used in verb clauses or as nouns or adjectives, the appropriate translation must make use of syntactical clues and context.

Let us first consider our lesson phrase שֹׁמֵעַ יוֹסֵף

יוֹסֵף is a name, *Joseph*. The participle modifies the noun Joseph. In this simple phrase the participle provides the action, the verbal component. You can translate: *Joseph was listening* or *Joseph is listening*. The tense will be decided by the main verb of the verse. Other possible translations exist for this construction, but this will suffice for the moment.

Sometimes the participle is used in a construction as a noun. A hypothetical phrase, here featuring the participle with the definite article, might be:

יוֹסֵף הַשֹּׁמֵעַ דִּבֵּר   *Joseph, the listener, spoke*

Joseph, the one who heard, spoke

Joseph, who was listening, spoke

Again, the larger context and syntax of the verse would help us decide on the translation (and a more exact description of the function of the participle). Whether used as verbal action or as a noun, <u>the participle always involves someone doing something</u>. Frequently you will be helped by having a noun or pronoun in the immediate vicinity of the participle, and will remember this rule.

> The participle never stands for the action of the verb in the abstract.

That means that the participle of שמע for example, would never mean the act of listening as in "listening is an art."

9.4 Translation of verse: _____

9.5 Extra Grammar

To identify the Qal participle, you must look for the ḥolem after the first root letter. Remember, this vowel can be written two ways in Hebrew: וֹ and ֹ Thus two spellings are possible for the Qal participle. For example:

defectiva	plene
שֹׁמֵעַ	שׁוֹמֵעַ

9.5a For hollow verbs (verbs whose middle letter is the vowel וֹ ו or ֵ ֵ [6.1a]), there is an irregular participle form. In this case the 3 m. sg. affix and the m. sg. participle are identical in the Qal: בָּא can be either the 3 m. sg. affix or the m. sg. participle.

Three hints can help you decide on the form used:

1. You have a participle if the ambiguous form is combined with another participle.

Joshua 6:1 אֵין יוֹצֵא וְאֵין בָּא

  ambiguous   regular

no one <u>was going out</u> and no one <u>was coming in</u>

2. You most likely have a participle if the ambiguous form is combined with an independent pronoun or a pronoun attached to הִנֵּה (10.3b)

Exodus 3:13 אָנֹכִי בָא אֶל־בְּנֵי יִשְׂרָאֵל

I <u>am coming</u> to the children of Israel

3. You have a participle if the definite article is attached to the ambiguous form, since the affix cannot be combined with the definite article.

Psalms 118:26 [בָּרוּךְ *blessed* (adj.)] בָּרוּךְ הַבָּא בְּשֵׁם יהוה

blessed is <u>he who comes</u> in the name of the Lord

Assignments

A. Vocabulary: words 1–90.

B. ⊙ ב א track 8: read Genesis 22:1–4.

C. 🔊 track 10: learn **Song of Songs 2:8** קוֹל דּוֹדִי שַׁבְּחִי. What is the form of בָּא in the first part of the verse? How will you make your decision? You should be able to translate the verse up to the atnaḥ (the accent that looks like ◡).

D. Analyze the following verbs:

הֹלֵךְ וְשָׁמַע הַנֹּתֵן וַיֹּאמֶר יוֹדֵעַ

E. Translate:

(In verses 4, 6, 7, and 9, be able to explain whether בָּא is a participle or an affix form.)

1 אֲנִי הֹלֵךְ אֵלָיו *2 Samuel 12:23*

✡2 וְשָׁמַע הַשֹּׁמֵעַ וְאָמַר *2 Samuel 17:9*

3 וַיָּמָת יוֹסֵף . . . וְכֹל הַדּוֹר [*generation* דּוֹר 6.1a וַיָּמָת] *Exodus 1:6*

4 וְלֹא־בָא שְׁמוּאֵל הַגִּלְגָּל *1 Samuel 13:8*

✡5 כִּי זֶה הַיּוֹם אֲשֶׁר נָתַן יְהוָה אֶת־סִיסְרָא בְּיָדֶךְ *Judges 4:14*

[בְּיָדֶךְ *into your hand*]

6 הוּא־בָא עַד־לֶחִי *Judges 15:14*

7 דּוֹר הֹלֵךְ וְדוֹר בָּא (דּוֹר ⟶ *generation*) *Qohelet 1:4*

8 זֶה־הַיּוֹם עָשָׂה יְהוָה *Psalms 118:24*

9 בָּא אִישׁ הָאֱלֹהִים *2 Kings 8:7*

10 כִּי־יוֹדֵעַ יְהוָה דֶּרֶךְ צַדִּיקִים [*righteous ones* צַדִּיקִים] *Psalms 1:6*

11 הֵם יָצְאוּ אֶת־הָעִיר *Genesis 44:4*

✡12 וַיִּקְרָא שֵׁם הָעִיר כְּשֵׁם בְּנוֹ *Genesis 4:17*

13 בְּנֵי־יִשְׂרָאֵל לֹא־שָׁמְעוּ אֵלַי [אֵלַי ⟶ + 1 c. sg. suffix אֶל] *Exodus 6:12*

LESSON 10

וַיָּבֹא אֶל־אָבִיו וַיֹּאמֶר אָבִי וַיֹּאמֶר הִנֶּנִּי

Genesis 27:18

10.1   וַיָּבֹא אֶל־אָבִיו

10.1a   Verb Analysis וַיָּבֹא (1.3b, 1.3c, 6.1a)

Root	Stem	Form	Person/Gender/Number	Special Features

10.1b   אֶל means _____ In אָבִיו | אָב is a noun meaning *father*. The ו____ at the end of the word is a _____ meaning _____ (2.9b) What kind of suffix is this? _____ אָבִיו means *his father*. Note the י between the noun and suffix. אָב has some irregular forms and is one of only two nouns, which in the singular require י before a suffix.

Translate the whole first clause: _____

10.2   וַיֹּאמֶר אָבִי

10.2a   Verb Analysis וַיֹּאמֶר (1.4)

Root	Stem	Form	Person/Gender/Number	Special Features

10.2b   אָבִי You should recognize the same noun you had just above: _____ Again the word has a suffix. What are its components? _____ Which person, gender, and number is it? _____ (8.3) Note that this time there is no connecting י between the noun and the suffix.

אָבִי means _____

57

10.2c Biblical Hebrew does not use quotation marks (or any other familiar punctuation marks). Sometimes it is difficult to tell where a speech begins. In this case, אָבִי is <u>what</u> he said, not the noun subject of the verb. This is clear from the larger context of the story. This context is the only clue you will have in deciding the structure of similar verses (unless you later memorize the whole accentual system).

10.2d Notice the ֡ under אָבִי This mark, called **atnaḥ**, indicates a break in the verse or sentence, equivalent to the break we mark with a period or semicolon. It indicates that the next word begins a new phrase, and it is one of the few clues you will have in punctuating a Hebrew verse in the Bible.

10.3 וַיֹּאמֶר הִנֶּנִּי

10.3a The new phrase begins with a familiar verb. וַיֹּאמֶר means _____

10.3b הִנֶּנִּי

הִנֵּה is a word that cannot be classed as either noun or verb. It is called a **predicator of existence**, emphasizing presence and immediacy; we have no comparable word function in English. _Behold, here_, and _now_ are all acceptable translations. When a suffix is added to this word—which happens frequently—the final ה is lost. נִי____ or נִי____ is a first person singular suffix. So הִנֶּנִּי is made up of two components; it can be translated _here I am_.

Compare this word with אָבִי which also has a first person singular suffix. Can you think of a reason why the suffixes are different? Nouns and most prepositions take י__ Verbs, particles like הִנֵּה and a few prepositions take נִי____

10.4 Translation of verse: _____

_____

Assignments

A. Vocabulary: words 1–100. Test yourself with ⊙אֵלֶּה הַדְּבָרִים tracks 3–12.

B. ⊙א ב track 8: read Genesis 22:1–8.

   ⊙שַׁבְּחוּ track 11: learn הִנֵּה מַה־טּוֹב **Psalm 133:1**.

C. Translate:

         1   הִנֵּה בְנֵי־הַמֶּלֶךְ בָּאוּ   _2 Samuel 13:35_

         ✡2   הִנְנִי־בָא   _Zechariah 2:14 (2:10 in some English Bibles)_

         ✡3   וְעַתָּה הִנְנִי הוֹלֵךְ לְעַמִּי   _Numbers 24:14_

4   הִנְנִי נֹתֵן לוֹ אֶת־בְּרִיתִי [covenant בְּרִית *Numbers 25:12*

5   וַיֹּאמֶר מֹשֶׁה מֹשֶׁה וַיֹּאמֶר הִנֵּנִי *Exodus 3:4*

6   וַיָּבֹא יַעֲקֹב אֶל־יִצְחָק אָבִיו *Genesis 35:27*

7   וְהִנֵּה אִישׁ מִבְּנֵי יִשְׂרָאֵל בָּא *Numbers 25:6*

REVIEW AND DRILL 3

I. Chart and translate the following verbs:

יָדְעוּ	שָׁמְעוּ	וַיְדַבְּרוּ
אָמְרוּ	וְהָלְכוּ	נָתְנוּ
וַיֵּדַע	בָּאוּ	יָדַע
שׁוֹמֵעַ	אָמַר	הוֹלֵךְ
בָּא	נָתַן	וַיִּשְׁלַח

II. Translate:

1   יהוה הוּא הָאֱלֹהִים   *1 Kings 18:39*

2   וּמֹשֶׁה עָלָה אֶל־הָאֱלֹהִים וַיִּקְרָא אֵלָיו יהוה מִן־הָהָר   *Exodus 19:3*
    (For help with וּמֹשֶׁה see 1.3a.)

3   אֶרֶץ כְּנַעַן אֲשֶׁר־אֲנִי נֹתֵן לִבְנֵי יִשְׂרָאֵל   *Numbers 13:2*

✡4   וְגַם הִנֵּה־הוּא יֹצֵא   *Exodus 4:14*

5   וַיֹּאמְרוּ לֹא־הוּא   *Jeremiah 5:12*

6   הוּא הַלֶּחֶם אֲשֶׁר נָתַן יהוה   [לֶחֶם *bread, food*]   *Exodus 16:15*

7   לַיהוה הָאָרֶץ   *Psalms 24:1*

8   הַלֶּחֶם אֲשֶׁר־הוּא אוֹכֵל   *Genesis 39:6*

✡9   וְאֵלָיו הוּא נֹשֵׂא אֶת־נַפְשׁוֹ   *Deuteronomy 24:15*

10   כִּי־יָדַע כָּל־יִשְׂרָאֵל   *2 Samuel 17:10*

11   כִּי אֶת־כָּל־הָאָרֶץ אֲשֶׁר־אַתָּה רֹאֶה לְךָ אֶתְּנֶנָּה   *Genesis 13:15*
    [לְךָ אֶתְּנֶנָּה *to you I will give it*]

✡12   אֱלֹהִים עִמְּךָ בְּכֹל אֲשֶׁר־אַתָּה עֹשֶׂה   *Genesis 21:22*
    [2 m. sg. object pronoun + עִם ⟷ עִמְּךָ]

III. Translate from English to Hebrew:

I am going	they entered	and he knew
he is walking	and they will know	

1. And he said, "My father, here I am."

2. The Lord is God. (two ways of saying this)

3. The earth is mine.

4. Here was the man of God coming on his way.

5. For my name is in (over) all the earth.

6. And God gave a covenant [בְּרִית] to Israel.

LESSON 11

וַיֵּצְאוּ לָלֶכֶת אַרְצָה כְּנַעַן וַיָּבֹאוּ אַרְצָה כְּנָעַן

Genesis 12:5

11.1 Verb Analysis **וַיֵּצְאוּ**

Root	Stem	Form	Person/Gender/Number	Special Features

How do you determine the root? _____ (3.1) Where and what is the missing letter? _____ (3.1) What are the components of the PGN? _____

Translation: _____

11.2 לָלֶכֶת

11.2a You need to separate at least one letter from the word to find the root. The root cannot be לֶלֶךְ because a root cannot start with the same two letters. (7.1a) This means that the initial ל must be something other than a root letter. It is the preposition meaning *to* or *for*. However, the letters that are left לֶכֶת do not constitute a root either. ת____ is frequently a special ending. In this case, it is the indicator of a 1st י infinitive. These infinitives drop the י of the root and end in ת Here, though, we are dealing with the exceptional case that we had in Lesson 3 where the first root letter is ה and so the root is הלך

11.2b Verb Analysis **לָלֶכֶת**

Root	Stem	Form	Person/Gender/Number	Special Features

62

וַיֵּצְאוּ לָלֶכֶת אַרְצָה כְּנַעַן וַיָּבֹאוּ אַרְצָה כְּנָעַן

<u>Note</u>: In English, "to" before a verb form usually indicates the infinitive. In Hebrew, a prefixed ל is not an integral part of the infinitive form, but when present it imparts a sense of purpose. In the Special Features column, put "preposition, ל" As in English, <u>Hebrew infinitives have no PGN</u>. What is the stem? _____

11.3 אַרְצָה כְּנַעַן

אֶרֶץ means _____ כְּנַעַן means *Canaan*.

Notice the הָ on the end of אֶרֶץ

> An extra, <u>unaccented</u> final הָ on a noun can be added to denote motion toward a place and is called a ה **directive**. It is usually translated *to* or *toward*.

What is the relationship of אַרְצָה to כְּנַעַן _____ (5.1b) Is כְּנַעַן definite? _____ (5.2a) Is the chain definite or indefinite? _____

Note that the ה directive can be placed on the construct noun just as any other preposition could be placed on the front of that noun.

Translate the phrase: _____

11.4 Verb Analysis וַיָּבֹאוּ

Root	Stem	Form	Person/Gender/Number	Special Features

11.5 Translation of the whole verse: _____

_____

Assignments

A. Vocabulary: words 1–105.

B. ⊙ב א track 8: read **Genesis 22:1–14**.

  ⊙ שַׁבְּחִי track 12: learn וּפָרַצְתָּ **Genesis 28:14**; note the four ה directives. Review הִנֵּי מַה־טּוֹב **Psalm 133:1** (track 11). Analyze שֶׁבֶת

C. Translate the sentences and analyze the verbs:

✡1   וַיֵּלְכוּ וַיָּבֹאוּ הָהָרָה [mountain הַר]   *Joshua 2:22*

2   וַיֵּצֵא לָלֶכֶת לְדַרְכּוֹ   *Judges 19:27*

3   יָצְאוּ מִן־הָעָם   *Exodus 16:27*

4   וַיָּבֹא עַד־הַיַּרְדֵּן וִיהוּדָה בָּא הַגִּלְגָּלָה [and Judah וִיהוּדָה]   *2 Samuel 19:16*

5   וַיֵּלְכוּ בְּנֵי־רְאוּבֵן ... לָלֶכֶת אֶל־אֶרֶץ הַגִּלְעָד   *Joshua 22:9*

6   וְכָל־הָעָם יָצְאוּ   *2 Samuel 18:4*

LESSON 12

וַיַּרְא כָּל־הָעָם וַיִּפְּלוּ עַל־פְּנֵיהֶם

1 Kings 18:39

12.1   Verb Analysis וַיַּרְא

Root	Stem	Form	Person/Gender/Number	Special Features

Only the root is a problem. Under what letter do you look for the clue to the missing letter?

_____ (3.1)

> When any vowel other than ◌ֵ (tsere) or ◌ָ (qamats) appears under the prefix pronoun,
>
> the missing letter is at the end of the root and is always ה

12.2   כָּל־הָעָם

הָעָם means _____ (4.5b) The relationship of this phrase to the first verb is

_____ Note that here "people" is treated as a collective noun and so has a

singular verb—thus emphasizing unity.

12.3   Verb Analysis וַיִּפְּלוּ

Root	Stem	Form	Person/Gender/Number	Special Features

What rule do you use to find the root? _____ (7.1a) You may be wondering

why the missing-letter rules weren't used here, why the root isn't פלה which is a rare, but

perfectly good, Biblical Hebrew root. The missing-letter rules come into play only when a letter

---

65

is <u>completely</u> missing. Assimilated letters leave a "footprint" behind by means of the dagesh forte. Always check for such a "footprint dagesh" before trying the missing-letter rules.[1]

נָפַל means *fall*.

12.3a The subject of וַיִּפְּלוּ is "they," which in this section of the verse focuses attention on the individual. Such switching between singular and plural, each with its distinct emphasis, is not at all uncommon in Biblical Hebrew.

12.4   פְּנֵיהֶם

> הֶם‏ַ‏ is the 3 m. pl. possessive or objective suffix. But if the word ends in a
>
> consonant, the suffix may be spelled ‏ָם‏

Compare with the independent subject pronoun in 9.1. When you remove the suffix, you are left with פְּנֵי Notice the similarity to בְּנֵי in 6.3c. The absolute form of בְּנֵי is _____ _____ So the absolute form of פְּנֵי will have the endiNG _____

פָּנִים means *face, faces*. Like אֱלֹהִים (2.4), almost without exception it is the plural of this noun that is used in Hebrew.

12.5 Translate the verse: _____

12.6 Extra Grammar

פָּנִים is frequently used to form prepositions. This word in its construct form פְּנֵי combines most frequently with the preposition לְ ⟶ לִפְנֵי Literally this combination means *to (the) face of*. In its present compound form, this word is equivalent to our preposition *before* or *in the presence of*.

Exodus 6:12 וַיְדַבֵּר מֹשֶׁה לִפְנֵי יהוה

and Moses spoke in the presence of the Lord

It is common in Hebrew to combine prepositions to create new prepositions. Thus the preposition מִן (3.4b) can be combined with לִפְנֵי to form a new preposition meaning *away from (the presence of)*:

Genesis 4:16 וַיֵּצֵא קַיִן מִלִּפְנֵי יהוה

and Cain went out from the presence of the Lord

---

1. The missing-letter rules can be found in Lessons 3.1, 6.1a, and 12.1.

וַיַּרְא כָּל־הָעָם וַיִּפְּלוּ עַל־פְּנֵיהֶם

Assignments

A. Vocabulary: words 1–110.

B. Using **א ב** 📀 track 8 if necessary, read Genesis 22:1–14.

On 📀**שַׁבְּחִי** review your songs and listen to אַל תַּשְׁלִיכֵנִי track 13. The words of this song are taken from Psalms.

C. Analyze these verbs:

יוֹצֵא   וַיְדַבְּרוּ   וַיָּבֹא   רָאָה   וַיִּרְאוּ

D. Translate:

1   וַיַּרְא־שָׁם אִשָּׁה   *Judges 16:1*

2   וַיְדַבְּרוּ לִפְנֵי מֹשֶׁה   *Numbers 36:1*

3   וַיָּבֹא אֶל־הַר הָאֱלֹהִים חֹרֵבָה   *Exodus 3:1*

4   וּשְׁמוּאֵל רָאָה אֶת־שָׁאוּל   *1 Samuel 9:17*

5   וַיִּרְאוּ אֵת אֱלֹהֵי יִשְׂרָאֵל   *Exodus 24:10*

6   וַיִּפְּלוּ עַל־פְּנֵיהֶם אָרְצָה   *Judges 13:20*

✡7   כִּי־הוּא יוֹצֵא וָבָא לִפְנֵיהֶם   *1 Samuel 18:16*

8   וַיֵּצֵא יוֹסֵף מִלִּפְנֵי פַרְעֹה   *Genesis 41:46*

✡9   וַיִּרְאוּ הַשֹּׁמְרִים אִישׁ יוֹצֵא מִן־הָעִיר   *Judges 1:24*

REVIEW AND DRILL 4

I. Referring to Lesson 12 if necessary, write the Qal prefix with vav conversive in the 3 m. sg. and 3 m. pl. for each of the following verbs.

(1) אמר

(3) הלך

שמע

(6) בוא

(7) נתן

(3) ידע

(12) ראה

(3) יצא

These verb forms are at the top of the list in frequency and are the key to analyzing most of the other regular and irregular prefix forms. Memorize them!

II. Write the Qal affix 3 m. sg. and 3 c. pl. for the following verbs. If you need help, for 3 m. sg. see 4.2a; for 3 c. pl. see 8.1c. The Qal affix is much more regular than the prefix. All you need here are the two sample forms listed to obtain the vowel pattern.

אמר

הלך

שמע

נתן

ידע

יצא

Note that יצא uses ◌ָ under the second root letter rather than ◌ַ in the 3 m. sg. This will be the case for every strong verb whose third root letter is either א or ה

III. For דבר write the Pi`el prefix 3 m. sg. ⎵ ⎵ ⎵ — 3 m. pl. —— ⎵ ◌ֲ ⎵ and the affix 3 m. sg. ⎵ ⎵ ⎵ 3 c. pl. —— ⎵ ◌ֲ ⎵ This verb also is used over 1000 times in the Hebrew Bible, and these are its most frequent forms. Memorize them.

68

IV. Write the Qal m. sg. participle form (9.3a) for:

(9.5a) בּוֹא   שׁמע   ידע (5.4)   הלך   אמר   נתן

V. Make up 20 construct chains using the following information:
Construct forms:

אֱלֹהֵי   מֶלֶךְ   עַם   דְּבַר   בֶּן   אֶרֶץ   אֲבִי   שֵׁם

Absolute forms:

אֱלֹהִים   יהוה   מֶלֶךְ   עַם   יִשְׂרָאֵל   אָב   דָּוִד

Identify each chain as definite or indefinite.

VI. Turn to your Hebrew Bible. Read Exodus 6:12–13 aloud. You will notice that some of the letters look slightly different in print from our script, and you will see many dots and lines in addition to the vowels. These are part of an elaborate accent system devised by the Masoretes. Many of these accents need not concern you at this stage. Each of these signs marks the syllable of the word that you must accent. As you read the verses aloud, check to see if you are accenting the proper syllable. Two marks are useful to learn at this stage: ‿ **atnah** occurs at the main pause in almost every verse in the Bible, roughly in the middle. You can think of it as equivalent to a period, semicolon, or important comma. (10.2d) Locate the atnaḥ in both verses here, and read them again with a pause at the atnaḥ. The final accent in a verse, usually on the last word, is ‿ called **silluq** and is followed by ׃‿ **sof passuq**, marking the end of the verse.

verse 12: שְׂפָתָיִם׃

verse 13: מִצְרָיִם׃

Translate the verses. Vocabulary you need:

saying (made up of what two elements?)	לֵאמֹר
how?	אֵיךְ
to bring forth	לְהוֹצִיא
and he charged them	וַיְצַוֵּם
uncircumcised lips	עֲרַל שְׂפָתָיִם

THE VERB

In these first twelve lessons, you have learned how to abstract a root and how to conjugate various roots in specific PGNs by changing vowels, adding letters, and so forth. You have expanded the pattern you learned with וַיֹּאמֶר and שָׁמַע to other verbs so that at this point you should be able to parse almost any 3 m. sg. or pl. Qal prefix or affix verb in the language. But since there are still stems, forms, and PGNs you have not studied, the following paragraphs will provide an overview of the verbal system so that you can become familiar with terminology as the various topics are presented.

Roots: All the Semitic languages build on triconsonantal and biconsonantal roots. There is disagreement as to whether the two-letter or the three-letter root is more primary in the emergence of these languages. Though many common words have only two letters and cannot be traced back to three-letter roots, all verbal roots are considered to have three letters and must be sought in the lexicon under the hypothetical triliteral root. The "missing letter" verbs represent three types of verbs in which only two strong letters are consistently present. In some instances, there is a strong case for arguing their derivation from three letters; in other cases, there is not. Each of the "missing letter" classes has its own designation. Verbs with the pattern of בּוֹא שִׂים or שׁוּב are called **hollow** verbs, because of the disappearing middle letter in some stems (e.g., Hif`il and Nif`al) and forms (e.g., affix and participle). Another way to describe such verbs is to identify the place where the weak letter occurs by number, and then the weak letter: **1st** י means "a verb with י in the first position." **3rd** ה means "a verb with ה in the third position." An older system accomplishes the same thing by using a paradigm verb פָּעַל in its designations. Any verb can be described by using פ ע and ל as equivalent to 1, 2, 3.

3	2	1
ל	ע	פ
ב	שׁ	י

In יֵשֵׁב the י occurs in the פ position, שׁ in the ע position, and ב in the ל position. יֵשֵׁב falls into the class of פ י (peh-yod) verbs. Other weak classes include ע ו (ayin-vav) and ל ה (lamed-heh). In this book, the former system (1st י etc.) is used; however, many paradigm charts use the older system, and you should understand this terminology as well.

Stems: Also characteristic of Semitic languages is the modification of the root meaning of verbs by the addition of letters (more properly, morphemes) at the beginning of or within the word. The modification patterns are similar within the Semitic language group, but Hebrew uses only four of the "families" or "systems" of stems. These modifications are identified in two ways: descriptively and with an invented name. For example, the most basic stem, closest to the root itself, we can describe as having no augment, only a set of characteristic vowels in each of its forms; or we can call it **Qal**, which is the name given this stem by classical grammarians of the Middle Ages. Qal is an appropriate name for this stem since it means "light," and was given to the pattern that had no additions. The other stem names were derived by these same grammarians by using the sound of the 3 m. sg. affix form of a sample verb in each family of modifications. Unfortunately the verb they chose for this honor was not a regular verb; it was פָּעַל and the ע cannot take a dagesh. This meant that while the names bear a relation to regular verbs in some stems, the names for the family in which the middle root letter is doubled are of little aid to the student. However, the system took hold and is now part of the shorthand terminology needed in studying Hebrew. Here is how the system works:

Stem	Name	Description	Meaning	Example
פָּעַל	**Qal**	simple stem	basic	פָּקַד
פִּעֵל	**Pi`el**	doubled middle root letter. In sample verb, doubling can't take place, so the vowel before ע is often lengthened	intensive, denominative, privative (15.6)	פִּקֵד
פֻּעַל	Pu`al	doubled middle root letter ◌ֻ under 1st root letter	passive of Pi`el (45.3)	פֻּקַד
הִפְעִיל	**Hif`il**	ה added before root	causative (28.2)	הִפְקִיד
הָפְעַל	Hof`al	ה + ◌ֳ ו or ◌ֻ following	passive of Hif`il (44.1)	הָפְקַד
נִפְעַל	**Nif`al**	נ added before root	passive, reflexive occurs mostly for verbs used basically in Qal (47.4)	נִפְקַד

Stems related to the Pi`el system

הִתְפָּעֵל	Hitpa'el	prefixed ה + infixed ת and doubled middle root letter	reflexive, passive, iterative (52.2; 53.1)	הִתְפַּקֵד
פֹּלֵל	Pol`el (+ Pol`al)	These are rather infrequent, and occur with verbs having only two strong letters		
הִתְפֹּלֵל	Hitpol`el			
פִּלְפֵּל	Pilp`el			

You have studied verbs only in the Qal and Pi`el systems so far and will not be studying the Hif`il or Nif`al systematically for some time yet. However, you should memorize the material in this chart now, especially since you will be studying Biblical passages while learning grammar.

Although the various stems are usually identified with specific meaning changes from the Qal, some things must be remembered about the whole system:

1. Few verbs in Biblical Hebrew occur in every stem.

2. Not every verb meaning seems to "fit" every stem in which it occurs. So, for example, although the Hif`il stem generally seems to yield a causative or transitive meaning, it does not always do so. And, of course, subtleties of meaning of the various stems may be lost in translation.

One further problem in terminology: the modification of the root system, which is so marked a characteristic of Semitic languages, is quite variously named. Besides stem, this same phenomenon is sometimes termed theme, conjugation, or pattern. The Hebrew term is בִּנְיָן

Forms: To use the term form for this part of the verb classification scheme admittedly is not precise. The stem modifications just described could as easily be called forms as the patterns about to be described. Most often, however, form is used by grammarians in describing the various patterns that result when a verb is conjugated with a subject pronoun within a stem system. In Hebrew, there are five of these forms:

affix   **prefix**   **imperative**   **participle**   **infinitive**

Attention has so far been devoted primarily to the prefix and affix forms. Notice that we do not say that the prefix and affix are future or past tenses, but only that we translate them in certain situations as English future or past tenses. Hebrew (and other Semitic languages) in the classical period did not use a tense system; rather the prefix and affix represent aspects of action.

Prefix forms without vav conversive present ongoing, incomplete action.

Prefix forms with vav conversive present completed action or temporal sequence.

Affix forms present completed action or description of state or condition.

The practical differences between the Hebrew system and our own must be absorbed. The prefix and affix forms cover a wide range of tenses in English, not always neatly divided between the two forms in Hebrew:

שָׁמַע	can mean	*he heard*	
		he has heard	completed actions
		he had heard	
		he will have heard	
יִשְׁמַע	can mean	*he will hear*	
		he hears, he is hearing	ongoing actions
		he would hear (constantly)	
		he was hearing, he used to hear	
אָהֵב	can mean	*he loved*	completed action
		he had loved	
		he loves	describing
		he would have loved	a state of being

The **vav conversive** with the prefix form was originally a separate form of the verb, a preterite conveying completed action. Before the classical Biblical period, however, this form had fallen together with the prefix form, so that for regular verbs in most stems, the prefix form is the same with or without the vav conversive. Hollow, 1st י and 3rd ה verbs have differences between the prefix form alone and the prefix form with vav conversive attached. Students should bear in mind that this form, like the other prefix and affix forms, has a broad range of translational possibilities because of syntactic variations.

Note: וּ + prefix form does not convert the tense.

The **vav reversive** arose by analogy to the vav conversive forms and does not represent an originally separate aspect.[1] While any וַ◌ can be identified as a vav conversive, there is no such clear marker for vav reversive. It is וְ + affix, which is usually translated as a future but can also be used to indicate repetitive action in the past.

1. vav reversive occurs only with the affix.

2. vav reversive has no unique marker. It is וְ + affix form.

As is often the case, the context will give indications of which translation is to be preferred.
For a range of uses of וְ see **S 43.3**.
Below is a simple synopsis:

שָׁמַע	*he heard*
וְשָׁמַע	*and he will hear, and he used to hear*
יִשְׁמַע	*he will hear*
וַיִּשְׁמַע	*and he heard*
וְיִשְׁמַע	*and he will hear*

Identify the stem (Qal, Piʿel, Nifʿal, Hifʿil, or Hitpaʿel) of each verb below and the root:

Root	Stem	Verb	Root	Stem	Verb
_____	_____	יָדְעוּ	_____	_____	נֶאֱחַז
_____	_____	הִתְבָּרְכוּ	_____	_____	יַחֲלֵק
_____	_____	וַיִּשָּׂא	_____	_____	שִׁלַּח
_____	_____	יָלַד	_____	_____	שִׁבְּרוּ
_____	_____	נִשְׁמְרוּ	_____	_____	הִתְהַלֵּךְ
_____	_____	שָׁמְרוּ	_____	_____	הִקְשִׁירוּ

---

1. For a more nuanced discussion on the formation of vav reversive, see Waltke and O'Connor, 32.1.2.

Give a possible translation for each of the augmented forms:

בּרך *bless*	הִתְבָּרְכוּ	_____
	נִבְרְכוּ	_____
שָׁבַר *break*	שִׁבֵּר	_____
קָטַר *burn*	הִקְטִֿירוּ	_____
שָׁפַך *pour out*	נִשְׁפַּך	_____
לבשׁ *dress*	הִלְבִּישׁ	_____
	נִלְבַּשׁ	_____
בּוא *come*	הֵבִיא	_____
בּנה *build*	נִבְנָה	_____
	הִתְבַּנָה	_____
	בָּנָה	_____

LESSON 13

וַיֹּאמֶר הִנְנִי כִּי קָרָאתָ לִי

1 Samuel 3:8

13.1 וַיֹּאמֶר means _____

13.2 הִנְנִי means _____ (10.3b) יִ___ is a _____ meaning
_____ What is the relationship between the first two words of this verse? _____
_____ (10.2c) After וַיֹּאמֶר or וַיְדַבֵּר you must learn to watch for **direct
speech**, such as we have here. Where does the speech end? In Biblical stories, the appearance of
another third person verb, often with vav conversive, signals the resumption of the narrative.

13.3 כִּי קָרָאתָ לִי
כִּי means _____ קָרָאתָ is a verb. The stem and form are likely to be _____
_____ because under the first root consonant there is a _____ (4.2a) In all affix forms
except 3 m. sg., a pronoun will be found _____

ךָ___ is the second masculine singular pronoun (2 m. sg.) in the affix form.

Root	Stem	Form	Person/Gender/Number	Special Features

קָרָא means _____ לִי means _____ (7.2c, 8.3)

13.4 Translation of the verse: _____
_____

13.5 Extra Grammar
It is now time to learn how to conjugate a verb in the Qal affix in all persons, genders, and numbers. We are using פָּקַד (which means *visit*) as the paradigm verb because it is a **strong verb**.

That means that all three of its root letters will always be present and each of them is able to receive a dagesh. We also chose it because it is one of the few verbs that is attested in Biblical Hebrew in all seven basic stems: Qal, Nif`al, Pi`el, Pu`al, Hitpa`el, Hif`il, and Hof`al.

Reminder:

The regular vowel of the Qal affix is qamats ָ under the first root letter.

Qal Affix Strong Verb

3 m. sg.	פָּקַד	3 c. pl.	פָּקְדוּ
3 f. sg.	פָּקְדָה		
2 m. sg.	פָּקַדְתָּ	2 m. pl.	פְּקַדְתֶּם ←
2 f. sg.	פָּקַדְתְּ	2 f. pl.	פְּקַדְתֶּן ←
1 c. sg.	פָּקַדְתִּי	1 c. pl.	פָּקַדְנוּ

13.5a Memorize the strong verb and then the variations on its patterns.

13.5b Notice how regular the vowels under the root letters stay as the different pronouns are added. The arrows point to the places where a vowel change takes place from the stem pattern. In both cases, the qamats has become a shewa.

13.5c Each dagesh in this paradigm is a dagesh lene. (3.3) Look at the 3 f. sg. and 3 c. pl. forms. You might expect such a dagesh in the ד because it follows a shewa ְ But this is a vocal shewa indicated by the meteg (8.1e) preceding it, and therefore a dagesh lene is not required. Remember that dagesh lene affects only pronunciation and there are a number of factors that can influence its appearance or nonappearance for that matter.

13.6 Variations on the strong verb pattern:

In the terminology of this book, a verb that shows all three root letters but has different vowels from the strong verb pattern (13.5) is said to be a **variation** on the strong pattern (roots with gutturals, e.g.). The term **weak** will apply to verbs that do not show all three root letters in each form or stem: 1st י 1st נ 3rd ה and hollows. The landmark signs (such as qamats ָ under the first root letter for the Qal affix) will usually be seen in variations of the strong verb and in weak verbs.

<u>Note</u>: Some grammars refer to the affix form as the perfect, perfective, or suffixed form.

13.6a Variation: **3rd** א

A verb like קָרָא which ends in א follows the pattern of the strong verb in the Qal affix except for three small changes:

1. Shewa is not written under the **א**

2. Dagesh lene cannot stand in the affixed pronoun

3. The second vowel in the stem pattern will be ־ָ rather than ־ַ

2 m. sg.

Strong	3rd **א**
	↓ 2nd vowel ־ָ
פָּקַדְתָּ	קָרָאתָ
	no dagesh ↑ ↑ no shewa

13.6b Variation: **1st guttural**

Verbs like **אָמַר** **הָלַךְ** or **עָבַד** which begin with a guttural normally do not take simple shewa under the first root letter. A composite shewa ־ֲ is therefore used in the 2 m. pl. and 2 f. pl. forms.

2 m. pl.

Strong	1st Guttural
פְּקַדְתֶּם	הֲלַכְתֶּם
	↑ composite shewa

13.6c Most verbs are regular in the Qal affix, following 13.5 or the pattern of **קָרָא** or **הָלַךְ** Two types of verbs that are not are hollow verbs (like **בּוֹא**) and verbs ending in **ה** These will be discussed in detail later. Complete paradigms for each type of variation and weak verb are given in the back of the book.

13.7 Referring to the paradigm for the strong verb in 13.5 and the variations noted in 13.6a and b, fill in the chart for the following verbs:

Qal Affix 3rd א

3 m. sg.	נָשָׂא	3 c. pl.	נָשְׂ א ___	
3 f. sg.	נָשְׂ א ___			
2 m. sg.	___ ⌴ ⌴ ⌴	2 m. pl.	___ ⌴ ⌴ ⌴ ⟵	
2 f. sg.	___ ⌴ ⌴ ⌴	2 f. pl.	___ ⌴ ⌴ ⌴ ⟵	
1 c. sg.	___ ⌴ ⌴ ⌴	1 c. pl.	___ ⌴ ⌴ ⌴	

Qal Affix 1st Guttural

3 m. sg.	עָ בַ ד	3 c. pl.	⎯ ⎵ ֖ ֖
3 f. sg.	⎯ ⎵ ֔ ֖		
2 m. sg.	⎯ ⎵ ⎵ ⎵	2 m. pl.	עֲ בַ דְ תֶּם ←
2 f. sg.	⎯ ⎵ ⎵ ⎵	2 f. pl.	⎯ ⎵ ⎵ ⎵ ←
1 c. sg.	⎯ ⎵ ⎵ ⎵	1 c. pl.	⎯ ⎵ ⎵ ⎵

Assignments

A. Vocabulary: words 1–115.

B. Memorize the paradigm for the Qal affix of the strong verb by listening to פָּקַד on ⊙ ב א track
9. Learn the variations for 1st guttural and 3rd א These verbs can be found conjugated in full in
Verb Charts A, B, and K, respectively.

C. Write out the Qal affix conjugation for:

הלך   אמר   ידע   יצא   קרא

D. Read and translate Genesis 22:1–2. During the course of Lessons 13–17 listen to and read out loud
the assigned verses on ⊙ ב א (track 8).

Each lesson from now on will have a reading assignment with it. If you can read the assigned
verses in your Hebrew Bible without further assistance, great. If you need help, refer to the appropriate section in Glosses to the Readings.

E. Translate the following verses:

1 נָתְנָה־לִּי מִן־הָעֵץ [עֵץ tree] *Genesis 3:12*

2 יָדַעְתִּי כִּי־נָתַן יהוה לָכֶם אֶת־הָאָרֶץ [לָכֶם to you m. pl.] *Joshua 2:9*

3 כִּי־לֹא שָׁמַעְתָּ בְּקוֹל יהוה [שמע listen to ב +] *Deuteronomy 28:45*

4 אֲשֶׁר לֹא־הָלַכְתָּ בְּדַרְכֵי יְהוֹשָׁפָט אָבִיךָ וּבְדַרְכֵי אָסָא
מֶלֶךְ־יְהוּדָה [ךָ —your m. sg.] *2 Chronicles 21:12*

5 וְאָמַרְתָּ אֶל־אַהֲרֹן *Exodus 7:9*

6 וְלֹא־הָלְכוּ בָנָיו בִּדְרָכוֹ בִּדְרָכָיו [Read the last word as if it were *1 Samuel 8:3*

7 וְלֹא שְׁמַעְתֶּם בְּקֹלוֹ *Deuteronomy 9:23*

8 שָׁמַעְנוּ אֶל־מֹשֶׁה *Joshua 1:17*

9 וַיֹּאמֶר לֹא־קָרָאתִי *1 Samuel 3:5*

10 וּקְרָאתֶם בְּשֵׁם אֱלֹהֵיכֶם [כֶם —your m. pl.] *1 Kings 18:24*

11 עַל־כֵּן אָמַרְתִּי לִבְנֵי יִשְׂרָאֵל [עַל־כֵּן therefore] *Leviticus 17:12*

A good Hebrew grammar for students beginning the study is still a desideratum. Our writers of Hebrew grammars have aimed to write for scholars rather than for students. They have been ambitious on most points to say all that could be said, without studying to say only that which is needful to be said.

"Hermeneutics and Homiletics"
Methodist Quarterly, 48 (1866), 372

LESSON 14

כִּי־תִשְׁמֹר אֶת־כָּל־הַמִּצְוָה הַזֹּאת לַעֲשֹׁתָהּ

Deuteronomy 19:9

14.1   כִּי־תִשְׁמֹר

For the first time, you see a prefix verb form without a vav conversive. Once you memorize all the prefix subject pronouns these will not be too difficult to recognize, even though you do not have the help of the vav.

תּ is the prefix pronoun for the second person masculine singular.

Root	Stem	Form	Person/Gender/Number	Special Features

Without the vav conversive, a prefix form is translated most often in the future tense, but ongoing present or imperfect are other possibilities as context suggests.

שׁמר means *keep, guard.* כִּי means _____

Translation of the first phrase: _____

14.2   אֶת־כָּל־הַמִּצְוָה הַזֹּאת

14.2a   אֵת is _____ (7.2) Which is the noun that is definite? _____
כָּל means _____ Note that this word functions here as a noun, as the first member of a construct chain. Why is it spelled here כָּל instead of כּוֹל (See 6.3a–b if you're not sure of the answer.)

14.2b   הַמִּצְוָה begins with _____ (4.3) Thus the noun itself is מִצְוָה This is a feminine noun, and its gender is signaled by the accented הָ ending.

80

> הָ ֶ is the regular feminine singular absolute noun endiNG.

מִצְוָה means *commandment*.

14.2c הַזֹּאת This word also begins with _____ (4.3) When you remove this article, you are left with זֹאת which means *this*. זֹאת is the feminine singular demonstrative adjective; its masculine counterpart is זֶה All adjectives must agree with the nouns they modify in gender and number. זֹאת must be used here rather than זֶה because מִצְוָה is feminine. In addition, when an adjective modifies a noun directly, it must follow the noun and agree with it in definiteness as well. We call this kind of adjective an **attributive adjective**.

> An **attributive adjective** modifies a noun directly; it follows the noun and agrees with it in gender, number, and definiteness.

Here מִצְוָה is definite, so זֹאת must also be definite—both therefore have the definite article. We would translate הַמִּצְוָה הַזֹּאת *this commandment*.

14.3 לַעֲשֹׂתָהּ

לְ is a preposition here; it means _____ הָ ֶ at the end of a word is the third feminine singular suffix "her." Note the dot in the הּ This is not a dagesh but a **mappiq** (which you may remember as the "feminine period"), and it marks this as a consonant rather than a vowel letter. An alternative way of writing this suffix is as the sounded consonant הָ ֶ Neither הּ ֶ nor הָ ֶ should be confused with the 3 f. sg. affix or f. sg. noun endiNG הָ ֶ (as in 13.5 and 14.2b), which <u>never</u> have a mappiq.

14.3a This leaves עֲשֹׂת (The dot for the שֹ is also functioning as the vowel ḥolem.) You must locate the root. The ע and שֹ must be part of the root, but according to what you have learned so far, ת_____ could be either part of the root or an ending. (11.2a) In this case, ת_____ is part of an ending: ת ָ or וֹת ָ is the regular Qal infinitive ending for verbs ending in ה So the root is עֲשֹׂה Fill in the chart.

Root	Stem	Form	Person/Gender/Number	Special Features
			See 11.2b	

> Verbs, the roots of which end in הָ, regularly lose the הָ and have תָ ָ or וֹתָ ָ in the infinitive construct.

This infinitive can be translated literally _____ The *her* refers back to what noun? _____ In English, nouns of this sort are considered neuter, and thus you can use the pronoun "it" in your translation of this Hebrew word.

14.4   Verse translation: _____

_____

14.5   Extra Grammar

You may have noticed from working with the prefix form + vav conversive that there are fewer regular verbs in the prefix than in the affix. All of the weak verbs: 1st י 1st נ 3rd הָ and hollows as well as 1st gutturals have distinctive features. However, the regular form is an important base from which to build.

Qal Prefix Strong Verb

3 m. sg.	יִפְקֹד	3 m. pl.	יִפְקְדוּ ←
3 f. sg.	תִּפְקֹד	3 f. pl.	תִּפְקֹדְנָה
2 m. sg.	תִּפְקֹד	2 m. pl.	תִּפְקְדוּ ←
2 f. sg.	תִּפְקְדִי ←	2 f. pl.	תִּפְקֹדְנָה
1 c. sg.	אֶפְקֹד ←	1 c. pl.	נִפְקֹד

The prefix pronoun at the beginning <u>and</u> the prefix complement at the end (6.1) together make up the subject pronoun. These pronoun elements (the consonants but not the vowels) remain the same in all prefix forms of the verb, regardless of stem, and recognizing them will help you to parse verbs whose vowel patterns differ.

Within the paradigm, the arrows indicate variations from the regular pattern. In addition, the vowel between the second and third root letters (here ḥolem) changes depending on the verb used. To conjugate a verb correctly in the prefix, you must see one of its PGNs to ascertain this vowel.

14.5a   <u>Note</u>: Other terms for the prefix form are the imperfect, imperfective, and future.

14.5b   For the strong verb the vav conversive form can be created simply by adding ◌ וַ to the forms on the chart. And conversely, the simple prefix for such a verb can be derived by removing ◌ וַ from a form. The one exception will be the first person singular. You cannot add ◌ וַ to אֶפְקֹד

because the **א** cannot take a dagesh. (3.3a) The vav conversive for this PGN will be וָאֶפְקֹד As you can see, removing the **וָ** leaves the proper prefix form. This is the only circumstance in which vav conversive is not pointed **וַ**

14.6   Exercises:

A. In addition to the endiNG of 2 f. pl. and 3 f. pl. prefix form verbs, you have now seen a number of things represented by הָ‍ 3 f. sg. affix, 3 m. sg. affix of 3rd ה verbs, f. sg. nouns, and ה directive. The following words end in הָ‍ and should be familiar to you from your vocabulary list and your reading in Genesis 22. Identify each הָ‍

הַמֹּרִיָּה	וַתֹּאמַרְנָה	אַרְצָה
בָּנָה	הָיָה	שָׁמְרָה
אַתָּה	נִסָּה	שָׁנָה
תֵּלַכְנָה	עֹלָה	נָתְנָה
אִשָּׁה	עָלָה	הָלְכָה

B. Conjugate שׁלח in the Qal prefix form. The pattern is begun for you:

Qal Prefix שׁלח

3 m. sg.	יִ שְׁ לַ ח	3 m. pl.	יִ שְׁ לְ ח וּ	
3 f. sg.	⎵ ⎵ ⎵	3 f. pl.	תִּ שְׁ לַ חְ נָה	
2 m. sg.	⎵ ⎵ ⎵	2 m. pl.	⎵ ⎵ ⎵	
2 f. sg.	⎵ ⎵ ⎵	2 f. pl.	⎵ ⎵ ⎵	
1 c. sg.	⎵ ⎵ ⎵ אֶ	1 c. pl.	⎵ ⎵ ⎵	

Conjugate מלך in the Qal prefix form. The 3 m. sg. יִמְלֹך gives you the pattern to follow.

Qal Prefix מלך

3 m. sg.	יִ מְ לֹ ך	3 m. pl.	יִ מְ לְ כ וּ	
3 f. sg.	⎵ ⎵ ⎵	3 f. pl.	תִּ מְ לֹ כְ נָה	
2 m. sg.	⎵ ⎵ ⎵	2 m. pl.	⎵ ⎵ ⎵	
2 f. sg.	⎵ ⎵ ⎵	2 f. pl.	⎵ ⎵ ⎵	
1 c. sg.	⎵ ⎵ ⎵ אֶ	1 c. pl.	⎵ ⎵ ⎵	

Assignments

A. Vocabulary: words 1–120.

B. Memorize the two most common paradigms for the Qal prefix of the strong verb. The יִפְקֹד pattern is illustrated in 14.5, in Chart A, and in song: ☉ﬡ track 10. The יִשְׁלַח pattern is shown in 14.6B and in Chart J.

C. Read and translate Genesis 22:3–5.

D. In the following verses, missing-letter verbs will be found as well as a few regular prefix forms. The missing letter rules work with the simple prefix forms as well as with vav conversive forms. Translate the verses, then analyze each prefix form verb.

1 *1 Samuel 28:12* וַתֹּאמֶר הָאִשָּׁה אֶל־שָׁאוּל

2 [The city name is regularly spelled without the 2nd יֹ] וָאָבוֹא אֶל־יְרוּשָׁלָ͏ִם
   Nehemiah 2:11

3 [כֶם— *you* m. pl.] כִּי תָבֹאוּ אֶל־אֶרֶץ כְּנַעַן אֲשֶׁר אֲנִי נֹתֵן לָכֶם
   Leviticus 14:34

4 *Numbers 21:22* בְּדֶרֶךְ הַמֶּלֶךְ נֵלֵךְ

5 *Exodus 7:17* בְּזֹאת תֵּדַע כִּי אֲנִי יהוה

✡6 *Isaiah 55:11* [פֹּי *thus* פִי *my mouth*] כֵּן יִהְיֶה דְבָרִי אֲשֶׁר יֵצֵא מִפִּי

7 *Genesis 13:1* [מִצְרַיִם *Egypt*] (12.1) וַיַּעַל אַבְרָם מִמִּצְרַיִם

✡8 *Jeremiah 32:22* וַתִּתֵּן לָהֶם אֶת־הָאָרֶץ הַזֹּאת

9 *Genesis 31:4* וַיִּשְׁלַח יַעֲקֹב וַיִּקְרָא לְרָחֵל וּלְלֵאָה

10 *1 Samuel 20:21* וְהִנֵּה אֶשְׁלַח אֶת־הַנַּעַר

11 *Genesis 43:3* [יֹ— *my.* See **S 8.3.** פָּנִים *is always plural.*] לֹא־תִרְאוּ פָנָי

12 *Deuteronomy 6:25* כִּי־נִשְׁמֹר לַעֲשׂוֹת אֶת־כָּל־הַמִּצְוָה הַזֹּאת

✡13 *Nehemiah 2:14* [שַׁעַר הָעַיִן *fountain gate*] וָאֶעֱבֹר אֶל־שַׁעַר הָעַיִן

14 *Numbers 20:20* וַיֹּאמֶר לֹא תַעֲבֹר

✡15 *Jeremiah 5:15* [לָשׁוֹן *language*] לֹא־תֵדַע לְשֹׁנוֹ וְלֹא תִשְׁמַע מַה־יְדַבֵּר

84

LESSON 15

וַיֹּאמֶר חִזְקִיָּהוּ אֶל־יְשַׁעְיָהוּ טוֹב דְּבַר־יהוה אֲשֶׁר דִּבַּרְתָּ

Isaiah 39:8

15.1 וַיֹּאמֶר חִזְקִיָּהוּ אֶל־יְשַׁעְיָהוּ

חִזְקִיָּהוּ is a proper name functioning as the _____ of the sentence.

יְשַׁעְיָהוּ is another proper name.

Translation: _____

Note the similarity in the endings of these names. Many Hebrew names are compounds with God's name יהוה as יְהוֹ____ or יָה____ as one element.

חָזַק means *be strong;* יָשַׁע means *rescue, save, deliver.* How might the two names be "translated?" _____

15.2 What do you expect to follow the first phrase? _____ (13.2)

טוֹב is an adjective meaning *good,* and דְּבַר־ is a noun. But this time the adjective precedes the noun. You cannot translate *the good word* [*of the Lord*] because an attributive adjective must _____ the noun. (14.2c) This new type of adjective, which precedes the noun, we call the **predicate adjective**.

A **predicate adjective** usually precedes the noun. It must agree with its noun in gender and number but not necessarily in definiteness.

A phrase consisting of an adjective preceding a noun or construct phrase is treated like a noun sentence (2.10b); you need to insert a form of the verb *to be.*

Translate the phrase: _____

15.3 אֲשֶׁר דִּבַּרְתָּ

אֲשֶׁר is the relative pronoun. (5.3a) The only new grammatical element in this sentence is the final verb: דִּבַּרְתָּ.

וַיֹּאמֶר חִזְקִיָּהוּ אֶל־יְשַׁעְיָהוּ טוֹב דְּבַר־יהוה אֲשֶׁר דִּבַּרְתָּ

Root	Stem	Form	Person/Gender/Number	Special Features

You should have no trouble finding the root, form, and PGN for this verb. Refer to 13.5 if necessary. Is this stem Qal? What is the stem indicator for the Qal affix? _____

_____ This is the other stem you have seen in the lessons.

What is its stem indicator? (2.3c) _____

Translation of the whole verse: _____

_____

15.4 Pi`el Affix

The major **stem** indicator of the Pi`el is the dagesh forte in the middle root letter:

       ◡ ◌ֹ ◡

The major **form** indicator for the Pi`el affix is ḥireq ◌ִ under the first root letter:

       ◡ ◌ֹ ◡

The subject pronoun endings you have learned for the Qal affix are the same ones used in the Pi`el; these endings are used in the affix form of every stem. If you haven't memorized them yet, do so **now**.

Pi`el Affix Strong Verb

3 m. sg.	דִּבֶּר	3 c. pl.	דִּבְּרוּ
3 f. sg.	דִּבְּרָה		
2 m. sg.	דִּבַּרְתָּ	2 m. pl.	דִּבַּרְתֶּם
2 f. sg.	דִּבַּרְתְּ	2 f. pl.	דִּבַּרְתֶּן
1 c. sg.	דִּבַּרְתִּי	1 c. pl.	דִּבַּרְנוּ

What kind of dagesh is in the first root letter of our example? You can see that much of the rest of the pointing is regular throughout the paradigm. This is the case for most Pi`el verbs.

15.4a Pi`el Affix for Middle א ה ח ע ר

These letters cannot take a dagesh, so either the vowel pattern stays the same and there is no dagesh: נֵהַג *he led,* or the vowel under the first root letter lengthens from ḥireq ◌ִ to tsere ◌ֵ as in בֵּרַךְ One way to remember this is to think of the dagesh forte as having gone from the middle root letter to join the expected hireq under the first root letter. You may think of this as the case of the traveling dagesh.

Complete the following paradigm using 15.4 as a guide, but compensating for the dagesh.

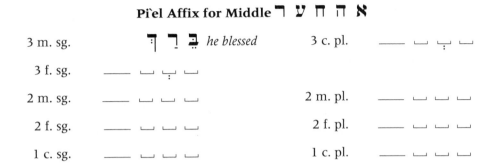

Pi'el Affix for Middle א ה ח ע ר

3 m. sg.	בֵּ רַ ךְ *he blessed*	3 c. pl.	⎵ ⎵ ⟂ ⎵
3 f. sg.	⎵ ⎵ ⟂ ⎵		
2 m. sg.	⎵ ⎵ ⎵ ⎵	2 m. pl.	⎵ ⎵ ⎵ ⎵
2 f. sg.	⎵ ⎵ ⎵ ⎵	2 f. pl.	⎵ ⎵ ⎵ ⎵
1 c. sg.	⎵ ⎵ ⎵ ⎵	1 c. pl.	⎵ ⎵ ⎵ ⎵

15.5 Pi'el Prefix

You construct the Pi'el prefix the same way as the Qal prefix. The prefix pronouns and prefix complements are the same for every stem of the verb.

> The form indicator for the Pi'el prefix is shewa ְ under the prefix pronoun. ⎵ ⎵ ⎵ | ְ

Fill in the chart for the Pi'el prefix of דבר Where something shows variation from the regular pattern, it has been filled in for you.

Pi'el Prefix Strong Verb

3 m. sg.	יְ דַ בֵּ ר	3 m. pl.	⎵ ⎵ ⟂ ⎵ ⎵
3 f. sg.	⎵ ⎵ ⎵ ⎵	3 f. pl.	⎵ ⎵ ⎵ ⎵
2 m. sg.	⎵ ⎵ ⎵ ⎵	2 m. pl.	⎵ ⎵ ⟂ ⎵ ⎵
2 f. sg.	⎵ ⎵ ⟂ ⎵ ⎵	2 f. pl.	⎵ ⎵ ⎵ ⎵
1 c. sg.	⎵ ⎵ ⎵ אֲ	1 c. pl.	⎵ ⎵ ⎵ ⎵

Can you explain the composite shewa under the prefix pronoun for the 1 c. sg.?

_____ (13.6b)

15.5a Pi'el Prefix for Middle א ה ח ע ר

The stem indicator for the Pi'el prefix of this group of verbs is shewa ְ under the prefix pronoun (the same as for verbs with dagesh forte in the middle root letter).

To compensate for the lack of doubling of the middle root letter, the vowel under the first root letter is lengthened, this time from pataḥ ⸯ to qamats ⸯ ⸯ ⸯ | ⸯ

doubled middle root letter	middle root letter cannot double
↓	↓
יְפַקֵּד	יְבָרֵךְ
pataḥ ↑↑ stem indicator	qamats ↑↑ stem indicator

Complete this paradigm using the 3 m. sg. as a model and refer to 15.5 if necessary.

Piʿel Prefix for Middle א ה ח ע ר

3 m. sg.	יְ בָ רֵ ךְ	3 m. pl.	ⸯ ⸯ ⸯ ⸯ
3 f. sg.	ⸯ ⸯ ⸯ ⸯ	3 f. pl.	ⸯ ⸯ ⸯ ⸯ
2 m. sg.	ⸯ ⸯ ⸯ ⸯ	2 m. pl.	ⸯ ⸯ ⸯ ⸯ
2 f. sg.	ⸯ ⸯ ⸯ ⸯ	2 f. pl.	ⸯ ⸯ ⸯ ⸯ
1 c. sg.	ⸯ ⸯ ⸯ ⸯ	1 c. pl.	ⸯ ⸯ ⸯ ⸯ

15.6 Meanings of the Piʿel Stem

You have learned that the Qal stem is the simple or basic meaning of the verb. (1.4a) The change from the Qal to the Piʿel varies from one verb to another but there are a few common relationships:

A. **Transitives:** Many verbs that are intransitive in the Qal have a transitive force in the Piʿel.

Qal		Piʿel	
אָבַד	*perish*	אִבֵּד	*destroy*
לָמַד	*learn*	לִמֵּד	*teach*

A subcategory of these verbs is called **factitive**. An adjective complement is needed to complete the meaning of the verb.

Qal		Piʿel	
צָדַק	*be just, righteous*	צִדֵּק	*declare just*

B. **Denominatives:** Some Piʿels seem to have been formed from nouns. You are already familiar with one of the most common of these: דִּבֶּר and its related noun דָּבָר

—

Noun		Pi`el	
סֵפֶר	document, record	סִפֵּר	recount, narrate

A subgroup of these denominatives is called **privative**: the verb relates to taking away or injuring the noun, in either a literal or figurative sense.[1]

Noun		Pi`el	
חֵטְא	sin	חִטֵּא	free from sin

C. **Strengthening**, **repetition**, or **intensification** of action ("pluralization") is the reason the Pi`el is used in other verbs:

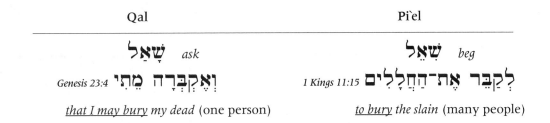

Qal		Pi`el	
שָׁאַל	ask	שִׁאֵל	beg
Genesis 23:4 וְאֶקְבְּרָה מֵתִי		1 Kings 11:15 לְקַבֵּר אֶת־הַחֲלָלִים	
that I may bury my dead (one person)		*to bury* the slain (many people)	

D. **Unidentified Nuances**: There are some Pi`el verbs for which Biblical Hebrew has no Qal. In other cases, Qal and Pi`el forms are both extant, but we do not know how to express the intended difference, if any, between the two.

No Qal		Pi`el	
בקש	_____	בִּקֵּשׁ	seek
צוה	_____	צִוָּה	give charge to

Qal		Pi`el	
Qohelet 2:8 כָּנַסְתִּי לִי גַּם־כֶּסֶף וְזָהָב		Psalms 147:2 נִדְחֵי יִשְׂרָאֵל יְכַנֵּס	
I also *gathered* for myself silver and gold		he *gathers* the outcasts of Israel	

---

1. The grammar of English food preparation has several of these noun/verb pairs: *skin, bone, seed, peel,* and so forth.

15.7   Hebrew Names

It is often intriguing to delve into a name either to learn the Hebrew root, as in the names in our lesson sentence, or to discover a cultural influence. The name of Sarah's maidservant הָגָר (Genesis 21) may be from an Arabic root: *forsake, retire*. It could also be a play on the word גֵּר *stranger*.

Hebrew proper names, both of people and of places, are often compounds. Many town names include the word בֵּית as in בֵּית אֵל בֵּית לֶחֶם and בֵּית How would you "translate" these?

_____

In some cases particular names are given for theological purpose. Hosea is told to name two of his children לֹא רֻחָמָה (Hosea 1:6) and לֹא עַמִּי (Hosea 1:9) The first name is *Not Pitied*. What is the second? _____

Many times, especially on the occasion of naming or changing the name of an individual, a reason for the name is given. Look at the poignant lines in Ruth 1:20. The names bespeak the difficulties Naomi has suffered.

$$\text{וַתֹּאמֶר אֲלֵיהֶן אַל־תִּקְרֶאנָה לִי נָעֳמִי קְרֶאןָ לִי מָרָא}$$
$$\text{כִּי־הֵמַר שַׁדַּי לִי מְאֹד:}$$

Then she said to them, "Do not call me נָעֳמִי *[root:* נעם *pleasant, delightful], call me* מָרָא *[root:* מרר *bitter], because God has made much bitterness for me."*

There are stories in which the names themselves set up our reactions to the characters. The story of David [root: דוד *beloved*] and Nabal [root: נבל *foolish*] (1 Samuel 25) is such an illustration. Look especially at 1 Samuel 25:25.

Of course not every name is pregnant with overtones, but in many cases names add dimensions of meaning and enjoyment to our reading of the text.

Assignments

A. Vocabulary: words 1–125.

B. Memorize the Piʿel affix and prefix paradigms for the strong verb (Verb Chart A) and for verbs whose middle root letter is א ה ח ע ר (Chart G).

⊙ א ב track 11: listen to and sing along with **Mr. Piʿel** (lyrics: pp. 464–465)

C. ⊙ שַׁבְּחִי track 14: listen to יְבָרֶכְךָ **Numbers 6:24–26.**

D. Read and translate Genesis 22:6–8.

וַיֹּאמֶר חִזְקִיָּהוּ אֶל־יְשַׁעְיָהוּ טוֹב דְּבַר־יהוה אֲשֶׁר דִּבַּרְתָּ

E. Translate the following verses:

Extra vocabulary: נָבִיא *prophet*

חָזַק Qal: *be strong, hard* Piʿel: *strengthen, harden*

1 וַיִּשְׁמַע שָׁאוּל אֶת־כָּל־הָעָם *1 Samuel 23:8*

2 אֲחַזֵּק אֶת־לִבּוֹ וְלֹא יְשַׁלַּח אֶת־הָעָם *Exodus 4:21*

3 וַיֹּאמֶר פַּרְעֹה אָנֹכִי אֲשַׁלַּח אֶתְכֶם [אֶתְכֶם ⟶ אֵת + 2 m. pl. object suffix]
Exodus 8:24

4 וַיְחַזֵּק יהוה אֶת־לֵב פַּרְעֹה וְלֹא שִׁלַּח אֶת־בְּנֵי־יִשְׂרָאֵל מֵאַרְצוֹ
Exodus 11:10 (Find the traveling dagesh in this verse. It isn't in a Piʿel verb this time.)

5 וְלֹא שִׁלַּח אֶת־הָעָם *Exodus 8:28*

6 ... וְשִׁלַּחְתֶּם אֹתוֹ וְהָלָךְ: [אֹתוֹ ⟶ DDO marker + 3 m. sg. obj. pronoun]
1 Samuel 6:8

✡7 כְּכֹל הַדְּבָרִים הָאֵלֶּה וּכְכֹל הֶחָזוֹן הַזֶּה כֵּן דִּבֶּר נָתָן אֶל־דָּוִיד:
1 Chronicles 17:15 [חָזוֹן *vision*. For segol ֶ as vowel for definite article see **S 21.3a**]

8 וַיֹּאמֶר לָהֶם הִנֵּה בֶן־הַמֶּלֶךְ יִמְלֹךְ כַּאֲשֶׁר דִּבֶּר יהוה עַל־בְּנֵי דָוִיד
2 Chronicles 23:3

9 זֶה הַדָּבָר אֲשֶׁר דִּבֶּר יהוה אֶל־מוֹאָב *Isaiah 16:13*

10 כִּי יהוה דִּבֶּר אֶת־הַדָּבָר הַזֶּה *Isaiah 24:3*

11 וַיִּשְׁלְחוּ וַיִּקְרְאוּ־לוֹ וַיָּבֹא יָרָבְעָם וְכָל־יִשְׂרָאֵל וַיְדַבְּרוּ אֶל־רְחַבְעָם
2 Chronicles 10:3

12 וְלֹא אֲדַבֵּר עוֹד בִּשְׁמוֹ *Jeremiah 20:9*

13 וְלֹא תִשְׁמַע מַה־יְדַבֵּר *Jeremiah 5:15*

14 וְאֶל־צִדְקִיָּה מֶלֶךְ־יְהוּדָה דִּבַּרְתִּי כְּכָל־הַדְּבָרִים הָאֵלֶּה *Jeremiah 27:12*

LESSON 16

—◆—

וַיִּפֹּל יוֹסֵף עַל־פְּנֵי אָבִיו וַיֵּבְךְּ עָלָיו וַיִּשַּׁק־לוֹ:

Genesis 50:1

16.1 From now on, atnaḥ ֑ and sof passuq ׃ (See Review and Drill 4, section VI.) will be written in full verses.

16.1a וַיִּפֹּל יוֹסֵף

Root	Stem	Form	Person/Gender/Number	Special Features

After accounting for the וַ how many consonants are left for the root? _____

If you forget why the root can't be נפל review 7.1a.

If you forget why the root isn't פלה review 12.3.

The root is _____ What is the stem? _____ It cannot be Pi'el because you have already accounted for the dagesh forte in the פ It is the assimilated נ of the root. Remember: A dagesh forte cannot stand for two letters simultaneously. (7.1a) Besides, if this were a Pi'el form, what vowel would you expect under the י ____ (15.5) You should be able to fill in the rest of the chart.

Translation of the phrase: _____

16.2 עַל־פְּנֵי אָבִיו

Translation: _____

16.3 וַיֵּבְךְּ עָלָיו

וַיִּפֹּל יוֹסֵף עַל־פְּנֵי אָבִיו וַיֵּבְךְּ עָלָיו וַיִּשַּׁק־לוֹ:

16.3a וַיֵּבְךְּ

Root	Stem	Form	Person/Gender/Number	Special Features

The PGN, stem, and form of this verb are straightforward; the trouble comes in determining the root. The י that is written cannot be part of the root because וַיּ begins a vav conversive construction, and therefore the י is a prefix pronoun.

> No letter of an affix pronoun, prefix pronoun, or prefix complement will ever assimilate.

That means that a footprint dagesh as in וַיִּפֹּל or a missing letter as in וַיֵּבְךְּ always tells you something about a <u>root</u> letter in a verb form.

According to 3.1, וַיֵּבְךְּ is a time when the missing letter rules can be used. According to the appropriate rule, the root needs _____ in the _____ position. But this is one of the 5% or so of cases where the convention for identifying the missing letter simply doesn't work.

The root here is בָּכָה which means *weep*. Sometimes בָּכָה will follow the missing letter rule (וַיִּבְכּוּ Gen. 33:4), sometimes it won't (וַתֵּבְךְּ Gen. 21:15). There are a few other 3rd ה verbs that sometimes take the prefix pronoun vowel of a 1st י The nonconforming instances tend to be in the singular when the prefix pronoun is י or ת

Verb		Expected Pointing		Ambiguous Pointing	
שׁתה	*drink*	וַיִּשְׁתֶּה	1 Kings 19:8	וַיֵּשְׁתְּ	Genesis 9:21
נטה	*stretch out, extend*	יִטֶּה	Job 15:29	וַיֵּט	Genesis 12:8
רעה	*pasture, tend*	יִרְעֶה	Isaiah 30:23	יֵרַע	Job 20:26[1]

16.3b עָלָיו This is a preposition and object suffix you have seen before.

Translation of phrase: _____

---

1. The root of יֵרַע is disputed. Some think it is רעע.

16.4   וַיִּשַּׁק־לוֹ

Root	Stem	Form	Person/Gender/Number	Special Features

16.4a   וַיִּשַּׁק means _____ (You will have to look up the root in the lexicon.)

16.4b   לוֹ Without any context, this would be translated *to him* or *for him*. In this sentence, it would make awkward English to say *he kissed to/for him.* This is an idiomatic use of the preposition לְ where we might expect אֵת It shouldn't be given a strictly literal English translation.

Translation of the whole verse: _____

_____

16.5a   The Qal affix of a 1st נ verb is completely regular, exactly like the pattern you learned in 13.5. Conjugate the Qal affix of נפל

Qal Affix נפל

3 m. sg.	⌴ ⌴ ⌴	3 c. pl.	⎯ ⌴ ְ ֽ
3 f. sg.	⎯ ⌴ ְ ֽ		
2 m. sg.	⎯ ⌴ ⌴ ⌴	2 m. pl.	⎯ ⌴ ⌴ ⌴ ←
2 f. sg.	⎯ ⌴ ⌴ ⌴	2 f. pl.	⎯ ⌴ ⌴ ⌴ ←
1 c. sg.	⎯ ⌴ ⌴ ⌴	1 c. pl.	⎯ ⌴ ⌴ ⌴

16.5b   Qal Prefix of 1st נ

Because the prefix pronoun causes the assimilation of the נ the Qal prefix does not follow exactly the pattern you learned in 14.5. However, the prefix pronouns and prefix complements themselves are the same.

Qal Prefix נפל

3 m. sg.	יִ פֹּ ל	3 m. pl.	⎯ ⌴ ְ ⎯
3 f. sg.	⌴ ⌴ ⎯	3 f. pl.	⎯ ⌴ ⌴ ⎯
2 m. sg.	⌴ ⌴ ⎯	2 m. pl.	⎯ ⌴ ְ ⎯
2 f. sg.	⎯ ⌴ ְ תִּ	2 f. pl.	⎯ ⌴ ⌴ ⎯
1 c. sg.	⌴ ⌴ אֶ	1 c. pl.	⌴ ⌴ ⎯

וַיִּפֹּל יוֹסֵף עַל־פְּנֵי אָבִיו וַיֵּבְךְּ עָלָיו וַיִּשַּׁק־לוֹ:

Just as is the case with strong verbs, the second vowel in the Qal prefix is not the same for every verb that is 1st נ The other pattern, pataḥ ַ under the second root letter, can be seen with these verbs, too, as exemplified by נגשׁ *draw near, approach.* Using the 3 m. sg. as a guide, finish this paradigm.

Qal Prefix נגשׁ

3 m. sg.	יִ גַּ שׁ	3 m. pl.	___ ⎵ ⎵ ___
3 f. sg.	⎵ ⎵ ___	3 f. pl.	___ ⎵ ⎵ ___
2 m. sg.	⎵ ⎵ ___	2 m. pl.	___ ⎵ ⎵ ___
2 f. sg.	___ ⎵ ⎵ תְ	2 f. pl.	___ ⎵ ⎵ ___
1 c. sg.	⎵ ⎵ ___	1 c. pl.	⎵ ⎵ ___

The 1 c. pl. needs careful consideration. The נ that is written is the prefix pronoun. The footprint of the first <u>root</u> letter is found in the dagesh forte of the middle root letter.

16.5c Some common 1st נ verbs that appear in the Qal are:

נתן	*give, permit*	נסע	*set out, journey*
נשׂא	*lift, carry*	נגשׁ	*draw near, approach*
נפל	*fall*	נשׁק	*kiss*
נגע	*harm, reach, touch*		

16.6 נָתַן

The most frequent of all the 1st נ verbs is נתן It is distinct because its third root letter נ behaves as its first נ does. That is, this נ also assimilates when its vowel would be shewa ְ and it is between two consonants. In those cases, the dagesh forte in the first letter of the affix pronoun will alert you to the identity of the unseen root letter. This is the only root that ends in a נ that regularly acts this way.

In the following paradigm, the arrows indicate those PGNs whose third root letter has assimilated. Pay special attention to the 3 c. pl. נָתְנוּ and the 1 c. pl. נָתַנּוּ How can they be distinguished?

וַיִּפֹּל יוֹסֵף עַל־פְּנֵי אָבִיו וַיֵּבְךְּ עָלָיו וַיִּשַּׁק־לוֹ׃

Qal Affix נתן

3 m. sg.	נָתַן		3 c. pl.	נָתְנוּ	
3 f. sg.	נָתְנָה				
2 m. sg.	נָתַתָּ	⟵	2 m. pl.	נְתַתֶּם	⟵
2 f. sg.	נָתַתְּ	⟵	2 f. pl.	נְתַתֶּן	⟵
1 c. sg.	נָתַתִּי	⟵	1 c. pl.	נָתַנּוּ	⟵

The prefix forms are regular according to 1st נ patterns, showing the second and third root letters in every case. (In the f. pl. the final נ assimilates into the נ of the prefix complement.) Thus the root can be identified after accounting for the dagesh forte, which represents ____________ ____________________

Fill in the Qal prefix paradigm.

Qal Prefix נתן

3 m. sg.	יִ תֵּ ן	3 m. pl.	____ __ ְ__ __
3 f. sg.	__ __ __	3 f. pl.	נָּה __ __
2 m. sg.	__ __ __	2 m. pl.	____ __ ְ__ __
2 f. sg.	____ __ ְ__ __	2 f. pl.	נָּה __ __
1 c. sg.	__ __ ֶ__	1 c. pl.	__ __ __

The participle is regular: ____________________

16.7 Extra Grammar
Idiomatic usage of certain verbs with certain prepositions.

16.7a Preposition instead of **את**
There are times when what we would consider a DDO is preceded not by the DDO marker but by a preposition. One such case occurs in the lesson sentence:

וַיִּשַּׁק־לוֹ

Another verb that commonly takes a preposition, this time בְּ is בחר *choose:*

1 Kings 8:16 לֹא־בָחַרְתִּי בְעִיר

I did not choose a city

וַיִּפֹּל יוֹסֵף עַל־פְּנֵי אָבִיו וַיֵּבְךְּ עָלָיו וַיִּשַּׁק־לוֹ׃

16.7b Sometimes a preposition will change the meaning of the verb it accompanies from what the verb usually means without the preposition. At times, different prepositions express different nuances; sometimes they seem to be interchangeable.

קָרָא *call, proclaim*

קָרָא לְ or קָרָא בְּ *call, give a name to, call unto, read*

Genesis 1:5 וַיִּקְרָא אֱלֹהִים לָאוֹר יוֹם

and God <u>called</u> (gave a name to) the light Day

Nehemiah 8:18 וַיִּקְרָא בְּסֵפֶר תּוֹרַת הָאֱלֹהִים

and he <u>read</u> (in) the scroll of the Torah of God

שָׁמַע *hear, listen*

שָׁמַע לְ or שָׁמַע אֶל or שָׁמַע בְּ *listen to*

2 Kings 18:12 לֹא־שָׁמְעוּ בְּקוֹל יהוה . . . וְלֹא שָׁמְעוּ וְלֹא עָשׂוּ

they did not <u>listen to</u> the voice of the Lord . . . and they did not <u>hear</u> (listen, obey) and they did not do

Exodus 16:20 וְלֹא־שָׁמְעוּ אֶל־מֹשֶׁה

and they did not listen to Moses

Assignments

A. Vocabulary: words 1–130.

B. Memorize the Qal affix and prefix conjugations of <div dir="rtl">נָפַל נָגַשׁ נָתַן</div> (Chart F).

C. ☺<div dir="rtl">שַׁבְּחִי</div> tracks 15 and 16: listen to and sing <div dir="rtl">וְיִתֶּן־לְךָ</div> **Genesis 27:28** and <div dir="rtl">אֶשָּׂא עֵינַי</div> **Psalm 121:1–2**.

D. Read and translate Genesis 22:9–11.

E. Translate:

1 <div dir="rtl">וְאֶת־כָּל־אֶחָיו נָתַתִּי לוֹ לַעֲבָדִים</div> *Genesis 27:37*

[<div dir="rtl">אֶחָיו</div> is the pl. of <div dir="rtl">אָח</div> + 3 m. sg. possessive suffix]

2 <div dir="rtl">וַיָּבֹא יְהוּדָה וְאֶחָיו בֵּיתָה יוֹסֵף . . . וַיִּפְּלוּ לְפָנָיו אָרְצָה</div> *Genesis 44:14*

☺3 <div dir="rtl">וַתָּבֹא וַתִּפֹּל עַל־רַגְלָיו . . . וַתִּשָּׂא אֶת־בְּנָהּ וַתֵּצֵא</div> [<div dir="rtl">רֶגֶל</div> *foot*] *2 Kings 4:37*

☺4 <div dir="rtl">דָּבָר שָׁלַח אֲדֹנָי בְּיַעֲקֹב וְנָפַל בְּיִשְׂרָאֵל</div> *Isaiah 9:7 (9:8 in some English Bibles)*

[<div dir="rtl">בְּ</div> can mean *against* here.]

וַיִּפֹּל יוֹסֵף עַל־פְּנֵי אָבִיו וַיֵּבְךְּ עָלָיו וַיִּשַּׁק־לוֹ:

☼5 וַיִּפֹּל הַבַּיִת עַל־הַסְּרָנִים וְעַל־כָּל־הָעָם אֲשֶׁר־בּוֹ *Judges 16:30*

[הַסְּרָנִים *the princes*]

6 וְאֶת־כָּל־יְהוּדָה אֶתֵּן בְּיַד מֶלֶךְ־בָּבֶל *Jeremiah 20:4*

7 וַיִּגַּשׁ דָּוִד אֶת־הָעָם *1 Samuel 30:21*

8 וַתֵּתֶן־לוֹ בֵן *1 Kings 3:6*

☼9 וְהִנֵּה־יָד נָגְעָה בִּי [*touch* נָגַע בְּ] *Daniel 10:10*

10 וּמִי יִתֵּן אֶת־הָעָם הַזֶּה בְּיָדִי *Judges 9:29*

98

LESSON 17

יהוה לִי לֹא אִירָא מַה־יַּעֲשֶׂה לִי אָדָם:

Psalms 118:6

17.1 יהוה לִי

The preposition ל was introduced in 7.2c, where you learned that it often acts as a marker of the indirect object (לוֹ *to* or *for him*) or as an indicator of the possessive (מֶלֶךְ לוֹ *he has a king*). In the phrase here, either use of ל would make sense.

Translation: _____

17.2 לֹא אִירָא

Root	Stem	Form	Person/Gender/Number	Special Features

אִירָא shows four consonants. When there are too many consonants for a root it is often helpful to begin by removing any vowel letters. That won't work here because:

אָרָא is not a root.

A prefix pronoun is never pointed with a plene ḥireq.

Take off the prefix pronoun and you are left with יָרָא which are the three root letters of the verb *fear.*

Translation of phrase: _____

The 1st י verbs you have already studied in the Qal prefix (presented in 3.1) are distinguished by the elision of the י of the root. The tsere ֵ under the prefix pronoun is the clue to the identity and location of the missing root letter.[1] You are familiar with forms such as יֵצֵא and יֵשֵׁב

---

1. Remember הלך follows the pattern of these 1st י verbs.

A second group of 1st **י** verbs is conjugated like **אִירָא** in the Qal prefix. In these, the **י** of the root quiesces (i.e., it appears but it has no vowel of its own), and the vowel ḥireq _ is under the prefix pronoun. **יִרָא** is the most common of these, but some others are **יָטַב** *be good*, **יָרַשׁ** *inherit*, **יָשַׁר** *be straight, upright*

17.3 מַה־יַּעֲשֶׂה לִי אָדָם

17.3a יַּעֲשֶׂה

Root	Stem	Form	Person/Gender/Number	Special Features

What letter is not part of the root? _____ The root is _____

There are two unusual things about יַּעֲשֶׂה The first is the vowel under the prefix pronoun.

> Roots that begin with the guttural **ע ח** or **ה** have the vowel pataḥ _ under the prefix pronoun in the Qal prefix except for the first person singular, whose prefix pronoun is also a guttural letter. In that case, the vowel is usually segol _

17.3b The second concerns the dagesh in the **י** It is called a **euphonic dagesh**. What its original melodic function was we do not know. It has no effect according to today's pronunciation conventions and has no apparent grammatical function. You can recognize one of these only by process of elimination; its most common occurrence is in the first consonant of a word following a final **ה** in the previous word.

The subject of this part of the verse is _____

17.3c לִי is the _____

17.3d אָדָם is most frequently used in the generic sense meaning *mankind, humanity* as opposed to **אִישׁ** *man*, which has a feminine counterpart **אִשָּׁה** *woman*.

Although the Qal prefix form is usually best translated as a simple future or ongoing present or past, it is the verb form that is often given modal force. Thus, יַּעֲשֶׂה could be translated *can do, might do, could do*, etc.

17.3e Translation of phrase: _____

17.4 Translation of entire verse: _____

_____

17.5 Following the pattern of אִירָא finish conjugating ירא in the Qal prefix. Remember to make the adjustment(s) that a 3rd א requires. (13.6a)

Qal Prefix ירא

3 m. sg.	⌣ ⌣ ⌣ _	3 m. pl.	___ ⌣ ⌸ ⌣ _
3 f. sg.	⌣ ⌣ ⌣ _	3 f. pl.	___ ⌣ ⌸ ⌣ _
2 m. sg.	⌣ ⌣ ⌣ _	2 m. pl.	___ ⌣ ⌸ ⌣ _
2 f. sg.	___ ⌣ ⌸ ⌣ _	2 f. pl.	___ ⌣ ⌸ ⌣ _
1 c. sg.	אִירָא	1 c. pl.	⌣ ⌣ ⌣ _

Following the pattern of אֵשֵׁב finish conjugating ישב in the Qal prefix.

Qal Prefix ישב

3 m. sg.	⌣ ⌣ _	3 m. pl.	___ ⌣ ⌸ _
3 f. sg.	⌣ ⌣ _	3 f. pl.	⌣ ⌸ ⌸ _
2 m. sg.	⌣ ⌣ _	2 m. pl.	___ ⌣ ⌸ _
2 f. sg.	___ ⌣ ⌸ _	2 f. pl.	___ ⌸ ⌸ _
1 c. sg.	אֵשֵׁב	1 c. pl.	⌣ ⌣ _

17.6 Qal Affix Vowel Patterns, A, I, and U

ירא differs from verbs you have seen so far not only in the Qal prefix but also in the Qal affix. Most strong verbs have either _ or _ as their second vowel in the 3 m. sg. Qal affix: אָמַר and קָרָא for example. They are called A class verbs because their second vowel, pataḥ or qamats, is an A class vowel. Two other patterns exist.

I class verbs have tsere _ as their second vowel, and U class verbs have ḥolem וֹ in the second vowel position. These three patterns, A, I, and U, correspond to the three classes of vowels as listed in the section Vowel Points (see p. 5). All three classes have _ under the first root letter, regardless of the second vowel.

Many of the I and U class verbs are intransitive and describe a state of being rather than an action. For example, יָרֵא means *be in awe, fear,* and קָטֹן means *be small.* In other words, they are often **stative**.

17.6a   **Qal Affix Vowel Patterns**

A class		I class	U class
יָצָא	שָׁמַע	יָרֵא	קָטֹן
2nd vowel ◌ָ	2nd vowel ◌ַ	2nd vowel ◌ֵ	2nd vowel וֹ

Below are Qal affix conjugations of verbs representative of the I and U patterns.

17.6b   **Qal Affix I Class**[2]

3 m. sg.	כָּבֵד	3 c. pl.	כָּבְדוּ
3 f. sg.	כָּבְדָה		
2 m. sg.	כָּבַדְתָּ	2 m. pl.	כְּבַדְתֶּם
2 f. sg.	כָּבַדְתְּ	2 f. pl.	כְּבַדְתֶּן
1 c. sg.	כָּבַדְתִּי	1 c. pl.	כָּבַדְנוּ

17.6c   **Qal Affix U Class**[3]

3 m. sg.	קָטֹן	3 c. pl.	קָטְנוּ
3 f. sg.	קָטְנָה		
2 m. sg.	קָטֹנְתָּ	2 m. pl.	קְטָנְתֶּם ←
2 f. sg.	קָטֹנְתְּ	2 f. pl.	קְטָנְתֶּן ←
1 c. sg.	קָטֹנְתִּי	1 c. pl.	קָטֹנּוּ

17.6d The **Qal prefix** of I and U class verbs tends to follow the pattern of יִשְׁלַח That is, these verbs have pataḥ ◌ַ under the second root letter: יִקְטַן יִכְבַּד etc. or qamats ◌ָ if the third letter is א as in יִירָא

---

2. In the Qal affix, only the 3 m. sg. demonstrates the I class vowel.

3. Notice that in קָטֹן the holem וֹ (written defectiva in our example) becomes a qamats ḥatuf in a closed, unaccented syllable. (6.3b)

17.6e The Qal participles of I and U class verbs do not have ḥolem after the first root letter; they build on the 3 m. sg. affix. Because I and U class verbs are usually stative, their participles are adjectives.

Qal Participle

I Class		U Class	
m. sg.	כָּבֵד	m. sg.	קָטֹן
f. sg.	כְּבֵדָה	f. sg.	קְטֹנָה
m. pl.	כְּבֵדִים	m. pl.	קְטֹנִים
f. pl.	כְּבֵדוֹת	f. pl.	קְטֹנוֹת

Assignments

A. Vocabulary: words 131–135.

B. Learn the Qal affix paradigms of I and U class verbs (see Verb Chart A).

C. On ☺ שַׁבְּחִי review your songs and listen to מִזְמוֹר שִׁיר **Psalm 92:1–5** (track 17).

D. Read and translate Genesis 22:12–14.

E. Read Genesis 21:1–7 and find the following:

Verse: 1   A verb in the Piʿel _____

             A DDO _____

             A Qal 3 m. sg. affix form _____

             A verb whose third root letter is ה _____

             A dagesh lene _____

             A proper noun _____

             A preposition _____

             A prefix pronoun _____

Verse: 2   A noun in the absolute _____

             A noun with a possessive suffix _____

             A vav conversive _____

             A 1st י verb _____

Verse: 3   A 3 f. sg. affix form _____

             A construct chain _____

יהוה לִי לֹא אִירָא מַה־יַּעֲשֶׂה לִי אָדָם:

—▶—

       A 3 m. sg. Qal prefix form _____

       The relative pronoun _____

Verse: 4   A noun that is present twice _____

       A verb that looks like a hollow verb _____

       A m. pl. noun in the absolute _____

       A Pi`el affix form _____

Verse: 5   A conjunction _____

Verse: 6   A 3 m. sg. Qal prefix form _____

       A 3 m. sg. affix form _____

       A 3 f. sg. prefix form _____

       A m. sg. Qal participle _____

       A 1 c. sg. pronominal suffix _____

Verse: 7   A 1 c. sg. affix form _____

       A dagesh forte _____

LESSON 18

שְׁמַע יִשְׂרָאֵל יהוה אֱלֹהֵינוּ יהוה אֶחָד:

Deuteronomy 6:4

18.1   Verb Analysis שְׁמַע

Root	Stem	Form	Person/Gender/Number	Special Features

18.1a   Is the form prefix? _____ Is it affix? _____ What is the sign of the Qal affix? _____ _____ (4.2a) Is the form participle? _____ What is the sign of the Qal participle? _____ _____ (9.3a) If this were an infinitve, you might see ל in front of the root. (11.2a) There is one other form: the **imperative** (command), which we have here.

> The **Qal imperative** is formed by removing the prefix pronoun from a second person prefix form. Thus, a shewa under the first root letter ‿ ‿ ‿ can indicate a Qal imperative form.

m. sg. imperative   2 m. sg. prefix

שְׁמַע   תִּשְׁמַע

18.1b   If the first root letter is a guttural, you can expect a composite shewa, for example, אֱמֹר

18.1c   Imperatives are always in the second person. When no other indicator is attached to the end of the imperative, the gender is masculine and the number is singular. Write 2 m. sg. in the PGN column.

18.2   יִשְׂרָאֵל means _____ Here it is the one addressed by the command: *(You) hear, O Israel!* This is called a **vocative**. Note that no special endings are used for the vocative. You can recognize its use only by the context.

18.3 יהוה אֱלֹהֵינוּ יהוה אֶחָד

18.3a יהוה means _____

18.3b אֱלֹהֵינוּ

> נוּ___ at the end of a word (noun, preposition, or verb) is the first person plural suffix (*us, our*).

אֱלֹהֵינוּ means _____

יהוה אֱלֹהֵינוּ can be treated as a noun sentence: _____ (2.10b)

18.3c אֶחָד יהוה | אֶחָד means *one* [feminine form: אַחַת]. Numbers in Hebrew do not all act the same way. "One" can be a regular adjective or it can be a substantive, in which case it is placed before the noun. This phrase is sometimes translated *one Lord*, with *one* as an adjective.

What kind of adjective? _____ (14.2c) Or it can be translated as a noun sentence: *the Lord is one*. Our entire phrase then has at least two possible translations. *the Lord is our God, one Lord*[1] or *the Lord is our God, the Lord is one*. Actually there are some other possibilities here, and you should notice at this point that we cannot always be sure there is a single "correct" translation.

18.4 Verse translation: _____

18.5 Extra Grammar: Some kinds and uses of adjectives

Attributive (definite)	הָאָרֶץ הַטּוֹבָה	*the good land*
Attributive (indefinite)	אֶרֶץ טוֹבָה	*a good land*
Attributive (demonstrative)	הָאָרֶץ הַזֹּאת	*this land*
Predicate	טוֹבָה הָאָרֶץ	*the land is good*
	וְהַמֶּלֶךְ ... זָקֵן	*and the king was old*
Predicate (demonstrative)	זֹאת הָאָרֶץ	*this is the land*
	אֵלֶּה אֱלֹהֶיךָ	*these are your gods*
Substantive	אַחַד מֵהֶם	*one of them*

---

1. I am not entirely comfortable with the use of אֶחָד as an attributive adjective for יהוה The reason is that since יהוה is a proper noun, its attributive adjective should have the definite article: יהוה הָאֶחָד

שְׁמַע יִשְׂרָאֵל יהוה אֱלֹהֵינוּ יהוה אֶחָד:

In addition to translating the following verses, identify types of adjectives involved using the framework of 18.5.

1   מִן־הָאָרֶץ הַהוּא אֶל־אֶרֶץ טוֹבָה   *Exodus 3:8*

2   מֵעַל הָאָרֶץ הַטֹּבָה אֲשֶׁר יהוה נֹתֵן לָכֶם   *Deuteronomy 11:17*

    [מֵעַל לָכֶם ⟶ *from on* ל + 2 m. pl. object suffix]

3   וַיֹּאמְרוּ טוֹבָה הָאָרֶץ אֲשֶׁר־יהוה אֱלֹהֵינוּ נֹתֵן לָנוּ   *Deuteronomy 1:25*

4   וְנָתַתִּי אֶת־הָאָרֶץ הַזֹּאת לְזַרְעֶךָ   *Genesis 48:4*

5   וַיֹּאמֶר לְזַרְעֲךָ אֶתֵּן אֶת־הָאָרֶץ הַזֹּאת   *Genesis 12:7*

Assignments

A.   Vocabulary: words 1–140.

B.   Read and translate Genesis 28:10–12. During Lessons 18–24, listen to the cantillation of Genesis 28:10–29:11: ⊙ א ב track 12.

C.   ⊙ שַׁבְּחִי track 18: sing and memorize שְׁמַע **Deuteronomy 6:4**.

D.   Translate:

1   שֵׁם הָאֶחָד פֶּלֶג   *Genesis 10:25*

2   שְׁמַע בְּקוֹל הָעָם לְכֹל אֲשֶׁר־יֹאמְרוּ אֵלֶיךָ   *1 Samuel 8:7*

3   שְׁמַע לְקוֹל דִּבְרֵי יהוה   *1 Samuel 15:1*

4   שְׁלַח־לִי אִישׁ־חָכָם [חָכָם *wise*]   *2 Chronicles 2:6*

5   אֱמֹר אֶל־בְּנֵי־יִשְׂרָאֵל [אָמַר 18.1b]   *Exodus 33:5*

6   שֵׁם אַחַת חַנָּה   *1 Samuel 1:2*

7   וּשְׁמַע אֵת כָּל־אֲשֶׁר יֹאמַר יהוה אֱלֹהֵינוּ   (27) *Deuteronomy 5:24*

8   קְרָא שְׁמוֹ יִזְרְעֶאל   *Hosea 1:4*

9   קוֹל אֹמֵר קְרָא   *Isaiah 40:6*

10   שְׁמֹר אֶת־הָאִישׁ הַזֶּה   *1 Kings 20:39*

11   אֱמֹר אֶל־כָּל־עַם הָאָרֶץ וְאֶל־הַכֹּהֲנִים   *Zechariah 7:5*

LESSON 19

וְאָמַרְתָּ דַּבֵּר יהוה כִּי שֹׁמֵעַ עַבְדֶּךָ

1 Samuel 3:9

19.1 Verb Analysis וְאָמַרְתָּ

What kind of dagesh is in the הּ _____ (3.3)

Root	Stem	Form	Person/Gender/Number	Special Features

Don't forget to note the type of vav in the Special Features column. (8.1d)

Translation: _____

19.2 דִּבֶּר יהוה

19.2a Verb Analysis דִּבֶּר

Root	Stem	Form	Person/Gender/Number	Special Features

What kind of dagesh is in the בּ _____ (1.2) Such a dagesh in the middle root letter of a verb indicates _____ (2.3c) Is the form affix? _____ (4.2a) What vowel would be under the first root letter if this were an affix? ____

> The **Pi`el imperative** is formed by removing the prefix pronoun from a second person prefix form. Thus, pataḥ under the first root letter ‿ ‿ ‿ can indicate a Pi`el imperative form.

וְאָמַרְתָּ דַּבֵּר יהוה כִּי שֹׁמֵעַ עַבְדֶּךָ

m. sg. Pi`el imperative	2 m. sg. Pi`el prefix
דַּבֵּר	תְּדַבֵּר

What will be the PGN of דַּבֵּר _____ (18.1c)

19.2b יהוה means _____ How is it related to the imperative just preceding it? _____
_____ (18.2)

Translate the entire phrase: _____

19.3 כִּי שֹׁמֵעַ עַבְדֶּךָ

19.3a Verb Analysis שֹׁמֵעַ

Root	Stem	Form	Person/Gender/Number	Special Features

Review 9.3a if you need help.

19.3b עַבְדֶּךָ

> ךָ ___ is the second person masculine singular possessive suffix for nouns and prepositions.

עֶבֶד means _____
Translation of phrase: _____

19.4 Sentence translation: _____
_____

19.5 Extra Grammar

The word עַבְדֶּךָ in the lesson sentence usually reads עַבְדְּךָ but here it is **in pause**. That means the word falls at a **major disjunctive accent**, which may cause a change in pointing. In the case of עַבְדֶּךָ the accent has moved from the last syllable ךָ to the second to last, and ךָ now bearing the accent, has become דֶּךָ

Noun	Noun with Suffix	Noun with Suffix (in pause)
עֶ֫בֶד	עַבְדְּךָ	עַבְדֶּ֑ךָ
דָּבָר	דְּבָרִי	דְּבָרָ֑י
כֶּ֫סֶף	כַּסְפְּךָ	כַּסְפֶּֽךָ׃

Preposition	Preposition with Suffix	Preposition with Suffix (in pause)
לְ	לְךָ	לָ֑ךְ
מִן	מִמְּךָ	מִמֶּ֑ךָּ

19.6   Exercise

Often it's the little words that will trip you up. Be sure you're confident of these, which may either look or sound similar.

	שֵׁם	שָׁם
	לֹא	לוֹ
אֶל	עַל	אֵל
עִם	אִם	עַם
	בַּת	בַּ֫יִת
	דִּבֶּר	דָּבָר
	הוּא	הִיא
	יוֹם	יָם
	מִי	מָה
	אֵין	עַ֫יִן
	עַתָּה	אַתָּה
	צָבָא	צִוָּה
יָרֵא	רָאָה	רָעָה
	עָשָׂה	נָשָׂא

Assignments

A.   Vocabulary: words 141–145.

B.   ☉שַׁבְּחִי track 12: review and memorize וּפָרַצְתָּ **Genesis 28:14**.

C.   Read and translate Genesis 28:13–15.

D. Translate:

1   שְׁמַע יַעֲקֹב עַבְדִּי *Isaiah 44:1*

2   וַיֹּאמֶר מֹשֶׁה כֵּן דִּבַּרְתָּ *Exodus 10:29*

3   מַה־דִּבַּרְתָּ אֶל־הַמֶּלֶךְ *Jeremiah 38:25*

4   דַּבֵּר אֶל־בְּנֵי יִשְׂרָאֵל וְאָמַרְתָּ אֲלֵהֶם *Leviticus 1:2*

5   כִּי־לֹא שָׁמַעְתָּ בְּקוֹל יהוה אֱלֹהֶיךָ *Deuteronomy 28:45*

6   שַׁלַּח אֶת־בְּנִי *Exodus 4:23*

7   דַּבֵּר אֶל־פַּרְעֹה מֶלֶךְ מִצְרָיִם *Exodus 6:29*

✡ 8   שַׁלַּח לַחְמְךָ עַל־פְּנֵי הַמָּיִם *Qohelet 11:1*

9   עֲמֹד בְּשַׁעַר בֵּית יהוה וְקָרָאתָ שָּׁם אֶת־הַדָּבָר הַזֶּה *Jeremiah 7:2*

10 וַיֹּאמֶר יהוה אֶל־מֹשֶׁה עֲבֹר לִפְנֵי הָעָם *Exodus 17:5*

11 שָׁמֹר וְשָׁמַעְתָּ אֵת כָּל־הַדְּבָרִים הָאֵלֶּה *Deuteronomy 12:28*

וְעַתָּה יהוה אֱלֹהֵי יִשְׂרָאֵל שְׁמֹר לְעַבְדְּךָ דָוִד אָבִי אֵת

✡12 אֲשֶׁר דִּבַּרְתָּ לוֹ *1 Kings 8:25*

LESSON 20

———◆———

וַיִּקְרָא פַרְעֹה אֶל־מֹשֶׁה וַיֹּאמֶר לְכוּ עִבְדוּ אֶת־יהוה

Exodus 10:24

20.1 וַיִּקְרָא פַרְעֹה אֶל־מֹשֶׁה

Verb Analysis וַיִּקְרָא

Root	Stem	Form	Person/Gender/Number	Special Features

קרא means _____

Translation of phrase: _____

20.2 וַיֹּאמֶר means _____

20.3 לְכוּ

This word begins the quotation—what Pharaoh said to Moses. Direct address of one person to another frequently means that imperatives will be used, as is the case here. לְכוּ is a plural im-perative (derived from תֵּלְכוּ [2 m. pl. Qal prefix]). 18.1a

---

ו___ is the second person masculine plural imperative ending.

This leaves only two letters for the root, and here there is no prefix with its vowel to help in determining the root. The loss of a root letter in the imperative can occur with all types of roots in which there is a weak letter. You simply have to guess the root, but the possibilities will be significantly reduced by your knowledge of vocabulary and the missing letter rules. Here the possibilities would be לכה ליך לוך נלך הלך ילך Which root is familiar? In this case, you may also remember from 11.2a that whenever the remaining two root letters are לכ the root is הלך

112

וַיִּקְרָא פַרְעֹה אֶל־מֹשֶׁה וַיֹּאמֶר לְכוּ עִבְדוּ אֶת־יהוה

Fill in the chart:

Root	Stem	Form	Person/Gender/Number	Special Features

20.4 Analyze עִבְדוּ

Is this an affix form? _____ Which form is it? (on the basis of elimination and context)

_____

Root	Stem	Form	Person/Gender/Number	Special Features

This is the regular vowel pattern for the masculine Qal plural imperative for verbs having three strong root letters. Translate: _____

20.5 Translate the verse: _____

_____

20.6 Extra Grammar

20.6a As already noted, the imperative is a derivative of the prefix form. This may not be immediately apparent in all four imperatives of every verb, but it is useful to note this feature as an aid in recognition and memorization.

Qal Imperatives

	Strong	3rd א	1st Guttural
m. sg.	שְׁמַע	קְרָא	עֲבֹד
f. sg.	שִׁמְעִי	קִרְאִי	עִבְדִי
m. pl.	שִׁמְעוּ	קִרְאוּ	עִבְדוּ
f. pl.	שְׁמַעְנָה	קְרֶאנָה	עֲבֹדְנָה

	1st י ישׁב	1st י ירא	3rd ה
m. sg.	שֵׁב	יְרָא	רְאֵה
f. sg.	שְׁבִי	יְרְאִי	רְאִי
m. pl.	שְׁבוּ	יְרְאוּ	רְאוּ
f. pl.	שֵּׁבְנָה	יְרֶאנָה	רְאֶינָה

	Hollow[1]	Hollow	Hollow
m. sg.	קוּם	בּוֹא	שִׂים
f. sg.	קוּמִי	בּוֹאִי	שִׂימִי
m. pl.	קוּמוּ	בּוֹאוּ	שִׂימוּ
f. pl.	קֹמְנָה ←	בֹּאנָה	שֵׂמְנָה ←

	1st נ	1st נ[2]	נתן
m. sg.	גַּשׁ	נְפֹל	תֵּן
f. sg.	גְּשִׁי	נִפְלִי	תְּנִי
m. pl.	גְּשׁוּ	נִפְלוּ	תְּנוּ
f. pl.	גַּשְׁנָה	נְפֹלְנָה	תֵּנָּה

20.6b

Pi'el Imperatives

	Strong	3rd Guttural	Mid-Guttural and ר
m. sg.	דַּבֵּר	שַׁלַּח	בָּרֵךְ
f. sg.	דַּבְּרִי	שַׁלְּחִי	בָּרְכִי
m. pl.	דַּבְּרוּ	שַׁלְּחוּ	בָּרְכוּ
f. pl.	דַּבֵּרְנָה	שַׁלַּחְנָה	בָּרֵכְנָה

---

1. The imperatives of hollow verbs whose middle letter is ו or י can be written plene or defectiva. Watch for spellings such as קֻם and בֹּא Note the variation from the pattern of the f. pl.

2. Some 1st נ verbs lose the נ of the root in the imperative form, and some act like strong verbs with all root letters present.

20.7   Exercises

A.   Write the four Qal imperatives for the verbs listed below:

הלך	עמד	שׁמר

m. sg.

f. sg.

m. pl.

f. pl.

B.   Write the root for each of the following Qal imperative forms:

דְּעִי	עֲנִי	עֲשֵׂה
עֲלוּ	מְצָא	בְּנֵה
קְרָא	שְׂאוּ	מֻת
צְאוּ	שְׁמַעְנָה	רֵד

Assignments

A.   Vocabulary: words 1–150. Test yourself using ◉אֵלֶּה הַדְּבָרִים tracks 3–17.

B.   Learn the imperatives presented in 20.6a and 20.6b.

C.   ◉שְׁבָחִי track 19: listen to and sing שׁוּבִי נַפְשִׁי **Psalm 116:7–8**.

D.   Read and translate Genesis 28:16–18.

E.   Translate:

1   קוּם צֵא מִן־הָאָרֶץ   *Genesis 31:13*

2   לְכִי וּבֹאִי אֶל־הַמֶּלֶךְ דָּוִד   *1 Kings 1:13*

3   לֵךְ וְאָמַרְתָּ אֶל־עַבְדִּי   *2 Samuel 7:5*

4   תְּנוּ־לָנוּ מַיִם   *Exodus 17:2*

5   דְּעוּ אֶת־יהוה   *Jeremiah 31:34*

6   בֹּא דַבֵּר אֶל־פַּרְעֹה מֶלֶךְ מִצְרָיִם וִישַׁלַּח אֶת־בְּנֵי־יִשְׂרָאֵל
מֵאַרְצוֹ׃   *Exodus 6:11*   [Read וִישַׁלַּח + יְשַׁלַּח as if it were written

7   דַּבְּרוּ אֶל־בְּנֵי יִשְׂרָאֵל   *Leviticus 11:2*

8   דְּעוּ כִּי־יהוה הוּא אֱלֹהִים   *Psalms 100:3*

115

LESSON 21

———

וַיִּקַּח יִשְׂרָאֵל אֵת כָּל־הֶעָרִים הָאֵלֶּה וַיֵּשֶׁב יִשְׂרָאֵל בְּכָל־עָרֵי הָאֱמֹרִי

Numbers 21:25

21.1 וַיִּקַּח יִשְׂרָאֵל

Verb Analysis וַיִּקַּח

Root	Stem	Form	Person/Gender/Number	Special Features

You should be able to fill in all but the root column. What kind of dagesh is in the קּ _____
_____ For root letters then, we have קקח ⟷ קח You would expect the root to be
נקח but this is the <u>one</u> instance where a footprint dagesh of an assimilated first root letter represents not a נ but a ל So the root is _____

21.2 אֵת is the sign of _____ (7.2a) Where is the direct object? _____

21.3 כָּל־הֶעָרִים הָאֵלֶּה

21.3a כָּל means _____ Look at the next word, הֶעָרִים What kind of endiNG does it have?
_____ (6.5a) If you take off the noun endiNG, you still do not have the root, however.
The הֶ at the beginning is the definite article. Usually before a guttural it is pointed הָ (4.5b),
but הֶ or sometimes even הַ is a possibility. Now you have עָר left — this is a form of the noun
עִיר one of a small group of irregular nouns. עָרִים is the plural form. This is all the more unusual because עִיר is a feminine noun (even though it lacks the feminine endiNG in the singular), and it takes the masculine plural noun endings. הֶעָרִים will mean _____

21.3b הָאֵלֶּה | הָ means _____ The dagesh associated with the definite article is lost because
_____ (4.5b) אֵלֶּה is a demonstrative adjective meaning *these*.

While you must choose the correct form, זֶה or זֹאת in the singular, אֵלֶּה is used for the plural with both masculine and feminine nouns. What do you call the type of adjectival construction in this phrase? _____ (14.2c)

Translation of the whole phrase: _____

21.4 וַיֵּשֶׁב יִשְׂרָאֵל

Verb Analysis וַיֵּשֶׁב

Root	Stem	Form	Person/Gender/Number	Special Features

Left with only שׁב for the root, how do you determine the missing letter?
_____ (3.1)

Phrase translation: _____

21.5 בְּכָל־עָרֵי הָאֱמֹרִי

21.5a בְּכָל means _____

21.5b עָרֵי | יִ _ at the end of a word indicates _____ (6.3c)

The plural absolute form of this word is _____ and means _____

הָאֱמֹרִי means *the Amorite* (to be construed in a collective sense).

What do you call the two-word phrase? _____

Is it definite or indefinite? _____

21.6 Sentence translation: _____

_____

21.7 Extra Grammar

21.7a לקח is a common irregular verb. But in the Qal affix it follows the pattern of the strong verb. You should be able to fill in the chart below:

117

וַיִּקַּח יִשְׂרָאֵל אֵת כָּל־הֶעָרִים הָאֵלֶּה וַיֵּשֶׁב יִשְׂרָאֵל בְּכָל־עָרֵי הָאֱמֹרִי

Qal Affix לקח

3 m. sg.	לָ קַ ח	3 c. pl.	— ⌴ ⌴ ⌴
3 f. sg.	— ⌴ ⌴ ⌴		
2 m. sg.	— ⌴ ⌴ ⌴	2 m. pl.	— ⌴ ⌴ ⌴
2 f. sg.	— ⌴ ⌴ ⌴	2 f. pl.	— ⌴ ⌴ ⌴
1 c. sg.	— ⌴ ⌴ ⌴	1 c. pl.	— ⌴ ⌴ ⌴

21.7b The Qal prefix of לקח follows the pattern of נגשׁ (16.5b) Complete the chart:

Qal Prefix לקח

3 m. sg.	יִ קַ ח	3 m. pl.	— ⌴ ⌴
3 f. sg.	⌴ ⌴ ⌴	3 f. pl.	— ⌴ ⌴ ⌴
2 m. sg.	⌴ ⌴ ⌴	2 m. pl.	— ⌴ ⌴ ⌴
2 f. sg.	— ⌴ ⌴	2 f. pl.	— ⌴ ⌴ ⌴
1 c. sg.	⌴ ⌴ אֶ	1 c. pl.	⌴ ⌴ ⌴

21.7c The Qal imperatives of לקח also follow the pattern of נגשׁ Complete the chart:

Qal Imperative לקח

m. sg.	קַ ח	m. pl.	— ⌴ ⌴
f. sg.	— ⌴ ⌴	f. pl.	— ⌴ ⌴

21.7d The m. sg. Qal participle of לקח is לֹקֵחַ The ַ is a furtive pataḥ. (5.4)

21.7e The Qal infinitive construct of לקח is קַ֫חַת

Assignments

A. Vocabulary: words 151–155.

B. Memorize the paradigms for the Qal of לקח

C. ☉שַׁבְּחִי track 20: suggested song is מַלְכוּתְךָ **Psalm 145:13.**

D. Read and translate Genesis 28:19–22.

E. Translate:

1 וַיֵּצְאוּ כְּאִישׁ אֶחָד *1 Samuel 11:7*

2 וְלֹא־לָקַ֫חְתָּ מִיַּד־אִישׁ מְא֫וּמָה [*anything*] *1 Samuel 12:4*

וַיִּקַּח יִשְׂרָאֵל אֵת כָּל־הֶעָרִים הָאֵלֶּה וַיֵּשֶׁב יִשְׂרָאֵל בְּכָל־עָרֵי הָאֱמֹרִי

---

3   וְלֹא־יָשַׁב אָדָם שָׁם   *Jeremiah 2:6*

4   וַיָּבֹא שָׁאוּל עַד־עִיר עֲמָלֵק   *1 Samuel 15:5*

5   וְהוּא יוֹשֵׁב בְּאֶרֶץ הַנֶּגֶב   *Genesis 24:62*

6   וְיָשַׁבְתָּ בְאֶרֶץ־גֹּשֶׁן   *Genesis 45:10*

7   וַיַּרְא וְהִנֵּה הָעָם יָצָא מִן־הָעִיר   *Judges 9:43*

8   וְדָוִד יוֹשֵׁב בִּירוּשָׁלָ͏ִם   *2 Samuel 11:1*

9   קַח אֶת־אַהֲרֹן וְאֶת־בָּנָיו   *Leviticus 8:2*

10   וַיִּבְנוּ אֶת־הֶעָרִים וַיֵּשְׁבוּ בָהֶם   *Judges 21:23*

11   כִּי־בָנָה יְהוָה צִיּוֹן [אֵת *note absence of*   *Psalms 102:17*

12   שְׁבוּ בָאָרֶץ וְעִבְדוּ אֶת־מֶלֶךְ בָּבֶל   *2 Kings 25:24*

LESSON 22

—

לֹא־תִקַּח אִשָּׁה לִבְנִי מִבְּנוֹת הַכְּנַעֲנִי אֲשֶׁר אָנֹכִי יֹשֵׁב בְּאַרְצוֹ

Genesis 24:37

22.1 Verb לֹא־תִקַּח

Root	Stem	Form	Person/Gender/Number	Special Features

You should be able to analyze this verb. (21.7b) The tense of the verb translation will be _____
_____ (14.1) Translate the verb phrase: _____

22.2 אִשָּׁה means _____ Relationship of noun to verb phrase: _____

22.3 לִבְנִי There are three parts to this word; can you break it down? ל means _____ בֵן means
_____ ִי means _____ (8.3) Notice the vowel changes in the noun when it is
combined in such a phrase. Translate the word: _____

22.4 מִבְּנוֹת ‖ ☐ מ means _____ (3.4b) בְּנוֹת means *daughters.* Minus the endiNG וֹת____
is the familiar root בַן The feminine singular of בְּנוֹת is בַּת an irregular noun.

> וֹת____ is the feminine plural noun endiNG for both the construct and absolute plural.

22.4a We can now make a chart for feminine nouns as we did for masculine nouns in 6.5a. נַחֲלָה
means *property, inheritance.*

	Absolute	Construct
Singular	נַחֲלָה	נַחֲלַת
Plural	נְחָלוֹת	נַחֲלוֹת

In the singular absolute, הָ or הֶ is a common endiNG for feminine nouns.

In the singular construct or with a suffix, these nouns will all end in תַ

Fill in the appropriate endiNGs (consonants and vowels) in the chart below.

מַלְכָּה means *queen*.

		Absolute		Construct
Singular		מַלְכּ____		מַלְכּ____
Plural		מַלְכּ____		מַלְכּ____

22.5 הַכְּנַעֲנִי

הַ in front of a word means _____ כְּנַעֲנִי is related to a place name you have already seen. The ending, a **gentilic**, is equivalent to *-ite* in English; הַכְּנַעֲנִי means *the Canaanite*.

How are מִבְּנוֹת and הַכְּנַעֲנִי related? _____ (5.1b)

Translation: _____

22.6 אֲשֶׁר אָנֹכִי יֹשֵׁב

אֲשֶׁר means _____ (5.3a) אָנֹכִי ⟷ אֲנִי which means _____

Verb Analysis יֹשֵׁב

Root	Stem	Form	Person/Gender/Number	Special Features

Translation of phrase: _____

22.7 בְּאַרְצוֹ

Again there are three parts to this word. בְּ means _____ אֶרֶץ means _____ וֹ ⟷ וֹ as

a suffix pronoun. Translation: _____

22.8 Sentence translation: _____

_____

22.8a Notice the way this subordinate אֲשֶׁר clause is constructed. It is a clause that further describes the Canaanite. In the clause in Hebrew, a pronoun is used that repeats this antecedent noun:

הַכְּנַעֲנִי │אֲשֶׁר│ אָנֹכִי יֹשֵׁב בְּאַרְצוֹ

*the **Canaanite**, **who** I am dwelling in **his** land*

This is a very common syntactical construction in Hebrew. English combines the וֹ . . . אֲשֶׁר to give:

*the **Canaanite**, in **whose** land I am dwelling*

22.9 Extra Grammar

You know from 5.3a that the relative particle אֲשֶׁר never changes. That is, its form will always be the same, regardless of what it modifies. It can fill any one of several functions and can be translated in many different ways, depending on its particular use in each instance. You have seen several of these uses in the readings from Genesis 22 and 28. In addition to what we usually think of as "relative" functions, אֲשֶׁר can be the subject of a verb, the object of a verb—with or without אֵת—or the object of a preposition.

A.   אֲשֶׁר as the subject of a verb:

Genesis 38:10 וַיֵּרַע בְּעֵינֵי יהוה אֲשֶׁר עָשָׂה

a)   *and it was evil in the eyes of the Lord—**what** he had done*

b)   *and **what** he had done was evil in the eyes of the Lord* [1]

B.   אֲשֶׁר as the direct object of a verb:

1.   Definite direct object with אֵת

Genesis 28:15 עָשִׂיתִי אֵת אֲשֶׁר־דִּבַּרְתִּי לָךְ

*I have done **(that about) which** I had spoken to you*

2.   Direct object without אֵת

Genesis 22:2 אֲשֶׁר־אָהַבְתָּ

__whom__ you love

C.   אֲשֶׁר as the object of a preposition:

1.   With אֶל

Ruth 1:16 כִּי אֶל־אֲשֶׁר תֵּלְכִי אֵלֵךְ

for (to) __where__ you go, I will go

---

1. Often the English will have different word order from the Hebrew, though the translation itself is straightforward. Here we are giving a literal translation followed by a more idiomatic rendering.

2. With **בְּ**

Isaiah 65:12 וּבַאֲשֶׁר לֹא־חָפַצְתִּי בְּחַרְתֶּם

you chose <u>that in which</u> I did not delight

3. With **מִן**

Genesis 31:1 וּמֵאֲשֶׁר לְאָבִינוּ עָשָׂה אֵת כָּל־הַכָּבֹד הַזֶּה

<u>*and from that which*</u> *was our father's, he has gotten all this glory*

D. **אֲשֶׁר** expressing a relative relationship:

m. sg. antecedent   *Genesis 29:9* הַצֹּאן אֲשֶׁר לְאָבִיהָ

the flock,<u>which</u> was her father's

f. sg.   *Genesis 28:18* וַיִּקַּח אֶת־הָאֶבֶן אֲשֶׁר־שָׂם מְרַאֲשֹׁתָיו

and he took the stone, <u>which</u> he had put at his head place

m. pl.   *Genesis 20:9* מַעֲשִׂים אֲשֶׁר לֹא־יֵעָשׂוּ

things <u>that</u> should not have been done

f. pl.   *Deuteronomy 4:2* אֶת־מִצְוֹת... אֲשֶׁר אָנֹכִי מְצַוֶּה אֶתְכֶם

the commandments . . . <u>which</u> I am commanding you

E. **אֲשֶׁר** in compounds:

אֲשֶׁר can be compounded with an attached or independent preposition. In these compounds, **אֲשֶׁר** converts the preposition into a conjunction but itself often need not be translated; its function is to signal that a clause is coming.

1. With attached preposition:

כֵּן תַּעֲשֶׂה כַּאֲשֶׁר דִּבַּרְתָּ *Genesis 18:5*

thus you will do <u>just as</u> you spoke

2. With independent preposition:

Judges 3:17 וְכָל־יִשְׂרָאֵל עֹבְרִים בֶּחָרָבָה עַד אֲשֶׁר־תַּמּוּ...לַעֲבֹר אֶת־הַיַּרְדֵּן

and all Israel was crossing over on dry land <u>until</u> they had finished crossing the Jordan

לֹא־תִקַּח אִשָּׁה לִבְנִי מִבְּנוֹת הַכְּנַעֲנִי אֲשֶׁר אָנֹכִי יֹשֵׁב בְּאַרְצוֹ

Assignments

A. Vocabulary: words 1–160.

B. Read and translate Genesis 29:1–3.

C. ☉שְׁבָחִי track 21: listen to רַבּוֹת מַחֲשָׁבוֹת **Proverbs 19:21** and **Psalm 33:11**. Also listen to and translate שִׁמְעָה **Psalm 97:8** (track 3).

D. Translate:

1   וַתְּדַבֵּר אֵלָיו כַּדְּבָרִים הָאֵלֶּה [כַּ + הַ ⟶ כָּ]   *Genesis 39:17*

2   תֵּדַע כִּי לַיהוה הָאָרֶץ   *Exodus 9:29*

3   וְלָקַחְתָּ אִשָּׁה לִבְנִי מִשָּׁם   *Genesis 24:7*

4   כִּי־תָבֹא אֶל־הָאָרֶץ אֲשֶׁר יהוה אֱלֹהֶיךָ נֹתֵן לָךְ   *Deuteronomy 17:14*

5   יָבֹאוּ בְּנֵי הָאֱלֹהִים אֶל־בְּנוֹת הָאָדָם   *Genesis 6:4*

✡6   וַיֹּאמֶר דָּוִיד אֶל־הָאֱלֹהִים חָטָאתִי מְאֹד אֲשֶׁר עָשִׂיתִי אֶת־הַדָּבָר הַזֶּה [חָטָא ⟶ sin]   *1 Chronicles 21:8*

7   יִצְחָק אֲשֶׁר תֵּלֵד לְךָ שָׂרָה   *Genesis 17:21*

✡8   אֶל כָּל־הַמָּקוֹם אֲשֶׁר נָבוֹא שָׁמָּה אִמְרִי־לִי אָחִי הוּא   *Genesis 20:13*

9   וַיָּקָם מֶלֶךְ־חָדָשׁ עַל־מִצְרָיִם אֲשֶׁר לֹא־יָדַע אֶת־יוֹסֵף: [חָדָשׁ new]   *Exodus 1:8*

✡10   וָאֹמַר אֲלֵכֶם בָּאתֶם עַד־הַר הָאֱמֹרִי אֲשֶׁר־יהוה אֱלֹהֵינוּ נֹתֵן לָנוּ:   *Deuteronomy 1:20*

11   וְלוֹ־אֶתֵּן אֶת־הָאָרֶץ אֲשֶׁר דָּרַךְ־בָּהּ וּלְבָנָיו [דֶּרֶךְ ⟶ verb related to]   *Deuteronomy 1:36*

12   כִּי עִמְּךָ יהוה אֱלֹהֶיךָ בְּכֹל אֲשֶׁר תֵּלֵךְ   *Joshua 1:9*

LESSON 23

◆

אֶת־הָאָרֶץ אֲשֶׁר־יהוה אֱלֹהֵיכֶם נֹתֵן לָכֶם וִירִשְׁתֶּם אֹתָהּ וִישַׁבְתֶּם־בָּהּ

Deuteronomy 11:31

23.1   אֶת־הָאָרֶץ אֲשֶׁר־יהוה אֱלֹהֵיכֶם נֹתֵן לָכֶם

23.1a   There is only one new element here: the suffix on the noun אֱלֹהֵי and on the   preposition
ל   (For preposition ל pointed לָ   see **S 11.2**.)

> כֶם_____ is the second person masculine plural suffix for nouns, prepositions, and verbs.

אֱלֹהֵיכֶם means _____
Suffixes are usually attached to the _____ form of a noun.

23.1b   You should be able to analyze נֹתֵן

Root	Stem	Form	Person/Gender/Number	Special Features

Participles take on "tense" from the context in which they occur. Here the sense may be present: *is giving*, or of imminent future: *is about to give*.

23.1c   Translation: _____

23.2   וִירִשְׁתֶּם אֹתָהּ וִישַׁבְתֶּם־בָּהּ

23.2a   תֶּם_____ is the sign of which PGN and which form? _____ וִישַׁבְתֶּם should
yield a familiar root. What is it? _____ Is there any augment to the root to suggest
a stem other than Qal? _____ So you would expect the first root letter to be pointed
with a _____ (13.5) But יְ + וְ (here for a vav reversive) results in there being two vocal shewas
in a row—something Hebrew does not tolerate—and so וְיְ becomes וִי

אֶת־הָאָרֶץ אֲשֶׁר־יְהוָה אֱלֹהֵיכֶם נֹתֵן לָכֶם וִירִשְׁתֶּם אֹתָהּ וִישַׁבְתֶּם־בָּהּ

(When the conjunction וְ is followed by a letter other than יְ that is pointed with a shewa, the conjunction becomes וּ e.g., וּלְיַעֲקֹב [Rule of shewa and vocalization of וְ are covered in **S 14.3.1–2.**])

יָרַשׁ means *inherit*.

23.2b אֹתָהּ is an interesting construction. It consists of אֵת the sign of the DDO combined with a pronoun, here הּ_____ When the DDO sign combines with pronouns, the segol ֶ usually becomes a ḥolem: וֹ or ֹ_

Sign of the DDO+Suffix

1 c. sg.	אֹתִי	1 c. pl.	אֹתָנוּ	
2 m. sg.	אֹתְךָ	2 m. pl.	אֶתְכֶם	←
2 f. sg.	אֹתָךְ	2 f. pl.	אֶתְכֶן	←
3 m. sg.	אֹתוֹ	3 m. pl.	אֹתָם	
3 f. sg.	אֹתָהּ	3 f. pl.	אֶתְהֶן	←

An object pronoun can be directly attached to a verb: וּשְׁמַרְתִּיךָ *and I will guard you*, or it can be attached to the DDO marker, as "her" is in our lesson sentence.

In our phrase, what is the antecedent for the pronoun הּ_____

23.2c There is a circumstance in which the mappiq may be missing from the feminine singular suffix. If the final ה is already consonantal because it has its own vowel, then a mappiq is not needed to give it that force.

Numbers 30:8 וְקָמוּ נְדָרֶיהָ וֶאֱסָרֶהָ אֲשֶׁר־אָסְרָה עַל־נַפְשָׁהּ יָקֻמוּ

mappiq↑ f. sg. affix↑ no mappiq↑ ↑no mappiq

and her vows will stand and her bonds, which she bound on her life, will stand

23.2d Translate the phrase: _____

23.3 Translate the verse: _____

_____

אֶת־הָאָ֫רֶץ אֲשֶׁר־יהוה אֱלֹהֵיכֶם נֹתֵן לָכֶם וִירִשְׁתֶּם אֹתָהּ וִישַׁבְתֶּם־בָּהּ

Assignments

A. Vocabulary: words 1–165.

B. Memorize sign of the DDO + suffix (23.2b), or learn אֹתִי **Me** on א ב ☉ track 13 (lyrics: p. 466).

D. Read and translate Genesis 29:4–7

E. No sentences. Night off. וְהָיִיתָ אַךְ שָׂמֵחַ (Dt. 16:15b)

LESSON 24

אֲנִי וְהָאִשָּׁה הַזֹּאת יֹשְׁבֹת בְּבַ֫יִת אֶחָד

1 Kings 3:17

24.1 אֲנִי וְהָאִשָּׁה הַזֹּאת

Translate the first three words of this sentence: _____

24.2 יֹשְׁבֹת

Root	Stem	Form	Person/Gender/Number	Special Features

This word contains a root you have seen a number of times: _____ (17.5, 21.4) The ending וֹת _____ however, is used on what kind of words? _____ (22.4) Only one verb form can take noun endiNGs—the participle. Up until now the only participles you have seen have been masculine singular, which have no special endiNGs, just as masculine singular nouns have no special endiNGs. But all other participles must take the appropriate noun endiNGs that tell us the gender and number of the participle. This participle is what gender and number? _____

How do participles use these endiNGs? They must agree with the noun(s) or pronoun(s) they modify. What words are modified by this participle? _____

_____

Are the nouns definite? _____ Is the participle? _____ Then what sort of adjective must it be in this case? _____ (15.2)

How do you fit this phrase together? Review 9.3b and then translate the whole first phrase of the sentence: _____

24.3 בְּבַ֫יִת אֶחָד | בְּ means _____ בַּ֫יִת means _____ אֶחָד means _____ (18.3c and 18.5) The type of grammatical construction you have here is called _____

_____

Translate the phrase: _____

128

24.4   Sentence translation: _____

_____

24.5   Extra Grammar

24.5a   The Qal participle of almost every verb is regular and can be recognized by the ḥolem (written plene or defectiva) after the first root letter plus the appropriate noun endiNG. Complete the chart below:

Qal Participle

	יֹשֵׁב	ר מ א	ל פ נ
m. sg.	יֹשֵׁב	א מ ר	נ פ ל
f. sg.	יֹשְׁבָה¹	___ ⎵ ⎵⃛ ⎵	___ ⎵ ⎵ ⎵
m. pl.	יֹשְׁבִים	___ ⎵ ⎵⃛ ⎵	___ ⎵ ⎵ ⎵
f. pl.	יֹשְׁבוֹת	___ ⎵ ⎵⃛ ⎵	___ ⎵ ⎵ ⎵

24.5b   Qal Participle of Hollow Verbs

The Qal participle of hollow verbs does not have ḥolem וֹ after the first root letter.

You learned in 9.5a that the m. sg. participle of a hollow verb looks exactly like the 3 m. sg. affix form. There is the same ambiguity between the f. sg. participle and the 3 f. sg. affix form of hollow verbs. The same clues given in 9.5a for removing the ambiguity of בָּא will also work for בָּאָה. The plural forms can be recognized by the noun endiNGs.

Qal Participle Hollow Verbs

	בּוֹא	קוּם	שִׂים
m. sg.	בָּא	קָם	שָׂם
f. sg.	בָּאָה	קָמָה	שָׂמָה
m. pl.	בָּאִים	קָמִים	שָׂמִים
f. pl.	בָּאוֹת	קָמוֹת	שָׂמוֹת

24.5c   Participles, as verbal nouns, can have not only the definite article but also any of the attached prepositions that a noun can have. Participles may occur in the construct or absolute state. Translate the words or phrases below:

עִירוֹ   שַׁעַר   כָּל־יוֹצְאֵי   הַיֹּצֵא   יֹצֵא   לַיּוֹצֵא   וְהַיּוֹצְאֹת

---

1. The f. sg. participle may also end in ת__ e.g., יֹשֶׁבֶת

אֲנִי וְהָאִשָּׁה הַזֹּאת יֹשְׁבֹת בְּבַיִת אֶחָד

Assignments

A. Vocabulary: words 1–170.

B. Read and translate Genesis 29:8–11.

C. ⊙ **אב** track 22: learn קָם קָמָה בָּא בָּאָה (hollow participle; lyrics: p. 475)

D. Translate:

1 וַיִּרְאוּ הַשֹּׁמְרִים אִישׁ יוֹצֵא מִן־הָעִיר [וַיִּרְאוּ ≠ וַיִּירְאוּ] *Judges 1:24*

2 וְהִנֵּה רִבְקָה יֹצֵאת *Genesis 24:15* [Remember ת___ is a f. sg. participle endiNG]

✿3 הִנֵּה שֶׁבַע שָׁנִים בָּאוֹת *Genesis 41:29*

4 קוֹל דְּבָרִים אַתֶּם שֹׁמְעִים *Deuteronomy 4:12*

✿5 וַיֹּאמֶר הַמֶּלֶךְ זֹאת אֹמֶרֶת זֶה־בְּנִי *1 Kings 3:23*

6 וּמַלְכַּת־שְׁבָא שֹׁמַעַת אֶת־שֵׁמַע שְׁלֹמֹה *1 Kings 10:1* [מַלְכַּת *report* שֵׁמַע review 22.4]

7 ...וּבְנֵי יִשְׂרָאֵל הַיֹּצְאִים מֵאֶרֶץ מִצְרָיִם: *Numbers 26:4*

✿8 שִׁמְעוּ אֵלַי יֹדְעֵי צֶדֶק [צֶדֶק *righteousness*] *Isaiah 51:7*

9 הִנֵּה בֵית־יִשְׂרָאֵל אֹמְרִים *Ezekiel 12:27*

10 קָרְאוּ...וְכָל־הָעָם הַבָּאִים מֵעָרֵי יְהוּדָה *Jeremiah 36:9*

11 הִנֵּה־עָם יוֹרֵד מֵרָאשֵׁי הֶהָרִים *Judges 9:36*

✿12 וְיָרַדְתָּ לְפָנַי... וְהִנֵּה אָנֹכִי יֹרֵד אֵלֶיךָ *1 Samuel 10:8*

13 וְשָׂרָה שֹׁמַעַת פֶּתַח הָאֹהֶל [פֶּתַח *opening*] *Genesis 18:10*

✿14 כִּי כֹה אָמַר־יהוה אֶל־שַׁלֻּם בֶּן־יֹאשִׁיָּהוּ מֶלֶךְ יְהוּדָה הַמֹּלֵךְ תַּחַת יֹאשִׁיָּהוּ אָבִיו אֲשֶׁר יָצָא מִן־הַמָּקוֹם הַזֶּה לֹא־יָשׁוּב שָׁם עוֹד: *Jeremiah 22:11*

130

THE NOUN

You have been introduced to an assortment of nouns, both masculine and feminine, with an array of endings. At this point we can summarize some information about nouns in Hebrew.

All nouns have three properties:

Gender: masculine or feminine

Number: singular or plural

State: absolute or construct (5.2)

The following chart shows the endiNGs that help in determining these three things:

	Masc. Absolute	Masc. Construct	Fem. Absolute	Fem. Construct
singular	— no special endiNGs —		הָ_ תַ_	תַ_
	דָּבָר	דְּבַר	שַׁבָּת בְּרָכָה	שַׁבַּת בִּרְכַּת
plural	ים_	ֵי_	וֹת_	וֹת_
	דְּבָרִים	דִּבְרֵי	שַׁבָּתוֹת בְּרָכוֹת	שַׁבְּתֹת בִּרְכוֹת

Nouns present two basic difficulties: The first lies in determining whether the word under consideration is, in fact, a noun. The second concerns vowel changes that nouns may undergo when they have suffixes, are in construct, or are plural. Unfortunately, there is no easy way around these difficulties since attempting to classify nouns by patterns of formation, by gender, and by variations to vowels caused by silent letters or gutturals produces well over one hundred different patterns for nouns. This does not even include those nouns that are simply irregular. Eventually you will want, and need, to know more about the forms or morphology of Hebrew nouns, but for now the information in this excursus should serve as a basic introduction. For somewhat more detailed information on the changes different vowels undergo as nouns change state, number, or have a suffix attached, see **S 5.1c–5.1c.3**.

A. Gender

It is safe to assume that a noun is masculine unless it ends in הָ֫_ תָ_ or תַ_ Two common feminine nouns that do not have these endiNGs are אֶרֶץ *land* and עִיר *city*. (עִיר even takes masculine plural endiNGs.)

If a noun ends in הֶ_ it is masculine. Common examples are מַחֲנֶה *camp,* שָׂדֶה *field,* מַטֶּה *staff, tribe.* <u>Note</u>: In the sg. const. these nouns end in הֵ__

131

While sometimes there seems to be no reason behind gender assignment, some classes of objects tend to fall into a particular gender:

אֶרֶץ is feminine, as are similar words such as אֲדָמָה *ground,* and תֵּבֵל *world.*

a) Pottery items are always feminine.

b) But containers of wood are usually masculine.

c) Boats, however, are feminine and have the הָ_ endiNG.

B. Many parts of the body—especially those occurring in pairs—are feminine even if they do not end in הָ_

יָד	*hand*	אֹזֶן	*ear*
עַיִן	*eye*	רֶגֶל	*foot*
בֶּטֶן	*belly*	נֶפֶשׁ	*self, soul*
רוּחַ	*breath, spirit*	שֵׁן	*tooth*

A notable exception to the rule of paired body parts being feminine is the masculine שַׁד *breast.* A few body parts, like לֵב *heart,* are considered masculine but use feminine plural endiNGs.

A special plural ending יִַם is used for these pairs or for two of something when that quantity is expressed without a numeral. In the construct or with a suffix, the dual looks the same as the masculine plural no matter what the gender of the word:

Dual Absolute		Dual Construct		Dual+Suffix	
עֵינַיִם	אָזְנַיִם	עֵינֵי	אָזְנֵי־	עֵינָיו	אָזְנָיו

C. Formation

Many nouns have more (or less) than three letters. Yet many lexicons require you to establish the hypothetical three-letter root in order to look up the noun. It is helpful, therefore, to learn to find the root of any noun.

1. Nouns may be formed from three-letter roots simply by adding ה at the end:

ברך	*bless*	בְּרָכָה	*blessing*
צדק	*be righteous*	צְדָקָה	*righteousness*

2. Nouns may be formed from three-letter roots by placing a מ in front of the root:

שׁפט	*judge*	מִשְׁפָּט	*judgment, justice*
קום	*arise, stand*	מָקוֹם	*place*

3. Nouns may be formed by adding a ה in front of the three-letter root:

ירה   *teach*   תּוֹרָה   *law, instruction*

4. Two-letter nouns tend to come from **geminate** or, more rarely, hollow roots:

√ עמם   עַם   *people*

√ הרר   הַר   *mountain*

5. 3rd ה roots tend to yield 3rd י nouns.

√ כלה   כְּלִי   *vessel*

√ חצה   חֲצִי   *half*

6. Some nouns are listed as two-letter or even four-letter words:

בֵּן   *son*   פֶּה   *mouth*   לָשׁוֹן   *tongue*

D. Many masculine nouns have feminine counterparts:

בֵּן   *son*   בַּת   *daughter*

אָח   *brother*   אָחוֹת   *sister*

מֶלֶךְ   *king*   מַלְכָּה   *queen*

אָדָם   *man*   אֲדָמָה   *earth*

(If this last pair seems strange to you, look at Gen. 2:7.)

E. Family relationships of nouns may be both helpful and confusing. For example, consider these nouns related to the root מלך

מֶלֶךְ   *king*   מַלְכָּה   *queen*   מַמְלָכָה   *kingdom*   מַלְכוּת   *reign*

Again, ability to pick out the root is an important asset in such times of confusion, since you can then use a lexicon to untangle the meanings.

F. One common noun pattern is the segolate noun, so called because almost every such noun of this class has segol as its second vowel. These nouns are always accented on the <u>first</u> syllable in the singular absolute. Some common examples are:

אֶרֶץ   *land*   מֶלֶךְ   *king*   כֶּסֶף   *silver*   סֵפֶר   *letter*   בֹּקֶר   *morning*

Some nouns—whose middle letter is a guttural—are considered to be segolates, even though the segol doesn't appear. They follow the other nouns of this class, however, in that the accent is on the first syllable:

נַעַר   *lad, youth*   בַּעַל   *Baal, master, owner, lord*   נַחַל   *stream, wadi, torrent*

G. Vowel Changes

When pronoun suffixes are added to nouns, the nouns may look similar to their construct forms:

	Absolute	Construct	Suffixed Form
m. sg.	דָּבָר	דְּבַר	דְּבָרֵנוּ דְּבָרִי
m. pl.	אֱלֹהִים	אֱלֹהֵי	אֱלֹהֵינוּ אֱלֹהָיו
f. sg.	תּוֹרָה	תּוֹרַת	תּוֹרָתִי תּוֹרָתוֹ
f. pl.	תּוֹרוֹת	תּוֹרוֹת	תּוֹרוֹתָם תּוֹרוֹתָיו

Segolate patterns are distinct:

	Absolute	Construct	Suffixed Form
m. sg.	מֶלֶךְ	מֶלֶךְ	מַלְכֵּנוּ מַלְכִּי
m. pl.	מְלָכִים	מַלְכֵי	מְלָכֵינוּ
f. sg.	אֶרֶץ	אֶרֶץ	אַרְצִי
f. pl.	אֲרָצוֹת	אַרְצוֹת	אַרְצוֹתֵיהֶם

One can see from the above sample that masculine plural nouns have a י after the root to denote the plural. Feminine plural nouns have their own plural endiNG and may, in addition, have a י before a suffix is added. The presence of a י between the noun and its suffix will distinguish plural from singular nouns with two exceptions:

Two important exceptions to the function of י after a noun:

1. אָב *father* and אָח *brother* have י in the singular before a suffix. (See **H** below.)

2. With the first person singular suffix, the vowel alone tells you whether the noun is singular or plural:

יָדִי   *my hand*   יָדַי   *my hands*

H.   **Common Irregular Nouns**[1]

	Absolute	Construct	With Suffix	
man	אִישׁ	אִישׁ	אִישָׁהּ	אִישִׁי
men	אֲנָשִׁים	אַנְשֵׁי	אֲנָשָׁי	אַנְשֵׁיכֶם
woman	אִשָּׁה	אֵשֶׁת	אִשְׁתְּךָ	אִשְׁתִּי
women	נָשִׁים	נְשֵׁי	נְשֵׁינוּ	נָשַׁי
house	בַּיִת	בֵּית	בֵּיתְךָ	בֵּיתִי
houses	בָּתִּים	בָּתֵּי	בָּתֵּיהֶם	בָּתֶּיךָ
daughter	בַּת	בַּת	בִּתּוֹ	בִּתִּי
daughters	בָּנוֹת	בְּנוֹת	בְּנוֹתֶיךָ	בְּנוֹתַי
father	אָב	אֲבִי	אָבִיו	אָבִי
fathers	אָבוֹת	אֲבוֹת	אֲבֹתָיו	אֲבֹתַי
brother	אָח	אֲחִי	אָחִי	אָחִינוּ
brothers	אַחִים	אֲחֵי	אַחֶיךָ	אַחַי
day	יוֹם	יוֹם	יוֹמָם	יוֹמוֹ
days	יָמִים	יְמֵי	יָמֵינוּ	יָמַי
city	עִיר	עִיר	עִירוֹ	עִירִי
cities	עָרִים	עָרֵי	עָרֶיהָ	עָרַי
name	שֵׁם	שֵׁם שֶׁם־	שְׁמָם	שְׁמִי
names	שֵׁמוֹת	שְׁמוֹת	שְׁמוֹתָם	שְׁמוֹתָן
mouth	פֶּה	פִּי	פִּי	פִּיךָ
heaven (dual)	שָׁמַיִם	שְׁמֵי	שְׁמֵיכֶם	שָׁמֶיךָ
water (dual)	מַיִם	מֵי מֵימֵי	מֵימַי	מֵימֶיהָ

---

1. Use 🎵 ＡＢ track 14, **So Is It אִישׁ** (lyrics on pp. 467–468) to study these irregular nouns.

LESSON 25

וְלֹא־נָתַן יְהוָה לָכֶם לֵב לָדַעַת וְעֵינַיִם לִרְאוֹת וְאָזְנַיִם לִשְׁמֹעַ עַד הַיּוֹם הַזֶּה׃

Deuteronomy 29:3

25.1   וְלֹא־נָתַן יְהוָה לָכֶם

25.1a   Analyze נָתַן

Root	Stem	Form	Person/Gender/Number	Special Features

25.1b   לְ | לָכֶם means _____   כֶם means _____
Translation of phrase: _____

25.2   לֵב לָדַעַת
לֵב means _____   לָדַעַת is a verb form. Analyze it.

Root	Stem	Form	Person/Gender/Number	Special Features

The key to the form is the לְ in front of the root. Which form of the verb usually occurs with the preposition *to*?_____ ת is the infinitive ending of one type of verb. (11.2a).
Do you remember a root with the letters דע in it? _____

> When a verb root begins with י the Qal infinitive construct usually drops the י and adds ת on the end.

Translation of phrase: _____

וְלֹא־נָתַן יְהוָה לָכֶם לֵב לָדַעַת וְעֵינַיִם לִרְאוֹת וְאָזְנַיִם לִשְׁמֹעַ עַד הַיּוֹם הַזֶּה:

___

25.3 וְעֵינַיִם לִרְאוֹת

25.3a וְעֵינַיִם Initial וְ means _____

> ◌יִם is the **dual** ending on nouns. This ending is used instead of the simple plural for referring to <u>two</u> of a noun, or for things that occur in pairs. (Review The Noun B.)

עַיִן means _____ so עֵינַיִם means _____ Note that the dual construct and the dual with a suffix look the same as the m. pl. construct and m. pl. with a suffix, but the gender for feminine nouns—such as body parts that come in pairs—remains feminine.

25.3b לִרְאוֹת

Root	Stem	Form	Person/Gender/Number	Special Features

> 3rd ה verbs in the Qal infinitive drop the ה and add ◌וֹת

25.4 וְאָזְנַיִם לִשְׁמֹעַ

What kind of endiNG is on וְאָזְנַיִם _____ אֹזֶן means *ear*.

אָזְנַיִם means _____

Analyze לִשְׁמֹעַ

Root	Stem	Form	Person/Gender/Number	Special Features

> A ḥolem after the <u>second</u> root letter indicates the Qal infinitive of the regular verb.

Translate phrase: _____

25.5 עַד הַיּוֹם הַזֶּה

What do you call this kind of adjective construction? _____

Translate phrase: _____

25.6 Translation of verse: _____

_____

25.7 Here is a summary of the **Qal infinitive construct**.[1]

Strong verb identifying feature: _____ (25.4)

שָׁמֹר   With attached preposition, לִשְׁמֹר

1st י including הלך form their infinitives by _____ (11.2b, 25.2)

ירד→רֶדֶת   יצא→צֵאת   ידע→דַּעַת

With attached preposition: ___ לְ   ___ לְ   ___ לְ

1st י verbs that retain the י of the root in the prefix (17.5) usually follow the pattern of the strong verb infinitive: ירא→יְרֹא

1st נ Some act like weak 1st י   נגש→גֶּשֶׁת
(לקח follows this pattern):   לקח→קַחַת

Some follow the pattern of strong verbs: נפל→נְפֹל
With attached preposition: לָגֶשֶׁת   לָקַחַת   לִנְפֹל

נתן The infinitive of נתן is תֵּת   With attached preposition: לָתֵת

3rd ה verbs form the infinitive by _____ (25.3b)

רְאוֹת   With attached preposition ___ לְ

Hollow verbs retain the middle י or ו in the Qal infinitive.

שִׂים→שִׂים   בוֹא→בוֹא   קוּם→קוּם
With attached preposition: ___ לְ   ___ לְ   ___ לְ

---

1. A second type of infinitive, the infinitive absolute, will be studied later.

וְלֹא־נָתַן יְהוָה לָכֶם לֵב לָדַעַת וְעֵינַיִם לִרְאוֹת וְאָזְנַיִם לִשְׁמֹעַ עַד הַיּוֹם הַזֶּה׃

Assignments

A. Vocabulary: words 1–175.

B. Memorize the Qal infinitive patterns in 25.7.

C. ☉ **ב א** track 14: review **So Is It** אִישׁ (The Noun H) (lyrics: p. 467–468).

☉ שַׁבְּחִי track 22: listen to אֶשָּׂא עֵינַי Psalm 121.

D. Translate Exodus 3:1–3. As you work through Lessons 25–29, listen to the cantillation of Exodus 3: 1–17 on ☉ **ב א** track 15.

E. Translate:

1   וַיָּקָם הָאִישׁ לָלֶכֶת   *Judges 19:7*

2   וַיִּשְׁלַח הַמֶּלֶךְ לִקְרֹא אֶת־אֲחִימֶלֶךְ   *1 Samuel 22:11*

3   לֹא אַתָּה תִּבְנֶה־לִּי הַבַּיִת לָשָׁבֶת׃ . . .   *1 Chronicles 17:4*

✡4   וַיִּמְלְאוּ יָמֶיהָ לָלֶדֶת   *Genesis 25:24*

5   וַיְדַבֵּר אֱלֹהִים אֶל־נֹחַ לֵאמֹר׃   *Genesis 8:15*

6   וַיֵּרֶד יְהוָה לִרְאֹת אֶת־הָעִיר   *Genesis 11:5*

7   וַיֹּאמֶר שְׁלֹמֹה לִבְנוֹת בַּיִת לְשֵׁם יְהוָה   *2 Chronicles 1:18*

8   וַיֵּלְכוּ . . . לָלֶכֶת לָבוֹא מִצְרָיִם׃ . . .   *Jeremiah 41:17*

9   וַיִּשְׁלַח שָׁאוּל מַלְאָכִים לָקַחַת אֶת־דָּוִד   *1 Samuel 19:14*

10   אֲנִי יְהוָה אֱלֹהֵיכֶם אֲשֶׁר־הוֹצֵאתִי אֶתְכֶם מֵאֶרֶץ מִצְרַיִם לָתֵת לָכֶם אֶת־אֶרֶץ כְּנַעַן [*I brought you out* הוֹצֵאתִי אֶתְכֶם]   *Leviticus 25:38*

11   עֵת לָלֶדֶת וְעֵת לָמוּת   *Qohelet 3:2*

12   וַיָּקָם יְהוֹשֻׁעַ וְכָל־עַם הַמִּלְחָמָה לַעֲלוֹת הָעָי [*place name* הָעָי]   *Joshua 8:3*

13   וַיָּשֶׂם חֲזָאֵל פָּנָיו לַעֲלוֹת עַל־יְרוּשָׁלָיִם   *2 Kings 12:18*

14   וַיֹּאמֶר יוֹסֵף אֶל־אֶחָיו אֲנִי יוֹסֵף . . . וְלֹא יָכְלוּ אֶחָיו לַעֲנוֹת אֹתוֹ [*be able* יכל]   *Genesis 45:3*

LESSON 26

וְאַתֶּם רְאִיתֶם אֵת כָּל־אֲשֶׁר עָשָׂה יהוה אֱלֹהֵיכֶם

Joshua 23:3

26.1 וְאַתֶּם means _____

When an independent pronoun is followed by a verb in the same person, gender, and number, it is used for emphasis.

26.2 Verb Analysis רְאִיתֶם

Root	Stem	Form	Person/Gender/Number	Special Features

תֶם is the 2 m. pl. affix ending. The root must therefore be found in the letters רְאִי How-ever, no Hebrew root ends in י

> When a verb root ends in a י before an affix pronoun, the last letter of the root is
>
> actually ה

What is the stem? _____ The form is Qal affix, even though ַ is not used. The change in pointing is due to the "heavy" ending תֶם which causes vowel shifts in the first part of the word. (Review 13.5) Translate verb: _____

26.3 אֵת כָּל־אֲשֶׁר עָשָׂה יהוה אֱלֹהֵיכֶם

This whole segment is the DDO of the main verb. Translate it: _____

_____

Analyze עָשָׂה

Root	Stem	Form	Person/Gender/Number	Special Features

140

26.4 Translate verse: _____

_____

26.5 Extra Grammar

3rd ה verbs present one of the very few irregular patterns in the Qal affix. The following chart shows how the ending of the root is affected by the addition of each affix pronoun. (In the second and first persons, the original י of the root is manifest.)

26.5a

Qal Affix 3rd ה

3 m. sg.	בָּנָה		3 c. pl.	בָּנוּ ←
3 f. sg.	בָּנְתָה ←			
2 m. sg.	בָּנִיתָ		2 m. pl.	בְּנִיתֶם
2 f. sg.	בָּנִית		2 f. pl.	בְּנִיתֶן
1 c. sg.	בָּנִיתִי		1 c. pl.	בָּנִינוּ

Note especially the 3 f. sg. and the 3 c. pl., which are unlike the others in the pattern. The chart uses בנה which has two strong letters at the beginning of the root. The most common 3rd ה verbs ראה היה עלה עשה are composed of weak and guttural letters, and thus may have other irregular vowel markings as well as those connected with the final ה

26.5b The Qal prefix of 3rd ה verbs loses the ה of the root before a prefix complement is added. In some PGNs, a י takes its place.

Qal Prefix 3rd ה

3 m. sg.	יִבְנֶה		3 m. pl.	יִבְנוּ
3 f. sg.	תִּבְנֶה		3 f. pl.	תִּבְנֶינָה
2 m. sg.	תִּבְנֶה		2 m. pl.	תִּבְנוּ
2 f. sg.	תִּבְנִי		2 f. pl.	תִּבְנֶינָה
1 c. sg.	אֶבְנֶה		1 c. pl.	נִבְנֶה

26.5c The Qal imperative of 3rd ה verbs was presented in 20.6a. Fill in the chart for בנה

Qal Imperative 3rd ה

m. sg.	⌐	⌐	⌐
f. sg.	——	⌐	⌐
m. pl.	——	⌐	⌐
f. pl.	——	יְ⌐	⌐

26.5d The Qal participle for 3rd ה verbs can be recognized by the usual feature for Qal participles: _____ Note that the m. sg. participle ends in הֶ and the f. sg. ends in הָ In the plurals the ה of the root is lost before the endings are added.

Qal Participle 3rd ה

m. sg.	בֹּנֶה
f. sg.	בֹּנָה
m. pl.	בֹּנִים
f. pl.	בֹּנוֹת

26.5e You have already learned the Qal infinitive for 3rd ה verbs. (14.3a, 25.7)

The Qal infinitive construct for בנה is _____ with an attached preposition _____

Assignments

A. Vocabulary: words 1–180.

B. Memorize the 3rd ה Qal paradigm (26.5a-e, or use Verb Chart L). The task of memorization will be facilitated by learning **If It's a Man** (3rd ה affix), **יִבְנֶה He** (3rd ה prefix), and בֹּנֶה בֹּנָה (3rd ה participle) on ⊕ ב א tracks 16–18; and imperative (lyrics: pp. 469–471).

D. Read and translate Exodus 3:4–6.

E. Translate:

Judges 1:24 וַעֲשִׂינוּ עִמְּךָ חָסֶד׃ ...	1
Numbers 13:18 וּרְאִיתֶם אֶת־הָאָרֶץ	2
Genesis 34:16 וְהָיִינוּ לְעַם אֶחָד	3
Numbers 3:4 וּבָנִים לֹא־הָיוּ לָהֶם	4
Genesis 31:12 כִּי רָאִיתִי אֵת כָּל־אֲשֶׁר לָבָן עֹשֶׂה לָּךְ׃ ...	5
Genesis 12:18 מַה־זֹּאת עָשִׂיתָ לִּי	6

וְאַתֶּם רְאִיתֶם אֵת כָּל־אֲשֶׁר עָשָׂה יהוה אֱלֹהֵיכֶם

———

☆7 וַיִּקְרָא יַעֲקֹב שֵׁם הַמָּקוֹם פְּנִיאֵל כִּי־רָאִיתִי אֱלֹהִים פָּנִים
אֶל־פָּנִים וַתִּנָּצֵל נַפְשִׁי: Genesis 32:31 [*has been saved*, i.e., נַפְשִׁי] וַתִּנָּצֵל

8 וַיִּקְרָא אֲבִימֶלֶךְ לְאַבְרָהָם וַיֹּאמֶר לוֹ מֶה־עָשִׂיתָ לָּנוּ
וּמֶה־חָטָאתִי לָךְ Genesis 20:9 [*sin* חָטָא מֶה ← מַה

9 וְאַתֶּם רְאִיתֶם אֵת כָּל־אֲשֶׁר עָשָׂה יהוה אֱלֹהֵיכֶם לְכָל־הַגּוֹיִם
הָאֵלֶּה מִפְּנֵיכֶם Joshua 23:3

10 וּבְנֵי רְאוּבֵן בָּנוּ אֶת־חֶשְׁבּוֹן Numbers 32:27

11 בַּת־שְׁלֹמֹה הָיְתָה לּוֹ לְאִשָּׁה 1 Kings 4:11

12 וְאֶרֶץ הַגִּלְעָד הָיְתָה לִבְנֵי־מְנַשֶּׁה Joshua 17:6

13 אַתֶּם רְאִיתֶם אֲשֶׁר עָשִׂיתִי לְמִצְרָיִם Exodus 19:4

14 וַיֹּאמֶר לָהֶם יוֹסֵף מָה־הַמַּעֲשֶׂה הַזֶּה אֲשֶׁר עֲשִׂיתֶם Genesis 44:15

15 וְאֵלֶּה הַכֹּהֲנִים וְהַלְוִיִּם אֲשֶׁר עָלוּ עִם־זְרֻבָּבֶל בֶּן־שְׁאַלְתִּיאֵל
Nehemiah 12:1 [Can you tell why there is a dagesh in וְהַלְוִיִּם]

16 וַיִּקְרָא מֹשֶׁה אֶל־כָּל־יִשְׂרָאֵל וַיֹּאמֶר אֲלֵהֶם אַתֶּם רְאִיתֶם אֵת
כָּל־אֲשֶׁר עָשָׂה יהוה לְעֵינֵיכֶם בְּאֶרֶץ מִצְרַיִם לְפַרְעֹה
וּלְכָל־עֲבָדָיו וּלְכָל־אַרְצוֹ: Deuteronomy 29:1

17 אַךְ בַּת־פַּרְעֹה עָלְתָה מֵעִיר דָּוִד אֶל־בֵּיתָהּ אֲשֶׁר בָּנָה־לָהּ
1 Kings 9:24 [אַךְ *surely, only*]

Here is a summary of the stem and form markers you should now know for strong verbs:

	Qal	**Pi`el**
Affix	⌣ ⌣ ָֽ	⌣ ֵ ֻ
Prefix	⌣ ⌣ ְ ֻ	⌣ ֵ ⌣ ְ
Imperative	⌣ ⌣ ְ	⌣ ֵ ֻ
Participle (active)	⌣ ⌣ וֹ ⌣	
Infinitive construct	⌣ ⌣ ְ	

Once these are committed to memory, the patterns for other sorts of verbs (3rd ה 1st נ hollow, and so on) are more easily worked out. Obviously the elements on the chart are not all that you will see on a particular verb. The additional things will help you sort out cases of potential ambiguity.

Why is it that יְדַעְתֶּם cannot be a Qal imperative even though it has a shewa under the first root letter? _____

Why isn't יִכְבַּד a Pi`el form even though the middle root letter has a dagesh? _____

_____

Classify the following verbs according to stem and form. Unfamiliar roots shouldn't be a hindrance to this exercise.

Stem	Form		Stem	Form	
____	____	סָבַב	____	____	צִוִּיתִי
____	____	בַּעֲבֹר	____	____	עִבְרִי
____	____	וַיְקַדְּשׁוּ	____	____	שָׁלַח
____	____	קִדְּשׁוּ	____	____	קַדֵּשׁ
____	____	קָדְשׁוּ	____	____	וַיְקַדֵּשׁ
____	____	שִׁלַּחְתָּ	____	____	לְשַׁלֵּחַ
____	____	וָאֶשְׁלַח	____	____	שׁוֹלֵחַ
____	____	שָׁמֹר	____	____	תִּמְכֹּרְנָה

You should know all the PGN indicators for affix and prefix by now. Participles and imperatives also have gender and number. Give the (P)GN for each of these verbs:

בְּחֵרוֹת	בְּחַרְנָה	בְחַרְתֶּן	תִּבְחַרְנָה

What do the following have in common (aside from root and stem)?

קַטֵּל	תְּקַטֵּל	תְּקַטֵּלְנָה	קָטַלְתְּ	קָטְלִי

None of the weak verbs present insurmountable problems in terms of recognizing (P)GN, although all the root letters may not be present. Give the (P)GN (or state lack thereof if the verb is an infinitive) and root for each of the following. Some may have more than one correct answer in this contextless exercise.

יִגְּשׁוּ	יוֹלֶדֶת	בָּנוֹת	בָּאָה
תָּבֹאנָה	אֶבְנֶה	אָבוֹא	בָּאוּ
בּוֹנֶה	בְּנוּ	נִגְּשׁוּ	תְּנוּ
אֵלֵד	לָלֶדֶת	בָּנִיתִי	נָשְׂאוּ
נִשְׂאוּ	שָׂא	שְׁבִי	יֵשֵׁב
שְׁבוּ	תָּשׁוּבִי	רָמוּ	תָּבִינוּ

Analyze the following:

וַיֵּצֵא	וַיֵּצֵא	סָר
תָּשֹׁבְנָה	וַיִּבֶן	וַיִּבֶן
יֵשֵׁב	גְּשׁוּ	עָשִׂיתִי
עֲלוּ	רָאִיתִי	יָרֵאתִי
עֲלוּ	עָנְתָה	עָנִיתָ

LESSON 27

וְלֹא־שָׁבוּ אֶל־יהוה אֱלֹהֵיהֶם

Hosea 7:10

27.1 וְלֹא־שָׁבוּ

Analyze שָׁבוּ

Root	Stem	Form	Person/Gender/Number	Special Features

The difficulty with this verb is finding the root, and this time it really is difficult because the form שָׁבוּ is morphologically ambiguous. It could be the 3 m. pl. affix of either a 3rd ה שׁבה *take into captivity* or a hollow שׁוב *return*. Here it happens to be שׁוב the more common of the two roots, since it is the only one that fits the need for an intransitive verb in the context of the verse segment.

In the Qal affix, hollow verbs use only the two strong letters of the root plus the affix pronouns. The vowel under the first root letter will be ָ for the third persons but ַ for the second and first persons.

Once you have determined the root and the form, it should not be difficult to fill in all the columns of the chart.

Translate phrase: _____

27.2 אֶל־יהוה אֱלֹהֵיהֶם

All the components of this phrase have been seen several times.

27.3 Translate the verse: _____

27.4 Extra Grammar

The Qal affix vowel pattern for קוּם conjugated just below, is also applied to hollow verbs whose middle letter is וֹ or יִ So you will see:

בּוֹא		שִׂים	
3 m. sg. בָּא		שָׂם	
3 f. sg. בָּאָה	etc.	שָׂמָה	etc.

27.4a <center>**Qal Affix Hollow**</center>

3 m. sg.	קָם	3 c. pl.	קָמוּ
3 f. sg.	קָמָה		
2 m. sg.	קַמְתָּ	2 m. pl.	קַמְתֶּם
2 f. sg.	קַמְתְּ	2 f. pl.	קַמְתֶּן
1 c. sg.	קַמְתִּי	1 c. pl.	קַמְנוּ

27.4b The Qal prefix of hollow verbs keeps the root vowel, but the for 2nd and 3rd feminine plurals, the root vowel is shortened.

Qal Prefix Hollow

3 m. sg.	יָ ק וּ ם	3 m. pl.	␣ ␣ ␣ ␣ —
3 f. sg.	␣ ␣ ␣ —	3 f. pl.	⟵ תָּ קֹ מְ —
2 m. sg.	␣ ␣ ␣ —	2 m. pl.	␣ ␣ ␣ ␣ —
2 f. sg.	— ␣ ␣ ␣	2 f. pl.	⟵ — ␣ ␣ —
1 c. sg.	␣ ␣ ␣ אָ	1 c. pl.	␣ ␣ ␣ ␣

27.4c The Qal imperatives of hollow verbs are regular (i.e., they are formed by removing the prefix pronoun from the corresponding second person prefix forms). Review 20.6a if necessary, then fill in the chart:

Qal Imperative Hollow

	ק ו ם	ב ו א	שׁ י ם
m. sg.			
f. sg.			
m. pl.			
f. pl.			ָ נ ָ

27.4d The Qal participles of hollow verbs do not follow the pattern of the strong verb participle. Review 24.5b and fill in the chart:

Qal Participle Hollow

	ק ו ם	ב ו א	שׁ י ם
m. sg.			
f. sg.			
m. pl.			
f. pl.			

27.4e The Qal infinitive of hollow verbs is formed by removing the prefix pronoun from the 3 m. sg. Review 25.7, then fill in the chart using the verbs בִּין בּוֹא קוּם

Qal Infinitive Hollow

	With attached preposition	לְ
		לְ
		לְ

Assignments

A. Vocabulary: words 1–185.

B. Memorize the Qal forms of the hollow verb (27.4a–e; also Verb Chart H). For help in memorizing, listen to א ב tracks 19–22: **Hello, New Haven!** (hollow affix), קָם קָמָה בָּא בָּאָה (hollow affix round), **It's All About the Hollow** (hollow prefix), and קָם קָמָה (hollow participle) (lyrics: pp. 472–475). Use the round to practice conjugating שִׂים קוּם and בּוֹא

C. שָׁבְחִי track 23: listen to אֶרֶץ Exodus 3:8.

D. Read and translate Exodus 3:7–9.

E. Translate:

1   וַיָּשׁוּבוּ הַמַּלְאָכִים אֵלָיו וַיֹּאמֶר אֲלֵיהֶם מַה־זֶּה שַׁבְתֶּם:

2 Kings 1:5

2   וְשַׂמְתִּי מָקוֹם לְעַמִּי לְיִשְׂרָאֵל

2 Samuel 7:10

3   שִׂים יְמִינְךָ עַל־רֹאשׁוֹ [*right hand* יָמִין]

Genesis 48:18

4   וַתֹּאמֶר נָעֳמִי ... לֵכְנָה שֹּׁבְנָה

Ruth 1:8

5   וְנִחְיֶה וְלֹא נָמוּת

Genesis 43:8

6   קוּמִי שְׂאִי אֶת־הַנַּעַר

Genesis 21:18

7   וַיָּשָׁב אַבְרָהָם אֶל־נְעָרָיו וַיָּקֻמוּ וַיֵּלְכוּ יַחְדָּו אֶל־בְּאֵר שָׁבַע

✡8   וַיֵּשֶׁב אַבְרָהָם בִּבְאֵר שָׁבַע:

Genesis 22:19

9   וּבָנִיתָ שָּׁם מִזְבֵּחַ לַיהוה אֱלֹהֶיךָ

Deuteronomy 27:5

10 וַיֵּרֶד יהוה לִרְאֹת אֶת־הָעִיר וְאֶת־הַמִּגְדָּל אֲשֶׁר בָּנוּ בְּנֵי הָאָדָם:

Genesis 11:5 [*tower* מִגְדָּל]

✡11 כִּי הָעֲמָלֵקִי וְהַכְּנַעֲנִי שָׁם לִפְנֵיכֶם וּנְפַלְתֶּם בֶּחָרֶב כִּי־עַל־כֵּן
שַׁבְתֶּם מֵאַחֲרֵי יהוה וְלֹא־יִהְיֶה יהוה עִמָּכֶם:

Numbers 14:43

[*because* כִּי־עַל־כֵּן]

<u>Hint</u>: the most common middle letter in hollow verbs is וֹ The rarest is י

149

LESSON 28

וְהַמֶּלֶךְ אָסָא הִשְׁמִיעַ אֶת־כָּל־יְהוּדָה

1 Kings 15:22

28.1   וְהַמֶּלֶךְ means _____ אָסָא is a name: _____

28.2   Verb Analysis הִשְׁמִיעַ

Root	Stem	Form	Person/Gender/Number	Special Features

Here you encounter a new stem. It is called **Hif`il** and is formed by adding ה before the root letters and by using a characteristic set of vowels. The key vowel to watch for comes between the second and third root letters and will usually be ִי ֵ ֶ or ֶ (an I class vowel), which you can refer to as a "dot vowel." This vowel does not occur in every PGN and form in the Hif`il but is in the most frequent ones (i.e., third persons).

The Hif`il most often gives a causative meaning to roots.

If you add the words "to cause" or "to make" before the Qal meaning, you will get the rough equivalent of the Hif`il in most cases. Sometimes a verb in the Hif`il may not transmit a causative sense into English but is translated as a simple transitive verb. Some Hif`ils, like some Pi`els, do not convey to us their reason for being in that stem. And some Hif`ils, also like some Pi`els, have no extant Qal.

The root in the case of הִשְׁמִיעַ once you have dealt with the signs of the Hif`il, is _____ This form, in which the ה clearly stands in front of the root, is the affix. As in the Qal, the affix is most clearly recognizable by the use of the affix pronouns you have seen. No affix pronoun means the PGN is _____

28.3   אֶת־כָּל־יְהוּדָה means _____

28.4 Sentence translation: _____

28.5 Memorize the chart below

Hif`il Affix Strong Verb

3 m. sg.	הִגְדִּיל		3 c. pl.	הִגְדִּילוּ
3 f. sg.	הִגְדִּילָה			
2 m. sg.	הִגְדַּלְתָּ		2 m. pl.	הִגְדַּלְתֶּם
2 f. sg.	הִגְדַּלְתְּ		2 f. pl.	הִגְדַּלְתֶּן
1 c. sg.	הִגְדַּלְתִּי		1 c. pl.	הִגְדַּלְנוּ

Note that for Hif`ils in the Qal affix, a preformative ה is constant, but that pataḥ ַ is the interior vowel for the first and second persons.

גדל in the Qal means *be great* or *be big.* In the Hif`il, it means _____

28.6 Extra Grammar: **Interrogative ה**

Aside from its function as a definite article marker (on nouns) and a Hif`il indicator (on verbs), ה on the front of a word can signify yet something else. One way of indicating a question in Hebrew is by the use of interrogative words—מָה or מִי —for example. Another way is by the use of the interrogative particle ה which is placed on the first word of a clause or phrase. This ה can be distinguished from the sign of the Hif`il and from the definite article by its usual pointing: הֲ It is sometimes pointed הַ and occasionally הֶ (<u>Note</u>: In Hebrew as in English, a question is sometimes assumed with no special interrogative component.)

> הֲ at the beginning of the first word of a phrase can be the interrogative ה

הֲ can be attached to a particle   *Exodus 4:11* הֲלֹא אָנֹכִי יהוה

a noun or pronoun   *Genesis 29:6* הֲשָׁלוֹם לוֹ

a verb   *1 Samuel 23:11* הֲיֵרֵד שָׁאוּל

a participle   *Genesis 4:9* הֲשֹׁמֵר אָחִי אָנֹכִי

Assignments

A. Vocabulary: words 1–190.

B. Memorize the Hif`il affix, presented in 28.5; also see Verb Chart A. During the course of Lessons 28–35, work with **The Stem was the Hif`il** on ☻ ב א track 23 (lyrics: pp. 476–479).

C. ☻שַׁבְּחִי track 24: learn מִן הַמֵּצַר **Psalm 118:5**.

D. Read and translate Exodus 3:10–13.

E. Translate:

1   וְהִקְרִיב אֹתוֹ לִפְנֵי יהוה   *Leviticus 3:7*

2   הִגְדִּיל יהוה לַעֲשׂוֹת עִמָּנוּ   *Psalms 126:3*

✡3   וַיָּבֶן דָּוִד כִּי מֵת הַיֶּלֶד וַיֹּאמֶר דָּוִד אֶל־עֲבָדָיו הֲמֵת הַיֶּלֶד
   וַיֹּאמְרוּ מֵת [מֵת *is dead*]   *2 Samuel 12:19*

4   אַתָּה הִמְלַכְתָּ אֶת־עַבְדְּךָ תַּחַת דָּוִד אָבִי   *1 Kings 3:7*

5   מִשָּׁמַיִם הִשְׁמַעְתָּ דִּין [דִּין *judgment*]   *Psalms 76:9*

6   הִקְרִיבוּ עֹלוֹת לֵאלֹהֵי יִשְׂרָאֵל   *Ezra 8:35*

7   וְהִקְרַבְתֶּם עֹלָה לַיהוה   *Numbers 29:8*

8   וַיִּשְׁמְעוּ כָל־שָׂרֵי הַחֲיָלִים אֲשֶׁר בַּשָּׂדֶה הֵמָּה וְאַנְשֵׁיהֶם כִּי־הִפְקִיד
   מֶלֶךְ־בָּבֶל אֶת־גְּדַלְיָהוּ בֶן־אֲחִיקָם בָּאָרֶץ   *Jeremiah 40:7*

LESSON 29

וְהָיָה אֱלֹהִים עִמָּכֶם וְהֵשִׁיב אֶתְכֶם אֶל־אֶרֶץ אֲבֹתֵיכֶם

Genesis 48:21

29.1 וְהָיָה אֱלֹהִים עִמָּכֶם

Verb Analysis וְהָיָה

Root	Stem	Form	Person/Gender/Number	Special Features

אֱלֹהִים means _____ עִמָּכֶם means _____ (23.1a)

Translation of this phrase: _____

29.2 Verb Analysis וְהֵשִׁיב

Root	Stem	Form	Person/Gender/Number	Special Features

A ה in front of a verb form can indicate _____ stem. (28.2) You see that the ִי

which accompanies the Hif`il affix in the third person, is present, but taking that into account

leaves only two root letters.

> In hollow verbs, the characteristic Hif`il stem vowel appears in place of the verb's middle
> root letter, and thus in the middle of the verb.

29.3 You have had all the components of the remaining phrase. If you need help with אֲבֹתֵיכֶם

review The Noun H. A reminder: Nouns using וֹת_____ plurals frequently have an extra י be-

tween the noun and the pronoun suffix.

אֲבוֹתֵ | י | כֶם

pronoun   plural ends in וֹת_____

29.4   Sentence translation: _____

_____

29.5   Extra Grammar

Verbs with weak letters[1] and 1st gutturals may deviate from the pattern of the strong verb in the Hif`il. (For more complete coverage, see the verb charts in the back of the book.)

3rd ה verbs: changes at the end are similar to those in the Qal (26.5): הִגְלִיתָ

1st נ verbs: נ assimilates into the second root letter, for example, הִגִּישׁ but other Hif`il characteristics are present.

1st Gutturals: the preformative ה may be pointed הֶ as in הֶחֱזִיק

Hollows: changes are more complicated and are shown below.

Hif`il Affix Hollow שׁוּב

3 m. sg.	הֵשִׁיב	3 c. pl.	הֵשִׁיבוּ
3 f. sg.	הֵשִׁיבָה		
2 m. sg.	הֲשִׁיבֹותָ	2 m. pl.	הֲשִׁיבֹותֶם
2 f. sg.	הֲשִׁיבֹות	2 f. pl.	הֲשִׁיבֹותֶן
1 c. sg.	הֲשִׁיבֹותִי	1 c. pl.	הֲשִׁיבֹונוּ

In the first and second persons, note the reduced vowel under the preformative ה and the addition of the וֹ before the affix pronouns. Because the א of בוא creates an open syllable, בוא does not use the extra וֹ (unless there is a suffix: הֲבִיאֹתַנִי הֲבֵיאתָ but).

29.6   Exercises:

You have now seen four uses of a ה at the beginning of a word. One is "first root letter." What are the other three?

_____ (4.3)

_____ (28.2)

_____ (28.6)

Explain the initial ה in the following words, and describe your reasoning process in each case

unless you don't have one; then just do the first part:

---

1. The Hif`ils of 1st י verbs are covered separately.

154

וְהָיָה אֱלֹהִים עִמָּכֶם וְהֵשִׁיב אֶתְכֶם אֶל־אֶרֶץ אֲבֹתֵיכֶם

הֵשִׁיב	הַהוּא	הָאָרֶץ
הָאֱלֹהִים	הָיָה	הַבָּשָׂר
הִגִּידָה	הִגִּישׁ	הֲקִימֹתִי
הֲשָׁלוֹם	הֲשִׁמְתָ	הֲשֹׁמֵר
הַהֹלֵךְ	הֲהֹלֵךְ	הָלַךְ

Assignments

A. Vocabulary: words 1–195.

B. Memorize the Hif`il affix paradigm of the hollow verb. (29.5; Verb Chart H).

C. ⊙ **א ב** track 23: listen to **The Stem was the Hif`il.**

D. ⊙ **שַׁבְּחִי** track 23: listen to **אֶרֶץ** **Exodus 3:8.**

E. Read and translate Exodus 3:14–17.

F. Translate:

1   וְהֵבִיאָה אֹתָם אֶל־הַכֹּהֵן   *Leviticus 15:29*

✡2   יהוה הֶעֱלִיתָ מִן־שְׁאוֹל נַפְשִׁי   *Psalms 30:4*

3   וְהֵבֵאתִי אֶתְכֶם אֶל־אַדְמַת יִשְׂרָאֵל   *Ezekiel 37:12*

4   וַהֲשִׁבֹתִי אֶתְכֶם דָּבָר כַּאֲשֶׁר יְדַבֵּר יהוה אֵלָי   *Numbers 22:8*

5   וְהִפַּלְתִּי אֶת־הַחֶרֶב מִיָּדוֹ   *Ezekiel 30:22*

6   הֵשִׁבוּ פְלִשְׁתִּים אֶת־אֲרוֹן יהוה   *1 Samuel 6:21*

7   וְהֶעֱמִיד הַכֹּהֵן אֶת־הָאִשָּׁה לִפְנֵי יהוה   *Numbers 5:18*

✡8   וַיִּתֵּן אֶת־יִשְׂרָאֵל בִּגְלַל חַטֹּאות יָרָבְעָם אֲשֶׁר חָטָא וַאֲשֶׁר הֶחֱטִיא
אֶת־יִשְׂרָאֵל׃   *1 Kings 14:16*   [בִּגְלַל *on account of*   חַטֹּאות super plene spelling]

9   יהוה אֱלֹהֵיכֶם הִרְבָּה אֶתְכֶם   *Deuteronomy 1:10*

10   וַיֹּאמֶר יִתְרוֹ בָּרוּךְ יהוה אֲשֶׁר הִצִּיל אֶתְכֶם מִיַּד מִצְרַיִם וּמִיַּד
פַּרְעֹה אֲשֶׁר הִצִּיל אֶת־הָעָם מִתַּחַת יַד־מִצְרָיִם׃   *Exodus 18:20*

[בָּרוּךְ ⟵ m. sg. Qal passive participle of ברך]

✡11   וְהִנֵּה הֶרְאָה אֹתִי אֱלֹהִים גַּם אֶת־זַרְעֶךָ   *Genesis 48:11*

LESSON 30

הַגִּידָה לִּי מֶה עָשִׂיתָה

1 Samuel 14:43

30.1 הַגִּידָה

Here we have another form of the Hif`il. Therefore the ה at the beginning of the word will be
_____ and not a letter of the root. (28.2) How many letters are left?
_____ What other letter is part of the characteristic Hif`il pattern? _____ Locating this tells
you something important, for this combination comes _____
_____ (28.2) What will the first root letter be? _____ (7.1a) What is the root?
_____ So the final ה must be some special ending. Note the vowel under the first ה In
the affix form the usual vowel under the ה stem indicator is ⷯ (Review 29.5 for variations.)

Patah ⷯ under the ה stem indicator is the sign of the Hif`il imperative.

30.1a We have accounted now for all the letters except the final ה This is not a PGN ending (review
imperatives, 20.6a, if necessary). It occurs at the end of the m. sg. imperative sometimes but not
always. It is usually called the **emphatic** ה although its actual function is a matter of specula-
tion. That it adds an extra syllable to the word may indicate its purpose is sonant or rhythmic.
In the case of הַגִּֽידָה לִּי it is interrupting the repetition of two ⷯ (ee) sounds. (Oddly
enough, the m. sg. imperative may, on occasion, do just the opposite and lose a syllable, e.g.,
הַעֲל a variant of the m. sg. Hif`il imperative of עלה)

Analyze הַגִּֽידָה

Root	Stem	Form	Person/Gender/Number	Special Features

נגד means *be conspicuous*. In the Bible, it is used exclusively in the Hif`il (or its passive counter-
part, the Hof`al), and we translate it *tell, declare*.

הַגִּֽידָה לִי מֶה עָשִׂיתָה

30.2 לִי What kind of dagesh is in the ל _____ (17.3b)

Translate phrase: _____

30.3 מֶה עָשִׂיתָה

מֶה ⟵ מַה and so means _____

Analyze עָשִׂיתָה

Root	Stem	Form	Person/Gender/Number	Special Features

What is the PGN? Determining that requires accounting for the י If you can't, review 26.5a and **S 26.5a**. Here the PGN is _____

What then is the final ה It is the plene spelling of the affix pronoun תָ

תָּה ⟵ תָ For some reason, it is not uncommon for the 2 m. sg. affix of 3rd ה verbs to have this plene spelling. Unlike the emphatic ה in הַגִּֽידָה the plene spelling does not add an extra syllable.

30.4 Translate sentence: _____

30.5 The sign of the Hif`il imperative, preformative הַ is constant for most types of verbs. One exception is hollows, whose preformative is usually pointed הָ

30.6 Give the form and PGN of the following Hif`ils:

Form	PGN		Form	PGN	
_____	_____	הֶאֱכַלְתֶּם	_____	_____	הַרְאֶֽינָה
_____	_____	הָבֵא	_____	_____	הַעֲלֵה
_____	_____	הַשְׁמִֽיעוּ	_____	_____	הִשְׁלַכְתִּי
_____	_____	וְהִגַּדְתָּ	_____	_____	הַגִּֽידוּ
_____	_____	וַהֲקִמֹתִי	_____	_____	הַעֲלוּ
_____	_____	הַקְרֵב	_____	_____	הָשִׁיבוּ
_____	_____	✡ הָעַל	_____	_____	וְהֵקִים

157

הַגִּידָה לִּי מֶה עָשִׂיתָה

Assignments

A. Vocabulary: words 1–200. Test yourself: אֵלֶּה הַדְּבָרִים☺ tracks 3–22.

B. Read and translate Genesis 37:1–4.

C. Suggested song: יהוה רֹעִי **Psalm 23** on שַׁבְּחִי╝ track 25.

D. Translate:

✡1 וַיֹּאמֶר דָּוִד מֶה עָשִׂיתִי עָתָּה הֲלוֹא דָּבָר הוּא: *1 Samuel 17:29*

2 הַשְׁמִיעוּ זֹאת *Isaiah 48:20*

3 וְאַתָּה הַקְרֵב אֵלֶיךָ אֶת־אַהֲרֹן אָחִיךָ וְאֶת־בָּנָיו *Exodus 28:1*

4 הָבֵא אֶת־הָאֲנָשִׁים הַבָּיְתָה *Genesis 43:16*

5 הֲלוֹא טוֹב לָנוּ שׁוּב מִצְרָיְמָה *Numbers 14:3*

6 הָשִׁיבוּ נָא לָהֶם *Nehemiah 5:11*

7 הַעַל אֶת־הָעָם הַזֶּה *Exodus 33:12*

8 עֲלֵה הָקֵם לַיהוה מִזְבֵּחַ *2 Samuel 24:18*

9 וְהֵקִים יהוה לוֹ מֶלֶךְ עַל־יִשְׂרָאֵל *1 Kings 14:14*

10 וַתֹּאמֶר אֵלָיו הֲלֹא צִוָּה יהוה אֱלֹהֵי־יִשְׂרָאֵל *Judges 4:6*

✡11 וַיֹּאמֶר הַמֶּלֶךְ אֶל־הַכּוּשִׁי הֲשָׁלוֹם לַנַּעַר לְאַבְשָׁלוֹם וַיֹּאמֶר הַכּוּשִׁי יִהְיוּ כַנַּעַר אֹיְבֵי אֲדֹנִי הַמֶּלֶךְ וְכֹל אֲשֶׁר־קָמוּ עָלֶיךָ לְרָעָה: *2 Samuel 18:32*

12 וַיָּבֹא שְׁמוּאֵל אֶל־שָׁאוּל וַיֹּאמֶר לוֹ שָׁאוּל בָּרוּךְ אַתָּה לַיהוה הֲקִימֹתִי אֶת־דְּבַר יהוה: (בָּרוּךְ *blessed*) *1 Samuel 15:13*

LESSON 31

הֵם הַמְדַבְּרִים אֶל־פַּרְעֹה מֶלֶךְ־מִצְרַיִם לְהוֹצִיא
אֶת־בְּנֵי־יִשְׂרָאֵל מִמִּצְרָיִם

Exodus 6:27

31.1 הֵם הַמְדַבְּרִים

הֵם means _____ הַמְדַבְּרִים is a verb form—a new one, but one which contains many familiar elements if you break it down.

Root	Stem	Form	Person/Gender/Number	Special Features

The endiNG ‏ִים‎ is _____ The initial ‏ה‎ cannot be interrogative because it is not attached to the first word of a phrase. It is not a Hif`il indicator because _____

_____ It must, therefore be the definite article. **(S 4.5b.2)** Only one verb form takes the trappings of nouns; it is the _____ (9.3a) Out of the five (count them) letters left, do you see a familiar root? _____ What stem will this be? Note the doubled root letter.

> The Pi`el participle uses a ‏מ‎ preformative in front of the root, in which the middle letter is doubled ‏מְ‎ ַ ּ ַ

Translation of phrase: _____

31.2 Verb Analysis ‏לְהוֹצִיא‎

Root	Stem	Form	Person/Gender/Number	Special Features

הֵם הַמְדַבְּרִים אֶל־פַּרְעֹה מֶלֶךְ־מִצְרַיִם לְהוֹצִיא אֶת־בְּנֵי־יִשְׂרָאֵל מִמִּצְרָיִם

The form is easy to identify because ל is used before it. The stem is not Qal but Hif`il. (28.2). The root letters appear to be ויצא and this actually was the root in a more archaic Hebrew. Later the ו became י in Qal forms, so that we know the root as יצא which means _____ _____ In the Hif`il (and other derived stems that have a preformative letter) the ancient ו takes the place of י in most verbs now beginning with י The Hif`il meaning of יצא will be _____ or more simply *bring forth*.

31.3 The rest of this sentence contains familiar words. Translate the whole sentence:

_____

31.4 Extra Grammar

The Hif`il infinitive of a 1st י verb looks the same as the 3 m. sg. affix form. So הוֹצִיא could be translated *to bring out* or *he brought out*. How will you know which is meant? The infinitive usually has an attached preposition, and of course the context will tell you which makes more sense. The other 1st י Hif`il affix PGNs don't cause this confusion because they have an affix pronoun at the end. Speaking of the Hif`il affix, try your skills by filling in the chart below. There is a vowel change caused by יצא being a 3rd א Tsere _ occurs where pataḥ _ appears in the strong verb. Check your answers against the 1st י chart at the back of the book.

31.5

Hif`il Affix 1st י

3 m. sg.	ה ו צִ י א	3 c. pl.	__ __ __ __
3 f. sg.	__ __ __ __		
2 m. sg.	__ אָ צֵ __ __	2 m. pl.	__ __ __ __
2 f. sg.	__ __ __ __ __	2 f. pl.	__ __ __ __
1 c. sg.	__ __ __ __ __	1 c. pl.	__ __ __ __

31.6 Exercise:
Give the root and form of the following Hif`ils:

Root	Form		Root	Form	
_____	_____	וְהוֹדַעְתֶּם	_____	_____	וְהוֹדַעְתָּ
_____	_____	וְהִזְכַּרְתֶּן	_____	_____	הוֹתַרְתִּי
_____	_____	וְהוֹשִׁיבוּ	_____	_____	הִזְכִּיר
_____	_____	הוֹתִיר	_____	_____	הוֹלִיד

Root	Form		Root	Form
_____	_____	הָקֵם	_____	_____	לְהָבִיא
_____	_____	לְהַקְרִיב	_____	_____	לְהַמְלִיךְ
_____	_____	הָשִׂימִי	_____	_____	הַקְרִיב
_____	_____	הֵבִיאוּ	_____	_____	הַזְכִּיר
_____	_____	הֲקִימֹתִי	_____	_____	הֵקִימוּ

Assignments

A. Vocabulary: words 1–205.

B. 🎵 שַׁבְּחִי track 26: listen to, translate, and sing רֶד־נָא מֹשֶׁה (lyrics: p. 480).

C. Revisit **Mr. Pi`el** on 🎵 א ב track 11 (lyrics: pp. 464–465).

D. Read and translate Genesis 37:5–8.

E. Translate:

1 וְהוֹדַעְתָּ לָהֶם אֶת־הַדֶּרֶךְ *Exodus 18:20*

2 וְהוֹדַעְתִּי לְךָ אֵת אֲשֶׁר תַּעֲשֶׂה *1 Samuel 10:8*

3 הִנְנִי מְשַׁלֵּחַ בָּם אֶת־הַחֶרֶב *Jeremiah 29:17*

4 שְׁמַע אֵת אֲשֶׁר־אֲנִי מְדַבֵּר אֵלֶיךָ *Ezekiel 2:8*

5 וְהוֹצֵאתָ לָהֶם מַיִם *Numbers 20:8*

6 כִּי־אֲנִי־הוּא הַמְדַבֵּר הִנֵּנִי *Isaiah 52:6*

7 הוֹצֵאתִי אֶתְכֶם מֵאֶרֶץ מִצְרַיִם *Leviticus 19:36*

8 וְחַנָּה הִיא מְדַבֶּרֶת עַל־לִבָּהּ [for מְדַבֶּרֶת see footnote to 24.5a] *1 Samuel 1:13*

9 וַיֹּצִיאוּ מִשָּׁם אֶת־הָאִשָּׁה וְאֶת־כָּל־אֲשֶׁר־לָהּ *Joshua 6:22*

10 וְהוֹדַעְתֶּם אֶת־בְּנֵיכֶם *Joshua 4:22*

11 וְהוֹצִיאוּ אֹתוֹ אֶל־זִקְנֵי עִירוֹ *Deuteronomy 21:19*

12 וְעָמְדוּ לְפָנַי לְהַקְרִיב לִי חֵלֶב וָדָם [fat] חֵלֶב *Ezekiel 44:15*

13 בָּאוּ חֶבְרוֹנָה לְהַמְלִיךְ אֶת־דָּוִיד עַל־כָּל־יִשְׂרָאֵל *1 Chronicles 12:39*

14 הַמֶּלֶךְ אֲחַשְׁוֵרוֹשׁ אָמַר לְהָבִיא אֶת־וַשְׁתִּי הַמַּלְכָּה לְפָנָיו *Esther 1:17*

LESSON 32

‎וַיַּגֵּד מֹשֶׁה אֶת־דִּבְרֵי הָעָם אֶל־יְהוָה

Exodus 19:9

32.1 Analyze ‎וַיַּגֵּד

Root	Stem	Form	Person/Gender/Number	Special Features

The focus of this lesson is on this first word of the sentence. Obviously we have here a prefix form of the verb. What is the root? _____ (7.1a) The stem is neither Qal nor Pi'el, but Hif'il. Where is the ‎ה that marks the Hif'il stem? It has elided:

‎וַיְהַגֵּד ⟵ וַיַּגֵּד original form

The ‎ה sound, merely a breath, was easily slid over and eventually dropped out altogether in the Hif'il prefix form. Only its vowel was left—pataḥ—which now stands under the prefix pronoun.

> The Hif'il prefix can be recognized by two characteristic vowels: pataḥ ‎ַ under the
> prefix pronoun and ‎ֵ ‎ֶ or ‎ִ (an I class or "dot" vowel) between the second and
> third root letters.

32.2 The remainder of this sentence is quite simple; translate the whole sentence:

_____

32.3 Fill in the chart for the Hif'il prefix of ‎גדל Why is there a dagesh in the ‎ד

וַיַּגֵּד מֹשֶׁה אֶת־דִּבְרֵי הָעָם אֶל־יהוה

Hif`il Prefix Strong Verb

3 m. sg.	יַ גְ דִּי ל	3 m. pl.	‿ ‿ ‿ ‿ ‿	
3 f. sg.	‿ ‿ ‿ ‿	3 f. pl.	‿ גְ דֵּ ל ‿	
2 m. sg.	‿ ‿ ‿ ‿	2 m. pl.	‿ ‿ ‿ ‿ ‿	
2 f. sg.	‿ ‿ ‿ ‿ ‿	2 f. pl.	‿ ‿ ‿ ‿ ‿	
1 c. sg.	‿ ‿ ‿ ‿	1 c. pl.	‿ ‿ ‿ ‿	

32.3a Extra Grammar

The verb for this lesson וַיַּגֵּד demonstrates a feature of some Hif`ils with vav conversive: the shortened form. The tsere ◌ֵ in וַיַּגֵּד is shorter than the plene ḥireq יִ◌ in the form without vav conversive: יַגִּיד (Plene ḥireq יִ◌ can also shorten to segol: תַּגִּיד ← וַתַּגֵּד)

Shortened forms with vav conversive also run through the Qal. This is most evident in hollow, 3rd ה and 1st י verbs for persons that have no prefix complement:

יֵשֵׁב ← וַיֵּשֶׁב	יָשׁוּב ← וַיָּשָׁב	יָשִׂים ← וַיָּשֶׂם
יִרְאֶה ← וַיִּרָא	יַעֲשֶׂה ← וַיַּעַשׂ	תִּבְנֶה ← וַתִּבֶן

32.3b The words וַיִּרָא and יַעֲשֶׂה and וַיַּעַשׂ (above) conflict with the recognition feature of the Hif`il prefix. The combination 1st guttural (or ר) + 3rd ה verb in the prefix form—with or without vav conversive—may look identical in the Qal and Hif`il. Your only clue to the correct stem in such a case is context. For example, with וַיִּרָא the question would be "Did the subject see (Qal) or did the subject cause someone else to see? (Hif`il)"

1st gutturals that don't end in ה may have ◌ֶ under the prefix pronoun in the Qal prefix. (17.3a) The stem of these verbs can be determined by going to the secondary key feature of the form. The Hif`il will have an I class ("dot") vowel between the 2nd and 3rd root letters; the Qal will not. Qal יַעֲמֹד Hif`il יַעֲמִיד

Assignments

A. Vocabulary: words 1–210.

B. Make sure you are confident of all the Hif`il signs presented so far. To learn this stem more thoroughly, consult the verb charts at the back of the book.

C. ☉ ב א track 23: review **The Stem was the Hif`il** (lyrics: pp. 476–479)

D. ☉ שַׁבָּחִי track 27: learn אַחַת שָׁאַלְתִּי **Psalm 27:4.**

E. Read and translate Genesis 37:9–12.

◆

F. Analyze:

אַגִּיד	וַיִּקְרַב	תַּקְרִיבוּ	תַּקְרִיב
תַּשְׁמִיעַ	וְיִשְׁמְעוּ	וַיַּגִּדוּ	הַגֵּד
הַשִּׁיא	תָּשׁוּב	תָּשִׁיב	תִּשְׁמַע
וָאֵשֶׁב	הָשֵׁב	הוֹשַׁבְתָּ	וַיֵּשֶׁב

G. Translate:

1 וְכֹל אֲשֶׁר בִּלְבָבְךָ אַגִּיד לָךְ *1 Samuel 9:19*

2 הוּא יַגִּיד לָךְ מַה־יִּהְיֶה לַנָּעַר *1 Kings 14:3*

3 וַיֵּלְכוּ וַיַּגִּדוּ לַמֶּלֶךְ דָּוִד *2 Samuel 17:21*

4 וְאֶת־אַהֲרֹן וְאֶת־בָּנָיו תַּקְרִיב אֶל־פֶּתַח אֹהֶל מוֹעֵד *Exodus 29:4*

5 לֹא־תַקְרִיבוּ אֵלֶּה לַיהוָה *Leviticus 22:22*

✡6 וְיִשְׁמְעוּ דְבָרַי אֶת־עַמִּי *Jeremiah 23:22*

7 וַיִּקְרַב אֹתְךָ וְאֶת־כָּל־אַחֶיךָ *Numbers 16:10*

8 וַתַּגֶּד־לוֹ אִשְׁתּוֹ אֶת־הַדְּבָרִים הָאֵלֶּה *1 Samuel 25:37*

9 וְלֹא־תַשְׁמִיעוּ אֶת־קוֹלְכֶם *Joshua 6:10*

10 וַיֹּאמֶר לִבְנֵי אַהֲרֹן הַכֹּהֲנִים לְהַעֲלוֹת עַל־מִזְבַּח יְהוָה *2 Chronicles 29:21*

LESSON 33

וָאוֹצִיא אֶת־אֲבוֹתֵיכֶם מִמִּצְרַיִם

Joshua 24:6

33.1 Analyze וָאוֹצִיא

Root	Stem	Form	Person/Gender/Number	Special Features

Can the וֹ here be a vav conversive? _____ Why or why not? _____

_____ (14.5a) What is the stem? _____ The clue here is the

יִ_ between the second and third letters of the root. (32.1) The root of the verb is _____

because in the Hifʿil the original first root letter was _____ (31.2) א is the prefix for which

PGN? _____

Translate: _____

> Holem וֹ after a prefix pronoun, combined with an I class ("dot") vowel after the middle
>
> root letter, is the sign of the Hifʿil prefix in this group of 1st יִ verbs.

33.2 אֶת־אֲבוֹתֵיכֶם means _____

מִמִּצְרַיִם means _____

33.3 Translate the whole sentence: _____

_____

33.4 Most different from the strong Hifʿil vocalization patterns are 1st יִ verbs. However, they are
consistently characterized by having וֹ between the preformative or prefix pronoun and the
root. This pattern can be seen in the participle as well. The Hifʿil participle of the strong verb can
be recognized by a מַ_ preformative (pataḥ being the favorite vowel for Hifʿil preformatives),
but for 1st יִ verbs it is מוֹ___

33.5 In the chart below, the m. sg. or 3 m. sg. is used even though its vocalization may not be the most representative of the form, but other PGNs have affix pronouns, prefix pronouns and/or complements, or endiNGs to help with identification.

Hif`il Synopsis

	Strong	Hollow	1st י
Affix	הִ ְ י ִ ַ	הֵ ִ י ַ	הוֹ ִ י ַ
Prefix	יַ ְ ִ י ִ ַ	יָ ִ י ַ	יוֹ ִ י ַ
Prefix/vav conv.	וַיַּ ְ ֵ ַ	וַ ֶ ִ ַ	וַיּוֹ ֶ ַ
Imperative	הַ ְ ֵ ַ	הָ ִ ֵ ַ	הוֹ ֵ ַ
Participle	מַ ְ ִ י ַ	מֵ ִ י ַ	מוֹ ִ י ַ
Infinitive	הַ ְ ִ י ַ	הָ ִ י ַ	הוֹ ִ י ַ

Assignments

A. Vocabulary: words 1–215.

B. Learn the Hif`il synopses.

C. 💿 שַׁבְּחִי track 5: listen to הוֹדוּ Analyze the word הוֹדוּ

D. Read and translate Genesis 37:13–16.

E. Translate:

1 יוֹדִיעַ דְּרָכָיו לְמֹשֶׁה *Psalms 103:7*

2 וַיּוֹשֶׁב שָׁם אֶת־בְּנֵי יִשְׂרָאֵל *2 Chronicles 8:2*

3 וְאֶת־שֵׁם קָדְשִׁי אוֹדִיעַ בְּתוֹךְ עַמִּי יִשְׂרָאֵל *Ezekiel 39:7*

4 כִּי־תוֹלִיד בָּנִים וּבְנֵי בָנִים *Deuteronomy 4:25*

5 וַיּוֹצֵא אֶת־בֶּן־הַמֶּלֶךְ *2 Kings 11:12*

6 תוֹצִיא הָאֲדָמָה *Haggai 1:11*

7 וְעֹבֵד הוֹלִיד אֶת־יִשַׁי וְיִשַׁי הוֹלִיד אֶת־דָּוִד: *Ruth 4:22*

8 וַיּוֹרֶד אֶת־הָעָם אֶל־הַמָּיִם *Judges 7:5*

9 וַתֵּלֶד שָׂרָה לְאַבְרָהָם בֵּן לִזְקֻנָיו *Genesis 21:2*

10 וְכִי אוֹצִיא אֶת־בְּנֵי יִשְׂרָאֵל מִמִּצְרָיִם *Exodus 3:11*

✡11 וְיָרְשׁוּ בֵּית יַעֲקֹב אֵת מוֹרָשֵׁיהֶם *Obadiah 1:17*

LESSON 34

———

וַיַּכּוּ אֶת־גְּדַלְיָהוּ בֶן־אֲחִיקָם בֶּן־שָׁפָן בַּחֶרֶב וַיָּמֶת אֹתוֹ

Jeremiah 41:2

34.1 Analyze וַיַּכּוּ

Root	Stem	Form	Person/Gender/Number	Special Features

After dealing with the vav conversive and the PGN of this verb, there is not much left. The first root letter will be _____ because the dagesh forte in the כ indicates _____ (7.1a) The final letter of the root must be _____ (use the missing-letter rule in 12.1). There are only a few verbs like this in Hebrew, but one or two occur with high frequency: נכה and נטה

> When only one consonant (doubled or not) shows for a root, you probably have a combination 1st נ 3rd ה verb.

What is the stem? That is easily determined. Since the first root letter is נ the pataḥ under the prefix pronoun is not being generated by a guttural. Therefore it is a sign of the Hifʿil stem.

34.2 אֶת־גְּדַלְיָהוּ בֶן־אֲחִיקָם בֶּן־שָׁפָן means _____

Now "translate" the names (שָׁפָן means *rock badger*) _____

34.3 בַּחֶרֶב means _____

34.4 וַיָּמֶת אֹתוֹ

Analyze וַיָּמֶת

Root	Stem	Form	Person/Gender/Number	Special Features

Determining stem: with hollow verbs, the vowel under the prefix pronoun continues to be $\underset{\tau}{}$ in the Hif`il, as it is in the Qal, (6.1a)[1] In this case, you must use the characteristic I class vowel to help you determine the stem. מוּת in the Qal means _____ so _____ in the Hif`il.

34.5 Translate sentence: _____

_____

34.6 Extra Grammar

The verb מוּת is a hollow I class verb. (I class verbs were covered in 17.6a.)

Extra credit: Why is there a dagesh forte in the ת of some PGNs?

Qal Affix Hollow I Class

3 m. sg.	מֵת	3 c. pl.	מֵתוּ
3 f. sg.	מֵתָה		
2 m. sg.	מַתָּה	2 m. pl.	מַתֶּם
2 f. sg.	מַתְּ	2 f. pl.	מַתֶּן
1 c. sg.	מַתִּי	1 c. pl.	מַתְנוּ

34.6a In the Hif`il, מוּת will follow the usual pattern for hollow verbs (see 33.5):

הֵמִית Hif`il affix     יָמִית  Hif`il prefix   וַיָּמֶת prefix + vav conversive

Assignments

A. Vocabulary: words 1–220.

B. Learn the Qal affix of מוּת (34.6, also Verb Chart H).

C. Suggested song: מִי הָאִישׁ **Psalm 34:13–14** on שְׁבָחִי track 7.

_____

1. In hollows, $\underset{\tau}{}$ is the vowel under the preformative ה in the infinitive and imperative, as well, e.g., הָמֵת m. sg. imperative; הָמִיתוּ m. pl. imperative; הָמִית infinitive construct.

D. Read and translate Genesis 37:17–20.

E. Translate:

✡1 וְנָבִא לְבַב חָכְמָה *Psalms 90:12*

2 ... לָמָּה תָּבִיאוּ אֹתוֹ אֵלָי: *1 Samuel 21:15*

3 וַיַּרְא אֹתָם אֶת־בֶּן־הַמֶּלֶךְ *2 Kings 11:4*

4 וַיָּבִיאוּ אֶת־הַנַּעַר אֶל־עֵלִי *1 Samuel 1:25*

5 וְאַתָּה תַּעֲלֶה אֹתָם יְרוּשָׁלָָם *2 Chronicles 2:15*

6 וַיַּעֲלוּ הַכֶּסֶף בְּיָדָם [silver כֶּסֶף *Judges 16:18*

7 וַיַּעַל דָּוִד עֹלוֹת לִפְנֵי יְהוָה *2 Samuel 6:17*

8 וַיָּבֹא יוֹסֵף וַיַּגֵּד לְפַרְעֹה *Genesis 47:1*

✡9 וַתָּקֶם אֶת־דְּבָרֶיךָ כִּי צַדִּיק אָתָּה *Nehemiah 9:8*

10 וַיָּקֶם יְהוָה אֶת־דְּבָרוֹ אֲשֶׁר דִּבֵּר *1 Kings 8:20*

11 וַיָּשֶׁב־יְהוָה לִי כְצִדְקִי *Psalms 18:25*

12 וְלֹא־יָשִׁיב אֶת־הָעָם מִצְרַיְמָה *Deuteronomy 17:16*

13 וַיָּשִׁבוּ אוֹתָם דָּבָר *Joshua 22:32*

14 אַעֲלֶה אֶתְכֶם מִמִּצְרַיִם וָאָבִיא אֶתְכֶם אֶל־הָאָרֶץ *Judges 2:1*

15 כִּי אַתָּה תָּבִיא אֶת־בְּנֵי יִשְׂרָאֵל אֶל־הָאָרֶץ *Deuteronomy 31:23*

16 וַתִּשָּׂא אֹתִי רוּחַ וַתָּבֵא אֹתִי אֶל־שַׁעַר בֵּית־יְהוָה *Ezekiel 11:1*

17 וַיִּקַּח אֶת־לֵאָה בִתּוֹ וַיָּבֵא אֹתָהּ אֵלָיו *Genesis 29:23*

18 וָאָקִים מִבְּנֵיכֶם לִנְבִיאִים *Amos 2:11*

169

LESSON 35

בִּהְיוֹת שָׁאוּל מֶלֶךְ אַתָּה הַמּוֹצִיא וְהַמֵּבִיא אֶת־יִשְׂרָאֵל

1 Chronicles 11:2

35.1 בִּהְיוֹת שָׁאוּל מֶלֶךְ

35.1a Analyze בִּהְיוֹת

Root	Stem	Form	Person/Gender/Number	Special Features

The key to analyzing this form is the בְּ What part of speech is this? _____ Only one form of the verb is <u>regularly</u> found with a preposition, although usually it is the preposition לְ What is this form? _____ (11.2b) This analysis is confirmed by the וֹת_____ ending, which is the regular infinitive ending for what sort of root? _____ (14.3a)

The translation of this infinitive is obviously different from the translation of one employing לְ The infinitive, used alone, names the <u>action</u> of the verb; the best way of achieving this in English is to add "–ing" to the meaning:

הָיָה *be*   הֱיוֹת *be-ing*

When an infinitive is used in this way, it can have a subject and object.

35.1b שָׁאוּל is a name. In the phrase we are studying, it is the <u>subject</u> of the infinitive. מֶלֶךְ is the <u>predicate</u> of the infinitive. Literally, with no attention to other grammatical facets, we have *in-being-Saul-king*. If we work with the idea of the infinitive as a verb with a subject and object, we can translate:

subject	verb	predicate (or object)
in Saul's	*being*	*king*

170

35.1c When either **בּ** or **כּ** is used with the infinitive, it functions as a temporal preposition; thus, the best translation is usually *when* + the past tense of the verb (infinitive):

when Saul was king

35.2 **אַתָּה הַמּוֹצִיא**

אַתָּה means _____

Analyze **הַמּוֹצִיא** (33.4)

Root	Stem	Form	Person/Gender/Number	Special Features

You have seen the elements of this form before. The stem is _____ because the vowels are

_____ (33.4) The root is therefore _____ **הַ‎ ☐** is the _____

_____ and this can occur only with a verb used as a noun, so the form is probably _____

_____ (9.3b) The **מ** here is _____

Translate phrase: _____

35.3 Analyze **וְהַמֵּבִיא**

Root	Stem	Form	Person/Gender/Number	Special Features

What is the root? _____ With hollow verbs in the Hif`il, the Hif`il vowels regularly

occur _____ (29.2)

35.4 Sentence translation: _____

_____

171

35.5 Exercise:
Analyze the following forms:

הֵשִׁיב	מֵקִים	מוֹשִׁיבִים
הַמַּעֲלֶה	בְּשָׁמְעוֹ	שָׁמְעוּ
וְשִׂים	רוֹאוֹת	הֶעֱלָה
הַמַּגִּיד	מַשְׁמִעַ	וַיִּשְׁמַע

35.6 Extra Grammar

An infinitive, with or without a prefixed preposition, can have a subject attached directly to it.

Psalm 63:1 בִּהְיוֹתוֹ בְּמִדְבַּר יְהוּדָה

when he was in the wilderness of Judah

35.6a When a Qal infinitive of the פָּקֹד type has a suffix attached, the vowel pattern usually changes. It is as if the holem retracts and is expressed as qamats ḥatuf.

Qal infinitive with suffix   Qal infinitive

↓ qamats ḥatuf   ↓ holem

Deuteronomy 6:6 וּבְשָׁכְבְּךָ   שָׁכֹב

and when you lie down   *to lie down*

Assignments

A. Vocabulary: words 1–225.

B. Listen to ☺שַׁבְּחִי track 28: שִׁיר הַמַּעֲלוֹת **Psalm 126**.

☺שַׁבְּחִי track 26: review רְד־נָא מֹשֶׁה (lyrics: p. 480)

C. Read and translate Genesis 37:21–24.

D. Translate:

1   *Jeremiah 28:3* אֲנִי מֵשִׁיב אֶל־הַמָּקוֹם הַזֶּה אֶת־כָּל־כְּלֵי בֵית יְהוָה

2   *Jeremiah 6:19* הִנֵּה אָנֹכִי מֵבִיא רָעָה אֶל־הָעָם הַזֶּה

3   כִּי יְהוָה אֱלֹהֵינוּ הוּא הַמַּעֲלֶה אֹתָנוּ וְאֶת־אֲבוֹתֵינוּ מֵאֶרֶץ מִצְרַיִם
מִבֵּית עֲבָדִים *Joshua 24:17*

4   וַיְהִי כִּשְׁמֹעַ כָּל־יִשְׂרָאֵל כִּי־שָׁב יָרָבְעָם וַיִּשְׁלְחוּ וַיִּקְרְאוּ אֹתוֹ
1 Kings 12:20

5   *Ezekiel 40:4* שְׁמַע וְשִׂים לִבְּךָ לְכֹל אֲשֶׁר־אֲנִי מַרְאֶה אוֹתָךְ

בִּהְיוֹת שָׁאוּל מֶלֶךְ אַתָּה הַמּוֹצִיא וְהַמֵּבִיא אֶת־יִשְׂרָאֵל

6   אֲנִי יְהוָה הַמַּעֲלֶה אֶתְכֶם מֵאֶרֶץ מִצְרַיִם לִהְיֹת לָכֶם לֵאלֹהִים

Leviticus 11:45

7   וַיֹּאמֶר דָּוִד אֶל־הַנַּעַר הַמַּגִּיד לוֹ   *2 Samuel 1:5*

8   אַף אֵין־מַגִּיד אַף אֵין מַשְׁמִיעַ [אַף *surely*]   *Isaiah 41:26*

9   אֲנִי יְהוָה מְקַדִּשְׁכֶם: הַמּוֹצִיא אֶתְכֶם מֵאֶרֶץ מִצְרַיִם   *Leviticus 22:32–33*

LESSON 36

כִּי־אַתָּה תְּבָרֵךְ צַדִּיק יהוה

Psalms 5:13

36.1 כִּי means _____ Note that כִּי frequently begins clauses in Biblical Hebrew, clauses that describe the result of preceding actions. כִּי may sometimes also be translated as *but* or *surely* when it introduces a clause that contrasts with a preceding statement.

36.2 אַתָּה means _____ What do you call this kind of pronoun? _____

36.3 Verb Analysis תְּבָרֵךְ

Root	Stem	Form	Person/Gender/Number	Special Features

תְ is the prefix pronoun for _____ (14.1) ברך appears almost always in the Pi'el stem. However, as you have learned, ר is a letter that cannot take the dagesh required in the formation of the Pi'el. It also happens to be a guttural that regularly demands compensation in the previous vowel for the missing dagesh. (15.4a) Not all mid-gutturals demand compensatory lengthening. In those cases, watch for the regular Pi'el vowels minus the dagesh forte in the middle root letter.

36.3a

	Pi'el Regular	Mid-Guttural and mid-ר with compensation	Mid-Guttural without compensation
Affix	דִּבֵּר	בֵּרַךְ בֵּרֵךְ	נִהַג
Prefix	יְדַבֵּר	יְבָרֵךְ	יְנַהֵג
Imperative	דַּבֵּר	בָּרֵךְ	נַהֵג
Participle	מְדַבֵּר	מְבָרֵךְ	מְנַהֵג
Infinitive	דַּבֵּר	בָּרֵךְ	נַהֵג

36.3b When the middle root letter of a Pi'el is pointed with a shewa ֱ the dagesh forte is sometimes not written. In such cases there is no compensation for the missing dagesh: תְּבַקְשֶׁנּוּ (Gen. 43:9) but תְּבַקְשֶׁנָּה (Gen. 31:39). Your clue to the stem will be the usual vocalization for the particular Pi'el form.

36.4 צַדִּיק means _____ This word is a **substantive adjective**; in other words, it is an adjective used as a noun, *righteous one.*

36.5 יהוה is related to the sentence in what way? _____ (18.2)

36.6 Sentence translation: _____

36.7 Extra Grammar
Independent subject pronouns are often used in Biblical Hebrew for emphasis, as is the case in this lesson sentence. They are also used as

1. The subject of a noun sentence: אֲנִי יהוה *(Genesis 15:7)*

2. The subject in a participial clause: כִּי־עֹשֶׂה אֲנִי *(Judges 15:3)*

Independent Subject Pronouns

1 c. sg.	אֲנִי אָנֹכִי	1 c. pl.	אֲנַחְנוּ
2 m. sg.	אַתָּה	2 m. pl.	אַתֶּם
2 f. sg.	אַתְּ	2 f. pl.	אַתֵּן אַתֵּנָה
3 m. sg.	הוּא	3 m. pl.	הֵם הֵמָּה
3 f. sg.	הִיא	3 f. pl.	הֵן הֵנָּה

36.8 Exercise
Analyze the following verbs:

אִכֵּל	קֵרַבְתִּי	קָרְבוּ
אִכְּלוּ	רַבָּה	יִשְׁאַל
פִּתַּח	וַיְבָרֶךְ	הַלִדְרֹשׁ
וַיֶּסְפָּה	שַׁחֵת	שִׁחֵת
וַיָּגֶל	יָכִין	בֵּרְכוּ
הוֹשִׁיעַ	יֶחֱטָא	מְצָאַת

Assignments

A. Vocabulary: words 1–230.

B. Study the Pi'el forms for regular and mid-guttural, mid-ר verbs using Verb Charts A and G and **Mr. Pi'el** on ☻ א ב track 11 (lyrics: pp. 464–465).

C. Memorize the independent subject pronoun; listen to אִתִּי Me א ב track 24.

D. ☻ שַׁבְּחִי tracks 14, 18, and 23 respectively: listen to and translate יְבָרֶכְךָ **Numbers 6:24–26**; sing שְׁמַע **Deuteronomy 6:4**; and listen to אֶרֶץ

E. Read and translate Deuteronomy 6:1–5. The full reading is cantillated on ☻ א ב track 25.

F. Translate:

1 וַיַּכֶּה יְהוֹשֻׁעַ אֶת־כָּל־הָאָרֶץ *Joshua 10:40*

2 וַיהוָה בֵּרַךְ אֶת־אַבְרָהָם בַּכֹּל *Genesis 24:1*

3 וַיְבָרֲכוּ אֱלֹהִים בְּנֵי יִשְׂרָאֵל *Joshua 22:33*

(Note absence of DDO marker. How will you determine the subject?)

4 כִּי עַם קָדוֹשׁ אַתָּה לַיהוָה אֱלֹהֶיךָ בְּךָ בָּחַר יְהוָה אֱלֹהֶיךָ
לִהְיוֹת לוֹ לְעַם סְגֻלָּה מִכֹּל הָעַמִּים אֲשֶׁר עַל־פְּנֵי הָאֲדָמָה
Deuteronomy 7:6 [סְגֻלָּה *possession, treasure*]

5 רוּחַ יְהוָה דִּבֶּר בִּי *2 Samuel 23:2*

6 וּבָרֵךְ אֶת־בֵּית עַבְדְּךָ לִהְיוֹת לְעוֹלָם לְפָנֶיךָ כִּי־אַתָּה אֲדֹנָי
יְהוָה דִּבַּרְתָּ *2 Samuel 7:29*

7 הִנְנִי נֹתֵן בּוֹ רוּחַ *2 Kings 19:7*

✡8 וּלְעוֹלָם כָּל־מִשְׁפַּט צִדְקֶךָ *Psalms 119:160*

9 כִּי הַמִּשְׁפָּט לֵאלֹהִים הוּא *Deuteronomy 1:17*

10 צַדִּיק יְהוָה בְּכָל־דְּרָכָיו *Psalms 145:17*

✡11 בָּרֲכִי נַפְשִׁי אֶת־יְהוָה וְכָל־קְרָבַי אֶת־שֵׁם קָדְשׁוֹ׃ *Psalms 103:1*

12 וְיָשַׁב שָׁם עַד־עוֹלָם *1 Samuel 1:22*

13 אַתָּה תִּהְיֶה עַל־בֵּיתִי *Genesis 41:40*

14 וַיַּרְא דָּוִד כִּי־יָצָא שָׁאוּל לְבַקֵּשׁ אֶת־נַפְשׁוֹ *1 Samuel 23:15*

LESSON 37

מֵאֵת יְהוָה הָיְתָה זֹּאת

Psalms 118:23

37.1 מֵאֵת יְהוָה

We have here a compound prepositional phrase. The first component is _____

אֵת is not the sign of the definite direct object here, but a preposition meaning *with*. Together with מִן it means *from with*, rendered more colloquially as *from*. Since this אֵת is identical in many cases to the sign of the DDO, you must decide by the context which you have. Here there is no problem—the sign of the DDO could never combine with a preposition.

Literal translation of the phrase: _____

37.1a When the preposition אֵת combines with a pronoun, it can be differentiated from the sign of the DDO + pronoun (23.2b) by its having a dagesh.

אֹתִי *me*   אִתִּי *with me*

37.2 הָיְתָה זֹּאת

הָיְתָה is a verb. Can you determine the root? There is one type of weak verb in which the 3 f. sg. affix looks like תָה ⏝ ⏝ When other affix endings are added to 3rd ה roots, the final ה either drops off or changes to י (26.5a)

Root	Stem	Form	Person/Gender/Number	Special Features

37.2a הָיָה is not a hollow verb. Its middle root letter is י but the letter before it has a vowel and the י has its own vowel; therefore, the י is functioning as a consonant. This י will not be lost in any stems or forms of היה The other letter that can be either the middle letter of a hollow verb or a consonant is _____ If the letter preceding it has a vowel already, the ו must be a consonant and will be pronounced "v." The confusion comes in a word like מִצְוָה in which ו is ו + dagesh and not the vowel shureq.

177

37.2b זֹאת is the feminine counterpart of זֶה. What is its relation to the verb? _____
_____ Note the order of the elements in this sentence. What is the effect of having the prepositional phrase at the beginning?

37.3 Translation: _____

37.4 Exercises:

In the following words, identify each י or ו as a consonant or vowel letter:

יַיִן	סוּר	וְעַתָּה
צִוָּה	קָדוֹשׁ	וַיֹּאמֶר
גְּבוּל	יִהְיֶה	אוֹר
אַיִן	אִישׁ	צַוּוּ
מָוֶת	הֵיכָל	וְאֶחְיֶה
מִצְוֹת	הַמִּצְוֹת	וְלָאָדָם

Translate:

רְבָתָה	הָיוּ	וַתִּהְיֶינָה
תִּהְיִי	הָיִיתָ	וְהָיִינוּ
יִרְאֶה	רָאִינוּ	רָאֲתָה
חָיָה	וּבָנִיתָ	וַיֵּשֶׁב
אָמְרָה	וְהָלְכָה	יִשָּׂא
עָשָׂה	וַתֵּצֵא	נָתְנָה

Assignments

A. Vocabulary: words 1–235.

B. Review the Qal affix of 3rd ה verbs: 26.5a, Verb Chart L, **S 37.2**, and **If It's a Man** ☉ ב א track 16.

C. Read and translate Deuteronomy 6:6–10.

D. Translate:

1 כִּי־יָצְאָה בִי יַד־יְהוָה *Ruth 1:13*

2 הִיא נָתְנָה־לִּי מִן־הָעֵץ וָאֹכֵל *Genesis 3:12*

3 וּלְדָוִד וּלְזַרְעוֹ וּלְבֵיתוֹ... יִהְיֶה שָׁלוֹם עַד־עוֹלָם *1 Kings 2:33*

4 וַיֵּצֵא הַשָּׂטָן מֵאֵת פְּנֵי יְהוָה [שָׂטָן just transliterate] *Job 2:7*

5 יִשָּׂא בְרָכָה מֵאֵת יְהוָה *Psalms 24:5*

6 וְלֹא־הָיִיתָ כְּעַבְדִּי דָוִד *1 Kings 14:8*

7   וַתֹּאמֶר הָאִשָּׁה הַזֹּאת אָמְרָה אֵלַי   *2 Kings 6:28*

8   עַיִן לֹא־רָאָתָה   *Isaiah 64:3*

9   כִּי־הָיוּ יָדָיו כִּידֵי עֵשָׂו   *Genesis 27:23*

10   וּבָנִיתָ בֵּית יְהוָה אֱלֹהֶיךָ   *1 Chronicles 22:11*

✡11   וְיָשְׁבָה הָעִיר־הַזֹּאת לְעוֹלָם   *Jeremiah 17:25*

12   וְגַם־בְּנֵי עֲנָקִים רָאִינוּ שָׁם   *Deuteronomy 1:28*

13   וְיָצְאָה מִבֵּיתוֹ וְהָלְכָה וְהָיְתָה לְאִישׁ־אַחֵר: *Deuteronomy 24:2*

14   כָּזֹאת וְכָזֹאת דִּבְּרָה הַנַּעֲרָה אֲשֶׁר מֵאֶרֶץ יִשְׂרָאֵל   *2 Kings 5:4*

15   הֲלוֹא רָאִיתָ מָה־הָעָם הַזֶּה דִּבְּרוּ   *Jeremiah 33:24*

16   וְאָמַרְתָּ לְבִנְךָ עֲבָדִים הָיִינוּ לְפַרְעֹה   *Deuteronomy 6:21*

17   ... וּבָנוּ בָתִּים וְלֹא יֵשֵׁבוּ וְנָטְעוּ כְרָמִים וְלֹא יִשְׁתּוּ אֶת־יֵינָם:

Zephaniah 1:13   [נטע plant   כֶּרֶם vineyard   יַיִן wine]

LESSON 38

◆

וַיִּקָּחֵהוּ שָׁאוּל בַּיּוֹם הַהוּא וְלֹא נְתָנוֹ לָשׁוּב בֵּית אָבִיו׃

1 Samuel 18:2

38.1 Verb Analysis וַיִּקָּחֵהוּ

Root	Stem	Form	Person/Gender/Number	Special Features

For help in determining the root, see 21.7b.

> הוּ___ at the end of a verb is another form of the 3 m. sg. suffix.

It is easy to confuse this with the masculine plural prefix complement and the third common plural affix subject pronoun. Always look to see if a הֵ precedes וּ If so, the chances are very good that you have a <u>suffix</u> (object of the verb).

Translation of phrase: _____

38.2 בַּיּוֹם הַהוּא

38.2a What is the initial בַּ _____ Notice the vowel under the בַּ Pataḥ represents the definite article *the* ☐הַ which has elided so that only the vowel of the definite article and the dagesh forte remain.

Thus, ☐בַּ ⟵ ☐הַבְּ *in the*

יוֹם☐ means _____

38.2b הַהוּא

What is the initial הַ_____ (21.3a) הוּא besides being the 3 m. sg. independent pronoun, is also used as a demonstrative adjective (*that*).

The adjective construction בַּיּוֹם הַהוּא is called _____

180

וַיִּקָּחֵהוּ שָׁאוּל בַּיּוֹם הַהוּא וְלֹא נְתָנוֹ לָשׁוּב בֵּית אָבִיו:

38.2c Summary of the **Demonstrative Adjectives**

	this	*that*
masculine	הַיּוֹם הַזֶּה	הַיּוֹם הַהוּא
feminine	הָאִשָּׁה הַזֹּאת	הָאִשָּׁה הַהִיא

	these	*those*
masculine	הַיָּמִים הָאֵלֶּה	הַיָּמִים הָהֵם
feminine	הַנָּשִׁים הָאֵלֶּה	הַנָּשִׁים הָהֵן

38.3 Verb Analysis וְלֹא נְתָנוֹ

וְלֹא means _____

Root	Stem	Form	Person/Gender/Number	Special Features

Until now, all the suffixes we have studied have been on nouns or on prepositions. Verbs can have suffixes, too. What is the suffix here? _____ (7.2c) In the Special Features column: 3 m. sg. suffix. נתן means _____

Here it means *give,* as in *give permission* or *allow.*

When a suffix is added to a verb, the verb behaves like a noun with regard to the vowel changes caused by pretonic lengthening and propretonic reduction. (**S 5.1c.1–3**) When a suffix causes the regular vowels of a verb to change, you must determine the form by other hints. Is the form prefix? Is the form imperative? What form fits the context best? Here the stem is Qal—even though the suffix has caused the landmark qamats under the first root letter to be reduced to shewa—since there are no other changes in the verb. So נְתָנוֹ is a 3 m. sg. Qal affix with a 3 m. sg. suffix.

38.4 Verb Analysis לָשׁוּב

Root	Stem	Form	Person/Gender/Number	Special Features

וַיִּקָּחֵהוּ שָׁאוּל בַּיּוֹם הַהוּא וְלֹא נְתָנוֹ לָשׁוּב בֵּית אָבִיו:

38.5 בֵּית אָבִיו is a _____ It means _____

Note that the context demands a preposition in front of the phrase. Occasionally there is no preposition in Biblical Hebrew with nouns toward which, or in which, action takes place. Supply the preposition when you translate.

38.6 Translate sentence: _____

_____

38.7a Extra Grammar

You have seen two ways of expressing a verb + pronominal DDO. One is by using the verb followed by אֵת + pronoun: וַיָּמִתוּ אֹתוֹ (23.2b) The other way we have seen in this lesson: the object pronoun can be attached directly to the conjugated form of the verb. Below is a chart showing the most common suffixes.

Verb Suffixes

1 c. sg.	נִי_		1 c. pl.	נוּ_
2 m. sg.	ךָ_		2 m. pl.	כֶם_
2 f. sg.	ךְ_		2 f. pl.	כֶן_
3 m. sg.	הוּ_ וֹ_ וֹ_		3 m. pl.	ם_ הֶם_
3 f. sg.	הָ_ ה_		3 f. pl.	הֶן_ ן_

38.7b As you have seen, there can be vocalization changes in the verb when a suffix is added. This does not mean that all identification keys totally disappear. Affix pronouns, prefix pronouns, and complements will remain, and so will any augmentation to the root. Most of the problems occur in the Qal.

1. Vowels at the beginning of the word may reduce:

   3 m. sg. Qal affix   **3 m. sg. Qal affix + 3 f. sg. suffix**

   שָׁמַר   שְׁמָרָהּ

2. Affix pronouns may lose their characteristic vocalization:

   2 m. sg. Qal affix   **2 m. sg. Qal affix + 1 c. sg. suffix**

   שָׁמַרְתָּ   שְׁמַרְתַּנִי

3. There may be an extra syllable in the word to facilitate pronunciation:

   3 m. sg. Qal prefix   **3 m. sg. Qal prefix + 1 c. sg. suffix**

   יִשְׁמֹר   יִשְׁמְרֵנִי

4. In cases of apparent ambiguity, you have to be astute:

3 m. sg. Qal affix + 2 m. sg. suffix	Qal infinitive + 2 m. sg. suffix
שְׁמָרְךָ	שָׁמְרְךָ

38.8 If you can analyze these verbs with confidence, or even with difficulty, you are well on your way to mastery of Hebrew verbs.

C	B	A	
פְּקַדְתִּי	פְּקַדְתִּיו	פְּקַדְתִּים	1
פְּקַדְתֶּם	פָּקְדוּ	יִפְקְדֵם	2
פּוּקַד	וַיַּפְקִידוּ	הִפְקַדְתִּיךָ	3
וַתָּבֵא	וַיָּבֹאוּ	תְּבִיאֶינָה	4
בְּבוֹא	הֲבִיאֹתַנִי	וַתְּבִיאֵם	5
וָאָבִיא	אָשִׁיב	וַיֵּשְׁבוּ	6
וַיֵּשְׁבוּ	יָשַׁב	יֵשֵׁב	7
אוֹשִׁיבְךָ	אֲשִׁיבְךָ	וָאֶעֱלֶה	8
וַיַּעֲלֵהוּ	וַיַּעֲלוּ	תַּעֲלֶה	9
יוֹרִידֵנִי	יִרְאֵהוּ	מְצָאתִי	10
מְצָאתִיו	נְתַתִּים	נְתָנִים	11
נְתַתִּיו	נְתַתִּיהוּ	נְתָנַנִי	12
נְתָתַנִי	צִוָּהוּ	צִוָּה	13
בֵּרְכוּ	בֵּרְכָנוּ	בֵּרְכוּנִי	14
יְבָרְכֵנוּ	וַיְבָרְכֵהוּ	וַיְבָרְכֵנוּ	15
תְּבָרְכֵנִי	בָּרְכוּ	יַעֲשֶׂה	16
יַעֲשֵׂהוּ	יַעֲשֶׂהָ	יַעֲשׂוּ	17
עָשׂוּ	עָשׂוּ	וַיַּעֲשׂוּנִי	18
עָשִׂיתִי	עָשְׂתָה	עָשִׂיתָה	19
וַעֲשִׂיתִיהוּ	עֲשִׂיתִים	עֲשִׂיתָנִי	20
עֲשִׂיתָה	עָשָׂהוּ	עָשָׂהוּ	21
עָשׂוּנוּ	עָשִׂינוּ	עָשׂוּנִי	22
עָשׂוּהוּ	שְׁלָחֻנוּ	שְׁלָחַנִי	23

וַיִּקָּחֵהוּ שָׁאוּל בַּיּוֹם הַהוּא וְלֹא נְתָנוֹ לָשׁוּב בֵּית אָבִיו׃

Assignments

A. Vocabulary: words 1–240.

B. Learn the verb suffixes in 38.7a.

C. 💿 track 2: learn the song שַׁבְּחִי Psalm 147:12.

D. Read and translate Deuteronomy 6:11–15.

E. Translate:

1	וַיִּרְאֶהָ יְהוּדָה *Genesis 38:15*
2	בַּיָּמִים הָהֵם אֵין מֶלֶךְ בְּיִשְׂרָאֵל *Judges 17:6*
3	אֲשֶׁר לְקָחָהּ לוֹ לְאִשָּׁה *Deuteronomy 24:3*
4	וַיָּשָׁב בַּיּוֹם הַהוּא עֵשָׂו לְדַרְכּוֹ *Genesis 33:16*
5	כֹּה אָמַר יְהוֹה שַׁבְתִּי אֶל־צִיּוֹן *Zechariah 8:3*
6	וַיִּשְׁלַח יָדוֹ וַיִּקָּחֶהָ *Genesis 8:9*
7	וַיִּתְּנֵהוּ יְהוֹה אֱלֹהֵינוּ לְפָנֵינוּ *Deuteronomy 2:33*
8	וְרוּחַ נְשָׂאַתְנִי וַתִּקָּחֵנִי וָאֵלֵךְ *Ezekiel 3:14*
9	וַיִּתְּנָהּ אֶל־הַכֹּהֲנִים בְּנֵי לֵוִי *Deuteronomy 31:9*
10	וּנְתַתִּיךָ בְּיַד מְבַקְשֵׁי נַפְשֶׁךָ (36.3b) *Jeremiah 22:25*
11	וּנְתַתִּיו לַיהוֹה כָּל־יְמֵי חַיָּיו *1 Samuel 1:11*
12	לָמָּה זֶּה שְׁלַחְתָּנִי *Exodus 5:22*
13	הִנֵּה בָּרְכוּ אֶת־יְהוֹה כָּל־עַבְדֵי יְהוֹה *Psalms 134:1*

LESSON 39

◆

וַיְצַו מֹשֶׁה וַיַּעֲבִירוּ קוֹל בַּמַּחֲנֶה לֵאמֹר אִישׁ וְאִשָּׁה
אַל־יַעֲשׂוּ־עוֹד מְלָאכָה לִתְרוּמַת הַקֹּדֶשׁ

Exodus 36:6

39.1 וַיְצַו מֹשֶׁה

Verb Analysis וַיְצַו

Root	Stem	Form	Person/Gender/Number	Special Features

According to the missing letter rule in 12.1, what is the missing root letter? _____

The tricky part of this analysis is the stem. What stem routinely has shewa ְ under the prefix

pronoun and pataḥ ַ under the first root letter? _____ (15.5) Where, then, is the

supporting dagesh forte to confirm this stem?

> Omission of dagesh forte occurs, almost always, at the end of a word.

צוה is a common verb and in the Bible is found almost exclusively in the Piʻel. Because it is a

3rd ה it may lose its third root letter in some forms; therefore, it will lose the dagesh forte when

ו appears as the last letter.

Translation of the phrase: _____

39.2 וַיַּעֲבִירוּ קוֹל בַּמַּחֲנֶה לֵאמֹר

39.2a Verb Analysis וַיַּעֲבִירוּ

Root	Stem	Form	Person/Gender/Number	Special Features

וַיְצַו מֹשֶׁה וַיַּעֲבִירוּ קוֹל בַּמַּחֲנֶה לֵאמֹר אִישׁ וְאִשָּׁה אַל־יַעֲשׂוּ־עוֹד מְלָאכָה לִתְרוּמַת הַקֹּדֶשׁ

Does the vowel under the prefix pronoun create an ambiguity? _____ (32.3b) Where will you look next to determine the stem? Pay particular attention to the PGN of this verb. A literal translation would be _____

How is קוֹל related to וַיַּעֲבִירוּ _____

You should be able to translate the next word in this phrase, but if you can't, where would you look in the dictionary? _____ (The Noun C.)

39.2b Verb Analysis לֵאמֹר

Root	Stem	Form	Person/Gender/Number	Special Features

What is the form of the verb _____ and how is it being used? (35.1a) _____

_____ Compare this to the uses of the participle. (9.3b) לֵאמֹר often comes immediately before a direct quotation and functions as an aural quotation mark.

Literal translation of the whole phrase: _____

_____

39.3   אִישׁ וְאִשָּׁה אַל־יַעֲשׂוּ־עוֹד מְלָאכָה

39.3a The compound subject of this phrase is composed of a masculine and a feminine noun: אִישׁ וְאִשָּׁה In such a case, you can expect a masculine verb. The conjunction linking the two nouns need not be translated *and*. After working out the verb, see how you can best link the subject to it.

אִישׁ can mean, in addition to *a man*, *each man* or *every man*. By extension, then, the phrase here is an idiom meaning *each man and woman*.

39.3b אַל־יַעֲשׂוּ

Root	Stem	Form	Person/Gender/Number	Special Features

> אַל is a negative particle used with a prefix form of the verb to express a negative command (**Don't . . .**).

In the Special Features column write "negative imperative."

The problem with analyzing the verb is determining the stem. What are the possibilities? _____ _____ (32.3b) Can you resolve the ambiguity in this case? עוֹד is an adverb meaning _____.

Translation of the phrase: _____

39.4 לִתְרוּמַת הַקֹּדֶשׁ

One thing to be determined about לִתְרוּמַת is whether it is a noun or a verb. In either case, which letter will be extraneous? _____ Of the letters left, is there a pattern that can confirm or eliminate one syntactical possibility? (Prefix pronoun/prefix complement, or noun preformative and state indicator.)

What part of speech is הַקֹּדֶשׁ _____ It means _____ קֹדֶשׁ may be a synecdoche (the naming of a part to represent the whole; not to be confused with a city in Upstate New York) referring to the sanctuary.

39.5   Translation of the verse: _____

_____

_____

39.6   In the sampling of translations below, you can see how editors handled what they perceived as idiom or awkward language in this verse. Consider whether you think such liberties as change in voice and change in placement of the negative are justified. Then there is the matter of some of the words themselves, the choice of which is probably the most interesting aspect of the different translations.

And Moses gave commandment, and they caused it to be proclaimed throughout the camp, saying, "Let neither man nor woman make any more work for the offering of the sanctuary."
> —Jewish Publication Society of America, 1917
> King James Version
> New King James Version

So Moses sent word round the camp that no man or woman should prepare anything more as a contribution for the sanctuary.
> —New English Bible

וַיְצַו מֹשֶׁה וַיַּעֲבִירוּ קוֹל בַּמַּחֲנֶה לֵאמֹר אִישׁ וְאִשָּׁה

אַל־יַעֲשׂוּ־עוֹד מְלָאכָה לִתְרוּמַת הַקֹּדֶשׁ

So Moses bade the crier give out that no man or woman should offer any more for the needs of the sanctuary.

—Knox

So Moses sent a command throughout the camp that no one was to make any further contribution for the sacred Tent.

—T E V American Bible Society

Moses thereupon had this proclamation made throughout the camp: "Let no man or woman make further effort toward gifts for the sanctuary."

—The Torah, A Modern Commentary

Assignments

A. Vocabulary: words 1–245.

B. Read and translate Deuteronomy 6:16–20.

C. ✺⊙ track 13: listen to אַל תַּשְׁלִיכֵנִי שַׁבְחִי

D. Translate:

1 הִנֵּה הַנְּבִאִים אֹמְרִים לָהֶם לֹא־תִרְאוּ חֶרֶב וְרָעָב לֹא־יִהְיֶה

לָכֶם כִּי־שָׁלוֹם אֱמֶת אֶתֵּן לָכֶם [רָעָב *famine*]   *Jeremiah 14:13*

2 וְכָל־הָעָם רֹאִים אֶת־הַקּוֹלֹת   *Exodus 20:18*

3 וַתֹּאמֶר בַּת־שֶׁבַע טוֹב אָנֹכִי אֲדַבֵּר עָלֶיךָ אֶל־הַמֶּלֶךְ:   *1 Kings 2:18*

✡4 וַיֹּאמֶר יְהוָה אֵלַי אַל־תֹּאמַר נַעַר אָנֹכִי כִּי עַל־כָּל־אֲשֶׁר

אֶשְׁלָחֲךָ תֵּלֵךְ וְאֵת כָּל־אֲשֶׁר אֲצַוְּךָ תְּדַבֵּר: אַל־תִּירָא

מִפְּנֵיהֶם כִּי־אִתְּךָ אֲנִי לְהַצִּלֶךָ נְאֻם־יְהוָה: [נְאֻם *utterance*]   *Jeremiah 1:7–8*

5 וְעַתָּה בָנִים שִׁמְעוּ־לִי וְאַל־תָּסוּרוּ מֵאִמְרֵי־פִי: *Proverbs 5:7*

LESSON 40

◆

גַּם עָשֹׂה תַעֲשֶׂה וְגַם יָכֹל תּוּכָל

1 Samuel 26:25

40.1 גַּם means _____

וְגַם . . . גַּם means *not only . . . but also,* or you could be more emphatic and say *not only . . . but moreover.*

40.2 עָשֹׂה תַעֲשֶׂה

40.2a What do you notice about these two words? We hope you notice that the root is repeated. The first word uses the root alone; the second word is a prefix form of the verb. Together they form an emphatic phrase—English usually renders this type of construction with the adverb *surely* + the verb used in the proper tense.

What we have here is actually a special type of the infinitive, the **infinitive absolute** (here in the Qal), and this is its major use in Hebrew prose. For the strong verb, the two infinitives look very much alike: פְּקֹד construct פָּקֹד absolute. But in the case of a 3rd ה the forms are more distinct: עֲשֹׂות infinitive construct עָשֹׂה infinitive absolute.

> The infinitive absolute + verb (usually prefix) is an emphatic construction conveyed in English by adding the word ***surely*** to the verb employed.

40.2b Analyze עָשֹׂה

Root	Stem	Form	Person/Gender/Number	Special Features

In the Special Features column, note the type of infinitive.

189

40.2c   Analyze תַעֲשֶׂה

Root	Stem	Form	Person/Gender/Number	Special Features

40.3   וְגַם יָכֹל תּוּכָל

You can see here a repetition of the previous construction. יָכֹל has several meanings: *be able, have power, prevail, endure.*

40.4   Translate the verse: _____

40.5   יָכֹל does not follow a 1st י pattern. Below are charts of its extant forms in the Bible.

Qal Affix יכל

3 m. sg.	יָכֹל	3 c. pl.	יָכְלוּ
3 f. sg.	יָכְלָה		
2 m. sg.	יָכֹלְתָּ	2 m. pl.	_____
2 f. sg.	_____	2 f. pl.	_____
1 c. sg.	יָכֹלְתִּי	1 c. pl.	_____

Qal Prefix יכל

3 m. sg.	יוּכַל	3 m. pl.	יוּכְלוּ
3 f. sg.	תּוּכַל	3 f. pl.	_____
2 m. sg.	תּוּכַל	2 m. pl.	תּוּכְלוּ
2 f. sg.	_____	2 f. pl.	_____
1 c. sg.	אוּכַל	1 c. pl.	נוּכַל

Qal Infinitives יכל

Construct	יְכֹלֶת	Absolute	יָכֹל

190

גַּם עָשֹׂה תַעֲשֶׂה וְגַם יָכֹל תּוּכָל

Assignments

A. Vocabulary: words 1–250. Test yourself: 💿 אֵלֶּה הַדְּבָרִים tracks 3–27.

B. Memorize the affix, prefix and infinitives of יכל

C. Read and translate Deuteronomy 6:21–25. Listen to the cantillation on 💿 א ב track 25.

D. 💿 שִׁבְחִי Enjoy your favorite songs.

E. Translate:

1   כִּי עָשֹׂה אֶעֱשֶׂה עִמְּךָ חֶסֶד   *2 Samuel 9:7*

2   וַאֲנַחְנוּ לֹא נֵדַע מַה־נַּעֲשֶׂה כִּי עָלֶיךָ עֵינֵינוּ   *2 Chronicles 20:12*

3   אָכוֹל תֹּאכְלוּ אֹתָהּ בַּקֹּדֶשׁ כַּאֲשֶׁר צִוֵּיתִי   *Leviticus 10:18*

4   בֹא־יָבוֹא מֶלֶךְ־בָּבֶל וְהִשְׁחִית אֶת־הָאָרֶץ הַזֹּאת   *Jeremiah 36:29*

5   וְכִי תֹאמְרוּ מַה־נֹּאכַל   *Leviticus 25:20*

6   הֲלֹא אַהֲרֹן אָחִיךָ הַלֵּוִי יָדַעְתִּי כִּי־דַבֵּר יְדַבֵּר הוּא   *Exodus 4:14*

7   אֶת־בְּנֹתָם נִקַּח־לָנוּ לְנָשִׁים וְאֶת־בְּנֹתֵינוּ נִתֵּן לָהֶם   *Genesis 34:21*

8   וְעֹזְבֵי יהוה יִכְלוּ   *Isaiah 1:28*

9   יָצֹא אֵצֵא גַם־אֲנִי עִמָּכֶם   *2 Samuel 18:2*

10   וַיֹּאמֶר יְהוּדָה מַה־נֹּאמַר לַאדֹנִי מַה־נְּדַבֵּר   *Genesis 44:16*

11   וּצְדָקָה תִּהְיֶה־לָּנוּ כִּי־נִשְׁמֹר לַעֲשׂוֹת אֶת־כָּל־הַמִּצְוָה הַזֹּאת

12   לִפְנֵי יהוה אֱלֹהֵינוּ כַּאֲשֶׁר צִוָּנוּ׃   *Deuteronomy 6:25*

13   וְנֵצֵא אֶל־מֶלֶךְ יִשְׂרָאֵל אוּלַי יְחַיֶּה אֶת־נַפְשֶׁךָ [אוּלַי *perhaps*]   *1 Kings 20:31*

14   כִּי מֵרָעָה אֶל־רָעָה יָצָאוּ וְאֹתִי לֹא־יָדָעוּ   *Jeremiah 9:2*

15   וְגַם־אֲנַחְנוּ נִהְיֶה לַאדֹנִי לַעֲבָדִים   *Genesis 44:9*

16   כִּי־כָלִינוּ בְאַפֶּךָ   *Psalms 90:7*

✡17   כִּי אָמַרְתִּי יֶשׁ־לִי תִקְוָה גַּם הָיִיתִי הַלַּיְלָה לְאִישׁ וְגַם יָלַדְתִּי בָנִים [תִּקְוָה *hope*]   *Ruth 1:12*

<u>Extra Credit</u>: Can you explain the dageshes in the two words beginning with נ in sentence 10? (Answer can be found at **S 17.3b.**)

LESSON 41

נֵלְכָה־נָּא דֶּרֶךְ שְׁלֹשֶׁת יָמִים בַּמִּדְבָּר

Exodus 3:18

41.1 Verb Analysis נֵלְכָה־נָּא

Root	Stem	Form	Person/Gender/Number	Special Features

In the first word נ is _____ Thus the root will be _____ The ending הָ can be an emphatic or rhythmic verb ending. (30.1a) Combined with a first person prefix pronoun, it is a sign of a specialized form of the prefix.

A first person prefix, singular or plural, +הָ ending constitutes a specialized construction called the **cohortative**.

The cohortative is a type of command—to oneself:

> "**Let us** do such and such."
>
> "I <u>will</u> do . . ."
>
> "We <u>will</u> do such and such."

(an exercise of will, not a mere statement about the future)

41.1a נָא is a particle attached almost exclusively to imperatives, cohortatives, and jussives (next lesson). Use this helpful bit of information to assist in locating these forms. It is sometimes also attached to הִנֵּה │ נָא is frequently translated as *please*, modernized from *prithee*, and just as frequently not translated at all. Some scholars treat it as a "modal particle," indicating action arising out of a preceding statement (translation: *now, as a result*). While this explanation will not work in every case, נָא usually has the force of *now* in אָסֻרָה־נָּא *I will turn aside now* (Ex. 3:3).

41.1b The cohortative ה is an extra ה‎ָ syllable, so it cannot be added to a verb that already ends in ה Thus, in a form such as נַעֲלֶה the mood has to be inferred from the context.

41.2 דֶּרֶךְ שְׁלֹשֶׁת יָמִים

דֶּרֶךְ means _____ שְׁלֹשֶׁת is a form of שָׁלֹשׁ *three*. יָמִים means _____

(The Noun H) Note the endiNGs on these words. Do they agree?

41.2a Numbers are the grand exception to all our adjective rules in Hebrew. In fact, they themselves do not follow one consistent scheme. The basic number words (cardinals) for the numbers from 1 to 10 are shown below. Note that the form given is identified as the word <u>modifying</u> masculine or feminine nouns—the words themselves often appear to be in the gender opposite to that of the noun modified.

	Modifying Masculine Nouns		Modifying Feminine Nouns	
	Before or After	Before Only (construct)	Before or After	Before Only (construct)
One	אֶחָד	אַחַד	אַחַת	אַחַת
Two	שְׁנַיִם	שְׁנֵי	שְׁתַּיִם	שְׁתֵּי
Three	שְׁלֹשָׁה	שְׁלֹשֶׁת	שָׁלֹשׁ	שְׁלֹשׁ
Four	אַרְבָּעָה	אַרְבַּעַת	אַרְבַּע	
Five	חֲמִשָּׁה	חֲמֵשֶׁת	חָמֵשׁ	חֲמֵשׁ
Six	שִׁשָּׁה	שֵׁשֶׁת	שֵׁשׁ	
Seven	שִׁבְעָה	שִׁבְעַת	שֶׁבַע	שְׁבַע
Eight	שְׁמֹנָה	שְׁמֹנַת	שְׁמֹנֶה	
Nine	תִּשְׁעָה	תִּשְׁעַת	תֵּשַׁע	תְּשַׁע
Ten	עֲשָׂרָה	עֲשֶׂרֶת	עֶשֶׂר	

Rules on use:

1. The number **one** always agrees with its noun in gender.

2. **Two** has a dual ending ◌ַיִם in both masculine and feminine forms. The noun used with the number two is plural. But if an item occurs in a pair, only the dual ending is used with the noun, without the use or the word *two*.

3. From **three** to **ten,** the plural of the noun is used with the number word, with few exceptions. (After number ten the singular of the noun is used, as a rule.)

Back to our phrase דֶּרֶךְ שְׁלֹשֶׁת יָמִים We have here a _____

This also helps us to understand how the number can be singular and the noun plural. Is the chain definite or indefinite? _____

Translate phrase: _____ בַּמִּדְבָּר means _____ (38.2c)

41.3 Translate verse: _____

41.4 You have seen that there are many things that הָ at the end of a word can be:

רָאָה	part of verb root
פְּקָדָה	3 f. sg. affix pronoun
תִּרְאֶינָה	2 and 3 f. pl. prefix complement
שְׁמֹרְנָה	f. pl. imperative
שָׁנָה	f. sg. noun endiNG
טוֹבָה	f. sg. adjective endiNG
פֹּקְדָה	f. sg. participle endiNG
עָרֶיהָ	f. sg. possessive suffix[1]
הַגִּידָה	extra syllable on a m. sg. imperative
נֵלְכָה	cohortative ה
אַרְצָה	locative or directional ה
עָשִׂיתָה	plene spelling
עַתָּה	part of another sort of word (pronoun, adverb, etc.)

Some clues to help you determine what the הָ is:

It may be part of a whole word you should recognize as it stands: עַתָּה

In other cases, you need to find the root. If it is a noun, knowing your vocabulary will be a great help.

If it is a verb form:

a) ḥolem וֹ after the first root letter is probably a sign of _____

b) shewa ְ under the first root letter and נ immediately before the הָ could be an indication of _____

---

1. Admittedly, הָ is not the same as הָ but it is included because it may be visually ambiguous.

c) a prefix pronoun, combined with **ו** immediately before the ה‬ָ could indicate _____

_____

What other hints can you think of to identify other things? ("Context" counts!)

41.5   Identify the function of the ה‬ָ or הָ‬ in each of the following words. In some cases, there is more than one possibility. In such potentially ambiguous cases, tell how you would decide among the options.

C	B	A	
רָעָה	וָאֹבְדָה	הַיַּרְדֵּנָה	1
עֶשְׂרֵה	הַבְּהֵמָה	הַבָּאָה	2
תִּרְאֶינָה	שְׁמֹרְנָה	וַיַּצִּילֵהָ	3
נֹאבְדָה	שְׁדָתָיהָ	טוֹבָה	4
רָאֲתָה	מִצְרַיְמָה	שִׁבְעָה	5
הָלְכָה	מֵאָה	עֵדָה	6
הַשְׁלֵכְנָה	עָשִׂיתָה	גָּלָה	7
מִלְחָמָה	הִרְבְּתָה	שָׁמָּה	8
שִׁשָּׁה	שׁוֹפְטָה	עַתָּה	9
אֶשְׁמְרָה	דִּבַּרְנָה	הֶרְאָה	10
מִשְׁפָּחָה	שָׁכְבָה	גָּלָה	11
נָבוֹאָה	וְנָשׁוּבָה	לָמָּה	12
תַּשְׁלֵכְנָה	אָמְרָה	מִנְחָה	13
וָאֹמְרָה	שָׁפְטָה	צִוָּה	14
הָאָמְרָה	אָמַרְנָה	אָמְרָה	15
עָלָה	גָּדְלָה	וְהַגְּדוֹלָה	16
חָכְמָה	הָרְשָׁעָה	הִטָּה	17
שָׁלַחְנָה	עָנָה	נַחֲלָה	18
לָיְמָה	אֲדָמָה	וַתֹּאבְדֵנָה	19
מַלְכָּה	חַיָּה	מַלְכָּה	20
מְצָאנָה	הִשְׁמַעְנָה	רָבָה	21
תִּכְלֶינָה	שָׁתָה	עָלֵינָה	22

Assignments

A.   Vocabulary: words 1–255.

B.   Learn the numbers 1–10 (41.5); memorize א ב ❂ אַחַת שְׁתַּיִם track 26.

C.   ❂ שַׁבְּחִי track 29: learn לֹא יִשָּׂא גוֹי Isaiah 2:4.

D.   Read and translate 1 Kings 17:1–5.

E.   Translate. Then identify the form and mood of each first person verb:

1	וְאָבוֹאָה אֶל־מִזְבַּח אֱלֹהִים *Psalms 43:4*
2	שִׁבְעַת יָמִים מַצּוֹת תֹּאכֵלוּ [*matzah*] מַצּוֹת *Exodus 12:15*
3	וַנֹּאמֶר בֹּאוּ וְנָבוֹא יְרוּשָׁלָ͏ִם *Jeremiah 35:11*
4	וָאֲבָרֵךְ אֶת־יהוה אֱלֹהֵי אֲדֹנִי *Genesis 24:48*
5	שָׂמַחְתִּי בְּאֹמְרִים לִי בֵּית יהוה נֵלֵךְ *Psalms 122:1*
6	וַיִּקַּח סֵפֶר הַבְּרִית וַיִּקְרָא בְּאָזְנֵי הָעָם וַיֹּאמְרוּ כֹּל אֲשֶׁר־דִּבֶּר יהוה נַעֲשֶׂה וְנִשְׁמָע: *Exodus 24:7*
7	וַיַּעֲשׂוּ־חָג שִׁבְעַת יָמִים [*celebration*] חָג *Nehemiah 8:18*
8	לְעוֹלָם אֶשְׁמוֹר־לוֹ חַסְדִּי [אֶשְׁמָר read as אֶשְׁמוֹר *Psalms 89:29*
9	וַנִּקַּח בָּעֵת הַהִוא אֶת־הָאָרֶץ מִיַּד שְׁנֵי מַלְכֵי הָאֱמֹרִי *Deuteronomy 3:8*
10	וַיִּגְּשׁוּ אֶל־זְרֻבָּבֶל וְאֶל־רָאשֵׁי הָאָבוֹת וַיֹּאמְרוּ לָהֶם נִבְנֶה עִמָּכֶם *Ezra 4:2*
11	וָאֶבְנֶה הַבַּיִת לְשֵׁם יהוה *1 Kings 8:20*
✿12	הִנֵּה־נָא לִי שְׁתֵּי בָנוֹת אֲשֶׁר לֹא־יָדְעוּ אִישׁ אוֹצִיאָה־נָּא אֶתְהֶן אֲלֵיכֶם וַעֲשׂוּ לָהֶן כַּטּוֹב בְּעֵינֵיכֶם *Genesis 19:8*
13	שְׁנֵי אֲנָשִׁים הָיוּ בְּעִיר אֶחָת *2 Samuel 12:1*
14	שֵׁשֶׁת יָמִים תַּעֲבֹד *Deuteronomy 5:13*
15	וַיִּהְיוּ־שָׁם שְׁלֹשָׁה בְּנֵי צְרוּיָה *2 Samuel 2:18*
16	וַיֹּאמְרוּ לָנוּ עֶשֶׂר פְּעָמִים *Nehemiah 4:6*
17	אֶת־יהוה אֱלֹהֵינוּ נַעֲבֹד וּבְקוֹלוֹ נִשְׁמָע *Joshua 24:24*
18	אֶעְבְּרָה־נָּא וְאֶרְאֶה אֶת־הָאָרֶץ הַטּוֹבָה *Deuteronomy 3:25*

LESSON 42

יְהִי יהוה אֱלֹהֶיךָ בָּרוּךְ

1 Kings 10:9

42.1   Verb Analysis יְהִי

Root	Stem	Form	Person/Gender/Number	Special Features

You have seen וַיְהִי many times. יְהִי is less common. It has the same root and prefix pronoun, but is a different form. This form is called the **jussive**.

> A third person prefix form, singular or plural, may be used as a **jussive**, a command given in the third person.

Examples of jussives:

"May he do such and such"

"Let them do such and such"

"He or they <u>shall</u> do such and such"

42.1a   The jussive form is ordinarily identical to the prefix form. However, if there are two forms of the prefix, as happens, for example, with 3rd ה verbs—יִהְיֶה and יְהִי — the jussive will use the shorter form. (32.3a) We have seen examples of these shortened forms with the vav conversive. Without the vav conversive, the shortened form must be a jussive.

42.2   יהוה אֱלֹהֶיךָ is related to the verb _____

Translation of the first three words: _____

197

42.3   בָּרוּךְ

Do you see a familiar root here? This form, in which a וּ appears between the second and third letters of the root, is called the **Qal passive participle**. In the Bible, it is regularly used as an adjective rather than as a verbal construction.

ברך means _____   בָּרוּךְ means _____

42.4   Translate sentence: _____

42.5   Our imperative picture is now complete:

Cohortative First Person	Imperative Second Person	Jussive Third Person
Let me/us do usually lengthens (41.1)	*Do* may lengthen (30.1a)	*Let him/her/them do* may shorten (42.1)

All of these are closely related to the prefix forms. Indeed, in some cases of the cohortative and jussive, the two forms may be indistinguishable. Sometimes נָא will be a broad hint for you; sometimes it is simply a matter of judgment.

Assignments

A.   Vocabulary: words 1–260.

B.   Read and translate 1 Kings 17:6–10.

C.   ☉אב track 27: learn בָּרוּךְ הַבָּא (lyrics: p. 481).

D.   ☉שַׁבְּחִי track 30: listen to אוֹר זָרוּעַ **Psalm 97:11.**

E.   Translate:

Ruth 1:8 [Read יַעֲשֶׂ as יַעַשׂ] יַעֲשֶׂה יהוה עִמָּכֶם חֶסֶד   1

Genesis 1:3 [אוֹר *light*] וַיֹּאמֶר אֱלֹהִים יְהִי אוֹר וַיְהִי־אוֹר: 2

Psalms 121:8 יהוה יִשְׁמָר־צֵאתְךָ וּבוֹאֶךָ מֵעַתָּה וְעַד עוֹלָם: 3

(Do you see the "scribal error" here?) יְהִי־נָא דְבָרְיךָ כִּדְבַר אַחַד מֵהֶם   4
1 Kings 22:13

Psalms 132:12 אִם־יִשְׁמְרוּ בָנֶיךָ בְּרִיתִי   5

2 Kings 7:13 וְיִקְחוּ־נָא חֲמִשָּׁה מִן־הַסּוּסִים   6

1 Chronicles 17:12 הוּא יִבְנֶה־לִּי בָּיִת   7

Genesis 24:27 בָּרוּךְ יהוה אֱלֹהֵי אֲדֹנִי אַבְרָהָם   8

Genesis 12:20 וַיְשַׁלְּחוּ אֹתוֹ וְאֶת־אִשְׁתּוֹ וְאֶת־כָּל־אֲשֶׁר־לוֹ   9

10 וַיֹּאמֶר יהוה אֶל־מֹשֶׁה בְּלֶכְתְּךָ לָשׁוּב מִצְרַיְמָה רְאֵה
כָּל־הַמֹּפְתִים אֲשֶׁר־שַׂמְתִּי בְיָדֶךָ וַעֲשִׂיתָם לִפְנֵי פַרְעֹה וַאֲנִי אֲחַזֵּק
אֶת־לִבּוֹ וְלֹא יְשַׁלַּח אֶת־הָעָם: מֹפְתִים [wonders] *Exodus 4:21*

11 יַעֲמָד־נָא דָוִד לְפָנַי כִּי־מָצָא חֵן בְּעֵינָי... חֵן [grace, favor] *1 Samuel 16:22*

12 וְיוֹאָב וְכָל־הַצָּבָא אֲשֶׁר־אִתּוֹ בָּאוּ וַיַּגִּדוּ לְיוֹאָב לֵאמֹר בָּא־אַבְנֵר
בֶּן־נֵר אֶל־הַמֶּלֶךְ וַיְשַׁלְּחֵהוּ וַיֵּלֶךְ בְּשָׁלוֹם: *2 Samuel 3:23*

13 וָאֶתְּנָה אֶת־הַלְוִיִּם נְתֻנִים לְאַהֲרֹן וּלְבָנָיו *Numbers 8:19*

14 וָאֶקַּח אֶת־רָאשֵׁי שִׁבְטֵיכֶם אֲנָשִׁים חֲכָמִים וִידֻעִים *Deuteronomy 1:15*

✡15 וְנַעֲמָן שַׂר־צְבָא מֶלֶךְ־אֲרָם הָיָה אִישׁ גָּדוֹל לִפְנֵי אֲדֹנָיו
וּנְשֻׂא פָנִים *2 Kings 5:1*

16 וַיֹּאמֶר הַמֶּלֶךְ לְהָמָן הַכֶּסֶף נָתוּן לָךְ וְהָעָם לַעֲשׂוֹת בּוֹ
כַּטּוֹב בְּעֵינֶיךָ: *Esther 3:11*

17 וַיֶּחֶרְדוּ כָּל־הַקְּרֻאִים אֲשֶׁר לַאֲדֹנִיָּהוּ וַיֵּלְכוּ אִישׁ לְדַרְכּוֹ *1 Kings 1:49*

18 פֶּן־תִּכְרֹת בְּרִית לְיוֹשֵׁב הָאָרֶץ וְזָנוּ אַחֲרֵי אֱלֹהֵיהֶם וְזָבְחוּ
לֵאלֹהֵיהֶם וְקָרָא לְךָ וְאָכַלְתָּ מִזִּבְחוֹ: זנה [prostitute oneself] *Exodus 34:15*

LESSON 43

וְהָיָה בִּקְרָב־אִישׁ לְהִשְׁתַּחֲוֹת לוֹ וְשָׁלַח אֶת־יָדוֹ וְהֶחֱזִיק לוֹ
וְנָשַׁק לוֹ:

2 Samuel 15:5

43.1 וְהָיָה בִּקְרָב־אִישׁ

Frequently וְהָיָה announces a future event, which is what you would expect when you see וֹ
followed by the affix. However, its secondary use is to introduce past events that were repeated
over a period of time. The feeling of future or **frequentative past** time must be ascertained
from the larger context of the story. Here the latter meaning fits best. וְהָיָה itself is usually left
untranslated, but it certainly could be: *And it used to be*

בִּקְרָב־ is composed of how many segments? _____ To determine the form, you have to first
determine the function of the qamats, which is on inspection, a qamats ḥatuf. The form is _____
_____ Literally בִּקְרָב־אִישׁ translates *in the approaching of a man*. The combination of the
temporal preposition (35.1c) and the frequentative וֹ could be more colloquially translated: *And
it used to be that whenever a man approached*

43.2 לְהִשְׁתַּחֲוֹת לוֹ

We have here a unique language "fossil"—a remnant of a once larger system that still survives
in other Semitic languages. This word is a verb. What form? _____ The stem is
called **Hishtaf`el**—the letters הֹשׁת were prefixed to the root. There is evidence that this stem
was extensively used in Semitic languages, but only one verb has survived in Biblical Hebrew in
which this stem is used (and this verb occurs in the Bible only in the Hishtaf`el). The root is
חוה *prostrate oneself in worship*, which you can find by taking off the stem letters הֹשׁת and the
3rd ה infinitive ending. In some older lexicons, the root is considered to be שׁחה and the stem
a Hitpa`el with metathesis (switching of the שׁ and ת sounds).

The infinitive, imperative, and affix of this verb can be recognized by the הֹשׁת prefix.

וְהָיָה בִּקְרָב־אִישׁ לְהִשְׁתַּחֲוֺת לוֹ וְשָׁלַח אֶת־יָדוֹ וְהֶחֱזִיק לוֹ וְנָשַׁק לוֹ:

Synopsis

Affix	3 m. sg.	הִשְׁתַּחֲוָה	3 m. pl.	הִשְׁתַּחֲווּ
Prefix	3 m. sg.	יִשְׁתַּחֲוֶה וַיִּשְׁתַּחוּ	3 m. pl.	יִשְׁתַּחֲווּ וַיִּשְׁתַּחֲווּ
Participle	m. sg.	מִשְׁתַּחֲוֶה	m. pl.	מִשְׁתַּחֲוִים

Analyze לְהִשְׁתַּחֲוֺת

Root	Stem	Form	Person/Gender/Number	Special Features

43.2a Translate the phrase: _____

43.3 וְשָׁלַח אֶת־יָדוֹ

The sense of frequentative past continues throughout the verse.

Translate the phrase: _____

43.4 וְהֶחֱזִיק לוֹ וְנָשַׁק לוֹ

Analyze וְהֶחֱזִיק

Root	Stem	Form	Person/Gender/Number	Special Features

Note the frequentative וֹ in the Special Features column.

After extracting the root, what function will you give the extra letters? _____

Why is the הֹ pointed with a segol? _____ (29.5)

The meaning of חזק in the Qal is _____ In the Hif`il, it can have several connotations: *make strong, take hold, seize.*

For the function of the preposition, review 16.4a if necessary. Translate the phrase:

_____

43.5 Translate the verse: _____

_____

וְהָיָה בִּקְרָב־אִישׁ לְהִשְׁתַּחֲוֺת לוֹ וְשָׁלַח אֶת־יָדוֹ וְהֶחֱזִיק לוֹ וְנָשַׁק לוֹ:

Assignments

A. Vocabulary: words 1–265.

B. Read and translate 1 Kings 17:11–15.

C. ☺ שַׁבְּחִי track 31: listen to and sing הַלְלוּ יָהּ **Psalm 150**.

D. Translate:

1   וַיִּקְרָא לִשְׁלֹמֹה בְנוֹ וַיְצַוֵּהוּ לִבְנוֹת בַּיִת לַיהוָה אֱלֹהֵי יִשְׂרָאֵל:
1 Chronicles 22:6

2   הִשְׁתַּחֲווּ־לוֹ כָּל־אֱלֹהִים
Psalms 97:7

3   עֲבָדֶיךָ יַעֲשׂוּ כַּאֲשֶׁר אֲדֹנִי מְצַוֶּה
Numbers 32:25

4   וַיִּפֹּל עַל־פָּנָיו וַיִּשְׁתָּחוּ
2 Samuel 9:6

5   לִפְנֵי הַמִּזְבֵּחַ הַזֶּה תִּשְׁתַּחֲווּ
2 Kings 18:22

6   וְהִשְׁתַּחֲוִיתָ לִפְנֵי יְהוָה אֱלֹהֶיךָ
Deuteronomy 26:10

7   כִּי־בָרֵךְ יְבָרֶכְךָ יְהוָה בָּאָרֶץ
Deuteronomy 15:4

8   נַפְשִׁי יָצְאָה בְדַבְּרוֹ
Song of Songs 5:6

9   וַיְהִי בְּשַׁלַּח פַּרְעֹה אֶת־הָעָם
Exodus 13:17

✡10   וַיְכַל יַעֲקֹב לְצַוֺּת אֶת־בָּנָיו
Genesis 49:33

11   וְהִשְׁתַּחֲווּ לַיהוָה בְּהַר הַקֹּדֶשׁ בִּירוּשָׁלָ͏ִם
Isaiah 27:13

12   וּצְבָא הַשָּׁמַיִם לְךָ מִשְׁתַּחֲוִים
Nehemiah 9:6

13   כִּי בֶאֱמֶת שְׁלָחַנִי יְהוָה עֲלֵיכֶם לְדַבֵּר בְּאָזְנֵיכֶם
Jeremiah 26:15

———◆———

אַתָּה הָרְאֵתָ לָדַעַת כִּי יהוה הוּא הָאֱלֹהִים אֵין עוֹד מִלְבַדּוֹ:

Deuteronomy 4:35

44.1 אַתָּה הָרְאֵתָ

The pronoun is used here to _____ the verb. (36.7) You should be able to pick out the root of the verb since it is a common one. This in turn suggests that the הָ in front of the root is a preformative and that the תָ at the end is _____ If this were a Hif`il affix, the preformative would be pointed הֶ (29.5) The first vowel in הָרְאֵתָ —being a qamats ḥatuf—is a U class vowel, and the stem is therefore not Hif`il but its passive counterpart, the **Hof`al**.

Active: you **showed** me

Passive: I **was shown** by you

When the first vowel in a Hif`il type of form does not seem to fit the regular pattern but is וֹ וּ ָ or ֻ in a closed unaccented syllable, you should think of the Hof`al.

Root	Stem	Form	Person/Gender/Number	Special Features

Translation of phrase: _____

44.2 Analyze לָדַעַת

Root	Stem	Form	Person/Gender/Number	Special Features

44.3 כִּי יהוה הוּא הָאֱלֹהִים means _____

44.4 אֵין means _____ עוֹד means _____

אַתָּה הָרְאֵתָ לָדַעַת כִּי יהוה הוּא הָאֱלֹהִים אֵין עוֹד מִלְבַדּוֹ׃

44.5 מִלְבַדּוֹ is formed from the noun בַּד *part, piece* (from the root בדד), but it usually appears with the preposition לְ to give לְבַד meaning *alone, by itself.* The attached pronoun indicates who is alone. מִן adds the sense of "except." The entire word means _____

44.6 The final three words of the verse mean _____

44.7 Sentence translation: _____

_____

Assignments

A. Vocabulary: words 1–270.

B. Read and translate 1 Kings 17:16–20.

C. א ב track 28: listen to **The Hebrew Blues.**

D. Analyze the following verbs:

יָדֹועַ	דְּעוּ	הוֹדַע
יְדַעְתִּיךָ	לְדַעְתּוֹ	יוֹדֵעַ
תֵּדָעֶוֹהָ	יוֹדִיעַ	לְהוֹדִיעֵךְ
הוֹדַעְתִּיךָ	מוֹדַעַת	וְהוּבָא
תְּבִיאֵם	הַמּוּבָא	מֻכִּים
הוֹרַד	וַיִּתֵּן	וּמַכֵּה
יוּמָת	מוֹת	יֻכֶּה

E. Translate:

1 הוֹדַע אֵלָיו חַטָּאתוֹ [Treat חַטָּאתוֹ as the subject] *Leviticus 4:23*

2 ...וְהוּבָא אֶל־אַהֲרֹן הַכֹּהֵן אוֹ אֶל־אַחַד מִבָּנָיו הַכֹּהֲנִים׃ *Leviticus 13:2*

3 וְהִנֵּה עֲבָדֶיךָ מֻכִּים *Exodus 5:16*

4 וְיוֹסֵף הוּרַד מִצְרָיְמָה *Genesis 39:1*

✿5 יֻתַּן אֶת־הָאָרֶץ הַזֹּאת לַעֲבָדֶיךָ *Numbers 32:5*

6 וּמַכֵּה אָבִיו וְאִמּוֹ מוֹת יוּמָת׃ *Exodus 21:15*

7 וְאִישׁ כִּי יַכֶּה כָּל־נֶפֶשׁ אָדָם מוֹת יוּמָת׃ *Leviticus 24:17*

8 יִהְיוּ־לְךָ לְבַדֶּךָ וְאֵין לְזָרִים אִתָּךְ׃ [זָר *stranger*] *Proverbs 5:17*

LESSON 45

◆

וָאַ֣עַשׂ בַּבֹּ֖קֶר כַּאֲשֶׁ֣ר צֻוֵּ֑יתִי

Ezekiel 24:18

45.1 Analyze וָאַ֣עַשׂ

Root	Stem	Form	Person/Gender/Number	Special Features

45.2 בַּבֹּ֖קֶר means _____   כַּאֲשֶׁ֣ר means _____

45.3 צֻוֵּ֑יתִי

Here again we have a variation of a more familiar stem. Think how this word is pronounced.

The ו is not a vowel but _____ (37.2a) What stem does this suggest? _____ The vowels are not the expected ones for the Pi'el affix, however.

> Qibbuts ◌ֻ under the first root letter plus doubling of the middle root letter are signs of the **Pu'al**, the passive of the Pi'el system.

Root	Stem	Form	Person/Gender/Number	Special Features

If the verb צוה were active, it would be translated _____

But the verb is passive, so the translation will be _____

45.4 Verse translation: _____

205

45.5 Some compounds with אֲשֶׁר are:

בַּאֲשֶׁר *in* (the place)	עַל אֲשֶׁר *to* (the place)	לַאֲשֶׁר *to him who*
עַד אֲשֶׁר *until*	כַּאֲשֶׁר *when, as*	שָׁם . . . אֲשֶׁר *where* or *whence*

Assignments

A. Vocabulary: words 1–275.

B. 🔊 track 9: learn שַׁבְּחִי דּוֹדִי לִי **Song of Songs 2:16** and **3:6**.

C. Read and translate 1 Kings 17:21–24.

D. Analyze the following verbs:

יְלוּדִים	יָלַדְתִּי	יָלַדְתִּי
יָלְדוּ	יוֹלֵדוֹת	יָלַד
יֵלֵד	לֶדֶת	יָלְדָה
תֵּלְדִי	הַמְיַלְּדוֹת	הוֹלִיד
מְבֹרָךְ	יְבָרֵךְ	מְבֹרָךְ
בּוֹרֵךְ	הֻגַּד	הָשְׁלַכְתְּ
יְצֻוֶּה	צִוִּיתָה	צֻוּוּ

E. Translate:

1 וּלְשֵׁת גַּם־הוּא יֻלַּד־בֵּן *Genesis 4:26*

2 אָרוּר הַיּוֹם אֲשֶׁר יֻלַּדְתִּי בּוֹ [אָרוּר *cursed* adj.] *Jeremiah 20:14*

✡3 וְאַתָּה צֻוֵּיתָה זֹאת עֲשׂוּ *Genesis 45:19*

4 אֵלֶּה יֻלְּדוּ לְדָוִד בְּחֶבְרוֹן *2 Samuel 3:5*

5 . . . יְהוָה נָתַן וַיהוָה לָקָח יְהִי שֵׁם יְהוָה מְבֹרָךְ: *Job 1:21*

6 יְבָרֵךְ בֵּית־עַבְדְּךָ לְעוֹלָם *2 Samuel 7:29*

7 וְדִבֶּר אֶל־בְּנֵי יִשְׂרָאֵל אֵת אֲשֶׁר יְצֻוֶּה *Exodus 34:34*

✡8 וְיָשַׁבְתָּ עִמּוֹ יָמִים אֲחָדִים עַד אֲשֶׁר־תָּשׁוּב חֲמַת אָחִיךָ: *Genesis 27:44* [אֲחָדִים pl. of אֶחָד Treat as *a few* חֵמָה *fury*]

9 וְאָמְרוּ עַל אֲשֶׁר עָזְבוּ אֶת־בְּרִית יְהוָה אֱלֹהֵי אֲבֹתָם אֲשֶׁר כָּרַת עִמָּם בְּהוֹצִיאוֹ אֹתָם מֵאֶרֶץ מִצְרָיִם: *Deuteronomy 29:24*

10 אַל־תִּירְאִי כִּי־שָׁמַע אֱלֹהִים אֶל־קוֹל הַנַּעַר בַּאֲשֶׁר הוּא־שָׁם *Genesis 21:17*

LESSON 46

וְרָאוּ כָּל־עַמֵּי הָאָרֶץ כִּי שֵׁם יהוה נִקְרָא עָלֶיךָ

Deuteronomy 28:10

46.1 וְרָאוּ כָּל־עַמֵּי הָאָרֶץ

Analyze וְרָאוּ

Root	Stem	Form	Person/Gender/Number	Special Features

46.1a Translate the phrase: _____

46.2 כִּי means _____

46.3 שֵׁם יהוה means _____

46.4 נִקְרָא

Here you meet the last family in the stem classification. It is called **Nif`al**, and the stem indicator is a נ added in front of the root letters. Its secondary recognition sign is often ◌ֵ or ◌ַ under the second root letter. (Hence the stem name Nif`a̱l, as in A class vowel.) The form here is affix—what is the PGN? _____

Root	Stem	Form	Person/Gender/Number	Special Features

The Nif`al is a passive stem. Qal is almost always active; Pi`el and Hif`il are active stems with related passive forms. For this reason, verbs that occur in the Qal for the most part usually occur in the Nif`al also, while verbs that occur mostly in the Pi`el or Hif`il systems use the passives of those stems.

קָרָא means _____   נִקְרָא means _____

207

46.5   עָלֶיךָ means _____

46.6   Sentence translation: _____

_____

46.7   The Nif`al affix is formed like the affix of most of the derived stems.

affix pronoun ⟵ root ⟵ stem preformative

תָּ   _ _ _   נ

You should be able to fill in the chart, making the internal vowel adjustments where necessary. The vowel under the preformative will not change.

Nif`al Affix Mid-Guttural and Mid-י

3 m. sg.	נִבְרַךְ	3 c. pl.	__ __ __ __
3 f. sg.	__ __ __ __		
2 m. sg.	__ __ __ __	2 m. pl.	__ __ __ __
2 f. sg.	__ __ __ __	2 f. pl.	__ __ __ __
1 c. sg.	__ __ __ __	1 c. pl.	__ __ __ __

46.7a   Nif`al affix variations

1st נ has dagesh forte in the second root letter to represent the assimilated נ of the root:

3 f. sg. Qal affix   3 f. sg. Nif`al affix

נָשְׂאָה   נִשְּׂאָה

1st י has וֹ between the preformative and the root:

3 f. sg. Qal affix   3 f. sg. Nif`al affix

יָדְעָה   נוֹדְעָה

Hollow has נָ preformative or נְ for the second and first persons, which persons also have an extra וֹ syllable before the affix pronoun:

3 f. sg. Qal affix   3 f. sg. Nif`al affix

רָמָה   נָרוֹמָה

1 c. pl. Qal affix   1 c. pl. Nif`al affix

רַמְנוּ   נְרוֹמוֹנוּ

$$\text{וְרָאוּ כָּל־עַמֵּי הָאָרֶץ כִּי שֵׁם יהוה נִקְרָא עָלֶיךָ}$$

1st guttural: the preformative is usually pointed **נֶ** but **נַ** or **נָ** is possible:

3 f. sg. Qal affix	3 f. sg. Nif`al affix
עָמְדָה	נֶעֶמְדָה

46.7b The **נ** preformative can create some ambiguities. The 3 m. sg. Nif`al affix, for example, can be identical to the Pi`el affix and to the 1 c. pl. Qal prefix of verbs that follow the יִשְׁלַח pattern. In such cases, context will indicate which stem and PGN are meant.

Jeremiah 8:3 וְנִבְחַר מָוֶת מֵחַיִּים לְכֹל הַשְּׁאֵרִית הַנִּשְׁאָרִים

3 m. sg. Nif`al affix

and death <u>shall be chosen</u> rather than life by all the residue of those who are left

1 Kings 9:11 חִירָם מֶלֶךְ־צֹר נִשָּׂא אֶת־שְׁלֹמֹה בַּעֲצֵי אֲרָזִים

3 m. sg. Pi`el affix

Hiram King of Tyre <u>furnished</u> Solomon with cedar trees

Lamentations 3:41 נִשָּׂא לְבָבֵנוּ אֶל־כַּפָּיִם אֶל־אֵל בַּשָּׁמָיִם:

1 c. pl. Qal prefix

<u>Let us lift up</u> our heart with our hands to God in the heavens.

Jeremiah 51:9 כִּי־נָגַע אֶל־הַשָּׁמַיִם מִשְׁפָּטָהּ וְנִשָּׂא עַד־שְׁחָקִים

3 m. sg. Nif`al affix   3 m. sg. Qal affix

for her judgment reaches heaven and <u>is lifted up</u> to the clouds

Assignments

A. Vocabulary: words 1–280.

B. Learn the Nif`al affix (46.7–46.7a and Verb Chart A). For 1st gutturals, 1st **י** 1st **נ** and hollows, see Charts B, D, F, and H, respectively. Also, listen to **Visible נ** (the Nif`al song) on ☉ ב א track 29 (lyrics: pp. 482–484).

C. ☉ שְׁבָחִי track 32: listen to מִמִּזְרַח־שֶׁמֶשׁ **Psalm 113:3–9**.

D. Read and translate 1 Kings 18:20–24.

E. Analyze the following verbs. If a form is ambiguous, note that.

יָדֹ֫ועַ	נֵדַע	נוֹדַע
וְנִבְנְתָה	נוֹדִיעַ	וְנִבְנוּ
נִבְנֶה	נִבְנֶה	נִתְּנָה
נֵתְּנָה	נִתֵּן	נִתְּנוּ
נוֹתֵן	נֶהְיָה	נֶהֶיְתָה
נֵעֲשׂוּ	יֵעָשׂוּ	הֵעָשׂוּ
נוֹלַד	נִרְאָה	נִרְאוּ

F. Translate:

1. וְנִקְרְאָה יְרוּשָׁלַ֫ם עִיר־הָאֱמֶת *Zechariah 8:3*

2. לֹא נוֹדַע מִי הִכָּ֫הוּ *Deuteronomy 21:1*

3. שִׁשָּׁה נוֹלַד־לוֹ בְחֶבְרוֹן *1 Chronicles 3:4*

4. וְנוֹדַע יהוה לְמִצְרַ֫יִם וְיָדְעוּ מִצְרַ֫יִם אֶת־יהוה בַּיּוֹם הַהוּא *Isaiah 19:21*

5. וּשְׁמִי יהוה לֹא נוֹדַ֫עְתִּי לָהֶם *Exodus 6:3* [Read שְׁמִי as if it had בְּ before it]

6. וְנִבְנְתָה הָעִיר לַיהוה *Jeremiah 31:38* (Lesson 37)

7. בִּדְבַר יהוה שָׁמַ֫יִם נַעֲשׂוּ *Psalms 33:6* (Lesson 46.7a)

8. כִּי לֹא־נִבְנָה בַ֫יִת לְשֵׁם יהוה *1 Kings 3:2*

9. הַיּוֹם יהוה נִרְאָה אֲלֵיכֶם *Leviticus 9:4*

10. וְהָעִיר נִתְּנָה בְּיַד הַכַּשְׂדִּים *Jeremiah 32:24*

11. נִרְאוּ רָאשֵׁי הֶהָרִים *Genesis 8:5*

12. כִּי מֵאִתִּי נִהְיָה הַדָּבָר הַזֶּה *1 Kings 12:24*

13. כִּי שִׁמְךָ נִקְרָא עַל־עִירְךָ וְעַל־עַמֶּ֑ךָ *Daniel 9:19*

14. וַאֲנִי לֹא נִקְרֵ֫אתִי לָבוֹא אֶל־הַמֶּ֫לֶךְ *Esther 4:11*

15. מָה הָרָעָה הַזֹּאת אֲשֶׁר נִהְיְתָה בָּכֶם *Judges 20:12*

16. נַעֲשָׂה הַפֶּ֫סַח הַזֶּה לַיהוה בִּירוּשָׁלָ֑ם׃ [Passover] פֶּסַח *2 Kings 23:23*

LESSON 47

—

וְעֲשֵׂה־שָׁם מִזְבֵּחַ לָאֵל הַנִּרְאֶה אֵלֶיךָ

Genesis 35:1

47.1 וְעֲשֵׂה־שָׁם מִזְבֵּחַ

Analyze וְעֲשֵׂה

Root	Stem	Form	Person/Gender/Number	Special Features

Translate phrase: _____

47.2 לָאֵל הַנִּרְאֶה

אֵל is a shorter form of אֱלֹהִים

הַנִּרְאֶה is a new verb form.

Root	Stem	Form	Person/Gender/Number	Special Features

הַ is the _____ and occurs with which verb form? _____

With this help, you should be able to analyze the rest of the verb. The נ in front of the root

indicates _____ (46.4)

Since no special endiNGs are added, the number and gender will be _____

Except for 3rd ה verbs, whose m sg. participle ends in הֶ the difference between the vowel

patterns of the 3 m. sg. Nif`al affix and the m. sg. Nif`al participle is slight. If the vowel under the

second root letter is ַ the form is affix as in נִבְרַךְ If the vowel is ָ it may be a participle as

in נִבְרָךְ But if the third root letter is א or ה or the word is in pause, the affix and the par-

ticiple will look the same: נִשְׁמַר נִקְרָא

211

> The Qal and the Nif`al are the only stems in which the participle does not have a preformative מ

47.3 Translate sentence: _____

_____

47.4 Meanings of the Nif`al Stem

The passive meaning of the Nif`al, like the causative meaning of the Hif`il, can allow more colloquial translations that obscure the stem function. Hif`il of רָאָה *cause to see* becomes *show*; the Nif`al of רָאָה *be seen* becomes *appear*.

Aside from its basic function of acting as the passive for the Qal, the Nif`al can impart a variety of meanings to a root.

A. A lot of verbs have a **reflexive** meaning in the Nif`al:

Qal	Nif`al
שָׁמַר *guard*	נִשְׁמַר *take heed to oneself*

B. It can be used to express **reciprocal** action:

Pi`el	Nif`al
דִּבֶּר *speak*	נִדְבַּר *speak to one another*

Qal	Nif`al
שָׁפַט *judge*	נִשְׁפַּט *enter into controversy with*

C. It can be the **active + to** or **for oneself**:

Qal	Nif`al
שָׁאַל *ask*	נִשְׁאַל *ask for oneself*

D. The Nif`al is often used to express an **emotional state**:

Pi`el	Nif`al
נִחַם יהוה עַמּוֹ *(Isaiah 49:13)*	נִחַם יהוה עַל־זֹאת *(Amos 7:3)*
comfort (someone else)	*be sorry, be regretful*

212

וַעֲשֵׂה־שָׁם מִזְבֵּחַ לָאֵל הַנִּרְאָה אֵלֶיךָ

Assignments

A. Vocabulary: words 1–285.

B. Listen to **Visible נ** on ⊙ **א ב** track 29 (lyrics: pp. 476–479).

C. Read and translate 1 Kings 18:25–29.

D. ⊙ **שַׁבְּחִי** track 19: listen to **שׁוּבִי נַפְשִׁי** Psalm 116:7–8.

E. Translate:

1. נוֹדָע בִּיהוּדָה אֱלֹהִים *Psalms 76:2*

2. וַיִּהְיוּ נִקְרָאִים לִפְנֵי הַמֶּלֶךְ *Esther 6:1*

3. הִנֵּה־בֵן נוֹלָד לְבֵית־דָּוִד *1 Kings 13:2*

4. וְנִבְרְכוּ בְךָ כֹּל מִשְׁפְּחֹת הָאֲדָמָה *Genesis 12:3*

5. ... וַיֹּאמֶר מִצְרַיִם אָנוּסָה מִפְּנֵי יִשְׂרָאֵל כִּי יהוה נִלְחָם לָהֶם בְּמִצְרָיִם׃ *Exodus 14:25*

6. וּפְלִשְׁתִּים נִלְחָמִים בְּיִשְׂרָאֵל וַיָּנֻסוּ אַנְשֵׁי יִשְׂרָאֵל מִפְּנֵי פְלִשְׁתִּים *1 Samuel 31:1*

7. וְהַקֹּל נִשְׁמַע בֵּית פַּרְעֹה לֵאמֹר בָּאוּ אֲחֵי יוֹסֵף וַיִּיטַב בְּעֵינֵי פַרְעֹה וּבְעֵינֵי עֲבָדָיו׃ *Genesis 45:16*

8. אֵין־קֹרֵא בְצֶדֶק וְאֵין נִשְׁפָּט בֶּאֱמוּנָה [*steadfastness* אֱמוּנָה] *Isaiah 59:4*

9. חָזְקוּ עָלַי דִּבְרֵיכֶם אָמַר יהוה וַאֲמַרְתֶּם מַה־נִּדְבַּרְנוּ עָלֶיךָ׃ *Malachi 3:13*

10. וַיִּקְרָא אַבְרָהָם אֶת־שֶׁם־בְּנוֹ הַנּוֹלַד־לוֹ אֲשֶׁר־יָלְדָה־לוֹ שָׂרָה יִצְחָק *Genesis 21:3*

11. וּבְכָל־דְּגֵי הַיָּם בְּיֶדְכֶם נִתָּנוּ [*fish* דָּג] *Genesis 9:2*

נִי___ is *me*

מִי is *who*

הוּא is *he*

הִיא is *she* and

דָּג is *fish*

LESSON 48

וְלֹא־יִשָּׁמַע בָּהּ עוֹד קוֹל בְּכִי

Isaiah 65:19

48.1 וְלֹא־יִשָּׁמַע

Analyze יִשָּׁמַע

Root	Stem	Form	Person/Gender/Number	Special Features

Do you recognize a familiar root? _____ The stem is the only problem. This is the Nif`al prefix, which has been formed in the following way:

dagesh forte ↓   ↓ stem indicator

יִ נְ שָׁמַע ←— יִשָּׁמַע

↑ prefix pronoun

That is, the נ of the Nif`al stem in the prefix form has been assimilated to the following consonantal sound. This form is usually not too difficult to recognize except when the first consonant cannot take a dagesh; in such a case there must be compensatory lengthening for the missing dagesh:

no dagesh ↓

וַיֹּאמֶר

↑
◌ִ lengthened to ◌ֵ

Translate the phrase: _____

48.2 בָּהּ עוֹד

בָּהּ means _____ The antecedent for הָ◌ is *Jerusalem,* which appears earlier in the verse. Translate the phrase: _____

214

וְלֹא־יִשָּׁמַע בָּהּ עוֹד קוֹל בְּכִי

48.3 קוֹל בְּכִי

קוֹל means _____ In the word בְּכִי the component יִ is not a suffix; it is part of the noun בְּכִי which means *weeping*. How does this phrase relate to the verb? _____

_____

48.4 Translate the verse: _____

48.5 Fill in the chart for the regular Nif`al prefix pattern. Do not forget the dagesh forte!

Nif`al Prefix Strong Verb

3 m. sg.	יִ שָּׁ מַ ע	3 m. pl.	⎵ ⎵ ָ ⎵
3 f. sg.	⎵ ⎵ ⎵	3 f. pl.	⎵ ָ ⎵ ⎵
2 m. sg.	⎵ ⎵ ⎵	2 m. pl.	⎵ ⎵ ⎵
2 f. sg.	⎵ ⎵ ְ ⎵	2 f. pl.	⎵ ⎵ ⎵
1 c. sg.	⎵ ⎵ ⎵ ֶ	1 c. pl.	⎵ ⎵ ⎵

48.5a Now fill in the chart for the Nif`al prefix of 1st guttural or 1st ר verbs.

Nif`al Prefix 1st Guttural

3 m. sg.	יֵ אָ מֵ ר	3 m. pl.	⎵ ⎵ ְ ⎵
3 f. sg.	⎵ ⎵ ⎵	3 f. pl.	⎵ ְ ⎵ ⎵
2 m. sg.	⎵ ⎵ ⎵	2 m. pl.	⎵ ⎵ ⎵
2 f. sg.	⎵ ⎵ ְ ֵ	2 f. pl.	⎵ ⎵ ⎵
1 c. sg.	⎵ ⎵ ⎵	1 c. pl.	⎵ ⎵ ⎵

48.5b Nif`al prefix for weak verbs:

1st נ the נ of the root stays: יִנָּגַע תִּנָּגַע

1st י the י reverts to the older ו that is now consonantal: יִוָּשֵׁב תִּוָּלֵד

3rd ה exhibits no change: יִבָּנֶה תִּבָּנֶה

48.6 Write the 3 m. pl. Nif`al prefix for the following verbs:

זכר	מלך	ידע
נטע	רדף	עמד
נטה	אכל	יתר

215

48.7 Extra Grammar

You have had plenty of practice finding the roots for nouns that have more than three letters. What about nouns with three or fewer letters?

1. Nouns that end in **י** come from roots that end in **ה**

root	noun
בכה	בְּכִי

2. Some two-letter nouns are found listed as two-letter nouns:

בֵּן   יָד   פֶּה   דָּם

3. Most two-letter nouns are listed as being from a hollow, geminate, or 3rd **ה** root:

root	noun
גור	גֵּר
הרר	הַר
אבה	אָב

Assignments

A. Vocabulary: words 1–290.

B. Memorize the Nifʿal prefix patterns in 48.5 and 48.5a (see Verb Charts A and C), and using
⊙ **א ב** track 29: listen again to **"Visible נ"**

C. Read and translate 1 Kings 18:30–34.

D. Review קוֹל דּוֹדִי **Song of Songs 2:8** on ⊙ שַׁבְּחִי track 10.

E. Translate:

1   וְאַתֶּם כֹּהֲנֵי יהוה תִּקָּרֵאוּ   *Isaiah 61:6*

2   יִוָּדַע הַנָּבִיא אֲשֶׁר־שְׁלָחוֹ יהוה בֶּאֱמֶת   *Jeremiah 28:9*

3   לֹא יַעֲקֹב יֵאָמֵר עוֹד שִׁמְךָ   *Genesis 32:29*

4   וָאֵרָא אֶל־אַבְרָהָם אֶל־יִצְחָק   *Exodus 6:3*

5   יֵרָאֶה אֶל־אֱלֹהִים בְּצִיּוֹן   *Psalms 84:8*

✡6   לְזֹאת יִקָּרֵא אִשָּׁה כִּי מֵאִישׁ לֻקֳחָה־זֹּאת   *Genesis 2:23*

(the verb יִקָּרֵא does not agree with its subject in what respect?)

7   אַל־יִוָּדַע כִּי־בָאָה הָאִשָּׁה   *Ruth 3:14*

8   כִּי לֹא־יֵעָשֶׂה כֵן בְּיִשְׂרָאֵל

2 Samuel 13:12

9   בְּחָכְמָה יִבָּנֶה בָּיִת

Proverbs 24:3

10   בְּיַד מֶלֶךְ־בָּבֶל תִּנָּתֵן

Jeremiah 37:17

11   וַיֵּרָא יהוה אֶל־אַבְרָם

Genesis 12:7

12   לֹא תִנָּתֵן יְרוּשָׁלִַם בְּיַד מֶלֶךְ אַשּׁוּר

2 Kings 19:10

13   כִּי־יֶלֶד יֻלַּד־לָנוּ בֵּן נִתַּן־לָנוּ

Isaiah 9:5

14   כִּי תִּמָּלֵא הָאָרֶץ לָדַעַת אֶת־כְּבוֹד יהוה כַּמַּיִם יְכַסּוּ עַל־יָם׃

Habakkuk 2:14

LESSON 49

וַיֹּאמֶר אֵלַי הִנָּבֵא אֶל־הָרוּחַ הִנָּבֵא בֶן־אָדָם

Ezekiel 37:9

49.1 וַיֹּאמֶר אֵלַי means _____

49.2 Analyze הִנָּבֵא

Root	Stem	Form	Person/Gender/Number	Special Features

Two Nif`al forms, the imperative and the infinitive, often give beginning students trouble because these forms are prefixed with the syllable ____הִ instead of simply ____נ In the present example, notice what happened to these Nif`al forms:

הִנָּבֵא ← נְבָא + הִנ

The form with the assimilated נ is now the regular form for the Nif`al imperative.

Note that the imperative cannot be confused with the affix in this stem, nor with the participle. You must be careful not to fall into the trap of thinking that you have a Hif`il form—remember the dagesh!

> The **Nif`al imperative** and the **Nif`al infinitive** can be recognized by the הִ☐ preformative.

נבא means *prophesy* and is translated in the active voice even in the Nif`al.

49.3 אֶל־הָרוּחַ means _____

49.4 הִנָּבֵא בֶן־אָדָם means _____

49.5 Sentence translation: _____

_____

49.6 The sample verb in this lesson shows how a 1st **נ** verb looks in the Nif`al imperative. Following the explanation in 49.2, write the m. sg. Nif`al imperative for the strong verb שׁפט _____

The changes you saw in the Nif`al prefix for compensatory lengthening in 1st gutturals (48.1) and the change in 1st **י** (48.5b) apply also to the Nif`al imperative.

Write the m. sg. Nif`al imperative for אמר _____ and ילד _____

Assignments

A. Vocabulary: words 1–295.

B. Read and translate 1 Kings 18:35–40.

C. After your **Visible נ** review on ⊛אב track 29, listen to and learn יִשְׂמְחוּ **Psalm 96:11**: ⊛שַׁבְּחִי track 33.

D. Translate:

1   לֵךְ הֵרָאֵה אֶל־אַחְאָב   *1 Kings 18:1*

2   הִשָּׁמֶר לְךָ מִדַּבֵּר עִם־יַעֲקֹב   *Genesis 31:29*

3   הִשָּׁמֶר מִפָּנָיו וּשְׁמַע בְּקֹלוֹ   *Exodus 23:21*

4   וְעַתָּה הִשָּׁבְעָה לִּי בֵאלֹהִים   *Genesis 21:23*

5   עַל־כֵּן קָרָא לַמָּקוֹם הַהוּא בְּאֵר שָׁבַע כִּי שָׁם נִשְׁבְּעוּ שְׁנֵיהֶם׃   *Genesis 21:31*

6   וַיֹּאמֶר יְהוָה הִנֵּה מָקוֹם אִתִּי וְנִצַּבְתָּ עַל־הַצּוּר׃ [*rock* צוּר]   *Exodus 33:21*

7   וִיהוֹנָתָן וַאֲחִימַעַץ עֹמְדִים בְּעֵין־רֹגֵל וְהָלְכָה הַשִּׁפְחָה וְהִגִּידָה לָהֶם וְהֵם יֵלְכוּ וְהִגִּדוּ לַמֶּלֶךְ דָּוִד כִּי לֹא יוּכְלוּ לְהֵרָאוֹת לָבוֹא הָעִירָה׃   *2 Samuel 17:17*

LESSON 50

וַיֹּסֶף יְהוָה לְהֵרָאֹה בְשִׁלֹה

1 Samuel 3:21

50.1 וַיֹּסֶף יְהוָה

The first word cannot be a name because it begins with _____ Pay careful attention to the stem of the verb; it may look as if you have a missing letter, but this is actually a case of a camouflaged letter. The ḥolem here is more commonly written plene וֹ and represents the first root letter, which has _____ (31.2)

Root	Stem	Form	Person/Gender/Number	Special Features

יסף means *add, continue, do again* and is used most often in the Hif`il stem.

Translate phrase: _____

50.2 Analyze לְהֵרָאֹה

Root	Stem	Form	Person/Gender/Number	Special Features

We said in 49.2 that the imperative and the infinitive of the Nif`al are marked by the combination הַנ ← הִ⬚ before the root. But before a letter that cannot take a dagesh the vocalization will be _____ (48.1) Here the form is _____ You would expect this word to end in _____ הֵרָאֹה is an alternative spelling. How can you distinguish this form from a Hif`il infinitive? What key vowel is different? _____ (Consult 1st guttural verb charts: Chart B.)

50.3 בְשִׁלֹה involves a place name: _____

50.4   יסף is almost always to be translated in coordination with another verb, either conjugated or in infinitive form. When so used, it means *do X again* or sometimes, *continue to do X*

50.5   Translate sentence: _____

Assignments

A. Vocabulary: words 1–300. Review words 201–300 on אֵלֶּה הַדְּבָרִים💿 tracks 23–32.

B. Review the signs of the Nif`al, Lessons 46–50, and listen to **Visible נ** one more time: אב💿

track 29.

C. 💿 שְׁבָחִי track 34: listen to הַלְלוּהוּ **Psalm 150:5–6.**

D. Read and translate 1 Kings 18:41–46.

E. Translate:

1   וַיֹּאמֶר הַמֶּלֶךְ לְהֵעָשׂוֹת כֵּן   *Esther 9:14*

2   כִּי הִנָּתֹן יִנָּתֵן בְּיַד מֶלֶךְ־בָּבֶל   *Jeremiah 32:4*

3   וַיֹּסֶף עוֹד לְדַבֵּר אֵלָיו וַיֹּאמַר אוּלַי יִמָּצְאוּן שָׁם   *Genesis 18:29*
[אוּלַי *perhaps*]

4   וַיֵּלֶךְ אֵלִיָּהוּ לְהֵרָאוֹת אֶל־אַחְאָב וְהָרָעָב חָזָק בְּשֹׁמְרוֹן: *1 Kings 18:2*

5   ...וְלֹא־יוֹסִפוּ לַעֲשׂוֹת כַּדָּבָר הָרָע הַזֶּה בְּקִרְבֶּךָ:   *Deuteronomy 13:12*

6   כֹּה יַעֲשֶׂה־לְּךָ אֱלֹהִים וְכֹה יוֹסִיף   *1 Samuel 3:17*

✡7   הָעָם הַזֶּה אָמְרוּ לֹא עֶת־בֹּא עֶת־בֵּית יְהוָה לְהִבָּנוֹת   *Haggai 1:2*

REVIEW AND DRILL 6

I. **Nif`al Synopses**

	Regular	1st Guttural	1st נ [3rd ע]
Affix	נִשְׁפַּט	נֶאֱמַר	נִטַּע
Prefix	יִשָּׁפֵט	יֵאָמֵר	יִנָּטַע
Imperative	הִשָּׁפֵט	הֵאָמֵר	הִנָּטַע
Participle	נִשְׁפָּט	נֶאֱמָר	נִטָּע
Infinitive	הִשָּׁפֵט	הֵאָמֵר	הִנָּטַע

	1st י	Hollow	3rd ה
Affix	נוֹלַד	נָבוֹן	נִבְנָה
Prefix	יִוָּלֵד	יִבּוֹן	יִבָּנֶה
Imperative	הִוָּלֵד	הִבּוֹן	הִבָּנֵה
Participle	נוֹלָד	נָבוֹן	נִבְנֶה
Infinitive	הִוָּלֵד	הִבּוֹן	הִבָּנוֹת

II. Now here is a comparison of the Qal, Nif`al, and Hif`il for **1st נ/3rd ה**

	Qal	Hif`il	Nif`al
Affix	נָטָה	הִטָּה	נִטָּה
Prefix	יִטֶּה	יַטֶּה	יִנָּטֶה
Imperative	נְטֵה	הַטֵּה	הִנָּטֵה
Participle	נוֹטֶה	מַטֶּה	נִטֶּה
Infinitive	לִנְטוֹת	לְהַטּוֹת	לְהִנָּטוֹת

222

III. In this exercise, some ambiguous forms are presented. Each is morphologically a Qal and can also be either a Hif`il, Nif`al, or Pi`el. Give the form and PGN for the Qal and the other stem(s).

נָבִין נְבָרֵךְ	יֵעָלֶה	
נֶשֶׁה	נַעֲשֶׂה	נִלְחַם

IV. Give the stem: Qal, Pi`el, Hif`il, or Nif`al, and form for the following forms of זכר

הַזְכִּיר	זוֹכֵר	נִזְכּוֹר
נַזְכִּיר	נִזְכָּר	בְּזֹכֵר
בְּהִזָּכֵר	בְּהַזְכִּיר	בְּזֹכֵר
הִזָּכְרוּ	תִּזָּכַרְנָה	תִּזְכֹּרְנָה
תִּזַּכַּרְנָה	תִּזְכֹּרְנָה	הִזְכִּירוּ
נִזְכָּרִים	זָכְרוּ	זִכְרוּ
מֻזְכָּרִים	זְכוּרוֹת	מַזְכִּירָה

V. In the verbs below, identify each נ as a root letter, prefix pronoun, prefix complement, affix pronoun, stem indicator, or suffix. Assimilated נs count.

נֵלֵךְ	נַגִּיעַ	הִנָּגְעִי
נֵהָלֵךְ	אֶנְגַּע	נַבִּיט
נוֹלִיךְ	נֻגַּעְנוּ	תִּנָּתֵן
נְתוּנִים	נָנוֹחַ	נָח
נוֹלַד	נֶהֶלְכוּ	נִפֹּל
הֻנַּחְנוּ	הִגַּעְתֶּן	מַגִּיעַ
נִנְגַּע	נָגְעוּ	נָגַעְנוּ
נֶאֱמָן	נָעֳמָד	נְתוּנוֹת
וַתְּכַסֵּנִי	נִכְתַּב	נוֹתְרוּ

VI. Analyze the following verbs:

קָרְבָה	הַקְרִיב	נִקְרַבְתֶּם
וַיִּקְרַב	קָרֵב	יִקְרְבוּ
יְקָרְבוּ	יִקְרְבוּ	יַקְרִיבוּ
מְקָרֵב	מַקְרִיב	הַקְרֵב
נוֹתַר	נוֹתִיר	הוֹתֵר
הוּתַר	מִיֻתַּר	יֶתֶר

בְּהֻוָתֵר	יִתַּֽרְנוּ	נוֹתַֽרְנוּ
הוֹתַֽרְנוּ	מוֹתִיר	בְּהוֹתִיר
בִּיַתֵּר	מִיַתְּרִים	מוֹתִירִים
נוֹתָרִים	נֹאכַל	אוֹכַל
נֵאָכֵל	אָכְלוּ	יֹאכַל
נֹאכַל	הַאֲכֵל	מַאֲכִיל
תֹּאכַל	נֶאֶכְֽלֶת	אֹכֵל

VII. Write the Hebrew for the following verbs:

שׁמע   3 m. pl. Nif`al affix   בוא   3 m. pl. Qal prefix

             3 m. sg. Hof`al affix                 3 f. sg. Hif`il affix

             1 c. pl. Hif`il prefix                 3 m. pl. Nif`il prefix

ראה   1 c. sg. Nif`al prefix   אסף   1 c. pl. Qal affix

             1 c. sg. Qal affix   1 c. pl. Pi`el prefix

             f. pl. Qal participle   3 m. sg. Nif`al prefix

שׁלח   m. sg. Pi`el participle      שׁלח    2 m. sg. Nif`il affix

             2 m. pl. Pi`el affix                 2 m. sg. Nif`al prefix

             3 c. pl. Hif`il affix                 m. sg. Hof`al participle

LESSON 51

וָֽנֵּסֶב אֶת־הַר־שֵׂעִיר יָמִים רַבִּים

Deuteronomy 2:1

51.1 Analyze וָֽנֵּסֶב

The final type of verb we will study is the **geminate,** so named because its second and third root letters twin. These verbs have no consistent patterns that are exclusively their own, but appear with patterns characteristic of several other verb types, especially hollows. וָֽנֵּסֶב for example, looks as if it could be a hollow but is actually a geminate, so its root is _____

Root	Stem	Form	Person/Gender/Number	Special Features

How is one to recognize such verbs?

1. You can memorize the basic patterns.

2. You can keep the possibility of a geminate in mind when you analyze a verb according to the basic rules but then cannot find it in the dictionary. Before you give up, try a geminate.

   סבב means *go around, surround.*

51.2 אֶת־הַר־שֵׂעִיר means _____ יָמִים means _____

   רַב is an adjective meaning _____

51.3 Translate the verse: _____

51.4 The chart below shows the most common Qal affix pattern for geminates. Note that in the second and first persons, the double ב is represented by a dagesh forte and that וֹ is inserted between the root and the affix pronoun.

51.4a Qal Affix סבב

3 m. sg.	סָבַב	3 c. pl.	סָבְבוּ	
3 f. sg.	סָבְבָה			
2 m. sg.	סַבּ֫וֹתָ	2 m. pl.	סַבּוֹתֶם	
2 f. sg.	סַבּוֹת	2 f. pl.	סַבּוֹתֶן	
1 c. sg.	סַבּ֫וֹתִי	1 c. pl.	סַבּ֫וֹנוּ	

51.4b In these, the two most common Qal prefix patterns, notice that:

1. Those PGNs that have no prefix complement do not show a doubled ב (analogous to the formation of וַיִּ֫צֶר 39.1).

2. The יִסֹּב pattern shows a doubled first root letter, making it look like a _____ _____

3. The יָסֹב pattern has the vowel under the prefix pronoun of _____

4. Here again ḥolem appears, but its position is different from that in the Qal affix.

Qal Prefix סבב

3 m. sg.	יָסֹב	יִסֹּב	3 m. pl.	יָסֹ֫בּוּ	יִסֹּ֫בוּ	
3 f. sg.	תָּסֹב	תִּסֹּב	3 f. pl.	תְּסֻבֶּ֫ינָה	תְּסֹ֫בְנָה	
2 m. sg.	תָּסֹב	תִּסֹּב	2 m. pl.	תָּסֹ֫בּוּ	תִּסֹּ֫בוּ	
2 f. sg.	תָּסֹ֫בִּי	תִּסֹ֫בִּי	2 f. pl.	תְּסֻבֶּ֫ינָה	תְּסֹ֫בְנָה	
1 c. sg.	אָסֹב	אֶסֹּב	1 c. pl.	נָסֹב	נִסֹּב	

51.4c **Qal imperatives** of סבב follow the pattern of יִסֹּב So the m. sg. imperative is סֹב Write these others: f. sg. _____ m. pl. _____

51.4d **Qal participles** follow the pattern of the strong verb. The m. sg. Qal active participle is סוֹבֵב Write the m. sg. Qal passive participle _____ (42.3)

51.4e **Qal infinitives** of סבב are סֹב (construct) and סָבוֹב (absolute).

51.5 Geminates have two equivalents of the Piʿel. The **Poʿlel** gets its name from the vowel וֹ after the first root letter: יְסוֹבֵב This stem is absolutely regular: you will always see the ḥolem and all three root letters, but unfortunately the configuration ⌣ ⌣ וֹ ⌣ can be other things as well. (See Verb Charts.)

226

The **Pilpʿel** is formed by doubling the two strong consonants: כִּלְכֵּל

Hollow verbs can do the same thing, so one cannot tell from looking at a Polʿel or Pilpʿel whether the root is geminate or hollow.

51.6   The **Hifʿil** and **Nifʿal** patterns have some of the characteristics of hollows in those stems. Below is a synopsis using סבב

	Hifʿil	Nifʿal
3 m. sg. Affix	הֵסֵב	נָסַב
2 m. sg. Affix	הֲסִבּ֫וֹתָ	נְסַבּ֫וֹתָ
3 m. sg. Prefix	יָסֵב	יִסַּב
3 m. pl. Prefix	יָסֵ֫בּוּ	יִסַּ֫בּוּ
m. sg. Imperative	הָסֵב	הִסַּב
m. pl. Imperative	הָסֵ֫בּוּ	הִסַּ֫בּוּ
m. sg. Participle	מֵסֵב	נָסָב
f. sg. Participle	מְסִבָּה	נְסַבָּה
Infinitive Construct	הָסֵב	הִסַּב
Infinitive Absolute	הָסֵב	הִסּוֹב

51.7   Analyze the following forms of סבב

סוֹבַ֫בְתִּי	תְּסוֹבֵב	הֲסִבּוֹתֶם
מְסוֹבֵב	אָסֵב	נְסַבּ֫וֹת
נְסַבּ֫וֹנוּ	תָּסֹ֫בִּי	תָּסֹ֫בִּי
תָּסֹ֫בִּי	סְבָב֫וּנִי	וַיִּסֹּ֫בְּנִי
נָסֵב	נְסַבָּה	יְסֹבְבֵ֫נִי

51.8   It will serve you well to memorize this list of common geminates:

הלל	*praise*	פלל	*pray*	חלל	*profane*
רבב	*become great*	תמם	*be complete*	רעע	*be evil*
המם	*make a noise*	רנן	*give a ringing cry*	חנן	*show favor*
חמם	*become warm*	ארר	*curse*	שמם	*be desolate*
שדד	*lay waste*	צרר	*be hostile*	מדד	*measure*

227

Assignments

A. Vocabulary: words 1–305.

B. Learn to identify geminates that follow the patterns of סׇבַב (51.4–6 and Verb Chart I).

C. 🔊 שַׁבְּחִי track 31: sing הַלְלוּ יָהּ **Psalm 150.**

D. Read and translate 1 Kings 19:1–5. Verses 1–12 are cantillated on 🔊 א ב track 30.

E. Translate:

1	וְסַבֹּתֶם אֶת־הָעִיר *Joshua 6:3*
2	סַבּוּנִי גַם־סְבָבוּנִי בְּשֵׁם יהוה *Psalms 118:11*
3	סוֹבֵב סֹבֵב הוֹלֵךְ הָרוּחַ *Qohelet 1:6*
4	וַיִּסֹּב וַיַּעֲבֹר וַיֵּרֶד הַגִּלְגָּל *1 Samuel 15:12*
5	סֹב אֶל־אַחֲרָי *2 Kings 9:18*
6	עִבְרוּ וְסֹבּוּ אֶת־הָעִיר *Joshua 6:7*
7	וַיָּסֹבּוּ בְּכָל־עָרֵי יְהוּדָה וַיְלַמְּדוּ בָּעָם *2 Chronicles 17:9*
8	בֵּאלֹהִים הִלַּלְנוּ כָל־הַיּוֹם *Psalms 44:9*
9	וַאֲסֹבְבָה אֶת־מִזְבַּחֲךָ יהוה *Psalms 26:6*
10	הַלְלוּ אֶת־יהוה כָּל־גּוֹיִם *Psalms 117:1*
11	וְהֵסֵב לֵב מֶלֶךְ־אַשּׁוּר עֲלֵיהֶם *Ezra 6:22*
12	מְהֻלָּל אֶקְרָא יהוה *2 Samuel 22:4*
13	וְהִלַּלְתֶּם אֶת־שֵׁם יהוה אֱלֹהֵיכֶם *Joel 2:26*
14	הַלְלוּ יָהּ הַלְלוּ אֶת־שֵׁם יהוה הַלְלוּ עַבְדֵי יהוה׃ *Psalms 135:1*
15	וְאַתָּה יהוה חָנֵּנִי וַהֲקִימֵנִי *Psalms 41:11*
16	וְאַנְשֵׁי הָעִיר ... נָסַבּוּ עַל־הַבַּיִת *Genesis 19:4*
17	וַיַּסֵּב אֱלֹהִים אֶת־הָעָם דֶּרֶךְ הַמִּדְבָּר *Exodus 13:18*
18	מִי יוֹדֵעַ יְחָנֵּנִי יהוה וְחַי הַיָּלֶד *2 Samuel 12:22*
19	שֻׁדְּדָה נִינְוֵה מִי יָנוּד לָהּ מֵאַיִן אֲבַקֵּשׁ מְנַחֲמִים לָךְ *Nahum 3:7*
	[נוד *wander* מֵאַיִן *from where*]

228

LESSON 52

אֵלֶּה אֲשֶׁר שָׁלַח יְהוָה לְהִתְהַלֵּךְ בָּאָרֶץ

Zechariah 1:10

52.1 ### אֵלֶּה אֲשֶׁר שָׁלַח יְהוָה

Note that אֲשֶׁר here stands for several words in English: *(the) ones who*

Translate phrase: _____

52.2 Analyze לְהִתְהַלֵּךְ

Root	Stem	Form	Person/Gender/Number	Special Features

Can you find a familiar root in the verb? Note the dagesh in the ל It is a dagesh _____
What stem does this suggest? _____ We have here yet another variation of the Pi`el
system. This one is called **Hitpa`el** and usually yields a reflexive/intensive or iterative meaning.
Its signs are the doubling of the middle root letter and the infixed ת "Infixed" means "fixed inside the word." Note that the ה is what infixes the ת here. The infinitive, imperative, and affix
infix the ת in the Hitpa`el by means of the ה So the Hitpa`el pattern is: הִת ַ ֵ _ The stem
meaning here seems to be iterative, conveying the notion of *walking about* or *walking to and fro*.

Translate the verb: _____

52.3 Translate sentence: _____

52.4 You have learned a lot of stems and verb types. Make sure you are confident of these. In this
exercise, identify the stem. Possibilities are: Qal, Pi`el, Pu`al, Pol`el, Pilp`el, Hif`il, Hof`al, Nif`al,
Hitpa`el, or Hishtaf`el.

גָּדַל	הִתְגַּדֵּל	גָּדְלוּ
הִגְדִּיל	יְהוֹלֵל	לְהִתְהַלֵּל
מְהַלָּל	תָּהֹלוּ	הוֹלְלִים

אֵלֶּה אֲשֶׁר שָׁלַח יְהוָה לְהִתְהַלֵּךְ בָּאָרֶץ

———

מִתְגּוֹרֵר	גָּר	יָקִים
מֵקִים	תְּקוֹמֵם	קוֹמֵם
כִּלְכֵּל	עוֹלֵל	מְעֹלֵל
הִתְרָאָה	הַרְאֵנִי	כְּהֵרָאוֹת
הֶרְאָה	מַרְאֶה	מַרְאֶה
וְהִשְׁתַּחֲוֵית	וְרַבָּה	הַרְע

Assignments

A. Vocabulary: words 1–310. Review words 101–200: אֵלֶּה הַדְּבָרִים💿 tracks 13–22.

B. Read and translate 1 Kings 19:6–10.

C. 💿 track 25: listen to שַׁבְּחִי יְהוָה רֹעִי **Psalm 23**.

D. Translate:

1 וְהִתְקַדִּשְׁתֶּם וִהְיִיתֶם קְדֹשִׁים כִּי קָדוֹשׁ אָנִי וְלֹא תְטַמְּאוּ
אֶת־נַפְשֹׁתֵיכֶם *Leviticus 11:44*

2 כִּי־חַסְדְּךָ לְנֶגֶד עֵינָי וְהִתְהַלַּכְתִּי בַּאֲמִתֶּךָ׃ *Psalms 26:3*

3 קוּם הִתְהַלֵּךְ בָּאָרֶץ *Genesis 13:17*

4 וַיְהִי בְּצֵאת הַכֹּהֲנִים מִן־הַקֹּדֶשׁ כִּי כָּל־הַכֹּהֲנִים הַנִּמְצְאִים
הִתְקַדָּשׁוּ אֵין לִשְׁמוֹר לְמַחְלְקוֹת [*division* מַחְלֶקֶת] *2 Chronicles 5:11*

5 הִתְהַלְלוּ בְּשֵׁם קָדְשׁוֹ יִשְׂמַח לֵב מְבַקְשֵׁי יְהוָה׃ *Psalms 105:3*

6 וְשָׁבוּ אֵלֶיךָ וְהוֹדוּ אֶת־שְׁמֶךָ וְהִתְפַּלְלוּ וְהִתְחַנְּנוּ אֵלֶיךָ
בַּבַּיִת הַזֶּה *1 Kings 8:33*

7 וְהִתְבָּרֵךְ בִּלְבָבוֹ לֵאמֹר שָׁלוֹם יִהְיֶה־לִּי כִּי בִּשְׁרִרוּת לִבִּי
אֵלֵךְ [*firmness* שְׁרִרוּת] *Deuteronomy 29:18*

8 וְהָאֲמֻצִּים יָצְאוּ וַיְבַקְשׁוּ לָלֶכֶת לְהִתְהַלֵּךְ בָּאָרֶץ וַיֹּאמֶר לְכוּ
הִתְהַלְּכוּ בָאָרֶץ וַתִּתְהַלַּכְנָה בָּאָרֶץ׃ [*steeds* אֲמֻצִּים] *Zechariah 6:7*

9 וַיֹּאמֶר אֵלָי יְהוָה אֲשֶׁר־הִתְהַלַּכְתִּי לְפָנָיו יִשְׁלַח מַלְאָכוֹ אִתָּךְ
וְהִצְלִיחַ דַּרְכֶּךָ וְלָקַחְתָּ אִשָּׁה לִבְנִי מִמִּשְׁפַּחְתִּי וּמִבֵּית אָבִי׃
[*make successful* צלח] *Genesis 24:40*

LESSON 53

◆

וַיִּתְהַלֵּךְ חֲנוֹךְ אֶת־הָאֱלֹהִים וְאֵינֶנּוּ כִּי־לָקַח אֹתוֹ אֱלֹהִים:

Genesis 5:24

53.1 Analyze וַיִּתְהַלֵּךְ

Root	Stem	Form	Person/Gender/Number	Special Features

Note that the prefix of the Hitpaʿel infixes the ת by use of the regular prefix pronouns. The participle is even simpler: it infixes the ת by the preformative מ

53.2 וַיִּתְהַלֵּךְ חֲנוֹךְ אֶת־הָאֱלֹהִים means _____

_____

53.3 וְאֵינֶנּוּ

What components can you find? אַיִן means _____ What kind of dagesh is in the נ _____ This is not the 1 c. pl. suffix, as you may have expected, but a different and rarer form of the 3 m. sg. suffix. Originally נְהוּ____ in time this suffix became נּוּ ֶ Such a form (which exists for other pronouns as well) is called an **energic** form. Watch for suffixes with dagesh forte. Translate: _____

53.4 כִּי־לָקַח אֹתוֹ אֱלֹהִים

Notice the two different meanings of את in this verse.

Translate the phrase: _____

Translate the verse: _____

_____

53.5 The suffixes with energic נ are object suffixes. They can be attached to verbs, most frequently in pause, and to some particles, most particularly הִנֵּה

231

You will also see energic **נ** on adverbs (which really are particles), but they are not suffixes for nouns. These energic forms of the suffix are not extant for every PGN.

<u>Note</u>: the 3 m. sg. and the 1 c. pl. suffix נּוּ֫ are the same only in the energic form.

53.5a   **Suffixes with Energic נ**

1 c. sg.	*me*	נִּי֫	נִי֫
2 m. sg.	*you*	נְּךָ֫	ךָ֫
3 m. sg.	*him*	נְהוּ֫	נּוּ֫
3 f. sg.	*her*	נָּה֫	
1 c. pl.	*us*	נּוּ֫	

53.5b Now we review the various forms of the regular object suffix. The suffixes for verbs, prepositions, and other particles are virtually the same except for two differences:

1. The 1 c. sg. suffix on a preposition may be simply יָ or יִ

2. Prepositions may have a connecting יֹ before the suffix. (See Chart O: Prepositions with Suffixes.)

Object Suffixes

1 c. sg.	*me*	נִי֫	נִ֫י	נִ֫י			
2 m. sg.	*you*	ךָ	ךָ	ךָ	ךָ֫		
2 f. sg.	*you*	ךְ	ךְ	ךְ	ךְ		
3 m. sg.	*him*	הוּ	וֹ	וֺ	וֹ▢	הוּ֫	הוּ֫
3 f. sg.	*her*	הָ	הָ	הָ֫			
1 c. pl.	*us*	נוּ	נוּ֫	נוּ֫			
2 m. pl.	*you*	כֶם	כֶם				
2 f. pl.	*you*	כֶן	כֶן				
3 m. pl.	*them*	הֶם	ם	ם	ם	ם	ם
3 f. pl.	*them*	הֶן	ן	ן			

232

53.5c Nouns take possessive suffixes. Review those lessons that discuss the construct and absolute states of the noun.

		Masculine Noun			Feminine Noun
			Singular		
	a horse	סוּס		*a mare*	סוּסָה
1 c. sg.	*my horse*	סוּסִי		*my mare*	סוּסָתִי
2 m. sg.	*your horse*	סוּסְךָ		*your mare*	סוּסָתְךָ
2 f. sg.	*your horse*	סוּסֵךְ		*your mare*	סוּסָתֵךְ
3 m. sg.	*his horse*	סוּסוֹ		*his mare*	סוּסָתוֹ
3 f. sg.	*her horse*	סוּסָהּ		*her mare*	סוּסָתָהּ
1 c. pl.	*our horse*	סוּסֵנוּ		*our mare*	סוּסָתֵנוּ
2 m. pl.	*your horse*	סוּסְכֶם		*your mare*	סוּסַתְכֶם
2 f. pl.	*your horse*	סוּסְכֶן		*your mare*	סוּסַתְכֶן
3 m. pl.	*their horse*	סוּסָם		*their mare*	סוּסָתָם
3 f. pl.	*their horse*	סוּסָן		*their mare*	סוּסָתָן
			Plural		
	horses	סוּסִים		*mares*	סוּסוֹת
1 c. sg.	*my horses*	סוּסַי		*my mares*	סוּסוֹתַי
2 m. sg.	*your horses*	סוּסֶיךָ		*your mares*	סוּסוֹתֶיךָ
2 f. sg.	*your horses*	סוּסַיִךְ		*your mares*	סוּסוֹתַיִךְ
3 m. sg.	*his horses*	סוּסָיו		*his mares*	סוּסוֹתָיו
3 f. sg.	*her horses*	סוּסֶיהָ		*her mares*	סוּסוֹתֶיהָ
1 c. pl.	*our horses*	סוּסֵינוּ		*our mares*	סוּסוֹתֵינוּ
2 m. pl.	*your horses*	סוּסֵיכֶם		*your mares*	סוּסוֹתֵיכֶם
2 f. pl.	*your horses*	סוּסֵיכֶן		*your mares*	סוּסוֹתֵיכֶן
3 m. pl.	*their horses*	סוּסֵיהֶם		*their mares*	סוּסוֹתֵיהֶם
3 f. pl.	*their horses*	סוּסֵיהֶן		*their mares*	סוּסוֹתֵיהֶן

53.6 When you know what's נו‍ ____ and who owns the horse, do the following exercise. Not every word will have a suffix, although most do.

C	B	A	
אֵלֶיךָ	הוֹלֵךְ	אֵלֶיךָ	1
אִשְׁתּוֹ	אִשָּׁה	אִשָּׁה	2
נְשֵׁיכֶם	אִשְׁתְּךָ	אֲנָשֶׁיהָ	3
אָחַי	אָחִיךְ	אָחִיךָ	4
אָחִי	אָחִיהָ	אֲחוֹתָם	5
אָבִיךָ	אֲבוֹתָיו	אֹהֲבִים	6
בָּתֶּיךָ	בְּנָהּ	בִּתִּי	7
בָּתַּי	בְּנוֹתֶיהָ	בַּתְּכֶם	8
יִשְׁמְרֵנוּ	שָׁמְרוּ	הִשָּׁמְרִי	9
הִשְׁלִיךְ	שְׁלַחְתַּנִי	וַיִּשְׁלְחֵם	10
וָאֶרְמְמֶנְהוּ	רִמְמוּ	מִנִּי	11
מִכֶּם	מֵהֵנָּה	מִמֶּךָ	12
קוּמִי	תַּחְתָּיו	מִמֶּנּוּ	13
בְּכִי	לְמַעַנְכֶם	עוֹדֶנִּי	14
עֲנֵנִי	וַעֲנֵנִי	יִתְּנֶהָ	15
תְּנוּ	יִתֶּנְךָ	יִתְּנֵנִי	16
לָכֶם	לֶחֶם	לְבַדְּהֶן	17
עֲשָׂהוּ	עֲשָׂתוֹ	עֲשָׂנִי	18
עֲשָׂיִךְ	יְבָרֵךְ	יְבָרֶכְךָ	19
תְּבָרֲכֵנִי	הִנְּךָ	הִנְּךָ	20
הִנֵּהוּ	הִנְנִי	הִנְנִי	21
הִנְנוּ	הִנֵּנוּ	הִנֶּנּוּ	22

234

Assignments

A. Vocabulary: review words 201–310 using 💿 אֵלֶּה הַדְּבָרִים tracks 23–33.

B. Read and translate 1 Kings 19:11–15.

C. 💿 שַׁבְּחִי tracks 4 and 22: review אֶשָּׂא עֵינַי Psalm 121 and אֵלִי אַתָּה Psalm 118:28. The two verbs in אֵלִי אַתָּה and the verb יַכְּכָה in Psalm 121:6 have energic נ suffixes, the נs of which have assimilated into the 2 m. sg. suffix. Also, in Psalm 121:6 note that the suffix has a plene spelling. For the root of the verb, see vocabulary word 222.

D. Translate:

1	*Deuteronomy 9:18* וָאֶתְנַפַּל לִפְנֵי יהוה
2	*1 Samuel 19:24* וַיִּתְנַבֵּא גַּם־הוּא לִפְנֵי שְׁמוּאֵל
3	*Jeremiah 26:20* וְגַם־אִישׁ הָיָה מִתְנַבֵּא בְּשֵׁם יהוה
4	*Psalms 34:3* בַּיהוה תִּתְהַלֵּל נַפְשִׁי
5	*2 Chronicles 18:7* כִּי אֵינֶנּוּ מִתְנַבֵּא עָלַי לְטוֹבָה
6	*1 Chronicles 15:14* וַיִּתְקַדְּשׁוּ הַכֹּהֲנִים וְהַלְוִיִּם
7	*Jeremiah 9:23* כִּי אִם־בְּזֹאת יִתְהַלֵּל הַמִּתְהַלֵּל
8	*Isaiah 44:17* [pray פלל] וְיִשְׁתַּחוּ וְיִתְפַּלֵּל אֵלָיו
9	*1 Samuel 12:2* הִנֵּה הַמֶּלֶךְ מִתְהַלֵּךְ לִפְנֵיכֶם
10	*Deuteronomy 9:26* וָאֶתְפַּלֵּל אֶל־יהוה וָאֹמַר
11	*Jeremiah 4:2* וְהִתְבָּרְכוּ בוֹ גּוֹיִם וּבוֹ יִתְהַלָּלוּ
12	*1 Kings 22:10* וְכָל־הַנְּבִיאִים מִתְנַבְּאִים לִפְנֵיהֶם
13	*2 Samuel 7:27* עַל־כֵּן מָצָא עַבְדְּךָ אֶת־לִבּוֹ לְהִתְפַּלֵּל אֵלֶיךָ
14	*Jeremiah 37:3* הִתְפַּלֶּל־נָא בַעֲדֵנוּ אֶל־יהוה אֱלֹהֵינוּ
15	*1 Chronicles 21:4* וַיֵּצֵא יוֹאָב וַיִּתְהַלֵּךְ בְּכָל־יִשְׂרָאֵל
16	*Psalms 116:9* אֶתְהַלֵּךְ לִפְנֵי יהוה בְּאַרְצוֹת הַחַיִּים:
17	*Psalms 30:9* אֵלֶיךָ יהוה אֶקְרָא וְאֶל־אֲדֹנָי אֶתְחַנָּן:
18	*Obadiah 7* עַד־הַגְּבוּל שִׁלְּחוּךָ כֹּל אַנְשֵׁי בְרִיתֶךָ

בִּשְׁנַת עֶשְׂרִים וָשֶׁבַע שָׁנָה לְיָרָבְעָם מֶלֶךְ יִשְׂרָאֵל מָלַךְ עֲזַרְיָה
בֶן־אֲמַצְיָה מֶלֶךְ יְהוּדָה: בֶּן־שֵׁשׁ עֶשְׂרֵה שָׁנָה הָיָה בְמָלְכוֹ
וַחֲמִשִּׁים וּשְׁתַּיִם שָׁנָה מָלַךְ בִּירוּשָׁלָם

2 Kings 15:1–2

54.1 In this very long lesson sentence there are several numbers. The cardinals from **one** to **ten** were presented in Lesson 41.2a. Review that section if necessary.

Note the following:

The numbers from **eleven** to **nineteen** combine the proper words for ten plus the other number between 1 and 10 with no "and" between the words. The smaller number precedes the ten in these combinations. For example, 16 is שֵׁשׁ עֶשְׂרֵה

The **tens** words are plurals of the basic words. 30: שְׁלֹשִׁים   40: אַרְבָּעִים and so on.

Twenty, however, is עֶשְׂרִים

With **numbers over ten**, the singular of the noun is most often used. That means these numbers do not agree in number and gender with the noun they modify. For example, fifty-two years: חֲמִשִּׁים וּשְׁתַּיִם שָׁנָה

Ordinals (first, second, third) are forms related to the cardinals and can be recognized by finding the relevant root: שְׁלִישִׁי שֵׁנִי Ordinals are attested only for the numbers 1 through 10, after which the cardinal numbers must be employed with ordinal meaning (by context).

A **hundred** has the following forms:

Absolute	Construct	Dual	Plural (for 100s over 200)
מֵאָה	מְאַת	מָאתַיִם	מֵאוֹת

A **thousand** is אֶלֶף   plural אֲלָפִים

Age formula: A person is *a son* (or *daughter*) *of X years* בֶּן (בַּת)... שָׁנָה

54.2 מָלַךְ as a verb means _____ Here the meaning of the first occurrence verges on *began to reign.*

בִּשְׁנַת עֶשְׂרִים וְשֶׁבַע שָׁנָה לְיָרָבְעָם מֶלֶךְ יִשְׂרָאֵל מָלַךְ עֲזַרְיָה
בֶּן־אֲמַצְיָה מֶלֶךְ יְהוּדָה: בֶּן־שֵׁשׁ עֶשְׂרֵה שָׁנָה הָיָה בְמָלְכוֹ
וַחֲמִשִּׁים וּשְׁתַּיִם שָׁנָה מָלַךְ בִּירוּשָׁלָ͏ִם

54.3 Translate verses: _____

_____

_____

_____

_____

Assignments

A. Vocabulary: Review all vocabulary words. Use אֵלֶּה הַדְּבָרִים as necessary.

B. Read and translate 1 Kings 19:16–21.

C. ⊙**ב א** track 26: review אַחַת שְׁתַּיִם

⊙**שַׁבְחִי** track 35: sing at least the chorus of הוֹדוּ לַיהוה **Psalm 136**.

D. Translate:

1 וּלְאַחְאָב שִׁבְעִים בָּנִים בְּשֹׁמְרוֹן
2 Kings 10:1

2 הִכָּה שָׁאוּל בַּאֲלָפָיו
1 Samuel 18:7

3 וְאַבְרָהָם בֶּן־מְאַת שָׁנָה בְּהִוָּלֶד לוֹ אֵת יִצְחָק בְּנוֹ:
Genesis 21:5

4 בִּשְׁנַת עֶשְׂרִים וְשָׁלֹשׁ שָׁנָה לְיוֹאָשׁ בֶּן־אֲחַזְיָהוּ מֶלֶךְ יְהוּדָה מָלַךְ
יְהוֹאָחָז בֶּן־יֵהוּא עַל־יִשְׂרָאֵל בְּשֹׁמְרוֹן שְׁבַע עֶשְׂרֵה שָׁנָה:
2 Kings 13:1

5 וַיְהִי־שֵׁת חָמֵשׁ שָׁנִים וּמְאַת שָׁנָה וַיּוֹלֶד אֶת־אֱנוֹשׁ: וַיִּהְיוּ
כָּל־יְמֵי־שֵׁת שְׁתֵּים עֶשְׂרֵה שָׁנָה וּתְשַׁע מֵאוֹת שָׁנָה וַיָּמֹת:
Genesis 5:6, 8

6 וַיְשַׁמַּע שָׁאוּל אֶת־הָעָם וַיִּפְקְדֵם בַּטְּלָאִים מָאתַיִם אֶלֶף רַגְלִי
וַעֲשֶׂרֶת אֲלָפִים אֶת־אִישׁ יְהוּדָה: [טְלָאִים name of a place]
1 Samuel 15:4

7 וְאָנֹכִי הֶעֱלֵיתִי אֶתְכֶם מֵאֶרֶץ מִצְרַיִם וָאוֹלֵךְ אֶתְכֶם בַּמִּדְבָּר
אַרְבָּעִים שָׁנָה לָרֶשֶׁת אֶת־אֶרֶץ הָאֱמֹרִי:
Amos 2:10

LESSON 55

Introduction to Biblical Hebrew Poetry

As you have already seen, much Biblical Hebrew prose is written in an elevated, elegant style, rife with such elements as euphony, repetition of roots and/or syntactical structures, inverted or chiastic word order, and evidence of careful phrasing. Sometimes these components blend so exquisitely that it is difficult not to label certain passages as poetry. In fact, James Kugel argues that it is impossible to make a precise and categorical distinction between Biblical prose and poetry. But we can look at some features that are characteristic of passages—Psalms, for example—that many moderns would consider to be poetry to see how these are like and yet different from Western poetry.

In English, we recognize traditional poetry by meter and rhyme scheme, and by the way the lines are set out on the page. Biblical poetry has no regular rhyme; it does have rhythm and certain structural indicators. We don't know what the metrical conventions were, and so the structural features—such things as כִּי clauses, use of independent subject pronouns, syntactical parallelism, for example—are important conceptual guides.

The basic structural characteristic of Biblical Hebrew poetry is **parallelism**. A line is paralleled by a statement that relates to the first one, and the poetry proceeds by means of couplets or, less frequently, triplets. This is a characteristic of all ancient Semitic poetry. (The examples below treat only one kind of parallelism—semantic—since that was the feature that scholars first noticed, but there are many other kinds of parallelism: syntactic, sonant, structural, grammatical, etc.) If the second line echoes the thought of the first line, then the parallelism is said to be **synonymous**:

מָה־אֱנוֹשׁ כִּי־תִזְכְּרֶנּוּ
וּבֶן־אָדָם כִּי תִפְקְדֶנּוּ׃ *Psalm 8:5*

> *What is man, that you are mindful of him?*
> *And the son of man that you visit him?*

If the second line contrasts with the first, the parallelism is called **antithetic**:

בַּבֹּקֶר יָצִיץ וְחָלָף
לָעֶרֶב יְמוֹלֵל וְיָבֵשׁ׃ *Psalm 90:6*

> *In the morning it flourishes and grows up;*
> *In the evening it is cut down and withers.*

The thought may continue from line to line to build up a cumulative effect; in this case, the parallelism is said to be **synthetic** (actually, it is synthetic when it does not fit any other category):

יהוה רֹעִי לֹא אֶחְסָר׃

בִּנְאוֹת דֶּשֶׁא יַרְבִּיצֵנִי

עַל־מֵי מְנֻחוֹת יְנַהֲלֵנִי׃

נַפְשִׁי יְשׁוֹבֵב

יַנְחֵנִי בְמַעְגְּלֵי־צֶדֶק לְמַעַן שְׁמוֹ׃ *Psalm 23:1–3*

The Lord is my shepherd; I shall not lack;

He causes me to crouch down in green pastures (fresh grass)

He leads me beside waters of rest

He restores my soul (life)

He guides me in paths of righteousness for his name's sake.

Very rarely will all the elements of one line be paralleled by the second. If they do, the parallelism is called **complete**:

| d | c | b | a |

בְּטֶרֶם אֶצּוֹרְךָ בַבֶּטֶן יְדַעְתִּיךָ

| d¹ | c¹ | b¹ | a¹ |

Jeremiah 1:5 וּבְטֶרֶם תֵּצֵא מֵרֶחֶם הִקְדַּשְׁתִּיךָ

Before I formed you in the belly I knew you;

And before you came out of the womb I sanctified you.

Most parallelism is **incomplete** with more elements in the first line than in the second:

| d | c | b | a |

וַתֹּאמֶר צִיּוֹן עֲזָבַנִי יְהוָה

| c¹ | d¹ |

Isaiah 49:14 וַאדֹנָי שְׁכֵחָנִי׃

But Zion said, "The Lord has forsaken me;

And my Lord has forgotten me."

Also there is incomplete parallelism with **compensation**:

         c   b   a

          אָכֵן שָׁמַע אֱלֹהִים

         e   d   b¹

Psalm 66:19 הִקְשִׁיב בְּקוֹל תְּפִלָּתִי׃

      But surely God has heard;
      He has attended to the voice of my prayer.

In ancient scrolls, such as those from Qumran, "poetry" was written out like prose. In other words, it was not laid out in lines or verses. But in many printed Bibles, there is a horizontal or vertical space between the two halves of a line or **couplet**. A section of a poem, which in English is called a stanza, is usually referred to in Hebrew poetry as a **strophe**.

Aside from a preponderance of parallelistic expressions, some of the other features of Biblical poetry are highly compressed expression, frequent absence of the DDO marker אֵת absence of particles, greater variety of word order, lots of vocatives, and the occurrence of much vocabulary not seen in prose literature. Lines tend to be short and rhythmic. We look at some of these poetic elements in Psalms 24 and 100.

Psalm 24:1

Psalm 24 begins with the words מִזְמוֹר לְדָוִד We simply do not know if this means that David wrote the psalm, that it was written during his period, or whether it was dedicated to him. It could mean that it is part of a collection of psalms belonging to him. *David* may not refer specifically to King David, but might refer to the House of David, that is, a Davidic King. We do not know the exact function of מִזְמוֹר לְדָוִד but it does open many psalms—though it usually appears with the words in reverse order: מִזְמוֹר לְדָוִד The term מִזְמוֹר is a technical term used only in regard to Psalms, and occurs in the heading of fifty-seven of them. Both in Hebrew and in Greek the root-meaning is *to play instrumental music* or *to sing to musical accompaniment.*

	c	b	a
The first line is	לַיהוה הָאָרֶץ וּמְלוֹאָהּ		

	c¹	b¹
The second is	תֵּבֵל וְיֹשְׁבֵי בָהּ:	

In the word וּמְלוֹאָהּ the feminine possessive suffix is referring to הָאָרֶץ and so it means *and its fullness*. Interestingly, a contrasting thought is expressed in Psalm 115:16:

הַשָּׁמַיִם שָׁמַיִם לַיהוָה
וְהָאָרֶץ נָתַן לִבְנֵי־אָדָם:

In the second line תֵּבֵל is a parallel for הָאָרֶץ It is a poetic term for world, but may refer specifically to the habitable parts of the earth. Like most terms for earth or world, it is feminine. Poetic convention allows the definite article ה to be dropped in front of תֵּבֵל The ה of הָאָרֶץ does "double duty." Notice that the more general noun is used first and the more specific one, second.

וְיֹשְׁבֵי בָהּ These words are parallel to וּמְלוֹאָהּ and so are identified as c¹. The ḥolem after the first root letter identifies יֹשְׁבֵי as a _____

בָהּ is a separate word, but its parallel lies in the suffix of וּמְלוֹאָהּ Note that both וּמְלוֹאָהּ and וְיֹשְׁבֵי בָהּ have four syllables.

The first colon maps out: a b c // b¹ c¹, an example of incomplete, synonymous parallelism.

Psalm 24:2

כִּי־הוּא   An emphatic use of the independent subject pronoun.

עַל־יַמִּים   Do not confuse יַמִּים with יָמִים (See The Noun H.) The word order of this couplet is: subject / adverbial phrase / verb + DO. The image here is that the earth rests upon the great cosmic ocean and is supported by pillars that are, at the same time, the underwater bases of mountains.

יְסָדָהּ   The suffix is still referring to the feminine תֵּבֵל or הָאָרֶץ If the verb did not have a suffix, it would be pointed _____

וְעַל־נְהָרוֹת   This begins the second half of the second couplet, and you can see that it is a parallel statement to עַל־יַמִּים There is no parallel for כִּי־הוּא the first phrase in the couplet, and so וְעַל־נְהָרוֹת is designated b¹. These נְהָרוֹת are likely the subterranean waters, and may be translated as *floodwaters*. Some interpreters take נְהָרוֹת to mean actual rivers such as the Jordan and Euphrates.

יְכוֹנְנֶהָ   This verb is in the _____ which is one of the ways to give a hollow verb Pi'el intensity. (51.5) The suffix is still the 3 f. sg. object suffix, but it does not have a mappiq because _____ _____ (23.2c) Text note 2b suggests reading כוֹנְנֶהָ instead of יְכוֹנְנֶהָ so that the aspects of the two verbs in this couplet would be the same.

Psalm 24:3

מִי־יַעֲלֶה   What stems are possible for the verb? _____ (32.3b) How will you decide? The verb עלה can be used to mean making a pilgrimage to the sanctuary.

בְּהַר־יהוה   Mountains feature prominently in the imagery of Psalms. They are thought to be a link between earth and heaven. Although the imagery in this psalm can be taken in an abstract sense, it probably is referring specifically to the temple in Jerusalem and *the mountain* is most likely Mt. Zion.

קָדְשׁוֹ   This is the noun קֹדֶשׁ + the 3 m. sg. possessive suffix; not the adjective קָדוֹשׁ Why, then, is the ק pointed קָ _____ The phrase בִּמְקוֹם קָדְשׁוֹ is a construct chain, which English treats as a noun and an adjective. This third couplet demonstrates complete parallelism:

c　　　b　　　a

מִי־יַעֲלֶה בְהַר־יְהוָה

c¹　　　b¹　　　a¹

וּמִי־יָקוּם בִּמְקוֹם קָדְשׁוֹ:

Psalm 24:4

נְקִי It is true that 3 f. sg. imperatives end in ‏ִי‏ but there is no antecedent for a f. sg. imperative here. What are two other possibilities for the ending? (8.3 and 48.7) Why is the first syllable pointed with shewa? **(S 5.2)**

כַּפַּיִם This is the dual of a vocabulary word. Why is there a dagesh in the פ _____

Verse 4 is a triplet and this first line contains its own internal parallelism:

b¹　　a¹　　　　b　　　a

נְקִי כַפַּיִם　וּבַר־לֵבָב

נְפְשִׁי There are two different Masoretic conventions not only for the reading of this word but also for the writing of it. Some texts have נַפְשׁוֹ If it is read נַפְשִׁי then the meaning is *who has not sworn deceitfully by my* נֶפֶשׁ (literally: *who has not lifted up my* נֶפֶשׁ *to vanity*) and נַפְשִׁי is taken to be a substitute for *my name*. This idea is expressed in the commandment לֹא תִשָּׂא אֶת־שֵׁם־יְהוָה אֱלֹהֶיךָ לַשָּׁוְא (Ex. 20:7).

If the word is taken to be נַפְשׁוֹ then the meaning becomes *who has not lifted up his* נֶפֶשׁ *to vanity*. Either one of the two meanings was likely intended, or just as likely, there was an attempt here to preserve a double tradition.

וְלֹא נִשְׁבַּע The word אֲשֶׁר introduced the previous clause and is understood in this one. It is an example of a word doing double duty, like the definite article ה in the word הָאָרֶץ (Ps. 24:1) Is the _____ נ a preformative or the 1 c. pl. subject pronoun?

לְמִרְמָה It is difficult to abstract the root of this word. Taking off the preposition leaves מרמה There are many possibilities with this combination of letters; you should be able to think of about four, but in order to get on with the psalm let it be known that the root is רמה

Psalm 24:5

יִשָּׂא בְרָכָה The use of the verb נשא is contrasted with its use in the previous verse.

מֵאֵת Discussed in 37.1.

יִשְׁעוֹ The fact that this word comes after a word in the construct form should tell you that you are looking at a noun. What part of it is not part of the root? _____

The parallelism in this couplet is incomplete with compensation. Diagram it:

יִשָּׂא בְרָכָה מֵאֵת יְהוָה

וּצְדָקָה מֵאֱלֹהֵי יִשְׁעוֹ:

Psalm 24:6

זֶה דּוֹר Why can this phrase not be *this generation?* (15.2)

דֹּרְשׁוֹ Note the כְּתִב קְרֵא It tells us that the participle is to be read as a plural. The verb דרשׁ can mean *seeking after*, that is, *knowing God's ways*. It is also the term used for consulting an oracle.

מְבַקְשֵׁי Analyze this word. The stem is a bit tricky. (36.3b)

יַעֲקֹב Vocative, but may be a shortened epithet for אֱלֹהֵי יַעֲקֹב *O God of Jacob*. It may mean *even Jacob.*

סֶלָה Nobody knows what סֶלָה means. It could mean "crash the cymbals here." It could represent a musical direction, some kind of interruption or change, or a word like *amen*. It is found in many psalms at the end of a strophe, but the word may not be intrinsic to the compositions. Notice here how it marks a break in the psalm. What follows seems to be a chorus or refrain.

This couplet is an example of synthetic parallelism. Diagram it:

זֶה דּוֹר דֹּרְשׁוֹ

מְבַקְשֵׁי פָנֶיךָ יַעֲקֹב סֶלָה:

Psalm 24:7

שְׂאוּ שְׁעָרִים רָאשֵׁיכֶם How do the words שְׁעָרִים רָאשֵׁיכֶם fit with the imperative שְׂאוּ The word רָאשֵׁיכֶם is a DO and שְׁעָרִים is a vocative. This is the third use of נשׂא in the psalm. In verse 4 it was used with לַשָּׁוְא *who has not lifted up his soul to deceit*. In verse 5 it is used with בְּרָכָה *he has lifted up a blessing*. Here it is used with *gates*. Most likely this is supposed to be a physical image and not a metaphor. According to tradition, this psalm was composed to celebrate the bringing of the ark into Jerusalem. At this point in the psalm, the bearers of the ark are at the gates and the address to the gates to *lift up your heads* means to extend their height because they are too low for the king of glory to enter.

וְהִנָּשְׂאוּ Another use of the verb נשא This time the stem is _____ (49.2)

פִּתְחֵי עוֹלָם The imagery may be either of the temple in Jerusalem or of the gates of heaven. It may very well be a double image.

מֶלֶךְ הַכָּבוֹד The concept expressed here, of God as king, is very ancient and was never challenged by the institution of the monarchy.

Verses 7–10 are all triplets. Verses 7 and 9 make a pair as do verses 8 and 10.

Psalm 24:8

מִי זֶה An interrogative noun sentence.

עִזּוּז וְגִבּוֹר Adjectives modifying יהוה

מִלְחָמָה English needs a preposition before this word. The images of God as warrior stem from the days when the ark used to be carried into battle.

Psalm 24:9

Not an exact repetition of verse 7.

Psalm 24:10

מִי הוּא זֶה Even more emphatic than מִי זֶה in verse 8.

יהוה צְבָאוֹת A problem (for moderns) with this phrase is the meaning of צְבָאוֹת
It can refer to the armies of Israel, but more likely refers to the heavenly bodies or heavenly armies.

Psalm 100

Psalm 100:1

מִזְמוֹר לְתוֹדָה This is the only one of the Psalms labeled לְתוֹדָה It is thought that it was originally intended to accompany the bringing of the sacrifice. It is sung, in contemporary Jewish liturgy, on days other than the Sabbath and Festivals.

הָרִיעוּ The stem and PGN are straightforward. Of the Hif`il forms, only three have the הֿ preformative. One obviously is the Hif`il affix, the others are the _____ Which fits here? What about the root? It looks like רִיע but if your dictionary doesn't list it that way, remember: In the Hif`il the middle letter of hollow verbs, which may be __ or __ is replaced by י (29.2) Explain the vowel under the preformative. (34.4, footnote 1)

Psalm 100:2

Diagram these lines and tell what type of parallelism they exemplify: _____

עִבְדוּ אֶת־יהוה בְּשִׂמְחָה

בֹּאוּ לְפָנָיו בִּרְנָנָה:

Psalm 100:3

דְּעוּ The mood is a continuation of that expressed in the verbs in the previous verse.

יהוה הוּא אֱלֹהִים Where else have you seen this phrase (with one slight difference)?

עָשָׂנוּ If this looks like an ambiguous form, study 26.5 and 53.5b.

הוּא עָשָׂנוּ וְלֹא אֲנַחְנוּ There are two conventions regarding this line. One takes it the way it is written and translates it *He made us and not we ourselves*. The other, and more widely accepted tradition, claims that וְלֹא is a scribal error and it should read וְלוֹ Then the line becomes *He made us and we are his*.

מַרְעִיתוֹ Roots that look as if they might end in י most likely end in _____ The image of God as shepherd is found frequently in Psalms.

Verse 3 is set out as a triplet. It is difficult to analyze this verse in terms of parallelism—at least of the semantic type. Sections b and c of the verse give a reason for the imperatives in the rest of the psalm. Just as those two segments offer a picture of protection, they are "protected" by being in the very center of the poem. Notice that sections a and b of the verse are connected by the repetition of וֹ sounds and that section c, which is in apposition to b, builds on b, moving to a greater degree of intimacy.

246

Psalm 100:4

שְׁעָרָיו Of the temple.

בְּתוֹדָה According to rabbinic interpretation, all forms of sacrifice and prayers of petition should become obsolete in the messianic era with the exception of thanksgiving offerings, because even in a perfect world people should show their appreciation to God.

חֲצֵרֹתָיו The temple had outer courts where the people gathered.

בִּתְהִלָּה A ת preformative noun. This type of prayer is recited aloud as opposed to תְּפִלָּה which is usually silent prayer.

הוֹדוּ Same root as תּוֹדָה

בָּרְכוּ 36.3a.

Psalm 100:5

וְעַד־דֹּר וָדֹר A frequently used expression to convey the idea of perpetuity, often translated *from generation to generation.*

אֱמוּנָתוֹ Knowing that this is a noun is the clue to abstracting the root.

Note that there is no verb in this verse. The effect is of timelessness. There are two ways to look at verse 5: as a couplet or as triplets. Would it make a conceptual difference if one read

כִּי־טוֹב יהוה לְעוֹלָם חַסְדּוֹ as one or two clauses?

About the structure of this psalm: it has a symmetrical structure. It is composed of two strophes. The first strophe (verses 1–3) has four plural imperatives and then a כִּי clause that proclaims the omnipotence of God. The second strophe (verses 4–5) has three plural imperatives followed by a כִּי clause that proclaims God's goodness. That there are seven imperatives is significant. It is common to see groups of either five or seven verbs or names for God in a Psalm.

Assignments

A. Review all vocabulary. Use ⊙אֵלֶּה הַדְּבָרִים to test yourself.

B. ⊙שְׁבָחַי (tracks 25, 28, and 35 respectively): listen to שִׁיר הַמַּעֲלוֹת יהוה רֹעִי Psalm 23, Psalm 126, and הוֹדוּ לַיהוה Psalm 136.

GLOSSES TO THE READINGS

Genesis 22:1 [Lesson 13]

וַיְהִי | וַיְהִי is a common way to begin a narrative. It is usually translated *And it happened* or *And it came to pass*. Is it a vav conversive? (2.12) _____ What is the root? (12.1) _____

אַחַר Vocabulary word.

הַדְּבָרִים הָאֵלֶּה What are the gender and number of the noun דְּבָרִים _____ (6.5a) What is the ☐ הַ in front of it? _____ (4.3)

הָאֵלֶּה is an adjective modifying הַדְּבָרִים The word אֵלֶּה means _____ An adjective that follows a noun and agrees with it in gender (m. or f.), number (sg. or pl.), and definiteness is called an **attributive adjective**. הַדְּבָרִים is masculine, plural, and definite, so its adjective הָאֵלֶּה must also be masculine, plural, and definite. Actually, the gender of הָאֵלֶּה is common (i.e., masculine or feminine). To review why the הָ of הָאֵלֶּה is pointed with a qamats ָ see 4.5b.

The Attributive Adjective *this*

זֶה	*this*	(m. sg.)
זוֹאת	*this*	(f. sg.)
אֵלֶּה	*these*	(c. pl.)

וְהָאֱלֹהִים It is not unusual to see the definite article in front of אֱלֹהִים English translation, however, tends not to distinguish between אֱלֹהִים and הָאֱלֹהִים What about the initial וְ When a verse begins with a temporal or circumstantial clause, the following clause is often introduced by וְ It can be translated *that* or *when*. (Syntactic uses of וְ are discussed in **S 43.3**. This is use number one.)

נִסָּה The dagesh in the סּ is a dagesh forte. (1.2, 3.3a) That means that the סּ is doubled either because it is denoting a Piʿel stem (2.3c) or because it is representing an assimilated letter. (7.1a) Do the easy thing first: look up נסה in a dictionary. The entry indicates that this root is found in the Bible exclusively in the Piʿel stem. Furthermore, a m. sg. affix works in the context of the verse.

249

Although אֱלֹהִים is plural, when it refers to "God" it takes a singular verb. (2.4) The usual word order in a Hebrew sentence is verb–subject. For emphasis, the subject may precede the verb, as it does here.

אֶת־אַבְרָהָם Why is אַבְרָהָם preceded by אֶת _____ (7.2)

וַיֹּאמֶר אֵלָיו אַבְרָהָם The question here is whether אַבְרָהָם is the subject of וַיֹּאמֶר or whether the subject of וַיֹּאמֶר is "he," that is, אֱלֹהִים in which case אַבְרָהָם would begin a quotation. (10.2c discusses the difficulties in identifying direct speech in the Hebrew Bible.)

Genesis 22:2 [Lesson 13]

קַח־נָא | קַח is the m. sg. imperative of the irregular verb לקח There is no exact equivalent in English for נָא It is a particle of entreaty or exhortation. Two possible translations are *pray* or *now*.

אֶת־בִּנְךָ The suffix ךָ__ is the 2 m. sg. possessive pronoun *your*. The addition of the suffix causes a change in vowel in the noun: בֵּן *son*, but בִּנְךָ *your son* and בְּנוֹ *his son*. The particular change will depend on the nature of the vowel, whether the suffix ends or begins a syllable, the length of the word, and the word's particular accent.

אֶת־יְחִידְךָ | אֶת־יְחִידְךָ further qualifying אֶת־בִּנְךָ is usually translated as *your only one*. This is a problematic rendering as you will see if you examine the root. First remove the suffix ךָ__ Four letters י ח י ד are left. Of these י can be either a consonant or a vowel letter. If it has a vowel, it is a consonant; if it does not, it is a vowel letter. Since vowel letters may or may not be part of the root, look to a vowel letter to remove something if there are more than three letters for the root. The first י has shewa __ under it, so it is a consonant. The second י is part of the vowel plene ḥireq י__ so it is a vowel letter. If you remove the second י you are left with the three-letter root יחד which means *be united, make as one*. יְחִיד (shewa __ under the first root letter here due to propretonic reduction [**S 5.1c.2**]) is a substantive derived from that root. The phrase would mean then *the-one-with-whom-you-are-one*. Some grammarians claim that יְחִיד is related to אֶחָד *one*, which accounts for the translation *only one*.

אָהַבְתָּ Affix form usually means past tense translation, but with verbs denoting affections or states of mind the affix form often requires present tense translation in English.

אֶת־יִצְחָק This is the third DDO in this verse. Give the reason for the definiteness of each.

The Three Ways in Which a Noun Can Be Definite

1. It has the definite article	הַדְּבָרִים
2. It is a proper noun	אַבְרָהָם
3. It has a possessive pronoun	בִּנְךָ

A word about the style of this part of the verse: notice how each phrase builds upon and intensifies the one before:

אֶת־יִצְחָק   אֲשֶׁר־אָהַבְתָּ   אֶת־יְחִידְךָ   אֶת־בִּנְךָ

וְלֶךְ־לְךָ | לֶךְ־לְךָ is another instance of a Qal imperative's losing a root letter; it is from the root _____ לְ imparts to the verb a reflexive nuance, which some translations (e.g., NRSV, JPS) ignore, saying simply *go* rather than *take yourself*. (Incidentally, the only other occurrence of לֶךְ־לְךָ is in Genesis 12:1, which verse has other structural and thematic similarities to Genesis 22:2.)

אֶרֶץ הַמֹּרִיָּה | מֹרִיָּה is usually transliterated, but its letters resonate with the roots רָאָה *see* and יָרֵא *fear, be in awe*, both of which are significant in this narrative. Resultant compounds could be יָהּ + מַרְאֶה *vision of God* or מוֹרָה + יָהּ *awe of God*.

וְהַעֲלֵהוּ To find the root, first take off the conjunction וְ in front. הוּ____ at the end is the 3 m. sg. object suffix *him*. It is a variation of the suffix וֹ or ֹ We are left with הַעֲל but no such root exists. לְ and עַ in an interior position are always root letters, so you have to assume that the הַ is not part of the root. The missing letter could be in the first, second, or third position. According to what you have learned so far, if the missing letter were in the first position it would probably be a יְ or a נְ and the root would be יָעַל or נָעַל In the second position, it would be a יְ or a וְ possible roots being עוּל or עִיל and in the third position it would be a הַ leading to the root עָלָה A few of the possible combinations are indeed roots, but עָלָה happens to be the root here. The הַ in front of the verb is a sign of the Hif`il stem. The Hif`il takes a basic root idea and makes it causative. The Hif`il of עָלָה is either *cause to go up* (as smoke of a sacrifice) or *bring up*. The form is imperative. The whole word וְהַעֲלֵהוּ means *and sacrifice him* or *and bring him up*.

Why could the final letter וּ____ not be the 3 m. pl. affix ending? Because verbs that end in הַ always lose the הַ before a subject or object pronoun is added to the verb. (The m. pl. Hif`il imperative of עָלָה would be הַעֲלוּ)

אֶחָד הֶהָרִים | אֶחָד means _____ הֶ is the pointing for the definite article in front of a guttural when the first syllable is propretonic (two syllables before the accent). After taking off the definite article and the m. pl. noun endiNG, you are left with הַר (vocabulary word). The phrase is a construct chain. Is it definite or indefinite? _____ (5.2)

אָמַר The ḥolem ◌ֹ after what appears to be the first root letter is usually the sign of the Qal participle. (9.3a) However, the prefix form of אמר has, along with four other 1st א verbs, ḥolem after the prefix pronoun. When the prefix pronoun is א we would expect to see אֶאֱמָר But when the prefix pronoun of a 1st א verb is also א the א of the root elides. Furthermore, the second vowel of אֹמַר is not tsere ◌ֵ which it would be in a Qal m. sg. participle. אֹמַר then, is the 1 c. Qal prefix of אמר *I will say.*

Synopsis of אמר

Verb	PGN/Form	Special Feature	Usual Translation
אָמַר	3 m. sg. affix	_____	past
אֹמֵר	m. sg. participle	_____	depends on context
אֹמַר	1 c. sg. prefix	_____	future or ongoing present
וְאָמַר	3 m. sg. affix	vav reversive	future or frequentative past
יֹאמַר	3 m. sg. prefix	_____	future or ongoing present
וַיֹּאמֶר	3 m. sg. prefix	vav conversive	past

אֵלֶיךָ The suffix ךָ ◌ has appeared three times already in this verse as the possessive pronoun *your.* Here as the object of the preposition אֶל it is translated *you.* Several prepositions take a י before a suffix is added. (2.9b) Four frequently seen are:

אֶל *to*   עַל *on*   תַּחַת *under*   אַחַר *behind* or *after*

Genesis 22:3 [Lesson 14]

וַיַּשְׁכֵּם | In BDB, שׁ and שׂ are treated as two different letters. Words beginning with שׂ are listed first in BDB (but not necessarily in other dictionaries). When you look up שׁכם you will notice that this verb is extant only in the Hifʿil even though it is not causative or transitive. In this verse, it is the 3 m. sg. prefix form with vav conversive. The Hifʿil prefix does not show a preformative ה but it does typically have two distinguishing characteristics:

1. The vowel pataḥ ◌ַ under the prefix pronoun

2. An I class ("dot") vowel ◌ֵ ◌ִ or ◌ֶ under the second root letter

<u>Note</u>: The properties of vav conversive ◌ַ וַ are the same regardless of the stem of the verb.

בַּבֹּקֶר | בֹּקֶר   means_____ בְּ is a prefixed preposition. To say *in the morning*, you need ◌ַ הַ + בְּ before the noun. Since that sound combination is hard to maintain, the הַ elides, leaving only the two other signs of the definite article: the vowel pataḥ ◌ַ and the following dagesh forte. Why is there a dagesh in the first בּ _____ (3.3a)

וַיַּחְבֹּשׁ   The vowel under the prefix pronoun looks like that of the Hif`il prefix (as in וַיַּשְׁכֵּם just above), but there is no I class ("dot") vowel between the second and third root letters to confirm a Hif`il prefix form. וַיַּחְבֹּשׁ is a Qal. It is the guttural ח which attracts the vowel pataḥ. The usual vowel under the prefix pronoun of a strong verb in the Qal is ____ (14.5, 14.6B, and Verb Charts)

חֲמֹרוֹ   The root חמר has four entries in BDB, each preceded by a large Roman numeral. The function of these Roman numerals is to indicate that each entry is considered to be from an entirely different root.

וַיִּקַּח   This is another form of the irregular verb לקח (see קַח־נָא [Gen. 22:2]). לקח acts like נתן (7.1a) and נפל (12.3) except that its assimilated root letter is ל

שְׁנֵי   The construct form of the number "two" can be translated *both* or *two*.

נְעָרָיו | נַעַר   means _____ י after a noun means _____ ו means _____

Synopsis of נַעַר

נַעַר	*youth*	נְעָרִים	*youths*
נַעֲרוֹ	*his youth*	נְעָרָיו	*his youths*

אִתּוֹ | אִתּוֹ   looks like the DDO marker אֵת but with the "accompanying" dagesh and a pronominal suffix, it means *with*. אֵת by itself can be either the sign of the DDO or the preposition *with*.

Synopsis of אֵת

אֶת־הַבֵּן	*the son* (DDO) or *with the son*
אֵת הַבֵּן	*the son* (DDO) or *with the son*
אֹתוֹ	*him* (DDO)
אִתּוֹ	*with him*

וַיְבַקַּע What is the stem _____ (2.3c) The root is _____

עֲצֵי עֹלָה For help with the construction, see 6.5a.

וַיָּקָם See 6.1a for help determining the root.

הַמָּקוֹם | Vocabulary word + definite article. מ in front of a root is a common way of forming nouns. מ preformative nouns are often nouns of place or instrument.

Genesis 22:4 [Lesson 14]

בַּיּוֹם הַשְּׁלִישִׁי | בַּיּוֹם is constructed like בַּבֹּקֶר (Gen. 22:3) שְׁלִישִׁי means _____ and is an attributive adjective because _____ _____ (See 14.2c and הַדְּבָרִים הָאֵלֶּה [Gen. 22:1].)

וַיִּשָּׂא For help determining the root, see 7.1a and 12.3.

אֶת־עֵינָיו The root of עֵינָיו is _____

וַיַּרְא 12.1 discusses the root.

מֵרָחֹק | רָחֹק is a noun. מֵרָחֹק is constructed like מִשָּׁם (3.4b) But since ר can't take a dagesh, the vowel under the מ is lengthened in compensation. As a mnemonic device, we can say that the dagesh that couldn't stand in the ר went under the מ turning the hireq ִ into tsere ֵ We call this "the case of the traveling dagesh."

Genesis 22:5 [Lesson 14]

שְׁבוּ־לָכֶם | שְׁבוּ is a m. pl. Qal imperative from the verb יָשַׁב and וֹ_____ is the m. pl. imperative endiNG. The suffix כֶם_ is the plural of the suffix ךְ_ (Gen. 22:2). After all, there are two נְעָרִים A literal translation might be *seat/stay yourselves.*

Every imperative you have seen in this reading comes from a verb with a weak root letter or a verb that acts as if it has a weak root letter. That letter is lost in the imperative form.

Synopsis of Imperatives

(Gen. 22:2)	קַח	from	לקח
	לֶךְ-לְךָ	from	הלך
	וְהַעֲלֵהוּ	from	עלה
(Gen. 22:5)	שְׁבוּ-לָכֶם	from	ישׁב

פֿה **פֹה** In BDB under פֹה

וַאֲנִי **וַאֲנִי** Why is this word not written וְאֲנִי? Because with that spelling there would be two vocal shewas in a row: וְ would be vocal because it is the first syllable of the word, and אֲ would be vocal as the second shewa in a row. To resolve that difficulty, when the second shewa is a composite shewa, the first shewa transforms to match the full vowel component in the composite shewa. (The rule of shewa is discussed in **S 14.3.1**.)

נֵלְכָה **נֵלְכָה** This is a new form of הלך. The נ is a prefix pronoun (14.5), and the ֵ under it indicates that this is a verb missing its first root letter. (3.1) Following the prefix pronoun and the root is a special ending ָה. This triple combination: 1) first person prefix pronoun (sg. or pl.) 2) verb root 3) special ending ָה means the form is **cohortative**.

כֹה **כֹה** In BDB under כֹה

וְנִשְׁתַּחֲוֶה **וְנִשְׁתַּחֲוֶה** The root of this verb is disputed and so is the name of its stem (it will be discussed later in the course), but the interior consonant cluster שׁתחו means we are dealing with a verb meaning *prostrate oneself in worship*. The נ is a prefix pronoun. The ending ֶה could indicate either a regular prefix form or a cohortative, but since the previous verb was cohortative (and the following verb is too), וְנִשְׁתַּחֲוֶה is likely cohortative as well.

וְנָשׁוּבָה **וְנָשׁוּבָה** This is the third cohortative. The root is _____

אֲלֵיכֶם **אֲלֵיכֶם** The suffix כֶם_ is the plural of ךָ_ (See אֶת-בִּנְךָ in Genesis 22:2.)

Genesis 22:6 [Lesson 15]

וַיִּקַּח **וַיִּקַּח** Discussed in comments to the same word in Genesis 22:3.

אֶת־עֲצֵי הָעֹלָה Compare with עֲצֵי עֹלָה (Gen. 22:3).

וַיָּשֶׂם What does the vowel under the prefix pronoun tell you? _____ (6.1a)

בְּיָדוֹ Identify the parts of this word: _____

הַמַּאֲכֶלֶת Is this word a noun or a verb? There is a feature that should tell you: the DDO sign אֵת in front of it. To find the root, take off the definite article ◌ הַ

A מ in front of a verb root can make it into a noun. ת at the end indicates the noun is feminine. You are left with the root אכל which means _____ In BDB, after all the words beginning with only the root letters—in this case א כ ל —are exhausted, the words beginning with preformatives to the root are listed according to the alphabetization of their preformative letter. That is where you will find the noun מַאֲכֶלֶת

שְׁנֵיהֶם The suffix is discussed in 12.4. For שְׁנֵי review vocabulary.

יַחְדָּו Vocabulary word.

Genesis 22:7 [Lesson 15]

וַיֹּאמֶר יִצְחָק Watch for direct speech in this verse; there are several changes of speakers.

אָבִיו . . . אָבִי 10.1b and 10.2b discuss these words. **S 10.1b** goes into more detail.

וְהָעֵצִים This word is made up of four components.

וְאַיֵּה הַשֶּׂה A literal translation would be *and where the sheep*? This is an interrogative noun sentence. (2.10b)

Genesis 22:8 [Lesson 15]

יִרְאֶה־לּוֹ הַשֶּׂה │ יִרְאֶה is the same root, stem, form, and PGN as וַיַּרְא (12.1 and above in verse 4) but without vav conversive. (Prefix forms with vav conversive often use shortened verb forms.) One question in the phrase יִרְאֶה־לּוֹ is how to translate the suffix וֹ of לוֹ The KJV considers it an indirect object, *God will provide himself a lamb;* NRSV treats it as an emphatic: *God himself will provide the lamb . . .;* JPS treats it as an adjective: *God will see to the sheep for His burnt offering;* and Everett Fox, translator of the *Shocken Bible*, vol. 1, has *God will see-for-himself, to the lamb,* a translation that stays closest to the reflexive of the previous uses of ל + suffix (Gen. 22:2 and 5). Another notable difference in these translations is the rendering of רָאָה The choice *provide* comes from the Vulgate's *providebit.*

The Latin word clearly preserves the root concept "see" (the "vide" in provident), so important to this story as well as the whole Abrahamic cycle, but the English "provide" does not.

Genesis 22:9 [Lesson 16]

וַיִּבֶן   12.1 tells how to find the root.

וַיַּעֲרֹךְ   The root is _____

וַיַּעֲקֹד   The root is _____

וַיָּשֶׂם   The root is _____ (6.1a)

אֹתוֹ   Holem is the vowel that goes with the DDO marker אֵת when an object pronoun (except for 2 m. and f. pl) is added. Compare אֹתוֹ with אִתּוֹ (Gen. 22:3).

מִן + מַעַל ‖ מִמַּעַל

Genesis 22:10 [Lesson 16]

לִשְׁחֹט   The preposition לְ in front of a verb is usually a sign of _____ (11.2b)

Genesis 22:11 [Lesson 16]

מַלְאַךְ   This is a noun; is it definite or indefinite? _____ (5.2a)

Genesis 22:12 [Lesson 17]

אַל־תִּשְׁלַח ‖ אַל + the prefix form of the verb expresses a negative command.

וְאַל־תַּעַשׂ   Another negative imperative. But here, a shortened (apocopated) form of the verb (as in a vav conversive construction) is used.

מְאוּמָה   means *anything*.

עַתָּה   Do not confuse this adverb with the independent subject pronoun אַתָּה

יָדַעְתִּי   See remarks to אָהַבְתָּ (Gen. 22:2). Affix would be appropriate for יָדַעְתִּי in any case because the action is taking place at a specific point in time.

יְרֵא   A form of the verb ירא which, being an I class (presented in this lesson), does not have a holem after the first root letter in its Qal participial form. The 3 m. sg. affix יָרֵא *he feared* and the m. sg. participial form יָרֵא *a fearer* are morphologically the same. Here we know that יְרֵא is the participle because it is in construct.

מִמֶּנִּי │ מִמֶּנִּי is the preposition מִן + 1 c. sg. suffix. (10.3b) But why does it take this long form? One explanation is that it arises from duplication of the preposition + suffix: מנ מנ ני

Another explanation is that it arises from an original מִנֶּנִּי which is the preposition

מִן + an **energic** נ suffix. (An energic נ suffix is an object suffix preceded and supposedly "energized," i.e., given vocal emphasis, by an accented נֶ‍ syllable.)

Genesis 22:13 [Lesson 17]

וַיַּרְא . . . וַיִּשָּׂא   A repetition of Genesis 22:4a. ("a" is the part of the verse up to the atnaḥ ‸)

אַיִל   Vocabulary word.

אַחַר │ אַחַר can be the preposition *after, behind* as in Genesis 22:1. It can also be an adverb of place: *hind part, back part* or of time: *after.*

נֶאֱחַז   The root אחז means *seize, grasp.* A נ in front of a root can be one of two things:

1.   The 1 c. pl. prefix pronoun

2.   The sign of some Nifʿal forms

A first person wouldn't make sense here, but the Nifʿal, which can give a verb a passive meaning, would. נֶאֱחַז is the 3 m. sg. Nifʿal affix.

בְּסֻבַךְ │ סֻבַךְ is a noun. ◻ַ בְ ⟵ ◻ הַ + בְ (Cf. בַּבֹּקֶר [Gen. 22:3].)

בְּקַרְנָיו   This word is composed of a preposition + noun + plural (or dual) indicator + suffix. The preposition בְ can express *means* or *instrument*, so here it would mean *by (means of).*

Some Uses of the Preposition בְ

Gen. 22:3	בַּבֹּקֶר
Gen. 22:4	בַּיּוֹם הַשְּׁלִישִׁי
Gen. 22:6	בְּיָדוֹ
Gen. 22:13	בְּקַרְנָיו

וַיַּעֲלֵהוּ   In Genesis 22:2 you saw וְהַעֲלֵהוּ a Hifʿil imperative + 3 m. sg. object suffix הוּ‎ וַיַּעֲלֵהוּ is a Hifʿil prefix + vav conversive with the same suffix. What happened to the characteristic ה in front of the root, marking the Hifʿil? As we saw in another Hifʿil prefix form, וַיַּשְׁכֵּם (Gen. 22:3), it elided. In וַיַּעֲלֵהוּ only one characteristic of the Hifʿil prefix is left: pataḥ under the prefix pronoun. Truth be told, with this particular verb in the prefix form, stem identification can be difficult because the vowel under the prefix pronoun may be pataḥ in the Qal of 1st gutturals as well. But the suffix helps because עלה is consistently intransitive in the Qal and transitive in the Hifʿil.

Genesis 22:14 [Lesson 17]

שֵׁם־הַמָּקוֹם הַהוּא   When הוּא functions as an attributive adjective, it takes the definite article. Literally: *the name of the place, the that one.* Idiomatically: *the name of that place.*

יהוה יִרְאֶה   These words can be translated *Adonai will see/sees.* Other translations or transliterations are: KJV: *Jehovah jireh;* JPS: *Adonai-yireh* ; NRSV: *The Lord will provide;* and Everett Fox: *YHWH sees.*

יֵאָמֵר   The root and prefix pronoun are familiar, but the vowel pattern indicates that יֵאָמֵר is neither the Qal nor the Hifʿil (see synopsis of אמר in Genesis 22:2). יֵאָמֵר is the 3 m. sg. Nifʿal prefix form. The Nifʿal affix form is distinctive because it has a preformative נ as the name Nifʿal suggests. But in the Nifʿal prefix, the preformative נ assimilates and is represented by dagesh forte in the first root letter. If the first root letter is a guttural, the vowel under the prefix pronoun lengthens to compensate. Despite the difficulties caused by the assimilated נ the Nifʿal prefix can be recognized by a characteristic vowel pattern:

Nifʿal Prefix Vowel Pattern

For roots beginning with a guttural   ◌ָ ◌ֳ ◌ָ | ◌ֵ

For other roots   ◌ַ ◌ֻ ◌ָֹ | ◌ִ

הַיּוֹם   Literally, *the day,* often translated idiomatically *today* or *until this day.*

בְּהַר יהוה יֵרָאֶה   There is more than one way to translate these words.

First, let us assume that the phrase בְּהַר יהוה is not a construct chain. בְּהַר would be *on a mountain,* and יהוה would be the subject of יֵרָאֶה another 3 m. sg. Nifʿal prefix (note the distinctive vowel pattern). The three words would then read: *on a mountain the Lord will be seen* (or *will appear*).

A more popular reading takes בְּהַר יהוה as a construct chain. The translation would then be *on the mountain of the Lord, he will be seen.*

A third approach is taken by some scholars who go with the construct chain, *on the mountain of the Lord,* but believe that the Nif`al יֵרָאֶה is a scribal error, that it should be יִרְאֶה a Qal and therefore active: *he will see* or *he will provide.*

No matter what one does with this clause, it's tricky. For the whole verse, here are the translations from the previously cited sources. Note how each deals with grammar and vocabulary.

KJV: *And Abraham called the name of that place Jehovah jireh: as it is said to this day, In the mount of the Lord, it shall be seen.*

NRSV: *So Abraham called the name of that place, "the Lord will provide"; as it is said to this day, "on the mount of the Lord, it shall be provided."*

JPS: *And Abraham named that site Adonai-yireh, whence the present saying, "on the mount of the Lord there is vision."*

Fox: *Avraham called the name of that place: YHWH Sees. As the saying is today: On YHWH'S mountain (it) is seen.*

My preference would be: *And Abraham called the name of the place "Adonai will see," because /where it is said today, "On the mountain of Adonai, he will be seen."*

בְּאֵר שֶׁבַע מִבְּאֵר שֶׁבַע | בְּאֵר שֶׁבַע is the name of a place. בְּאֵר means *well.* שֶׁבַע is a vocabulary word. A construct chain will solve the grammatical connection, and Genesis 21:24–34 can explain the semantic connection.

חָרָנָה The name of a place plus ה directive. (11.3)

וַיִּפְגַּע What kind of dagesh is in the ג _____ (3.3) The stem is _____

וַיָּלֶן If you are having trouble determining the root, refer to 6.1a.

כִּי־בָא הַשֶּׁמֶשׁ What are the two possible forms for בָא _____ (9.5a) Do you think either verb form could be used here? בוֹא הַשֶּׁמֶשׁ is an image of the sun entering the earth.

מֵאַבְנֵי The root is _____ The preposition is pointed מֵ instead of מִ because _____ (see מֵרָחֹק Gen. 22:4). מִן is being used in the partitive sense to mean *some of.*

מְרַאֲשֹׁתָיו The root is _____ (vocabulary word). This noun appears rarely, but always in the plural and with a suffix.

סֻלָּם This word, whose only occurrence (academic term is hapax legomenon) in the Hebrew Bible is here, is most often translated *ladder.* It is probably from the root סלל which means *lift up* or *cast up.* So even if *ladder* is not precise, we can assume from associated words and the context that some sort of thing-that-goes-up is meant.

מֻצָּב At this stage, מֻצָּב is too difficult for you to analyze. It is a Hof`al (passive of the Hif`il) participle of נצב a root that means *take one's stand.* Since English does not use the phraseology *caused to be set up,* translators go with *set up* or *stationed.* It so happens that מֻצָּב can be found listed as a noun meaning *palisade,* but that meaning does not literally fit the context here (or perhaps it does to the extent that a palisade's verticality enhances the image of the verb).

אַרְצָה The unaccented ה_ ending can be ה directive (11.3) or ה locative. Some grammarians consider these to be the same construction; others think they are completely different. The important thing is that both *place to which* and *place at which* or *on which* can be expressed by unaccented final

וְרֹאשׁוֹ_הָ To what does the suffix refer? _____

מַגִּיעַ Like מֻצָּב just previous, מַגִּיעַ is also a participle. (All participles except those in the Qal and Niʿfal have a preformative מ) As the dagesh in the צ of מֻצָּב represents the assimilated נ of the root, so does the dagesh in the ג of מַגִּיעַ The root of מַגִּיעַ then, is נגע which means *touch* or *reach*. However, the stems of מֻצָּב and מַגִּיעַ are different, as the vowel patterns might indicate. Pataḥ under a preformative element and an I class vowel between the second and third root letters are strong indicators of the Hifʿil in the prefix, imperative, participle, and infinitive forms (see, e.g., וַיַּשְׁכֵּם Gen. 22:3). Although the Hifʿil is usually causative or transitive, נגע is a verb that sometimes has an intransitive meaning in the Hifʿil, as it seems to here: *touching* or *reaching*.

הַשָּׁמָיְמָה The components of this word are _____

עֹלִים The ḥolem __ after the first root letter identifies the form as a _____ (9.3a) The endiNG is _____ (6.5a) That leaves two letters for the root. If you can't figure out the root, re-read the comments about וְהַעֲלֵהוּ (Gen. 22:2) and study your vocabulary.

בוֹ Preposition + suffix.

Genesis 28:13 [Lesson 19]

נִצָּב The same root as מֻצָּב (Gen. 28:12), but what is the stem? It looks a lot like a Piʿel, but a Piʿel affix would not have a qamats __ as the second vowel in a closed syllable (see under the Piʿel column of Verb Chart A). נִצָּב is a Nifʿal participle; *stationed* would be a good translation. Remember: all participles (as in the Hofʿal מֻצָּב and the Hifʿil מַגִּיעַ [Gen. 28:12]) have a preformative מ except those in the Qal and Nifʿal. Also, הִנֵּה frequently announces a participle. The visible נ in נִצָּב is the stem indicator of the Nifʿal affix and participle. The dagesh represents the assimilated נ of the root. (16.1a)

ננצב

נ of the root ↑↑ נ preformative of the Nifʿal affix and participle

וַיֹּאמַר Starting in Genesis 28:12 there has been a series of constructions made up of הִנֵּה followed by a participle. The reappearance of a finite verb means that the main narrative has resumed. (13.2) (The מ is pointed with pataḥ __ because of the strong disjunctive accent.)

יִצְחָק There is a major break in the sense of the verse after the atnaḥ __

שֹׁכֵב ‎| הָאָ֫רֶץ אֲשֶׁר אַתָּה שֹׁכֵב עָלֶ֫יהָ has the vowel pattern of a _____
(9.5) עָלֶ֫יהָ is the feminine counterpart of עָלָיו The suffix refers to _____

Why does the ה of עָלֶ֫יהָ not have a mappiq? _____ (**S 14.3**) Translating the Hebrew, the result is: *the ground, which you are lying on her.* English would turn that to *the ground on which you are lying.*

לָךְ See 19.3b.

אֶתְּנֶ֫נָּה At this point in the verse, a verb is needed, and since this is direct speech in the first person (clear from the אֲנִי earlier in the verse), it would make sense to take the א as a first person prefix pronoun. That the verb is נתן then becomes clear from the dagesh forte in the תּ and the following נ But what about the נֶ֫נָּה at the end of the word? It is the 3 f. sg. energic נ suffix, which is characterized by an accented penultimate נֶ֫ syllable. (מִמֶּ֫נִּי in Genesis 22:12 has a 1 c. sg. energic נ suffix). In the word אֶתְּנֶ֫נָּה the suffix נֶ֫נָּה is 3 f. sg., referring to הָאָ֫רֶץ

וּלְזַרְעֶ֫ךָ ‎| וּ is the same conjunction as וְ but will appear as וּ in most cases when the next letter is shewa. (**S 14.3.1**) In English, four words are needed for this one in Hebrew. Look at its components: conjunction + preposition + noun + suffix.

A comment on the word order in the "b" part of this verse: הָאָ֫רֶץ standing at the front is emphasized and לָךְ placed in front of the verb is also emphasized.

Genesis 28:14 [Lesson 19]

כֶּעֲפַר Here כֶּ is not analogous to בַּ in בַּבֹּ֫קֶר (Gen. 22:3). כֶּעֲפַר being in construct cannot have the definite article. It is pointed כֶּעֲפַר instead of כְּעֲפַר to obviate the problem of there being two vocal shewas in a row (see וַאֲנִי in Genesis 22:5 and the rule of shewa **S 14.3.1**).

וּפָרַצְתָּ For וּ ← וְ see **S 14.3.2**.

יָ֫מָּה וָקֵ֫דְמָה וְצָפֹ֫נָה וָנֶ֫גְבָּה Aside from providing four nice examples of ה directive, these words are the names of the four directions. (For vocalization of the ו see **S 11.2**.) Imagine yourself standing in Israel:

יָם	West	⟷	sea
קֶדֶם	East	⟷	in front of, before
צָפוֹן	North	⟷	hide (beyond the mountains)
נֶגֶב	South	⟷	be dry

וְנִבְרְכוּ Remove the conjunction and the 3 m. pl. affix pronoun to get closer to the root. Which of the remaining letters do you think is "extra?" Root letters are found together in a cluster. (There is no reason to discard the כ because if it were part of a suffix it would come after everything else.) That leaves נ which can be either the 1 c. pl. prefix pronoun or the sign of the Nif`al. If it were the 1 c. pl. prefix pronoun, ו at the end of the word would be extraneous. That leaves us with a Nif`al preformative. The form is affix + vav reversive and the PGN is _____

מִשְׁפְּחֹת This is a מ preformative noun; it is also a vocabulary word. The endiNG ת‍ֹ is feminine plural.

וּבְזַרְעֶךָ This word is like the last word in Genesis 28:13. Note that in both cases the vowel under the ע is a segol ‍ֶ Normally the vowel would be a shewa ‍ְ but, as discussed in this lesson (19.5), at a strong disjunctive accent there can be a change in the vowel.

Genesis 28:15 [Lesson 19]

עִמָּךְ The usual pointing for this word is עִמְּךָ But as with וּבְזַרְעֶךָ it is in pause (19.5) (another term for strong disjunctive accent). In this case, though, the vowel retreats a syllable (common with ‍ָךְ in pause). Why is there a dagesh in the מ Many two-letter nouns and some prepositions are derived from geminate roots. When a suffix is added to such words, their geminate origins are manifested by actual doubling or more often by a dagesh forte. Note: יָמָּה (in Genesis 28:14) has a dagesh for the same reason.

וּשְׁמַרְתִּיךָ A verb with a suffix acts like a noun with respect to vowel changes. The most common progression is that the pretonic vowel (the one just before the accent) is long and the propretonic vowel (two before the accent) is short. (S 5.1c.2–3). What this means for a verb in the Qal is that the identifying qamats ‍ָ under the first root letter shortens to a shewa. But you can deduce that this isn't one of the derived stems because there is no stem preformative or dagesh forte in the middle root letter.

וַהֲשִׁבֹתִיךָ The beginning and ending of this word are almost identical to the beginning and ending of וּשְׁמַרְתִּיךָ Here the וּ is pointed with a patah because _____ (**S 14.3.1**) After dealing with the conjunction, suffix and affix pronoun, you are left with הֹשֵׁב but that is not a root. The הֹ is a Hif`il indicator, and the root is the hollow verb שׁוּב Note the second Hif`il feature: the I class vowel, ḥireq ִ in place of the middle root vowel וּ Hollow verbs in the second and first persons in the Hif`il affix have an extra וֹ syllable added before the affix pronoun. Just why is not clear. The Hif`il of שׁוּב is *cause to return* or *bring back*.

אֶעֱזָבְךָ After the כִּי a switch is made from affix + vav conversive to prefix form. Take note of the vowels in אֶעֱזָבְךָ The ḥolem that would normally be between the second and third root letters of a Qal prefix has been shortened to qamats ḥatuf.

עַד אֲשֶׁר אִם These three words can be translated *until*. In other words, it is the preposition עַד that carries the meaning. אֲשֶׁר signals that a clause is coming but after a preposition is not translated, and אִם here is pleonastic (it has no specific meaning of its own), but BDB suggests that after a negative clause it emphasizes a contrasting idea.

עָשִׂיתִי You can take off the ־תִי as an affix subject pronoun, but the root cannot be עשׂי because no Biblical Hebrew root ends in י The י is there because at an earlier stage of the language, many verb roots that are now 3rd ה were 3rd י That ancient י reasserts itself in the affix form of the second and third persons or, put another way, before an affix pronoun that begins with a consonant.

דִּבַּרְתִּי If this poses a problem, do not party Saturday night. Do not pass *Go*. Do not collect $200.00.

לָךְ See 19.5.

Genesis 28:16 [Lesson 20]

וַיִּיקַץ 17.2 discusses this type of verb.

מִשְּׁנָתוֹ | שֵׁנָה is the noun *sleep* (found in BDB under ישׁן). When feminine nouns that end in ה have a suffix added to them, the final ה becomes ת

אָכֵן An adverb.

יֵשׁ A predicator of existence, *there is*.

יָדַ֫עְתִּי For tense, see יָדַ֫עְתִּי Genesis 22:12. It is worth repeating that a function of the affix is to express completed action or action with a fixed sense of time; past tense is not the only way to capture that feature of the form. For example, in Genesis 22:12 the adverb עַתָּה denotes the time, and in this verse Jacob is referring to the moment of his awakening.

Genesis 28:17 [Lesson 20]

מַה־נּוֹרָא │ מָה מָה is the interrogative pronoun *what? which?* It is also an exclamation *how! what!* What about the root of נּוֹרָא In an earlier stage of the language, most 1st י verbs used to be 1st ו That ancient ו takes the place of the present י in stems other than Qal, after a preformative letter or prefix pronoun. In נּוֹרָא the נ is a Nif`al preformative and the root is יָרֵא נּוֹרָא is a m. sg. Nif`al participle. The phrase מַה־נּוֹרָא means *How awesome* or *how to be feared.* KJV: *how dreadful*; NRSV and JPS: *how awesome*; Fox: *how awe-inspiring.*

אֵין │ אֵין אֵין is the negative of יֵשׁ (Gen. 28:16). יֵשׁ is what it is. אֵין is what it ain't!

כִּי אִם │ כִּי אִם After a negative, כִּי אִם means *but, but indeed, except.*

וְזֶה שַׁ֫עַר Why does the adjective precede the noun? _____ (15.2)

Three Uses for an Adjective

1. **Attributive:** Modifies a noun. It follows the noun and must agree with it in gender, number, and definiteness: הָאֲדָמָה הַזֹּאת (Gen. 28:15)   סֻלָּם מֻצָּב (Gen. 28:12)

2. **Predicate:** It functions as the predicate of a noun sentence: וְהָאֶבֶן גְּדֹלָה (Gen. 29:2)

3. **Substantive:** Makes a noun out of an adjective: יְרֵא אֱלֹהִים (Gen. 22:12)

Genesis 28:18 [Lesson 20]

וַיַּשְׁכֵּם For a discussion of the stem, see Genesis 22:3, same word.

מְרַאֲשֹׁתָיו Genesis 28:11, same word.

אֹתָהּ When אֵת is followed by an object pronoun, the pointing changes to ḥolem (in all PGNs except 2 m. and f. pl.). You will see it both plene אוֹתָהּ and defectiva as it is here.

מַצֵּבָה A מ preformative noun from the root נצב seen earlier in מֻצָּב (Gen. 28:12) and in נִצָּב (Gen. 28:13). It means *pillar* —the type used in worship (which, in later times, the Israelites were told not to set up). This word fits in with the phrase immediately preceding, either by our assuming a comma after אַתָּה or adding a link such as *as a*.

וַיִּצֹק According to the missing-letter rules, this looks like it should be missing its third root letter (12.1), but it isn't. יצק is one of a small class of 1st י verbs that act like 1st נ (**S 17.2** discusses types of 1st י verbs.) But in this occurrence of וַיִּצֹק there is not even a dagesh forte in the צ to compensate for the י of the root.

עַל־רֹאשָׁה To what is the suffix ה referring? _____

Genesis 28:19 [Lesson 21]

אוּלָם *But*

לוּז שֵׁם־הָעִיר A noun sentence (2.10b) + a construct chain. (5.1b)

לָרִאשֹׁנָה An adverb meaning *at first, formerly* from the root _____

Genesis 28:20 [Lesson 21]

וַיִּדַּר . . . נֶדֶר It is common Hebrew style to use the same root in different ways close together. It strengthens the idea and is euphonic.

לֵאמֹר A preposition in front of a verb root almost certainly signals an infinitive (tsere ֵ under the attached preposition occurs only in the words לֵאמֹר and לֵאלֹהִים).

In Hebrew, an infinitive is not always translated "to + verb." It can be "verb + ing," that is, a gerund. It gives the idea of the verb in the abstract sense. Both infinitives and participles have verb and noun-like qualities, but there is a distinction between the two.

> The **participle** stresses the doer of the action.

> The **infinitive** focuses on the action itself.

אִם | אִם is introducing a string of clauses.

עִמָּדִי A lengthened form of עִם with the 1 c. sg. object suffix.

וּשְׁמָרַנִי | נִי ____ is another form of the 1 c. sg. object suffix. (10.3b) The verb is a 3 m. sg. Qal affix with vav reversive. Without the suffix, the verb would be vocalized שָׁמַר But a verb with a suffix tends to lead to pretonic lengthening and propretonic reduction of vowels, so the מ of שָׁמַר now pretonic in וּשְׁמָרַ֫נִי is lengthened to מָ and שְׁ now propretonic is reduced to שְׁ The question is: Could the 3 m. sg. affix + suffix be confused with an imperative + suffix? Not if you know what to look for. Patah ַ before the suffix is the vowel the 3 m. sg. affix takes; in the m. sg. imperative, the vowel before the suffix is most likely to be tsere ֵ *Guard me* would be שָׁמְרֵ֫נִי (the qamats under the שׁ is a qamats ḥatuf). In unpointed texts, both forms would look the same.

הוֹלֵךְ Notice the plene spelling.

לֶאֱכֹל For the vowel under the preposition, see **S 14.3.1**. A Qal infinitive construct usually has a simple shewa under the first root letter, but when the first root letter is a guttural, it takes a composite shewa.

לִלְבֹּשׁ Here the problem of there being two vocal shewas in a row is resolved in the most usual way:
ִ ְ ← ְ ְ (**S 14.3.1**)

Genesis 28:21 [Lesson 21]

וְשַׁבְתִּי After removing the conjunction and affix pronoun, you are left with two letters for the root. In the Qal affix, 3rd ה and hollow verbs may show only two root letters. But only hollow verbs have the vowel patah ַ (instead of qamats ָ) under the first root letter in the first and second persons. Thus the root here is _____

בְּשָׁלוֹם When you are looking for a root, remember that a plene spelling does not introduce a new consonant.

Question: How far does the conditional אִם continue to govern the verbs? If one takes the אִם to this point and begins the next clause with "then," it seems that the promises God offered (verse 15) will have been met. There is nothing in the grammar, though, that determines which verb begins the apodosis (main clause of a conditional sentence). One of my translations leaves the apodosis until the beginning of the next verse!

וְהָיָה יהוה לִי לֵאלֹהִים 7.5 talks about some uses of ל BDB devotes some sixteen columns to that preposition.

Genesis 28:22 [Lesson 21]

וְהָאֶבֶן Note: אֶבֶן is feminine (well, almost always). How do we know that it is here?

שַׂמְתִּי For help with the root, see וְשַׁבְתִּי (Gen. 28:21).

268

מַצֵּבָה   For help with the syntax, see Genesis 28:18.

תִּתֶּן־לִי   16.6 concentrates on this verb. The second vowel has been shortened from tsere ֵ to segol ֶ because of the maqqef.

עַשֵּׂר אֲעַשְּׂרֶנּוּ   Notice that the consonants ר שׂ ע are common to both words.

First look at אֲעַשְּׂרֶנּוּ An א in front of a root can be a prefix pronoun, which is what is here. That means that נוּ ֶ at the end cannot be an affix subject pronoun; it must have some other function. Note that the end of the word is not simply נוּ ֶ but נּוּ ֶ an energic נ suffix (as in אֶתְּנֶנָּה [Gen. 28:13]). The suffix נּוּ ֶ (not to be confused with plain נוּ ֶ) actually has two possible meanings: it can be the 1 c. pl. object pronoun *us* or it can be the 3 m. sg. object pronoun *him/it*. That it could mean *us* is apparent; that it could mean *him* or *it* is not. The reason it can be is because נּוּ ֶ can be a contraction of a fuller spelling נְהוּ ֶ whose ה has elided. (For an example of the endiNG with ה see Exodus 15:2.)

Now look at the word עַשֵּׂר Hebrew has two infinitives. You have already seen the infinitive construct. As its name implies, you can build with it: prepositions on the front, suffixes at the end. עַשֵּׂר is an example of the other infinitive, the **infinitive absolute**, here in the Pi`el. The infinitive absolute serves to intensify the idea of the root. It most commonly stands right before the conjugated verb, usually in the same stem. English has no corresponding construction that uses the verb twice, so most translators use the verb and an adverb such as *surely* or *indeed* to convey the intensification. Everett Fox is one translator who regularly keeps the double use of the verb. The whole clause עַשֵּׂר אֲעַשְּׂרֶנּוּ לָּךְ translates *I shall tithe, tithe it to you* or *surely I will tithe it to you*.

Genesis 29:1 [Lesson 22]

רַגְלָיו   Constructed like נְעָרָיו (Gen. 22:3).

בְּנֵי | בְּנֵי־קֶדֶם   בְּנֵי in front of a name is one of the ways of referring to a people. The most common example is בְּנֵי־יִשְׂרָאֵל translated variously as *the sons of Israel, the children of Israel, the people of Israel,* or *Israelites.*

Genesis 29:2 [Lesson 22]

שָׂדֶה | ה ֶ is a m. sg. noun ending; a feminine noun ending is ה ָ

שְׁלֹשָׁה עֶדְרֵי־צֹאן   What you are seeing is not a feminine adjective modifying a m. pl. noun and, what would be even more irregular, preceding the noun! Numbers in Hebrew have a complicated and varied grammar. Here the number שְׁלֹשָׁה is being used as a substantive: *a triad, flocks of sheep* → *three flocks of sheep*.

עָלֶיהָ For the suffix, see 14.3.

הַהוּא This word is really הַהִיא When a word in the Hebrew Bible is spelled "incorrectly," the consonants are not changed, but the correct spelling is noted in the margin. The word is to be pronounced <u>not</u> the way it is written but according to the marginal notation. This system is called כְּתִב (ketiv: written) קְרֵא (qere: read). Some words are so commonly spelled "incorrectly" that the error is not noted. This is called qere perpetuum. Such is the case for הַהוּא which appears as it does here all but some twelve times in the Bible.

יַשְׁקוּ Why can this not be a 3 m. pl. Qal affix? _____ (13.5) Furthermore, ישׁק is not a root, so the י is likely a prefix pronoun. That leaves only two letters for the root. Since the vowel under the prefix pronoun is not tsere ֵ the root is probably not a 1st י And since the vowel under the prefix pronoun is not qamats ָ the root is probably not hollow. It is not a 1st נ because _____ (Although shewa can make dagesh forte disappear and נשׁק is a root, it is not the root here.) That leaves 3rd ה שׁקה means *to give drink* →*to water* and it occurs almost exclusively in the Hifʿil. In יַשְׁקוּ only one feature of the Hifʿil prefix is manifest: patah under the prefix pronoun. There is no I class vowel between the second and third root letters because there is no third root letter. A word about tense: Prefix form is usually translated in the future, but it has a dominant imperfective sense, and in the context of this narrative *they used to water* is an effective translation.

וְהָאֶבֶן גְּדֹלָה The conjunction וְ on a noun, especially when the noun (or pronoun) is the subject of a new clause, can have a contrasting sense such as *now* or *but*. The adjective follows the noun, but is it an attributive adjective? (14.2c and 15.2)

פִּי See vocabulary word פֶּה

Genesis 29:3 [Lesson 22]

וְנֶאֶסְפוּ Like וְנִבְרְכוּ (Gen. 28:14), but the guttural א frequently attracts segol ֶ at the beginning of a word. All the verbs in this verse are affix forms + vav reversive, but they are not translated in the future. (As you read on in the narrative, you will see why.) These verbs use the other function of vav reversive, which is for actions that were repeated over a period of time.

שָׁמָּה | שָׁם with ה directive or locative has a dagesh forte in the מ It just does!

כָּל־הָעֲדָרִים Text note 3ª in BHS, indicated by the ª at the end of הָעֲדָרִים points to some manuscripts that read הָרֹעִים instead. After finishing the rest of the verse, go back to this phrase to see why there might be such a reading. (There is an explanation on the use of text notes after the comments to Exodus 3:1.)

וְגָלֲלוּ A root cannot begin with the same two letters, but the second and third root letters can twin. Such roots are called geminates, and, as you will discover, they can cause no end of trouble. Here, fortunately, the components are straightforward.

מֵעַל A compound preposition. For the vowel under the מ see מֵרָחֹק (Gen. 22:4).

וְהִשְׁקוּ Hif`il affix of שׁקה with vav reversive. (The same verb appeared in the Hif`il prefix in Genesis 29:2.)

וְהֵשִׁיבוּ The Hif`il affix of שׁוּב with vav reversive. The preformative הֵ and an I class ("dot) vowel between the second and third root letters (in the case of hollow verbs, the I class vowel takes the place of the middle root letter) are the stem indicators.

לִמְקֹמָהּ Components: preposition + noun + suffix. The הָ cannot be the ה directive because:

1. It has a mappiq, which is always the sign of _____ (14.3)

2. It is the accented syllable.

3. The preposition לְ gives the meaning of direction toward.

To what is the הָ referring? _____ Notice the defectiva spelling: לִמְקֹמָהּ Plene would be לִמְקוֹמָהּ (For the vowel under the לְ see **S 14.3.1**.)

Genesis 29:4 [Lesson 23]

וַיֹּאמֶר לָהֶם יַעֲקֹב Compare this to וַיֹּאמֶר אֵלָיו אַבְרָהָם (Gen. 22:1). The components are the same in both cases, but they don't translate the same way.

אַחַי This word is in the vocative. (18.2) As was the case in that lesson sentence, there are no guidelines here other than context to identify that part of speech. About the suffix—you have already seen that יִ is the sign of the 1 c. sg. possessive suffix.

If the noun is singular, you will see יִ as in אָחִי *my brother.*

If the noun is plural, you will see יַ as in אַחַי *my brothers.*

Two Common but Irregular Nouns: אָב and אָח

אָבִי	*my father*	אָחִי	*my brother*
אֲבִי	*father of*	אֲחִי	*brother of*
אֲבוֹתַי	*my fathers*	אַחַי	*my brothers*
אֲבוֹתֵי	*fathers of*	אֲחֵי	*brothers of*

מֵאַיִן   A compound preposition *from where.* Found in BDB under [אַיִן], a sublisting of אַי

Genesis 29:5 [Lesson 23]

הַיְדַעְתֶּם   The PGN is _____ The form is _____ The root is _____

That leaves the הַ unaccounted for. Is it the sign of the Hif`il? Not here. In 1st י verbs, the addition of a stem preformative causes the י of the root to appear as a וֹ so the 2 m. pl. Hif`il affix of ידע for example, would be הוֹדַעְתֶּם A הַ in front of a verb or noun can be the interrogative particle (see the particle section at the beginning of the vocabulary list). Usually the interrogative הַ is pointed הֲ but it may be pointed הַ or rarely הֶ In הַיְדַעְתֶּם a full vowel is needed under the interrogative הַ to avoid there being two vocal shewas in a row. Context would indicate present tense translation even though הַיְדַעְתֶּם is an affix form. This is discussed in the phrase כִּי עַתָּה יָדַעְתִּי (Gen. 22:12).

לְבָן בֶּן־נָחוֹר   This is how a person's full name is expressed in Hebrew: *so-and-so* בֶּן (or בַּת) *so-and-so.*

יְדָעְנוּ   What about the נוּ____ Is it the 1 c. pl. affix pronoun (13.5) or the 1 c. pl. suffix *us?* (18.3b) Which makes more sense? (It cannot be the 3 m. sg. suffix as in אֲעַשְּׂרֶנּוּ [Gen. 28:22] because the only time נוּ____ can be a 3 m. sg. suffix is when it is the energic נּוּ__) Note that although English might add an object pronoun here, Hebrew doesn't require one.

Genesis 29:6 [Lesson 23]

הֲשָׁלוֹם   The noun שָׁלוֹם is in Genesis 28:21. It is a word with a broad range of meanings: *completeness, wholeness, well-being, welfare, peace.* What about the הֲ in front? You have seen a הַ in front of a word as a sign of the Hif`il, as the definite article, and as an interrogative particle. You should be able to eliminate two of these possibilities here. ("Context" doesn't count as a sufficient reason this time.) The phrase הֲשָׁלוֹם לוֹ should be treated as an interrogative noun sentence.

בִּתּוֹ ‖ בַּת is an irregular noun; בִּתּוֹ shows the change in vocalization when a suffix is added. Why the dagesh forte? Because the original consonants of בַּת were בִּנְת The נ has assimilated and shows as a dagesh forte when a suffix is added. It does not show in בַּת because dagesh forte rarely occurs in the last letter of a word.

בָּאָה Both the 3 m. and f. sg. Qal affix and the m. and f. sg. Qal participle of a hollow verb look the same. (9.5a and for further explanation **S 9.5a**) Which is the intended form here? Well, הִנֵּה intro-duces the clause, which points to its being a participle. Also, the accent can be a clue. If it is placed with the first syllable, the form is probably affix. So here, the accent is supporting the participial form, and in this context a participle makes more sense.

Genesis 29:7 [Lesson 23]

הֵן A shortened form of הִנֵּה

הַיּוֹם גָּדוֹל What kind of adjective is גָּדוֹל here? _____ (15.2) Compare with וְהָאֶבֶן גְּדֹלָה (Gen. 29:2)

עֵת Vocabulary word.

הֵאָסֵף What will you take off to find the root? This is yet another use of a preformative ה It is the in-dicator of two Nif`al (yes, Nif`al) forms: the imperative and the infinitive. Here הֵאָסֵף is the infinitive construct in construct. Starting with לֹא עֵת the translation reads *it is not time for the gathering together of the sheep* → *for the sheep to be gathered*. The vowel pattern ⌣⌣⌣ֳ | ָ or ⌣⌣⌣ֳ | ֵ before a guttural or ר (or at least the beginning of the pattern) is the signpost of the Nif`al in the prefix, imperative, and in-finitive forms. ( יֵאָמֵר in Genesis 22:14 is an example of the Nif`al prefix.)

הַמִּקְנֶה The root letters are _____

הַשְׁקוּ This is the third occurrence of שׁקה in this chapter. A preformative ה or _ under a prefix pronoun has been a consistent identifier:

יַשְׁקוּ 3 m. pl. Hif`il prefix (Gen. 29:2)

וְהִשְׁקוּ 3 m. pl. Hif`il affix (Gen. 29:3)

הַשְׁקוּ m. pl. Hif`il imperative (Gen. 29:7)

וְרְעוּ The PGN is _____ That leaves _____ for root letters. 20.3 explains that in an imperative form missing a root letter, the missing letter can be in the first, second, or third position. In the case of this word, there is a root for all those possibilities. As a reward for so much hard work so far, here's a suggestion: try the third position first.

Genesis 29:8 [Lesson 24]

נוּכַל The root of נוּכַל is יכל *be able* (an irregular verb). It can be recognized in the prefix form by the vowel וּ after the prefix pronoun. No one understands the formation, so it's best to just learn to recognize it.

עַד אֲשֶׁר When a preposition is in front of אֲשֶׁר the preposition is translated and אֲשֶׁר becomes "silent." So עַד אֲשֶׁר means *until*. What, then, is the function of the אֲשֶׁר It indicates that a clause is coming. (See also עַד אֲשֶׁר אִם in Genesis 28:15.)

יֵאָסְפוּ This is the third occurrence in this chapter of the verb אסף in the Nif`al.

נֶאֶסְפוּ	3 m. pl. Nif`al affix (Gen. 29:3)
הֵאָסֵף	Nif`al infinitive (Gen. 29:7)
יֵאָסְפוּ	3 m. pl. Nif`al prefix (Gen. 29:8)

You saw the same stem and form in יֵאָמֵר and יֵרָאֶה (Gen. 22:14). Note the meteg after the vowel qamats אָ It is there to keep the syllable open; otherwise the qamats could be read as qamats ḥatuf. You should hear four syllables in יֵאָסְפוּ

וְגָלֲלוּ Genesis 29:3, same word.

וְהִשְׁקִינוּ Glance back to הַשְׁקוּ (Gen. 29:7). The summary there should be of value in determining the stem and form of this verb. The discussion in Genesis 28:15 of the י after the second root letter in וְהִשְׁקִינוּ applies to עָשִׂיתִי

Genesis 29:9 [Lesson 24]

עוֹדֶנּוּ מְדַבֵּר | עוֹדֶנּוּ is עוֹד + energic נ suffix (seen in מִמֶּנִּי [Gen. 22:12], אֶתְּנֶנָּה [Gen. 28:13], and אֲעַשְּׂרֶנּוּ [Gen. 28:22]). In עוֹדֶנּוּ the suffix is 3 m. sg. referring to Jacob. Now for מְדַבֵּר All participles except those in the Qal and Nif`al begin with מ So what is the stem here? _____ The two words are translated *while he was still speaking*.

עִמָּם The ה of the 3 m. pl. suffix הֶם_ often elides, leaving only the ם_

וְרָחֵל When a temporal clause precedes the main clause, the main clause is regularly introduced by וֹ (See, e.g., Genesis 22:1. For the range of uses of וֹ see **S 43.3**.)

בָּאָה In Genesis 29:6, same word, there is a discussion of the form.

לְאָבִיהָ For help with the suffix, see 14.3 or עָלֶיהָ (Gen. 28:13). Why the י (10.1b)

רֹעָה This is a f. sg. participle of a 3rd הֹ verb. The m. sg. would be רֹעֶה To review the functions of participles, see 9.3b.

הִוא For the spelling, see discussion of הַהוּא at Genesis 29:2.

Genesis 29:10 [Lesson 24]

וַיְהִי כַּאֲשֶׁר | *And it was as . . .* often rendered more colloquially *and when.*

For the construction and function of כַּאֲשֶׁר see עַד אֲשֶׁר (Gen. 29:8).

אֲחִי If necessary, consult the chart: Two Common but Irregular Nouns אָח and אָב at Genesis 29:4.

אִמּוֹ There is a conjunction אִם which does not take a suffix, and there is a noun אֵם from the root אמם which can.

Synopsis

אִם	*if*
עִם	*with*
עִמּוֹ	*with him*
עַם	*people*
עַמּוֹ	*his people*
אֵם	*mother*
אִמּוֹ	*his mother*

וַיִּגַּשׁ Featured in 16.5b.

וַיָּגֶל This verb appears in the Qal affix form וְגָלְלוּ in Genesis 29:3 and 8. Here it is a Qal prefix. The qamats under the prefix pronoun makes it look like a hollow verb (6.1a), but in some forms geminates often masquerade as hollows. Why is the second ל missing? Final letters are often not doubled.

וַיַּשְׁקְ See יַשְׁקוּ (Gen. 29:2) for the stem. In יַשְׁקוּ the third root letter ה is missing because of the prefix complement. Here it is missing because this is a shortened form with vav conversive. The 3 m. sg. Hif`il prefix form without vav conversive is יַשְׁקֶה

Genesis 29:11 [Lesson 24]

וַיִּשַּׁק Where is the missing root letter? _____ (7.1a) This is not a form of שׁקה If you mix up these two verbs, you will have Jacob watering Rachel and kissing the sheep.

קֹלוֹ Defectiva spelling.

וַיֵּבְךְּ 16.3a discusses this verb. The sound of ךְּ is a hard, catch-in-the-throat "k" sound. (4.4a)

הָיָה רֹעֶה   The combination of הָיָה in the affix form + participle gives emphasis to ongoing action in the past. רֹעֶה being a participle, can be translated verbally, *was shepherding,* or as the noun *shepherd.* The choice will depend on context.

אֶת־צֹאן   This is a DDO but there is no definite article. Looking ahead to the next few words, you can see that צֹאן is the first part of a construct chain and the definiteness of the word in the absolute makes the whole chain definite. (5.2)

חֹתְנוֹ   The root is _____

וַיִּנְהַג   Prefix form + vav conversive means that the action took place at a specific time or occasion. Together with the participle just before, we get *he was a shepherd* or *and he was shepherding . . . and he led.*

אֶת־הַצֹּאן   Here the definite article *is* used because there is no other element to make the noun definite.

אַחַר הַמִּדְבָּר   KJV: *to the backside of the desert;* NRSV: *beyond the wilderness;* JPS: *into the wilderness;* Fox: *behind the wilderness.* However one renders אַחַר הַמִּדְבָּר its sense is to emphasize the isolation of Moses.

חֹרֵב אֶל־הַר הָאֱלֹהִים חֹרֵבָה   is a proper noun. Notice that two different ways of expressing "direction toward" are used in this segment of the verse. In translating, you can think of there being a comma between הָאֱלֹהִים and חֹרֵבָה

Text Criticism

↓

Note the small superscript "a" after ªהָאֱלֹהִים It refers to BHS text note "a" for this verse, found at the bottom of the page. (This assumes you are using *Biblia Hebraica Stuttgartensia.*)

Cp 3, 1ª	is what to look for first.
‖	is the division mark between text notes.
Cp	chapter
3,1	chapter and verse are divided by a comma. The chapter number is given only for the first note in the chapter. After that, only the verse numbers are given.
a	is the first note for this verse.

Before you interpret this particular note, there is another matter to be considered. There are many more textual variants that could be listed, many more observations from the ancient versions that could be noted, than could possibly be included in a volume this size. So we begin with the presumption that the editors were selective, not haphazard, in deciding which to print and which to omit. Presumably these notes are here to aid the reader in some way, to help with a difficulty, whether it be grammatical, lexical, stylistic, theological, or whatever. When looking at textual notes, it is a good habit to begin by asking yourself what the editors are trying to fix. Sometimes the difficulty is plain; sometimes it is esoteric. At other times you may even be reminded of that great maxim, "If it ain't broke, don't fix it." Students and scholars alike approach these text critical notes with varying degrees of skepticism or enthusiasm. Whether or not the notes sway us to consider an alternative reading, they are nonetheless valuable as an insight into other text traditions.

The notes are given in a compressed, sometimes even cryptic, form. The note we are considering, 3ᵃ, consists of three symbols:

> G*

Consulting the key at the front of BHS, you can "translate" the note to read, literally, "not in / Septuagint / original" or "not in the original Septuagint."

Some questions to think about:

1. What is the difficulty with הָאֱלֹהִים in this context? In other words, why do you think the editor selected this word for comment? Do you think his concern is grammatical, stylistic, or theological?

2. What is the Septuagint [LXX]?

3. What is the "original" LXX?

4. Where is the "original" LXX today?

5. How could the determination be made that something was not in the "original" LXX? (Remember that the language of the LXX is Greek, not Hebrew.)

6. Are there any other extant sources which seem to find this phrase a problem?

7. If all you had was the Hebrew text, could you make sense of the passage as it stands?

Exodus 3:2 [Lesson 25]

וַיֵּרָא According to the missing-letter rule in 3.1, this verb looks as if it should be a 1st י The "rules" are valuable, and they work most of the time but not this time. וַיֵּרָא is the 3 m. sg. Nif`al + vav conversive of רָאָה We encountered this verb, stem, and form in יֵרָאֶה (Gen. 22:14) and, in the same verse, using the verb יֵאָמֵר discussed the Nif`al prefix vowel pattern. But with vav conversive, there is often a shortened form for verbs with weak letters, so וַיֵּרָא shows only the first two syllables of the ־ֵ ־ָ ־ֶ pattern.

בְּלַבַּת   There is a noun לֶהָבָה *flame* (לַהֶבֶת in construct) to which our word seems to be related, and flame fits the context: *in a flame of fire*, but the dagesh forte in the בּ is a problem because intervocalic הּ elides; it does not leave a footprint dagesh as does נ That said, most readers take לַבַּת as some form of לֶהָבָה anyway. Another attractive thought is that the root is לבב (which accounts for the dagesh but not the final הּ), in which case בְּלַבַּת אֵשׁ would read *in the heart of the fire*. (See Rashi on this.)

וַיֵּרָא   Be sure you can distinguish וַיֵּרָא from וַיֵּרָא at the beginning of the verse.

אֵין אֵינֶנּוּ   אֵין is the particle of nonexistence (see Gen. 28:17 and vocabulary); נּוּ is the 3 m. sg. energic נ suffix (For an explanation of how נּוּ can be a 3 m. sg. object suffix, see Genesis 28:22 at אֲעַשְׂרֶנּוּ)

אֻכָּל   The first thing to determine is the function of the dagesh. Either it is an assimilated נ (in which case the א would be a 1 c. sg. prefix pronoun) or it is strengthening of the middle root letter. נכל is a root but is not extant in a stem or form that would fit the vocalization, and a 1 c. sg. prefix form does not suit the narrative here. So the root is _____ There are few verbs in the Pu'al in the Hebrew Bible. Qibbuts ֻ under the first root letter and the dagesh forte in the middle root letter are sure signs of that stem. אֻכָּל may be an irregular spelling of the Pu'al participle, which should read מְאֻכָּל It could be a 3 m. sg. Pu'al affix, but the verb form that follows אֵין is usually the participle. Another way some grammarians have read אֻכָּל is as an archaic Qal passive form. However, that leaves the dagesh unaccounted for. Most grammarians consider אֻכָּל to be a m. sg. Pu'al participle missing its preformative מ

Exodus 3:3 [Lesson 25]

אָסֻרָה־נָּא   One clue to this verb form is נָא at the end of the phrase. It is seen with imperatives as in קַח־נָא (Gen. 22:2) and imperative-like forms. In the word אָסֻרָה the prefix pronoun א and the ending ה‍ָ are indicators of the cohortative (as in נֵלְכָה Gen. 22:5). Removing those two letters leaves only two letters for the root. The vowel under the prefix pronoun is the indicator of the missing root letter. (6.1a) Qibbuts ֻ is a defectiva spelling for וּ so the root is _____

וְאֶרְאֶה אֶת־הַמַּרְאֶה   A comment about the syntax of the first part of the verse: The verb sequence imperative (or imperative-like form) followed by ו + prefix form gives the prefix form verb a sense of purpose or result: *I will turn now that I may see* . . .

מַדּ֫וּעַ   Some dictionaries list the word just this way. BDB has it under יָדַע

יְבְעַר   Reminder: Prefix form conveys incompleted action, not simply future tense.

Exodus 3:4 [Lesson 26]

סָר   One way to determine the root is to recognize that this verb appears in Exodus 3:3 in the phrase אָסֻרָה־נָּא Another is to know that when there are two strong letters, qamats ָ under the first one, and a verb is needed, you most likely have a 3 m. sg. Qal affix of a hollow verb. A word about the verb sequence in 4a: A verb with past tense translation, for example וַיַּ֫רְא followed by a dependent clause whose verb has affix form, for example כִּי סָר sets up a perfect//pluperfect temporal relationship: *and he saw that he had turned*.

לִרְא֫וֹת   25.3b discusses this very word.

Exodus 3:5 [Lesson 26]

אַל אַל־תִּקְרַב   + prefix form of a verb indicates negative imperative: *don't* . . .

הֲלֹם   An adverb.

שַׁל   is a verb. How can you tell? You can't really, but there was just a negative imperative in direct speech, so there are likely to be other imperatives as the speech continues. Verbs whose first root letter is weak (1st י 1st נ) may lose that weak letter in the imperative. (20.6a) Only one type shows the vocalization of שַׁל in the m. sg. imperative.

מֵעָלֶ֫יךָ . . . רַגְלֶ֫יךָ   What are the gender and number of these nouns? Look at text note 5[a]. That note may be not so much the editor's solution to a problem as his giving us an interesting bit of information. Again, using the key, we can "translate" the note:

many / manuscripts / Samaritan Pentateuch / Septuagint / Vulgate / נַעַלְךָ

1. How many manuscripts are represented by "many"?
2. Could the LXX or the Vulgate really say נַעַלְךָ
3. How might this change (from plural to singular) have come about?
4. 5[b] seems to support 5[a] for a change to the singular, but strangely cites different sources: it adds one, subtracts two, and keeps one the same.

אֲשֶׁר אַתָּה עוֹמֵד עָלָיו   The syntax is discussed in 22.8a.

אַדְמַת־קֹדֶשׁ   This is a construct chain. The first link is the feminine noun אֲדָמָה undergoing the regular change for the construct form. (22.4a) קֹדֶשׁ is a noun. Using two nouns in a construct chain, rather than a noun and an adjective, is common Hebrew style.

Exodus 3:6 [Lesson 26]

אָבִיךָ   Note 6ᵃ cites some sources where a plural is used instead of the singular *father*.

וַיַּסְתֵּר   Is this a Pi'el? Don't let the dagesh in the ת sway you too quickly; check the vowel before it first. Also check the vowel under the prefix pronoun. This is a classic Hif'il prefix: patah under the prefix pronoun and an I class vowel between the second and third root letters. סתר is not extant in the Qal.

יָרֵא   An I class Qal affix. (See 17.6.)

מֵהַבִּיט   In this word, the ב and ט are definitely root lettters. בִּיט is not a root, so the ה cannot be part of the definite article; it is a Hif'il preformative. The dagesh in the ב is representing the assimilated נ of the root נבט The initial מֵ is the preposition מִן The whole word is a Hif'il infinitive + preposition. Even though grammatically one could translate מֵהַבִּיט *from looking*, translators seem to opt for *to look*. However, Exodus 3:4 reports that Moses had turned to look, so maybe *from looking* is worth some consideration.

Exodus 3:7 [Lesson 27]

עַשֵּׂר אֲעַשְּׂרֶנּוּ רָאֹה רָאִיתִי   See (Gen. 28:22) for a discussion of this construction. Lesson 26.5 treats the conjugated form of the verb. Note that the infinitive absolute for a 3rd ה does not have the וֹת ending of the infinitive construct. The infinitive absolute is a stable form, and most verbs follow the pattern of the strong verb, which in the Qal is ַ וֹ ָ

עֳנִי   This sounds like, but does not look like, the 1 c. sg. independent pronoun אֲנִי It is a vocabulary word, however.

עַמִּי   What is the root? _____ What is the function of the י _____

צַעֲקָתָם Could the last two letters תָם__ be the 2 m. pl. affix pronoun? NO! That pronoun is consistently spelled תֶם__ What else, then could those letters be? (See 22.4a, The Noun G, and 12.4.)

נֹגְשָׂיו Be careful not to confuse the root here with the more common נגשׁ You may have noticed that this is a plural noun with a singular suffix and that just before was צַעֲקָתָם a singular noun with a plural suffix. Both of these words refer to the collective עַם Switching between singular (focus on the individual) and plural (focus on the people) is common Biblical Hebrew style. There is another frequently used stylistic device in this verse, chiasm. What effect would that arrangement of words have?

יָדַ֫עְתִּי For a discussion of the translation of the affix form of ידע see Genesis 22:12.

אֶת־מַכְאֹבָיו Identify the four components of מַכְאֹבָיו _____

Exodus 3:8 [Lesson 27]

וָאֵרֵד 14.5a discusses the pointing of the conjunction. Look at text note 8ᵃ. Can you see the different nuance the alternative reading would impart?

לְהַצִּילוֹ This word is structurally similar to מַהִבִּיט (Ex. 3:6). The root is _____ and the stem is _____ The antecedent for the suffix is the collective עַם of the previous verse.

מִצְרַ֫יִם The name of the country is also used for the name of the people.

וּלְהַעֲלֹתוֹ Another Hifʻil infinitive, with the same preposition and suffix as לְהַצִּילוֹ just previous. The infinitive of what kind of root ends in וֹת__ _____ (14.3a or 25.3b) There is no I class ("dot") vowel between the second and third root letters because in 3rd ה words 3rd ה features regularly dominate.

הַהוּא For the spelling, see the same word in Genesis 29.2.

זָבַת Here are three strong letters, but they do not compose a root. The only letter of זָבַת that could be extraneous to the root is the ת which could have emerged from a ה (22.4a) Replacing the ת with a ה yields זָבָה which is not a root either. זָבָה could be a 3 f. sg. Qal affix or a f. sg. participle of a hollow root. (9.5a) As luck would have it, there is a verb זוּב *flow* or *gush*, so now we have to determine whether זָבָה is an affix or a participle. Affix form can be ruled out because it does not explain the ת A participle, since it acts like a noun, will have final feminine ה becoming ת when it is in construct. (22.4a) That is what זֶבַח is. Usually *of* works best to link the construct with the absolute, but here *with* works better.

הַכְּנַעֲנִי   22.5 discusses the gentilic ending.

Exodus 3:9 [Lesson 27]

בָּ֫אָה   The subject is _____ Potential ambiguity of the form is discussed in Genesis 29:6, same word.

רָאִ֫יתִי   Learn the chart in 26.5a if you had to refer to it.

לֹחֲצִים   The ל is not a preposition here. Although prefixed prepositions take different vowels, they are never pointed with ḥolem. The vowel pattern and endiNG indicate that לֹחֲצִים is a _____ _____ (9.3a) What is its subject? _____

אֹתָם   23.2b discusses the vocalization.

Exodus 3:10 [Lesson 28]

לְכָה │ לְכָ֫ה   לְכָה is a lengthened form of the m. sg. imperative לֵךְ Some grammarians posit that the added הָ is analogous to the cohortative ending. (See נֵלְכָה [Gen. 22:5].) Whether it is or it isn't, the lengthened m. sg. imperative is quite common. The extra syllable may be there for no other reason than because it sounds better in a particular context.

וְאֶשְׁלָחֲךָ   This word may be harder to pronounce than to analyze. For the narrative sequence: imperative (or an imperative-like form) followed by וְ + prefix form, see comments to וְאֶרְאֶה אֶת־הַמַּרְאֶה (Ex. 3:3).

וְהוֹצֵא   Visually this looks like a m. sg. Qal participle, but הצא is not a root. When a word proper begins וֹהֹ and it isn't a Qal participle, then Hif`il of a 1st י is a good bet. At נוֹרָא in Genesis 28:17, we mentioned that in an earlier form of the language, many 1st י roots were 1st ו and that in stems with preformatives (most commonly Nif`al and Hif`il) that ancient ו comes back in place of the י The root of וְהוֹצֵא then is _____ The Hif`il of יצא means *cause to go out* or *bring out*. The form here is imperative.

Exodus 3:11 [Lesson 28]

כִּי אֵלֵךְ Prefix form can carry modal sense: *that I should . . .*

אוֹצִיא Again, if ḥolem after the first consonant is not an indicator of a Qal participle, then the word is likely a Hifʻil of a 1st י The I class vowel, here a plene ḥireq יִ between the second and third root letters, confirms the stem. א indicates that the form is _____

Exodus 3:12 [Lesson 28]

כִּי כִּי־אֶהְיֶה עִמָּךְ כִּי can express absolute certainty. Note how some translations consider that nuance and others prefer to disregard it: KJV: *certainly I will be with thee . . .*; NRSV and JPS: *I will be with you . . .*; Fox: *indeed I will be-there with you.* For the vocalization of עִמָּךְ see 19.5.

הָאוֹת וֹת ◌ וֹת looks like the ending of a 3rd ה infinitive (25.3b) or a f. pl. noun (22.4), but there is no root האת The ה is the definite article and אוֹת is a noun, listed in BDB under אוה

אָנֹכִי Emphatic use of the independent subject pronoun.

שְׁלַחְתִּיךָ The landmark vowel of the Qal affix, qamats ◌ָ under the first root letter, has been shortened because the addition of a suffix has led to propretonic reduction. (See **S 5.1c.2–3.**)

בְּהוֹצִיאֲךָ Removing the preposition and suffix leaves הוֹצִיא In Exodus 3:10 we saw a similar looking word, הוֹצֵא which was a m. sg. Hifʻil imperative of יצא The word in this verse is a Hifʻil infinitive of the same verb. As we have seen, infinitives can take prepositions and suffixes. The preposition בְּ gives the infinitive a temporal sense. The literal translation of בְּהוֹצִיאֲךָ is *in-your-causing-to-go-out* → *when you bring out.*

תַּעַבְדוּן The final ן at the end of the word is called **paragogic** ן By making a fuller sound, this always accented וּן◌ ending is thought to add emphasis to the word.

Exodus 3:13 [Lesson 28]

הִנֵּה אָנֹכִי בָא How many reasons can you give to support your choice of meaning for the morphologically ambiguous verb form? (9.5a) _____

_____ The sense is of imminent action: *about to.*

אֲבוֹתֵיכֶם See 22.4a and The Noun H.

שְׁלָחַנִי For the structure and vocalization, see comments to וּשְׁמָרַנִי at Genesis 28:20.

שְׁמוֹ *Name* is often a synonym for *power*. מַה־שְּׁמוֹ implies the question, *What are his great deeds? What is his power?* as well as, *What is his name/identity?*

אָמַר This verb form appears in Genesis 22:2. There are five common first א verbs in which the א of the root regularly elides in the 1 c. sg. prefix form. They are:

אמר *say*   אבה *be willing*   אכל *eat*   אפה *bake*   אבד *perish*

They can be remembered by this little ditty:

The bride **said** to the bridegroom, "I am **willing** to **eat** what you **bake** though I **perish**."

Review of Terms

Elide: A letter disappears without a trace: אָמַר for אאמר

Assimilate: A letter disappears, but leaves a footprint dagesh: וַיִּתֵּן for וינתן

Quiesce: A letter loses its vowel and its own sound. Though it can still be seen in the word, it cannot be heard: the א in וַיֹּאמֶר

> Quiesce, Elide, and Assimilate
>
> Went out for a stroll about half past eight.
>
> Quiesce was seen, but never heard.
>
> Elide disappeared without a word.
>
> Whatever happened to assimilate?
>
> A footprint dagesh points to its fate.

Exodus 3:14 [Lesson 29]

אֶהְיֶה אֲשֶׁר אֶהְיֶה Problems: how to render the tense of the verbs and how to understand אֲשֶׁר Here is a sample of translations:

KJV: *I AM THAT I AM*

NRSV: *I AM WHO I AM*

JPS: *Eheyeh-Asher-Eheyeh*

Fox: *EHEYEH-ASHER-EHEYEH/I will be-there howsoever I will be-there.*

אֶהְיֶה resonates with יהוה which itself resonates with היה and could be denoting either constant presence or being, or a Hif`il sense of causing to be—or both. Both of those ideas have been entertained by commentators. In BDB, see יהוה under the root הוה Also Fox's comments on p. 270 of his *The Five Books of Moses* for the notion of presence contained in the verb. Brevard Childs treats the clause in the context of the history of Protestant scholarship in his commentary on Exodus, pp. 60–70.

Exodus 3:15 [Lesson 29]

לְדֹר דֹּר Two words repeated can convey continuity. English would put the preposition on the second word: *generation to generation.*

Exodus 3:16 [Lesson 29]

לֵךְ וְאָסַפְתָּ . . . וְאָמַרְתָּ Two choices for translation: retain the imperative + vav reversive: *Go and you will gather . . . and you will say,* or treat as a sequence of imperatives: *Go and gather . . . and say.*

נִרְאָה Why could this not be a 1 c. pl. prefix form of ראה _____ (If you don't know, study Chart L, the 3rd ה Verb Chart.) What else can a נ be at the front of a word? נִרְאָה is a 3 m. sg. Nif`al affix of ראה

פָּקֹד פָּקַדְתִּי There is a discussion of this construction with the phrase עַשֵּׂר אֲעַשְּׂרֶנּוּ (Gen. 28:22). What is the stem this time? _____

הֶעָשׂוּי This is a new form: it is a Qal passive participle, the identifying characteristic of which is a shureq וּ between the second and third root letters. The root of הֶעָשׂוּי is עשה What we are seeing in הֶעָשׂוּי is the ancient 3rd י in place of the present 3rd ה The initial ה is the definite article, pointed הֶ because it is propretonic before a word beginning with a guttural. הֶעָשׂוּי is m. sg. (there being no f. or pl. additions) and means *the thing done* or *what is being done.*

Exodus 3:17 [Lesson 29]

וָאֹמַר See אמר (Gen. 22:2) and for the conjunction, וָאֵרֵד (14.5a) Text note 17ᵃ points out that the Septuagint has a 3 m. sg. subject pronoun here.

אַעֲלֶה אֶתְכֶם Although 1st gutturals, especially ע can attract pataḥ ⎵ under the prefix pronoun in the Qal, when the pronoun is א its vowel is segol אֶ so *I will go up* would be אֶעֱלֶה (See Verb Chart B.) In אַעֲלֶה the pataḥ under the prefix pronoun is a Hifʻil indicator, and furthermore, the DDO אֶתְכֶם indicates that the verb is transitive; the Qal of עלה is intransitive.

מֵעֳנִי Vocabulary word + preposition.

זָבַת See Exodus 3:8, same word.

וַיֵּשֶׁב You have seen many shortened forms of the prefix with vav conversive. Below is a sample of such forms seen in the readings so far. Identify the root in each.

_____	וַיֵּלֶן	(Gen. 28:10)	_____	וַיְהִי	(Gen. 22:1)
_____	וַיָּגֶל	(Gen. 29:10)	_____	וַיָּקָם	(Gen. 22:3)
_____	וַיֵּשְׁק	(Gen. 29:10)	_____	וַיַּרְא	(Gen. 22:4)
_____	וַיֵּבְךְ	(Gen. 29:11)	_____	וַיָּשֶׂם	(Gen. 22:6)
_____	וַיֵּרָא	(Ex. 3:2)	_____	וַיִּבֶן	(Gen. 22:9)

בְּאֶרֶץ Is this word definite or indefinite? _____ (5.2a)

מְגוּרֵי The endiNG reveals that you are looking at what form of the word? _____ If your dictionary does not list this word under מ where would you look next? _____

אֵלֶּה תֹּלְדוֹת | תֹּלְדוֹת is a ת preformative f. pl. noun. The ḥolem (here defectiva spelling) is actually an indicator of the root. Genesis 28:17 at מַה־נּוֹרָא discussed the effect of stem preformatives on 1st י roots, that being י → ו That reversion to the "original" first root letter can be effected by any preformative, so the root of תֹּלְדוֹת is _____ The word means *descendents* or *successors* even though here the focus is only on Joseph. How is אֵלֶּה related to תֹּלְדוֹת _____ (15.2)

בֶּן־שְׁבַע־עֶשְׂרֵה שָׁנָה The idiom for telling someone's age is *a son / daughter of X number of years*. The number is composed much the same way as it is in English, but שָׁנָה is singular.

אֶת־ | הָיָה רֹעֶה אֶת־אֶחָיו can be a DDO indicator; it can also be the preposition *with*. Perhaps in this context there is an intended ambiguity.

אֶחָיו An unscientific but practical way to tell the singular from the plural of אָח with a 3 m. sg. endiNG is:

אֶחָיו אָחִיו

one dot, one brother ↑   ↑ more than one dot, more than one brother

בַּצֹּאן If you translated אֶת־אֶחָיו as *with his brothers*, then the preposition בּ here would be marking a transitive use of the verb. If you chose אֵת as the DDO indicator, then the בּ could be *among*.

אֶת־בְּנֵי Again think of the two possibilities for אֵת

נְשֵׁי See The Noun H.

וַיָּבֵא | וַיָּבֹא looks a lot like וַיָּבֵא It should be no surprise that they both come from the same root. The I class vowel taking the place of the root vowel indicates the Hif`il. Hollows in the Hif`il have qamats ָ under their prefix pronouns where the strong verb has pataḥ ַ

דִּבָּתָם The root of דִּבָּתָם is the geminate דבב (ergo the dagesh forte in the ב). If you have difficulty finding the noun form in the dictionary, review 22.4a. For the suffix, see 12.4.

רָעָה This word certainly looks like it might be related to רֹעֶה further back in the verse, but in this context it isn't. This רָעָה is a feminine adjective from the root רעע The translational difficulty is reconciling an indefinite adjective with a suffixed noun, which is definite. Most translators go with *their evil report,* but רָעָה is not, strictly speaking, an attributive adjective (it is not definite and דִּבָּתָם is). Grammatically, the phrase is *their report, an evil one.*

Genesis 37:3 [Lesson 30]'

וְיִשְׂרָאֵל אָהַב אֶת־יוֹסֵף מִכָּל־בָּנָיו One use of the preposition מִן is to denote the comparative degree.

זְקֻנִים The root is _____ זְקֻנִים is a m. pl. noun meaning *old age.*

לוֹ To what is the suffix referring? KJV, NRSV, JPS: *his old age;* Fox: *of old age to him.*

וְעָשָׂה לוֹ Use of the affix + vav reversive can refer to repeated action in the past. Is its use here implying that Jacob made more than one garment for Joseph? You can see from text note 3[a] that the difficulty of the verb form has not gone unnoticed.

כְּתֹנֶת פַּסִּים This phrase occurs five times in the Bible: three times in the Joseph story (Gen. 37:3, 23, and 32) and twice in the story of Tamar (2 Sa. 13:18 and 19). The noun פַּס means *flat of hand or foot.* So where does the famous image of a many-colored coat come from? It is as old as some of the earliest translations. Ancient Egyptian tomb paintings show that there was indeed a striped garment worn by Hebrew dignitaries. Later evidence from Middle Eastern countries shows that coats into which colored threads were woven were worn by young boys of rank. Whether Joseph's coat was colorful, long, or both, it certainly had to have been special!

Genesis 37:4 [Lesson 30]

וַיִּרְאוּ Be able to defend your choice of root. Consult 12.1 and 17.5.

אֹתוֹ Notice the emphatic position of אֹתוֹ in this part of the verse.

יָכְלוּ Of the consonants in this word, it is sure that כֹל is part of the root. וֹ ָ ֻ indicates what PGN? _____ The potentially ambiguous component is the initial יְ It could be the first root letter of a Qal affix (4.2 and 8.1), and in fact, it is. But perhaps you were thinking, "hollow verb, Qal prefix." (6.1) But in the Qal prefix of a hollow verb, the middle root letter will appear:

שׁ י ם	ב ו א	כ ו ל
יָשִׂימוּ	יָבוֹאוּ	יָכוּלוּ

דִּבְּרוֹ The root, stem, and suffix are familiar. What vowel would you expect under the first root letter if this were a Pi'el affix? _____ (15.4) Every other Pi'el form has pataḥ under the first root letter. You have seen several already: וַיְדַבֵּר (prefix + vav conversive, 2.3c); דַּבֵּר (m. sg. imperative, 19.2a); מְדַבֵּר (m. sg. participle, Gen. 29:9). What form remains? _____ BHS note 4ᵇ is a nice help.

לְשָׁלֹם This is an example of yet another use of the preposition לְ in front of a noun. Some English translations have the לְ give the noun an adverbial sense.

Genesis 37:5 [Lesson 31]

וַיַּחֲלֹם If the pataḥ under the prefix pronoun seems to be an ambiguous stem identifier, check the vowel between the second and third root letters and then 17.3a if you are still stumped. (The next lesson, at 32.3b, actually addresses the very difficulty posed by וַיַּחֲלֹם)

חֲלוֹם You can see that the DO and the verb are built from the same root. Why is this DO not preceded by אֵת_____

וַיַּגֵּד When you are looking for a missing root letter, what do you do first? (The answer is not "cry.") First, look for a footprint dagesh. Only if that doesn't work do you try the missing letter rules. (16.1a) So the root is _____ The next issue is the stem. Several times now you have seen pataḥ under the prefix pronoun and an I class vowel between the second and third root letters as the characteristics of a Hif'il prefix, and that is what this is. This particular verb, which is quite common, occurs exclusively in the Hif'il or in its passive counterpart, the Hof'al.

אֶחָיו לְאֶחָיו   Is אֶחָיו sg. or pl.? _____ (See The Noun H, vocabulary list, or אֶחָיו [Gen. 37:2].) Note that sometimes English wants a pronominal direct object, *he made it known to his brothers,* although Hebrew does not require it.

וַיּוֹסִפוּ | ו between the prefix pronoun and two root letters means the root is _____ (31.2) (Does this root not evoke the name of the leading persona in this drama?) Look at the vowel between the second and third root letters. What stem most often has this type of vowel in this position in the prefix form? _____

שְׂנֹא   25.4 discusses the pointing of this form.

Now look at the whole phrase וַיּוֹסִפוּ עוֹד שְׂנֹא אֹתוֹ The words make sense individually but don't flow well in English. Although יסף means *increase* or *add,* it is very often used, as it is here, to mean *to do something more strongly.* Thus there are two strengthenings—in the verb and the adverb—to the basic idea: שְׂנֹא אֹתוֹ

Genesis 37:6 [Lesson 31]

שִׁמְעוּ־נָא   For help with the form, see 20.6a.

הַחֲלוֹם   21.3a explains the pointing of the definite article before a guttural. ח is a "strong" guttural and often does not cause compensatory lengthening of the preceding vowel.

Genesis 37:7 [Lesson 31]

מְאַלְּמִים   The root is _____ If you can't figure out the rest, study this lesson.

קָמָה   If the root cannot be קמה which consonant can you remove? _____ What familiar root contains the two remaining consonants? _____ Re-read the notes to בָּאָה (Gen. 29:6b) for a refresher on the form.

אֲלֻמָּתִי   Does seeing תִי_____ at the end of the word cause the reflex response, "1 c. sg. affix pronoun"? Why could it not be here? What else could these components be? (22.4a) _____

וְנִצָּבָה   Perhaps this word looks familiar. The root appears in מֻצָּב (Gen. 28:12), in נִצָּב (Gen. 28: 13), and in מַצֵּבָה (Gen 28:18). וְנִצָּבָה is a 3 f. sg. Nifʿal affix.

תְּסֻבֶּינָה A prefix pronoun pointed with shewa ְ and a dagesh forte in the second root letter should signal "Pi'el," in which case the third root letter would be ה (26.2). However, there is no such root. The root is סבב a geminate verb, so you can see that the dagesh is representing the doubled ב of the root. The י is a connecting letter in this case. Incidentally, תְּסֻבֶּינָה does read exactly like a 3rd ה Pu'al. Geminates are notoriously difficult, so when all else fails to yield a root, think of the possibility of a geminate.

וַתִּשְׁתַּחֲוֶיןָ The root and stem were discussed with וְנִשְׁתַּחֲוֶה *and we will prostrate ourselves in worship* (Gen. 22:5). The endiNG you see here ֶןָ is a defectiva spelling of the f. pl. prefix complement נָה. What element constitutes the prefix pronoun? What is the subject of the verb?

לַאֲלֻמָּתִי The root of this word appears five times in this verse. Look especially at the phrase מְאַלְּמִים אֲלֻמִּים and then at אֲלֻמֹתֵיכֶם The root generates both masculine and feminine nouns that seem to have the same meaning.

Genesis 37:8 [Lesson 31]

אֶחָיו Is the noun sg. or pl.? _____ (See the same word, Gen. 37:2.)

הֲמָלֹךְ תִּמְלֹךְ What is the function of the הֲ _____ (Choices to consider are definite article, Hif'il preformative, and interrogative ה) What are the stem, form, and PGN of the conjugated verb form?_____ For a review of the whole construction, see עַשֵּׂר אֲעַשְּׂרֶנּוּ (Gen. 28:22).

אִם The basic meaning of אִם is *if*, but when preceded by the interrogative particle ה as it is here, it can be expressing a question with an alternative: Do you really mean to X or do you really mean to Y? Since the verbs in this verse are synonyms, the construction is simply emphatic.

מָשׁוֹל תִּמְשֹׁל A repetition of the same construction seen earlier in the verse with the root מלך with the interrogative still holding. Although most translators render the infinitive absolute by an adverb, one can retain the duplication of the root: *Rule? Will you rule over us?*

בָּנוּ Morphologically, a 3 c. pl. Qal affix of a 3rd ה or hollow, or a preposition + DO. Appeal to context.

וַיּוֹסִפוּ עוֹד שְׂנֹא אֹתוֹ An exact repetition of the phrase in Genesis 37:5.

עַל־חֲלֹמֹתָיו | עַל here gives the sense of *because of* or *on account of*.
If you cannot identify the components of חֲלֹמֹתָיו see The Noun G.

Genesis 37:9 [Lesson 32]

אַחֵר Not the same as אַחַר but both are vocabulary words.

אֹתוֹ To what is the suffix referring? _____

וְאַחַד עָשָׂר Add these two numbers together.

מִשְׁתַּחֲוִים The root and stem are discussed with וְנִשְׁתַּחֲוֶה (Gen. 22:5). The preformative מ indicates which form? _____ The endiNG is _____

Genesis 37:10 [Lesson 32]

וַיִּגְעַר־בּוֹ 16.7a discusses the combination: verb + preposition + DO.

הֲבוֹא נָבוֹא Like הֲמָלֹךְ תִּמְלֹךְ (Gen. 37:8). What is the PGN of נָבוֹא _____

וְאִמְּךָ Why is there a dagesh in the מ _____ (See אִמּוֹ [Gen. 29:10] and vocabulary.)

לְהִשְׁתַּחֲוֺת | וֹת_____ can be the f. pl. noun endiNG or the sign of a 3rd ה infinitive. Which fits the context?

אָֽרְצָה Need a reminder about the ending? See comments in Genesis 28:12, same word.

Genesis 37:11 [Lesson 32]

וַיְקַנְאוּ The difficulty with this word is the identity of its stem. Shewa ְ under the prefix pronoun indicates _____ (15.5) But there is no dagesh in the middle root letter. The combination dagesh forte + shewa ְ can make dagesh forte disappear, which actually happens twice in וַיְקַנְאוּ

וְאָבִיו When ו in front of a noun or pronoun introduces a change in subject and begins a new part of a verse, it may have a contrastive sense: *but*. (**S 43.3** discusses uses of ו)

הַדָּבָר Suggestions for meanings of this noun occupy four columns in BDB.

Genesis 37:12 [Lesson 32]

לִרְעוֹת What are your choices for the ending וֹת ְ _____ (14.3a and 22.4)

אֶת־ Note the two heavy dots over this word (this assumes you are using BHS). They are one of ten instances of puncta extraordinaria in the Torah (there are five other occurrences elsewhere in the corpus). The purpose of these marks is not well understood. Any one explanation, such as that the puncta mark words that should be deleted, simply does not fit all instances. It so happens that the marks over the אֶת־ in this verse are one of the most enigmatic occurrences.

Genesis 37:13 [Lesson 33]

הֲלוֹא | לוֹא is the plene spelling for לֹא

לְכָה See 30.1a and comments to the same word, Exodus 3:10.

וְאֶשְׁלָחֲךָ The sequence imperative followed by וְ + prefix form may give to the prefix form verb the sense of purpose or result.

Genesis 37:14 [Lesson 33]

רְאֵה If the form is difficult, study the 3rd ה Verb Chart: Chart L.

וַהֲשִׁבֵנִי The נִי at the end of the word is the 1 c. sg. object suffix. After accounting for that and after removing the initial וְ the consonants ה שׁ ב are left. They do not make a root. The consonant that could be something else is _____ Two familiar roots containing שׁב are ישׁב and שׁוּב If the verb here were ישׁב and it had a ה preformative, what would have happened to the י of the root? _____ _____ (31.2) The root then is _____ and the ה is a Hif`il preformative. But why the reduced vowel? Because a verb with a suffix will, if it can, have the progression pretonic lengthening and propretonic reduction of vowels.

Genesis 37:15 [Lesson 33]

תֹעֶה Pointed like a 3rd ה m. sg. participle, and that is what it is.

Genesis 37:16 [Lesson 33]

אֶת־אַחַי Here the distinction between singular and plural is not conveyed by dots. It is explained in The Noun G 2. Note the direct object placed in front of the verb for emphasis.

מְבַקֵשׁ The stem and form are discussed in 31.1.

הַגִּידָה־נָּא The verb is featured in 30.1.

אֵיפֹה Can be found in BDB under אֵי It is a compound made up of אֵי (where) and פֹּה (here), so it means *where* as *in which place* (as opposed to *to* or *from which place*).

Genesis 37:17 [Lesson 34]

מִזֶּה | זֶה is functioning as a substantive meaning *this place*.

שָׁמַ֫עְתִּי   Text note 17ᵃ cites sources that read שְׁמַעְתִּים here. What is the difference, and what is the purpose of the difference?

נֵלְכָה   Genesis 22.5 same word.

אַחַר אָחִיו | אַחַר has appeared in different contexts in the readings:

אַחַר הַדְּבָרִים הָאֵלֶּה   (Gen. 22:1)

וְהִנֵּה־אַיִל אַחַר נֶאֱחַז בַּסְּבַךְ בְּקַרְנָיו   (Gen. 22:13)

וַיִּנְהַג אֶת־הַצֹּאן אַחַר הַמִּדְבָּר   (Ex. 3:1)

Genesis 37:18 [Lesson 34]

וַיִּרְאוּ   Is the root more likely to be יָרֵא (17.5) or רָאה

וּבְטֶרֶם   A temporal adverb, in BDB under טֶרֶם   It is most followed by the prefix form no matter what the "tense" of the verb in translation.

וַיִּתְנַכְּלוּ   The stem of this verb is the Hitpaʿel. It can be recognized in the prefix form by the prefix pronoun followed by ת and by its doubled middle root letter. The root is _____ The Hitpaʿel is often intensive and usually either reflexive and/or interactive. Here *they planned deceitfully among themselves* seems to make the point.

אֹתוֹ   This is the DDO for which verb?

לַהֲמִיתוֹ   If this word is a problem, re-read comments at וַהֲשִׁבֵ֫נִי (Gen. 37:14).

Genesis 37:19 [Lesson 34]

וַיֹּאמְרוּ אִישׁ אֶל־אָחִיו   The question here is why the plural verb. אִישׁ meaning *a man* can imply *each man*. The sense is: *and they said, each to his brother*.

בַּעַל הַחֲלֹמוֹת הַלָּזֶה   First look at הַלָּזֶה It is an expanded form of הַזֶּה and so can only be an attributive adjective (predicate adjectives do not have the definite article). Which word is it modifying? It cannot be הַחֲלֹמוֹת because הַחֲלֹמוֹת is f. pl. and הַלָּזֶה is m. sg. It is modifying בַּעַל When the construct segment of a construct chain takes a modifier, the modifier can only be positioned after the absolute because theoretically nothing should come between the word(s) in the construct and the word in the absolute. The construction is: *the master of dreams, the this one* → *this master of dreams*.

בָּא Will you treat this as a participle or an affix form?

Genesis 37:20 [Lesson 34]

לְכוּ וְנַהַרְגֵהוּ וְנַשְׁלִכֵהוּ English uses "come" as an expression of exhortation. Hebrew some-times uses "go." What are the stems of the verbs in this cluster? _____

הַבֹּרוֹת There is a feminine noun בְּאֵר meaning *well* and a masculine noun בּוֹר also meaning *well* and also listed in BDB under בָאר Both nouns take the f. pl. endiNG.

חַיָּה רָעָה Is חַיָּה a 3 m. sg. Qal affix? Check the vowel under the first root letter. Would a Qal affix have a dagesh forte in the middle root letter? The root is חיה (not היה), and חַיָּה is a noun. Now take a look at רָעָה In this chapter, we have seen רֹעֶה and רָעָה (v. 2), לִרְעוֹת (v. 12), and רֵעִים (v. 13). The root in each of these words is either רעע or רעה Which root fits here?

אֲכָלָתְהוּ Remove the suffix; remember: הו is a unit that is only very rarely not a single compo-nent. The question now is, of the consonants left, which is extraneous to the root? Both feminine nouns that end in הָ and 3 f. sg. verbs in the affix undergo a similar change when a suffix is added: feminine ה becomes ת Since כלת is not a root, the root must be either כלה or אכל If כלה then the א would be a prefix pronoun, but we are not in a first person mode here. Furthermore, the vowels don't work for a prefix form. So the root is אכל the subject of which is provided by the f. sg. רָעָה חַיָּה Final question: Why is the vowel under the א not qamats ָ _____
Answer: פרפרסנק רדקשן

וְנִרְאֶה Is the נ the 1 c. pl. prefix pronoun or a Nif`al preformative? _____

יִהְיוּ For the dagesh, see 17.3b and **S 17.3b**.

חֲלֹמֹתָיו | חֲלֹם has a f. pl. endiNG even though it is a masculine noun.

Genesis 37:21 [Lesson 35]

רְאוּבֵן Text note 21ᵃ proposes יהודה in place of רְאוּבֵן to harmonize with verse 26. There is no textual support for the suggestion, but it is provocative. Later on in the story, at Genesis 44:18, it is יְהוּדָה who speaks on behalf of the brothers.

וַיִּצְלָהוּ Take care of the dagesh forte to get the root, which is _____ What is the stem? _____

מִיָּדָם ‖ יָד is a two-letter noun that is not from a geminate root. For help with the suffix, see דִּבָּתָם (Gen. 37:2). As one student pointed out, it's hard not to hear דָּם (*blood*) in this word. Pun intended?

לֹא נַכֶּנּוּ The best place to start may be at the end. נּוּ is an energic נ suffix and can mean *him* or *us* (explained in the phrase עֲשֵׂר אֲעַשְּׂרֶנּוּ [Gen. 28:22]). The next task is to figure out the function of the dagesh in the כ It is either designating the Pi'el or it is an assimilated נ of the root. Suppose a Pi'el: then the root would be נכה and the form would be imperative. We can stop there because there is no construction לֹא + imperative. (Negative imperative is presented in 39.3b.) So the dagesh represents an assimilated נ and the נ you see is a prefix pronoun. The root is נכה in this case, too! The pataḥ under the pronoun would indicate the Hif'il, though this is a Hif'il that does not have a causative sense. The phrase translates: *we will not smite him.*

נָפֶשׁ This word further qualifies the DO, which is the suffix of the verb. Why the qamats ָ under the נ Because when segol is at a major disjunctive accent (and the end of a verse is the most major), it almost always becomes the long vowel of its class: vowel class is determined by the vowel the segolate takes when it has a suffix: נַפְשִׁי → נֶפֶשׁ In pause, ֶ → ָ (**S 4.4b** has a brief discussion of segolate nouns.)

Genesis 37:22 [Lesson 35]

אַל אַל־תִּשְׁפְּכוּ ‖ אַל + the prefix form → negative imperative.

הַשְׁלִיכוּ There is a discussion of the form at 30.1.

וְיָד אַל־תִּשְׁלְחוּ־בוֹ The difficulty here is to determine how יָד is related to the verb.

Compare this phrase with אַל־תִּשְׁלַח יָדְךָ (Gen. 22:12).

Note that in verses 13–24 שׁלח is used three times and שׁלך twice. Is there a difference between the verbs? BDB distinguishes between them thus: שׁלח *send, stretch out, extend* → *don't lay a hand on him;* שׁלך *throw, throw away, send* → *throw him into the well.*

לְמַעַן הַצִּיל The same verb was in the verse just previous, but there in the prefix form. Here the form is _____ לְמַעַן is a vocabulary word.

לְהָשִׁיבוֹ Morphologically the same as לַהֲמִיתוֹ (Gen. 37:18).

Genesis 37:23 [Lesson 35]

וַיְהִי כַּאֲשֶׁר | וַיְהִי sets the action in the past. כְּ gives the sense of *as* or *just as* and אֲשֶׁר signals that a clause is coming, but the word itself, when compounded, is not translated. (22.9)

אֶת־יוֹסֵף אֶת־כֻּתָּנְתּוֹ אֶת־כְּתֹנֶת הַפַּסִּים How many direct objects are there here? _____ Review 5.2a if you cannot come up with a different reason for the definiteness of each. Text note 23ᵃ cites two sources, the Septuagint and the Syriac versions of the text, which omit the segment אֶת־כֻּתָּנְתּוֹ How unfortunate! It is an essential part of the crescendo. A similar intensive style is used in Genesis 22:2:

$$קַח־נָא אֶת־בִּנְךָ אֶת־יְחִידְךָ אֲשֶׁר־אָהַבְתָּ אֶת־יִצְחָק$$

אֲשֶׁר עָלָיו Like a noun sentence, in the sense that English would add a form of the verb "to be" to connect these words.

Genesis 37:24 [Lesson 35]

וַיִּקָּחֻהוּ The vowel ֻ is the defectiva spelling for _____

וַיַּשְׁלִכוּ Compare with וְנַשְׁלִכֵהוּ (Gen. 37:20) and הַשְׁלִיכוּ (Gen. 37:22).

הַבֹּרָה Very economical use of language! For the root see comments to הַבֹּרוֹת (Gen. 37:20).

רֵק This is a real specialty item, an I class hollow. One other verb of that kind is מוּת covered in 34.4. Its 3 m. sg. Qal affix is מֵת

בּוֹ The antecedent is _____

וְזֹאת הַמִּצְוָה What kind of adjective is זֹאת _____ (15.2) In the singular, מִצְוָה can mean *set of commandments*.

הַחֻקִּים The root חקק means *inscribe* or *engrave* and so may refer to enactments passed by an authoritative body and engraved on a tablet. There is the masculine noun חֹק from this root and also a feminine noun חֻקָּה They have such possible meanings as *prescribed portion* or *allowance of food* (Gen. 47:22), *an offering due to the priests* (Lev. 6:11), *a specific decree* (Gen. 47:26), *law in general* (Ps. 94:20). According to traditional thinking, חֻקִּים also include precepts, the reason for the observance of which we do not know, such as which foods may not be eaten (Lev. 11). (For the vowel under the definite article, see **S 4.5b**.)

וְהַמִּשְׁפָּטִים | מִשְׁפָּט deals with matters pertaining to the relationship between person and person, that is, civil and criminal law, and not to precepts governing the relationship between oneself and God, for example, the laws of Passover.

For purposes of consistency, we will use the following terms:

מִצְוָה	*commandment*
חֹק	*statute*
מִשְׁפָּט	*judgment*

לַעֲשׂוֹת For the body of the word, see 14.3a.

אַתֶּם עֹבְרִים שָׁמָּה The question here is what tense to give the participle. The sense is of the imminent future *about to*. Also notice that ה directive can be attached to an adverb.

לְרִשְׁתָּהּ The suffix is _____ (14.3) The fact that neither לרש nor רשת is a root reveals that neither ל nor ת is a root letter, so each must have some other function. The ל is _____ ת before a suffix could be a f. sg. noun ending; another thing it could be is a special verb ending. What kind of verb and what kind of ending?_____ (11.2a, 25.2)

לְמַעַן Vocabulary word. Although the verb form that often follows a preposition is the infinitive, a prefix form is another possibility.

תִּירָא   The verb form is discussed in 17.2. A feature of Deuteronomy is the frequent switching between second person singular and plural: "you" the individual as in תִּירָא as opposed to "you" the group as in אַתֶּם עֹבְרִים (Dt. 6:1).

אֶת־כָּל־חֻקֹּתָיו   Compare to חֻקִּים (Dt. 6:1).

וּמִצְוֹתָיו   The ו after the צ is a consonant. How do we know? Because the צ already has a vowel in the shewa ָ

מְצַוְּךָ   31.1 discusses the stem and form.

יַאֲרִכֻן   The ending וּן is called paragogic ן (see תַּעַבְדוּן at the end of Exodus 3:12) and is a favorite of Deuteronomic style. The root is _____ The stem is _____ (32.1) Qibbuts ֻ is the defectiva spelling of shureq וּ so the PGN of the verb is _____ Note that the causative sense of the Hif`il is not apparent in this use of אָרך

יָמֶיךָ   An irregular noun (see The Noun H) with a possessive suffix. Could this be confused with the plural of יָם sea? Not if you think of there being a "fish" in the יָמִים sea. What is the relationship of יָמֶיךָ to the verb יַאֲרִכֻן which comes just before it?

Deuteronomy 6:3 [Lesson 36]

וְשָׁמַעְתָּ יִשְׂרָאֵל   For syntax see 18.2.

וְשָׁמַרְתָּ לַעֲשׂוֹת   KJV: *and observe to do [it]*; NRSV: *and observe them diligently*; Fox: *And you are to take care to observe them.* JPS's translation: *Obey, O Israel, willingly and faithfully* treats these words as modifiers of וְשָׁמַעְתָּ יִשְׂרָאֵל

אֲשֶׁר אֲשֶׁר יִיטַב   אֲשֶׁר here is not functioning as the relative pronoun; it is functioning more like כִּי *that* it will be good . . .

וַאֲשֶׁר תִּרְבּוּן   A continuation of the use of אֲשֶׁר just previous. For ן__ see יַאֲרִכֻן (Dt. 6:2). The root is _____ (26.5) Why is there a dagesh in the ב _____

לָךְ   When does לְךָ become לָךְ _____ (19.5) It is interesting that in this verse the accent zaqef qaton once changes the vocalization of לָךְ and once does not of לְךָ That accent usually does cause a vowel, or in this case a syllabic, change.

אֶרֶץ זָבַת חָלָב וּדְבָשׁ Same phrase as in Exodus 3:8 and 17.

Deuteronomy 6:4 [Lesson 36]

Lesson 18 is devoted to the grammar of this verse. The orthography is another matter. Note that the ע of שְׁמַע and the ד of אֶחָד are written in large script. The number of letters in the Torah written large varies depending on the manuscript from as few as three to as many as more than a dozen. The reasons for all of them are not clear. A large letter may mark the beginning of a book (though only some books are so marked) or draw attention to a significant point, such as the midpoint of the Torah. The large letters in Deuteronomy 6:4 may be to safeguard the reading. The large ד keeps אֶחָד from being confused with אַחֵר The large ע could be to keep the pronunciation of שְׁמַע distinct from שְׁמָא a Mishnaic word meaning *perhaps*. The problem with that explanation is that there are many words in an unpointed scroll that could be ambiguous. An observation by some commentators is that the enlarged letters ע and ד form the word עֵד which means *testimony* or *witness*. Whatever the reason, the large letters make the verse stand out.

Deuteronomy 6:5 [Lesson 36]

וְאָהַבְתָּ   An imperative followed by the affix + vav reversive gives the affix imperative force: *you shall* . . . The imperative שְׁמַע is in the previous verse; the 2 m. sg. affix forms + vav reversive continue until verse 9.

בְּכָל־לְבָבְךָ וּבְכָל־נַפְשְׁךָ וּבְכָל־מְאֹדֶךָ | KJV, NRSV, and JPS translate: *(thou) you (shalt) will love the Lord (thine) your God with all (thine) your heart, with all (thy) your soul, and with all (thy) your might.* Fox has: *Now you are to love YHWH your God with all your heart, with all your being, with all your substance!* He points out that "soul" "while stirring . . . gives the impression of something contrasted to the body—not an idea that appears in the Hebrew Bible."

Deuteronomy 6:6 [Lesson 37]

וְהָיוּ   Refer to 26.5 and 37.2a if you need help with the root.

הַיּוֹם   In addition to its literal translation, הַיּוֹם can be an idiom meaning *today*.

(See also the clause אֲשֶׁר יֵאָמֵר הַיּוֹם in Genesis 22:14.)

Deuteronomy 6:7 [Lesson 37]

וְשִׁנַּנְתָּם How many נs are in this word? _____ The root is geminate. The stem is _____ Is the subject sg. or pl.? _____ (Answers: 3, Pi'el, sg.) If this were the 2 m. pl. affix form, the subject pronoun would be תֶּם ‿ It is true that the addition of a suffix can cause a change in pointing, but תָּם ‿ at the end of a <u>verb</u> will always be 2 m. sg. affix subject + 3 m. pl. object pronoun. A translation of שׁן suggested by a student that I think is effective is *incise* since that captures the root meaning *sharpen* as well as the noun שֵׁן *tooth*. Most translators tend to go with more abstract choices: KJV: *And thou shalt teach them diligently*; NRSV: *Recite them*; JPS: *Impress them*; Fox: *You are to repeat them*.

לְבָנֶיךָ Is the noun singular or plural? Compare with וּבָנֶךָ (Dt. 6:2).

וְדִבַּרְתָּ בָּם The preposition בְּ is sometimes used with verbs of speaking or to mean *about* or *of*.

בְּשִׁבְתְּךָ Refer to 35.1c and בְּהוֹצִיאֲךָ (Ex. 3:12b) for a discussion of the syntax; see 11.2b, 25.2, and **S 4.4b** for the spelling of the form. In Lesson 35 the subject of the infinitive is a separate word. Here the subject is expressed by the pronominal suffix ךָ _____ Another difference from the similar construction in Lesson 35 is the tense that would make the most sense in English. Obviously a past tense does not work here.

וּבְלֶכְתְּךָ This is a repetition of the construction just above. You can start from the inside, with a familiar consonant cluster and work out, or you can go from the ends to the middle. In either case, you should end up with four components.

Deuteronomy 6:8 [Lesson 37]

וּקְשַׁרְתָּם The components are like those in וְשִׁנַּנְתָּם (Dt. 6:7).

לְאוֹת Could אוֹת be the plene spelling of the DDO marker as אֹתִי No. The DDO marker takes that form only when a suffix is added, and it never takes an attached preposition. אוֹת is a noun from the root אוה *describe with a mark*. (Notice that the consonant ו of the root becomes a vowel letter in the noun.)

עַל־יָדֶךָ The usual pointing of יָדְךָ is _____ (19.5)

לְטֹטָפֹת Very few Hebrew words have the same first two root letters. When they do, as in this case and in יַיִן for example, they are thought to be loan words. The origin and derivation of טֹטָפֹת are uncertain. The word might best be left untranslated, although *frontlets* or *bands* are common English translations.

Deuteronomy 6:9 [Lesson 37]

מְזוּזֹת   Generally this word is transliterated or else is given the English term *doorpost*. It is another word whose origin is not certain. There is a root זוז which means *move* or *rise* , so it is possible that the mezzuzah was originally part of a tent.

בֵּיתֶךָ   The usual spelling of this word is בֵּיתְךָ The plural would be בָּתֶּיךָ Why תָ ← תֶ is not clear. The accent is disjunctive but not a strong disjunctive. Text note 9ᵇ cites sources that have the plural— a reading that would account for the תֶ but would require that the rest of the word have a different shape. If one checks the reference in that note to Deuteronomy 11:20, one finds that MT has בֵּיתֶךָ there, too; that verse's text note cites two of the three sources of 6:9—the Syriac and Septuagint—and adds a third source, Targum Jonathan, all of which have the plural *houses*. Furthermore, the note at 11:20 adds the comment that the texts cited are more "correct."

Synopsis of בַּיִת and בַּת

בַּיִת	sg. absolute	בַּת
בֵּית	sg. construct	בַּת
בֵּיתְךָ	sg. with suffix	בִּתְּךָ
בֵּיתֶךָ	sg. with suffix, in pause	בִּתֶּךָ
בָּתִּים	pl. absolute	בָּנוֹת
בָּתֶּיךָ	pl. with suffix	בְּנוֹתֶיךָ

וּבִשְׁעָרֶיךָ   Presumably of cities.

Deuteronomy 6:10 [Lesson 37]

יְבִיאֲךָ   This verb does not have consistent signs of any stem. It has shewa ְ under the prefix pronoun, which usually indicates _____ stem. (15.5) But there is no other sign of that stem. It has an interior I class ("dot") vowel, which is a sign of _____

Hint: The accented suffix is causing propretonic reduction from qamats ָ to shewa ְ

וְנִשְׁבַּע   The נ here looks as if it could be the 1 c. pl. prefix pronoun or a Nif`al preformative, but see word 139 in the vocabulary list.

לָתֶת   What is notable about this form is that the first נ of the root does not assimilate; it does not leave a "footprint dagesh;" it elides. The third root letter נ would not assimilate in this case because the last letters of words rarely take dagesh forte. (25.7)

עָרִים גְּדֹלֹת וְשֹׁבֹת   At first glance it may seem as if the adjectives do not agree in gender with the noun, but עִיר is feminine. (It is also irregular; see The Noun H.) It is interesting that some masculine nouns such as אָב have f. pl. endiNGs and feminine nouns such as עִיר have m. pl. endiNGs.

לֹא־בָנִיתָ   Lesson 26.5a features this very verb.

Deuteronomy 6:11 [Lesson 38]

וּבָתִּים מְלֵאִים   For בָתִּים see the synopsis of בַּיִת at Deuteronomy 6:9. מָלֵא is a stative or I class verb. (17.6a) A characteristic of statives is that adjectives can be formed from the 3 m. sg. Qal affix. The phrase וּבָתִּים מְלֵאִים looks as if it could be a noun sentence or a noun and an attributive adjective. You have to go further into the verse to see which works out better.

טוּב   The root טוב yields three nouns: טוּב and טוֹב (m.) and טוֹבָה (f.)

מְלֵאת   Here is an illustration of a verb that is usually intransitive in the Qal and transitive in the

---

וּבֹרֹת   The root of this noun appears variously as בְּאֵר (Gen. 29:2) and בּוֹר (Gen. 37:20, where it is discussed). בּוֹר is a masculine noun with a feminine endiNG in the plural.

חֲצוּבִים   The root will be readily apparent if you read ahead just two words. The stem of the verb here is Qal, the form is participle, and the voice is passive. You saw a Qal passive participle before in הֶעָשׂוּי (Ex. 3:16). The indicator is וּ between the second and third root letters.

וְשָׂבַעְתָּ   Does this word contain the same root as נִשְׁבַּע (Dt. 6:10)?

Deuteronomy 6:12 [Lesson 38]

הִשָּׁמֶר   This is a Nif`al imperative. It is believed that in the early stages of the language the preformative of the Nif`al was הִנ This syllable is still seen in the imperative and infinitive forms, but with the

נ assimilated. That is why there is a dagesh forte (footprint dagesh) in the first root letter of these two forms. The other distinctive characteristic of some Nif`al forms is their vowel pattern (illustrated at יֵאָמֵר [Gen. 22:14]).

A Synopsis of Three Forms and Four Stems of the Strong Verb

Prefix		Imperative		Infinitive Construct	
3 m. sg. Qal	יִפְקֹד	m. sg. Qal	פְּקֹד	Qal	פְּקֹד
3 m. sg. Pi`el	יְפַקֵּד	m. sg. Pi`el	פַּקֵּד	Pi`el	פַּקֵּד
3 m. sg. Hif`il	יַפְקִיד	m. sg. Hif`il	הַפְקֵד	Hif`il	הַפְקִיד
3 m. sg. Nif`al	יִפָּקֵד	m. sg. Nif`al	הִפָּקֵד	Nif`al	הִפָּקֵד

הִשָּׁמֶר לְךָ ׀ הִשָּׁמֶר לְךָ   is the same construction as לֶךְ־לְךָ (Gen. 22:2).

תִּשְׁכַּח   Is this a Pi`el? _____

הוֹצִיאֲךָ   The root is _____ The stem is _____ The subject is _____

בֵּית עֲבָדִים   A noun in the plural can represent an abstract idea (as in זְקֻנִים [Gen. 37:3]), so בֵּית עֲבָדִים can mean either *house of slavery* or *house of slaves*. Although there is no sign of definiteness attached to the phrase, it may be definite by implication. This was <u>the</u> house of slaves/slavery.

Deuteronomy 6:13 [Lesson 38]

אֶת־יְהוָה אֱלֹהֶיךָ תִּירָא   Notice the word order: DDO followed by verb. The same inverted word order is used for emphasis in כִּי־אֹתוֹ אָהַב אֲבִיהֶם (Gen. 37:4).

וְאֹתוֹ תַעֲבֹד   A continuation of the emphatic construction. The pointing of אֹת is discussed in 23.2b. Why is there a patah ֲ under the prefix pronoun of תַעֲבֹד _____
_____ (**S 14.3.1.**)

וּבִשְׁמוֹ   The style of the verse should be your clue that this phrase is related to the verb that follows it in a way similar to the patterns —DO followed by verb—that precede it. A word about the vowels: both the בּ and the ו would normally have shewa ְ under them. If you don't understand why or how those vowels have changed, see **S 14.3.1–2.**

תִּשָּׁבֵעַ The root of this verb appears in וְשָׁבַע (Dt. 6:10), and you probably discovered at that point that this verb occurs almost exclusively in the Nif`al. Note again the dagesh forte in the first root letter (representing the assimilated נ of the stem preformative) and the vowel pattern ‿‿ ְִַ | ַ The pataḥ ַ with the ע is _____ (5.4)

Deuteronomy 6:14 [Lesson 38]

תֵלְכוּן Another paragogic ן (see יַאֲרִכֻן [Dt. 6:2] and תִּרְבּוּן [Dt. 6:3]). Notice that this passage started with its address in the 2 m. pl., switched to the 2 m. sg., and now is back to the 2 m. pl.

אַחֲרֵי אֱלֹהִים אֲחֵרִים The preposition has two forms: אַחַר (as in Gen. 22:1) and אַחֲרֵי as it is here.

מֵאֱלֹהֵי Here the preposition מִן means *from among* as it did in מֵאַבְנֵי (Gen. 28:11).

סְבִיבוֹתֵיכֶם When the preposition סָבִיב has a suffix, it takes the plural. That is not so unusual. אַחַר תַּחַת עַל אֶל among others, do the same. סָבִיב stands out because it has a f. pl. ending; the others are masculine.

Deuteronomy 6:15 [Lesson 38]

אֵל One of the titles used for God. There is no agreement as to whether אֵל is etymologically related to אֱלֹהִים

קַנָּא As a verb קנא can have a human being or God as a subject. As an adjective, it is used with reference to God only.

יֶחֱרֶה אַף First the verb: why the segol ֱ under the prefix pronoun? In the Qal of a 1st guttural, the vowel under the prefix pronoun is either pataḥ ַ or segol ֱ (the reasons why one or the other are related to vowel patterns, open and closed syllables, and "original" vowels). Now the noun: There are two words spelled אַף The one we are working with here means *nose* and is from the root אנף The other is a particle meaning *also, indeed, even* (it is not assigned a three-letter root). The expression יֶחֱרֶה אַף *his nose will burn* is usually translated more abstractly: *he [will]be angry.*

בְּךָ One of the many uses for the preposition בְּ is adversative, that is, *against.* However, staying with *in* leads to a legitimate interpretation also. בָּךְ ← בְּךָ because _____ (19.5) <u>Note</u>: BHS, which has בָּךְ for בְּךָ is in error.

306

Deuteronomy 6:16 [Lesson 39]

תְּנַסּוּ Spelled out, this would read תְּנַסְסוּ Is נסס a root? Yes it is. Could the root be anything else? _____ What are the stem indicators? _____ (36.3a) Read on in the verse and you will see the same root used again, but in the affix form. In fact the root is used three times in this verse. The reference is to Exodus 17:7. (You encountered this root in Genesis 22:1.)

Deuteronomy 6:17 [Lesson 39]

עָשֹׂר אֲעַשְּׂרֶנּוּ שָׁמוֹר תִּשְׁמְרוּן See (Gen. 28:22) for a discussion of the construction and תַּעַבְדוּן (Ex. 3:12) for an discussion of the final ן

וְעֵדֹתָיו Another word for a kind of law, עֵדוֹת or עֵדֹת from the root עוד *bear witness* or *testify.*

צִוָּךְ To translate this word, you have to determine whether the three letters are a root or whether you are dealing with more than one component. What is the stem? _____

Deuteronomy 6:18 [Lesson 39]

הַיָּשָׁר וְהַטּוֹב יָשָׁר and טוֹב are substantive adjectives.

יִיטַב Used as in Deuteronomy 6:3.

נִשְׁבַּע The same word appears in Deuteronomy 6:10.

Deuteronomy 6:19 [Lesson 39]

אֹיְבֶיךָ Holem after the first root letter indicates what stem and form? _____ (9.3a) Colloquial English often prefers a noun over the more verb-like force of a participle. The definition of a participle "someone doing something" still holds: *those-being hostile-to-you* can also be translated as *your enemies.*

Deuteronomy 6:20 [Lesson 39]

כִּי Text note 20ᵃ may be of some help in choosing an appropriate translation for כִּי here.

יִשְׁאָלְךָ בִנְךָ Observe that one ךְ____ is an object suffix and the other is a possessive suffix. More interesting, though, is the qamats under the א It is a result of pretonic lengthening—שאל in the Qal prefix form uses the pattern יִשְׁאַל—so it is not a qamats ḥatuf although it looks as if it is in a closed syllable. Texts made from the Second Rabbinic Bible tradition have a meteg after the א which tells us

307

that **א** is an open syllable. There is not one in BHS either because it was absent from the manuscript or because the editor chose not to retain it.

מָחָר Could this be a 3 m. sg. Qal affix? Other than the fact that that would not make much sense at this point in the verse, it is unlikely for another reason. The vowel qamats ‿ under the second root letter would appear instead of patah ‿ if the syllable were open (last letter ה or **א**) or at a strong disjunctive accent. True, מָחָר is at a disjunctive accent, but it is not one that changes the vowel. ‿ ‿ ‿ is a common noun pattern, דָּבָר for example. מָחָר can be specific or can refer to time in the future in a general sense.

מָה הָעֵדֹת וְהַחֻקִּים וְהַמִּשְׁפָּטִים אֲשֶׁר צִוָּה יהוה אֱלֹהֵינוּ אֶתְכֶם At the Passover seder, these questions (analogous to Exodus 13:14) are asked. The answers, which consist mainly of passages from Exodus and Deuteronomy, with midrashic interpretations, deal with the deliverance from Egypt.

Deuteronomy 6:21 [Lesson 40]

עֲבָדִים הָיִינוּ Notice the word order. If הָיִינוּ is a problem, see 37.2.

וַיּוֹצִיאֵנוּ 33.1 deals with the stem. נוּ‿ cannot be the subject because that function is taken up by the prefix pronoun. Then נוּ‿ must be a _____ Can it be 3 m. sg. or 1 c. pl.? No. That ambiguity exists only when the suffix is in the nunated form נוּ‿

בְּיָד חֲזָקָה Does חֲזָקָה meet the criteria for an attributive adjective? (See 14.2c and The Noun B.)

Deuteronomy 6:22 [Lesson 40]

אֹתֹת See לְאֹת (Dt. 6:8). The gender and number of אֹתֹת are _____

וּמֹפְתִים BDB lists this noun under the root אפת

גְּדֹלִים וְרָעִים The consonant cluster רע leads one to think of a couple of possible roots. (See Genesis 37:2a and b for examples.) But only one of those roots has an adjective that can generate the plural רָעִים and context will support one meaning over the other. רָעִים and גְּדֹלִים refer to מֹפְתִים and אֹתֹת Although אֹתֹת has a f. pl. endiNG, it functions as either a masculine or feminine noun. Furthermore, a masculine noun and a feminine noun in combination take masculine modifiers.

בְמִצְרַ֫יִם בְּפַרְעֹה וּבְכָל־בֵּיתוֹ לְעֵינֵ֫ינוּ Here the prepositions בְּ and לְ require some thought. Nuance is the translator's choice.

Deuteronomy 6:23 [Lesson 40]

וְאוֹתָ֫נוּ The noun אוֹת (Dt. 6:8 and 22) does not take a suffix in the singular, so אוֹתָ֫נוּ must be _____ (23.2b)

הֵבִיא Root _____ Stem _____ Form _____

לָתֶת 25.7 and gloss to Deuteronomy 6:10 discuss this word.

נִשְׁבַּע Stem discussed at Deuteronomy 6:10. Who is the subject?

Deuteronomy 6:24 [Lesson 40]

וַיְצַוֵּ֫נוּ The root צוה has occurred several times in this reading:

וּמִצְוֹתָיו (Dt. 6:2)		הַמִּצְוָה (Dt. 6:1)
מְצַוְּךָ		צִוָּה
מִצְוֹת (Dt. 6:17)		מְצַוְּךָ (Dt. 6:6)
צִוְּךָ		

לְיִרְאָה Context and the attached preposition לְ suggest an infinitive, and it is. The infinitive construct of ירא takes several forms. Without an attached preposition or suffix, it appears only once, just as one would expect it to: יְרֹא With a prefixed לְ it is לְיִרְאָה Almost every occurrence of לְיִרְאָה is followed by אֵת It is possible that the ה was added to the infinitive here so that two אs would not be next to each other.

שׂוֹב | לְטוֹב שׂוֹב can be a verb or a noun.

לְחַיֹּתֵ֫נוּ Morphologically לְחַיֹּתֵ֫נוּ reads like either a f. pl. noun + suffix or an infinitive + suffix. If you consult a dictionary you will see that the noun חַיָּה is not extant in the plural with a suffix. So then, what are the form (14.3a) and stem (15.6) of the verb ? _____ The factitive function—which means that an adjective complement is needed to complete the verb—of the Piʻel (15.6) is demonstrated in לְחַיֹּתֵ֫נוּ _keep_ us _alive_.

כְּהַיּוֹם If you are wondering why the ה has not elided to give כַּיּוֹם you are astute. Normally the definite article does elide after a preposition. Gesenius § 35 *n* explains that for the particular noun יוֹם a distinction is preserved between כְּהַיּוֹם *at about this time*, and כַּיּוֹם *first of all*. However, the elision is also a sign of later Hebrew, an explanation that better suits the context.

Deuteronomy 6:25 [Lesson 40]

וּצְדָקָה Although this word has come to mean *charity*, its primary meaning is *righteousness*.

נִשְׁמֹר לַעֲשׂוֹת This combination of verbs is seen in Deuteronomy 6:3.

הַמִּצְוָה הַזֹּאת As in Deuteronomy 6:1, the sense of a body of law is implied.

אֵלִיָּהוּ "Translate" the components of this name.

הַתִּשְׁבִּי One way to read this word is as a gentilic. (22.5) In the apocryphal literature (Tobit 1:2), there is reference to a place, Tishbe, in Northern Galilee. The *Oxford Bible Atlas* puts Tishbe on the brook of כְּרִית (very near Jabesh Gilead), the place where אֵלִיָּהוּ is told to go (1 Ki. 17:2–3). Some commentators claim there was no such place and read הַתִּשְׁבִּי as a variant of the noun תּוֹשָׁב *sojourner* under the root יָשַׁב Text note Cp 17,1a offers yet another approach by pointing out that some versions of the Septuagint have הַנָּבִיא *the prophet* instead of הַתִּשְׁבִּי

מִתֹּשָׁבֵי גִלְעָד The problem of how to read the word הַתִּשְׁבִּי continues into this phrase. Text note 17[b] suggests changing the vocalization to read מִתִּשְׁבֵּי *from Tishbe [of Gilead]*. Part of the difficulty of the words lies in the interpretation of מִ It can be *from* [the place] or *from among* [the people].

חַי־יְהוָה | חַי is a vocabulary word from the root _____ The phrase חַי־יְהוָה introduces an **oath formula**. The formula consists of three parts:

1. The deity by whom the person is swearing, which here is יהוה אֱלֹהֵי יִשְׂרָאֵל

2. A clause introduced by אִם which is understood as a negative, even though a negative particle as such doesn't appear: that is that such-and-such <u>won't</u> happen.

3. כִּי אִם which begins the third clause and is translated as *but, except,* or *unless.*

An oath formula, found mostly in Kings, may consist of only the first two components. Here, though, we have a complete example:

1   חַי־יְהוָה אֱלֹהֵי יִשְׂרָאֵל אֲשֶׁר עָמַדְתִּי לְפָנָיו
2   אִם־יִהְיֶה הַשָּׁנִים הָאֵלֶּה טַל וּמָטָר
3   כִּי אִם־לְפִי דְבָרִי

עָמַדְתִּי In direct speech, the affix form of the verb is sometimes used even though the action is taking place in the present. Just a reminder: Affix form is used for actions that have a specific beginning and a specific end regardless of the tense.

הַשָּׁנִים הָאֵלֶּה The difficulty is where to find הַשָּׁנִים in the dictionary. Fortunately for you, it is a vocabulary word. It is, however, somewhat irregular in that it is feminine but has a m. pl. endiNG in the plural.

שַׁל can be found under the root שָׁלַל Two-letter nouns are usually formed from geminate or hollow roots.

וּמָטָר The מ is not a preformative here. It is actually part of the root. Hebrew has many words for rain, each having to do with the season in which it falls and the type of rain that it is. מָטָר is the most general term for rain. שַׁל is a very fine rain, like a mist or dew. גֶּשֶׁם is heavy rain. The early, light rain is יוֹרֶה and the later, heavier rain is מַלְקוֹשׁ

לְפִי | פֶּה פִּי in construct → פִּי *To the mouth of* is commonly rendered *according to*. In a different context, what else could פִּי mean? _____ (See vocabulary.)

דְּבָרִי Why is there a shewa ְ under the ד _____ (**S 5.1c.2**) Is this word singular or plural? _____ (The Noun G 2)

1 Kings 17:2 [Lesson 41]

דְּבַר־יהוה אֵלָיו Such a phrase is common in prophetic narratives. It can be read as a noun sentence, but the verb *came* is often used instead of *was* to make it flow better in English.

1 Kings 17:3 [Lesson 41]

לֵךְ וּפָנִיתָ לְךָ . . . לֵךְ The sequence here, imperative followed by affix + vav reversive, gives the affix form imperative force. (See שְׁמַע יִשְׂרָאֵל . . . וְאָהַבְתָּ [Dt. 6:4–5].) לְךָ used precisely as it is here, appears in וְלֶךְ־לְךָ (Gen. 22:2).

מִזֶּה | זֶה זֶה is being used as a substantive adjective: *this* → *this place*.

וְנִסְתַּרְתָּ The consonant cluster סתר can be extracted to supply the root; that leaves three other elements. וְ is _____ Now you have תָּ ְ ַ ְ נ Which of these consonants must be the subject pronoun? What will the other one be? _____ וְנִסְתַּרְתָּ is still part of the sequence imperative + affix + vav reversive.

בְּנַחַל The word נַחַל is a segolate noun (see The Noun F), but it is pointed with pataḥ ַ instead of segol ֶ because of the middle guttural. Gutturals have a propensity for the vowel ַ under them, before them, and even after them.

1 Kings 17:4 [Lesson 41]

תִּשְׁתֶּה What will you take off to find the root? Does either dagesh represent doubling?

הָעֹרְבִים In BDB, there are six root meanings for עֹרֵב The sixth means *be black,* which is where the translation *raven* comes from. Some of the other roots don't make sense here, but others you might find possible.

לְכַלְכֶּלְךָ Remove the preposition and the suffix. You are left with the two letters כל which are repeated. Doubling the two strong consonants is one way that a hollow verb can be intensified because the middle letter, being a vowel letter, is almost never doubled. This stem is called the Pilpèl and is a variant of Pìel.

1 Kings 17:5 [Lesson 41]

כִּדְבַר Are you dealing with a noun or a verb here? (Check vocabulary list for answer.)

1 Kings 17:6 [Lesson 42]

מְבִיאִים This word has the same endiNG as the word וְהָעֹרְבִים just before it, an indication that the two words are probably connected in some way. It cannot be an attributive adjective because it is not definite. There is one verb form that has a מ preformative in most stems and takes adjective endiNGs. The vowel under the preformative suggests Pìel (31.1), but the I class vowel between the ב and the א suggests Hifìl, which is what the stem is.

Remember: 1.   Hollow verbs do not go into a standard Pìel. They use the Polèl or the Pilpèl.

2.   Propretonic reduction can make landmark vowels disappear.

Review question: How would the m. sg. of this word be pointed? _____ (33.5)

בָּעֶרֶב The root עֹרֵב is being used to mean something different from what it does at the beginning of the verse.

יִשְׁתֶּה An example of the prefix form as an imperfect: *was drinking* or *would drink.*

1 Kings 17:7 [Lesson 42]

מִקֵּץ The first thing to figure out is what the dagesh is for. מִקֵּץ is not a root, so the dagesh most likely represents _____ (3.4b) That leaves only two visible root letters. Two-letter nouns tend to come from geminate or hollow roots. There is a root קוץ and also a root קצץ but only one yields a noun קֵץ

מִקֵּץ יָמִים The preposition מִן occasionally gives a temporal sense. יָמִים is the plural of an irregular noun. (See יָמֶיךָ [Dt. 6:2] and The Noun H.) A literal translation of the phrase yields an apocalyptic-sounding *at an end of days*. Translators tend to go with something like *after a while* (KJV) or *after some time* (JPS).

1 Kings 17:9 [Lesson 42]

קוּם לֵךְ The form of these words is _____ (20.6a)

צָרְפַּֽתָה The root may be hinting at the motifs of testing and purifying with fire in the Elijah narratives.

וְיָשַׁבְתָּ Is the י a root letter or a prefix pronoun? _____

צִוִּ֫יתִי What are the root, stem, form, and PGN of this verb? _____

אִשָּׁה אַלְמָנָה Why isn't אֵת in front of this phrase? You will have to determine whether the root letters for אַלְמָנָה are אלם or למן

לְכַלְכְּלֶֽךָ See לְכַלְכֶּלְךָ (1 Ki. 17:4). The reason for the slightly different spelling of these words is due to the accent each receives.

1 Kings 17:10 [Lesson 42]

אֶל־פֶּתַח הָעִיר This description reveals that צָרְפַת was most likely a walled city.

מְקֹשֶׁ֫שֶׁת There are two possibilities for the root of this word. One is that it is hollow; the other is that it is a geminate. מְקֹשֶׁ֫שֶׁת happens to be from a geminate root. The hollow possibility comes up because there are two ways to intensify hollows. One is to repeat the two strong letter cluster as in לְכַלְכְּלֶֽךָ (1 Ki. 17:4) The other is to double the second strong letter. מ preformative indicates

———————— form in stems other than the Qal and Nif`al. The endiNG tells you that the gender and number are ———— (24.5a, footnote 1)

Warning: The introduction of a female character means that you should be on the lookout for feminine singular verb forms and suffixes.

אֵלֶ֫יהָ Suffix discussed at 23.2c.

קְחִי־נָא If the form of the verb is not obvious, review 21.7c.

בִכְלִי The יֽ_ ending on this word looks like the 1 c. sg. possessive pronoun, but, alas, it is not. Like עֳנִי (Ex. 3:7), כְּלִי is a noun (and a vocabulary word).

וְאִשְׁתֶּה Following the imperative קְחִי־נָא this וֽ + prefix form gives to the verb a sense of purpose or result.

Review

Imperative + affix+vav rev. → affix has imperative force: לֵךְ מִזֶּה וּפָנִיתָ לְךָ קֵ֫דְמָה

Imperative + וֽ+prefix → prefix expresses purpose: קְחִי־נָא לִי מְעַט־מַ֫יִם...וְאִשְׁתֶּה

For more syntactical possibilities of וֽ see **S 43.3**

1 Kings 17:11 [Lesson 43]

לָקַ֫חַת 25.7 discusses the form. Is the ל here a root letter or a preposition?

וַיֹּאמָ֑ר וַיֹּאמֶר is וַיֹּאמָ֑ר in pause.

לְקִחִי This is an "irregular" imperative. קְחִי in the previous verse is the regular form. The Masoretic note cites this as the sole occurrence of such a spelling. Text note 11[b], seeking to account for this unusual spelling, suggests it may be meant to be read לָהּ קְחִי *[and he said] to her, "Take . . ."*

פַּת To find the root, see comment on טַל (1 Ki. 17:1).

בְּיָדֵךְ ךְ_ is the 2 f. sg. possessive suffix.

1 Kings 17:12 [Lesson 43]

חַי־יְהוָה See the discussion about the oath formula at 1 Kings 17:1.

אִם־יֶשׁ־לִי This begins the second part of the oath. The shorter יֶשׁ is used instead of יֵשׁ in this phrase because of the maqqef.

אֱלֹהֶיךָ It is worth noting that the widow, a Phoenician and presumably therefore a worshiper of Baʿal, swears by the God of Elijah.

מָעוֹג There is a noun עֻגָה which means *cake*, and in fact that word is used in 1 Kings 18:5. מָעוֹג seems to mean the same thing. (The root עוּג in Hebrew and other cognate languages means *circle* or *something curved*.) Text note 12ᵃ tells us that the Syriac and Targum(s) read a completely different word here מְאוּמָה as in: וְאַל־תַּעַשׂ לוֹ מְאוּמָה (Gen. 22:12).

כִּי אִם Introduces the third part of the oath.

מְלֹא Morphologically מְלֹא could be a m. sg. Qal imperative, an infinitive construct, or a noun.

בַּכַּד Figure out the function of each dagesh. To determine the root refer to שַׁל (1 Ki. 17:1).

שְׁנָיִם This word is from a root of שׁנה different from that of הַשְּׁנִים (1 Ki. 17:1) The question is, "Just how many sticks is this?" Rather than referring to a precise number, שְׁנַיִם may be *a few*.

וּבָאתִי There are four verbs from here until the end of the verse; all of them are affix forms with vav reversive. Not one of the conjunctions is pointed with a shewa, either because of the first root letter or its vowel, or in the case of וְמָתְנוּ because of the location of tone (accent). For more detail on the vowels that וְ takes, see **S 14.3.2–3**.

וַעֲשִׂיתִהוּ The suffix is referring to _____ Analyze this verb: _____ For vocalization of the initial וְ see **S 14.3.1**.

וְלִבְנִי Five letters comprising four components.

וַאֲכַלְנֻהוּ Qibbuts ֻ is a defectiva shureq וּ

וְמָתְנוּ Why the qamats ָ under the וְ Because initial וָ ← וְ when it is pretonic, especially if the next vowel is an A class. The qamats ָ under the מ would normally be pataḥ ַ but it is at a strong accent and so has lengthened.

1 Kings 17:13 [Lesson 43]

אַל־תִּירְאִי 39.3b discusses the grammar of the phrase.

בֹּאִי עֲשִׂי 20.6a covers the form.

כִּדְבָרֵךְ   The suffix ךְ ֵ is 2 f. sg. as in בְּיָדֵךְ just above in 1 Kings 17:11.

אַךְ   An adverb found in BDB under אַךְ Despite the three-letter-root theory, some words are found under a two-letter listing.

בָּרִאשֹׁנָה   An adverb formed from the feminine form of the adjective רִאשׁוֹן + the preposition בְּ

וְהוֹצֵאת   The root and stem are the topic of 31.2, but by this time you should be familiar with such forms as הוֹצִיא מוֹצִיא and יוֹצִיא We expect a DO to follow because of the transitive meaning of the verb, but one doesn't.

וְלָךְ   **S 43.3** discusses syntactical uses of וְ We have seen לָךְ many times before, but always as the m. sg. form of לְךָ in pause. Here it is the regular combination of the preposition לְ with a 2 f. sg. object suffix ךְ ָ (ךְ ָ is another vowel consonant combination for the 2 f. sg. suffix.) Text note 13ᶜ tells us that two other extant Hebrew manuscripts understood it differently. Can you see how the other reading is possible?

בָּאַחֲרֹנָה   Approach this the same way as בָּרִאשֹׁנָה earlier in the verse.

1 Kings 17:14 [Lesson 43]

תִכְלֶה   Is this ה ֶ + תכל or כלה + ת Once you determine that, you might wonder why the final vowel is qamats ָ and not segol ֶ The marginal Masoretic note informs that תִכְלֶה occurs three times, twice with a ה and once with a final א It seems, then, that תִכְלֶה is a mixed form, taking the vowel of the 3rd א but retaining the 3rd ה What is the subject of תִכְלֶה

<u>Note</u>: Pottery items are feminine (The Noun A).

תֶחְסָר | תֶחְסַר   חָסֵר is an I class verb (17.6b). I and U class verbs tend to take the יִשְׁלַח pattern (rather than the יִפְקֹד pattern) in the prefix form. In תֶחְסָר the pataḥ has become a qamats ָ ← ַ because it is at a strong disjunctive accent. Segol ֶ under the prefix pronoun of a 1st guttural in the Qal is not uncommon, especially in a closed syllable. The other vowel that can be under the prefix pronoun of a Qal prefix for a 1st guttural is pataḥ ַ

תִתֵּן   The Masoretic note cites this word as a כְּתִב (written) קְרָא (read). It is written תתן but should be read תֵּת (הַהִוא in Gen. 29:2 is another example. See also Glossary entry ketiv-qere.)

1 Kings 17:15 [Lesson 43]

וַתֹּאכַל Often when there are a lot of subjects, as there are here, the verb agrees with the first one. So far the subject has been 3 f. sg., but after וַתֹּאכַל another subject is introduced.

הִוא־וָהִיא Another כְּתִב קְרֵא supported by text note 15[b]. There is a dagesh in the י to stand for ו Read this as הִיא־וָהוּא The verb is 3 f. sg. so we can assume that הִיא comes first. Here both the Masoretic notation and text critical note are commenting on and saying the same thing. They frequently attend to completely different matters.

וּבֵיתָה The widow's household has not been mentioned before, and this did not escape the eye of the BHS editor, who proposes וּבְנָה in place of וּבֵיתָה

יָמִים English needs the addition of a preposition.

1 Kings 17:16 [Lesson 44]

כָּלָתָה An affix form from the same root as תִכְלֶה (1 Ki. 17:14), but why the ָ ָ ָ The first and third vowels are expected. The middle vowel is usually a shewa ְ Again it is the strong disjunctive accent that stimulates the vowel change.

חָסֵר Why the tsere ֵ as the second vowel? _____ (17.6) This verb, in the Qal prefix, appears in 1 Kings 17:14.

1 Kings 17:17 [Lesson 44]

וַיְהִי אַחַר הַדְּבָרִים הָאֵלֶּה This expression is the sign of a new story. Genesis 22 starts the same way. The 3 m. sg. Qal prefix of וַיְהִי without ו conversive is _____

בַּעֲלַת הַבַּיִת This phrase is qualifying הָאִשָּׁה Remember that the construct of a feminine noun ends in ת____ though the absolute may end in _____ (22.4a)

חָלְיוֹ The question here concerns the function of the י It could indicate a plural or be the remnant of a 3rd ה root. Hint: The root occurs earlier in the verse. How will you pronounce the first syllable?

עַד אֲשֶׁר When a preposition is followed by אֲשֶׁר the word אֲשֶׁר serves to convert the preposition into a conjunction, but itself is not translated. (45.5)

נוֹתְרָה־ The root is יתר and the נ is a Nif`al preformative. The י of a 1st י verb in the Nif`al is affected the same way it is in the Hif`il; it becomes the primitive ו Could נוֹתְרָה also be a f. sg. Qal participle of the verb נָתַר *spring* or *startup*? Yes.

נְשָׁמָה is close in meaning to נֶפֶשׁ (Dt. 6:5), but נְשָׁמָה is one's actual breath.

1 Kings 17: 18 [Lesson 44]

מַה־לִּי וָלָךְ Literally *What [is it] to me and to you?* More colloquially, *What is there between you and me?* For the dagesh in the לּ see 17.3b and especially **S 17.3b.**

אִישׁ הָאֱלֹהִים The same grammatical case as יִשְׂרָאֵל in שְׁמַע יִשְׂרָאֵל (Dt. 6:4).

אֵלַי If this is a problem see Chart O: Prepositions with Suffixes.

לְהַזְכִּיר The text is not explicit as to just who is doing the remembering or who is being reminded.

עֲוֺנִי The root is עוה Although 3rd ה roots tend to yield 3rd י nouns, they don't always. Hebrew has many words for sin. Some are:

עָוֺן *iniquity* or *guilt,* from the root עוה *bend* or *twist*

חַטָּאת *sin,* from a root meaning *miss the mark, err, offend*

רֶשַׁע *acting wickedly,* with the connotation of especially gross or crass wickedness.

פֶּשַׁע *rebellion, revolt, transgression*

Trivia question: When is וֹ a defectiva ḥolem? (Answer at the end of this verse.)

וּלְהָמִית The stem is _____ The form is _____ The root is _____ (The root appears in 1 Kings 17:12.)

Answer to trivia question: When the ו is a consonant as in עָוֺן

1 Kings 17:19 [Lesson 44]

תְּנִי Is the dagesh standing for the assimilated נ of the root? (Answer at the end of this verse.)

בְּנֵךְ The suffix ֵךְ is 2 f. sg., as in בְּיָדֵךְ (1 Ki. 17:11).

וַיִּקָּחֵהוּ The root is _____ (21.1) The suffix is _____ (Gen. 22:2)

Synopsis of Common 3 m. sg. Suffixes

———

וֹ֫____ וֹ____ 3 m. sg. possessive suffix on a noun

חָלְיוֹ *his sickness* (1 Ki. 17:17) נְעָרָיו *his youths* (Gen. 22:3)

וֹ____ וֹ____ 3 m. sg. object suffix on a preposition

אֵלָיו *to him* (Gen. 22:1) וַיִּגְעַר־בּוֹ *and he rebuked him* (Gen. 37:10)

נּוּ֫____ הוּ____ וֹ____ 3 m. sg. object suffix on a verb

לַהֲמִיתוֹ *to kill him* (Gen. 37:18) לֹא נַכֶּ֫נּוּ *let us not smite him* (Gen. 37:21)

וַיִּקָּחֵ֫הוּ *and he took him* (1 Ki. 17:19)

מֶחֱיָקָה Hollow roots often have biforms. This noun may be listed under חִיק חוק or חוק

וַיַּעֲלֵ֫הוּ Is וַיַּעֲלֵ֫הוּ ambiguous? _____ (See Genesis 22:13.)

הָעֲלִיָּה A noun (with the definite article) from the same root as וַיַּעֲלֵ֫הוּ Review question: Why is the initial ה pointed הָ _____ (4.5b)

אֲשֶׁר־הוּא יֹשֵׁב שָׁם For syntax, see 22.8a.

וַיַּשְׁכִּבֵ֫הוּ Pay particular attention to stem indicators.

מִטָּתוֹ There are two challenges to this word. One is the reason for the dagesh. The second is the reason for the ת

Answer: No. The dagesh in תֵּן is not standing for the assimilated נ of the root. It is lene in a בגדכפת letter. Since dagesh forte requires a full vowel immediately before it, it cannot be in the first letter of a word.

1 Kings 17:20 [Lesson 44]

וַיִּאמַר What is the subject of the verb? The atnaḥ suggests that what comes next starts a new thought.

אֱלֹהַי The usual pointing would be אֱלֹהַי but the accent over this word (two vertical dots) is a strong disjunctive, and so the vowel is lengthened.

הֲגַם   Can the הֲ here be the sign of the Hif`il or the definite article? _____ If not, why not? _____
_____ What else could it be? _____ (28.6) There is a long אֲשֶׁר clause
(22.8a) before the main verb.

מִתְגּוֹרֵר   The Hitpa`el (see Glossary or The Verb: stems related to the Pi`el) participle can be recognized by the מִתְ‎ָ preformative. The Hitpa`el, like the Pi`el, requires a doubling of the middle root letter, which, as we have seen, is a problem with hollow verbs. The root here is גּוּר and the intensification is achieved by doubling the third—or second—(depending on how you look at it) root letter. To be
technically correct, we have to call this the Hitpol`el rather than the Hitpa`el because of the pointing.
(See לְכַלְכְּלֶךָ 1 Ki. 17:4 for another solution to making a hollow root into a kind of Pi`el.)

הֲרֵעוֹתָ   This time הֲ is not the interrogative; it is a Hif`il preformative, and the formation is similar to
that of וַהֲשִׁבֹתִיךָ (Gen. 28:15). However, the root of הֲרֵעוֹתָ is geminate, not hollow.

1 Kings 17:21 [Lesson 45]

וַיִּתְמֹדֵד   This Hitpol`el prefix form could result from either a geminate or hollow root (as in
מִתְגּוֹרֵר 1 Ki. 17:20). As opposed to its handling of מְקֹשֶׁשֶׁת (1 Ki. 17:10), BDB assigns וַיִּתְמֹדֵד
a hollow root, but cites a geminate root as a secondary form. Note the reflexive character of וַיִּתְמֹדֵד

יהוה אֱלֹהַי   Same syntax as אִישׁ הָאֱלֹהִים (1 Ki. 17:20).

תָּשָׁב נָא   What is the root of the verb? _____ (6.1a) The form is tricky. The Qal prefix form of
a 3 f. or 2 m. sg. of שׁוּב is תָּשׁוּב   When the verb is written in a shortened form (the way it would be
with vav conversive as is תָּשָׁב), then it is jussive (42.1) and the PGN in that case can only be 3 f. sg.
(M. sg. imperatives may lengthen—see Lesson 30—but they do not shorten.) What, then, is the subject? _____

נֶפֶשׁ   Note that in 1 Kings 17:17 נְשָׁמָה is used.

עַל־קִרְבּוֹ   The prepositions אֶל and עַל seem to interchange in later writings. One theory is that ע
and א had come to sound alike and when the material was dictated the letters were sometimes confused. (The problem with that theory is that the material may not have been dictated; it may have been
copied.) Another possibility is that we don't understand the whole range of meaning of the words.

Prepositions tend to be highly idiomatic, each having a multitude of nuances related to context. English has not escaped this problem. Look at a sampling of the preposition "in": To come <u>in</u> a rage, <u>in</u> a car, <u>in</u> a door, <u>in</u> a minute, <u>in</u> a suit, <u>in</u> a hurry, <u>in</u> spite of it all! קׇרְבּוֹ is an I class segolate noun + suffix. (See **S 4.4b**.)

1 Kings 17:22 [Lesson 45]

וַיִּשְׁמַע יהוה בְּקוֹל אֵלִיָּהוּ   16.7b discusses the use of a preposition before a DO.

וַיְּחִי   The usual spelling and accentuation of this word is וַיְחִי So in וַיְּחִי both the place of the accent and the vowel have been changed.

1 Kings 17:23 [Lesson 45]

וַיֹּרִדֵהוּ   This is a defectiva spelling, so you can assume ו between the prefix pronoun and the root. The suffix tells us that the verb must be transitive. The stem is _____ In the Qal, this verb means

_____

הַבַּיְתָה   What is the ending הָ here? _____ (11.3)

וַיִּתְּנֵהוּ   Constructed like וַיִּקָּחֵהוּ (1 Ki. 17:19).

לְאִמּוֹ   Why is there a dagesh in the מ _____ (See עִמָּךְ [Gen. 28:14].)

רְאִי   For help with the form, review 20.6a.

חַי   Thematically, one can connect the living boy to the living God in 1 Kings 17:1.

1 Kings 17:24 [Lesson 45]

בְּפִיךָ   There is a vocabulary word lurking in בְּפִיךָ

אֱמֶת   Vocabulary word.

וַיִּשְׁלַח אַחְאָב Is אַחְאָב the subject or the object of the verb? Although "send" is transitive in English, it doesn't always require an object in Hebrew.

הַנְּבִיאִים BHS text note 20[b] tells us that a few texts insert כָּל before הַנְּבִיאִים Because כָּל precedes בְּנֵי יִשְׂרָאֵל earlier in the verse, its presence before הַנְּבִיאִים would balance the verse. One of the things the editor of BHS looks for is stylistic consistency; look for other notes like this one in the chapter (and elsewhere, of course).

עַד־מָתַי | מָתַי is listed precisely this way in the dictionary.

אַתֶּם What purpose is this pronoun serving? _____ (9.3b, 36.7)

פֹּסְחִים Whether פסח has two distinct roots is a point of controversy.

עַל־שְׁתֵּי For שְׁתֵּי see 41.2a.

אִם . . . אִם *Either . . . or*

יהוה הָאֱלֹהִים What is this construction called? _____ (2.10b)

אַחֲרָיו What is the function of the י _____ (See אֵלֶיךָ [Gen. 22:2].)

אֹתוֹ דָּבָר The אֵת identifies the suffix וֹ as the DDO. Where, then, does דָּבָר fit into the phrase? It is also a DO: Answer *him* (DDO) *a word* (DO). In English grammar, *him* would be called the indirect object.

אֲנִי Is this pronoun serving the same function as אַתֶּם in 1 Kings 18:21? _____

נוֹתַרְתִּי If you have trouble with the root or stem, study 46.7a and look over the remarks to נוֹתְרָה at 1 Kings 17.17. This is another example of the affix form used in direct speech to convey present time, as in עָמַדְתִּי (1 Ki. 17:1) and יָדַעְתִּי (1 Ki. 17:24).

לְבַדִּי Vocabulary word + suffix.

אַרְבַּע־מֵאוֹת וַחֲמִשִּׁים Vocabulary words or derivatives all.

אִישׁ   After the number 100, the noun associated with a number is usually in the singular. Two ways of translating the phrase אַרְבַּע־מֵאוֹת וַחֲמִשִּׁים אִישׁ are: *450 men* or *450 to a man.*

1 Kings 18:23 [Lesson 46]

וְיִתְּנוּ־לָנוּ   Jussive mood (42.1) works best for וְיִתְּנוּ and all the verbs up to the atnaḥ, but must be inferred because none has a shortened form. Notice that both words in this phrase end in וּנ___ In וְיִתְּנוּ the נ is part of the root; in לָנוּ it is part of the suffix. Can the suffix be ambiguous? _____ (See וַיּוֹצִיאֵנוּ [Dt. 6:21].) In this long verse, use each ו as a syntactical division marker.

שְׁנַיִם פָּרִים   The numerals from 3–10 may stand before the noun either in the construct state or in the absolute (as here), or in the absolute after the noun.

לָהֶם   The suffix has a reflexive meaning in this context.

הַפָּר הָאֶחָד   The numeral one acts like a regular adjective.

וַיְנַתְּחֻהוּ   There is no vowel under the י because _____ (23.2a)

Analyze this verb: _____

וְיָשִׂימוּ | שִׂים like שָׁלַח does not always take a DO.

וְאֵשׁ   Remember that *and* is not the only meaning for the conjunction ו Attached to a noun or pronoun that introduces a new subject, ו can be contrastive: *but.* (**S 43.3** for the range of uses of initial ו)

1 Kings 18:24 [Lesson 46]

בְשֵׁם־יהוה   Text note 24[a] notes that the Septuagint, Syriac, and Vulgate add the equivalent of *my God* after יהוה perhaps to balance the verse.

יַעֲנֶה   What about the stem? יַעֲנֶה is pointed for _____ or _____ If you look in a dictionary, you will see that only one possibility is extant.

בָאֵשׁ   The preposition is being used as it is in בְּקַרְנָיו (Gen. 22:13).

הוּא הָאֱלֹהִים   Granted, this could be a noun sentence (2.10b), but a verbless clause also allows for a sense of timelessness.

וְלֹא־עָנוּ כָל־הָעָם   This time עַם is taking a singular verb. (See וַיַּעַן הָעָם

[1 Ki. 18:21].) But go one word further וַיֹּאמְרוּ and the verb becomes plural.

שׁוֹב הַדָּבָר When an adjective precedes the noun, it is functioning as _____

(15.2) A couple of translations: KJV and NRSV: *Well spoken*! JPS: *Very good!*

1 Kings 18:25 [Lesson 47]

בַּחֲרוּ If the form is giving you trouble, read through the rest of the verse; that may help reveal the mood. The pointing could be either Qal or Pi'el. Since the verb is not elsewhere attested in the Pi'el and has only one occurrence in the Pu'al, it is considered to be a Qal. That being so, why pataḥ ◌ַ under the first root letter? _____ **(S 14.3.1)**

לָכֶם is functioning like לָהֶם in verse 23.

וַעֲשׂוּ Why does the ו have a pataḥ ◌ַ **(S 14.3.1)**

רִאשֹׁנָה Same word discussed in 1 Kings 17:13.

1 Kings 18:26 [Lesson 47]

אֲשֶׁר־נָתַן An affix form in a subordinate clause is often referring to an action that occurred before the main action of the verse, so would be expressed by the pluperfect in English.

הַבַּעַל It is common to see ◌ַ ה in front of a proper name, although the article may not be acknowledged in English translation. Two other occurrences of this convention that we have seen are הָאֱלֹהִים (Gen. 22:1) and הַמֹּרִיָּה (Gen. 22:2).

עֲנֵנוּ What is the root? ענ are root letters, but what about נוּ ◌ Is the נ part of the root or does it go with the ו There are two ענן roots, but one has no verbal development, and the other is extant only in the Po'el. Since the root is not ענן the נוּ ◌ is a single component. Furthermore, it must be an object suffix because there is no root and stem that would have such a vowel pattern in the 1 c. sg. affix form. Also, before a suffix, there will usually be an accented penultimate ◌ֵ syllable on imperative or prefix form verbs in those PGNs that have no prefix complement. Since there is no prefix pronoun on עֲנֵנוּ it must be a m. sg. imperative. Back to the original question. What is the root? _____ (It is a vocabulary word.)

וַיְפַסְּחוּ This verb in another stem and form appeared in 1 Kings 18:21.

אֲשֶׁר עָשָׂה The tense relationships in this clause parallel אֲשֶׁר נָתַן at the beginning of the verse. (There are some tense relationships in the story, too.)

1 Kings 18:27 [Lesson 47]

כִּי שִׂיחַ The conjunction, which is repeated in the following phrases, conveys the idea of certainty. Sarcasm is no doubt intended, as implied by the verb וַיְהַתֵּל

וְכִי־שִׂיג לוֹ וְכִי־דֶרֶךְ לוֹ English sometimes uses noun phrases the way they are being used here—for example, "Surely so-and-so has a pressing engagement." שִׂיג is found in BDB under סוּג

אוּלַי Listed precisely this way in the dictionary.

יָשֵׁן Do you recognize this verb type? If not, see 17.6.

וְיִקָץ This is not a 3rd ה or a geminate. יקץ is a 1st י verb like ירא in that it retains the י of the root in most forms. Here, unfortunately, the י of the root has elided (the י you see is a prefix pronoun), so the root's identifying characteristic is lost. The Masoretic note cites וְיִקָץ as a singular occurrence and confirms the defectiva spelling. (In Genesis 28:16 יקץ appears in the Qal prefix with vav conversive and is written וַיִּיקַץ the way one would expect to see it.)

1 Kings 18:28 [Lesson 47]

וַיִּתְגֹּדְדוּ Another Hitpol'el of a geminate verb like וַיִּתְמֹדֵד (1 Ki. 17:21). Both reflexive (*they cut themselves*) and interactive (*they cut each other*) meanings might be appropriate here.

כְּמִשְׁפָּטָם Although *judgment* is the primary meaning of מִשְׁפָּט *custom* and *fashion* are also possibilities. Identify the four components of the word _____

בַּחֲרָבוֹת The preposition is functioning like that in בָּאֵשׁ (1 Ki. 18:24) and בְּקַרְנָיו (Gen. 22:13). What is וֹת ⌣ here? _____

עַד־שְׁפָךְ־דָּם A word about שְׁפָךְ It is an infinitive construct in construct. The ḥolem of the Qal infinitive construct has been reduced to a qamats ḥatuf because the syllable is closed and unaccented. This clause is grammatically similar to בִּהְיוֹת שָׁאוּל (35.1c) except that here the preposition is not attached to the verb.

1 Kings 18:29 [Lesson 47]

כְּעֲבֹר הַצָּהֳרַ֫יִם This phrase is constructed like עַד־שְׁפָךְ־דָּם In both cases, there is a preposition + infinitive + subject.

וַיִּֽתְנַבְּאוּ Some scholars believe that one of the meanings of the Hitpaʿel is to feign something, like *to play the prophet.* But it is a major interpretational difference to say *they prophesied* or *they feigned prophesy.* Other possibilities could be *they prophesied to each other, they prophesied to themselves* (a bit far out perhaps but "correct"), *they prophesied over and over.* KJV: *they prophesied*; NRSV and JPS: *they raved on.*

לַעֲלוֹת הַמִּנְחָה This is yet another infinitive construct in construct + noun. The מִנְחָה was probably an offering that was given late in the afternoon because it fits the context, and later in Judaism it became the term for the late afternoon service. Because the verb עלה is used, it seems likely that this was a burnt offering, although some interpreters think the term applies to any offering made to God.

וְאֵין Note the repetition and extension of the וְאֵין clauses here and also in 1 Kings 18:26.

1 Kings 18:30 [Lesson 48]

גְּשׁוּ If you don't recognize the root, read a little further into the verse and it may become apparent. Is the dagesh in the ג lene or forte? (For the answer, see comments to תְּנִי in 1 Kings 17:19.)

הֶהָרוּס Lesson 42.3 discusses the form. הֶהָרוּס is modifying מִזְבַּח which is the first word in a construct chain. Because nothing comes between the construct and the absolute, a modifier of the construct must come after the whole chain. You saw this arrangement in בַּ֫עַל הַחֲלֹמוֹת הַלָּזֶה (Gen. 37:19).

1 Kings 18:31 [Lesson 48]

שְׁתֵּים עֶשְׂרֵה After the numbers 11–19, the singular or the plural of the noun is used. The number itself can precede or follow the noun.

כְּמִסְפַּר שִׁבְטֵי בְנֵי־יַעֲקֹב A phrase with three words in construct.

יַעֲקֹב אֲשֶׁר הָיָה דְבַר־יהוה אֵלָיו For syntax see 22.8a. A second point: since the verb in the main clause is past tense, the affix form verb in the אֲשֶׁר clause can be pluperfect.

1 Kings 18:32 [Lesson 48]

אֶת־הָאֲבָנִים מִזְבֵּחַ Hebrew handles this as a double DO or what we might call a DO and an object complement. English needs something like *into an* between the two nouns.

תְּעָלָה A ת preformative noun.

בְּבֵית בֵית in this context has the sense of *receptacle*.

סָאתַיִם סָאתַיִם is the dual (see The Noun B) of סְאָה and can be transliterated as *two seahs*.

1 Kings 18:33 [Lesson 48]

וַיַּעֲרֹךְ אֶת־הָעֵצִים Compare this section with Genesis 22:9.

וַיְנַתַּח The stem is _____

וַיָּשֶׂם If you need help, glance back at the note to וַיֵּשֶׁב (Gen. 37:1). This is yet another case where English would add a DO.

1 Kings 18:34 [Lesson 48]

מִלְאוּ The Qal of מָלֵא can be either stative: *be full* or transitive: *fill*.

כַדִּים Can't find the root? See בַּכַּד (1 Ki. 17:12).

וַיִּצְקוּ This verb, in the phrase וַיִּצֹק שֶׁמֶן עַל־רֹאשָׁהּ (Gen. 28:18), was acting like a 1st נ whose נ elided rather than assimilated. Here it is acting like a strong 1st י The meteg after the prefix pronoun is the indicator that the י of the root is not being written. It is interesting that יצק and יקק (1 Ki. 18:27), whose letters are metathetic (transposed), are both irregularly spelled 1st י verbs. (See **S 17.2** for a fuller discussion of 1st י verbs.)

וַיֹּאמֶר שְׁנוּ וַיִּשְׁנוּ וַיֹּאמֶר שַׁלֵּשׁוּ וַיְשַׁלֵּשׁוּ A magnificent example of compressed, parallel expression. Notice also that the first set of verbs (from the root שׁנה) is in the Qal, but the second set, being denominative, is in the Piʿel. (15.6)

1 Kings 18:35 [Lesson 49]

וַיֵּלְכוּ הַמַּיִם מַיִם is a dual noun and always takes a plural verb. Why it is dual is not clear— perhaps because originally it referred to the water above and the water below the רָקִיעַ

מְלֵא־מָיִם What is the subject of מָלֵא (It cannot be מַיִם for the reason stated just above.) The stem of מָלֵא is _____ so it must be transitive. For help with the grammar of וְגַם אֶת־הַתְּעָלָה מְלֵא־מָיִם see the comment to אֶת־הָאֲבָנִים מִזְבֵּחַ (1 Ki. 18:32).

1 Kings 18:36 [Lesson 49]

בַּעֲלוֹת הַמִּנְחָה Is this phrase more analogous to בַּעֲלַת הַבַּיִת (1 Ki. 17:17) or to לַעֲלוֹת הַמִּנְחָה (1 Ki. 18:29)? For help with the prepositional phrase, see 35.1c.

אֵלִיָּהוּ הַנָּבִיא This is the only time in this cluster of stories when Elijah is referred to as הַנָּבִיא

יִוָּדַע A ו between the prefix pronoun and the verb means the first root letter is _____ The stem is more difficult. What does the dagesh forte in the ו represent? _____ (48.5b) Only part of the characteristic Nif`al vowel pattern is seen because of the guttural ע Jussive mood best fits the sense here with an impersonal *it* as the subject.

וּבִדְבָרֶיךָ Another instance of כְּתִב קְרֵא See the marginal notation and text note 36[f].

1 Kings 18:37 [Lesson 49]

עֲנֵנִי Similar to עֲנוּנוּ (1 Ki. 18:26).

הֲסִבֹּתָ The form and PGN are straightforward, but the rest is not quite so obvious. We have here another configuration of the geminate root סבב There is a similarly constructed word, הֲרֵעוֹתָ in 1 Kings 17:20, derived from רעע The difference is that הֲסִבֹּתָ shows the gemination of the root; הֲרֵעוֹתָ shows compensation for the nondoubled ע in the longer vowel tsere ‗

לִבָּם Compare with לְבָבְךָ (Dt. 6:5).

אֲחֹרַנִּית This is an adverb whose root you have seen many times before.

The meaning of the second half of this verse is puzzling. KJV: *Thou hast turned their heart back again*; NRSV: *You have turned their hearts back*; JPS: *You have turned their heart backward*.

1 Kings 18:38 [Lesson 49]

וַתִּפֹּל Is there a noun subject to clear up the ambiguous prefix pronoun? _____

אֵשׁ־יהוה Does the variation put forth in text note 38[a] change the image?

לְחָכָה Both חכה and לחך are roots. So you have to figure out whether the ל or the ה is extraneous to the root. What is the stem? _____ The atnaḥ ‿ sets off this portion from the string of consumptions in the first part of the verse, but the subject is the same in a and b.

1 Kings 18:39 [Lesson 49]

וַיַּרְא Is the root ירא or ראה _____

וַיֹּאמְרוּ Note 39ᶜ tells us that the Septuagint inserts the equivalent of אָמֵן here.

יהוה הוּא הָאֱלֹהִים The use of the independent pronoun and the repetition of the entire phrase create the highest degree of emphasis.

1 Kings 18:40 [Lesson 49]

תִּפְשׂוּ Decision: Is this word constructed ו + תפשׂ or ו + פשׂ + ת In the second case, there would be a missing root letter. <u>Hint:</u> Always try the easiest possibility first.

אַל־יִמָּלֵט Since אַל negates an imperative (39.3b), we can assume that יִמָּלֵט is a jussive *let him not . . .* The stem and form are presented in this lesson.

וַיִּתְפְּשׂוּם At first glance, this looks as if it might be a Hitpaʿel prefix form (see וַיִּתְנַבְּאוּ [1 Ki. 18:29]), but it is missing one key ingredient: a dagesh forte in the second root letter. The root appears in another form earlier in the verse.

וַיּוֹרִדֵם 1. ו between a prefix pronoun and the root means _____ 2. The root is _____ 3. An I class ("dot") vowel between the second and third root letters means _____ 4. This verb is a) transitive b) intransitive 5. ם____ is one spelling of the object suffix for which PGN? _____ Notice that even though וַיִּתְפְּשׂוּם and וַיּוֹרִדֵם are joined by a conjunction they do not have the same subject.

1 Kings 18:41 [Lesson 50]

עֲלֵה אֱכֹל וּשְׁתֵה These three verbs have the same form, but each has different pointing because of the characteristics of its root letters.

כִּי־קוֹל הֲמוֹן הַגָּשֶׁם This is a clause because it is introduced by כִּי Since there is no verb, treat it as a noun sentence. The one difficult word in the clause is הֲמוֹן It is a noun in construct from the root הָמָה *murmur, growl, roar.* (Interestingly, there is a root הָמֵן meaning *rage, be turbulent,* but it doesn't yield a noun with this vowel pattern.) The word הַגֶּשֶׁם is in pause as indicated by the silluq. If pointed regularly, it would read הַגֶּשֶׁם

1 Kings 18:42 [Lesson 50]

וַיַּעֲלֶה   If you read this verb in context, the stem will not be ambiguous.

לֶאֱכֹל   Why the segol ֶ under the לֶ _____ (**S 14.3.1**)

וְלִשְׁתּוֹת   What is the root? _____ (14.3a)

בִּרְכֹּו   The Masoretic note and text note 42[b] agree that this spelling represents a scribal error. Without consulting the notes, can you identify the problem?

1 Kings 18:43 [Lesson 50]

הַבֵּט   What kind of dagesh is in the בֵּ _____ You have to discern its function. Is הבט a root? If the dagesh is the footprint of an assimilated letter, what letter is it most likely to be?

דֶּרֶךְ־יָם   A literal translation gets the idea across. דֶּרֶךְ־יָם may be referring to the major road along the coast, which became known in Roman times as the Via Maris (Road of the Sea).

מְאוּמָה   Some identify the root as אום This would allow the assumption that the מ is a noun identifier and the ה ָ the f. sg. endiNG. Others identify the root as מאם which is where you will find it in BDB. (This word occurs also in Genesis 22:12.)

שֻׁב   Remember that ֻ is a defectiva _____

1 Kings 18:44 [Lesson 50]

בַּשְּׁבִעִית   The ordinal form of שֶׁבַע + preposition + definite article.

וַיֹּאמֶר   When a temporal clause precedes the main verb, ו introduces the main verb and need not be translated. (**S 43.3** treats the translational possibilities of ו)

עָב   Do not confuse with אָב speaking of which, אָב is derived from a 3rd ה root, but עָב is not. What kinds of roots (two choices here) tend to yield two-letter nouns? _____
(See טַל [1 Ki. 17:1].)

בְּכַף־אִישׁ A phrase further modifying עָב קְטַנָּה

מַיִם Not to be confused with מִים

וַיֵּרֶד Context should reveal the form. Explain the vowel under the ו _____(S 14.3.3b)

יַעַצָרְכָה Obviously too many letters for a root, but three can be nothing else. The endiNG כָה_ is a plene spelling of ךָ_ The usual ḥolem of the Qal prefix form has been shortened to a qamats ḥatuf in the syllable צָרְ Such a change is not uncommon in a Qal prefix + suffix. Note that the PGN of this verb is not the same as that of the two previous verbs.

הַגֶּשֶׁם How is הַגֶּשֶׁם related to the verb? _____

1 Kings 18:45 [Lesson 50]

עַד־כֹּה וְעַד כֹּה The expression עַד־כֹּה appears in Genesis 22:5 and is usually translated as a spatial adverb: *hither, yonder, over there.* Here it is usually given a temporal sense: *in a little while, meanwhile.*

הִתְקַדְּרוּ A _ הִתְ preformative and doubled middle root letter identify the Hitpaʿel affix, imperative and infinitive forms.

עָבִים Hebrew doesn't need a preposition before this word; English does.

וַיְהִי גֶּשֶׁם גָּדוֹל For a thematic and geographic parallel, read the story of Deborah, Judges 4:4–5:28, especially 5:21.

1 Kings 18:46 [Lesson 50]

אֶל־אֵלִיָּהוּ Although English would prefer עַל instead of אֶל the same use of אֶל is in Genesis 22 12.

עַד־בֹּאֲכָה An infinitive with a 2 m sg. suffix, plene spelling: *until your coming* → *until the entrance of.*

וַיַּגֵּד   This verb is featured in Lesson 32.

אֵת כָּל־אֲשֶׁר עָשָׂה   At 1 Kings 18:26, there is a discussion of the English tenses involved in translating an affix followed by אֲשֶׁר followed by yet another affix.

וְאֵת כָּל־אֲשֶׁר הָרַג   This clause parallels the one just before it.

אֵת־כָּל־הַנְּבִיאִים   Qualifies the previous אֲשֶׁר

בֶּחָרֶב   For this use of the preposition, see בָאֵשׁ (1 Ki. 18:24). The structure of this verse is an elaboration of the style of Genesis 22:2a and Genesis 37:23b, where the tension of the verse is prolonged and the DDO heightened by the repetition of אֵת phrases, each of which further specifies the one before.

מַלְאָךְ   The root is _____

כֹּה־יַעֲשׂוּן אֱלֹהִים   The beginning of an oath formula. (See 1 Ki. 17:1 where its components are discussed and 1 Ki. 17:12 for a variant example.) Note that אֱלֹהִים has a plural verb because Jezebel, who may be a foil for the widow woman (1 Ki. 17), is swearing by her gods. The final ן in יַעֲשׂוּן is _____ (See תַּעַבְדוּן [Ex. 3:12].) Since the prefix form can include the use of modal auxiliaries—can, may, must, ought, shall, should, will, and would— it is fine to read *So may the gods do,* etc., if desired, and the mood chosen may be extended to the next verb.

וְכֹה יוֹסִפוּן   To translate the verb, see 50.4 or refer to וַיּוֹסִפוּ עוֹד שְׂנֹא אֹתוֹ (Gen. 37:5). In this verse, oratorical impact is achieved by balanced phrasing and repetition of the paragogic ן in adjacent phrases.

כִּי־כָעֵת   The second part of the oath is introduced by כִּי rather than אִם (1 Ki. 17:1).

כָעֵת is a compound word: עֵת + כְּ meaning *at about this time.* Note that this vow has only two clauses.

מֵהֶם   The reference is to the four hundred and fifty prophets of Ba`al massacred in the previous chapter.

1 Kings 19:3 [Lesson 51]

וַיַּרְא Text note 3ᵃ cites sources that read וַיִּרָא (an alternate spelling of וַיֵּירָא) instead of וַיַּרְא

אֶל־נַפְשׁוֹ Even if we are dealing with an אֶל עַל ambiguity, as suggested by note 3ᵇ, we are still left with an idiom that means something like *for his life.*

וַיַּנַּח | וַיַּנַּח simply does not yield to the missing-letter or any other kind of "rule." Look at vocabulary word 238. It shows that for the Hif`il of נוּחַ BDB lists an **A** and a **B**. Hif`il **A**s look as one would expect; Hif`il **B**s (to which group our word belongs) are characterized by a dagesh forte in the נ and pataḥ rather than an I class vowel between the second and third root letters.

אֶת־נַעֲרוֹ Trivia question: How many נְעָרִים did Abraham and Elijah each have?

1 Kings 19:4 [Lesson 51]

וְהוּא־הָלַךְ S **43.3** catalogues uses of ו

דֶּרֶךְ יוֹם Compare with דֶּרֶךְ־יָם (1 Ki. 18:43).

וַיֵּשֶׁב If you are not sure about וַיֵּשֶׁב and וַיָּשָׁב refer to S **28.5**, Weak Verb Review of יָשַׁב שׁוּב שָׁבָה and listen to "The Hebrew Blues" on the CD to find out the trouble you could get into if you can't keep these verbs straight.

רֹתֶם Identifying vegetation can be a problem. רֹתֶם is variously translated *juniper* or *broom tree*, or left transliterated as *rotem*.

אַחַת What is the problem with אַחַת (Look at the Masoretic marginal note, text note 4ᵃ, and this word in the next verse.)

וַיִּשְׁאַל אֶת־נַפְשׁוֹ לָמוּת KJV: *and he requested for himself that he might die.* NRSV: *he asked that he might die.* JPS: *and prayed that he might die.* A request to die contradicts Elijah's having fled to save his נֶפֶשׁ (1 Ki. 19:3).

רַב An adjective. Found under I. רַב רָבַב 1.

יְהוָה If not the subject of רַב what other syntactical function might it have?

מִן כִּי־לֹא־טוֹב אָנֹכִי מֵאֲבֹתַי | מִן can have a comparative function.

1 Kings 19:5 [Lesson 51]

תַּחַת רֹתֶם אֶחָד Note 5ᵃ finds this phrase redundant and would prefer us to read שָׁם instead. Such an objection to the text without major citation is more a reflection of the editor's literary taste than anything else.

וְהִנֵּה־זֶה מַלְאָךְ נֹגֵעַ בּוֹ KJV: *Behold, then an angel touched him;* NRSV and JPS: *Suddenly an angel touched him.* My suggestion: *And behold this: an angel! touching him!* (Note: מַלְאָךְ has a disjunctive accent, which separates it slightly from נֹגֵעַ) What form is נֹגֵעַ _____ For help with verb + preposition + DO, see 16.7b.

אֱכוֹל This word occurs in 1 Kings 18:41 but with defectiva spelling.

1 Kings 19:6 [Lesson 52]

וַיַּבֵּט Compare with הַבֵּט (1 Ki. 18:43).

מְרַאֲשֹׁתָיו Discussed in Genesis 28:11, same word.

עֻגַת רְצָפִים In English, something like *baked on* has to be inserted between these two words. עֻגָה comes from the same root as מָעוֹג (1 Ki. 17:12).

וַיֵּשְׁתְּ A 3rd ה with identifying features of a 1st י (16.3a).

וַיָּשָׁב | שׁוּב can be used to convey doing something again. (יסף can be used to convey doing something more intensely.)

1 Kings 19:7 [Lesson 52]

רַב מִמְּךָ The preposition מִן + suffix has two forms. You saw one in Genesis 22:12 for the word מִמֶּנִּי where the preposition has an energic נ suffix. מִמְּךָ is the other form the preposition takes with a suffix. (See Chart O: Prepositions with Suffixes.) The function of the preposition is comparative as it is in לֹא שׁוֹב . . . מֵאֲבֹתָי (1 Ki. 19:4).

1 Kings 19:8 [Lesson 52]

וַיִּשְׁתֶּה A full spelling of a 3rd ה verb with vav conversive. What usually happens? _____ _____ (12.1) Note how the same verb is written in 1 Kings 19:6.

בְּכֹחַ Preposition + vocabulary word.

מַאֲכֶלֶת ‖ הָאֲכִילָה (Gen. 22:6) is another noun from the same root.

הַהִיא How does this word relate to the word before it? _____

אַרְבָּעִים יוֹם Why is יוֹם singular? Peek ahead to Lesson 54.

עַד הַר הָאֱלֹהִים חֹרֵב Text note 8ᵃ is reminiscent of Exodus 3:1 text note 1ᵃ.

1 Kings 19:9 [Lesson 52]

הַמְּעָרָה The ה is the definite article; the מ is a מ preformative; the final הָ is a feminine endiNG, leaving two letters for a root. For help with the third letter, see שָׁל (1 Ki. 17:1).

מַה־לְּךָ פֹה אֵלִיָּהוּ NRSV: *What are you doing here, Elijah?* JPS: *Why are you here Elijah?* Why the dagesh in the לְ _____ (See 17.3b and **S 17.3b**.)

1 Kings 19:10 [Lesson 52]

קַנֹּא קִנֵּאתִי 40.2a presents the construction. What is the stem of these verbs? _____

בְּרִיתְךָ If you didn't know this word (minus the suffix), where would you find it in the dictionary? Shortcut: Check the vocabulary list.

מִזְבְּחֹתֶיךָ Analyze this word _____

וָאִוָּתֵר אֲנִי לְבַדִּי About וָאִוָּתֵר First remove the conjunction. The vowel pattern of the rest of the word should ring a bell. If there are no bells, review 48.5b. לְבַדִּי is discussed in 1 Kings 18:22. The three words here constitute a highly emphatic construction. The first person is expressed first in the prefix pronoun of the verb, then by the independent subject pronoun, and then again in the suffix of לבד

וַיְבַקְשׁוּ What is the stem? _____ If you need a refresher, see **S 3.3a.2**.

לְקַחְתָּהּ Is the ל functioning as a root letter here or a preposition? _____ (25.7) What is the role of the ה _____ (25.2) And one more question: To what is the suffix referring?

_____

1 Kings 19:11 [Lesson 53]

צֵא Problem? See 20.6a.

וְהִנֵּה יְהוָה עֹבֵר   There is heavy use of participles in this verse. A participle may be used instead of a finite form of the verb to express a single continuous event.

וְרוּחַ גְּדוֹלָה וְחָזָק   This is a curious combination of a noun, which is usually feminine but may at times be masculine, taking one feminine and one masculine adjective. What is it about the pointing of וְחָזָק that precludes its being a verb?

מְפָרֵק   The vowel under the preformative מ is the stem identifier. (31.1) This stem usually has another indicator. Why is it missing here? (36.3a, **S 3.3a.2**)

לִפְנֵי יְהוָה   The accent over יְהוָה is a strong disjunctive; it acts as a natural separation from the next phrase.

לֹא בָרוּחַ יְהוָה   English handles the phrases from here until the end of the next verse as a string of noun sentences.

1 Kings 19:12 [Lesson 53]

קוֹל דְּמָמָה דַקָּה   KJV: *a still small voice*; NRSV: *a sound of sheer silence*; JPS: *a soft murmuring sound.* קוֹל דְּמָמָה is a construct chain; דַקָּה is a feminine adjective modifying דְּמָמָה.

1 Kings 19:13 [Lesson 53]

כִּשְׁמֹעַ אֵלִיָּהוּ   כ like בְּ in front of an infinitive is a temporal indicator. (35.1c)

הַמְּעָרָה   This word appears in 1 Kings 19:9 and is discussed there.

וַיֹּאמֶר מַה־לְּךָ פֹה אֵלִיָּהוּ   This segment through verse 14 repeats 1 Kings 19:9b-10.

1 Kings 19:15 [Lesson 53]

אֶת־חֲזָאֵל לְמֶלֶךְ   BDB's fourth use of לְ is *into*, as into a new state or condition, which seems to fit here.

1 Kings 19:16 [Lesson 54]

יֵהוּא   This word must be a noun because it follows אֵת It is the first component of a name.

אֱלִישָׁע מֵאָבֵל מְחוֹלָה   Where אֱלִישָׁע is from.

תַּחְתֶּיךָ | תַּחַת ‎ is a preposition that takes **י** before a suffix is added. What others can you think of?

_____

1 Kings 19:17 [Lesson 54]

הַנִּמְלָט ‎ 47.2 discusses the stem and form. Why is there a dagesh in the **נ** _____

(9.3a) This verb appears in the prefix form 1 Kings 18:40.

יָמִית ‎ Stem? _____ (29.2) Qal prefix would be _____ (27.4b)

יֵהוּא ‎ Is this the subject or the object of יָמִית

1 Kings 19:18 [Lesson 54]

שִׁבְעַת אֲלָפִים ‎ 41.2a treats numbers 1 to 10; this lesson treats numbers above 10.

כָּל־הַבִּרְכַּיִם ‎ This phrase is in apposition to the phrase just previous, and it is the subject of the following אֲשֶׁר ‎ clause. How many knees are there? _____

לֹא־נָשַׁק לוֹ ‎ This is clear visually but is a great aural pun.

1 Kings 19:19 [Lesson 54]

חֹרֵשׁ ‎ There are two ways to proceed after this participle: tie the participle to the next phrase with a preposition: _with,_ or treat the zaqef qaton (the accent) as demanding a comma.

שְׁנֵים־עָשָׂר צְמָדִים ‎ Like שְׁתֵּים עֶשְׂרֵה אֲבָנִים ‎ (1 Ki. 18:31), but different gender.

וְהוּא בִּשְׁנֵים הֶעָשָׂר ‎ The ordinal and the cardinal are the same for this number.

וַיִּשְׁלֵךְ ‎ Stem? _____ (32.1)

אַדַּרְתּוֹ ‎ The concrete and abstract meanings of this word create a rich image.

אֵלָיו ‎ Look at BHS text note 19[b]. Does the other preposition affect the meaning?

1 Kings 19:20 [Lesson 54]

אֶשְּׁקָה־נָּה ‎ Why is there a dagesh in the **שׁ** _____

אֶשְּׁקָה־נָּא ... וְאֵלֵכָה ‎ Two cohortatives, same person speaking each time. Question: What nuance to give them? KJV, NRSV: *Let me, I pray thee (you), kiss my father and my mother, and then I will follow thee (you).* JPS: *Let me kiss my father and mother good-bye and I will follow you.*

לֵ֤ךְ שׁוּב֙ כִּ֣י מֶה־עָשִׂ֖יתִי לָ֑ךְ A few difficulties here: What does שׁוּב mean? Is מֶה introducing a question or is כִּי introducing an indirect statement? KJV, NRSV, and JPS all agree on: *Go back again; for what have I done to you?* Classic Jewish commentators are mixed in their interpretations. Rashi and Redak interpret as the translation above suggests: that Elisha could still go back and not follow Elijah—that Elijah's casting his mantle over Elisha was meant to be a test to see whether Elisha intended to follow him wholeheartedly. Mezudath David and Ralbag suggest that *return* means that Elisha should return to Elijah—that Elijah's act of throwing his mantle over him was meant to inspire him to follow him (Elijah) as a prophet.

1 Kings 19:21 [Lesson 54]

וַיָּ֖שׇׁב מֵאַחֲרָ֑יו This is not so much a problem to translate; it's a problem to know what it means.

וַיִּזְבָּחֵ֔הוּ צֶ֧מֶד הַבָּקָ֣ר The צֶמֶד הַבָּקָר is treated as a collective, as reflected in the use of the object pronoun.

וּבִכְלִ֤י Analyze this word. <u>Hint</u>: It appears in 1 Kings 17:10, but the meaning is different here. How will you treat בּ here?

בִּשְּׁלָ֣ם הַבָּשָׂ֗ר First a word about בִּשְּׁלָם The consonant that is not part of the root is either the first or the last. שׁלם בשׁל and even נשׁל (if you were thinking assimilated נ for the dagesh) are all roots. Which works here? _____

The difficulty is the function of the ם_____ To what is it referring? There is no m. pl. antecedent. There are two arguments:

1. Treat the ם_____ as an indirect object: *he cooked for them* and the following word הַבָּשָׂר becomes the direct object (a DDO not preceded by אֵת is not uncommon.)

2. The ם_____ refers to the yoke of oxen, which, granted, received a singular suffix in וַיִּזְבָּחֵהוּ but we have seen many times that switching between singular and plural is not uncommon style. If we go with the second possibility, then the following הַבָּשָׂר further qualifies the oxen: *he cooked them, the meat.*

וַיֹּאכֵ֑לוּ Normally this word would read וַיֹּאכְלוּ It is the strong accent (atnaḥ) that brings on the tsere ◌ֵ

וַיְשָׁרְתֵֽהוּ Stem? _____ (36.3a)

GLOSSARY

---

a and b

That part of a verse in the Hebrew Bible up to and including the word with the **atnaḥ** is designated **a**; the portion following to the end of the verse is **b**.

$$\text{Deuteronomy 6:4} \quad \boxed{\text{שְׁמַ֖ע יִשְׂרָאֵ֑ל}} \quad \boxed{\text{יְהוָ֥ה אֱלֹהֵ֖ינוּ יְהוָ֥ה אֶחָֽד:}}$$

b   a

Absolute

The plain, independent form of a noun; the form that is the last word of a construct chain. (5.2) A noun is listed in its absolute form in the dictionary, although you may have to look it up under its three root letters.

noun   root   noun

מַאֲכֶלֶת   ⟵   אכל   ⟶   אֲכִלָה

knife   *eat*   *meal*

Accentual System

The nonvowel marks over and under the letters make up the accentual system. These marks, usually placed just to the left of the syllable to be accented, serve to break up each verse into small syntactical segments. Each accent is either conjunctive—joining a word to the next or disjunctive—creating a major or minor pause. The accentual markings are used to chant the Torah, Prophets, and some of the Writings. (**S 10.2d**)

Active Voice

That state of the verb in which the subject of the verb is doing the action.
(See also *Passive Voice*)

1 Kings 18:39   וַיַּרְא כָּל־הָעָם

subject   active verb

and all the people <u>saw</u>

★ Affix Form

The affix is the Hebrew verb form in which the subject pronoun is "affixed" to the end of the root. For example, the 2 m. sg. Qal affix of שמר is שָׁמַ֫רְ‌תָּ and the 2 m. sg. Hif`il affix is הִשְׁמַ֫רְ‌תָּ Some textbooks refer to this form as the "perfect" because affix form usually implies past tense translation. However, since this form is used to signify completed actions, sometimes present or even future tense translation is possible.

(Affix pronouns: 13.5; 💿 ב א track 9)

341

Antecedent

The word, phrase, or clause to which a pronoun refers or for which it has been substituted.

Exodus 3:5   כִּי הַמָּקוֹם אֲשֶׁר אַתָּה עֹמֵד עָלָיו

pronoun ⬆ *it*   antecedent ⬆ *the place*

Literally: <u>*the place*</u>, *which you are standing* <u>*on it*</u>

Colloquially: <u>*the place*</u> <u>*on which*</u> *you are standing*

Apocope

A form that is shortened at the end. This is seen, for example, in 3rd ה s, which tend to be apocopated in the prefix with vav conversive and in the jussive. (32.3a and 42.1a)

יְהִי ⟵ וַיְהִי ⟵ יִהְיֶה

jussive   prefix/vav conv.   prefix

Aspect

Hebrew does not employ a tense system comparable to the tenses in English and most other Indo-European languages. Rather the verbs refer to completed action (affix) or incompleted action (prefix). (See **Mood** and the excursus on The Verb, which follows Lesson 12.)

Assimilation

The adaptation of two adjacent sounds so that one consonant has come to sound like its neighbor. The original consonant does not disappear completely; it leaves a footprint in the form of a dagesh.

יִשָּׂא ⟵ יִשְׂשָׂא ⟵ יִנְשָׂא

The נ is assimilating to the שׂ

Atnaḥ

In all except very short Hebrew prose verses, this caret-shaped sign ⎯ marks the main syntactical division of a verse.

וַיֵּשֶׁב יַעֲקֹב בְּאֶרֶץ מְגוּרֵי אָבִיו בְּאֶרֶץ כְּנָעַן׃   *Genesis 37:1*

And Jacob dwelled in the land of his father's sojournings, in the land of Canaan.

Attributive Adjective

This type of adjective follows the noun it modifies and agrees with it in gender, number, and definiteness. (14.2c)

Genesis 21:26   מִי עָשָׂה אֶת־הַדָּבָר הַזֶּה

m. sg. definite adjective ⬆   ⬆ m. sg. definite noun

Who did <u>this thing</u>?

Exodus 3:8

f. sg. indefinite adjectives ↑   ↑   ↑ f. sg. indefinite noun

to <u>a good and big land</u>

BeGaDKePHaT Letters

A mnemonic device to remember the six letters ת פ כ ד ג ב which are the most common to contain a dagesh lene. Speakers of Modern Hebrew distinguish the sounds of only three of these letters פ כ ב with and without dagesh, but some readers of Biblical Hebrew still differentiate the pronunciation of plain and dageshed ת ד ג as well.

Bible

In this textbook, "Bible" refers to the Hebrew Bible, which consists of the five books of the Torah, Prophets, and Writings: תּוֹרָה נְבִיאִים כְּתוּבִים **TaNaKh**. Jewish, Protestant, and Roman Catholic Bibles are different in their ordering of books (Prophets follows Kings in Jewish Bibles, but comes after the Writings in Protestant and Catholic Bibles), and classification (e.g., Daniel is included in the Writings in the TaNaKh but is a prophet in Protestant and Catholic Bibles). They also differ in their collections: The Apocrypha are included in Catholic Bibles and may be inserted as a special section in some Protestant Bibles, but are not in Jewish Bibles.

Bicolon

The two parallel segments of a line of Biblical Hebrew poetry.

colon   colon

Isaiah 1:3

←——bicolon——→

the ox knows its owner, and the ass its master's crib

BuMP Letter

A mnemonic device to remind us of the letters פ מ ב before which the conjunction וּ is pointed וּ

1 Kings 7:8 וּבַיִת   *Genesis 28:14* וְנִבְרְכוּ

pointing of וּ for word beginning with ב ↑   regular pointing ↑ for conjunction

Chiasm

A rhetorical inversion of the second of two parallel structures. Such a word order creates an intensification in the center of a verse, an effect which may be lost in translation.

וַתֹּאמֶר צִיּוֹן עֲזָבַנִי יְהוָה וַאדֹנָי שְׁכֵחָנִי: Isaiah 49:14

Adonai repeated in the center of the line

But Zion has said, the Lord has forsaken me,
And my Lord has forgotten me.

Clause

A sentence or part of a sentence that contains both subject and predicate. "Clause" is often used in describing Hebrew grammar and syntax in place of "sentence," because there is no clear definition of the sentence in Hebrew, as there is in English. כִּי and אֲשֶׁר frequently introduce subordinate clauses.

Cognate

Words in different languages derived from a common origin are cognates.

Hebrew	אָב	Aramaic	אַבָּא	French	*abbe*
Phoenician	אב	Greek	αββα	Assyrian	*abu*
Sabean	אב	Old English	*abbod*		

Cognate Accusative

A direct object (noun) built from the same root as the verb.

Genesis 37:5 וַיַּחֲלֹם יוֹסֵף חֲלוֹם

cognate accusative   verb

and Joseph <u>dreamed</u> a <u>dream</u>

Cognate Language

Cognate languages are related through the same origin. Hebrew is related to the other Semitic languages: Arabic, Ugaritic, Aramaic, etc. The more closely related languages are, the more cognate words they share. Hebrew and Aramaic have a multitude of cognates; Hebrew and English virtually none. (Words in English such as *Amen* and *Hallelujah* are more properly termed "loan words.")

Cohortative

The cohortative is a first person strong future and/or a mood of encouragement. It is sometimes referred to as the "first person imperative." It can be translated as a regular, but emphatic future, *I <u>will</u> go.* It can have a wishful sense, *that I might go,* or be frankly encouraging, *let us go!* It is formed by adding an extra הָ syllable to the end of a prefix form. (41.1)

Genesis 22:5 וַאֲנִי וְהַנַּעַר נֵלְכָה עַד־כֹּה וְנִשְׁתַּחֲוֶה וְנָשׁוּבָה אֲלֵיכֶם

There are several ways you could translate this passage, have it be grammatically correct, and yet have different shades of meaning.

Collective Noun

A collective noun is singular in form although it refers to more than one individual. In Hebrew, it may take either singular or plural modifiers and either a singular or plural verb.

1 Kings 18:39 וַיַּרְא כָּל־הָעָם

collective subject — singular verb

and all the people saw

Though the subject of the sentence *all the people* refers to many individuals, it designates the group as a unit and so the verb is singular. It is, of course, possible to have a plural verb with כָּל־הָעָם in which case the emphasis is on each individual within the group.

Exodus 19:8 וַיַּעֲנוּ כָל־הָעָם יַחְדָּו וַיֹּאמְרוּ

plural verb — collective subject — plural verb

and all the people (they) answered as one and (they) said

Common [Gender]

Common is the gender designation that includes both masculine and feminine. This can be seen in some verb and adjective forms. So, for example, the third person plural subject of the affix form פָּקְדוּ *they visited*, could be *they* the women, *they* the men, or *they* both men and women. The prefix form, however, has both a 3 m. pl. יִפְקְדוּ and a 3 f. pl. תִּפְקֹדְנָה Mixed groups are usually represented by masculine verbs. The one common adjective in Hebrew is the plural demonstrative adjective אֵלֶּה *these*.

Comparative Degree

The comparative degree implies *more than* as in *prettier than, faster than, taller than.*

In Hebrew, this sense of comparison may be expressed by using the particle מִן in front of a noun or adjective.

Genesis 37:4 וַיִּרְאוּ אֶחָיו כִּי־אֹתוֹ אָהַב אֲבִיהֶם מִכָּל־אֶחָיו

and his brothers saw that their father loved him more than all his brothers

Compensatory Lengthening

When a letter cannot accept a needed dagesh forte the vowel before it is often lengthened to make up or compensate for the lack of the doubled consonant. (4.5b, **S 4.5b.1–2**; 5.2, **S 5.2.1**; 15.4a, 15.5a; 48.1)

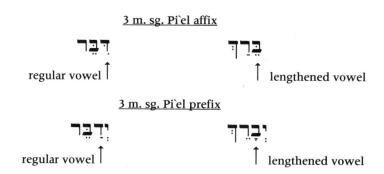

3 m. sg. Pi`el affix

דִּבֵּר   בֵּרֵךְ

regular vowel ↑   ↑ lengthened vowel

3 m. sg. Pi`el prefix

יְדַבֵּר   יְבָרֵךְ

regular vowel ↑   ↑ lengthened vowel

Composite Shewa

A shewa ֽ and either pataḥ ַ segol ֶ or qamats ָ to give the half vowels ֲ ֱ and ֳ A composite (compound) shewa is used when a vocal shewa is needed, usually under a guttural letter and sometimes ר It is pronounced like the corresponding full vowel, only shorter in duration.

Compound Preposition

Two prepositions combining to form a new preposition.

מֵאֵת ⟵ אֵת + מִן *from (with)*

מֵעַל ⟵ עַל + מִן *(from) on*

Compound Subject

Two or more elements composing the subject of a sentence. They usually take a plural verb:

Genesis 22:5 וַאֲנִי וְהַנַּעַר נֵלְכָה

plural   compound
verb   subject

and I and the youth will go

Then again, they may take a singular verb:

Genesis 17:9 אֶת־בְּרִיתִי תִּשְׁמֹר אַתָּה וְזַרְעֲךָ

compound   2 m. sg.
subject   verb

my covenant you will keep, you and your seed

Conjugate/conjugation

The methodical presentation of the inflected forms of a verb according to person, gender, and number. In Hebrew, the only forms of the verb that are fully conjugated are the prefix and affix. By convention, the conjugation in Biblical Hebrew has the order 3 m., 3 f., 2 m., 2 f., 1 c. in the singular and then in the plural. This is because the 3 m. sg. sets the basic pattern from which all the others are built.

Conjunction

A conjunction connects words, phrases, clauses, or sentences and expresses the relation between the two. The most common conjunction in Biblical Hebrew is **וֹ** *and*. Other common conjunctions are **אֲשֶׁר** *who, which;* **כִּי** *that, because, for,* and **פֶּן** *lest.* When a preposition and a conjunction join, the two are considered a single conjunction **כַּאֲשֶׁר ⟷ אֲשֶׁר + כְּ**

Construct; Construct Chain

A word or words that depend(s) on the following word, the **absolute**, for completion of concept and definiteness. Such a grammatical construction is called a construct chain. In translation the most common, but not the only, way to link the construct to the absolute is by inserting *of* between the elements. In terms of English grammar, a construct chain represents a genitive relationship. (5.1b-5.2)

אֱלֹהֵי הָאֱלֹהִים *Dt. 10:17*

absolute   construct

the God of gods

Many nouns have a shortened form for the construct (**S 5.1c-5.1c.1**); it is also the form of the word to which a suffix is appended. (**S 5.1c.2, 3; S 18.3b**)

Genesis 37:2 אֶת־בְּנֵי בִלְהָה וְאֶת־בְּנֵי זִלְפָּה נְשֵׁי אָבִיו

initial vowels in construct shortened

Genesis 37:2 אֵלֶּה תֹּלְדוֹת יַעֲקֹב

initial vowel in construct not shortened

Genesis 37:4 כִּי־אֹתוֹ אָהַב אֲבִיהֶם

construct form of noun + suffix הֶם ַ

Copula

A linking word, usually between the subject and the predicate. It can be a pronoun or a verb. The element identified as a copula is sometimes used not so much to link as to provide emphasis.
Pronoun being used as a copula:

1 Kings 18:39 יהוה הוּא הָאֱלֹהִים

noun   copula   noun

Adonai (He) is God

In many cases, a form of היה serves as a copula:

וּמֹשֶׁה הָיָה רֹעֶה אֶת־צֹאן *Exodus 3:1*

copula

and Moses was shepherding the sheep

In a Hebrew noun sentence, the copula needn't be present at all:

וְהִנֵּה דְבַר־יהוה אֵלָיו *1 Kings 19:9*

and behold, the word of Adonai (was/came) to him

Dagesh

A dot inside a letter. However, a dot inside a final ה is called a **mappiq**.

1 Kings 19:10 לְקַחְתָּהּ

mappiq ↑ ↑ dagesh

Dagesh Forte

A dagesh that has grammatical significance, doubling the consonant in which it appears. It must be preceded by a full vowel. (1.2 and 3.3b)

כֹּל אֲשֶׁר יִתֵּן מִמֶּנּוּ לַיהוה *Leviticus 27:9*

strengthened נ ↑ ↑ —↑ assimilated נs

Dagesh Lene

A dagesh that has no apparent grammatical significance but may indicate a difference in pronunciation. It is most often found in the six BeGaDKePHaT letters: ת פ כ ד ג ב when they begin a word or follow a silent shewa.

Note carefully: A dagesh in one of these letters may be a dagesh forte. (3.3a)

וַתִּכְתֹּב סְפָרִים בְּשֵׁם אַחְאָב *1 Kings 21:8*

lene ↑   lene ↑ ↑ forte

A subcategory of dagesh lene is the *euphonic dagesh*.

DDO

See *Definite Direct Object*

Defectiva

Sometimes a word can be spelled either with a vowel letter or without. The shorter spelling is termed, from the Latin, *defectiva*. The Hebrew term is כְּתָב חָסֵר *writing in want of.* It is unfortunate that the English "defective" carries the connotation of wrong, broken, or incorrect because its grammatical opposite isn't right, but *plene* means full or complete. (The terminology is part of our legacy from European grammarians, who gave Latin names to Hebrew constructions.) Sometimes the difference in spelling is used for approximate dating of material because plene spellings were used more frequently in later Biblical and post-Biblical times.

יָלֶדֶת

הוֹלַדְתָּ

defectiva spelling, no vowel letter ⌐

⌐ plene spelling, vowel letter

Definite Article

In English "the," in Hebrew הַ attached to the front of a noun with a dagesh forte in the next letter: הַ ⬚ Sometimes הָ is used to compensate if the letter following the definite article cannot take a dagesh. The only verb form that can take the definite article is a participle. (4.3; 4.5b; 21.3a and **S 21.3a.1; S 30.1**)

Genesis 1:7 וַיַּבְדֵּל בֵּין הַמַּיִם

dagesh forte ⌐ ⌐ definite article

and He divided between the waters

Isaiah 41:13 הָאֹמֵר לְךָ אַל־תִּירָא

guttural can't take dagesh ⌐ ⌐ compensatory lengthening

the one saying to you, "Do not fear"

Definite Direct Object (DDO)

The direct object of a verb can be definite or indefinite. A definite DDO is usually, but not always, designated by having אֶת־ or אֵת (which itself is not translated) in front of it.

Exodus 34:1 פְּסָל־לְךָ שְׁנֵי־לֻחֹת . . . וְכָתַבְתִּי עַל־הַלֻּחֹת אֶת־הַדְּבָרִים

DDO sign of DDO   indefinite DO

hew for yourself two tablets . . . and I will write upon the tablets the words

1 Kings 16:25 וַיַּעֲשֶׂה עָמְרִי הָרַע בְּעֵינֵי יְהוָה

DDO in prose without אֵת

and Omri did what was evil in the eyes of the Lord

Definite Noun; Definiteness

A noun is definite if has the definite article ⬜ הַ in front of it, if it has a possessive pronoun attached to it, or if it is a proper noun. A noun in the construct state will be definite if the absolute is definite, although a construct noun never has in itself the marks of definiteness. (5.2, 5.2a)

Definite nouns:

הַבֵּן   בְּנוֹ   יִשְׂרָאֵל

the son   *his son*   *Israel*

Definite nouns in construct chains:

Genesis 1:2 עַל פְּנֵי הַמָּיִם

noun in construct made definite by noun in absolute having definite article

on the face of the water

Joshua 1:3 כַּף־רַגְלְכֶם

noun in construct governed by noun in absolute that has a possessive pronoun

the sole of your foot

Joshua 1:1 בִּן־נוּן

noun in construct governed by noun in absolute, which is a proper noun

the son of Nun

Demonstrative Adjective

An adjective that points out or specifies: *this* or *that*. It may be used as an **attributive** or a **predicate adjective**. In the latter use, it often functions as a pronoun and is sometimes referred to as a demonstrative pronoun. (38.2c)

this זֹאת f. sg.   זֶה m. sg.   *that* הִיא f. sg.   הוּא m. sg.

these אֵלֶּה c. pl.   *those* הֵנָּה f. pl.   הֵם m. pl.

Genesis 22:1 אַחַר הַדְּבָרִים הָאֵלֶּה

demonstrative adjective used as an attributive adjective

after these words

Exodus 19:6 אֵלֶּה הַדְּבָרִים אֲשֶׁר תְּדַבֵּר

demonstrative adjective used as a pronoun and functioning as a predicate adjective

these are the words that you will speak

Denominative

A verb formed from a noun. The verb סָפַר *recount, relate* is thought to be derived from the noun סֵפֶר *document, letter.* These verbs are usually in the Pi῾el.

Derived Stem

The term "derived" refers to all the stems except the Qal.

Directive ה

See ה *Directive*

Direct Object (DO)

That which receives the action of a transitive verb. A DO may be either definite or indefinite.

Genesis 1:26   וַיֹּאמֶר אֱלֹהִים נַעֲשֶׂה אָדָם בְּצַלְמֵנוּ

      indefinite DO   verb

and God said, "Let us make אָדָם *in our image"*

Genesis 1:27   וַיִּבְרָא אֱלֹהִים אֶת־הָאָדָם בְּצַלְמוֹ

      DDO   verb

and God created the אָדָם *in his image*

A verb may have more than one direct object. If they are definite, אֵת is usually repeated:

Genesis 1:1   בָּרָא אֱלֹהִים אֵת הַשָּׁמַיִם וְאֵת הָאָרֶץ

      DDO   DDO

God created the heaven and the earth

The direct object may be an entire phrase or clause:

Genesis 1:25   וַיַּעַשׂ אֱלֹהִים אֶת־חַיַּת הָאָרֶץ

      DDO phrase

and God made the beasts of the earth

Genesis 1:31   וַיַּרְא אֱלֹהִים אֶת־כָּל־אֲשֶׁר עָשָׂה

      DDO clause

and God saw everything that he had made

The same DO may be expressed twice: as an object suffix on the verb, and by the specific object or objects being named:

Psalms 89:13 צָפוֹן וְיָמִין אַתָּה בְּרָאתָם

object suffix   DO

the <u>north and the south</u>, you have created <u>them</u>

★ *Dot Vowel*

This term, more properly called an I class vowel, is used specifically to remember the vowels ִ ֵ and ֶ which are characteristically found between the second and third root letters of many Hif`il forms.

Judges 6:8 אָנֹכִי הֶעֱלֵיתִי אֶתְכֶם מִמִּצְרַיִם

dot vowel ↑ sign of Hif`il

I brought you up from Egypt

Dual

Hebrew has a special ending יִם ַ for things that come in pairs: יָדַיִם *hands,* רַגְלַיִם *feet,* etc., or to denote two of something. יוֹם for example, has some occurrences of יוֹמַיִם The dual ending is the same for masculine and feminine nouns.

Exodus 21:21 אַךְ אִם־יוֹם אוֹ יוֹמַיִם יַעֲמֹד

dual   singular

but if he endures a day or <u>two days</u>

Elide

When a letter falls out of a word and leaves no trace in the form of a dagesh forte (footprint dagesh), it is said to have elided. The most common letters to elide are א ה ו י

אֵצֵא

1 c. sg. Qal prefix of יצא the י of the root has elided

לְ + הַבֹּקֶר ⟶ לַבֹּקֶר

the ה of the definite article has elided

Emphatic Construction

Some of the devices used in Biblical Hebrew prose to achieve emphasis are:
A change in the normal word order:

Genesis 37:4 כִּי־אֹתוֹ אָהַב אֲבִיהֶם

DO before verb

because him their father loved

The use of an independent pronoun when it is not necessary to avoid ambiguity:

1 Kings 18:39 יְהוָה הוּא הָאֱלֹהִים

independent pronoun

the Lord (he) is God

Repetition of a word or phrase:

Genesis 7:19 וְהַמַּיִם גָּבְרוּ מְאֹד מְאֹד עַל הָאָרֶץ

repetition of adverb

and the water prevailed mightily, mightily upon the earth

1 Kings 18:39 יְהוָה הוּא הָאֱלֹהִים יְהוָה הוּא הָאֱלֹהִים

repetition of entire clause

Adonai he is God; Adonai he is God

Using a verb and noun from the same root (cognate accusative):

Genesis 37:5 וַיַּחֲלֹם יוֹסֵף חֲלוֹם

root of noun and verb is חלם

and Joseph dreamed a dream

Using two verbs from the same root:

Genesis 37:8 הֲמָלֹךְ תִּמְלֹךְ עָלֵינוּ אִם־מָשׁוֹל תִּמְשֹׁל בָּנוּ

repeated construction of infinitive absolute + conjugated verb

Do you mean to be king (be king?!) over us and even to have dominion (dominion?!) over us?

★ *EndiNG*

This type of ending is specific because it gives **N**umber and **G**ender information about nouns, adjectives, and participles. An endiNG comes between the root and a suffix, if present.

Genesis 29:2 עֶדְרֵי־צֹאן

construct endiNG יִ___ indicates the noun עֵדֶר is m. pl.

עֹלֹת שֶׁבַע פָּרוֹת יְפוֹת *Genesis 41:2*

participle, noun, and adjective have f. pl. endiNG וֹת‏ ‎

אֶת־יְהוָה אֱלֹהֶיךָ *Deuteronomy 6:13*

m. pl. noun endiNG before 2 m. sg. suffix

★ Ending, Special

We are using this term to refer to a letter or letters at the end of a word that add(s) either special information or emphasis to the word: cohortative הָ imperative הָ locative הָ הָ directive, gentilic ending יִ‏ ‎ dual ending םַיִ‏ ‎ paragogic ן

Energic ן

There is a special set of suffixes with an accented נַ‏ ‎ syllable as their first component. This syllable is thought to add emphasis to the suffix. (53.3 and 53.5–5a) Various names given to this nunated suffix include: nun energicum, energetic nun, nun demonstrativum, nun epentheticum, or epenthetic nun. This brings us to our first principle of terminology: The more names something has, the less well it is understood.

עֲשֵׂר אֲעַשְּׂרֶנּוּ *Genesis 28: 22*

m. sg. object suffix with energic ן on a verb

עוֹדֶנּוּ מְדַבֵּר עִמָּם *Genesis 29:9*

suffix with energic ן on an adverb

Ethical Dative

A terminology oddly imposed onto a language that doesn't have a case system. In expressions such as לֶךְ־לְךָ (Gen. 22:2) and שְׁבוּ־לָכֶם פֹּה (Gen. 22:5), the "ethical dative" component is the לְ + object pronoun. Such an addition to the imperative is thought to give emphasis to or show concern for the one doing the action. Taking a sample of four English translations, we find that two acknowledge the Hebrew לְךָ and two ignore it. KJV: *get thee*; JPS and NRSV: *go*; Fox: *go-you-forth*.

Etymology

Etymologists study the origin and derivation of words, tracing a word back as far as possible, generally by the methods of comparative linguistics. (Not to be confused with entomologists, who study insects.)

Euphonic Dagesh

When a word ending in an open syllable is connected to the next word by either a **maqqef** or a conjunctive accent, then the first letter of the next word will usually have a dagesh if it is not a **BeGaDKePHaT** letter; if it is a BeGaDKePhat letter, it won't. The euphonic effect of the dagesh is not known. (**S 17.3b**)

מַה־לִּי וָלָךְ *1 Ki. 17:18*

↑ euphonic dagesh

Factitive

The addition of an adjective to a verb to designate its meaning. This use of an adjective complement applies only to the English; Hebrew conveys this notion by using the Pi`el. The use of an entirely different verb in English may mask the factitive quality.

Exodus 23:7 כִּי לֹא־אַצְדִּיק רָשָׁע

DO — verb root and adjective complement

for I will not <u>declare innocent</u> (acquit) the wicked

Exodus 1:16 וַיֹּאמֶר בְּיַלֶּדְכֶן

verb root ילד in Pi`el meaning *help bear*

and he said, "When you <u>do the office of midwife</u>"

Feminine

A grammatical distinction is made between masculine and feminine with nouns, pronouns, adjectives, and second and third person verbs. For some things—words for "girl" and "queen," for example—the feminine designation is obvious. For others—"city" or "year"—there doesn't seem to be any reason. But since Hebrew has no grammatical neuter, all objects must be assigned a gender. If a group is mixed, then the masculine form is used. (See The Noun B)

Esther 2:4 וְהַנַּעֲרָה . . . תִּמְלֹךְ תַּחַת וַשְׁתִּי

3 f. sg. prefix pronoun ↑   ה_ f. sg. noun endiNG

and let <u>the girl</u> . . . <u>be queen</u> instead of Vashti

Joshua 6:2 נָתַתִּי בְיָדְךָ אֶת־יְרִיחוֹ וְאֶת־מַלְכָּהּ

f. sg. possessive pronoun ↑   feminine noun

I have given into your hand Jericho and <u>its</u> (her) king

★Feminine Period

Because the mappiq in a suffixed ה is always the sign of a feminine singular object or possessive pronoun, we call it the "feminine period" as a reminder of both its use and its position in a word.

Genesis 2:15 וַיַּנִּחֵהוּ בְגַן־עֵדֶן לְעָבְדָהּ וּלְשָׁמְרָהּ

↑ 3 f. sg.   ↑ suffix
object

and he set him to rest in the Garden of Eden to till <u>it</u> (her) and to keep <u>it</u> (her)

Finite Verb

In Hebrew grammar, this term refers to the **prefix** and **affix** forms of the verb.

Genesis 28:12 וַיַּחֲלֹם וְהִנֵּה סֻלָּם מֻצָּב אַרְצָה

מֻצָּב Hofʻal participle, ≠ finite verb form   3 m. sg. Qal prefix, finite verb

and <u>he dreamed</u> and behold, (there was) a ladder set up on the earth

★ Form

There are five verb forms in Hebrew: affix (perfect), prefix (imperfect, future), imperative, participle, infinitive. (Jussive and cohortative are considered to be subgroups of the imperative.) These forms are traditionally referred to as inflections or the principal parts of the verb.

★ Form Indicator

Any consonant and/or vowel that is a sign of a certain verb form.

Psalms 18:22 כִּי שָׁמַרְתִּי דַּרְכֵי יהוה

subject pronoun at the end of a verb root → sign of affix form

for <u>I have kept</u> the ways of the Lord

Jonah 2:9 מְשַׁמְּרִים הַבְלֵי־שָׁוְא

preformative מ and noun ending ◌ִים → signs of participle

<u>they that guard</u> lying vanities

Formulaic Language

Phrases that occur in different passages according to a fixed pattern, such as:

Exodus 3:6, 15; 4:5, etc. אֱלֹהֵי אַבְרָהָם אֱלֹהֵי יִצְחָק וֵאלֹהֵי יַעֲקֹב

Frequentative Past

See *Vav Reversive*

Full Vowel

Any of the vowels except shewa and the composite shewa vowels.

אֱלֹהִים

◌ֱ and ◌ֹ full vowels | half vowel

Furtive Pataḥ

A pataḥ ◌ַ written just to the right of a final ה or ע which consonant is immediately preceded by a long vowel. The pataḥ in this case is pronounced before the consonant.

רֹוּחַ

furtive pataḥ ↑ word pronounced ru-aḥ

Geminate Verb

A verb whose root has the same second and third root letters: גלל סבב רעע (51)

Gender

Hebrew uses two genders, **masculine** and **feminine**. There is no neuter "it." All nouns, pronouns and adjectives have gender; particles, prepositions, conjunctions, and infinitives do not. Gender determination for nouns is discussed in The Noun sections A and B. A few nouns in Hebrew are masculine in some occurrences and feminine in others. For example, Genesis 1:1 reads וְרוּחַ אֱלֹהִים מְרַחֶפֶת There the noun רוּחַ is feminine, as shown by the **endiNG** on the participle. 1 Kings 19:11 reads רוּחַ . . . מְפָרֵק which shows the same noun using a masculine participle. Those verb forms that do not have separate masculine and feminine designators are called **common**.

Gentilic

A classification that refers to members of the same class, usually in terms of nationhood. One way of expressing nationality in Hebrew is by the use of a special gentilic ending יִ_ Some peoples are referred to this way with the יִ_ ending and some, such as the Egyptians, מִצְרַיִם usually are not.

Exodus 34:11 הִנְנִי גֹרֵשׁ מִפָּנֶיךָ אֶת־הָאֱמֹרִי וְהַכְּנַעֲנִי וְהַחִתִּי

behold, I am driving out before you the Amorite(s) and the Canaanite(s), and the Hittite(s)

Guttural Letter

ע ח ה א are the gutturals, even though in Modern Hebrew the throat sound is not heard in all of them. Gutturals cannot accept a dagesh forte. (The dot sometimes seen in a final ה as in וְעַמָּהּ [Isaiah 65:18] is not a dagesh but a **mappiq**.) When a dagesh is needed—in the middle root letter of a Piʿel or the first root letter of a Nifʿal prefix, for example—a guttural often causes the previous vowel to lengthen, a phenomenon termed "compensatory lengthening." Gutturals may cause other vowel changes, too.

Genesis 29:26 יֵעָשֶׂה |

3 m. sg. Nifʿal prefix

_ lengthened to _ because dagesh needed in ע

1 Samuel 3:7 יִגָּלֶה |

3 m. sg. Nifʿal prefix

_ under prefix pronoun regular pointing

A guttural takes a composite shewa instead of a simple shewa when that syllable is to be pronounced:

Isaiah 66:3 בְּחֲרוּ |

composite shewa ↑

Genesis 14:24 אָכְלוּ |

vocal shewa ↑

Gutturals have a propensity for pataḥ ◌ַ before, under, and sometimes even after them:

Jeremiah 25:30 יַעֲנֶה   *1 Samuel 20:2* יִגְלֶה

Qal prefix of a 1st guttural has ◌ַ under prefix pronoun   ◌ִ usual vowel for Qal prefix pronoun

The letter ר is not classified as a guttural although it shares some of the gutturals' peculiarities, such as not being able to take a dagesh.

Half Vowel

A vocal shewa and the composite shewas are considered to be half or ḥatef vowels. (See Vocalization B)

Deuteronomy 5:8 לֹא־תַעֲשֶׂה־לְךָ

half vowels ↑   ↑

Hapax Legomenon

The single occurrence of a word in a language. It is a Greek term meaning *thing said only once* and thus a word or form used only once in the Bible. Examples from the readings are סֻלָּם (Gen 28:12) and טֹטָפֹת (Dt. 6:8).

ה *Directive and* ה *Locative*

An unaccented ◌ָה on the end of a noun indicating direction toward a place, <u>never</u> toward a person. (11:3; 💿 שָׁבְחִי track 12)

Genesis 28:14 וּפָרַצְתָּ יָמָּה וָקֵדְמָה וְצָפֹנָה וָנֶגְבָּה

four examples of ה directive

and you will spread abroad <u>to the west</u>, and <u>to the east</u>, <u>to the north</u>, and <u>to the south</u>

The construction אֶל + place name can also carry this meaning.

2 Samuel 24:7 וַיֵּצְאוּ אֶל־נֶגֶב יְהוּדָה בְּאֵר שָׁבַע

אֶל־נֶגֶב used to express direction toward

and they went out <u>to the south</u> of Judah (which is) Be'er-Sheva

Some grammarians use the term ה locative (place in which) to mean the same as ה directive; some use the term more narrowly to refer only to place *in* or *on which*.

Genesis 28:12 וַיַּחֲלֹם וְהִנֵּה סֻלָּם מֻצָּב אַרְצָה

↑ ה locative

and he dreamed and behold, a ladder set up <u>on the earth</u>

Hif`il

The stem that, primarily, takes the basic root meaning (Qal) and makes it causative. Verbs that are in-transitive in the Qal may take on a transitive force in the Hif`il: צָעַק (Qal) *cry* → Hif`il *call together* or *assemble*. (28–33; 💿 **א ב** track 23)

(See also **Hof`al**)

וַיִּרְכַּב אַחְאָב וַיֵּלֶךְ יִזְרְעֶאלָה *1 Kings 18:45*

Qal Qal

and Ahab rode and he went to Yizre'el

1 Kings 1:38 אֶת־שְׁלֹמֹה עַל־פִּרְדַּת הַמֶּלֶךְ דָּוִד וַיַּרְכִּבוּ

Hif`il

and they caused Solomon to ride on King David's mule

Hishtaf`el

A stem characterized by having the preformative ____שׁת [ה] It is found in the Hebrew Bible applied only to the root חוה giving that root an intensive, reflexive meaning *prostrate oneself in worship*. (43.2)

Genesis 22:5 וְנִשְׁתַּ֖חֲוֶה וְנָשׁוּבָה אֲלֵיכֶם

שׁת sign of the Hishtaf`el

and we will prostrate ourselves in worship and we will return to you

Hitpa`el

This stem is related to the **Pi`el** because its middle root letter is doubled. The preformative ____הת im-parts a reflexive and/or reciprocal meaning to the root. (52, 53)

Ezekiel 38:23 וְהִתְגַּדִּלְתִּי וְהִתְקַדִּשְׁתִּי

↑ dagesh forte   ↑ + preformative

and I will magnify myself and I will sanctify myself

Hof`al

The Hof`al functions as the passive of the **Hif`il**. It is one of the more difficult stems to recognize, but then again it is not seen very often. Its distinguishing feature is a U class vowel (shureq וּ qamats ḥatuf ָ qibbuts ֻ) under the preformative consonant. (44)

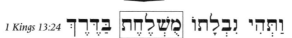

Hof`al participle with ָ under preformative מ

and its carcass was thrown down in the road

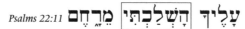

Hof`al 1 c. sg. affix with ָ under preformative ה

I was cast upon you from the womb

Hollow Verb

When ו or י appears as the middle root letter of a verb and does not have consonantal value, as in שׁוּב and שִׂים בּוֹא it functions as a weak letter. That is, it may fall out in some forms and so the verb appears to be hollow in the middle. Thus a hollow verb is a type of weak verb. Roots such as חָיָה and צָוָה are not hollow because there ו and י do have consonantal value. (27; 💿 ב א tracks 19–22)

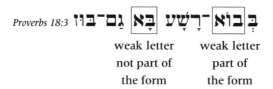

weak letter	weak letter
not part of	part of
the form	the form

when wickedness comes, contempt comes also

Imperative

The verb form used to express commands. It applies only to the second person. Other ways of expressing imperative force are by using an infinitive or the sequence: imperative + affix + vav reversive.

Exodus 19:24 לֵךְ־רֵד וְעָלִיתָ

affix	m. sg.
+ vav	impera-
reversive	tives

go, (get yourself) down and (you will) come up

Exodus 20:8 זָכוֹר אֶת־יוֹם הַשַּׁבָּת

infinitive used to convey imperative

remember the Shabbat day

Imperfect

A term used by many grammarians to refer to the **prefix** form.

Indefinite

Not specifying or limiting. *A* and *an* are indefinite articles. Hebrew does not have a designator for indefinite articles or pronouns. You can assume indefiniteness if there are no signs of the definite article or anything else, such as a possessive pronoun, that makes a word definite.

וַיֵּרָא מַלְאַךְ יהוה אֵלָיו בְּלַבַּת־אֵשׁ מִתּוֹךְ הַסְּנֶה *Exodus 3:2*

definite   indefinite   definite

in construct with a proper noun

and the angel of the Lord appeared to him in a flame of fire from the midst of the bush

Independent Subject Pronoun

A pronoun that is not attached to another word. (36.7;  **א ב** track 24)

וְאַתָּה אָמַרְתָּ *Exodus 33:12*

subject pronoun affixed to verb: not independent ⌐   independent

subject pronoun

Indirect Object

The person or thing to which something is given, shown, or told or for whom something is done. In Hebrew, the preposition אֶל or לְ may introduce an indirect object.

(See also *Ethical Dative*)

וַיֹּאמֶר יהוה אֶל־מֹשֶׁה פְּסָל־לְךָ *Exodus 34:1*

2 m. sg.   noun as

pronoun as   indirect

indirect object   object

and God said <u>to Moses</u>, *"Make* <u>for yourself</u> *. . ."*

Infinitive

The form of the verb that expresses the action or state of the verb without any indication of person, gender, or number. In English, an infinitive is a verb always preceded by *to,* as in *to go* or *to do.* Not necessarily so in Hebrew. To know more, read the next two entries.

Infinitive Absolute

The infinitive absolute rarely has anything added to it. (40.2a) Some of its common uses are to:

1)   emphasize the idea of a verb in the abstract:

אַל־תִּירְאוּ מֵהֶם כִּי־לֹא יָרֵעוּ וְגַם־הֵיטֵיב אֵין אוֹתָם *Jeremiah 10:5*

Hif`il infinitive absolute

do not fear them because they will not do evil, nor is it in them <u>to do good</u>

2)   intensify another form of the verb:

שָׁמוֹר תִּשְׁמְרוּן אֶת־מִצְוֹת *Deuteronomy 6:17*

infinitive absolute, intensifying the verb following

you will <u>diligently keep</u> *the commandments*

3)   represent the imperative:

Deuteronomy 5:12   שָׁמוֹר אֶת־יוֹם הַשַּׁבָּת

infinitive absolute expressing imperative idea

<u>keep</u> the Shabbat day

Infinitive Construct

Of the two infinitives, the infinitive construct is the more common and flexible. Most often it appears with a preposition, which may be attached or unattached, and it may have a suffix. (25) Like the infinitive absolute, it can:

1)   express the abstract and noun-like quality of a verb:

1 Samuel 18:23   הַנְקַלָּה בְעֵינֵיכֶם הִתְחַתֵּן בַּמֶּלֶךְ

is it a small thing in your eyes, <u>becoming son-in-law</u> to the king?

2)   serve as the main verbal idea in a temporal clause:

Deuteronomy 6:7   בְּשִׁבְתְּךָ בְּבֵיתֶךָ

preposition + infinitive construct + 2 m. sg. suffix

<u>when you sit</u> in your house

3)   express purpose:

Deuteronomy 13:13   אֲשֶׁר יהוה אֱלֹהֶיךָ נֹתֵן לְךָ לָשֶׁבֶת שָׁם

which the Lord your God is giving you <u>to dwell</u> there

Interrogative

Asking a question. There is no question mark in Hebrew, and so sometimes interrogative mood is inferred from the context. There are some interrogative indicators, however, such as interrogative הַ and words such as מִי *who*   מֵאַיִן *from where*   מַדּוּעַ *why*

Genesis 27:24   אַתָּה זֶה בְּנִי עֵשָׂו

interrogative inferred from context

Is this you? my son? Esau?

Genesis 29:5   הַיְדַעְתֶּם אֶת־לָבָן בֶּן־נָחוֹר

interrogative הַ

Do you know Laban, the son of Naḥor?

Genesis 29:4 וַיֹּאמֶר לָהֶם יַעֲקֹב אַחַי מֵאַיִן אַתֶּם

interrogative adverb

And Jacob said to them, "My brothers, from where are you?"

Intransitive

A verb that cannot take a direct object to complete its meaning.

Genesis 29:1 וַיִּשָּׂא יַעֲקֹב רַגְלָיו וַיֵּלֶךְ אַרְצָה בְנֵי־קֶדֶם:

intransitive   DO   transitive
verb   verb

And Jacob went on his journey (picked up his feet) and went to the land of the children of the east

★ Irregular Verb

Some classifiers would call any verb irregular that does not follow exactly the pattern of the strong verb. We are reserving the term to capture those verbs that do not fit into any of the strong or weak patterns.

Genesis 29:8 לֹא נוּכַל

prefix form of יָכוֹל *be able*

Iterative

Done frequently or repeatedly. The infinitive absolute of הלך can impart this meaning to a verb, as can using either of the intensive stems: the Pi̇'el or Hitpȧ'el.

2 Samuel 18:25 וַיֵּלֶךְ הָלוֹךְ וְקָרֵב

infinitive absolute giving the sense of keeping on walking

and he kept on walking and drew near

1 Samuel 12:2 וַאֲנִי הִתְהַלַּכְתִּי לִפְנֵיכֶם מִנְּעֻרַי

Hitpȧ'el giving iterative meaning

and I have walked before you since my childhood

Jussive

A verb form expressing a command in the third person: *let him do . . .; that they may do . . .*

It may look no different from the prefix (which means that its use may be an interpretation of the translator) or it may be a shortened form of the prefix as in 3rd ה verbs, for example. (42)

יִשָּׁבַע־לִי כַיּוֹם הַמֶּלֶךְ שְׁלֹמֹה *1 Kings 1:51*

jussive looking the same as Nifʿal 3 m. sg. prefix form

let king Solomon swear to me today

וַיֹּאמֶר אֱלֹהִים יְהִי אוֹר *Genesis 1:3*

shortened form of Qal prefix יִהְיֶה

And God said, "Let there be light"

Ketiv-Qere כְּתִב קְרֵא

There are places in the Biblical text where there is either a scribal error or variant traditions that the Masoretes wished to preserve. In these cases, the desired pronunciation is noted in the margin; the correct reading is written over a קְ and usually in a footnote where the instruction is **Q**. This is known as כְּתִב *it is written* קְרֵא *to be read.* (כְּתִב and קְרֵא are Aramaic passive participles. All the marginal notes are Aramaic; most like קְ for קְרֵא are abbreviations.) In the phrase רֹתֶם אַחַת (1 Ki. 19:4), the word אַחַת [כְּתִב] is referenced to a note that tells us to read אֶחָד [קְרֵא] The "error" there is that the vowels ַ ַ are for the masculine form of the word, but the ending ת is for the feminine form. When a scribal "error" occurs frequently, it may not be noted, as in the words יְרוּשָׁלַם and הוּא This is called qere perpetuum.

Lexicon

The same thing as a dictionary, but often used to refer to a dictionary of an ancient language.

Locative ה

(See ה *Directive*)

Major Disjunctive Accent

Silluq in the last word of a verse and **atnaḥ**, which marks the major break within the verse, are the two most important major disjunctive accents. A third is **zaqef qaton,** which looks like a shewa on top of a letter: אֲ (We are not discussing the whole accentual system in this course.) There may be a change in vowel at these accent points, where the word is said to be in **pause**.

וַיַּעֲשׂוּ אֶת־הַפֶּסַח *Numbers 9:5*

regular pointing for פֶּסַח

וַיְדַבֵּר מֹשֶׁה אֶל־בְּנֵי יִשְׂרָאֵל לַעֲשֹׂת הַפָּסַח׃ *Numbers 9:4*

ֶ becomes ָ because of the silluq. פָּסַח is in pause

Mappiq

A mappiq, like a dagesh, is a dot within a consonant. It is a sign that the letter is to be regarded as a full consonant and not a vowel letter. Most usually it is seen in a הַ at the end of a word where it identifies the 3 f. sg. possessive or object suffix.

(See *Feminine Period*)

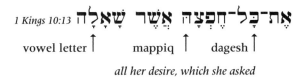

1 Kings 10:13 אֶת־כָּל־חֶפְצָהּ אֲשֶׁר שָׁאָלָה

vowel letter ↑   mappiq ↑   dagesh ↑

all her desire, which she asked

Maqqef

The mark that looks like a hyphen and joins two or more words together into a single accentual unit. The vowels in the first word(s) of the unit may be shortened. (2.5)

Exodus 29:12 וְאֶת־כָּל־הַדָּם

A phrase with two maqqefs. Only the word הַדָּם has an accent.

Masculine

Of the two genders in Hebrew, it is considered to be the prior gender. This means that if a group is composed of masculine and feminine nouns, masculine verb forms are used. Likewise, a group of masculine and feminine nouns will be referred to by a masculine pronoun. Occasionally even a feminine plural subject will take a masculine verb.

(See *Common*, *Feminine*, and *Gender*)

Genesis 18:11 וְאַבְרָהָם וְשָׂרָה זְקֵנִים

m. pl.   f.   m.
adjective   noun   noun

Abraham and Sarah were old

Genesis 1:27 זָכָר וּנְקֵבָה בָּרָא אֹתָם

3 m. pl.   f.   m.
object pronoun   noun   noun

male and female he created them

1 Kings 11:3 וַיַּטּוּ נָשָׁיו אֶת־לְבּוֹ

f. pl. subj.   3 m. pl. Hif`il prefix of נטה

and his wives turned away his heart

Masora

In its fullest sense, this term is indefinable because it refers first to an oral tradition concerning the transmission of the Bible as it developed through the ages. Later, the term came to refer to the total orthography of the Hebrew Bible. It includes such issues as writing materials, sizes and shapes of the letters, length of lines, spaces between words, and proper pronunciation. In the narrow sense, "Masora" refers to everything that is written outside the Biblical text but accompanies it. The common technical division is between the **Masora Magna** and **Masora Parva**.

Masora Magna

A detailed explanation of the Masora Parva including some additional notes. These notes were written at the top and bottom of each page, and if there was not enough room the scribes would continue their notation at the end of the book. The purpose of these meticulously detailed notes was to guard the text from scribal changes.

Masora Parva

These brief and often abbreviated notes are found in the margins of the text. There may be a small circle over a word in the text to which the note of the Masora is directed. The notes catalogue such things as corrected pronunciations, unusual spellings, rare usages of words, the number of occurrences of a particular form, and the number of words in a book.

Masoretes

The Masoretes were those scholars who were responsible for the creation of the entire Masora. Their activities date from the fourth century CE, but are based on an oral tradition that goes back centuries earlier. Most of the Masoretes are anonymous; among the few known to us, perhaps the most prominent were the ben Asher family.

Masoretic Text

This is the Biblical Hebrew text accepted by both Jews and Christians. The oldest, complete, extant manuscript is the Leningrad Codex (1009 CE), written by Aaron ben Moses ben Asher. This codex arose from earlier traditions of the Masoretic Text.

Matres Lectionis

A Latin phrase that translates as *mothers of reading*. Before the dot-dash vowel system was developed, the letters י ו ה and rarely א were the only vowel indicators in Hebrew. This is still the case for Torah scrolls used in worship services.

י stands for hireq ִ tsere ֵ and segol ֶ

ו for holem וֹ shureq וּ and qibbuts ֻ

ה at the end of a word for qamats ָ pataḥ ַ segol ֶ

א in the middle, or at the end of a word, can stand for qamats ָ

Spellings with vowel letters are called scriptio plene or כְּתָב מָלֵא (*full writing*): קוֹל

The omission of vowel letters is scriptio defectiva or כְּתָב חָסֵר (*writing in want of*): קֹל

Remember, vowel letters also function as full consonants, which was, of course, their original use. In יִהְיֶה the final ה is a vowel letter; the three other letters are consonants.

Metathesis

The transposition of letters: כֶּשֶׂב instead of כֶּבֶשׂ or שַׂלְמָה instead of שִׂמְלָה The verb stem in which metathesis is most likely to occur is the **Hitpa`el**, so you will see הִשְׁתַּמֵּר instead of הִתְשַׁמֵּר

Meteg

A small vertical stroke, usually to the left of a vowel, whose purpose is to separate the vowel syllabically from the following vowel (often a shewa). This is especially important in distinguishing qamats from qamats ḥatuf. In the word אָכְלָה for example, the meteg identifies the 3 f. sg. affix *she ate*. אָכְלָה without the meteg is the noun *food*.

★*Missing-Letter Rule*

An aid to help identify a missing root letter in a verb. It is usually the identification of a particular vowel under the prefix pronoun or, in the affix, under the first root letter. These "rules" are definitely worth memorizing. They can be found in 3.1, 6.1a, and 12.1.

Mood

That state of a verb that has to do with the speaker's attitude toward the action or state expressed: indicative → statement; interrogative → question; imperative → command. In English some moods, such as the subjunctive, may be expressed by using an auxiliary verb such as *might, may, should*. In Hebrew, mood may be expressed by the form, but most often is inferred from the context.

1 Kings 17:10 וַיֹּאמֶר קְחִי־נָא לִי מְעַט־מַיִם בַּכְּלִי וְאֶשְׁתֶּה

subjunctive   imperative indicative

And he said, "Bring me, pray, a little water in the vessel that I may drink"

Morphology

Morphology has to do with the shape of a word. Morphologically בָּנוּ could mean *among us, they built,* or *they perceived*. If it had no vowels, one could add to that list *his son*.

Nif`al

The Nif`al is often considered to be the passive of the **Qal**, but like the other derived stems it has a variety of functions. It may express reflexive action: נִסְתַּר *he hid himself;* reciprocal or mutual action: נִלְחַם *he engaged in warfare*. Its forms are characterized by a נ or ◻ ה **preformative**. Fortunately, in pointed texts, the distinctive vowel patterns of this stem often help reduce seeming ambiguity: הִזָּכֶרְכֶם (Nif`al infinitive with suffix). הַזְכִּרְכֶם (Hif`il infinitive with suffix).

(46–50.2, Review and Drill 5, and song on ⊘ ב א track 29)

Noun

A word used to denote a person, place, quality, action, or thing. A proper noun is the name of a place or a person. In Hebrew, nouns are either masculine or feminine, singular or plural. They can occur in the absolute or construct states and have prepositions and suffixes attached to them.

(See: The Noun pp. 131–135; The Noun H ⊛ בֿ א track 15)

Genesis 37:1   וַיֵּשֶׁב יַעֲקֹב בְּאֶרֶץ מְגוּרֵי אָבִיו בְּאֶרֶץ כְּנָעַן

יַעֲקֹב	m. sg. proper noun
בְּאֶרֶץ	f. sg. noun with a preposition and in construct
מְגוּרֵי	m. pl. noun in construct
אָבִיו	m. sg. noun with m. sg. suffix
כְּנָעַן	m. sg. proper noun

Noun Sentence

Two nouns, a noun and a pronoun, or a noun and an adjective. In English, a verb, most often a form of *to be,* is often used between the elements to make a smoother sentence.

Deuteronomy 14:1   בָּנִים אַתֶּם לַיהוה

pronoun   noun

you are children of the Lord

Deuteronomy 14:4   זֹאת הַבְּהֵמָה אֲשֶׁר תֹּאכֵלוּ

demonstrative pronoun as predicate adjective + noun

this is the animal (life) that you may eat

Deuteronomy 16:8   וּבַיּוֹם הַשְּׁבִיעִי עֲצֶרֶת לַיהוה אֱלֹהֶיךָ

noun   (adjective)   noun

on the seventh day <u>shall be</u> a solemn assembly to the Lord your God

Number

Refers to singular, plural, or dual. Nouns, pronouns, adjectives, and most verb forms have number. Adverbs, infinitives, prepositions, conjunctions, and particles do not.

(For numbers, as in 1, 2, 3, see 41.2a and 54 and listen to ⊛ בֿ א track 26.)

Genesis 22:6   וַיִּקַּח בְּיָדוֹ אֶת־הָאֵשׁ

(f.) sg. noun with (m.) sg. suffix

and he took the fire in <u>his hand</u>

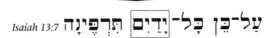

Isaiah 13:7

f. noun + dual ending

therefore, every (pair of) hands will be weak

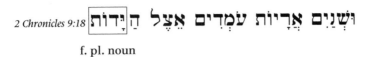

2 Chronicles 9:18

f. pl. noun

and two lions standing by the <u>arms</u> (hands)

Nunated Form

See *Energic* **נ**

Object of Preposition

The noun or pronoun that follows a preposition. This is not the same as a **direct object**.

Genesis 22:3 וַיֵּלֶךְ אֶל־הַמָּקוֹם

noun as object of preposition

And he went to the place

Genesis 22:3 וַיִּקַּח אֶת־שְׁנֵי נְעָרָיו אִתּוֹ

pronoun **ו** object of preposition **אֵת**

and he took his two youths with him

Object Pronoun

A suffixed pronoun that receives the action of a verb or follows a preposition. Object pronouns have **person, gender, and number. Independent pronouns** cannot be object pronouns.

Genesis 37:3 וְעָשָׂה לוֹ כְּתֹנֶת פַּסִּים

ו__ 3 m. sg. object pronoun; **ל** preposition

and he made for him a כְּתֹנֶת פַּסִּים

Isaiah 48:5 פֶּן־תֹּאמַר עָצְבִּי עָשָׂם

ם__ 3 m. pl. object pronoun of verb עָשָׂה

lest you should say, "My idol has done <u>them</u>"

Paradigm

An example of a conjugation or a declension giving all the forms of a verb, noun, or pronoun. The paradigmatic strong verb for this course is פָּקַד

Paragogic נ

Paragogic refers to an extra sound added to the end of a word. A paragogic נ may be seen after a long vowel usually in prefix forms, for example: תַּעַבְדוּן Such a נ does not appear to have grammatical significance, but it does enhance the sound of the word.

Parse

To parse is to break down a word into its component parts. To give a few examples: וְאָהַבְתִּי is a Qal affix of אהב with a 1 c. sg. subject and vav reversive: לְךָ is the preposition לְ with a 2 m. sg. suffix; בְּנֵי is the m. pl. construct of the noun בֵּן

Participle

The verb form that functions sometimes like a noun and sometimes like a verb, which emphasizes the agent of the action. Participles are declined like nouns. They have **number** and **gender**, which are displayed in their **endiNGs**. In all stems except the Qal and Nif`al, participles have a preformative מ In the Qal, the identifying feature is holem וֹ after the first root letter. (9.5) In the Nif`al, there is a preformative נ and usually qamats ָ under the second root letter. (47.2)

הִנֵּה הַמֶּלֶךְ מִתְהַלֵּךְ לִפְנֵיכֶם *1 Samuel 12:2*

m. sg. Hitpa`el participle

behold, the king is walking before you

זֹאת אֹמֶרֶת זֶה־בְּנִי הַחַי *1 Kings 3:23*

f. sg. Qal participle

and this one is saying, "This is my son, the living one"

הֵם הַמְדַבְּרִים אֶל־פַּרְעֹה *Exodus 6:27*

m. pl. Pi`el participle

they were the ones speaking to Pharaoh

Particle

A short and indeclinable part of speech, such as the definite article הַ interjection הוֹי preposition בְּ לְ בְּ מִן etc., conjunction וְ כִּי לָכֵן כִּי etc., expression of entreaty נָא בִּי etc., *predicator of existence* יֵשׁ הִנֵּה etc.

Passive Voice

That state of the verb in which the subject is the recipient of the action rather than the agent. The stems in Hebrew that communicate passive action are the **Pu`al**, and **Hof`al**, and often the **Nif`al**. The **Qal** has a passive participle, which can be recognized by the shureq וּ between the second and third root letters. (Qal Passive Participle: ⊘ ‎ב‎ ‎א‎ track 27.)

Genesis 6:21 וְאַתָּה קַח־לְךָ מִכָּל־מַאֲכָל אֲשֶׁר יֵאָכֵל וְאָסַפְתָּ אֵלֶיךָ

3 m. sg. Nif`al prefix

take for yourself of all the food <u>that may be eaten</u> and gather (it) to yourself

Ezekiel 2:9 וְהִנֵּה־יָד שְׁלוּחָה אֵלָי

f. sg. Qal passive participle

behold a hand <u>was sent</u> to me

Pause

The stress laid on the word at a **major disjunctive accent**. There may be a change of vowel and even of accent position at these points.

Malachi 3:23 הִנֵּה אָנֹכִי שֹׁלֵחַ לָכֶם

אָנֹכִי not in pause; accented on last syllable

Jeremiah 1:6 כִּי־נַעַר אָנֹכִי

אָנֹכִי in pause; accent on נ rather than on כ

Jeremiah 22:29 אֶרֶץ אֶרֶץ אָרֶץ שִׁמְעִי דְּבַר־יְהוָה׃

vowel change due to pause ↑

Numbers 11:17 וְיָרַדְתִּי וְדִבַּרְתִּי עִמְּךָ שָׁם

↑ vowel in usual position

Exodus 34:10 אֲשֶׁר אֲנִי עֹשֶׂה עִמָּךְ׃

↑ shift in vowel position due to accent

Pentateuch

The Greek word, still commonly used, for the first five books of the Bible (the Torah).

Perfect

The term some grammarians use for the affix form.

Person

There are three grammatical "persons." First person refers to the speaker or speakers and is demonstrated by such pronouns as *I, we, me, us, my, mine,* and *our.* Second person refers to the person spoken to, designated by *you* or *your.* Third person refers to the person or thing spoken about. Some third person pronouns are *he, she, them, their.* In Hebrew, person is designated by affix pronouns, and by prefix pronouns and complements; by the use of independent pronouns; and by possessive and object suffixes. (Independent subject pronouns: 36:7; ☺ בֿ אֿ track 24. Sign of DDO + object pronouns: 23.2b; ☺ בֿ אֿ track 13.)

וְזֹאת הַמִּצְוָה הַחֻקִּים וְהַמִּשְׁפָּטִים אֲשֶׁר צִוָּה יהוה אֱלֹהֵיכֶם לְלַמֵּד

2 m. pl. possessive suffix   3 m. sg. verb

Deuteronomy 6:1   אֶתְכֶם לַעֲשׂוֹת בָּאָרֶץ אֲשֶׁר אַתֶּם עֹבְרִים שָׁמָּה לְרִשְׁתָּהּ׃

3 f. sg. object suffix   2 m. pl. independent subject pronoun   2 m. pl. object suffix

PGN (Person, Gender, Number)

Person is first, second, or third. **G**ender is masculine or feminine. **N**umber is singular, plural, or dual. Verbs, pronouns, and suffixes have PGN. Nouns, adjectives, and participles have only gender and number. Infinitives, particles, prepositions, and conjunctions have no PGN.

m. sg. predicate adjective

1 Kings 18:24   וַיַּעַן כָּל־הָעָם וַיֹּאמְרוּ טוֹב הַדָּבָר

m. sg. noun   3 m. pl. verb   3 m. sg. verb

Phrase

In English, a phrase is a group of two or more words, forming a separate part of a sentence but not containing both a subject and a verb. In Hebrew, a phrase such as וּבְכָל־מְאֹדֶךָ *and with all your might* coincides with this definition. But because of the way Hebrew is built, a phrase that may need several words in English translations may be expressed by a single Hebrew word: וּבִשְׁעָרֶיךָ *and within your gates.*

Piʿel

One of the verb stems in Hebrew characterized by the strengthening of the middle root letter by means of a **dagesh forte**. The basic meaning of the stem is intensified: שָׁבַר *break* in the Qal becomes *smash* in the Piʿel. בָּחַר *choose* becomes *prefer.* The Piʿel may give a transitive meaning to many verbs that are intransitive in the Qal. מָלֵא *be full* means *fill* in the Piʿel. יָשַׁב *sit* or *dwell*, in the Piʿel means *colonize.* (15.4–15.7a; ☺ בֿ אֿ track 11.)

Pilpʿel

The Pilpʿel refers to the strengthening of the two strong root letters of hollow verbs and geminates to give them the intensity of the Piʿel. גָּלַל *roll* would become גִּלְגֵּל

Plene

The spelling of a word that includes the vowel letter ו ה י plus the dot or dash vowel. הַגָּדוֹל as opposed to **defectiva** spelling הַגָּדֹל The Hebrew term for this fuller spelling is כְּתָב מָלֵא *full writing.* Some scholars believe that text heavily sprinkled with plene spellings is indicative of late composition.

Pluperfect

This tense can also be referred to as the past perfect. It refers to actions that have taken place before the main action of the verse. In English, it is recognized by the auxiliary verb *had* plus a past tense. In Hebrew, the pluperfect is rendered by the affix form and must be inferred from the context, but often אֲשֶׁר followed by the affix is an indication of pluperfect time.

Genesis 2:2 וַיְכַל אֱלֹהִים בַּיּוֹם הַשְּׁבִיעִי מְלַאכְתּוֹ אֲשֶׁר עָשָׂה

pluperfect translation   past tense translation

and God finished on the seventh day his work that he <u>had made</u>

Pointing/Points

The vowels that were inserted into the consonantal text can also be called points (hence the Hebrew term נְקֻדּוֹת). Such a text is vocalized or pointed. Vocalization also refers to the other marks such as dagesh, meteg, sof passuq, and, of course, all the other accents. This system was developed after everyday usage of the language had died out and there was danger that correct pronunciation might be lost. Most of this work was done in the sixth and seventh centuries CE by Masoretic scholars. The insertion of the dot-dash vowel system is in itself an interpretation of the text. If you look at a sample of unvocalized text, you can see that for many words there is more than one way to point the text.

ויקרא אברהם שם המקום ההוא יהוה יראה אשר יאמר

Genesis 22:14 היום בהר יהוה יראה

וַיִּקְרָא אַבְרָהָם שֵׁם־הַמָּקוֹם הַהוּא יְהוָה יִרְאֶה אֲשֶׁר יֵאָמֵר

Genesis 22:14 הַיּוֹם בְּהַר יְהוָה יֵרָאֶה׃

Torah scrolls used for public reading of the text are not pointed.

Possessive Pronoun

A suffixed pronoun used to show ownership: *my, mine, your, yours,* etc. In Hebrew, possessive pronouns can be attached to nouns, and sometimes to infinitives. They have **person**, **gender**, and **number**.

Deuteronomy 6:2 תִּירָא אֶת־יהוה אֱלֹהֶיךָ לִשְׁמֹר אֶת־כָּל־חֻקֹּתָיו וּמִצְוֹתָיו

3 m. sg. possessive pronoun   2 m. sg. possessive pronoun

you will fear the Lord <u>your</u> God to keep all <u>his</u> statutes and <u>his</u> commandments

Predicate

The predicate may be simply a verb, or the term may refer to everything in a sentence other than the subject and its modifiers.

1 Kings 10:2 וַתָּבֹא יְרוּשָׁלַ֫מָה בְּחַ֫יִל כָּבֵד מְאֹד גְּמַלִּים נֹשְׂאִים בְּשָׂמִים

And she came to Jerusalem with a very great retinue, with camels bearing spices

The predicate could be the בֹא component of וַתָּבֹא or the בֹא component and all the phrases following.

Predicate Adjective

This is another way of referring to an adjective that is part of a **noun sentence**. A predicate adjective often precedes the noun (or pronoun) it modifies. (15.2)

1 Kings 19:4 כִּי־לֹא־טוֹב אָנֹכִי מֵאֲבֹתָי

pronoun   predicate adjective

because I __am__ no __better__ than my fathers

Predicator of Existence

An indeclinable word that indicates the being of something, יֵשׁ or הִנֵּה for example, or its nonexistence, אֵין These words may have a suffix attached.

Genesis 37:24 וְהַבּוֹר רֵק אֵין בּוֹ מָיִם

predicator of nonexistence

but the well was empty; __there was no__ water in it

Genesis 37:13 וַיֹּאמֶר לוֹ הִנֵּנִי

predicator of existence with 1 c. sg. suffix attached

And he said to him, "__Here I am__"

★ Prefix Form

The prefix is the Hebrew verb form in which the subject pronoun is "prefixed" to the front of the root. Part of the subject pronoun may also follow the root; that component of the pronoun is called the prefix complement.

(Prefix pronouns 14.5; ◉ בֹ א track 10)

3 m. pl.	Hif'il prefix	3 m. sg.
יַמְלִ֫יכוּ		יַמְלִיךְ

prefix complement ↑   ↑ prefix pronoun   ↑ prefix pronoun

The prefix form is called the imperfect by many grammarians because it refers to incomplete action. It is usually given a future or present tense translation. The prefix form may carry the notion of *could, should, would,* or *might.* (Prefix pronouns and complements: 14.5 and ⊘ ℶ א track 10.)

Deuteronomy 6:2 לְמַ֫עַן תִּירָא אֶת־יהוה אֱלֹהֶ֫יךָ

prefix form, many possibilities for "correct" translation

Preformative

A letter or letters in front of a root that affect the meaning of the root in some way. For example, נ in front of a root can turn a Qal into a Nif`al: אָמַר *he said;* נֶאֱמַר *it was said.* A preformative ה can signal a Hif`il: עָלָה *he went up;* הֶעֱלָה *he caused (X) to go up,* and so on. Two common preformatives that can turn a root into a noun are מ and ת as in מַאֲמָר *word* and תְּעָלָה *water-course.* Add-ons such as prefixed **prepositions** or **interrogative** ה are not preformatives because they do not change the form of the word.

Preposition

An indeclinable word that introduces a phrase or clause. A preposition can be an independent word: אֶל or it can be attached to another word: לְבֵן

It may join with another preposition to create a new preposition: מִן + עַל ⟶ מֵעַל

It may be combined with a conjunction, in which case the two words together create a single conjunction: עַל אֲשֶׁר ⟶ *because.*

Prepositions are among the most difficult elements one has to cope with in trying to get the feel of a foreign language. Example: עַל fills thirteen-plus columns in a standard dictionary, לְ sixteen.

Prepositional Phrase

In English, a prepositional phrase consists of at least two words, but that is not necessarily the case in Hebrew because the preposition may be attached to its object.

(See also *Phrase*)

Genesis 22:3 וַיָּ֫קָם וַיֵּ֫לֶךְ אֶל־הַמָּקוֹם אֲשֶׁר־אָֽמַר־לוֹ הָאֱלֹהִים

attached preposition + pronoun   independent preposition + noun

And he arose and he went <u>to the place</u> which God had said <u>to him</u>

Pronoun

A word used in place of a noun. The adjective for pronoun is "pronominal," as in the question, "In the example below, how many pronominal suffixes are there?"

וְזֹאת הַמִּצְוָה הַחֻקִּים וְהַמִּשְׁפָּטִים אֲשֶׁר צִוָּה יְהוָה אֱלֹהֵיכֶם

2 m. pl. possessive pronoun	relative pronoun	demonstrative pronoun

לְלַמֵּד אֶתְכֶם לַעֲשׂוֹת בָּאָרֶץ אֲשֶׁר אַתֶּם עֹבְרִים שָׁמָּה לְרִשְׁתָּהּ:

3 f. sg. object pronoun	2 m. pl. independent pronoun	2 m. pl. object pronoun

לְמַעַן תִּירָא אֶת־יְהוָה אֱלֹהֶיךָ   *Deuteronomy 6:1–2*

2 m. sg. possessive pronoun	2 m. sg. prefix pronoun

See also **Independent Subject Pronoun, Subject Pronoun, Object Pronoun, Possessive Pronoun, Relative Pronoun**

Proper Noun

Proper nouns are the names of particular people or places. It's easy to recognize them in English because they begin with a capital letter, but in Hebrew only the meaning or context will identify proper nouns.

דִּבְרֵי יִרְמְיָהוּ בֶן־חִלְקִיָּהוּ מִן־הַכֹּהֲנִים אֲשֶׁר בַּעֲנָתוֹת בְּאֶרֶץ בִּנְיָמִן: *Jeremiah 1:1*

← four proper nouns →

The words of <u>Jeremiah</u>, *son of* <u>Hilkijahu</u> *of the kohanim, who were in* <u>Anatoth</u> *in the land of* <u>Benjamin</u>

Pu`al

The Pu`al stem is the passive of the **Pi`el**. Like the Pi`el, the middle root letter is doubled by means of a dagesh forte, and the **preformatives** have shewa ְ under them. The Pu`al makes similar adjustments to those of the Pi`el for things such as middle guttural. A regular feature of this stem is the vowel qibbuts ֻ under the first root letter. (45.3)

וַיִּפְקֹד אֹתָם מֹשֶׁה עַל־פִּי יְהוָה כַּאֲשֶׁר צֻוָּה: *Numbers 3:16*

Pu`al 3 m. sg. affix form

And Moses numbered them according to the word of the Lord, <u>as he had been commanded</u>.

וְדִבֶּר אֶל־בְּנֵי יִשְׂרָאֵל אֵת אֲשֶׁר יְצֻוֶּה   *Exodus 34:34*

Pu`al 3 m. sg. prefix form

and he would speak to the children of Israel that which <u>he had been commanded</u>

Qal

The Qal is the basic stem of the verb, sometimes called the ground-form. The root Qal קלל means *light*. The derived stems are called כְּבֵדִים *heavy* because they have additions, in terms either of preformatives or strengthening, to the basic stem.

Genesis 12:10 כִּי־‌כָבֵד‌ הָרָעָב‌ בָּאָרֶץ

3 m. sg. Qal affix

because the famine <u>was heavy</u> (severe) in the land

כַּבֵּד‌ אֶת־אָבִיךָ‌ וְאֶת־אִמֶּךָ *Exodus 20:12*

3 m. sg. Pi`el affix, middle root letter strengthened

<u>*honor*</u> *your father and your mother*

Qere
See **Ketiv-Qere**

Quiescent
A letter that is seen but not heard. This most often occurs with the vowel letters י ו ה and the letters א and ע when they are at the end of a syllable and have no vowel.

יָדַע   קָרָא   הָיָה

quiescent ע ↑   quiescent א ↑   quiescent ה ↑   ↑ vocal ה

Examples of quiescent letters in English are the *k* and *g* in *knight*.

Radical
Another term for root letter. In אמר   א would be the first radical, מ the second, and ר the third. "The three radicals" refer then to the three root letters, not to a singing group.

Rashi
Rashi was a leading Jewish Bible commentator who lived in France, 1040–1105. He drew heavily from rabbinic sources, but also gave a number of philological explanations. His analyses of language are meticulous and he makes many comments on syntax, tenses, moods, stems, roots, etc. At Genesis 3:8, Rashi states his purpose in writing his commentary: "I am only concerned with the literal meaning of Scriptures and with such aggadot as explain the biblical passages in a fitting manner."

Reflexive
An action that is turned back upon the subject of the verb. In Hebrew the **Nif`al** and **Hitpa`el** are the verb stems that may most commonly impart a reflexive meaning to an action. Pronouns can also fulfill this function.

Deuteronomy 8:11 הִשָּׁמֶר‌ לְךָ‌ פֶּן־תִּשְׁכַּח‌ אֶת־יְהוָה‌ אֱלֹהֶיךָ

reflexive use of pronoun and of Nif`al imperative

take heed (upon yourself) lest you forget the Lord your God

וְהִתְגַּדִּלְתִּי וְהִתְקַדִּשְׁתִּי וְנוֹדַעְתִּי לְעֵינֵי גּוֹיִם רַבִּים *Ezekiel 38:23*

reflexive meanings of Nif'al and Hitpa'el affix

and I will <u>magnify myself</u> and <u>sanctify myself</u> and I will <u>make myself known</u> in the eyes of many nations

Regular Verb
See **Strong Verb**

Relative Clause

A clause often introduced by the relative particle אֲשֶׁר Sometimes when Hebrew uses a definite article before a participle, the "best" English translation employs a relative clause to express the idea.

Psalms 1:1 אַשְׁרֵי הָאִישׁ אֲשֶׁר לֹא הָלַךְ בַּעֲצַת רְשָׁעִים

relative clause introduced by אֲשֶׁר

Happy is the man <u>who does not walk in the council of the wicked</u>

Psalms 118:26 בָּרוּךְ הַבָּא בְּשֵׁם יְהוָה

הַ in front of a participle

Blessed is he <u>who comes in the name of the Lord</u>

Relative Pronoun

A word that introduces a clause and refers to an antecedent. In Hebrew, this function is absorbed by the all-purpose relative pronoun אֲשֶׁר

Genesis 22:2 קַח־נָא אֶת־בִּנְךָ אֶת־יְחִידְךָ אֲשֶׁר־אָהַבְתָּ אֶת־יִצְחָק

relative pronoun referring to בִּנְךָ and יְחִידְךָ

<u>whom</u> you love

Root

A three-letter consonant cluster—called שֹׁרֶשׁ in Hebrew—that represents the base from which verbs and nouns develop. So, for example, מלך would represent the concept of ruling. From this root come the verb מָלַךְ *rule* and such nouns as מֶלֶךְ *king* and מַלְכוּת *royalty*. There are those who do not agree entirely with this concept but reason instead that some roots are originally from a two-letter or a four-letter base. They believe such a hypothesis better explains such phenomena as hollow and geminate verbs. This is the stuff of advanced **etymology**.

Segolate Noun

A two-syllable noun having the emphasis on the first syllable. Its vowels are most often segol $\_\_$ אֶ֫רֶץ

מֶ֫לֶךְ בֹּ֫קֶר If the middle letter of a segolate noun is a guttural, then the vowels change to patah $\_\_$

נַ֫עַר (See **S 4.4b** and **S 11.3**.)

Semitic Language

A major group of languages of southwestern Asia and northern Africa. The subgroups are East Semitic (Akkadian), Northwest Semitic (Phoenician, Punic, Aramaic, Hebrew), and Southwest Semitic (Arabic, Ethiopic, Amharic).

Septuagint

A Greek translation of the Hebrew Bible so called because it was said to be the work of seventy-two Jews who completed the work in seventy days in the third century BCE. Contrary to this lovely legend, the actual work was done by many people over a long period of time. The original document no longer exists. The reason for the translation was that the Jews were moving into Greek-speaking areas, adopting that language as the vernacular, and wanted to be able to read the Bible in that tongue.

Silluq

A small vertical line $\_\_$ (it looks just like a **meteg**) in the last word of a verse that marks where the tone or accent is. It is one of the **major disjunctive accents**.

Deuteronomy 5:17–19 לֹא תִּרְצָֽח׃ וְלֹא תִּנְאָֽף׃ וְלֹא תִּגְנֹֽב׃

Simple Vav

Actually, ו is rarely simple. But when it is attached to a noun, adjective, or particle, less often when attached to a prefix form of the verb, and rarely on an affix form, it can mean simply *and*. However, ו has a wide range of meanings, some of which are *then, but, both . . . and*. (For other vocalizations of ו see **S 14.3.2**; for its syntactical range, **S 43.3**.

See also *Vav Conversive* and *Vav Reversive*.)

1 Kings 17:4 וְהָיָ֞ה מֵהַנַּ֣חַל תִּשְׁתֶּ֑ה וְאֶת־הָעֹרְבִ֣ים צִוִּ֔יתִי לְכַלְכֶּלְךָ֖ שָֽׁם

simple vav ↑   vav reversive ↑

And it shall be that you will drink of the wadi, <u>and</u> the ravens I have commanded to feed you there

Sof Passuq

The sign ׃ which marks the end of a verse. Like the vowels, it is not indigenous to the text but was added when the text (for use outside of the synagogue) began to be written with vocalization markings. (See also *Pointing/Points*)

Special Ending
See *Ending, Special*

Stative

Stative verbs denote the state of the subject rather than describe an action. In English, this state is usually expressed by using a form of *to be* with a predicate adjective such as *old, afraid, heavy*. Many of the statives in Hebrew have tsere ◌ֵ (an I class vowel) or holem וֹ (a U class vowel) as their second vowel in the **Qal** and only a few are **transitive**. (17.6)

1 Kings 1:1 וְהַמֶּלֶךְ דָּוִד ‬זָקֵן‭

stative verb

and King David <u>was old</u>

Genesis 37:4 וַיִּשְׂנְאוּ ‬אֹתוֹ‭

stative verb taking a DO

and they hated him

Stem

The seven major patterns בִּנְיָנִים of the verb. The stems other than Qal are called derived stems and are formed either by internal intensification of the root or by the addition of preformatives. Most verbs do not exist in all stems.

Qal	basic stem	פָּקַד	*attend, visit, muster, appoint*
Nif`al	passive or reflexive	נִפְקַד	*be visited (upon), be appointed*
Pi`el	intensive	פִּקֵּד	*muster (a host)*
Pu`al	passive of Pi`el	פֻּקַּד	*be passed in review*
Hif`il	causative	הִפְקִיד	*make overseer*
Hof`al	passive of Hif`il	הָפְקַד	*be made overseer*
Hitpa`el	intensive reflexive	הִתְפַּקֵּד	*be mustered*

Stem Indicator

A distinctive **preformative, dagesh forte**, or vowel that helps to identify the stem of a verb. So, for example, in the 3 m. sg. Pi`el affix form פִּקֵּד the dagesh forte in the middle root letter is a stem indicator. In the Hif`il הִפְקִיד the preformative ה and the I class vowel ḥireq ◌ִ between the second and third root letters are stem indicators.

Strong Verb

Some classify as a strong verb one whose root is made up of three consonants that follow the **paradigm** exactly such as קטל and פקד It is difficult to give a definition of the strong or regular verb since there is not an agreed-upon classification. So rather than define we will advise: Learn the paradigms and be prepared for arguments on this topic.

Subject

The noun or pronoun that does the action of the verb or about which something is said. In Hebrew, the subject may be indicated within the verb form and/or it may be a separate word.

1 Kings 17:5 וַיֵּ֣לֶךְ וַיַּ֔עַשׂ כִּדְבַ֖ר יְהוָ֑ה

two 3 m. sg. Qal prefix verbs: the subject is indicated by the prefix י

and <u>he</u> went and <u>he</u> did according to the word of the Lord

1 Kings 19:2 וַתִּשְׁלַ֤ח אִיזֶ֙בֶל֙ מַלְאָ֔ךְ אֶל־אֵלִיָּ֖הוּ

subject a proper noun, and also indicated by prefix pronoun ת

and <u>Jezebel</u> <u>(she)</u> sent a messenger to Elijah

Subject Pronoun

The pronoun (I, they, you, etc.) that does the action of the verb. In the affix and prefix forms, the subject pronoun is carried by the verb; in the imperative, it is understood to be second person; with a participle, it is indicated by another word, either a noun or an independent subject pronoun; and if an infinitive has a subject pronoun, it will be a possessive suffix or an independent noun (most likely a proper noun). Independent subject pronouns are often used for emphasis.

(Affix pronouns 13.5; ☉ ב א track 9. Prefix pronouns 14.5; ☉ ב א track 10. Independent subject pronouns 36.7; ☉ ב א track 24.)

Deuteronomy 9:1 שְׁמַ֣ע יִשְׂרָאֵ֗ל אַתָּ֨ה עֹבֵ֤ר הַיּוֹם֙ אֶת־הַיַּרְדֵּ֔ן

Qal m. sg. imperative שְׁמַע subject pronoun implied

m. sg. participle עֹבֵר subject indicated by independent subject pronoun אַתָּה

<u>(you)</u> hear, O Israel: <u>you</u> are about to pass over the Jordan this day

Genesis 22:14 אֲשֶׁ֨ר יֵאָמֵ֣ר הַיּ֔וֹם

3 m. sg. Nifʿal prefix. Subject pronoun *it* indicated by prefix pronoun

as <u>it</u> is said (to) this day

Subordinate Clause

See *Clause*

Substantive
A word—usually an adjective but sometimes a preposition—that is used for the equivalent of a noun.

Deuteronomy 6:18 וְעָשִׂ֫יתָ הַיָּשָׁ֥ר וְהַטּ֖וֹב

and (you will) do what is <u>upright</u> and <u>good</u>

★ Suffix
We are reserving this term to refer specifically to object pronouns and possessive pronouns that are attached to verbs, nouns, and prepositions. Suffixes have **person**, **gender**, and **number**.

Deuteronomy 6:10 וְהָיָה כִּי יְבִיאֲךָ יְהוָה אֱלֹהֶ֫יךָ אֶל־הָאָ֫רֶץ

2 m. sg. possessive suffix attached to noun   2 m. sg. object suffix attached to a verb

and it will be that the Lord <u>your</u> God will bring <u>you</u> to the land

Syllable
A unit of pronunciation. In Hebrew, a syllable starts with a consonant (except when a word starts with the conjunction vocalized as וּ). If it ends in a consonant, it is a closed syllable and if it ends in a vowel sound, it is an open syllable.

(See **S C-D**)

זֹאת   וַ יְ פֶ נֶה

monosyllabic word of one closed syllable   trisyllabic word: open   closed   open

Syntax
The branch of grammar that deals with the arrangement of words and how the arrangement and the meaning conveyed are related. Syntax addresses such issues as the construction and placement of phrases, clauses, direct speech, agreement of nouns and adjectives, and use of tenses.

Targum
The root תרגם means both *to explain* and to *translate*. In Biblical Studies, the term is commonly used to refer to Aramaic translations of the Bible. Targum Onkelos, the official translation of the first five books, was made in the second century CE. Targum Jonathan, from the early centuries of the common era, is the official Targum to the Prophets. There are Aramaic translations of the Writings, but they originate from a later period and none, except for Esther, have enjoyed official recognition. ("Official recognition" refers to use in the synagogue service.)

Text Criticism
Full text criticism would be an examination of all extant manuscripts to try to determine the best text. It is a concern of text criticism to try to explain how existing variants may have arisen. There is a modest discussion of this topic in the glosses to Exodus 3:1.

Tone
Tone is another term for the accented syllable in a word.

Torah

In its most specific sense, the word "Torah" refers to the books Genesis, Exodus, Leviticus, Numbers, and Deuteronomy. The word "Torah" is derived from the root יָרֹה which, in the Hif`il, means *instruct, point out, show*. It is <u>not</u> synonymous with *law* as in *legislate*. In its fullest sense, Torah refers to all learning that has its source in scripture.

Transitive

A verb that takes a **direct object** (DO) to complete its meaning.

Genesis 28:18 וַיַּשְׁכֵּם יַעֲקֹב בַּבֹּקֶר וַיִּקַּח אֶת־הָאֶבֶן

DDO   transitive verb   intransitive verb

And Jacob got up early in the morning and <u>he took</u> the stone

Triliteral

"Three letters." A term used to describe the Hebrew hypothetical three-letter root. Some dictionaries, such as BDB, are organized around this concept. Some grammarians believe that there were also biliteral and quadraliteral roots. (See **Root**)

Trope

The musical symbols used to chant the Torah, Prophets, and some of the Writings. The sound patterns are indicated by the accent marks over and under the words.

Ultima

The last syllable in a word. It generally receives the accent or **tone**.

Genesis 1:1 בְּרֵאשִׁית בָּרָא אֱלֹהִים אֵת הַשָּׁמַיִם וְאֵת הָאָרֶץ׃

In this verse, all the words except for הָאָרֶץ and הַשָּׁמַיִם are accented on the ultima.

Vav Consecutive

What we are calling the **vav conversive**. Each term takes into account one use of this construction. Consecutive implies "This happened and then . . . " and so describes its narrative function. Conversive is descriptive of the tense being converted in translation from future or present to past.

★ Vav Conversive

A construction formed by vav-patah-dagesh forte ☐ וַ in front of the prefix form of the verb: וַתְּדַבֵּר (but shewa <u>can</u> make dagesh forte disappear as in וַיְדַבֵּר) Some 1st י 3rd ה hollows, and Hif`ils have a shortened form in the vav conversive for some PGNs:

יֵשֵׁב ←— וַיֵּשֶׁב   יָקוּם ←— וַיָּקָם   יִרְאֶה ←— וַיַּרְא   יַרְכִּיב ←— וַיַּרְכֵּב

1st י   Hollow   3rd ה   Hif`il

It is a stylistic device of Biblical Hebrew when narrating a series of past events to begin the narration with an affix form of the verb and to continue it with a series of verbs in the prefix form with vav conversive.

וְהָאָדָם יָדַע אֶת־חַוָּה אִשְׁתּוֹ ‎וַתַּהַר וַתֵּלֶד אֶת־קַיִן‎ וַתֹּאמֶר

prefix forms with vav conversive   affix form

Genesis 4:1 קָנִיתִי אִישׁ אֶת־יהוה׃

direct speech, so affix form

And אָדָם *knew* חַוָּה *his wife and (then) she conceived and (then) she bore* קַיִן *and (then) she said,*
"I have acquired a man (child) with (the help of) the Lord."

A new section of a narrative often is introduced by a vav conversive:

Genesis 6:5 ‎וַיַּרְא‎ יהוה כִּי רַבָּה רָעַת הָאָדָם בָּאָרֶץ

and (then) the Lord saw that the wickedness of man was great on the earth

★ *Vav Reversive*

When a vav ‎ו‎ is attached to the front of the affix form of the verb, it usually serves to give it a future tense translation. Hence the vav "reverses" the tense. The name vav reversive is an analogic extension of vav conversive for the affix. In the narration of future events, the first verb will often be a prefix form and the following ones will be affix form plus vav reversive. There are instances of the vavs not changing the tense from past to future; in that case, the ‎ו‎ is called a **simple vav**. Such occurrences are mostly in the later books.

Deuteronomy 2:28 אֹכֶל בַּכֶּסֶף תַּשְׁבִּרֵנִי ‎וְאָכַלְתִּי‎

affix form + vav reversive   prefix form

you will sell me food for money <u>that I may eat</u> (and I will eat)

וְרָאִיתִי וְהִנֵּה־עֲלֵיהֶם גִּדִים וּבָשָׂר עָלָה *Ezekiel 37:8*

arguably a simple vav

<u>*and (as) I beheld*</u>*, lo, sinews and flesh (came) upon them*

Vav on an affix form can also denote repetitive action in the past. (43.1)

Genesis 29:3 וְנֶאֶסְפוּ־שָׁמָּה כָל־הָעֲדָרִים וְגָלֲלוּ אֶת־הָאֶבֶן מֵעַל פִּי הַבְּאֵר

and all the flocks <u>used to gather</u> there and they <u>would roll</u> the stone from on the mouth of the well

Verb

A word or words that express(es) action, existence, or occurrence. In Hebrew, the verb has five **forms**: affix, prefix, participle, imperative, and infinitive. It has seven major **stems**: Qal, Nif`al, Pi`el, Pu`al, Hif`il, Hof`al, and Hitpa`el. Because Biblical Hebrew uses so few adjectives and adverbs, the impact and color of the language are conveyed particularly through the verb. The fact that the verb can be built up in front with preformatives, strengthened in the middle by a dagesh or infix, and lengthened by the addition of pronominal suffixes enhances its conspicuousness. The verbs in Deuteronomy 6:7 are a representative example of the strength of highly inflected verbs. English needs about four times as many words to communicate ideas expressed by the verbs in this verse.

וְשִׁנַּנְתָּם לְבָנֶיךָ וְדִבַּרְתָּ בָּם בְּשִׁבְתְּךָ בְּבֵיתֶךָ וּבְלֶכְתְּךָ בַדֶּרֶךְ
וּבְשָׁכְבְּךָ וּבְקוּמֶךָ׃ *Deuteronomy 6:7*

And you will inculcate them in your children, and you will speak about them when you sit in your house, when you walk by the way, when you lie down, and when you rise up.

Vocalization
See *Pointing*

Vocative

The direct address of a person or thing. The vocative has no special marker in Hebrew.

Deuteronomy 6:4 שְׁמַע יִשְׂרָאֵל יְהוָה אֱלֹהֵינוּ יְהוָה אֶחָד׃
vocative

Hear, (O) Israel, Adonai is our God; Adonai is one

Isaiah 49:13 רָנּוּ שָׁמַיִם וְגִילִי אָרֶץ
vocative vocative

sing, (O) heavens; and be joyful, (O) earth

Voice
See *Active Voice* and *Passive Voice*

Vowel Class

There are three classes of vowels in Hebrew A _ _ _ I _ _ _ and U וּ וֹ _ _

Segol _ substitutes for either A or I. Qamats _ is an A class vowel, but in a closed, unaccented syllable it is a shortened U class vowel. When vowels shorten or lengthen, they tend to do so within their own class. (For more on vowels, see **S A-B**.)

qamats ḥatuf ⬆

Vowel Letter

The letters א ה ו י (See *Matres Lectionis*)

Vulgate

The Latin translation of the Hebrew Bible plus the Apocrypha and New Testament prepared primarily by St. Jerome in the fourth century CE. This translation enjoyed wide acceptance in Western Christendom during the Middle Ages, and thus became known as the *Vulgata Versio* (Common Version.) Until recently, it was the only authorized version of the Bible for the Roman Catholic Church.

★ Weak Verb

A verb with a root letter that may not appear in all forms: 1st י 1st נ 3rd ה hollow verbs, and geminates fall into this category. Some grammars include in this group verbs that contain a guttural letter. In the following Qal prefix forms of weak verbs, note the missing root letter: (17.6)

תֵּצֵא	תִּתֵּן	וַתָּקָם	וַתֵּרֶא	תֵּרַע
1st י missing	1st נ assimilated	middle ו missing	final ה missing	final ע missing

Word Order

The usual word order of a Biblical verse is: verb followed by its subject (if there is an independent subject), then the indirect object followed by the direct object. Other features such as adjectives and adverbs, which may be single words, phrases, or clauses, are fitted in, of course. Word order is often varied for emphasis or euphony.

וְיִשְׂרָאֵל אָהַב אֶת־יוֹסֵף מִכָּל־בָּנָיו כִּי־בֶן־זְקֻנִים הוּא לוֹ

placement of הוּא לוֹ emphatic   note: subject יִשְׂרָאֵל precedes verb אָהַב

וְעָשָׂה לוֹ כְּתֹנֶת פַּסִּים: וַיִּרְאוּ אֶחָיו כִּי־אֹתוֹ אָהַב אֲבִיהֶם

placement of DO אֹתוֹ before the verb is emphatic   usual word order

מִכָּל־אֶחָיו וַיִּשְׂנְאוּ אֹתוֹ

Genesis 37:3 and 4a

usual word order

Zagef Qaton

A *major disjunctive accent*, represented by two vertical dots over a letter. It often causes vowel changes.

הֱ

VOCABULARY

Particles

Single-letter particles are always attached to another word.

a   בְּ   **in,** *at, by means of*

     בְּבַיִת   *in a house*

b   הֲ   **?** (interrogative)

     הֲלֹא   *not?*

c   וְ   **and,** *but, then, or*

     וְלֹא   *and not*

d   כְּ   **as, like,** *according to*

     כְּאִישׁ   *like/as a man*

e   לְ   **to, for,** *of*

     לְבֵן   *to/for a son*

f   שֶׁ   **who, which, that**

     שֶׁשָּׁם   *which/who [is/was] there*

g   מִ   מִן   **from, out of,** *more than*

h   הַ   **the** (definite article)

     הַבֵּן   *the son*

VOCABULARY

Words

1	[הוה]	become	7a	בַּת	daughter (f.) ⓘ
	יהוה	Adonai, Lord		בִּתִּי	sg. + suffix
				בָּנוֹת	pl. abs.
2	I. כָּלַל	complete, perfect		בְּנוֹת	pl. const.
	כֹּל כּוֹל	the whole, all		בְּנוֹתָיו	pl. + suffix
	כָּל-	const.			
			8	עָלָה	go up, ascend
3	אֲשֶׁר	who, whom, which,			Q. he went up
		that, because		יַעֲלֶה וַיַּעַל	Q. prefix
		(introduces a clause)		נַעֲלָה	Ni. he was taken up
				הֶעֱלָה	Hi. he brought up;
4	אֶל	to, toward			offered up
		(takes י before suffix)			
	אֵלָיו אֵלֶיךָ	+ suffix	8a	עֹלָה	burnt offering (f.)
				עֹלַת	sg. const.
5	אָמַר	say		עֹלָתוֹ	sg. + suffix
		Q. he said		עֹלוֹת	pl. abs./const.
	יֹאמַר וַיֹּאמֶר	Q. prefix		עֹלוֹתֶיךָ	pl. + suffix
	יֵאָמֵר	Ni. it will be said			
			8b	II. עַל	on, upon, concerning
6	לֹא לוֹא	not			(takes י before suffix)
		(negates what follows)		עָלָיו עָלֶיךָ	+ suffix
	אֲשֶׁר לֹא הָיָה	who was not			
			8c	מַעַל	above (substantive)
7	בֵּן	son		מִמַּעַל	from on top of (prep.)
	בֶּן	sg. const.			
	בְּנוֹ בִּנְךָ	sg. + suffix	9	כִּי	that, because, surely
	בָּנִים	pl. abs.			(conj.)
	בְּנֵי	pl. const.			(introduces a clause)
	בָּנָיו	pl. + suffix			

10	הָיָה	be, happen
		Q. *he/it was, it happened*
	יִהְיֶה וַיְהִי	Q. prefix
11	I. עָשָׂה	make, do
		Q. *he made, did*
	יַעֲשֶׂה וַיַּעַשׂ	Q. prefix
	נַעֲשָׂה	Ni. *it was done*
11a	מַעֲשֶׂה	*deed, work*
	מַעֲשֵׂה	sg. const.
	מַעֲשֵׂהוּ מַעֲשֵׂנוּ	sg. + suffix
	מַעֲשִׂים	pl. abs.
	מַעֲשֵׂי	pl. const.
	מַעֲשָׂיו	pl. + suffix
12	I. אלה	see discussion of √ in BDB
	II. אֵל	*God*, also proper name *El*
	אֵלִי	+ suffix
	אֵלִים	pl. abs.
12a	אֱלֹהַּ	*God*
	אֱלֹהִים	*God, gods*
	אֱלֹהֵי	const.
	אֱלֹהָיו	+ suffix

13	בּוֹא	enter, come in (Q. infin.)
	בָּא	**Q.** *he entered/came*
	יָבוֹא וַיָּבֹא	Q. prefix
	הֵבִיא	Hi. he brought in
14	I. מלך	√ dubious
	מֶלֶךְ	*king*
	מַלְכּוֹ	sg. + suffix
	מְלָכִים	pl. abs.
	מַלְכֵי	pl. const.
	מְלָכָיו	pl. + suffix
14a	מַלְכָּה	*queen*
	מַלְכַּת	sg. const.
	מְלָכוֹת	pl. abs.
15	II. מָלַךְ	*become king or queen; reign*
		Q. *he was king; he ruled*
	יִמְלֹךְ וַיִּמְלֹךְ	Q. prefix
	הִמְלִיךְ	Hi. *he caused to reign*
15a	מַלְכוּת	*royalty, royal power*
15b	מַמְלָכָה	*kingdom* (f.)
	מַמְלֶכֶת	sg. const.
	מַמְלַכְתִּי	sg. + suffix
	מַמְלָכוֹת	pl. abs.

16	אֶרֶץ	earth, land (f.)	20	בַּיִת	house ⓘ
	אַרְצוֹ	sg. + suffix		בֵּית	sg. const.
	אֲרָצוֹת	pl. abs.		בֵּיתוֹ	sg. + suffix
	אַרְצוֹת	pl. const.		בָּתִּים	pl. abs.
				בָּתֵּי	pl. const.
17	יוֹם	day ⓘ		בָּתֵּיהֶם	pl. + suffix
	יוֹמוֹ	sg. + suffix			
	יָמִים	pl. abs.	21	נָתַן	give, put, set (16.6)
	יְמֵי	pl. const.			**Q.** *he gave*
	יָמָיו	pl. + suffix		יִתֵּן וַיִּתֵּן	Q. prefix
				תֵּת	Q. infin.
18	אוש איש	see discussion of √ in BDB			
			22	I. עמם	those united/related
	אִישׁ	man → husband ⓘ			(E.K.)
	אִישִׁי	sg. + suffix		עַם עָם	people
	אֲנָשִׁים	pl. abs.		עַם	sg. const.
	אַנְשֵׁי	pl. const.		עַמּוֹ	sg. + suffix
	אֲנָשָׁיו	pl. + suffix		עַמִּים	pl. abs.
				עַמֵּי	pl. const.
19	פָּנָה	turn			
		Q. *he turned*	23	יָד	hand → strength (f.)
	יִפְנֶה וַיִּפֶן	Q. prefix		יַד	sg. const.
	פִּנָּה	Pi. *he turned away; cleared away*		יָדוֹ	sg. + suffix
				יָדַיִם	du.
	הִפְנָה	Hi. *he made a turn*		יְדֵי	du. const.
				יָדָיו	du. + suffix
19a	פָּנִים [פָּנֶה]	face → presence			
	פְּנֵי	const.	24	הָלַךְ	go, walk
	פָּנָיו פָּנֶיךָ	+ suffix			**Q.** *he went, walked*
				יֵלֵךְ וַיֵּלֶךְ	Q. prefix
				לֶכֶת	Q. infin.

וְהִתְהַלֵּךְ Ht. *and he will walk about*

הוֹלִיךְ Hi. *he caused to go; led*

25 [דָּבַר] *speak*

דִּבֶּר **Pi.** *he spoke*

יְדַבֵּר וַיְדַבֵּר Pi. prefix

25a דָּבָר *word, thing, affair*

דְּבַר sg. const.

דְּבָרוֹ sg. + suffix

דְּבָרִים pl. abs.

דִּבְרֵי pl. const.

דְּבָרָיו pl. + suffix

25b II. מִדְבָּר *wilderness*

מִדְבַּר sg. const.

26 הוּא *he, that one* (subj.)

הַהוּא *that* (attrib. adj.)

26a הִיא *she, that one* (subj.)

הַהִיא הַהוּא *that* (attrib. adj.)

27 רָאָה *see, look at*

Q. *he saw*

יִרְאֶה וַיַּרְא Q. prefix

נִרְאָה Ni. *he was seen, appeared*

הֶרְאָה Hi. *he caused to see; showed*

27a מַרְאֶה *sight, appearance*

מַרְאֵה sg. construct

מַרְאֵהוּ מַרְאָהּ sg. + suffix

מַרְאֵיהֶם pl. + suffix

28 I. עָדָה *pass on, advance*

III. עַד *as far as, until* (prep.)

29 II. אבה ? formal connection with noun

אָב *father, ancestor* ⓘ

אֲבִי אַב sg. const.

אֲבִי אָבִיו sg. + suffix

אָבוֹת pl. abs.

אֲבוֹת pl. const.

אֲבֹתֵיהֶם pl. + suffix

30 שָׁמַע *hear, listen to*

Q. *he heard*

יִשְׁמַע וַיִּשְׁמַע Q. prefix

הִשְׁמִיעַ Hi. *he caused to hear; proclaimed*

31 זֶה *this, this one* (subj.)

הַזֶּה *this* (attrib. adj.)

| 31a | זֹאת | *this*, *this one* (subj. f.) | 37 | הִנֵּה הֵן | *behold! see! here!* |
| | הַזֹּאת | *this* (attrib. adj.) | | הִנְנִי | *Here I am! Behold me!* |

| 32 | אֵלֶּה | *these* (subj. m./f.) | 38 | עִם | *with* |
| | הָאֵלֶּה | *these* (attrib. adj.) | | עִמּוֹ עִמָּהֶם | *+ suffix* |

33	II. עִיר	*city, town* (f.) ⓘ	39	לָקַח	*take, receive*
	עִירוֹ	sg. + suffix			ⓘ (21.a–d)
	עָרִים	pl. abs.			**Q.** *he took*
	עָרֵי	pl. const.		יִקַּח וַיִּקַּח	Q. prefix
	עָרָיו עָרֶיהָ	pl. + suffix		לָקַחַת	Q. infin.

34	יָשַׁב	*sit, remain, dwell*	40	אֶחָד	*one* (noun/adj.)
		Q. *he sat, remained*		אַחַת	(f.)
	יֵשֵׁב וַיֵּשֶׁב	Q. prefix			
	שֶׁבֶת	Q. infin.	41	יָדַע	*know*
	הוֹשִׁיב	Hi. *he caused to sit,*			**Q.** *he knew*
		dwell		יֵדַע וַיֵּדַע	Q. prefix
				דַּעַת	Q. infin.
				נוֹדַע	Ni. *he/it was made*
35	יָצָא	*go forth, come out*			*known*
		Q. *he went forth*		הוֹדִיעַ	Hi. *he made known*
	יֵצֵא וַיֵּצֵא	Q. prefix			
	צֵאת	Q. infin.	42	אִם	*if*
	הוֹצִיא	Hi. *he caused to go forth*			

36	שׁוּב	*return, turn back*	43	I. [שָׁנָה]	*change*
		(Q. infin.)		שָׁנָה	*year* (f.) ⓘ
	שָׁב	**Q.** *he turned back*		שְׁנַת	sg. const.
	יָשׁוּב וַיָּשָׁב	Q. prefix		שְׁנָתוֹ	sg. + suffix
	הֵשִׁיב	Hi. *he caused to return*		שָׁנִים	pl. abs.

	שְׁנֵי שְׁנוֹת	pl. const.	47a	II. עַיִן	spring, fountain (f.)
	שְׁנוֹתָיו שָׁנֵינוּ	pl. + suffix		עֵין	sg. const.
				עֲיָנוֹת	pl. abs.
44	III. שָׁנָה	repeat, do again		עֵינוֹת	pl. const.
	שְׁנַיִם	two	48	I. שָׁלַח	send
	שְׁנֵי	const.			Q. he sent
	שְׁנֵיהֶם	+ suffix: the two of them		יִשְׁלַח וַיִּשְׁלַח	Q. prefix
	שְׁתַּיִם	(f.)		שִׁלַּח	Pi. he cast out
	שְׁתֵּי	const.	49	מוּת	die (Q. infin.)
	שְׁתֵיהֶם	+ suffix		מֵת	Q. he died, is dead
44a	שֵׁנִי	second			(34.6)
	שֵׁנִית	(f.)		יָמוּת וַיָּמָת	Q. prefix
				הֵמִית	Hi. he caused to die; put to death
45	1. שֵׁם	name → fame ⓘ			
	שֵׁם שֶׁם	sg. const	49a	מָוֶת	death
	שְׁמוֹ	sg. + suffix		מוֹת	sg. const.
	שֵׁמוֹת	pl. abs.		מוֹתוֹ	sg. + suffix
	שְׁמוֹת	pl. const.	50	שָׁם	there
	שְׁמוֹתָם	pl. + suffix		שָׁמָּה	+ directive ה thither
46	אֲנִי	I	51	אָכַל	eat, consume
46a	אָנֹכִי	I (poetic)			Q. he ate
47	1. עַיִן	eye (f.)		יֹאכַל וַיֹּאכַל	Q. prefix
	עֵין	sg. const.		נֶאֱכַל	Ni. it was eaten
	עֵינוֹ	sg. + suffix		הֶאֱכַלְתִּי	Hi. I caused to eat; fed
	עֵינַיִם	du.			
	עֵינֵי	du. const.			
	עֵינָיו עֵינֵיהֶם	du. + suffix			

52	עָבַד	*serve; do work*		נְפָשׁוֹת	pl. abs.
		Q. *he served*		נַפְשֹׁתֵינוּ	pl. + suffix
	יַעֲבֹד וַיַּעֲבֹד	Q. prefix			
	הֶעֱבִיד	Hi. *he caused to serve*	56	II. אַיִן	*nothing*
					(particle of negation)
52a	1. עֶבֶד	*slave, servant*		אֵין	**const.:** *is not; are not*
	עַבְדּוּ	sg. + suffix		אֵינְךָ	+ suffix
	עֲבָדִים	pl. abs.		אֵינֶנּוּ	+ energic נ suffix
	עַבְדֵי	pl. const.			(53.3–5a)
	עֲבָדָיו עַבְדֵיהֶם	pl. + suffix			
			57	אָדוֹן	*master, lord*
52b	עֲבֹדָה	*service, labor* (f.)		אֲדוֹן	sg. const.
	עֲבֹדַת	sg. const.		אֲדֹנִי	sg. + suffix
	עֲבֹדָתִי	sg. + suffix		אֲדֹנָי	pl. + suffix
				אֲדֹנָי	*Lord*
53	III. אנש	*soft, delicate* (BDB);			
		√ uncertain (E.K.)	58	כהן	? √ כון (E.K.)
	אִשָּׁה	*woman* → *wife* (f.) ⓘ		כֹּהֵן	*priest*
	אֵשֶׁת	sg. const.		כֹּהֲנִים	pl. abs.
	אִשְׁתּוֹ	sg. + suffix		כֹּהֲנֵי	pl. const.
	נָשִׁים	pl. abs.			
	נְשֵׁי	pl. const.	59	מָה	*what? how!*
	נְשֵׁיכֶם	pl. + suffix			
			59a	4. d. לָמָּה	*why?*
54	גמם	*much, many*			
	גַּם	*moreover, also, even*	60	אנת	
				אַתָּה	*you* (m. sg.)
55	נפש	√ *throat, neck*			
	נֶפֶשׁ	*living being, person,*	60a	אַתֶּם	*you* (m. pl.)
		life (f.)			
	נַפְשׁוֹ נַפְשִׁי	sg. + suffix	61	I. קָרָא	*call, proclaim*
					Q. *he called*

יִקְרָא וַיִּקְרָא Q. prefix

נִקְרָא Ni. he/it has been proclaimed

62 II. [קָרָא] encounter, befall
same meaning as
קרה

קְרָאַנִי Q. affix + suffix

יִקְרָא Q. prefix

לִקְרַאת Q. infin. *to meet, encounter*

63 אָחַר remain behind, tarry

1. אַחֵר *another, different, other*

אַחֶרֶת (f.)

אֱלֹהִים אֲחֵרִים other gods

63a אַחַר אַחֲרֵי *behind, after*
adv./prep./substantive
(takes ֵ before suffix)

אַחֲרָיו + suffix

64 דָּרַךְ tread, march

דֶּרֶךְ *road, way* (m./f.)

דַּרְכּוֹ sg. + suffix

דְּרָכִים pl.abs.

דַּרְכֵי pl. const.

דְּרָכָיו pl. + suffix

65 I. כֵּן *thus, so*

65a 3d. לָכֵן *therefore*

66 I. רָעַע *be evil, bad* (E.K.)

רַע *evil, distress, misery*

66a רָעָה *evil, distress, misery* (f.)

רָעַת sg. const.

רָעָתִי sg. + suffix

רָעוֹת pl. abs.

רְעוֹתֵיכֶם pl. + suffix

67 I. רָעָה *pasture, tend, graze*
Q. he pastured, it (the flock) grazed

יִרְעֶה Q. prefix;

וַיִּרְעֵם vav conv. + suffix

רֹעֶה Q. part.

רֹעָה Q. part. (f.)

68 II. רָעָה *associate with*

רֵעַ *friend, companion*

רֵעִי רֵעֵהוּ sg. + suffix

רֵעִי pl. abs.

רֵעָיו pl. + suffix

69 נָשָׂא *lift, carry*
Q. *he lifted, carried*

יִשָּׂא וַיִּשָּׂא Q. prefix

69a 1. נָשִׂיא *prince*

נְשִׂיא sg. const.

395

נְשִׂיאִים   pl. abs.

נְשִׂיאֵי   pl. const.

70	אחה	see discussion of √ in BDB		לָבוֹת	pl. abs.
				לְבוֹתָם	pl. + suffix
	1. אָח	*brother* ⓘ	72a	לֵבָב	*heart, inner self →* *mind, will*
	אֲחִי	sg. const.		לְבַב	sg. const.
	אָחִי אָחִיו	sg. + suffix		לְבָבוֹ	+ suffix
	אַחַי	pl. abs.		לְבָבוֹת	pl. abs.
	אֲחֵי	pl. const.	73	רֹאשׁ	*head, top, chief*
	אַחַי אֶחָיו	pl. + suffix		רֹאשׁוֹ	+ suffix
70a	אָחוֹת	*sister* ⓘ		רָשִׁים	pl. abs.
	אֲחֹתִי	sg. + suffix		רָאשֵׁי	pl. const.
	אַחְיוֹתָיו	pl. + suffix		רָאשֵׁיהֶם	pl. + suffix
			73a	רִאשׁוֹן	*former, first* (adj.)
71	קוּם	*arise, stand* (Q. infin.)		רִאשֹׁנָה	(f.)
	קָם	**Q. he stood up**			
	יָקוּם וַיָּקָם	Q. prefix	74	I. מֵאָה	*hundred* (f.)
	הֵקִים	Hi. *he established;* *erected*		מְאַת	sg. const.
				מֵאוֹת	pl. abs.
71a	מָקוֹם	*place* (noun)		מָאתַיִם	du. *two hundred*
	מְקוֹם	sg. const.			
	מְקוֹמוֹ	sg. + suffix	75	שִׂים	*put, set* (Q. infin.)
	מְקוֹמוֹת	pl. abs./const.		שָׂם	**Q. he put, set**
				יָשִׂים וַיָּשֶׂם	Q. prefix
72	לבב				
	לֵב	*heart, inner self →* *mind, will*	76	[מִי]	
	לִבּוֹ	+ suffix		מַיִם	*water, waters*
				מֵי מֵימֵי	const.

77	כֹּה	*thus*		81	עָבַר	*pass over, through, by, on*

81 עָבַר — *pass over, through, by, on*
Q. he passed by

יַעֲבֹר וַיַּעֲבֹר	Q. prefix
הֶעֱבִיר	Hi. *he caused to pass by*

78 גוה — project, be convex ? (? related to body, thus denoting ethnic body. E.K.)

גּוֹי	*nation*
גּוֹיִי	sg. + suffix
גּוֹיִם	pl. abs.
גּוֹיֵי	pl. const.
לְגוֹיֵיהֶם	pl. + suffix

82 עָשַׂר — *gather, unite*

עֶשֶׂר	*ten* (with f. nouns)
עֲשָׂרָה	(with m. nouns)

82a עֶשְׂרִים — *twenty*

79 אדם — ? connected to √ meaning *be red.*

I. אָדָם	*man, humankind, Adam*

83 גָּדַל — *grow up; become great*
Q. he grew up; became great

יִגְדַּל וַיִּגְדַּל	Q. prefix
גִּדֵּל גִּדַּל	Pi. *he raised, reared (a child); he made great*
וְהִתְגַּדִּלְתִּי	Ht. *and I will magnify myself*
הִגְדִּיל	Hi. *he made great, magnified*

79a

אֲדָמָה	*ground, land* (f.)
אַדְמַת	sg. const.
אַדְמָתִי	sg. + suffix
אֲדָמוֹת	pl. abs.

83a גָּדוֹל — *big, great* (adj.)

גְּדַל גְּדָל-	m. sg. const.
גְּדוֹלִים	m. pl. abs.
גְּדֹלֵי	m. pl. const.
גְּדֹלָיו	m. pl. + suffix
גְּדוֹלָה	f. sg. abs.
גְּדוֹלֹת	f. pl. abs.

80 הרר

הַר	*mountain, hill*
הֲרָרִי הַרְכֶם	sg. + suffix
הָהָר	sg. + def. art.
הָרִים	pl. abs.
הָרֵי הַרְרֵי	pl. const.
הֶהָרִים	pl. + def. art.

84	עָמַד	stand		יֻלַּד	Pu. *he was born*
		Q. *he stood*		הוֹלִיד	Hi. *he begot*
	יַעֲמֹד וַיַּעֲמֹד	Q. prefix			
	הֶעֱמִיד	Hi. *he caused to stand firm; stationed*	88	II. אֶלֶף	***thousand, military unit***
				אַלְפִּי	+ suffix
84a	עַמֻּד עַמּוּד	***pillar, column***		אַלְפַּיִם	du.: *two thousand*
	עַמּוּדוֹ	sg. + suffix		אֲלָפִים	pl. abs.
	עַמּוּדִים	pl. abs.		אַלְפֵי	pl. const.
	עַמּוּדֵי	pl. const.			
	עַמּוּדָיו	pl. + suffix	89	תַּחַת	***under, in place of*** (takes יִ before suffix)
85	הֵם הֵמָּה	***they*** (subj.)		תַּחְתָּיו	+ suffix
	הָהֵם	*those* (attrib. adj.)			
			90	חָיָה	*live*
85a	הֵן הֵנָּה	***they*** (f. subj.)			**Q. *he lived***
	הָהֵנָּה	*those* (f. attrib. adj.)		יִחְיֶה וַיְחִי	Q. prefix
				חִיָּה	Pi. *he preserved alive; let live; revived*
86	קוֹל	in cognate languages: *speak, sound, shout*		הֶחֱיָה	Hi. *he preserved alive; let live, revived*
	קוֹל	***voice, sound***			
	קוֹלִי	sg. + suffix	90a	חַי	***alive, living, living one*** (adj.)
	קֹלוֹת	pl. abs./const.		חַיִּים	pl. abs.
				חַיָּה	(f.)
87	יָלַד	*bear, give birth to*			
		Q. *he bore* (!)	90b	חַיָּה	***living being, animal*** (f.)
	תֵּלֶד וַתֵּלֶד	Q. prefix		חַיַּת	sg. const.
	לֶדֶת	Q. infin.			
	נוֹלַד	Ni. *he was born*			
	מְיַלֶּדֶת	Pi. f. part.: *act as midwife*			

	חֲזִיתִי	sg. + suffix		יְצַוֶּה וַיְצַו	Pi. prefix
	חַיּוֹת	pl. abs.		צַו צַוּוּ	Pi. m. sg./pl. imperative
90c	חַיִּים	*life*	94a	מִצְוָה	*commandment* (f.)
	חַיֵּי	const.		מִצְוַת	sg. const.
	חַיֵּי	+ suffix		מִצְוָתוֹ	sg. + suffix
				מִצְוֹת	pl. abs./const.
91	[עוד]	*return, go about, repeat*		מִצְוֹתָיו	pl. + suffix
	עוֹד	**still, yet, again**	95	קדשׁ	denotes separation
	עוֹדֶנּוּ מְדַבֵּר	+ suffix: *while he was still speaking*		קֹדֶשׁ	**holiness, sacredness**
				קָדְשׁוֹ	sg. + suffix
92	פֶּה	**mouth** ⓘ		קָדָשִׁים	pl. abs.
	פִּי	sg. const.		קָדְשֵׁי	pl. const.
	פִּי פִּיךָ פִּיו	sg. + suffix		קָדְשֵׁי קָדָשָׁיו	pl. + suffix
	פִּיהוּ פִּימוֹ				
	פִּיּוֹת פֵּיוֹת	pl. abs.	95a	קָדוֹשׁ	*sacred, holy* (adj.)
				קְדוֹשׁ	sg. const.
93	[צָבָא]	*wage war*		קְדוֹשִׁי	sg. + suffix
	צָבָא	**army, warfare; heavenly bodies**		קְדֹשִׁים	pl. abs.
				קְדֹשָׁיו	pl. + suffix
	צְבָא	sg. const.			
	צְבָאוֹ	sg. + suffix	95b	קָדַשׁ	**Q.** *he/it was set apart*
	צְבָאוֹת	pl. abs.		יִקְדַּשׁ	Q. prefix
	צִבְאוֹת	pl. const.		נִקְדַּשׁ	Ni. *he/it was consecrated*
	צִבְאוֹתָם	pl. + suffix		קִדֵּשׁ	**Pi.** *he consecrated*
94	[צָוָה]	*charge, command, order*		וַיְקַדֵּשׁ	Pi. prefix + vav conv.
	צִוָּה	**Pi.** *he gave charge to/ over*		הִתְקַדִּשְׁתִּי	Ht. *I kept myself apart; showed myself sacred*

	הִקְדִּישׁ	Hi. *he set apart; consecrated*	99c	[מַעַן]	*purpose, intent*
				לְמַֽעַן	**for the sake of, in order that, on account of**
96	שָׁמַר	*keep watch, guard* **Q. he guarded**			
	יִשְׁמֹר וַיִּשְׁמֹר	Q. prefix	100	III. [עָנָה]	*be bowed down, afflicted* **Q. he was afflicted**
	נִשְׁמַר	Ni. *he took heed*		יֵעָנֶה	*prefix*
	הִשָּֽׁמֶר	Ni. imperative: *guard yourself*		עִנָּה	Pi. *he humbled*
97	מָצָא	*find* **Q. he found**	100a	עָנִי	*afflicted, poor* (adj.)
	יִמְצָא	Q. prefix		עֲנִיִּים	pl. abs.
	נִמְצָא	Ni. *he/it was found*		עֲנִיֵּי	pl. const.
				עֲנִיֶּֽיךָ	pl. + suffix
98	III. עלם	? √ *hidden* + *unknown time* or ? *remote time*	100b	עֳנִי	*affliction, poverty*
	עוֹלָם	*eternity; a long time back; future time*		עָנְיִי עָנְיֶֽךָ	+ suffix
99	I. עָנָה	*answer, respond* **Q. he answered**	101	נָפַל	*fall* **Q. he fell**
	יַעֲנֶה וַיַּֽעַן	Q. prefix		יִפֹּל וַיִּפֹּל	Q. prefix
				הִפִּיל	Hi. *he caused to fall*
99a	עֵת	*time, season* (f./m.)			
	עִתּוֹ	sg. + suffix	102	שׁלשׁ	√ unknown
	עִתּוֹת עִתִּים	pl. abs.		שָׁלֹשׁ	*three* (with f. nouns)
	עִתֹּתַי עִתֶּֽיךָ	pl. + suffix		שְׁלֹשׁ	const.
				שְׁלֹשָׁה	(with m. nouns)
99b	עַתָּה	*now*		שְׁלֹשֶׁת	const.

102a	שְׁלִישִׁי	*third*	106	שׂמה
	שְׁלִישִׁית	*(f.)*		

√ prob. *high place or height (or may be secondary)*

102b	שְׁלֹשִׁים	*thirty*

שָׁמַ֫יִם [שָׁמֵי] — *heaven(s), sky*
שְׁמֵי — *const.*
שָׁמֶ֫יךָ — *+ suffix*

103	I. [רָבַב]	*become much or many*
	1. רַב	*much, many, great (adj.)*
	רַבִּים	*m. pl.*
	רַבָּה	*f. sg.*
	רַבַּת	*f. sg. const.*
	רַבּוֹת	*f. pl.*

107	שׂרר	*be strong, firm* (E.K.)
	שַׂר	*ruler, chieftain*
	שַׂרְכֶם	*sg. + suffix*
	שָׂרִים	*pl. abs.*
	שָׂרֵי	*pl. const.*
	שָׂרֵיכֶם	*pl. + suffix*

103a	רֹב	*multitude, abundance*

104	מִי	*who?*

108	תָּ֫וֶךְ	*midst, middle*
	תוֹךְ	*const. (the) midst of*
	תוֹכוֹ	*+ suffix*
	בְּתוֹךְ מִתּוֹךְ	*+ prep. in/from the midst of*

105	שָׁפַט	*judge*
		Q. *he judged*
	יִשְׁפֹּט וַיִּשְׁפֹּט	*Q. prefix*
	נִשְׁפַּ֫טְתִּי	*Ni. I entered into controversy*

109	III. חֹ֫רֶב	*attack*
	חֶ֫רֶב	*sword* (f.)
	חַרְבּוֹ	*sg. + suffix*
	חֲרָבוֹת	*pl. abs.*
	חַרְבוֹת	*pl. const.*
	חַרְבֹתֵיהֶם	*pl. + suffix*

105a	מִשְׁפָּט	*judgment, justice; custom*
	מִשְׁפַּט	*sg. const.*
	מִשְׁפָּטִי	*sg. + suffix*
	מִשְׁפָּטִים	*pl. abs.*
	מִשְׁפְּטֵי	*pl. const.*
	מִשְׁפָּטֶ֫יךָ	*pl. + suffix*

110	יָרֵא	*fear, be in awe*
		Q. *he feared; was in awe*

		Q. part.: *a fearer, fearing*	113b	מִזְבֵּחַ	*place of sacrifice, altar*
	יְרֵא אֱלֹהִים	*a fearer of God*		מִזְבַּח	sg. const.
	יִירָא יִרְאוּ וַיִּירָא	Q. prefix		מִזְבְּחִי	sg. + suffix
	נוֹרָא	Ni. part. *awe-inspiring*		מִזְבְּחוֹת	pl.
				מִזְבְּחוֹתֶיךָ	pl. + suffix
111	I. נָא	*please, now, pray* (particle of entreaty)	114	אָהֵב אָהַב	*love* **Q.** *he loved*
				יֶאֱהַב וַיֶּאֱהַב	Q. prefix
112	[יָחַד]	*be united*			
	יַחַד	*unitedness, together*	115	II. עצה	√ dubious
				עֵץ	*tree(s), wood*
112a	יַחְדָּו	*together*		עֵצִים	pl. abs.
				עֲצֵי	pl. const.
112b	יָחִיד	*only one, unique*			
	יְחִידְךָ	+ suffix	116	III. נַעַר	*boy, youth, servant*
				נַעֲרוֹ	sg. + suffix
113	זָבַח	*slaughter for sacrifice* **Q.** *he sacrificed; slaughtered for sacrifice*		נְעָרִים	pl. abs.
				נַעֲרֵי	pl. const.
				נְעָרָיו נְעָרַי	pl. + suffix
	יִזְבַּח וַיִּזְבַּח	Q. prefix			
	זִבַּח	Pi. *he sacrificed abundantly*	117	יָרַד	*go down, descend* **Q.** *he went down*
				יֵרֵד וַיֵּרֶד	Q. prefix
113a	זֶבַח	*sacrifice* (noun)		הוֹרִד	Hi. *he caused to go down; brought down*
	זִבְחוֹ	sg. + suffix			
	זְבָחִים	pl. abs.			
	זִבְחֵי	pl. const.	118	[בָּקַר]	*inquire, seek* (orig. *divide; discern*)
	זִבְחֵיכֶם	pl. + suffix		לְבַקֵּר	pi. infinitive: *to seek*

118a	בָּקָר	cattle, herd, ox (m./f.)		124	דָּם	blood
	בְּקַר	sg. const.			דַּם	sg. const.
	בְּקָרְךָ	sg. + suffix			דָּמוֹ דִּמְכֶם	sg. + suffix
	בְּקָרִים	pl. abs.			דָּמִים	pl. abs.
	בְּקָרֵינוּ	pl. + suffix			דְּמֵי	pl. const
					דָּמָיו דָּמֶיהָ	pl. + suffix
118b	בֹּקֶר	morning				
	בַּבֹּקֶר	in the morning		125	I. אהל	settle down ?
					אֹהֶל	tent
119	רוּחַ	wind, spirit, breath (f./m.)			אָהֳלוֹ	sg. + suffix
					אֹהָלִים	pl. abs.
	רוּחִי רוּחֲךָ	sg. + suffix			אָהֳלֵי	pl. const.
	רוּחוֹת	pl.			אֹהָלֶיךָ	pl. + suffix
120	אֵשׁ	fire (f./m.)		126	I. חמש	√ dubious
	אִשּׁוֹ אֶשְׁכֶם	+ suffix			חָמֵשׁ	five (with f. nouns)
					חֲמֵשׁ	const.
121	II. איל אול	be in front of, precede			חֲמִשָּׁה	(with m. nouns)
	1. אַיִל	ram			חֲמֵשֶׁת	const.
	אֵיל	sg. const.				
	אֵילִים	pl. abs.		126a	חֲמִישִׁים	fifty
122	בָּנָה	build		127	II. טוֹב	good (adj.)
		Q. he built			טוֹבִים	m. pl.
	יִבְנֶה וַיִּבֶן	Q. prefix			טוֹבָה	f. sg.
	נִבְנָה	Ni. it was (re)built			טוֹבוֹת	f. pl.
123	I. שער	cognate with crack, rift, door (E.K.)		127a	III. טוֹב	benefit (noun)
	שַׁעַר	gate		128	לאך	send (E.K.)
					מַלְאָךְ	messenger, angel

מַלְאַךְ sg. const.

מַלְאָכִי sg. + suffix

מַלְאָכִים pl. abs.

מַלְאֲכֵי pl. const.

מַלְאָכֶיךָ pl. + suffix

128a מְלָאכָה **work**, *occupation*

(f.)

מְלֶאכֶת sg. const.

מְלַאכְתּוֹ sg. + suffix

מְלָאכוֹת pl. abs.

מַלְאֲכוֹתֶיךָ pl. + suffix

129 [בָּרַךְ] *kneel, bless*

Q. he knelt, blessed

בָּרוּךְ Q. pass. part.: *blessed*

בֵּרֵךְ **Pi. he blessed**

יְבָרֵךְ וַיְבָרֶךְ Pi. prefix

130 I. זָרַע *sow, scatter seed*

זֶרַע **seed** → *offspring*

זַרְעוֹ sg. + suffix

131 I. [לָחַם] *fight, do battle*

נִלְחַם **Ni. he waged war**

יִלָּחֵם Ni. prefix

131a מִלְחָמָה *battle, war* (f.)

מִלְחֶמֶת sg. const.

מִלְחַמְתִּי sg. + suffix

מִלְחָמוֹת pl. abs.

מִלְחֲמוֹת pl. const.

132 II. לָחַם use as food

לֶחֶם *bread, food*

לַחְמְךָ + suffix

133 II. אַל adv. of **negation**

(+ prefix to form neg.

imperative)

אַל־תִּשְׁלַח יָד *Do not send a hand*

134 I. רבע

אַרְבַּע *four* (with f. nouns)

אַרְבָּעָה (with m. nouns)

134a אַרְבָּעִים *forty*

135 עָזַב *abandon, forsake, leave*

Q. he abandoned

יַעֲזֹב Q. prefix

נֶעֱזַב Ni. *he was forsaken*

136 שָׁכַב *lie down*

Q. he lay down;

lay with

יִשְׁכַּב וַיִּשְׁכַּב Q. prefix

137 שמש for root suggestions

see E.K.

שֶׁמֶשׁ *sun* (f./m.)

138	אֶבֶן	stone (f.)	מִשְׁפַּחְתִּי	sg. + suffix
	אַבְנוֹ	sg. + suffix	מִשְׁפָּחוֹת	pl. abs.
	אֲבָנִים	pl. abs.	מִשְׁפְּחוֹת	pl. const.
	אַבְנֵי	pl. const.	מִשְׁפְּחוֹתֶיהָ	pl. + suffix

139 I.	שֶׁבַע	seven (with f. nouns)	143 I.	עפר	√ common in cognate languages
	שִׁבְעָה	(with m. nouns)			
	שִׁבְעַת	const.		עָפָר	dust, dry earth
				עֲפַר	sg. const.
139a	[שָׁבַע]	swear		עֲפָרוֹ	sg. + suffix
	נִשְׁבַּע	**Ni. he swore, took an oath**			
			144	צָפַן	hide
	יִשָּׁבַע וַיִּשָּׁבַע	Ni. prefix		צָפוֹן	north (f.)
	הִשְׁבִּיעַ	Hi. he caused to swear, adjured			
			145	נגב	be dry
				נֶגֶב	southland, Negev (the dry land)
140	נָגַע	touch, reach, strike			
		Q. he touched, reached			
			146	לָבַשׁ לָבֵשׁ	put on clothes, dress
	יִגַּע וַיִּגַּע	Q. prefix			**Q. he wore; was clothed**
	הִגִּיעַ	Hi. he caused to touch			
				יִלְבַּשׁ וַיִּלְבַּשׁ	Q. prefix
141	ימם	√ dubious		הִלְבִּישַׁנִי	Hi. + suffix: he clothed me
	יָם	sea, west			
	יָם יָם	sg. const.			
	יַמִּים	pl.	147	[אָיַב]	be hostile to
	יָמָּה	+ ה directive		אוֹיֵב	enemy (Q. part.)
				אוֹיְבִי	sg. + suffix
142	שׁפח	pour out, spill		אוֹיְבִים	pl. abs.
	מִשְׁפָּחָה	clan, family (f.)		אֹיְבֶיךָ	pl. + suffix
	מִשְׁפַּחַת	sg. const.			

148	I. [קָרַב] קָרֵב	draw near, approach	153	[בָּשַׂר]
		Q. *he drew near*		bear tidings (K-B and
	יִקְרַב וַיִּקְרְבוּ	Q. prefix		E.K. have two בשׂר
	הִקְרִיב	Hi. *he brought near;*		roots)
		presented		

<table>
148 I. [קָרַב] קָרֵב — draw near, approach; **Q. he drew near**
יִקְרַב וַיִּקְרְבוּ — Q. prefix
הִקְרִיב — Hi. he brought near; presented

149 II. קרב — midst, interior; ? connected to Arabic word for heart
קֶרֶב — **midst, inward part**
קִרְבִּי — sg. + suffix
בְּקֶרֶב — + prep.: in the midst, among

150 [בָּגַד] — deal treacherously
II. בֶּגֶד — **garment, covering**
בִּגְדוֹ — sg. + suffix
בְּגָדִים — pl. abs.
בִּגְדֵי — pl. const.
בְּגָדֶיךָ — pl. + suffix

151 אָסַף — gather, assemble; **Q. he gathered**
יֶאֱסֹף — Q. prefix
נֶאֱסַף — Ni. be gathered, assemble

152 צֹאן — maybe from יצא (E.K.)
צֹאן — flock (sheep/goats) (f.)
צֹאנְךָ — + suffix

153 [בָּשַׂר] — bear tidings (K-B and E.K. have two בשׂר roots)
בָּשָׂר — flesh (of animals or humans)
בְּשַׂר — sg. const.
בְּשָׂרִי — sg. + suffix

154 רֹשַׁע — see K-B discussion
רָשָׁע — **wicked, guilty of sin**
רְשָׁעִים — pl. abs.
רִשְׁעֵי — pl. const.

155 נָטָה — stretch out, extend, incline
נָטָה — **Q. he stretched out, inclined**
יִטֶּה וַיֵּט — Q. prefix
הִטָּה — Hi. he turned, inclined; perverted justice

155a מַטֶּה — rod, staff, tribe
מַטֵּה — sg. const.
מַטְּךָ מַטֵּהוּ — sg. + suffix
מַטּוֹת — pl. abs.
מַטָּיו מַטּוֹתָם — pl. + suffix

155b מִטָּה — bed, couch (f.)
מִטַּת — sg. const.
מִטָּתוֹ — sg. + suffix
מִטּוֹת — pl. abs./const.
</table>

156	מָלֵא	be full, fill	
		Q. *he/it was full, filled*	
	יִמְלְאוּ	Q. prefix	
	נִמְלָא	Ni. *it was filled*	
	יִמָּלֵא	Ni. prefix	
	מִלֵּא מָלֵא	Pi. *he filled*	
157	[חָסֵד]	*be good, kind*	
	1. חֶסֶד	*kindness, goodness*	
	חַסְדּוֹ	sg. + suffix	
	חֲסָדִים	pl. abs.	
	חַסְדֵי	pl. const.	
	חֲסָדַי	pl. + suffix	
158	רֶגֶל	*foot, leg* (f.)	
	רַגְלִי	sg. + suffix	
	רַגְלַיִם	du. abs.	
	רַגְלֵי	du. const.	
	רַגְלַי	du. + suffix	
159	II. [חיל חול]	*be strong*	
	חַיִל	*strength, wealth, army*	
	חֵיל	sg. const.	
	חֵילוֹ	sg. + suffix	
	חֲיָלִים	pl. abs.	
160	לַיְלָה לֵיל	*night* (m.) ⓘ	
	לֵיל	sg. const.	
	לֵילוֹת	pl. abs.	

161	גבל	? orig. *twist, wind* (a cord)	
	גְּבוּל	*border, territory*	
	גְּבוּלִי גְּבֻלְךָ	sg. + suffix	
	גְּבוּלֶיךָ	pl. + suffix	
162	אֲנַחְנוּ	*we*	
163	[שָׁלֵם]	*be complete, sound* (see in K-B)	
	שִׁלֵּם	**Pi.** *he completed; made compensation*	
	יְשַׁלֵּם	Pi. prefix	
163a	שָׁלוֹם	*welfare, wholeness, peace*	
	שְׁלוֹם	sg. const.	
	שְׁלוֹמִי	sg. + suffix	
164	זָכַר	*remember*	
		Q. *he remembered*	
	יִזְכֹּר וַיִּזְכֹּר	Q. prefix	
	הִזְכִּיר	Hi. *he caused remembrance, reminded*	
164a	זָכָר	*male*	
	זְכָרִים	pl. abs.	
165	יָרַשׁ	*take possession of; inherit*	
		Q. *he took possession*	

יִירַשׁ וַיִּירַשׁ   Q. prefix

הוֹרִישׁ   Hi. *he caused to inherit*

166   [נָגַשׁ]   *draw near, approach*

   Q. he drew near

יִגַּשׁ וַיִּגַּשׁ   Q. prefix

נִגַּשׁ   Ni. *he drew near*

הִגִּישׁ   Hi. *he brought near*

תַּגִּישׁ וַיַּגֵּשׁ   Hi. *prefix*

167   יָכוֹל יָכֹל   *be able, prevail* ⓘ

   Q. he was able,

   prevailed (40.5)

יוּכַל   **prefix**

168   I. [רָבָה]   *be/become many*

רָבוּ   **Q. they became many**

יִרְבֶּה וַיִּרֶב   Q. prefix

הִרְבָּה   Hi. *he made numerous;*

   he made great

169   [בָּקַשׁ]   *seek, desire*

בִּקֵּשׁ   **Pi. he sought**

יְבַקֵּשׁ   Pi. *prefix*

170   I. אמם   *be wide, roomy* (BDB;

   cf. K-B and E.K.)

אֵם   *mother*

אִמִּי   sg. + suffix

אִמֹּתֵנוּ   pl. + suffix

170a 11.   אַמָּה   *cubit* (f.)

אַמַּת   sg. const.

אַמָּתַיִם   du.

אַמּוֹת   pl. abs.

171   אָבַד   *perish*

   Q. he perished,

   was lost

יֹאבַד   Q. prefix

אִבֵּד   Pi. *he destroyed,*

   caused to perish

וְהַאֲבִיד   Hi. *and he will destroy;*

   put to death

172   כָּתַב   *write*

   Q. he wrote

יִכְתֹּב וַיִּכְתֹּב   Q. prefix

יִכָּתֵב   Ni. *it will be written*

173   יָעַד   *appoint*

עֵדָה   *congregation* (f.)

עֲדַת   sg. const.

173a   מוֹעֵד   *appointed time,*

   or place, assembly,

   festival

מוֹעֲדוֹ   sg. + suffix

מוֹעֲדִים   pl. abs.

מוֹעֲדֵי   pl. const.

מוֹעֲדֶיהָ   pl. + suffix

174	סוּר	turn aside (Q. infin.)		שִׁשָּׁה	(with m. nouns)
	סָר	**Q. he turned aside**		שֵׁשֶׁת	const.
	יָסוּר וַיָּסַר	Q. prefix			
	הֵסִיר	Hi. he caused to turn	180	לֵוִי	Levite
		aside; removed		לְוִיִּם	pl. abs.

175	יָרָה	throw, shoot (Hi. teach)	181	יָסַף	add
	תּוֹרָה	**Torah, teaching →**			**Q. he added,**
		law (f.)			**increased**
	תּוֹרַת	sg. const.		הֹסִיף	**Hi. he added to,**
	תּוֹרָתִי	sg. + suffix			**increased;**
	תּוֹרוֹת	pl. abs.			**did again/more**
	תּוֹרֹתַי	pl. + suffix		יוֹסִיף וַיּוֹסֶף	Hi. prefix

176	1. [כּוּן]	be firm	182	חָנָה	encamp
	נָכוֹן	**Ni. part.** (m. sg.)			**Q. he encamped**
		ready, established		יַחֲנוּ וַיִּחַן	Q. prefix
	יִכּוֹן	Ni. prefix			
	הֵכִין	Hi. he established	182a	מַחֲנֶה	**camp, encampment**
	יָכִין	Hi. prefix		מַחֲנֵה	sg. const.
	כּוֹנֵן	Po. he established		מַחֲנֵהוּ מַחֲנְךָ	sg. + suffix
	יְכוֹנֵן	Po. prefix		מַחֲנוֹת	pl. abs./const.
				מַחֲנֵיהֶם	sg. + suffix

177	שָׁתָה	drink	183	דּוּר	move in a circle,
		Q. he drank			go about, surround
	יִשְׁתֶּה וַיֵּשְׁתְּ	Q. prefix		1. דּוֹר	**generation, age,**
					period
178	אוֹ	or		דֹּרוֹת דּוֹרִים	pl. abs.
				דֹּרֹתָיו	pl. + suffix
179	שֵׁדֶשׁ				
	שֵׁשׁ	six (with f. nouns)			

184   פָּקַד   visit, attend to

    Q. he visited,

    attended

יִפְקֹד וַיִּפְקֹד   Q. prefix

נִפְקַד   Ni. *he was missed; called*

    to account

פִּקַּד   Pi. *he mustered*

הִפְקִיד   Hi. *he appointed*

185   [נָצַל]   *tear away* (E.K.)

יִנָּצֵל   **Ni. prefix** *he will be*

    delivered

נִצַּלְתֶּם   **Pi.** *you stripped off;*

    plundered

הִצִּיל   **Hi.** *he delivered;*

    snatched away

186   זקן   *to be bearded*

    (K-B, E.K.)

זָקָן   *chin, beard* (m./f.)

186a   זָקֵן   *be or become old*

    (verb)

186b   זָקֵן   *old, old man, elder*

    (adj./noun)

זְקַן   sg. const.

זְקֵנִים זְקֵנוֹת   pl. abs. m./f.

זִקְנֵי   m. pl. const.

187   חָטָא   miss (a goal or way);

    do wrong

    Q. he sinned

יֶחֱטָא וַיֶּחֱטָא   Q. prefix

הֶחֱטִיא   Hi. *he caused to sin*

187a   חַטָּאת   *sin, sin offering* (f.)

חַטַּאת   sg. const.

חַטָּאתִי   sg. + suffix

חַטָּאוֹת   pl. abs.

חַטֹּאת   pl. const.

חַטֹּאתַי   pl. + suffix

188   I. כָּלָה   *be complete; finished,*

    spent

    Q. he/it was

    completed

יִכְלֶה וַתֵּכֶל   Q. prefix

כִּלָּה   Pi. *he completed,*

    finished

188a   כְּלִי   *vessel, article, utensil*

כֶּלְיְךָ   sg. + suffix

כֵּלִים   pl. abs.

כְּלֵי   pl. const.

כֵּלֶיךָ כֵּלַי   pl. + suffix

189   צדק   *be just, righteous* (E.K.)

צֶדֶק   *righteousness,*

    rightness

צִדְקִי   + suffix

189a	צְדָקָה	*righteousness*
	צִדְקַת	sg. const.
	צִדְקָתִי	sg. + suffix
	צְדָקוֹת	pl. abs.
	צִדְקוֹת	pl. const.
	צִדְקוֹתֶיךָ	sg. + suffix
189b	צַדִּיק	*just, righteous* (adj.)
	צַדִּיקִים	pl. abs.
190	[יָשַׁע]	*deliver* (so BDB; K-B *give help, save*)
	נוֹשַׁע	Ni. *he was delivered (helped)*
	הוֹשִׁיעַ	**Hi.** *he delivered, saved*
	יוֹשִׁיעַ וַיּוֹשַׁע	Hi. prefix
	הוֹשַׁע	Hi. imperative
191	II. אֲרֹן	*chest* in cognate languages
	אֲרוֹן	*ark, chest, coffin*
	הָאָרוֹן	+ def. art.
192	נבא	see BDB for related cognates
	נָבִיא	*prophet*
	נְבִיאִים	pl. abs.
	נְבִיאֵי	pl. const.
	נְבִיאֶיךָ	pl. + suffix

192a	[נבא]	*prophesy* (verb)
	נִבָּא	**Ni.** *he prophesied*
	יִנָּבֵא וַיִּנָּבֵא	Ni. prefix
	הִנָּבֵא	Ni. m. sg. imperative
193	כָּבֵד	*be heavy, weighty* **Q.** *it was heavy*
	יִכְבַּד	Q. prefix
	נִכְבַּד	Ni. *he was honored*
	כִּבְּדוּ	Pi. *they made honorable, honored*
	הִכְבִּיד	Hi. *he made heavy (a yoke)*
193a	כָּבוֹד	*heaviness, splendor, honor*
	כְּבוֹד	sg. const.
	כְּבוֹדִי	sg. + suffix
194	רוּם	*be high, exalted* (Q. infin.)
	רָם	**Q.** *he was exalted*
	יָרוּם וַיָּרָם	Q. prefix
	הֵרִים	Hi. *he raised up, exalted*
195	שָׂנֵא	*hate* **Q.** *he hated*
	יִשְׂנָא וַיִּשְׂנָאוּ	Q. prefix

196	כָּפַף	bend, be bent
	כַּף	**palm of hand, sole of foot** (f.)
	כַּפִּי	sg. + suffix
	כַּפַּיִם	dual
	כַּפֵּי	du. const.
	כַּפֵּיהֶם	du. + suffix
197	I. [שָׁמֵן]	grow fat
	שֶׁמֶן	**oil, fat**
	שַׁמְנִי	sg. + suffix
	שְׁמָנִים	pl. abs.
	שְׁמָנֶיךָ	pl. + suffix
198	גָּלָה	uncover, reveal, remove
		Q. he uncovered (the ear or eyes)
	יִגְלֶה וַיִּגֶל	Q. prefix
	נִגְלָה	Ni. he uncovered himself, was uncovered; it was revealed
	גִּלָּה	Pi. he uncovered; disclosed
	הִגְלָה	**Hi. he took into exile**
199	שָׁבַט	strike, smite
	שֵׁבֶט	**rod, staff; tribe**
	שִׁבְטִי	sg. + suffix
	שְׁבָטִים	pl. abs.
	שִׁבְטֵי	pl. const.
	שְׁבָטֶיךָ	pl. + suffix

200	I. אזן	(pointed, sharp?)
	אֹזֶן	**ear** (f.)
	אָזְנִי	sg. + suffix
	אָזְנַיִם	dual
	אָזְנֵי	du. const.
	אָזְנֵיהֶם	du. + suffix
201	בהם	cognate √ impeded in speech
	בְּהֵמָה	**beast, animal, cattle** (f.)
	בֶּהֱמַת	sg. const.
	בֶּהֶמְתְּךָ	sg. + suffix
	בְּהֵמוֹת	pl. abs.
202	סֵפֶר	**letter, document**
	סִפְרִי	sg. + suffix
	סְפָרִים	pl. abs.
202a	סָפַר	count, number
		Q. he counted
	סִפֵּר	**Pi. he recounted, declared**
	יְסַפֵּר וַיְסַפֵּר	Pi. prefix
	יִסָּפֵר	Ni. it will be counted
202b	מִסְפָּר	**number**
	מִסְפַּר	sg. const.
	מִסְפָּרָם	sg. + suffix

203	שָׂדֶה	√ disputed: *mountain* or *arable ground*		יִוָּתֵר	Ni. prefix
	שָׂדֶה	*field*		הוֹתִיר	Hi. *he left over*
	שְׂדֵה	sg. const.		יוֹתִיר	Hi. prefix
	שָׂדִי שָׂדֵהוּ	sg. + suffix	207	בָּחַר	*choose*
	שָׂדוֹת	pl. abs.		בָּחַר (+ בְּ)	**Q. *he chose***
	שְׂדוֹת שְׂדֵי	pl. const.		יִבְחַר	Q. prefix

204	[נָגַד]	*be conspicuous*	208	שָׁאַל	*ask, inquire*
	הִגִּיד	**Hi. *he announced,* *declared***			**Q. *he asked, inquired***
	יַגִּיד וַיַּגֵּד	Hi. prefix		יִשְׁאַל וַיִּשְׁאַל	Q. prefix
	הֻגַּד וַיֻּגַּד	**Ho. *it was announced***	209	בִּין	*perceive, discern* (Q. infin.)
204a	נֶגֶד	*in front of, in sight of, opposite*		יָבִין וַיָּבֶן	**Q. prefix: *he will* *perceive*** (with eyes, ears, touch, taste)
	נֶגְדִּי	+ suffix		נָבוֹן	Ni. part.: *discerning*
205	שׂפה	*lip*		הֵבִין	Hi. *he gave understanding*
	שָׂפָה	*lip, edge, language* (f.)		הִתְבּוֹנֵן	Ht. *he considered diligently*
	שְׂפַת	sg. const.			
	שְׂפָתַיִם	du.	210	[בַּיִן]	*space between*
	שִׂפְתֵי	du. const.		בֵּין	*between* (prep.)
	שְׂפָתָיו	du. + suffix		בֵּינִי וּבֵינֶךָ	*between me and you*
	שִׂפְתוֹת	pl. const.			
206	[יָתַר]	*remain, be left over*	211	מְאֹד	*related to roots meaning be many* (E.K.)
	הַיּוֹתֵר	**Q. part.:** *the remainder*			
	נוֹתַר	**Ni. *it was left over***			

מְאֹד — strength, force (noun)
very, exceedingly
(adv.)

212 בָּעַל — marry, rule over
1. בַּעַל — **Baal, owner, lord**
בַּעְלָהּ — sg. + suffix
בְּעָלִים — pl.abs.
בַּעֲלֵי — pl. const.
בְּעָלֶיהָ בַּעֲלֵיהֶן — pl. + suffix

213 הָרַג — kill, slay
Q. he killed
יַהֲרֹג וַיַּהֲרֹג — Q. prefix

214 I. חוּץ — related to חִיץ
partition (E.K.)
חוּץ — **outside**

215 I. פָּתַח — open
Q. he opened
יִפְתַּח — Q. prefix
נִפְתַּח — Ni. it was opened, loosened
פִּתַּח — Pi. he set free, ungirded

215a פֶּתַח — **opening, entrance**
פִּתְחוֹ — sg. + suffix
פְּתָחִים — pl. abs.
פִּתְחֵי — pl. const.

216 דָּרַשׁ — resort to, seek
Q. he sought, consulted
יִדְרֹשׁ — Q. prefix
נִדְרַשׁ — Ni. he let himself be inquired of or consulted (only of God)

217 סָבַב — turn around, surround
Q. he/it turned about
יָסֹב וַיִּסֹב — Q. prefix
נָסַב — Ni. he closed round upon
הֵסֵב — Hi. he caused to turn, turn back, led around

217a סָבִיב — [the area] **round about, surrounding**
סְבִיבוֹת — prep.
סְבִיבוֹתֶיךָ — prep. + suffix

218 שָׁפַךְ — pour out
Q. he poured out
יִשְׁפֹּךְ וַיִּשְׁפֹּךְ — Q. prefix

219 I. נָסַע — pull out/up [stakes] → set out, journey
Q. he set out
יִסַּע — Q. prefix
תַּסִּיעַ — Hi. you will lead out
וַיַּסַּע — Hi. and he led out

220	נוּס	flee, escape (Q. infin.)
	נָס	**Q. he escaped**
	יָנוּס וַיָּנָס	Q. prefix
221	גָּבַר	be strong, mighty
	גִּבּוֹר	**warrior, mighty man**
	גִּבּוֹרָם	sg. + suffix
	גִּבּוֹרִים	pl. abs.
	גִּבּוֹרֵי	pl. const.
	גִּבּוֹרֶיךָ	pl. + suffix
222	[נָכָה]	smite
	הִכָּה	**Hi. he smote**
	יַכֶּה וַיַּךְ	**Hi. prefix**
223	I. [בדד]	be separated, isolated
	11. בַּד	separation
	1. לְבַד	**alone, by oneself**
	1. b. לְבַדִּי לְבַדּוֹ	+suffix
224	חָכַם	be wise
	חָכָם	*wise, skillful, clever*
	חֲכַם	sg. const.
	חֲכָמִים	pl. abs.
	חַכְמֵי	pl. const.
	חֲכָמֶיךָ	pl. + suffix
	חֲכָמָה	f. sg. abs.
	חַכְמַת	f. sg. const.
	חֲכָמוֹת	f. pl. abs.
	חַכְמוֹת	f. pl. const.

224a	חָכְמָה	wisdom, skill (f.)
	חָכְמַת	sg. const.
	חָכְמָתִי	sg. + suffix
225	שָׂמַח	rejoice, be glad
		Q. he rejoiced
	יִשְׂמַח	Q. prefix
	שִׂמַּח	Pi. he gladdened
226	מנח	give a gift
	מִנְחָה	**gift, offering, tribute**
		(f.)
	מִנְחַת	sg. const.
	מִנְחָתִי	sg. + suffix
	מְנָחוֹת	pl. abs.
	מִנְחֹתֵיכֶם	pl. + suffix
227	חָזַק	be strong, firm
		Q. he became strong
	יֶחֱזַק וַיֶּחֱזַק	Q. prefix
	חִזַּק	Pi. he made strong, firm
	הִתְחַזֵּק	Ht. he strengthened himself
	הֶחֱזִיק	Hi. he seized, grasped
228	[חָקַק]	cut in, inscribe
	חֹק	*statute* (m.)
	חָק־	sg. const.
	חֻקּוֹ חֻקִּי	sg. + suffix
	חֻקִּים	pl. abs.

חוּקֵי חֻקֵּי   pl. const.

חֻקָּיו   pl. + suffix

228a   חֻקָּה   *statute* (f.)

חֻקַּת   sg. const.

חֻקּוֹת חֻקֹּת   pl abs.

חֻקֹּתַי   pl. + suffix

229   כְּ   *like, as, when*

כְּמוֹ   *as, like* (poetic or with suffix)

כְּמוֹ הַשַּׁחַר עָלָה   *as dawn broke*

כָּמֹוךָ   + suffix: *like you* (Chart O)

230   [יָטַב]   *be well, be pleasing*

יִיטַב   **Q. prefix:** *it will be well*

הֵיטִיב   **Hi.** *he dealt well, did good*

יֵיטִיב וַיּיֵטֶב   Hi. prefix

231   [שָׁחַת]   *go to ruin*

נִשְׁחַת   **Ni.** *he/it was spoiled; corrupted*

שִׁחֵת   **Pi.** *he spoiled, ruined*

הִשְׁחִית   **Hi.** *he spoiled, ruined*

232   [אָנַף אָנֵף]   *breathe, snort → be angry*

אַף   *nostril* (m.) → *anger*

אַפּוֹ   sg. + suffix

אַפַּיִם   du. *face, countenance → anger*

אַפָּיו   du. + suffix

233   שָׁבַר   *break* **Q.** *he broke*

יִשְׁבֹּר   Q. prefix

נִשְׁבַּר   **Ni.** *it was broken*

שִׁבֵּר   **Pi.** *he broke, shattered*

234   I. [אָמַן]   *confirm, support*

נֶאֱמַן   **Ni.** *he was proven; shown to be faithful*

יֵאָמֵן   Ni. prefix

הֶאֱמִין   **Hi.** *he trusted, believed*

יַאֲמִין   Hi. prefix

234a   אֱמֶת   *firmness, constancy, trustworthiness, truth* (f.)

אֲמִתּוֹ   + suffix

235   I. חָצֵר   *enclosed area* (E.K.)

1. חָצֵר   *court, enclosure* (f./m.)

חֲצַר   sg. const.

חֲצֵרוֹ   sg. + suffix

חֲצֵרוֹת	pl. abs.	
חַצְרוֹת חַצְרֵי	pl. const.	
חֲצֵרֹתָיו חֲצֵרֶיךָ	pl. + suffix	

	וְרָדְפָה	Pi. *and she will pursue* *ardently*	
242	שָׁכַן	*settle down, abide*	
		Q. *he dwelled,* **settled down**	
236	שָׁכַח	*forget*	
		Q. *he forgot*	
	יִשְׁכַּח	Q. prefix	
	יִשְׁכֹּן	Q. prefix	
	שִׁכֵּן	Pi. *he caused to dwell*	
	הִשְׁכַּנְתִּי	Hi. *I placed, set*	
237	אָז	*at that time, then*	
242a	מִשְׁכָּן	*dwelling place* *(of God); tabernacle*	
238	נוּחַ	*rest* (Q. infin.)	
	מִשְׁכַּן	sg. const.	
	נָחָה	Q. *she rested, remained*	
	מִשְׁכָּנוֹת	pl. abs.	
	יָנוּחַ וַיָּנַח	Q. prefix	
	מִשְׁכְּנֵי מִשְׁכְּנוֹת	pl. const.	
	הֵנִיחַ	**Hi. A. *he gave rest to***	
	מִשְׁכְּנוֹתֶיךָ	pl. + suffix	
	הִנִּיחַ	**Hi. B. *he caused*** **to rest, set down**	
243	פֶּן	*lest*	
239	II. [הָלַל]	*be boastful*	
244	II. סוּס	*horse*	
	הִלֵּל	**Pi. *he praised***	
	סוּסִים	pl. abs.	
	יְהַלְלוּ	Pi. prefix	
	סוּסֵי	pl. const.	
	יִתְהַלֵּל	Ht. *he will glory*	
	סוּסֵי סוּסֶיךָ	pl. + suffix	
240	יַיִן	origin not known	
245	יָמַן	? related to אמן *confirm* (only BDB)	
	יַיִן	*wine*	
	יֵין	const.	
	יָמִין	*right hand* (f.)	
	יֵינִי	+ suffix	
	יְמִין	const.	
241	רָדַף	*pursue*	
	יְמִינוֹ	+ suffix	
		Q. *he pursued*	
	יִרְדֹּף וַיִּרְדֹּף	Q. prefix	
	נִרְדַּף	Ni. *he was pursued*	

246	יֵשׁ יֶשׁ־	*there is, there are* (particle of existence)
	הֲיֵשׁ	+ interrogative ה
	יֶשְׁךָ	+ suffix
247	III. נחשׁ	root meaning not known
	נְחֹשֶׁת	*copper, bronze*
	נְחֻשְׁתָּם נְחֻשְׁתִּי	+ suffix
248	I. חמה	protection
	חוֹמָה	*wall* (f.)
	חוֹמַת	sg. const.
	חוֹמָתָהּ	sg. + suffix
	חוֹמוֹת	pl. abs.
	חֹמֹתֶיךָ	pl. + suffix
249	כִּסֵּא כִּסֵּה	*throne, seat*
	כִּסְאוֹ	sg. + suffix
	כִּסְאוֹת	pl. abs.
250	I. נחל	√ gift
	נַחֲלָה	*property, possession, inheritance* (f.)
	נַחֲלַת	sg. const.
	נַחֲלָתִי	sg. + suffix
	נְחָלוֹת	pl. abs.
251	II. נָחַל	√ meaning not known
	נַחַל	*wadi, torrent*

	נְחָלִים	pl. abs.
	נַחֲלֵי	pl. const.
	נְחָלֶיהָ	pl. + suffix
252	I. שָׁאַר	*remain, be left over*
	נִשְׁאַר	**Ni.** *it/he was left over* → *he survived*
	יִשָּׁאֵר	Ni. prefix
	הִשְׁאִיר	**Hi.** *he left over* → *spared*
253	קָבַר	*bury*
		Q. *he buried*
	וַיִּקְבֹּר	Q. prefix + vav conv.
	יִקָּבֵר	Ni. *he will be buried*
	לְקַבֵּר	Pi. *to bury* (large numbers of dead)
254	כָּרַת	*cut, cut off, cut down*
		Q. *he cut*
	יִכְרֹת	Q. prefix
	נִכְרַת	Ni. *he was cut off*
	הִכְרִית	Hi. *he cut off*
255	II. ברה	? √ *bind, eat bread* (BDB, E. K.)
	בְּרִית	*covenant* (f.)
256	V. ערב	*enter* (E. K.)
	עֶרֶב	*sunset, evening*

257   [חָלַל]   *defile, profane, pollute*

חִלֵּל   **Pi.** *he defiled, profaned*

יְחַלֵּל   Pi. prefix

הֵחֵל   **Hi. 2. affix:** *he began*

יָחֵל   **Hi. prefix**

---

258   III. פַּר   *bull, young bull*

פָּרִים   pl. abs.

---

259   כחח   √ likely כוח *(strength, power)*

11 כֹּחַ כּוֹחַ   **strength, power**

כֹּחִי כֹּחֲךָ   + suffix

---

260   קָבַץ   *gather, collect*

Q. *he gathered, collected*

יִקְבֹּץ וַיִּקְבֹּץ   Q. prefix

נִקְבְּצוּ   Ni. *they assembled*

קִבְּצָם   Pi. *he gathered them together*

---

261   [שׁחח]   *prostrate oneself in worship* (BDB)

חוה   alternate root (43.2, also see K-B)

הִשְׁתַּחֲוָה   **affix:** *he prostrated himself in worship*

יִשְׁתַּחוּ   **prefix: 3 m. sg.**

יִשְׁתַּחֲווּ   **prefix: 3 m. pl.**

---

262   [מָעַט]   *become small*

מְעַט   *a little, a few*

---

263   I עָצַם   *be vast, mighty*

עֶצֶם   *bone, substance → self* (f.)

עַצְמִי   sg. + suffix

עֲצָמוֹת   pl. abs.

עַצְמוֹת   pl. const.

עַצְמֹתַי   pl. + suffix

---

264   [שָׁלַךְ]   *throw, cast*

הִשְׁלִיךְ   **Hi.** *he threw, cast*

יַשְׁלִיךְ   Hi. prefix

הָשְׁלַךְ   Ho. *he/it was thrown, cast down*

---

265   [חָדַשׁ]   *renew*

1. חֹדֶשׁ   *new moon, month*

חָדְשׁוֹ   sg. + suffix

חֳדָשִׁים   pl. abs.

חָדְשֵׁי   pl. const.

חֳדָשָׁיו   pl. + suffix

---

266   חָצָה   *divide*

חֲצִי   *half, middle*

חֶצְיָה   + suffix

---

267   קהל   ? orig. קול *call together* (so E.K. contra K-B)

קָהָל   *assembly,* *congregation*

קְהַל   sg. const.

קְהַלְכֶם   sg. + suffix

קְהָלֶיךָ   pl. + suffix

268   II. עוה   *bend, twist* (E.K.)

עָוֹן   *sin*, *guilt, punishment*

עֲוֹן   sg. const.

עֲוֹנִי   sg. + suffix

עֲוֹנוֹת   pl. abs./const.

עֲוֹנֹתֶיךָ   pl. + suffix

269   [אור]   *be or become light*

אוֹר   *light* (f.)

אוֹרִי אוֹרֵהוּ   sg. + suffix

אוֹרִים   pl. abs.

270   חָשַׁב   *think, account, plan*
     Q. he thought

יַחְשֹׁב   Q. prefix

נֶחְשַׁב   Ni. *it was reckoned*

יֵחָשֵׁב   Ni. prefix

חִשֵּׁב   Pi. *he considered,* *planned*

271   [יָחַם]   *be hot* (sexually excited)

חֵמָה   *heat, rage,* **fury** (f.)

חֲמַת   sg. const.

חֲמָתִי   sg. + suffix

חֵמוֹת חֵמֹת   pl. abs.

272   I. בָּטַח   *trust, be confident*
     Q. he trusted

יִבְטַח   Q. prefix

273   לָכַד   *capture, seize*
     Q. he captured

יִלְכֹּד וַיִּלְכֹּד   Q. prefix

נִלְכַּד   Ni. *he was captured*

274   I. [נָהַר]   *flow, stream*

נָהָר   **river, stream** (m.)

נְהַר   sg. const.

נְהָרוֹת נְהָרִים   pl. abs.

נַהֲרוֹת נַהֲרֵי   pl. const.

נַהֲרוֹתֶיךָ   pl. + suffix

275   רָכַב   *mount and ride, ride*

רֶכֶב   **chariot,** **group of chariots**

רִכְבּוֹ   sg. + suffix

רִכְבֵי   pl. const.

276   יָשַׁר   *be smooth, straight*

יָשָׁר   **upright, straight** (adj.)

יְשַׁר   m. sg. const.

יְשָׁרִים   m. sg. abs.

יִשְׁרֵי	m. pl. const.	
יְשָׁרוֹת	f. pl. abs.	

277	[פָּרָה]	*bear fruit*	
	פְּרִי	**fruit**	
	פִּרְיוֹ פִּרְיִי	+ suffix	

278	[פָּעַם]	*strike, beat → thrust, impel, move*
	פַּעַם	**beat, foot → occurrence, time** (f.)
	פַּעֲמַיִם	du.
	פְּעָמִים	pl. abs.
	פַּעֲמֵי	pl. const.
	פְּעָמֵי פַּעֲמֹתָיו	pl. + suffix

279	לִשֵּׁן	*lick*
	לָשׁוֹן	**tongue → language** (f./m.)
	לְשׁוֹנוֹ	sg. + suffix
	לְשׁוֹן	sg. const.
	לְשֹׁנוֹת	pl. abs.
	לְשֹׁנֹתָם	pl. + suffix

280	שָׂרַף	*burn*
		Q. he burned
	יִשְׂרֹף וַיִּשְׂרֹף	Q. prefix
	יִשָּׂרֵף	Ni. *he/it will be burned*

281	תָּעַב	? √ יעב *be faulty* (K-B)

תּוֹעֵבָה	*abomination* (f.)	
תּוֹעֲבַת	sg. const.	
תּוֹעֵבוֹת	pl. abs.	
תּוֹעֲבוֹת	pl. const.	
תּוֹעֲבוֹתָיו	pl. + suffix	

282	I. קָטַר	*smoke*
	לְקַטֵּר	Pi. infin.: *to burn incense*
	יְקַטֵּר	Pi. prefix
	הִקְטִיר	**Hi. he burned incense**
	יַקְטִיר וַיַּקְטֵר	Hi. prefix

283	בָּכָה	*weep, bewail*
		Q. he wept
	תִּבְכֶּה וַתֵּבְךְּ	Q. prefix

284	[יָדָה]	*throw, cast*
	הוֹדוּ	Hi. affix: *they gave thanks*
	הוֹדוּ	**Hi. imp.: give thanks!**
	הִתְוַדָּה	Ht. *he confessed, gave thanks*

285	[בָּלָה]	*become old and worn out*
	[בְּלָת]	*failure*
	בִּלְתִּי	**not, except**

286	רוּץ	run (Q. infin.)	293	בּוֹשׁ	be ashamed (Q. infin.)
	רָץ	**Q. he ran**		בֹּשׁ	**Q. he was ashamed**
	יָרוּץ וַיָּ֫רָץ	Q. prefix		יֵבוֹשׁ	**Q. prefix**

287	שִׁקֵּר	deceive	294	כָּנָף	wing
	שֶׁ֫קֶר	**lie, falsehood**		כָּנָף	wing → skirt, extremity, edge (f.)
	שְׁקָרִים	pl. abs.		כְּנַף	sg. const.
	שִׁקְרֵיהֶם	pl. + suffix		כְּנָפִי	sg. + suffix
288	I. רַקְק	thin		כְּנָפַ֫יִם	du. abs.
	2. רַק	**only, save, except**		כַּנְפֵי	du. const.
				כַּנְפֵיהֶן	du. + suffix
289	שָׁבַת	cease		כַּנְפוֹת	pl. const.
	שַׁבָּת	Sabbath (f./m.)			
	שַׁבָּתוֹת	pl. abs.	295	II. שׁמני שׁמן	
	שַׁבְּתוֹת	pl. const.		שְׁמֹנָה	**eight** (with f. nouns)
	שַׁבְּתוֹתַי	pl. + suffix		שְׁמֹנֶה	(with m. nouns)

290	I. כפר	cover, cleanse ritually	296	[כָּסַף]	long (for)
	כִּפֶּר	**Pi. he covered over →** made propitiation		כֶּ֫סֶף	**silver**
				כַּסְפִּי	+ suffix
	יְכַפֵּר	Pi. prefix	297	זהב	√ dubious
				זָהָב	**gold**
291	אַךְ	**surely, only; but yet**		זְהַב	const.
				זְהָבוֹ	+ suffix
292	[בָּכַר]	bring forth E.K.)			
	בְּכוֹר	**first-born**	298	כֶּ֫בֶשׂ	**lamb**
	בְּכֹרִי	sg. + suffix		כְּבָשִׂים	pl. abs.
	בְּכוֹרֵי	pl. const.			
	בְּכוֹרֵיהֶם	pl. + suffix	299	[נחם]	**be sorry, console oneself**
	בְּכֹרוֹת	f. pl. const			

נִחַם **Ni.** *he was sorry,
repented*

יִנָּחֵם וַיִּנָּחֶם Ni. prefix

נִחַם **Pi.** *he comforted*

יְנַחֵם Pi. prefix

300 I. [צָרַר] *show hostility toward*

II. צַר *adversary, foe*

צָרִי sg. + suffix

צָרִים pl. abs.

צָרֵי pl. const.

צָרַי צָרֶיךָ pl. + suffix

301 בַּעַד *denotes separation*

בַּעַד בְּעַד *away from,
through, behind;
on behalf of* (prep.)

בַּעֲדִי + suffix

302 בָּמָה *high place* (f.)

בָּמוֹת pl. abs.

בָּמֳתֵי pl. const.

בָּמֳתֵי pl. + suffix

303 I. גָּאַל *redeem, act as kinsman*

Q. *he redeemed*

יִגְאַל Q. prefix

304 I. טָמֵא *be, become unclean*

Q. *he was/became
unclean*

יִטְמָא Q. prefix

נִטְמָא Ni. *he defiled himself,
was defiled*

טִמֵּא Pi. *he defiled*

יִטַּמָּא Ht. *he defiled himself*

305 I. מוד *prob. secondary form
of* מדד *measure*

תָּמִיד *continually, daily*
(adv.)

306 I. [כָּסָה] *cover*

כִּסָּה **Pi.** *he covered,
concealed*

יְכַסֶּה וַיְכַס Pi. prefix

307 II. אַף *also, indeed, even*

אַף כִּי *indeed, furthermore*

308 נאם *speak* (E.K.)

נְאֻם *utterance, oracle*

309   רָחַב   *be wide or large*   310   רָעֵב   *be hungry*

         רֹחַב   **breadth, width**   רָעָב   **famine, hunger**

         רָחְבּוֹ   + suffix   רְעָבָם   + suffix

ALPHABETIC VOCABULARY

29	אָב	4	אֶל	13	בּוֹא
171	אָבַד	32	אֵלֶּה	293	בּוֹשׁ
138	אֶבֶן	12a	אֱלֹהִים	207	בָּחַר
57	אָדוֹן	88	אֶלֶף	272	בָּטַח
79	אָדָם	42	אִם	209	בִּין
79a	אֲדָמָה	170	אֵם	210	בֵּין
114	אָהַב	170a	אָמָה	20	בַּיִת
114	אָהֵב	234	אָמַן	283	בָּכָה
125	אֹהֶל	5	אָמַר	292	בְּכוֹר
178	אוֹ	234a	אֱמֶת	285	בִּלְתִּי
269	אוֹר	162	אֲנַחְנוּ	302	בָּמָה
237	אָז	46	אֲנִי	7	בֵּן
200	אֹזֶן	46a	אָנֹכִי	122	בָּנָה
70	אָח	151	אָסַף	301	בְּעַד
40	אֶחָד	232, 307	אַף	212	בַּעַל
40	אַחַת	134	אַרְבַּע	118a	בָּקָר
70a	אָחוֹת	134	אַרְבָּעָה	118b	בֹּקֶר
63a	אַחַר	134a	אַרְבָּעִים	169	בִּקֵּשׁ
63a	אַחֲרֵי	191	אָרוֹן	255	בְּרִית
63	אַחֵר	16	אֶרֶץ	129	בָּרַךְ
147	אוֹיֵב	120	אֵשׁ	129	בֵּרֵךְ
121	אַיִל	53	אִשָּׁה	293	בֹּשׁ
56	אַיִן	3	אֲשֶׁר	153	בָּשָׂר
56	אֵין	60	אַתָּה	7a	בַּת
18	אִישׁ	60a	אַתֶּם		
291	אַךְ			303	גָּאַל
51	אָכַל	13	בָּא	161	גְּבוּל
112	אַל	150	בֶּגֶד	221	גִּבּוֹר
12	אֶל	201	בְּהֵמָה	83	גָּדַל

425

83a	גָּדוֹל	238	הִנִּיחַ	224a	חָכְמָה
78	גּוֹי	185	הִצִּיל	257	חָלַל
198	גָּלָה	282	הִקְטִיר	271	חֵמָה
54	גַּם	80	הַר	126a	חֲמִשִּׁים
		213	הָרַג	126	חָמֵשׁ
25	דִּבֶּר	264	הִשְׁלִיךְ		חֲמִשָּׁה
25a	דָּבָר	261	הִשְׁתַּחֲוָה	182	חָנָה
183	דּוֹד			157	חֶסֶד
124	דָּם	31a	זֹאת	266	חֲצִי
64	דֶּרֶךְ	113	זֶבַח	235	חָצֵר
216	דָּרַשׁ	113a	זֶבַח	228	חֹק
		31	זֶה	228a	חֻקָּה
234	הֶאֱמִין	297	זָהָב	109	חֶרֶב
204	הִגִּיד	164	זָכַר	270	חָשַׁב
284	הוֹדוּ	164a	זָכַר		
181	הוֹסִיף	186a/b	זָקֵן	127–127a	טוֹב
26	הוּא	130	זֶרַע	304	טָמֵא
190	הוֹשִׁיעַ				
257	חִלֵּל	265	חֹדֶשׁ	209	יָבִין
26a	הִיא	261	חַוָּה	23	יָד
230	הֵשִׁיב	214	חוּץ	284	יָדָה
10	הָיָה	248	חוֹמָה	41	יָדַע
222	הִכָּה	227	חָזַק	1	יהוה
24	הָלַךְ	187	חָטָא	17	יוֹם
239	הִלֵּל	187a	חַטָּאת	112	יַחַד
85	הֵם	90	חַי	112a	יַחְדָּו
85	הֵמָּה	90a	חָיָה	112b	יָחִיד
37, 85a	הֵן	90b	חָיָה	271	יָחַם
37, 85a	הֵנָּה	90c	חַיִּים	230	יָשַׁב
37	הִנֵּה	159	חַיִל	240	יַיִן
238	הִנִּיחַ	224	חָכַם	167	יָכוֹל יָכֹל

87	יֶלֶד	249	בִּסָּא בִּסֵּה	59	מָה
141	יָם	306	בִּסָּה	173a	מוֹעֵד
245	יָמִין	296	כֶּסֶף	49	מוּת
181	יָסֵף	196	כַּף	49a	מָוֶת
35	יָצָא	290	כִּפֶּר	113b	מִזְבֵּחַ
110	יָרֵא	254	כָּרַת	182a	מַחֲנֶה
110	יִרְאָה	172	כָּתַב	155a	מַטֶּה
117	יָרַד			155b	מַטֶּה
165	יָרַשׁ			104	מִי
246	יֵשׁ	6	לֹא לוֹא	76	מַיִם
34	יָשַׁב	72	לֵב	156	מָלֵא
190	יָשַׁע	72a	לֵבָב	128	מַלְאָךְ
276	יָשָׁר	223	לְבַד	128a	מְלָאכָה
261	יִשְׁתַּחוּ	146	לָבַשׁ	131a	מִלְחָמָה
206	יֶתֶר	146	לְבֻשׁ	14	מֶלֶךְ
		180	לֵוִי	14a	מַלְכָּה
		131	לֶחֶם	15	מָלַךְ
193	כָּבֵד	132	לֶחֶם	15a	מַלְכוּת
193a	כָּבוֹד	160	לַיְלָה	15b	מַמְלָכָה
298	כֶּבֶשׂ	160	לַיִל	226	מִנְחָה
77	כֹּה	273	לָכַד	202b	מִסְפָּר
58	כֹּהֵן	65a	לָכֵן	262	מְעַט
176	כוּן	59a	לָמָּה	8c	מַעַל
259	כֹּחַ כֹּחַ	99c	לְמַעַן	11a	מַעֲשֶׂה
9	כִּי	39	לָקַח	97	מָצָא
2	כֹּל	62	לִקְרַאת	94a	מִצְוָה
188	כָּלָה	279	לָשׁוֹן	71a	מָקוֹם
188a	כְּלִי			27a	מַרְאֶה
229	כְּמוֹ	211	מְאֹד	242a	מִשְׁכָּן
65	כֵּן	74	מֵאָה	105a	מִשְׁפָּט
294	כָּנָף	25b	מִדְבָּר		

142	מִשְׁפָּחָה	185	נָצַל	8a	עָלָה
49	מֵת	139a	נִשְׁבַּע	22	עִם
		252	נִשְׁאַר	38	עַם
111	נָא	69	נָשָׂא	84	עָמַד
308	נְאֻם	69a	נָשִׂיא	84a	עָמַד עַמּוּד
234	נֶאֱמָן	21	נָתַן	99, 100	עָנָה
192a	נִבָּא			100a	עָנִי
192	נָבִיא	217	סָבַב	100b	עָנִי
145	נֶגֶב	217a	סָבִיב	143	עָפָר
204	נָגַד	244	סוּס	115	עֵץ
204a	נֶגֶד	174	סוּר	263	עֶצֶם
140	נָגַע	202a	סָפַר	256	עֶרֶב
166	נָגַשׁ	202a	סֵפֶר	11	עָשָׂה
274	נָהָר	202	סֹפֶר	82	עֶשֶׂר
238	נוּחַ	174	סַר	82	עֲשָׂרָה
220	נוּס			82a	עֶשְׂרִים
206	נוֹתַר	52	עָבַד	99a	עֵת
251	נָחַל	52a	עֶבֶד	99b	עַתָּה
250	נַחֲלָה	52b	עֲבֹדָה		
299	נָחַם	81	עָבַר	92	פֶּה
247	נְחֹשֶׁת	28	עַד	243	פֶּן
155	נָטָה	173	עֵדָה	19	פָּנָה
222	נָכָה	91	עוֹד	19a	פָּנִים
176	נָכוֹן	98	עוֹלָם	278	פַּעַם
131	נִלְחַם	268	עָוֹן	184	פָּקַד
220	נָס	135	עָזַב	258	פַּר
219	נָסַע	47, 47a	עַיִן	277	פְּרִי
116	נַעַר	33	עִיר	215	פָּתַח
101	נָפַל	8b	עַל	215a	פֶּתַח
55	נֶפֶשׁ	8	עָלָה	152	צֹאן

93	צָבָא	241	רָדַף	163a	שָׁלוֹם
189b	צַדִּיק	309	רֹחַב	48	שָׁלַח
189	צֶדֶק	119	רוּחַ	102a	שְׁלִישִׁי
189a	צְדָקָה	194	רוּם	102b	שְׁלֹשִׁים
94	צִוָּה	286	רוּץ	264	שָׁלַךְ
144	צָפוֹן	275	רֶכֶב	163	שָׁלֵם
300	צַר	194	רָם	163	שָׁלֵם
		68	רֵעַ	102	שָׁלֹשׁ
253	קָבַר	310	רָעֵב	102	שְׁלֹשָׁה
260	קָבַץ	66	רַע	50	שָׁם
95a	קָדוֹשׁ	66a, 67,68	רָעָה	45	שֵׁם
95b	קָדַשׁ	66	רעע	106	שָׁמַיִם
95b	קָדַשׁ	286	רָץ	197	שֶׁמֶן
95	קֹדֶשׁ	288	רַק	295	שְׁמֹנֶה
267	קָהָל	154	רָשָׁע	295	שְׁמֹנָה
86	קוֹל			30	שָׁמַע
71	קוּם	208	שָׁאַל	96	שָׁמַר
282	קָשַׁר	252	שָׁאַר	137	שֶׁמֶשׁ
71	קָם	36	שָׁב	43	שָׁנָה
61, 62	קָרָא	199	שֵׁבֶט	44a	שֵׁנִי
148	קָרַב	139a	שָׁבַע	44	שְׁנַיִם
148	קָרֵב	139	שֶׁבַע	123	שֵׂעָר
149	קֶרֶב	139	שִׁבְעָה	105	שָׁפַט
		233	שָׁבַר	218	שָׁפַךְ
27	רָאָה	289	שַׁבָּת	287	שֶׁקֶר
73	רֹאשׁ	36	שׁוּב	179	שֵׁשׁ
73a	רִאשׁוֹן	261	שָׁחָה	179	שִׁשָּׁה
103	רַב	231	שִׁחֵת	177	שָׁתָה
103a	רֹב	136	שָׁכַב	44	שְׁתַּיִם
168	רָבָה	236	שָׁכַח		
158	רֶגֶל	242	שָׁכַן	203	שָׂדֶה

75	שִׂים	107	שַׂר	281	תּוֹעֵבָה
75	שָׂם	280	שָׂרַף	175	תּוֹרָה
225	שָׂמֵחַ			89	תַּ֫חַת
195	שָׂנֵא	108	תָּ֫וֶךְ	305	תָּמִיד
205	שָׂפָה	108	תּוֹךְ		

CHARTS

			Qal A	Qal I	Qal U	Nifʿal
Affix	Sg.	3 m.	פָּקַד	כָּבֵד	קָטֹן	נִפְקַד
		3 f.	פָּקְדָה	כָּבְדָה	קָטְנָה	נִפְקְדָה
		2 m.	פָּקַדְתָּ	כָּבַדְתָּ	קָטֹנְתָּ	נִפְקַדְתָּ
		2 f.	פָּקַדְתְּ	כָּבַדְתְּ	קָטֹנְתְּ	נִפְקַדְתְּ
		1 c.	פָּקַדְתִּי	כָּבַדְתִּי	קָטֹנְתִּי	נִפְקַדְתִּי
	Pl.	3 c.	פָּקְדוּ	כָּבְדוּ	קָטְנוּ	נִפְקְדוּ
		2 m.	פְּקַדְתֶּם	כְּבַדְתֶּם	קְטָנְתֶּם	נִפְקַדְתֶּם
		2 f.	פְּקַדְתֶּן	כְּבַדְתֶּן	קְטָנְתֶּן	נִפְקַדְתֶּן
		1 c.	פָּקַדְנוּ	כָּבַדְנוּ	קָטֹנּוּ	נִפְקַדְנוּ
Prefix	Sg.	3 m.	יִפְקֹד	יִכְבַּד	יִקְטֹן	יִפָּקֵד
		3 f.	תִּפְקֹד	תִּכְבַּד	תִּקְטֹן	תִּפָּקֵד
		2 m.	תִּפְקֹד	תִּכְבַּד	תִּקְטֹן	תִּפָּקֵד
		2 f.	תִּפְקְדִי	תִּכְבְּדִי	תִּקְטְנִי	תִּפָּקְדִי
		1 c.	אֶפְקֹד	אֶכְבַּד	אֶקְטֹן	אֶפָּקֵד
	Pl.	3 m.	יִפְקְדוּ	יִכְבְּדוּ	יִקְטְנוּ	יִפָּקְדוּ
		3 f.	תִּפְקֹדְנָה	תִּכְבַּדְנָה	תִּקְטֹנָּה	תִּפָּקַדְנָה
		2 m.	תִּפְקְדוּ	תִּכְבְּדוּ	תִּקְטְנוּ	תִּפָּקְדוּ
		2 f.	תִּפְקֹדְנָה	תִּכְבַּדְנָה	תִּקְטֹנָּה	תִּפָּקַדְנָה
		1 c.	נִפְקֹד	נִכְבַּד	נִקְטֹן	נִפָּקֵד
Imperative	Sg.	2 m.	פְּקֹד	כְּבַד	קְטֹן	הִפָּקֵד
		2 f.	פִּקְדִי	כִּבְדִי	קְטְנִי	הִפָּקְדִי
	Pl.	2 m.	פִּקְדוּ	כִּבְדוּ	קְטְנוּ	הִפָּקְדוּ
		2 f.	פְּקֹדְנָה	כְּבַדְנָה	קְטֹנָּה	הִפָּקַדְנָה
Participle	Sg.	m.	פֹּקֵד	כָּבֵד	קָטֹן	נִפְקָד
		f.	פֹּקְדָה	כְּבֵדָה	קְטַנָּה	נִפְקָדָה
	Pl.	m.	פֹּקְדִים	כְּבֵדִים	קְטַנִּים	נִפְקָדִים
		f.	פֹּקְדוֹת	כְּבֵדוֹת	קְטַנּוֹת	נִפְקָדוֹת
Infinitive Construct			פְּקֹד	כְּבֹד	קְטֹן	הִפָּקֵד
Infinitive Absolute			פָּקוֹד	כָּבוֹד	קָטוֹן	הִפָּקֵד נִפְקֹד
Prefix/vav conversive			וַיִּפְקֹד	וַיִּכְבַּד	וַיִּקְטֹן	וַיִּפָּקֵד

432

Pi`el	Pu`al	Hif`il	Hof`al
פִּקֵּד פִּקַּד	פֻּקַּד	הִפְקִיד	הֻפְקַד הָפְקַד
פִּקְּדָה	פֻּקְּדָה	הִפְקִידָה	הֻפְקְדָה
פִּקַּדְתָּ	פֻּקַּדְתָּ	הִפְקַדְתָּ	הֻפְקַדְתָּ
פִּקַּדְתְּ	פֻּקַּדְתְּ	הִפְקַדְתְּ	הֻפְקַדְתְּ
פִּקַּדְתִּי	פֻּקַּדְתִּי	הִפְקַדְתִּי	הֻפְקַדְתִּי
פִּקְּדוּ	פֻּקְּדוּ	הִפְקִידוּ	הֻפְקְדוּ
פִּקַּדְתֶּם	פֻּקַּדְתֶּם	הִפְקַדְתֶּם	הֻפְקַדְתֶּם
פִּקַּדְתֶּן	פֻּקַּדְתֶּן	הִפְקַדְתֶּן	הֻפְקַדְתֶּן
פִּקַּדְנוּ	פֻּקַּדְנוּ	הִפְקַדְנוּ	הֻפְקַדְנוּ
יְפַקֵּד	יְפֻקַּד	יַפְקִיד	יֻפְקַד יָפְקַד
תְּפַקֵּד	תְּפֻקַּד	תַּפְקִיד	תֻּפְקַד
תְּפַקֵּד	תְּפֻקַּד	תַּפְקִיד	תֻּפְקַד
תְּפַקְּדִי	תְּפֻקְּדִי	תַּפְקִידִי	תֻּפְקְדִי
אֲפַקֵּד	אֲפֻקַּד	אַפְקִיד	אֻפְקַד
יְפַקְּדוּ	יְפֻקְּדוּ	יַפְקִידוּ	יֻפְקְדוּ
תְּפַקֵּדְנָה	תְּפֻקַּדְנָה	תַּפְקֵדְנָה	תֻּפְקַדְנָה
תְּפַקְּדוּ	תְּפֻקְּדוּ	תַּפְקִידוּ	תֻּפְקְדוּ
תְּפַקֵּדְנָה	תְּפֻקַּדְנָה	תַּפְקֵדְנָה	תֻּפְקַדְנָה
נְפַקֵּד	נְפֻקַּד	נַפְקִיד	נֻפְקַד
פַּקֵּד		הַפְקֵד	
פַּקְּדִי		הַפְקִידִי	
פַּקְּדוּ		הַפְקִידוּ	
פַּקֵּדְנָה		הַפְקֵדְנָה	
מְפַקֵּד	מְפֻקָּד	מַפְקִיד	מֻפְקָד מָפְקָד
מְפַקְּדָה ‗ֶדֶת	מְפֻקָּדָה ‗ֶדֶת	מַפְקִידָה	מֻפְקָדָה
מְפַקְּדִים	מְפֻקָּדִים	מַפְקִידִים	מֻפְקָדִים
מְפַקְּדוֹת	מְפֻקָּדוֹת	מַפְקִידוֹת	מֻפְקָדוֹת
פַּקֵּד		הַפְקִיד	
פַּקֵּד פַּקֹּד	פֻּקֹּד	הַפְקֵד	הֻפְקֵד הָפְקֵד
וַיְפַקֵּד		וַיַּפְקֵד	

433

			Qal		Nif`al	Hif`il	Hof`al
Affix	Sg.	3 m.	עָמַד		נֶעֱמַד	הֶעֱמִיד	הָעֳמַד
		3 f.	עָמְדָה		נֶעֶמְדָה	הֶעֱמִידָה	הָעֳמְדָה
		2 m.	עָמַׁדְתָּ		נֶעֱמַׁדְתָּ	הֶעֱמַׁדְתָּ	הָעֳמַׁדְתָּ
		2 f.	עָמַדְתְּ		נֶעֱמַדְתְּ	הֶעֱמַדְתְּ	הָעֳמַדְתְּ
		1 c.	עָמַׁדְתִּי		נֶעֱמַׁדְתִּי	הֶעֱמַׁדְתִּי	הָעֳמַׁדְתִּי
	Pl.	3 c.	עָמְדוּ		נֶעֶמְדוּ	הֶעֱמִידוּ	הָעֳמְדוּ
		2 m.	עֲמַדְתֶּם		נֶעֱמַדְתֶּם	הֶעֱמַדְתֶּם	הָעֳמַדְתֶּם
		2 f.	עֲמַדְתֶּן		נֶעֱמַדְתֶּן	הֶעֱמַדְתֶּן	הָעֳמַדְתֶּן
		1 c.	עָמַׁדְנוּ		נֶעֱמַׁדְנוּ	הֶעֱמַׁדְנוּ	הָעֳמַׁדְנוּ
Prefix	Sg.	3 m.	יַעֲמֹד	יֶחֱזַק	יֵעָמֵד	יַעֲמִיד	יָעֳמַד
		3 f.	תַּעֲמֹד	תֶּחֱזַק	תֵּעָמֵד	תַּעֲמִיד	תָּעֳמַד
		2 m.	תַּעֲמֹד	תֶּחֱזַק	תֵּעָמֵד	תַּעֲמִיד	תָּעֳמַד
		2 f.	תַּעַמְדִי	תֶּחֶזְקִי	תֵּעָמְדִי	תַּעֲמִׁידִי	תָּעֳמְדִי
		1 c.	אֶעֱמֹד	אֶחֱזַק	אֵעָמֵד	אַעֲמִיד	אָעֳמַד
	Pl.	3 m.	יַעַמְדוּ	יֶחֶזְקוּ	יֵעָמְדוּ	יַעֲמִׁידוּ	יָעֳמְדוּ
		3 f.	תַּעֲמֹׁדְנָה	תֶּחֱזַׁקְנָה	תֵּעָמַׁדְנָה	תַּעֲמֵׁדְנָה	תָּעֳמַׁדְנָה
		2 m.	תַּעַמְדוּ	תֶּחֶזְקוּ	תֵּעָמְדוּ	תַּעֲמִׁידוּ	תָּעֳמְדוּ
		2 f.	תַּעֲמֹׁדְנָה	תֶּחֱזַׁקְנָה	תֵּעָמַׁדְנָה	תַּעֲמֵׁדְנָה	תָּעֳמַׁדְנָה
		1 c.	נַעֲמֹד	נֶחֱזַק	נֵעָמֵד	נַעֲמִיד	נָעֳמַד
Imperative	Sg.	2 m.	עֲמֹד	חֲזַק	הֵעָמֵד	הַעֲמֵד	
		2 f.	עִמְדִי	חִזְקִי	הֵעָמְדִי	הַעֲמִׁידִי	
	Pl.	2 m.	עִמְדוּ	חִזְקוּ	הֵעָמְדוּ	הַעֲמִׁידוּ	
		2 f.	עֲמֹׁדְנָה	חֲזַׁקְנָה	הֵעָמַׁדְנָה	הַעֲמֵׁדְנָה	
Participle	Sg.	m.	עֹמֵד	חָזֵק	נֶעֱמָד	מַעֲמִיד	מָעֳמָד
		f.	עֹמְדָה ־ֶ֫דֶת	חֲזָקָה	נֶעֱמָדָה	מַעֲמִידָה	מָעֳמָדָה
	Pl.	m.	עֹמְדִים	חֲזָקִים	נֶעֱמָדִים	מַעֲמִידִים	מָעֳמָדִים
		f.	עֹמְדוֹת	חֲזָקוֹת	נֶעֱמָדוֹת	מַעֲמִידוֹת	מָעֳמָדוֹת
Infinitive Construct			עֲמֹד		הֵעָמֵד	הַעֲמִיד	
Infinitive Absolute			עָמוֹד		נַעֲמוֹד הֵאָסֹף	הַעֲמֵד	הָעֳמֵד
Prefix/vav conversive			וַיַּעֲמֹד		וַיֵּעָמֵד	וַיַּעֲמֵד	

			Qal	Nif'al	Hif'il	Hof'al
Affix	Sg.	3 m.	אָכַל	נֶאֱכַל	הֶאֱכִיל	הָאֳכַל
			אָכְלָה	נֶאֶכְלָה	הֶאֱכִילָה	הָאֳכְלָה
			אָכַלְתָּ	נֶאֱכַלְתָּ	הֶאֱכַלְתָּ	הָאֳכַלְתָּ
			אָכַלְתְּ	נֶאֱכַלְתְּ	הֶאֱכַלְתְּ	הָאֳכַלְתְּ
			אָכַלְתִּי	נֶאֱכַלְתִּי	הֶאֱכַלְתִּי	הָאֳכַלְתִּי
Prefix	Sg.	3 m.	יֹאכַל	יֵאָכֵל	יַאֲכִיל	יָאֳכַל
		3 f.	תֹּאכַל	תֵּאָכֵל	תַּאֲכִיל	תָּאֳכַל
		2 m.	תֹּאכַל	תֵּאָכֵל	תַּאֲכִיל	תָּאֳכַל
		2 f.	תֹּאכְלִי	תֵּאָכְלִי	תַּאֲכִילִי	תָּאֳכִיל
		1 c.	אֹכַל	אֵאָכֵל	אַאֲכִיל	אָאֳכַל
	Pl.	3 m.	יֹאכְלוּ	יֵאָכְלוּ	יַאֲכִילוּ	יָאֳכְלוּ
		3 f.	תֹּאכַלְנָה	תֵּאָכַלְנָה	תַּאֲכֵלְנָה	תָּאֳכַלְנָה
		2 m.	תֹּאכְלוּ	תֵּאָכְלוּ	תַּאֲכִילוּ	תָּאֳכְלוּ
		2 f.	תֹּאכַלְנָה	תֵּאָכַלְנָה	תַּאֲכֵלְנָה	תָּאֳכַלְנָה
		1 c.	נֹאכַל	נֵאָכֵל	נַאֲכִיל	נָאֳכַל
Imperative	Sg.	2 m.	אֱכֹל	הֵאָכֵל	הַאֲכֵל	
		2 f.	אִכְלִי	הֵאָכְלִי	הַאֲכִילִי	
	Pl.	2 m.	אִכְלוּ	הֵאָכְלוּ	הַאֲכִילוּ	
		2 f.	אֱכֹלְנָה	הֵאָכַלְנָה	הַאֲכֵלְנָה	
Participle	Sg.	m.	אֹכֵל	נֶאֱכָל	מַאֲכִיל	מָאֳכָל
		f.	־ֶלֶת אֹכְלָה	נֶאֱכֶלֶת	מַאֲכִילָה	מָאֳכָלָה
	Pl.	m.	אֹכְלִים	נֶאֱכָלִים	מַאֲכִילִים	מָאֳכָלִים
	Pl.	f.	אֹכְלוֹת	נֶאֱכָלוֹת	מַאֲכִילוֹת	מָאֳכָלוֹת
Infinitive Construct			אֱכֹל אֲכָל	הֵאָכֵל	הַאֲכִיל	הָאֳכַל
Infinitive Absolute			אָכוֹל	הֵאָכֵל	הַאֲכֵל	הָאֳכֵל
Prefix/vav conversive			וַיֹּאכַל וַיֹּאמֶר	וַיֵּאָכֵל	וַיַּאֲכֵל	וַיָּאֳכַל

			Qal	Nif`al	Hif`il	Hof`al
Affix	Sg.	3 m.	יָשַׁב	נוֹשַׁב	הוֹשִׁיב	הוּשַׁב
		3 f.	יָשְׁבָה	נוֹשְׁבָה	הוֹשִׁיבָה	הוּשְׁבָה
		2 m.	יָשַׁבְתָּ	נוֹשַׁבְתָּ	הוֹשַׁבְתָּ	הוּשַׁבְתָּ
		2 f.	יָשַׁבְתְּ	נוֹשַׁבְתְּ	הוֹשַׁבְתְּ	הוּשַׁבְתְּ
		1 c.	יָשַׁבְתִּי	נוֹשַׁבְתִּי	הוֹשַׁבְתִּי	הוּשַׁבְתִּי
	Pl.	3 c.	יָשְׁבוּ	נוֹשְׁבוּ	הוֹשִׁיבוּ	הוּשְׁבוּ
		2 m.	יְשַׁבְתֶּם	נוֹשַׁבְתֶּם	הוֹשַׁבְתֶּם	הוּשַׁבְתֶּם
		2 f.	יְשַׁבְתֶּן	נוֹשַׁבְתֶּן	הוֹשַׁבְתֶּן	הוּשַׁבְתֶּן
		1 c.	יָשַׁבְנוּ	נוֹשַׁבְנוּ	הוֹשַׁבְנוּ	הוּשַׁבְנוּ
Prefix	Sg.	3 m.	יֵשֵׁב	יִוָּשֵׁב	יוֹשִׁיב	יוּשַׁב
		3 f.	תֵּשֵׁב	תִּוָּשֵׁב	תּוֹשִׁיב	תּוּשַׁב
		2 m.	תֵּשֵׁב	תִּוָּשֵׁב	תּוֹשִׁיב	תּוּשַׁב
		2 f.	תֵּשְׁבִי	תִּוָּשְׁבִי	תּוֹשִׁיבִי	תּוּשְׁבִי
		1 c.	אֵשֵׁב	אִוָּשֵׁב	אוֹשִׁיב	אוּשַׁב
	Pl.	3 m.	יֵשְׁבוּ	יִוָּשְׁבוּ	יוֹשִׁיבוּ	יוּשְׁבוּ
		3 f.	תֵּשַׁבְנָה	תִּוָּשַׁבְנָה	תּוֹשֵׁבְנָה	תּוּשַׁבְנָה
		2 m.	תֵּשְׁבוּ	תִּוָּשְׁבוּ	תּוֹשִׁיבוּ	תּוּשְׁבוּ
		2 f.	תֵּשַׁבְנָה	תִּוָּשַׁבְנָה	תּוֹשֵׁבְנָה	תּוּשַׁבְנָה
		1 c.	נֵשֵׁב	נִוָּשֵׁב	נוֹשִׁיב	נוּשַׁב
Imperative	Sg.	2 m.	שֵׁב דַּע	הִוָּשֵׁב	הוֹשֵׁב	
		2 f.	שְׁבִי	הִוָּשְׁבִי	הוֹשִׁיבִי	
	Pl.	2 m.	שְׁבוּ	הִוָּשְׁבוּ	הוֹשִׁיבוּ	
		2 f.	שֵׁבְנָה	הִוָּשַׁבְנָה	הוֹשֵׁבְנָה	
Participle	Sg.	m.	יֹשֵׁב	נוֹשָׁב	מוֹשִׁיב	מוּשָׁב
		f.	יֹשֶׁבֶת יֹשְׁבָה	נוֹשָׁבָה	מוֹשִׁיבָה	מוּשָׁבָה
	Pl.	m.	יֹשְׁבִים	נוֹשָׁבִים	מוֹשִׁיבִים	מוּשָׁבִים
		f.	יֹשְׁבוֹת	נוֹשָׁבוֹת	מוֹשִׁיבוֹת	מוּשָׁבוֹת
Infinitive Construct			שֶׁבֶת	הִוָּשֵׁב	הוֹשִׁיב	הוּשַׁב
Infinitive Absolute			יָשׁוֹב		הוֹשֵׁב	
Prefix/vav conversive			וַיֵּשֶׁב	וַיִּוָּשֵׁב	וַיּוֹשֶׁב	

		Qal A	Qal I	Hif`il
Affix	Sg. 3 m.	יָטַב	יָרֵא	הֵיטִיב
	3 f.	יָטְבָה	note changes יָרְאָה	הֵיטִיבָה
	2 m.	יָטַבְתָּ	for 3rd א ⟶ יָרֵאתָ	הֵיטַבְתָּ
	2 f.	יָטַבְתְּ	יָרֵאת	הֵיטַבְתְּ
	1 c.	יָטַבְתִּי	יָרֵאתִי	הֵיטַבְתִּי
	Pl. 3 c.	יָטְבוּ	יָרְאוּ	הֵיטִיבוּ
	2 m.	יְטַבְתֶּם	יְרֵאתֶם	הֵיטַבְתֶּם
	2 f.	יְטַבְתֶּן	יְרֵאתֶן	הֵיטַבְתֶּן
	1 c.	יָטַבְנוּ	יָרֵאנוּ	הֵיטַבְנוּ
Prefix	Sg. 3 m.	יֵיטַב	יִירָא	יֵיטִיב
	3 f.	תֵּיטַב	תִּירָא	תֵּיטִיב
	2 m.	תֵּיטַב	תִּירָא	תֵּיטִיב
	2 f.	תֵּיטְבִי	תִּירְאִי	תֵּיטִיבִי
	1 c.	אִיטַב	אִירָא	אִיטִיב
	Pl. 3 m.	יֵיטְבוּ	יִירְאוּ	יֵיטִיבוּ
	3 f.	תֵּיטַבְנָה	תִּירֶאנָה	תֵּיטִבְנָה
	2 m.	תֵּיטְבוּ	תִּירְאוּ	תֵּיטִיבוּ
	2 f.	תֵּיטַבְנָה	תִּירֶאנָה	תֵּיטִבְנָה
	1 c.	נֵיטַב	נִירָא	נֵיטִיב
Imperative	Sg. 2 m.	יְטַב	יְרָא	הֵיטֵב
	2 f.	יְטְבִי	יִרְאִי	הֵיטִיבִי
	Pl. 2 m.	יְטְבוּ	יִרְאוּ	הֵיטִיבוּ
	2 f.	יְטַבְנָה	יְרֶאנָה	הֵיטֵבְנָה
Participle	Sg. m.	יֹטֵב	יָרֵא	מֵיטִיב
	f.	יֹטְבָה	יְרֵאָה	מֵיטִיבָה
	Pl. m.	יֹטְבִים	יְרֵאִים	מֵיטִיבִים
	s.	יֹתְבוֹת	יְרֵאוֹת	מֵיטִיבוֹת
Infinitive Construct		יְטֹב	יְרֹא לְיִרְאָה	הֵיטִיב
Infinitive Absolute		יָטוֹב	יָרוֹא	הֵיטֵב
Prefix/vav conversive		וַיֵּיטַב	וַיִּירָא וַיִּרָא	וַיֵּיטֶב

			Qal			Nifʿal	Hifʿil	Hofʿal
Affix	Sg.	3 m.	נָגַשׁ	נָפַל	נָתַן	נִגַּשׁ	הִגִּישׁ	הֻגַּשׁ
		3 f.	נָגְשָׁה	נָפְלָה	נָתְנָה	נִגְּשָׁה	הִגִּישָׁה	הֻגְּשָׁה
		2 m.	נָגַשְׁתָּ	נָפַלְתָּ	נָתַתָּ	נִגַּשְׁתָּ	הִגַּשְׁתָּ	הֻגַּשְׁתָּ
		2 f.	נָגַשְׁתְּ	נָפַלְתְּ	נָתַתְּ	נִגַּשְׁתְּ	הִגַּשְׁתְּ	הֻגַּשְׁתְּ
		1 c.	נָגַשְׁתִּי	נָפַלְתִּי	נָתַתִּי	נִגַּשְׁתִּי	הִגַּשְׁתִּי	הֻגַּשְׁתִּי
	Pl.	3 c.	נָגְשׁוּ	נָפְלוּ	נָתְנוּ	נִגְּשׁוּ	הִגִּישׁוּ	הֻגְּשׁוּ
		2 m.	נְגַשְׁתֶּם	נְפַלְתֶּם	נְתַתֶּם	נִגַּשְׁתֶּם	הִגַּשְׁתֶּם	הֻגַּשְׁתֶּם
		2 f.	נְגַשְׁתֶּן	נְפַלְתֶּן	נְתַתֶּן	נִגַּשְׁתֶּן	הִגַּשְׁתֶּן	הֻגַּשְׁתֶּן
		1 c.	נָגַשְׁנוּ	נָפַלְנוּ	נָתַנּוּ	נִגַּשְׁנוּ	הִגַּשְׁנוּ	הֻגַּשְׁנוּ
Prefix	Sg.	3 m.	יִגַּשׁ	יִפֹּל	יִתֵּן	יִנָּגֵשׁ	יַגִּישׁ	יֻגַּשׁ
		3 f.	תִּגַּשׁ	תִּפֹּל	תִּתֵּן	תִּנָּגֵשׁ	תַּגִּישׁ	תֻּגַּשׁ
		2 m.	תִּגַּשׁ	תִּפֹּל	תִּתֵּן	תִּנָּגֵשׁ	תַּגִּישׁ	תֻּגַּשׁ
		2 f.	תִּגְּשִׁי	תִּפְּלִי	תִּתְּנִי	תִּנָּגְשִׁי	תַּגִּישִׁי	תֻּגְּשִׁי
		1 c.	אֶגַּשׁ	אֶפֹּל	אֶתֵּן	אֶנָּגֵשׁ	אַגִּישׁ	אֻגַּשׁ
	Pl.	3 m.	יִגְּשׁוּ	יִפְּלוּ	יִתְּנוּ	יִנָּגְשׁוּ	יַגִּישׁוּ	יֻגְּשׁוּ
		3 f.	תִּגַּשְׁנָה	תִּפֹּלְנָה	תִּתֵּנָּה	תִּנָּגַשְׁנָה	תַּגֵּשְׁנָה	תֻּגַּשְׁנָה
		2 m.	תִּגְּשׁוּ	תִּפְּלוּ	תִּתְּנוּ	תִּנָּגְשׁוּ	תַּגִּישׁוּ	תֻּגְּשׁוּ
		2 f.	תִּגַּשְׁנָה	תִּפֹּלְנָה	תִּתֵּנָּה	תִּנָּגַשְׁנָה	תַּגֵּשְׁנָה	תֻּגַּשְׁנָה
		1 c.	נִגַּשׁ	נִפֹּל	נִתֵּן	נִנָּגֵשׁ	נַגִּישׁ	נֻגַּשׁ
Imperative	Sg.	2 m.	גַּשׁ	נְפֹל	תֵּן	הִנָּגֵשׁ	הַגֵּשׁ	
		2 f.	גְּשִׁי	נִפְלִי	תְּנִי	הִנָּגְשִׁי	הַגִּישִׁי	
	Pl.	2 m.	גְּשׁוּ	נִפְלוּ	תְּנוּ	הִנָּגְשׁוּ	הַגִּישׁוּ	
		2 f.	גֵּשְׁנָה	נְפֹלְנָה	תֵּנָּה	הִנָּגַשְׁנָה	הַגֵּשְׁנָה	
Participle	Sg.	m.	נֹגֵשׁ	נֹפֵל	נֹתֵן	נִגָּשׁ	מַגִּישׁ	מֻגָּשׁ
		f.	נֹגְשָׁה	נֹפְלָה	נֹתְנָה	נִגָּשָׁה	מַגִּישָׁה	מֻגָּשָׁה
	Pl.	m.	נֹגְשִׁים	נֹפְלִים	נֹתְנִים	נִגָּשִׁים	מַגִּישִׁים	מֻגָּשִׁים
		s.	נֹגְשׁוֹת	נֹפְלוֹת	נֹתְנוֹת	נִגָּשׁוֹת	מַגִּישׁוֹת	מֻגָּשׁוֹת
Infinitive Construct			גֶּשֶׁת	נְפֹל	תֵּת	הִנָּגֵשׁ	הַגִּישׁ	הֻגַּשׁ
Infinitive Absolute			נָגוֹשׁ	נָפֹל	נָתֹן	הִנָּגֵשׁ	הַגֵּשׁ	הֻגֵּשׁ
Prefix/vav conversive			וַיִּגַּשׁ	וַיִּפֹּל	וַיִּתֵּן	וַיִּנָּגֵשׁ	וַיַּגֵּשׁ	וַיֻּגַּשׁ

		Qal	Nif'al	Pi'el	Pu'al
Affix	Sg. 3 m.	גָּאַל	נִגְאַל	בֵּרַךְ בֵּרֵךְ	בֹּרַךְ
	3 f.	גָּאֲלָה	נִגְאֲלָה	בֵּרְכָה	בֹּרְכָה
	2 m.	גָּאַלְתָּ	נִגְאַלְתָּ	בֵּרַכְתָּ	בֹּרַכְתָּ
	2 f.	גָּאַלְתְּ	נִגְאַלְתְּ	בֵּרַכְתְּ	בֹּרַכְתְּ
	1 c.	גָּאַלְתִּי	נִגְאַלְתִּי	בֵּרַכְתִּי	בֹּרַכְתִּי
	Pl. 3 c.	גָּאֲלוּ	נִגְאֲלוּ	בֵּרְכוּ	בֹּרְכוּ
	2 m.	גְּאַלְתֶּם	נִגְאַלְתֶּם	בֵּרַכְתֶּם	בֹּרַכְתֶּם
	2 f.	גְּאַלְתֶּן	נִגְאַלְתֶּן	בֵּרַכְתֶּן	בֹּרַכְתֶּן
	1 c.	גָּאַלְנוּ	נִגְאַלְנוּ	בֵּרַכְנוּ	בֹּרַכְנוּ
Prefix	Sg. 3 m.	יִגְאַל	יִגָּאֵל	יְבָרֵךְ	יְבֹרַךְ
	3 f.	תִּגְאַל	תִּגָּאֵל	תְּבָרֵךְ	תְּבֹרַךְ
	2 m.	תִּגְאַל	תִּגָּאֵל	תְּבָרֵךְ	תְּבֹרַךְ
	2 f.	תִּגְאֲלִי	תִּגָּאֲלִי	תְּבָרְכִי	תְּבֹרְכִי
	1 c.	אֶגְאַל	אֶגָּאֵל	אֲבָרֵךְ	אֲבֹרַךְ
	Pl. 3 m.	יִגְאֲלוּ	יִגָּאֲלוּ	יְבָרְכוּ	יְבֹרְכוּ
	3 f.	תִּגְאַלְנָה	תִּגָּאַלְנָה	תְּבָרֵכְנָה	תְּבֹרַכְנָה
	2 m.	תִּגְאֲלוּ	תִּגָּאֲלוּ	תְּבָרְכוּ	תְּבֹרְכוּ
	2 f.	תִּגְאַלְנָה	תִּגָּאַלְנָה	תְּבָרֵכְנָה	תְּבֹרַכְנָה
	1 c.	נִגְאַל	נִגָּאֵל	נְבָרֵךְ	נְבֹרַךְ
Imperative	Sg. 2 m.	גְּאַל	הִגָּאֵל	בָּרֵךְ	
	2 f.	גַּאֲלִי	הִגָּאֲלִי	בָּרְכִי	
	Pl. 2 m.	גַּאֲלוּ	הִגָּאֲלוּ	בָּרְכוּ	
	2 f.	גְּאַלְנָה	הִגָּאַלְנָה	בָּרֵכְנָה	
Participle	Sg. m.	גֹּאֵל	נִגְאָל	מְבָרֵךְ	מְבֹרָךְ
	f.	גֹּאֶלֶת	נִגְאָלָה	מְבָרֶכֶת	מְבֹרָכָה
	Pl. m.	גֹּאֲלִים	נִגְאָלִים	מְבָרְכִים	מְבֹרָכִים
	f.	גֹּאֲלוֹת	נִגְאָלוֹת	מְבָרְכוֹת	מְבֹרָכוֹת
Infinitive Construct		גְּאֹל	הִגָּאֵל	בָּרֵךְ	
Infinitive Absolute		גָּאוֹל	הִגָּאֵל נִגְאוֹל	בָּרֵךְ	בֹּרֵךְ
Prefix/vav conversive		וַיִּגְאַל	וַיִּגָּאֵל	וַיְבָרֵךְ	וַיְבֹרַךְ

			Qal A		Qal A	Qal A	Qal I
Affix	Sg.	3 m.	קָם	note	בָּא	שָׂם	מֵת
		3 f.	קָ֫מָה	changes	בָּ֫אָה	שָׂ֫מָה	מֵ֫תָה
		2 m.	קַ֫מְתָּ	for 3rd א	בָּ֫אתָ	שַׂ֫מְתָּ	מַ֫תָּה
		2 f.	קַמְתְּ	→	בָּאת	שַׂמְתְּ	מַתְּ
		1 c.	קַ֫מְתִּי		בָּ֫אתִי	שַׂ֫מְתִּי	מַ֫תִּי
	Pl.	3 c.	קָ֫מוּ		בָּ֫אוּ	שָׂ֫מוּ	מֵ֫תוּ
		2 m.	קַמְתֶּם		בָּאתֶם	שַׂמְתֶּם	מַתֶּם
		2 f.	קַמְתֶּן		בָּאתֶן	שַׂמְתֶּן	מַתֶּן
		1 c.	קַ֫מְנוּ		בָּ֫אנוּ	שַׂ֫מְנוּ	מַ֫תְנוּ
Prefix	Sg.	3 m.	יָקוּם		יָבוֹא	יָשִׂים	יָמוּת
		3 f.	תָּקוּם		תָּבוֹא	תָּשִׂים	תָּמוּת
		2 m.	תָּקוּם		תָּבוֹא	תָּשִׂים	תָּמוּת
		2 f.	תָּק֫וּמִי		תָּב֫וֹאִי	תָּשִׂ֫ימִי	תָּמ֫וּתִי
		1 c.	אָקוּם		אָבוֹא	אָשִׂים	אָמוּת
	Pl.	3 m.	יָק֫וּמוּ		יָב֫וֹאוּ	יָשִׂ֫ימוּ	יָמ֫וּתוּ
		3 f.	תָּק֫וּמְנָה		תָּב֫וֹאנָה	תָּשֵׂ֫מְנָה	תָּמֹ֫תְנָה
		2 m.	תָּק֫וּמוּ		תָּב֫וֹאוּ	תָּשִׂ֫ימוּ	תָּמ֫וּתוּ
		2 f.	תָּק֫וּמְנָה		תָּב֫וֹאנָה	תָּשֵׂ֫מְנָה	תָּמֹ֫תְנָה
		1 c.	נָקוּם		נָבוֹא	נָשִׂים	נָמוּת
Imperative	Sg.	2 m.	קוּם		בּוֹא	שִׂים	מוּת
		2 f.	ק֫וּמִי		בּ֫וֹאִי	שִׂ֫ימִי	מ֫וּתִי
	Pl.	2 m.	ק֫וּמוּ		בּ֫וֹאוּ	שִׂ֫ימוּ	מ֫וּתוּ
		2 f.	קֹ֫מְנָה		בֹּ֫אנָה	שֵׂ֫מְנָה	מֹ֫תְנָה
Participle	Sg.	m.	קָם		בָּא	שָׂם	מֵת
		f.	קָמָה		בָּאה	שָׂמָה	מֵתָה
	Pl.	m.	קָמִים		בָּאִים	שָׂמִים	מֵתִים
		f.	קָמוֹת		בָּאוֹת	שָׂמוֹת	מֵתוֹת
Infinitive Construct			קוּם		בּוֹא	שִׂים	מוּת
Infinitive Absolute			קוֹם		בּוֹא	שׂוֹם	מוֹת
Prefix/vav conversive			וַיָּ֫קָם		וַיָּבֹא	וַיָּ֫שֶׂם	וַיָּ֫מָת

Qal U	Nif`al	Hif`il	Hof`al	Pol`el
בּוֹשׁ	נָקוֹם	הוּקַם	הוּקַם	קוֹמֵם
בֹּושָׁה	נָקֹומָה	הֵקִימָה	הוּקְמָה	קוֹמְמָה
בֹּשְׁתָּ	נְקוּמֹֿותָ	הֲקִימֹֿותָ	הוּקַמְתָּ	קוֹמַמְתָּ
בֹּשְׁתְּ	נְקוּמֹות	הֲקִימֹות	הוּקַמְתְּ	קוֹמַמְתְּ
בֹּשְׁתִּי	נְקוּמֹֿותִי	הֲקִימֹֿותִי	הוּקַמְתִּי	קוֹמַמְתִּי
בֹּושׁוּ	נָקֹומוּ	הֵקִימוּ	הוּקְמוּ	קוֹמְמוּ
בָּשְׁתֶּם	נְקוּמֹותֶם	הֲקִימֹותֶם	הוּקַמְתֶּם	קוֹמַמְתֶּם
בָּשְׁתֶּן	נְקוּמֹותֶן	הֲקִימֹותֶן	הוּקַמְתֶּן	קוֹמַמְתֶּן
בֹּשְׁנוּ	נְקוּמֹֿונוּ	הֲקִימֹֿונוּ	הוּקַמְנוּ	קוֹמַמְנוּ
יֵבוֹשׁ	יִקּוֹם	יָקִים	יוּקַם	יְקוֹמֵם
תֵּבוֹשׁ	תִּקּוֹם	תָּקִים	תּוּקַם	תְּקוֹמֵם
תֵּבוֹשׁ	תִּקּוֹם	תָּקִים	תּוּקַם	תְּקוֹמֵם
תֵּבֹֿושִׁי	תִּקֹּֿומִי	תָּקִֿימִי	תּוּקְמִי	תְּקוֹמֵמִי
אֵבוֹשׁ	אֶקּוֹם	אָקִים	אוּקַם	אֲקוֹמֵם
יֵבֹֿושׁוּ	יִקֹּֿומוּ	יָקִֿימוּ	יוּקְמוּ	יְקוֹמְמוּ
תֵּבֹשְׁנָה	תִּקֹּומְנָה	תָּקֵמְנָה	תּוּקַמְנָה	תְּקוֹמֵֿמְנָה
תֵּבֹֿושׁוּ	תִּקֹּֿומוּ	תָּקִֿימוּ	תּוּקְמוּ	תְּקוֹמֵמוּ
תֵּבֹשְׁנָה	תִּקֹּומְנָה	תָּקֵמְנָה	תּוּקַמְנָה	תְּקוֹמֵֿמְנָה
נֵבוֹשׁ	נִקּוֹם	נָקִים	נוּקַם	נְקוֹמֵם
בּוֹשׁ	הִקּוֹם	הָקֵם		קוֹמֵם
בֹּֿושִׁי	הִקֹּֿומִי	הָקִֿימִי		קוֹמְמִי
בֹּֿושׁוּ	הִקֹּֿומוּ	הָקִֿימוּ		קוֹמְמוּ
בֹּשְׁנָה	הִקֹּומְנָה	הָקֵמְנָה		קוֹמֵֿמְנָה
בּוֹשׁ	נָקוֹם	מֵקִים	מוּקָם	מְקוֹמֵם
בּוֹשָׁה	נְקוֹמָה	מְקִימָה	מוּקָמָה	מְקוֹמְמָה
בּוֹשִׁים	נְקוֹמִים	מְקִימִים	מוּקָמִים	מְקוֹמְמִים
בּוֹשׁוֹת	נְקוֹמֹות	מְקִימֹות	מוּקָמֹות	מְקוֹמְמֹות
בּוֹשׁ	הִקּוֹם	הָקִים	הוּקַם	קוֹמֵם
בּוֹשׁ	הִקּוֹם	הָקֵם		
וַיֵּבֹשׁ	וַיִּקּוֹם	וַיָּֿקֶם	וַיּוּקַם	וַיְקוֹמֵם

Chart I   **Geminate**

			Qal	**Nif`al**
Affix	Sg.	3 m.	סָבַב תַּם	נָסַב נָמֵס
		3 f.	סָבְבָה תַּמָּה	נָסַבָּה
		2 m.	סַבּוֹתָ	נְסַבּוֹתָ
		2 f.	סַבּוֹת	נְסַבּוֹת
		1 c.	סַבּוֹתִי	נְסַבּוֹתִי
	Pl.	3 c.	סָבְבוּ תַּמּוּ	נָסַבּוּ
		2 m.	סַבּוֹתֶם	נְסַבּוֹתֶם
		2 f.	סַבּוֹתֶן	נְסַבּוֹתֶן
		1 c.	סַבּוֹנוּ	נְסַבּוֹנוּ
Prefix	Sg.	3 m.	יָסֹב יִמַּל יֵקַל יִסֹּב	יִסַּב
		3 f.	תָּסֹב תִּסֹּב	תִּסַּב
		2 m.	תָּסֹב תִּסֹּב	תִּסַּב
		2 f.	תָּסֹבִּי תִּסֹּבִי	תִּסַּבִּי
		1 c.	אָסֹב אֶסֹּב	אֶסַּב
	Pl.	3 m.	יָסֹבּוּ יִסֹּבוּ	יִסַּבּוּ
		3 f.	תָּסֻבֶּינָה תִּסֹּבְּינָה	תִּסַּבֶּינָה
		2 m.	תָּסֹבּוּ תִּסֹּבוּ	תִּסַּבּוּ
		2 f.	תָּסֻבֶּינָה תִּסֹּבְּינָה	תִּסַּבֶּינָה
		1 c.	נָסֹב נִסֹּב	נִסַּב
Imperative	Sg.	2 m.	סֹב	הִסַּב
		2 f.	סֹבִּי	הִסַּבִּי
	Pl.	2 m.	סֹבּוּ	הִסַּבּוּ
		2 f.	סֻבֶּינָה	הִסַּבֶּינָה
Participle	Sg.	m.	סֹבֵב	נָסָב
		f.	סֹבְבָה	נְסַבָּה
	Pl.	m.	סֹבְבִים	נְסַבִּים
		f.	סֹבְבוֹת	נְסַבּוֹת
Infinitive Construct			סֹב	הִסַּב
Infinitive Absolute			סָבוֹב	הִסּוֹב הִמֵּס
Prefix/vav conversive			וַיָּסֹב	

Hif`il	Hof`al	Pol`el
הֵסַב הֵסֵב	הוּסַב	סוֹבֵב
הֵסַׄבָּה	הוּסַׄבָּה	סוֹבְבָה
הֲסִבֹּוֹתָ	הוּסַבֹּוֹתָ	סוֹבַׄבְתָּ
הֲסִבּוֹת	הוּסַבּוֹת	סוֹבַׄבְתְּ
הֲסִבֹּוֹתִי	הוּסַבֹּוֹתִי	סוֹבַׄבְתִּי
הֵסֵׄבּוּ הֵחֵׄלּוּ	הוּסַׄבּוּ	סוֹבְבוּ
הֲסִבּוֹתֶם	הוּסַבּוֹתֶם	סוֹבַבְתֶּם
הֲסִבּוֹתֶן	הוּסַבּוֹתֶן	סוֹבַבְתֶּן
הֲסִבֹּוֹנוּ	הוּסַבֹּוֹנוּ	סוֹבַׄבְנוּ
יָסֵב יַסֵב	יוּסַב יֻסַב	יְסוֹבֵב
תָּסֵב	תּוּסַב	תְּסוֹבֵב
תָּסֵב	תּוּסַב	תְּסוֹבֵב
תָּסֵׄבִּי	תּוּסַׄבִּי	תְּסוֹבְבִי
אָסֵב	אוּסַב	אֲסוֹבֵב
יָסֵׄבּוּ יַסֵׄבּוּ	יוּסַׄבּוּ	יְסוֹבְבוּ
תְּסִבֶּׄינָה	תּוּסַבֶּׄינָה	תְּסוֹבֵׄבְנָה
תָּסֵׄבּוּ	תּוּסַׄבּוּ	תְּסוֹבְבוּ
תְּסִבֶּׄינָה	תּוּסַבֶּׄינָה	תְּסוֹבֵׄבְנָה
נָסֵב	נוּסַב	נְסוֹבֵב
הָסֵב		סוֹבֵב
הָסֵׄבִּי		סוֹבְבִי
הָסֵׄבּוּ		סוֹבְבוּ
הָסִבֶּׄינָה		סוֹבֵׄבְנָה
מֵסֵב	מוּסָב	מְסוֹבָב
מְסִבָּה		מְסוֹבָבָה
מְסִבִּים		מְסֹבְבִים
מְסִבּוֹת		מְסֹבְבוֹת
הָסֵב	הוּסַב	סוֹבֵב
הָסֵב		סוֹבֵב
וַיָּׄסַב		

			Qal	Nif`al	Pi`el
Affix	Sg.	3 m.	שָׁלַח	נִשְׁלַח	שִׁלַּח
		3 f.	שָׁלְחָה	נִשְׁלְחָה	שִׁלְּחָה
		2 m.	שָׁלַ֫חְתָּ	נִשְׁלַ֫חְתָּ	שִׁלַּ֫חְתָּ
		2 f.	שָׁלַ֫חַתְּ	נִשְׁלַ֫חַתְּ	שִׁלַּ֫חַתְּ
		1 c.	שָׁלַ֫חְתִּי	נִשְׁלַ֫חְתִּי	שִׁלַּ֫חְתִּי
	Pl.	3 c.	שָׁלְחוּ	נִשְׁלְחוּ	שִׁלְּחוּ
		2 m.	שְׁלַחְתֶּם	נִשְׁלַחְתֶּם	שִׁלַּחְתֶּם
		2 f.	שְׁלַחְתֶּן	נִשְׁלַחְתֶּן	שִׁלַּחְתֶּן
		1 c.	שָׁלַ֫חְנוּ	נִשְׁלַ֫חְנוּ	שִׁלַּ֫חְנוּ
Prefix	Sg.	3 m.	יִשְׁלַח	יִשָּׁלַח	יְשַׁלַּח
		3 f.	תִּשְׁלַח	תִּשָּׁלַח	תְּשַׁלַּח
		2 m.	תִּשְׁלַח	תִּשָּׁלַח	תְּשַׁלַּח
		2 f.	תִּשְׁלְחִי	תִּשָּׁלְחִי	תְּשַׁלְּחִי
		1 c.	אֶשְׁלַח	אֶשָּׁלַח	אֲשַׁלַּח
	Pl.	3 m.	יִשְׁלְחוּ	יִשָּׁלְחוּ	יְשַׁלְּחוּ
		3 f.	תִּשְׁלַ֫חְנָה	תִּשָּׁלַ֫חְנָה	תְּשַׁלַּ֫חְנָה
		2 m.	תִּשְׁלְחוּ	תִּשָּׁלְחוּ	תְּשַׁלְּחוּ
		2 f.	תִּשְׁלַ֫חְנָה	תִּשָּׁלַ֫חְנָה	תְּשַׁלַּ֫חְנָה
		1 c.	נִשְׁלַח	נִשָּׁלַח	נְשַׁלַּח
Imperative	Sg.	2 m.	שְׁלַח	הִשָּׁלַח	שַׁלַּח
		2 f.	שִׁלְחִי	הִשָּׁלְחִי	שַׁלְּחִי
	Pl.	2 m.	שִׁלְחוּ	הִשָּׁלְחוּ	שַׁלְּחוּ
		2 f.	שְׁלַ֫חְנָה	הִשָּׁלַ֫חְנָה	שַׁלַּ֫חְנָה
Participle	Sg.	m.	שֹׁלֵחַ	נִשְׁלָח	מְשַׁלֵּחַ
		f.	שֹׁלְחָה חַת ַ ֫	נִשְׁלָחָה	מְשַׁלְּחָה
	Pl.	m.	שֹׁלְחִים	נִשְׁלָחִים	מְשַׁלְּחִים
		f.	שֹׁלְחוֹת	נִשְׁלָחוֹת	מְשַׁלְּחוֹת
Infinitive Construct			שְׁלֹחַ	הִשָּׁלַח	שַׁלַּח
Infinitive Absolute			שָׁלוֹחַ	נִשְׁלֹוחַ	שַׁלֵּחַ
Prefix/vav conversive			וַיִּשְׁלַח	וַיִּשָּׁלַח	וַיְשַׁלַּח

Pu`al	Hif`il	Hof`al
שֻׁלַּח	הִשְׁלִיחַ	הֻשְׁלַח הָשְׁלַח
שֻׁלְּחָה	הִשְׁלִיחָה	הֻשְׁלְחָה
שֻׁלַּחְתָּ	הִשְׁלַחְתָּ	הֻשְׁלַחְתָּ
שֻׁלַּחְתְּ	הִשְׁלַחְתְּ	הֻשְׁלַחְתְּ
שֻׁלַּחְתִּי	הִשְׁלַחְתִּי	הֻשְׁלַחְתִּי
שֻׁלְּחוּ	הִשְׁלִיחוּ	הֻשְׁלְחוּ
שֻׁלַּחְתֶּם	הִשְׁלַחְתֶּם	הֻשְׁלַחְתֶּם
שֻׁלַּחְתֶּן	הִשְׁלַחְתֶּן	הֻשְׁלַחְתֶּן
שֻׁלַּחְנוּ	הִשְׁלַחְנוּ	הֻשְׁלַחְנוּ
יְשֻׁלַּח	יַשְׁלִיחַ	יֻשְׁלַח יָשְׁלַח
תְּשֻׁלַּח	תַּשְׁלִיחַ	תֻּשְׁלַח
תְּשֻׁלַּח	תַּשְׁלִיחַ	תֻּשְׁלַח
תְּשֻׁלְּחִי	תַּשְׁלִיחִי	תֻּשְׁלְחִי
אֲשֻׁלַּח	אַשְׁלִיחַ	אֻשְׁלַח
יְשֻׁלְּחוּ	יַשְׁלִיחוּ	יֻשְׁלְחוּ
תְּשֻׁלַּחְנָה	תַּשְׁלַחְנָה	תֻּשְׁלַחְנָה
תְּשֻׁלְּחוּ	תַּשְׁלִיחוּ	תֻּשְׁלְחוּ
תְּשֻׁלַּחְנָה	תַּשְׁלַחְנָה	תֻּשְׁלַחְנָה
נְשֻׁלַּח	נַשְׁלִיחַ	נֻשְׁלַח
	הַשְׁלַח	
	הַשְׁלִיחִי	
	הַשְׁלִיחוּ	
	הַשְׁלַחְנָה	
מְשֻׁלָּח	מַשְׁלִיחַ	מֻשְׁלָח מָשְׁלָח
מְשֻׁלָּחָה ַחַת	מַשְׁלִיחָה	מֻשְׁלָחָה
מְשֻׁלָּחִים	מַשְׁלִיחִים	מֻשְׁלָחִים
מְשֻׁלָּחוֹת	מַשְׁלִיחוֹת	מֻשְׁלָחוֹת
	הַשְׁלִיחַ	
	הַשְׁלֵחַ	הֻשְׁלֵחַ
וַיְשֻׁלַּח	וַיַּשְׁלַח	וַיֻּשְׁלַח

			Qal A	Qal I	Nif`al	Pi`el
Affix	Sg.	3 m.	מָצָא	מָלֵא	נִמְצָא	מִצֵּא
		3 f.	מָצְאָה	מָלְאָה	נִמְצְאָה	מִצְּאָה
		2 m.	מָצָאתָ	מָלֵאתָ	נִמְצֵאתָ	מִצֵּאתָ
		2 f.	מָצָאת	מָלֵאת	נִמְצֵאת	מִצֵּאת
		1 c.	מָצָאתִי	מָלֵאתִי	נִמְצֵאתִי	מִצֵּאתִי
	Pl.	3 c.	מָצְאוּ	מָלְאוּ	נִמְצְאוּ	מִצְּאוּ
		2 m.	מְצָאתֶם	מְלֵאתֶם	נִמְצֵאתֶם	מִצֵּאתֶם
		2 f.	מְצָאתֶן	מְלֵאתֶן	נִמְצֵאתֶן	מִצֵּאתֶן
		1 c.	מָצָאנוּ	מָלֵאנוּ	נִמְצֵאנוּ	מִצֵּאנוּ
Prefix	Sg.	3 m.	יִמְצָא	יִמְלָא	יִמָּצֵא	יְמַצֵּא
		3 f.	תִּמְצָא	תִּמְלָא	תִּמָּצֵא	תְּמַצֵּא
		2 m.	תִּמְצָא	תִּמְלָא	תִּמָּצֵא	תְּמַצֵּא
		2 f.	תִּמְצְאִי	תִּמְלְאִי	תִּמָּצְאִי	תְּמַצְּאִי
		1 c.	אֶמְצָא	אֶמְלָא	אֶמָּצֵא	אֲמַצֵּא
	Pl.	3 m.	יִמְצְאוּ	יִמְלְאוּ	יִמָּצְאוּ	יְמַצְּאוּ
		3 f.	תִּמְצֶאנָה	תִּמְלֶאנָה	תִּמָּצֶאנָה	תְּמַצֶּאנָה
		2 m.	תִּמְצְאוּ	תִּמְלְאוּ	תִּמָּצְאוּ	תְּמַצְּאוּ
		2 f.	תִּמְצֶאנָה	תִּמְלֶאנָה	תִּמָּצֶאנָה	תְּמַצֶּאנָה
		1 c.	נִמְצָא	נִמְלָא	נִמָּצֵא	נְמַצֵּא
Imperative	Sg.	2 m.	מְצָא	מְלָא	הִמָּצֵא	מַצֵּא
		2 f.	מִצְאִי	מִלְאִי	הִמָּצְאִי	מַצְּאִי
	Pl.	2 m.	מִצְאוּ	מִלְאוּ	הִמָּצְאוּ	מַצְּאוּ
		2 f.	מְצֶאנָה	מְלֶאנָה	הִמָּצֶאנָה	מַצֶּאנָה
Participle	Sg.	m.	מֹצֵא	מָלֵא	נִמְצָא	מְמַצֵּא
		f.	מֹצֵאה	מְלֵאָה	נִמְצָאָה	מְמַצֵּאָה
	Pl.	m.	מֹצְאִים	מְלֵאִים	נִמְצָאִים	מְמַצְּאִים
		f.	מֹצְאוֹת	מְלֵאוֹת	נִמְצָאוֹת	מְמַצְּאוֹת
Infinitive Construct			מְצֹא	מְלֹא	הִמָּצֵא	מַצֵּא
Infinitive Absolute			מָצוֹא	מָלוֹא	נִמְצֹא	מַצֹּא
Prefix/vav conversive			וַיִּמְצָא	וַיִּמְלָא	וַיִּמָּצֵא	וַיְמַצֵּא

446

Pu`al	Hif`il	Hof`al
מֻצָּא קֹרָא	הִמְצִיא	הֻמְצָא
מֻצְּאָה	הִמְצִיאָה	הֻמְצְאָה
מֻצֵּאתָ	הִמְצֵּאתָ	הֻמְצֵאתָ
מֻצֵּאת	הִמְצֵאת	הֻמְצֵאת
מֻצֵּאתִי	הִמְצֵּאתִי	הֻמְצֵאתִי
מֻצְּאוּ	הִמְצִיאוּ	הֻמְצְאוּ
מֻצֵּאתֶם	הִמְצֵּאתֶם	הֻמְצֵאתֶם
מֻצֵּאתֶן	הִמְצֵּאתֶן	הֻמְצֵאתֶן
מֻצֵּאנוּ	הִמְצֵּאנוּ	הֻמְצֵאנוּ
יְמֻצָּא	יַמְצִיא	יֻמְצָא
תְּמֻצָּא	תַּמְצִיא	תֻּמְצָא
תְּמֻצָּא	תַּמְצִיא	תֻּמְצָא
תְּמֻצְּאִי	תַּמְצִיאִי	תֻּמְצְאִי
אֲמֻצָּא	אַמְצִיא	אֻמְצָא
יְמֻצְּאוּ	יַמְצִיאוּ	יֻמְצְאוּ
תְּמֻצֶּאנָה	תַּמְצֶּאנָה	תֻּמְצֶאנָה
תְּמֻצְּאוּ	תַּמְצִיאוּ	תֻּמְצְאוּ
תְּמֻצֶּאנָה	תַּמְצֶּאנָה	תֻּמְצֶאנָה
נְמֻצָּא	נַמְצִיא	נֻמְצָא
	הַמְצֵא	
	הַמְצִיאִי	
	הַמְצִיאוּ	
	הַמְצֶאנָה	
מְמֻצָּא	מַמְצִיא	מֻמְצָא
מְמֻצָּאָה	מַמְצִיאָה	מֻמְצָאָה
מְמֻצָּאִים	מַמְצִיאִים	מֻמְצָאִים
מְמֻצָּאוֹת	מַמְצִיאוֹת	מֻמְצָאוֹת
	הַמְצִיא	
	הַמְצֵא	
וַיְמֻצָּא	וַיַּמְצֵא	וַיֻּמְצָא

447

Chart L   **3rd ה**

			Qal	Nif`al	Pi`el
Affix	Sg.	3 m.	גָּלָה	נִגְלָה	גִּלָּה
		3 f.	גָּלְתָה	נִגְלְתָה	גִּלְּתָה
		2 m.	גָּלִיתָ	נִגְלֵיתָ נִגְלֵיתָ	גִּלִּיתָ
		2 f.	גָּלִית	נִגְלֵית	גִּלִּית
		1 c.	גָּלִיתִי	נִגְלֵיתִי	גִּלִּיתִי
	Pl.	3 c.	גָּלוּ	נִגְלוּ	גִּלּוּ
		2 m.	גְּלִיתֶם	נִגְלֵיתֶם	גִּלִּיתֶם
		2 f.	גְּלִיתֶן	נִגְלֵיתֶן	גִּלִּיתֶן
		1 c.	גָּלִינוּ	נִגְלֵינוּ	גִּלִּינוּ
Prefix	Sg.	3 m.	יִגְלֶה	יִגָּלֶה	יְגַלֶּה
		3 f.	תִּגְלֶה	תִּגָּלֶה	תְּגַלֶּה
		2 m.	תִּגְלֶה	תִּגָּלֶה	תְּגַלֶּה
		2 f.	תִּגְלִי	תִּגָּלִי	תְּגַלִּי
		1 c.	אֶגְלֶה	אֶגָּלֶה אִגָּלֶה	אֲגַלֶּה
	Pl.	3 m.	יִגְלוּ	יִגָּלוּ	יְגַלּוּ
		3 f.	תִּגְלֶינָה	תִּגָּלֶינָה	תְּגַלֶּינָה
		2 m.	תִּגְלוּ	תִּגָּלוּ	תְּגַלּוּ
		2 f.	תִּגְלֶינָה	תִּגָּלֶינָה	תְּגַלֶּינָה
		1 c.	נִגְלֶה	נִגָּלֶה	נְגַלֶּה
Imperative	Sg.	2 m.	גְּלֵה	הִגָּלֵה הִגָּל	גַּלֵּה גַּל
		2 f.	גְּלִי	הִגָּלִי	גַּלִּי
	Pl.	2 m.	גְּלוּ	הִגָּלוּ	גַּלּוּ
		2 f.	גְּלֶינָה	הִגָּלֶינָה	גַּלֶּינָה
Participle	Sg.	m.	גֹּלֶה	נִגְלֶה	מְגַלֶּה
		f.	גֹּלָה	נִגְלָה	מְגַלָּה
	Pl.	m.	גֹּלִים	נִגְלִים	מְגַלִּים
		f.	גֹּלוֹת	נִגְלוֹת	מְגַלּוֹת
Infinitive Construct			גְּלוֹת	הִגָּלוֹת	גַּלּוֹת
Infinitive Absolute			גָּלֹה	נִגְלֹה הִנָּקֵה	גַּלֵּה
Prefix/vav conversive			וַיִּגֶל	וַיִּגָּל	וַיְגַל

Pu`al	Hif`il	Hof`al
גֻּלָּה	הֻגְלָה	הָגְלָה
גֻּלְּתָה	הֻגְלְתָה	הָגְלְתָה
גֻּלֵּיתָ	הֻגְלֵיתָ הֻגְלֵית	הָגְלֵיתָ
גֻּלֵּית	הֻגְלֵית הֻגְלֵית	הָגְלֵית
גֻּלֵּיתִי	הֻגְלֵיתִי הֻגְלֵיתִי	הָגְלֵיתִי
גֻּלּוּ	הֻגְלוּ	הָגְלוּ
גֻּלֵּיתֶם	הֻגְלֵיתֶם	הָגְלֵיתֶם
גֻּלֵּיתֶן	הֻגְלֵיתֶן	הָגְלֵיתֶן
גֻּלֵּינוּ	הֻגְלֵינוּ	הָגְלֵינוּ

יְגֻלֶּה	יֻגְלֶה	יָגְלֶה
תְּגֻלֶּה	תֻּגְלֶה	תָּגְלֶה
תְּגֻלֶּה	תֻּגְלֶה	תָּגְלֶה
תְּגֻלִּי	תֻּגְלִי	תָּגְלִי
אֲגֻלֶּה	**אֻגְלֶה**	**אָגְלֶה**
יְגֻלּוּ	יֻגְלוּ	יָגְלוּ
תְּגֻלֶּינָה	תֻּגְלֶינָה	תָּגְלֶינָה
תְּגֻלּוּ	תֻּגְלוּ	תָּגְלוּ
תְּגֻלֶּינָה	תֻּגְלֶינָה	תָּגְלֶינָה
נְגֻלֶּה	נֻגְלֶה	נָגְלֶה

	הַגְלֵה	
	הַגְלִי	
	הַגְלוּ	
	הַגְלֶינָה	

מְגֻלֶּה	מַגְלֶה	מָגְלֶה
מְגֻלָּה	מַגְלָה	מָגְלָה
מְגֻלִּים	מַגְלִים	מָגְלִים
מְגֻלּת	מַגְלוֹת	מָגְלוֹת

גֻּלּוֹת	הַגְלוֹת	
גֻּלֹּה	הַגְלֵה	הָגְלֵה

וַיְגֻלֶּה	וַיַּגֶל	וַיָּגְלֶה

Suffix			1 sg.	2 m. sg.	2 f. sg	3 m. sg.
Affix	Sg.	3 m.	פְּקָדַ֫נִי שְׁכֵחַ֫נִי	פְּקָדְךָ	פְּקָדֵךְ	פְּקָדֹ֫הוּ פְּקָדוֹ
		3 f.	פְּקָדַ֫תְנִי	פְּקָדַתְךָ	פְּקָדָתֶךְ	פְּקָדָ֫תְהוּ פְּקָדָ֫תוּ
		2 m.	פְּקַדְתַּ֫נִי			פְּקַדְתָּ֫הוּ
		2 f.	פְּקַדְתִּ֫ינִי			פְּקַדְתִּ֫יהוּ
		1 c.		פְּקַדְתִּ֫יךָ	פְּקַדְתִּיךְ	פְּקַדְתִּ֫יו פְּקַדְתִּ֫יהוּ
	Pl.	3 c.	פְּקָדוּ֫נִי	פְּקָדוּךָ אֲהֵבוּךָ	פְּקָדוּךְ	פְּקָדוּ֫הוּ
		2 m.	פְּקַדְתּוּ֫נִי			פְּקַדְתּוּהוּ
		1 c.		פְּקַדְנ֫וּךָ	פְּקַדְנוּךְ	פְּקַדְנ֫וּהוּ
Prefix	Sg.	3 m.	יִפְקְדֵ֫נִי יִלְבָּשֵׁ֫נִי	יִפְקָדְךָ יִלְבָּשְׁךָ	יִפְקְדֵךְ יִלְבָּשֵׁךְ	יִפְקְדֵ֫הוּ יִלְבָּשֵׁ֫הוּ
energic ו		3 m.	יִפְקְדֵ֫נִי		יִפְקְדֶ֫ךָּ	יִפְקְדֶ֫נּוּ
	Pl.	3 m	יִפְקְדוּ֫נִי	יִפְקְדוּךָ	יִפְקְדוּךְ	יִפְקְדוּ֫הוּ יִגְאָל֫וּהוּ
Imperative	Sg.	2 m.	פָּקְדֵ֫נִי שְׁלָחֵ֫נִי			פָּקְדֵ֫הוּ
	Pl.	2 m.	שִׁמְע֫וּנִי			
Infinitive			פָּקְדִי פָּקְדֵ֫נִי	כָּתְבְּךָ פָּקְדְךָ	פָּקְדֵךְ	פָּקְדוֹ

3 f. sg.		1 c. pl.		2 m. pl.	2 f. pl.	3 m. pl.		3 f. pl.
פְּקָדָהּ	פְּקָדָ֫נוּ					פְּקָדָם		פְּקָדָן
						לְבֵשָׁם		
פְּקָדַ֫תָּה	פְּקָדַ֫תְנוּ					פְּקָדַ֫תַם		
פְּקַדְתָּהּ	פְּקַדְתָּ֫נוּ					פְּקַדְתָּם		
פְּקַדְתִּ֫יהָ	פְּקַדְתִּ֫ינוּ					פְּקַדְתִּים		
פְּקַדְתִּ֫יהָ				פְּקַדְתִּיכֶם		פְּקַדְתִּים		פְּקַדְתִּין
פְּקָד֫וּהָ	פְּקָד֫וּנוּ					פְּקָד֫וּם		פְּקָד֫וּן
	פְּקַדְת֫וּנוּ							
פְּקָד֫וּהָ				פְּקָד֫וּכֶם		פְּקָד֫וּם		
יִפְקְדֶ֫הָ	יִפְקְדֵ֫נוּ			יִפְקָדְכֶם		יִפְקְדֵם		
יַלְבִּשֶׁ֫הָ	יַלְבִּשֵׁ֫נוּ							
יִפְקְדֶ֫הָ								
יִפְקְדֶ֫נָּה	יִפְקְדֶ֫נּוּ							
יִפְקְד֫וּהָ	יִפְקְד֫וּנוּ			יִפְקְד֫וּכֶם		יִפְקְד֫וּם		
פָּקְדֶ֫הָ	פָּקְדֵ֫נוּ					פָּקְדֵם		
פָּקְדֵ֫הּ								
פָּקְדָהּ	פָּקְדֵ֫נוּ			כָּתְבְכֶם		פָּקְדָם		פָּקְדָן
				פָּקְדְכֶם				

Suffix			1 sg.	2 m. sg.	2 f. sg.
Affix	Sg.	3 m.	נְחֵ֫נִי	רָאֲךָ עָשְׂךָ	
			עָשָׂ֫נִי	קָנְךָ עָנָ֑ךְ	
		3 f.	עָשָׂ֫תְנִי		
			עָשָׂ֫תְנִי		
		2 m.	רְאִיתַ֫נִי		
		2 f.	Pi. רְמִיתַ֫נִי		
		1 c.		רְאִיתִ֫יךָ	Pi. עֲנִתָךְ
	Pl.	3 c.	עָשׂ֫וּנִי	רָא֫וּךָ	Pi. כִּסּ֫וּךְ
		1 c.		Pi. קִוִּינ֫וּךָ	
Prefix	Sg.	3 m.	יִרְאֵ֫נִי	יִפְדְּךָ	
				יַחְתְּךָ	
		3 f.		energic נ תִּשְׁבֶּ֑ךָּ	
		2 m.	תִּרְאֵ֫נִי		
		2 f.			
		1 c.		energic נ אֶרְאֶ֫ךָּ	אֶעְדֵּךְ
				אֶעֶנְךָ	
	Pl.	3 m.	יַעֲשׂ֫וּנִי	Pi. יְפַתּ֫וּךָ	
		2 m.	Pi. תְּצַוֻּ֫נִי		
		1 c.			
Imperative	Sg.	2 m.	נְחֵ֫נִי עֲנֵ֫נִי	יִפְתּ֫וּךָ	
		2 f.		Hif. הַרְאִ֫ינִי	
	Pl.	2 m.	Pi. כַּסּ֫וּנִי		

3 m. sg.	3 f. sg.	1 c. pl.	3 m. pl.
עָשָׂ֫הוּ	רָאָה	עָשָׂ֫נוּ	עָשָׂם
Pi. כִּלָּ֫תוּ	צִוַּ֫תָּה		Hif. הֶעֱלָ֫תַם
Pi. כִּסִּ֫תוּ	עֲשִׂיתָהּ	Pi. דִּכִּיתָ֫נוּ	עֲנִיתָם
עֲשִׂיתִ֫יהוּ	רְאִיתִ֫יהָ		רְעִיתִים
רְאִיתִיו			
עָשׂ֫וּהוּ	רָא֫וּהָ		שָׁב֫וּם
Pi. קִוִּ֫נֻהוּ			
יִרְאֵ֫הוּ	יִרְאֶ֫הָ	Pi. יְצַוֶּ֫נּוּ	יַחְצֵם
energic (יִלְוֶ֫נּוּ	energic (יִרְאֶ֫נָּה		יַעֲשֵׂם
Hif. תַּשְׁקֵ֫הוּ			
energic (תַּעֲשֵׂ֫נּוּ	תַּעֲשֶׂהָ	Hif. תַּתְעֵ֫נוּ	תְּזֹרֵם
			Pi. תְּכַסֵּ֫ים
energic (אֶרְאֶ֫נּוּ	אֶעֱשֶׂ֫נָּה		אֶפְדֵם
אֶעֱנֵ֫הוּ			
Pi. יְפַתּ֫וּהוּ	יַעֲשׂ֫וּהָ	Pi. יְעַנּ֫וּנִי	
			Pi. תְּצַוֵּ֫ם
נַשְׁקֵ֫נוּ	נַעֲשֶׂ֫נָּה		
		Hif. הַרְאֵ֫נוּ	רְעֵם
תְּל֫וּהוּ			הַכּוּם

	לְ *to*	כְּ *like, as*	מִן *from*
1 c. sg.	לִי	כָּמֹ֫ונִי	מִנִּי מִמֶּ֫נִּי מֶ֫נִּי
2 m. sg.	לְךָ (לְכָה) לָ֫ךְ	כָּמֹ֫וךָ	מִמְּךָ מִמֶּ֑ךָּ
2 f. sg.	לָ֫ךְ		מִמֵּ֑ךְ
3 m. sg.	לֹו לָמֹו	כָּמֹ֫והוּ	מִמֶּ֫נּוּ מֶ֫נְהוּ (מִנְהוּ)
3 f. sg.	לָהּ	כָּמֹ֫והָ	מִמֶּ֫נָּה
1 c. pl.	לָ֫נוּ	כָּמֹ֫ונוּ	מִמֶּ֫נּוּ
2 m. pl.	לָכֶם	כָּמֹוכֶם	מִכֶּם
2 f. pl.	לָכֶן לָכֵ֫נָה		מִכֶּן
3 m. pl.	לָהֶם לָהֵ֫מָּה לָמֹו	כָּמֹוהֶם כָּהֶם	מֵהֶם מִנְהֶם (מֵהֵ֫מָּה)
3 f. pl.	לָהֶן לָהֵ֫נָּה	כָּהֵ֫נָּה	מֵהֶן מֵהֵ֫נָּה

	אַחַר *after*	בֵּין *between*	סָבִיב *around*
1 c. sg.	אַחֲרַי	בֵּינִי	סְבִיבֹותַי
2 m. sg.	אַחֲרֶ֫יךָ	בֵּינְךָ	סְבִיבֹותֶ֫יךָ סְבִיבֶ֫יךָ
2 f. sg.	אַחֲרַ֫יִךְ		סְבִיבֹותַ֫יִךְ סְבִיבַ֫יִךְ
3 m. sg.	אַחֲרָיו	בֵּינֹו	סְבִיבֹותָיו סְבִיבָיו
3 f. sg.	אַחֲרֶ֫יהָ		סְבִיבֹותֶ֫יהָ סְבִיבֶ֫יהָ
1 c. pl.	אַחֲרֵ֫ינוּ	בֵּינֵ֫ינוּ בֵּינֹותֵ֫ינוּ	סְבִיבֹותֵ֫ינוּ
2 m. pl.	אַחֲרֵיכֶם	בֵּינֵיכֶם	סְבִיבֹותֵיכֶם
2 f. pl.	אַחֲרֵיכֶן	בֵּינֵיכֶן	סְבִיבֹותֵיכֶן
3 m. pl.	אַחֲרֵיהֶם	בֵּינֵיהֶם	סְבִיבֹותֵיהֶם
3 f. pl.	אַחֲרֵיהֶן	בֵּינֵיהֶן	סְבִיבֹותֵיהֶן

454

	תַּחַת *under*	אֶל *to*	עַל *on*	עִם *with*
1 c. sg.	תַּחְתַּי	אֵלַי	עָלַי	עִמִּי
2 m. sg.	תַּחְתֶּ֫יךָ	אֵלֶ֫יךָ	עָלֶיךָ	עִמְּךָ עִמָּךְ
2 f. sg.	תַּחְתַּ֫יִךְ	אֵלַיִךְ	עָלַיִךְ	עִמָּךְ
3 m. sg.	תַּחְתָּיו	אֵלָיו	עָלָיו	עִמּוֹ
3 f. sg.	תַּחְתֶּ֫יהָ	אֵלֶ֫יהָ	עָלֶיהָ	עִמָּהּ
1 c. pl.	תַּחְתֵּ֫ינוּ	אֵלֵ֫ינוּ	עָלֵ֫ינוּ	עִמָּ֫נוּ
2 m. pl.	תַּחְתֵּיכֶם	אֲלֵיכֶם	עֲלֵיכֶם	עִמָּכֶם
2 f. pl.	תַּחְתֵּיכֶן	אֲלֵיכֶן	עֲלֵיכֶן	עִמָּכֶן
3 m. pl.	תַּחְתֵּיהֶם	אֲלֵיהֶם	עֲלֵיהֶם	עִמָּהֶם עִמָּם
3 f. pl.	תַּחְתֵּיהֶן	אֲלֵיהֶן	עֲלֵיהֶן	עִמָּהֶן

	אֵת *with*	אֵת *sign of DDO*	אֵין *there isn't*	הִנֵּה *behold*
1 c. sg.	אִתִּי	אֹתִי	אֵינֶ֫נִּי	הִנְנִי הִנֵּ֫נִי הִנְנִי
2 m. sg.	אִתְּךָ אִתָּ֫ךְ	אֹתְךָ אֹתָ֫ךְ	אֵינְךָ	הִנְּךָ הִנֶּ֫ךָ
2 f. sg.	אִתָּךְ	אֹתָךְ	אֵינֵךְ	הִנָּךְ
3 m. sg.	אִתּוֹ	אֹתוֹ	אֵינֶ֫נּוּ	הִנּוֹ
3 f. sg.	אִתָּהּ	אֹתָהּ	אֵינֶ֫נָּה	הִנָּהּ
1 c. pl.	אִתָּ֫נוּ	אֹתָ֫נוּ	אֵינֶ֫נּוּ	הִנֶּ֫נּוּ הִנְנוּ הִנֵּ֫נוּ
2 m. pl.	אִתְּכֶם	אֶתְכֶם	אֵינְכֶם	הִנְּכֶם
2 f. pl.	אִתְּכֶן	אֶתְכֶן	אֵינְכֶן	הִנְּכֶן
3 m. pl.	אִתָּם	אֶתְהֶם אֹתָם	אֵינָם	הִנָּם
3 f. pl.	אִתָּן	אֶתְהֶן		

BIBLIOGRAPHY

Barr, James. *Comparative Philology and the Text of the Old Testament.* Winona Lake, Ind.: Eisenbrauns, 1987.

Brown, Francis, S. R. Driver, and Charles A. Briggs. *The New Brown-Driver-Briggs-Gesenius Hebrew and English Lexicon with an Appendix Containing the Biblical Aramaic.* Peabody, Mass.: Hendrickson, 1979.

Childs, Brevard S. *The Book of Exodus: A Critical, Theological Commentary.* Philadelphia: Westminster 1974.

Fox, Everett, trans. *The Five Books of Moses: Genesis, Exodus, Leviticus, Numbers, Deuteronomy: A New Translation with Introductions, Commentary, and Notes.* Vol. 1. of *The Shocken Bible.* New York: Shocken, 1995.

Joüon, Paul. *A Grammar of Biblical Hebrew.* 2 vols. Translated and revised by T. Muraoka. Rome: Editrice Pontifico Istituto Biblico, 1991.

Kautzsch, E., ed. *Gesenius' Hebrew Grammar.* Translated and revised by A. E. Cowley. Oxford: Clarendon, 1983.

Klein, Ernst. *A Comprehensive Etymological Dictionary of the Hebrew Language for Readers of English.* New York: Macmillan, 1987.

Koehler, Ludwig, and Walter Baumgartner. *The Hebrew and Aramaic Lexicon of the Old Testament.* 4 vols. Translated and edited by M. E. J. Richardson. Leiden: Brill, 1994.

Kugel, James. *The Idea of Biblical Poetry: Parallelism and Its History.* New Haven: Yale University Press, 1981.

Lambdin, Thomas O. *Introduction to Biblical Hebrew.* New York: Scribner's, 1971.

Waltke, Bruce K., and M. O'Connor. *An Introduction to Biblical Hebrew Syntax.* Winona Lake, Ind.: Eisenbrauns, 1990.

Yeivin, Israel. *Introduction to the Tiberian Masorah.* Translated and edited by E. J. Revell. Scholars Press, 1980.

CD TRACKS

—◆—

🔘 אב

Readings, Cantillations, and Conjugations

1. **copyright statement**

2. **Aleph Bet**   Music: Debbie Friedmann
                 Vocals: Michael Peppard (soloist), Ingrid Lilly,
                         Mary Jane Donohue, and Michael Sullivan

3. **Vowels**

4. **Lesson Sentences 1–5**

5. **Lesson Sentences 6–10**

6. **Lesson Sentences 11–15**

7. **Lesson Sentences 16–20**

8. **Genesis 22 1–14**   Reader: Victoria Hoffer

9. **פָּקַד**   Music: Mary Jane Donohue
   (Qal affix strong verb)   Vocals and vocal percussion: Ian Doescher

10. **יִפְקֹד**   Music: Mary Jane Donohue
   (Qal prefix strong verb)   Vocals: Michael Peppard (soloist), Mary Jane Donohue,
                         Ingrid Lilly, and Michael Sullivan

11. **Mr. Pi`el**   Lyrics, music, vocals, and vocal percussion: Ian Doescher

12. **Genesis 28:10–29:11**   Cantillation: Victoria Hoffer

13. **אֹתִי Me**   Lyrics: Mary Jane Donohue
   (sign of DDO + suffix)   Music: Knowing Me Knowing You, by Abba
                         Vocals: Ian Doescher
                         Keyboards: Matthew Croasmun

14. **So Is It אִישׁ**   Lyrics: Mary Jane Donohue
   (The Noun H)   Music: America, by Neil Diamond
                       Vocals: Mary Jane Donohue
                       Keyboards: Matthew Croasmun

15. **Exodus 3:1–17**   Cantillation: Daniel Lovins

16. **If It's a Man**   Lyrics: Mary Jane Donohue
   (3rd ה affix)   Music: Excite, by Rupert Holmes
                 Vocals: Mary Jane Donohue
                 Keyboards: Matthew Croasmun

17. **יִבְנֶה He**   Lyrics: Mary Jane Donohue
   (3rd ה prefix)   Music: Matthew Croasmun
                 Vocals: Mary Jane Donohue
                 Keyboards: Matthew Croasmun

18. **בּוֹנֶה בּוֹנֶה**
(3rd ה participle and imperative)

Music: Pop Goes the Weasel
Arrangement and vocals: Mary Jane Donohue

19. **Hello, New Haven!**
(hollow affix)

Lyrics: Victoria Hoffer
Music: Frere Jacques
Arrangement: Michael Sullivan
Vocals: Michael Sullivan (soloist), Mary Jane Donohue, Ingrid Lilly, Michael Peppard, Kristin Dunn, and Christine Luckritz
Guitar: Michael Hirsch

20. **קָם קָמָה בָּא בָּאָה**
(hollow affix round)

Lyrics: Victoria Hoffer
Music: Frere Jacques
Vocals: Mary Jane Donohue, Ingrid Lilly, Michael Peppard, Michael Sullivan, Kristin Dunn, and Christine Luckritz

21. **It's All About the Hollow**
(hollow prefix)

Lyrics, music, vocals, and vocal percussion: Ian Doescher

22. **קָם קָמָה**
(hollow participle)

Lyrics: Victoria Hoffer
Music: Frere Jacques
Vocals: Mary Jane Donohue, Ingrid Lilly, Michael Sullivan, and Michael Peppard

23. **The Stem was the Hif`il**

Lyrics: Victoria Hoffer; flourishes: Ian Doescher
Music: Ian Doescher and Matthew Croasmun
Arrangment: Ian Doescher
Vocals and vocal percussion: Ian Doescher
Guitar: Matthew Croasmun

24. **אֲנִי אָנֹכִי**
(independent subject pronouns)

Music: Mary Jane Donohue
Vocals: Mary Jane Donohue and Ingrid Lilly

25. **Deuteronomy 6**   Cantillation: Victoria Hoffer

26. **אַחַת שְׁתַּיִם**
(counting: 1 to 10)

Music: Yemenite traditional
Arrangement: Victoria Hoffer
Vocals: Ingrid Lilly and Michael Peppard

27. **בָּרוּךְ הַבָּא**
(Qal passive participle)

Lyrics: Victoria Hoffer
Music: Lubovitch ḥassidic
Arrangement: Victoria Hoffer
Vocals: Mary Jane Donohue and Ingrid Lilly

28. **The Hebrew Blues**

Lyrics and music: Ian Doescher
Guitar: Michael Hirsch

29. **Visible נ**
(Nif`al)

Lyrics: Victoria Hoffer; flourishes: Ian Doescher
Music: Old MacDonald
Arrangement: Ian Doescher
Vocals: Ian Doescher, Chandler Poling, Michael Peppard, and Michael Hirsch

30. **1 Kings 19:1–12**   Cantillation: Daniel Lovins

CD TRACKS

שַׁבְּחִי 💿
Sing Praises!

1. **copyright statement**

2. שַׁבְּחִי **Psalm 147:12**   Music: Rabbi Seymour Rockoff
    Vocals: Alvin Wainhaus
    Guitar: Michael Hirsch

3. שָׁמְעָה **Psalm 97:8**   Music: Linda Hirschhorn
    Vocals: Dorothy Goldberg

4. אֵלִי אַתָּה **Psalm 118:28**   Music: Lubovitch ḥassidic
    Vocals: Michael Sullivan

5. הוֹדוּ **Psalms**   Music: medieval
    Arrangement: Stephen Richards
    Vocals: Dorothy Goldberg

6. אָנָּה יהוה **Psalm 118:25**   Music: liturgical
    Vocals: Alvin Wainhaus

7. מִי הָאִישׁ **Psalm 34:13–15**   Music: Baruch Chait
    Vocals: Alvin Wainhaus
    Guitar: Michael Hirsch

8. מַה־טֹּבוּ **Numbers 24:5**   Music: traditional
    Vocals: Michael Peppard and Maya Wainhaus

9. דּוֹדִי לִי **Song of Songs**   Music: Steven Sher
    2:16 : 3:6   Arrangement and vocals: Dorothy Goldberg

10. קוֹל דּוֹדִי **Song of Songs 2:8**   Music: Sephardic traditional
    Vocals: Alvin Wainhaus
    Guitar: Michael Hirsch

11. הִנֵּה מַה־טּוֹב **Psalm 133:1**   Music: traditional
    Vocals: Michael Peppard and Maya Wainhaus

12. וּפָרַצְתָּ **Genesis 28:14**   Music: traditional
    Arrangement: Ian Doescher
    Vocals: Ian Doescher, Chandler Poling, Michael Peppard,
    and Michael Hirsch

13. אַל תַּשְׁלִיכֵנִי **Psalms**   Music: Velvel Pasternak
    Vocals: Dorothy Goldberg

14. יְבָרֶכְךָ **Numbers 6:24 - 26**   Cantillation: Alvin Wainhaus

15. וְיִתֶּן־לְךָ **Genesis 27:28**   Music: Modzitz ḥasidic
    Vocals: Alvin Wainhaus

16. **אֶשָּׂא עֵינַי** Psalm 121:1–2   Music: Shlomo Carlbach
   Vocals: Alvin Wainhaus

17. **מִזְמוֹר שִׁיר** Psalm 92:1–5   Music: Shlomo Carlbach
   Vocals: Alvin Wainhaus
   Guitar: Michael Hirsch

18. **שְׁמַע** Deuteronomy 6:4   Music: Zvika Pick
   Vocals: Mary Jane Donohue, Ingrid Lilly, Michael Peppard,
      Michael Sullivan, Kristin Dunn, and Christine Luckritz

19. **שׁוּבִי נַפְשִׁי** Psalm 116:7–8   Music: Rabbi Ner Bresler
   Vocals: Alvin Wainhaus
   Guitar: Michael Hirsch

20. **מַלְכוּתְךָ** Psalm 145:13   Music: Diaspora Yeshiva
   Vocals: Alvin Wainhaus
   Guitar: Michael Hirsch

21. **רַבּוֹת מַחֲשָׁבוֹת** Proverbs 19:21   Music: Rabbis' Sons
    Psalm 33:11   Vocals: Alvin Wainhaus
   Guitar: Michael Hirsch

22. **אֶשָּׂא עֵינַי** Psalm 121   Music: Ashley Grant
   Arrangement: Matthew Croasmun
   Vocals: Michael Peppard
   Keyboards: Matthew Croasmun

23. **אֶרֶץ** Exodus 3:8   Music: Matthew Croasmun
   Vocals: Mica Darley and Daniel Lovins
   Bass: Sean McClowry
   Guitar: Mark Dancigers
   Marimba: Tod Meehan
   Piano: Matthew Croasmun

24. **מִן־הַמֵּצַר** Psalm 118:5   Music: Baruch Chait
   Vocals: Mary Jane Donohue and Ingrid Lilly
   Percussion: Mary Jane Donohue

25. **יהוה רֹעִי** Psalm 23   Music: Robert Gay
   Arrangement and vocals: Charissa Wilson

26. **רֶד־נָא מֹשֶׁה**   Lyrics: Victoria Hoffer
   Music: traditional gospel
   Arrangement: Ian Doescher
   Vocals: Michael Peppard (soloist), Ian Doescher, Chandler Poling,
      and Michael Hirsch

27. **אַחַת שָׁאַלְתִּי** Psalm 27:4   Music: Izzie Katz
   Vocals: Alvin Wainhaus

28. **שִׁיר הַמַּעֲלוֹת** Psalm 126   Music: traditional
   Arrangement and vocals: Dorothy Goldberg

29. לֹא יִשָּׂא גוֹי **Isaiah 2:4**   Music: traditional
Vocals: Michael Peppard and Maya Wainhaus
Guitar: Michael Hirsch

30. אוֹר זָרֻעַ **Psalm 97: 11**   Music: Jeff Klepper
Arrangement and Vocals: Dorothy Goldberg

31. הַלְלוּ יָהּ **Psalm 150**   Music: traditional gospel
Vocals: Victoria Hoffer (soloist), Michael Peppard,
Mary Jane Donohue, Ingrid Lilly, and Michael Sullivan

32. מִמִּזְרַח־שֶׁמֶשׁ **Psalm 113:3–9**   Music: Sol Zim
Vocals: Dorothy Goldberg

33. יִשְׂמְחוּ **Psalm 96:11**   Music: The Pittsburgher Rebbe
Vocals: Michael Peppard and Maya Wainhaus
Guitar: Michael Hirsch

34. הַלְלוּהוּ **Psalm 150:-6**   Music: traditional
Arrangement and vocals: Dorothy Goldberg

35. הוֹדוּ לַיהוה **Psalm 136**   Music: Sam Asher
Arrangement: Alvin Wainhaus
Vocals: Alvin Wainhaus (soloist), Maya Wainhaus,
Michael Peppard, Brian McDonald
Percussion: Alvin Wainhaus and Matthew Croasmun

אֵלֶּה הַדְּבָרִים ⊙

These Are the Words

Ian Doescher and Victoria Hoffer

SELECTED SONG LYRICS

Mr. Pi'el

Lyrics and music: Ian Doescher

I'm Mr. Pi'el, and I'm a mean sort of man,
You think that you know me? Well, catch me if you can!
Usually dagesh forte's in my middle root letter,
With ‿ under the first, oh, what could be better?

But I'm Mr. Pi'el, and I'm here to cause you some trouble!
Sometimes that middle root letter can't double!
(For instance) if the middle root letter is א or ר
Then the first vowel is ‿ א and ר don't take dagesh!

I'm Mr. Pi'el, and just to confuse you once again,
If my middle root letter's   ה
                ח
             or ע
Then you'll still see a ‿ under letter number one!
But no dagesh forte in the middle—ain't this fun?

I'm the meanest little stem that you ever did see,
Scaring Hebrew students from New York to Laramie!
You think that you can count on that dagesh forte,
But you better know your rules to see when it goes away!

In the prefix, imperative, participle and infinitive,
There's ‿ under the first root letter—sure as you live!
But if א or ר is in the middle of the root,
Then ‿ is the first vowel—don't you think that's cute?

I'm Mr. Pi'el, and a headache to you I'll give,
'Cause that prefix, imperative, participle, and infinitive:
If it's   ה
         ח
        Or ע as the middle root letter,
The first vowel is still ‿ not ‿ does that fetter?

464

I'm Mr. Pi'el, and when, under that middle root letter,
You've got a ⤷ oh, you'd better remember,
That with ⤷ you always have to live in fear,
Because ⤷ can make dagesh forte disappear!

I'm the meanest little stem that you ever did see,
Scaring Hebrew students from Detroit to Tennessee!
You think that you can count on that dagesh forte,
But you better know your rules to see when it goes away!

I'm Mr. Pi'el, and I'm slippery and fast,
'Cause when the middle root letter is also the last,
Though you might expect to find a dagesh forte,
Last letters rarely take them—they're funny that way!

I'm Mr. Pi'el, and now that we've been introduced,
I hope that this song will make you feel induced,
To study your Hebrew, learn your Pi'el really well,
Then maybe you'll know me—I'm Mr. Pi'el!

אוֹתִי Me
Sign of the DDO + Suffix

Lyrics: Mary Jane Donohue
Music: Knowing Me Knowing You, by Abba

אוֹתִי	Me	אוֹתָנוּ	That's **Us**
אוֹתְךָ	You	אֶתְכֶם	**You**
אוֹתָךְ		אֶתְכֶן	**You** girls
אתוֹ	Him	אוֹתָם	**Them** for men
אוֹתָה	Her	אֶתְהֶן	**Them** girls will do

So is it אִישׁ
The Noun H

Lyrics: Mary Jane Donohue
Music: America, by Neil Diamond

So is it   אִישׁ

Or   אֲנָשִׁים

Or is the **man** in construct?

'Cause if it's   אִישׁ

Or it's   אַנְשֵׁי

Then that **man's** in construct!

אִשָּׁה נָשִׁים

The **woman** seems not to be in construct!

אֵשֶׁת נְשֵׁי

I have to say, this **woman** is in construct!

בַּיִת בָּתִּים

בֵּית בָּתֵּי

Is your **house** in construct?

בַּת בָּנוֹת

בַּת בְּנוֹת

Your **daughter** is in construct!

אָב אָבוֹת

My **daddy** says

אֲבִי אֲבוֹת

Is construct!

אָח אָחִים

Those **boys** are mean

But they are not in construct!

אֲחִי אֲחֵי

I have to say

These **guys** are cleared for construct!

יוֹם יָמִים

The **day** is clean

יוֹם יְמֵי

Is construct!

עִיר עָרִים

The **city** scene

עִיר עָרֵי

Is construct!

שֵׁם שֵׁמוֹת

That is your **name**

שֵׁם שֵׁם שֵׁמוֹת

Is construct!

פֶּה פִּי

Sing out **mouth** in construct!

If It's a Man
3rd ה Affix

Lyrics: Mary Jane Donohue
Music: Excite, by Rupert Holmes

If it's a **man** then it's בָּנָה

Or בָּנְתָה for a **she**

How 'bout **you** you're בָּנִיתָ

or בָּנִית

But for **me** בָּנִיתִי

3rd common plural build is בָּנוּ

בְּנִיתֶם **you** the **hes**

בְּנִיתֶן **you** the **sheilas**

And בָּנִינוּ is **we**

Don't forget the י in one and two,

Don't forget the י whatever you do.

יִבְנֶה He

3rd ה Prefix

Lyrics: Mary Jane Donohue
Music: Matthew Croasmun

יִבְנֶה	he	יִבְנוּ	they
תִּבְנֶה	she	תִּבְנֶינָה	
תִּבְנֶה	for **you**!	תִּבְנוּ	**you** too
תִּבְנִי	**you** lady, and	תִּבְנֶינָה	**you** ladies, and
אֶבְנֶה	**me** too!	נִבְנֶה	**we're** through

בּוֹנֶה בּוֹנֶה

3rd ה Participle and Imperative

Arrangement: Mary Jane Donohue
Music: Pop Goes the Weasel

בּוֹנוֹת	בּוֹנִים	בּוֹנֶה	בּוֹנֶה
	בּוֹנִים	בּוֹנֶה	בּוֹנֶה
בּוֹנוֹת	בּוֹנִים	בּוֹנֶה	בּוֹנֶה

Qal participle

בְּנֶינָה	בְּנוּ	בְּנִי	בְּנֵה
	בְּנוּ	בְּנִי	בְּנֵה
בְּנֶינָה	בְּנוּ	בְּנִי	בְּנֵה

3rd ה imperative

Hello, New Haven!
Hollow Affix

Lyrics: Victoria Hoffer
Music: Frere Jacques

Hello, New Haven!
Are you ready to rock and roll?
What do you want to study?
Hebrew!

Third person hollow affix,
Has a ⟝ has a ⟝
One and two have ⟝
⟝ threw my game off!
But what can you do,
With one and two?

קָמָה קָם

קָמָה קָם

קַמְתָּ קַמְתְּ

Now I'm really stumped!

קַמְתִּי

That's me!

קַמְתִּי

That's me!

אֲנִי אָנֹכִי אָנֹכִי אֲנִי

קָמוּ קָמוּ

Conjugation not through,
Two and one then we're done,

קַמְתֶּם קַמְתֶּן

⟝ in the stem again?

קַמְנוּ

We got up too.

קַמְנוּ

We got up too.

קָם קָמָה בָּא בָּאָה
Hollow Affix Round

Lyrics: Victoria Hoffer
Music: Frère Jacques

שָׁם	בָּא	קָם
שָׁמָה	בָּאָה	קָמָה
שָׁם	בָּא	קָם
שָׁמָה	בָּאָה	קָמָה
שַׁמְתָּ	בָּאתָ	קַמְתָּ
שַׁמְתְּ	בָּאת	קַמְתְּ
שַׁמְתָּ	בָּאתָ	קַמְתָּ
שַׁמְתְּ	בָּאת	קַמְתְּ
שַׁמְתִּי	בָּאתִי	קָמְתִּי
that's me!	that's me!	that's me!
שַׁמְתִּי	בָּאתִי	קָמְתִּי
that's me!	that's me!	that's me!

אֲנִי אָנֹכִי אָנֹכִי אֲנִי

שָׁמוּ שָׁמוּ	בָּאוּ בָּאוּ	קָמוּ קָמוּ

Conjugation not through,
Two and one then we're done:

שַׁמְתֶּם	בָּאתֶם	קַמְתֶּם
שַׁמְתֶּן	בָּאתֶן	קַמְתֶּן
שַׁמְתֶּם	בָּאתֶם	קַמְתֶּם
שַׁמְתֶּן	בָּאתֶן	קַמְתֶּן
שַׁמְנוּ שַׁמְנוּ	בָּאנוּ בָּאנוּ	קַמְנוּ קַמְנוּ

It's All About the Hollow
Hollow Prefix

Lyrics and music: Ian Doescher

Ooo bop it's all about the hollow,
Ooo bop it's more than you can swallow,
Ooo bop in despair you won't wallow,
Ooo bop there are rules that you can follow.

So you're thinkin' about the prefix hollow verb,
And it's got you upset—oh yeah—you're real disturbed,
But just relax because we'll give you a guide,
And then the prefix hollow will be a free ride.

יָקוּם תָּקוּם תָּקוּם תָּקוּמִי
יָקוּם תָּקוּם תָּקוּם תָּקוּמִי

And I'll get up, too אָקוּם
And I'll get up, too, yeah!

יָקוּם תָּקוּם תָּקוּם תָּקוּמִי
יָקוּם תָּקוּם תָּקוּם תָּקוּמִי

And I'll get up, too אָקוּם
And I'll get up, too, yeah, kick it!

Ooo bop it's all about the hollow,
Ooo bop it's more than you can swallow,
Ooo bop in despair you won't wallow,
Ooo bop there are rules that you can follow.

יָקוּמוּ תָּקֹמְנָה תָּקוּמוּ תָּקֹמְנָה

And we'll get up, too נָקוּם

יָקוּמוּ תָּקֹמְנָה תָּקוּמוּ תָּקֹמְנָה

And we'll get up, too נָקוּם

יָקוּמוּ תָּקֹמְנָה תָּקוּמוּ תָּקֹמְנָה

And we'll get up, too נָקוּם

יָקוּמוּ תָּקֹמְנָה תָּקוּמוּ תָּקֹמְנָה

And we'll get up, too נָקוּם

Ooo bop it's all about the hollow,
Ooo bop it's more than you can swallow,
Ooo bop in despair you won't wallow,
Ooo bop there are rules that you can follow.

יָקוּם תָּקוּם תָּקוּם תָּקוּמִי

And I'll get up, too אָקוּם

קָם קָמָה

Hollow Participle

Lyrics by Victoria Hoffer
Melody: Frere Jacques

קָם

קָמָה

בָּא

בָּאָה

Hollow participle
Really is despicable!

קָמִים

קָמוֹת

בָּאִים

בָּאוֹת

Strike a better note

With the ים

And the וֹת

קָמִים

and

קָמוֹת

Strike a better note

With the ים

And the וֹת

The Stem was the Hif`il

Lyrics: Victoria Hoffer
Flourishes: Ian Doescher
Music: Ian Doescher and Matthew Croasmun

Woke up in the mornin' 'fore my final exam,
Desperate for some help though the prof. said don't cram,
Determined not deterred I vowed to take a good look,
At my interesting, scintillating Hebrew book.

Happened upon a page of verbs,
The stem was the Hif`il,
Made me perturbed.

אָמַרְתִּי בְּלִבִּי

Get organized,
And find me some patterns to make me wise!

הִפְקִיד the **affix 3 m. s g**.

Gave its name to the Hif`il, don't you see?
Man that's cool, that's the name of the game,
But what about the other dudes? Are they the same?

הִפְקִידָה
and הִפְקִידוּ

Have ⤸ in the middle, too—oh, don't you know that?

But the persons **I, we, you**,

Have ⤸ instead like הִפְקַדְנוּ

They do? Oh no!

Now in the **prefix** and on down the line,
There's a honey of a pattern, elegant and fine,
It'll be there for you all of the time,
In the strong verb so listen to the rhymes:

⤸ under the preformative,

Is the first articulating sign it gives,
Then going on to the middle of the word,
Where an I class vowel is gonna be heard.

An I class vowel in the middle of the verb?
What's an I class vowel? Tell a grammar-hungry nerd!

I'm glad you asked; now it can be told,

It's   ـֲ

          ـֱ

Or even   ـֲ

Again it's   ـֲ

         ـֱ

Or even   ـֲ

That's an I class vowel—it's as good as gold!

You have   יַפְקִיד

         תַּפְקִיד

And so on to the plural,

Where girls who תַּפְקֵדְנָה could take you for a whirl.

What happened to the ה   Does the prefix need revision?
No. The prefix pronoun turned it into an elision!

We'll hear it now in the **imperative** form,

That pattern with a ה which is the Hif`il norm.

     הַפְקֵד

     הַפְקִידִי

Hand over or appoint,

פקד   as a verb could put you out of joint!

The sign of the **participle** form is מ

Add to it a ـַ and you're into the stem;

מַפְקִיד he'll install as a superior,

Other folks need endings at the posterior!

Oh, I get it, Hif`il participles take a מ with a ـַ

This is easy!

הַפְקֵד is an **infinitive** of the construct kind,

But the other keeps the rule we put in mind,

ـַ in the first place I class in the middle,

With these two signs you don't want to fiddle!

1st **י** has its own sort of sound,

You'll hear הוֹצִיא

יוֹצִיא

מוֹצִיא all around,

וֹ in the front and I class in the middle,

Don't alter that combo a jot or a tittle!

Hollows in the Hif`il are a weird sort of bird,

To their peculiarities you have to be inured,

So study the chart, it would be folly to say nay,

Because הֲקִימוֹתִי is here to stay!

Happened upon a page of verbs,

The stem was the Hif`il,

Made me perturbed.

אָמַרְתִּי בְּלִבִּי

Get organized,

And find me some patterns to make me wise!

There is one sad exception to our observation,

About the I class vowel in the middle position,

When the **third root letter** is ח

ר

or ע

It may attract a ◌ַ and keep you cryin'.

When the third root letter is ע or ח

◌ַ may take over חַנַּח may be what you get.

Just study your Hebrew, it will be a cinch

That final exam will never make you flinch.

Oh this is so much better,

Now the Hif`il makes sense, I get it! Thank you!

Happened upon a page of verbs,

The stem was the Hif`il,

Made me perturbed.

אָמַרְתִּי בְּלִבִּי

Get organized,
And find me some patterns to make me wise!

Oh, I happened upon a page of verbs,
The stem was the Hif`il,
Made me perturbed.

אָמַרְתִּי בְּלִבִּי

Get organized,
And find me some patterns to make me wise!

רֵד־נָא מֹשֶׁה

Lyrics: Victoria Hoffer
Music: traditional gospel

עוֹד יִשְׂרָאֵל בְּמִצְרַיִם
הוֹצֵא אֶת עַמִּי
לַחוּץ מְאֹד לֹא־יָכְלוּ לָקוּם
הוֹצֵא אֶת עַמִּי

רֵד־נָא מֹשֶׁה אֶל אֶרֶץ מִצְרַיִם
דַּבֵּר אֶל פַּרְעֹה לְהוֹצִיא אֶת־עַמִּי

נְאֻם יהוה אָמַר־מֹשֶׁה הַגֶּבֶר
הוֹצֵא אֶת עַמִּי

אִם לֹא אַכֶּה־מֵת אֶת בְּכֹרְכֶם
הוֹצֵא אֶת עַמִּי

רֵד־נָא מֹשֶׁה אֶל אֶרֶץ מִצְרַיִם
דַּבֵּר אֶל־פַּרְעֹה לְהוֹצִיא אֶת־עַמִּי

לֹא עוֹד יֵעָנוּ בְּסִבְלֹתָם
הוֹצֵא אֶת עַמִּי
יֵצְאוּ הֵם אֶת־מִצְרַיִם יִנָּצְלוּ
הוֹצֵא אֶת עַמִּי

רֵד־נָא מֹשֶׁה אֶל אֶרֶץ מִצְרַיִם
דַּבֵּר אֶל־פַּרְעֹה לְהוֹצִיא אֶת־עַמִּי

בָּרוּךְ הַבָּא
Qal Passive Participle

Lyrics: Victoria Hoffer
Music: Lubovitch ḥassidic

בָּרוּךְ הַבָּא בְּשֵׁם יהוה

בְּרוּכָה הַבָּאָה בְּשֵׁם יהוה

בְּרוּכִים הַבָּאִים

בְּרוּכוֹת הַבָּאוֹת

בְּשֵׁם יהוה

Visible נ
Nif`al

Lyrics: Victoria Hoffer
Flourishes: Ian Doescher
Music: Old MacDonald

Visible נ in the Nif`al is quite fickle —oh so fickle—it only preforms in the affix and participle.

With a נִפְקַד he
And a נִפְקְדָה she
And so it goes to נִפְקַדְתִּי

Visible נ in the Nif`al is quite fickle; it only preforms in the affix and participle.

נִפְקְדוּ
נִפְקַדְתֶּם
הֵן ⌣ ⌣ ⌣ —
נִפְקַדְנוּ

That's us again!

Visible נ in the Nif`al is quite fickle; it only preforms in the affix and participle.

הִנֵּה־הוּא נִפְקַד
הִיא נִפְקָדָה

The ⌣ helps avoid a flaw.

הֵם נִפְקָדִים
הֵן נִפְקָדוֹת

Those **participles** float my boat!

Participle boat! Soon we'll be learning our Hebrew well;
Participle boat! Then we'll sing all our praises to El.

Visible נ in the Nif`al is quite fickle; it only preforms in the affix and participle.

And when that נ assimilates,
A vowel pattern takes its place.
Say:

⌣ ⌣ —

ḥireq—qamats—tsere
Because those vowels will save the day.
Here I come to save the day!

יִפָּקֵד

and תִּיפָקֵד

Those **prefix** folks have got it made.

Visible נ in the Nif`al is quite fickle; it only preforms in the affix and participle.

Now when that ה comes in to play,

It's quite OK just say: ‿ ָ ֵ

‿ ָ ֵ

‿ ָ ֵ

Have you got it? It's ‿ ָ ֵ

הִפָּקֵד

הִפָּקְדִי

Imperatives could make you flee!

Visible נ in the Nif`al is quite fickle; it only preforms in the affix and participle.

Infinitive like the command ,

And הִפָּקֵד is still on hand.

Visible נ in the Nif`al is quite fickle; it only preforms in the affix and participle.

In places where the patterns brief,

You still get vowels to save you grief.

So if

‿ ָ ֵ

All three can't stay, then

ָ ֵ

Still will light the way.

Should it ever be more bad than that—

It's bad, it's really bad. So bad, it's bad, its really bad,

An I class vowel still will take first spot.

With an

‿ ָ ֵ

ḥireq—qamats—tsere

Those Nif`al vowels are here to stay.

So when you have a **guttural**,

Say:

ֶ ָ ֲ

Don't shy away;

With a יֵאָמֵר here

And a תֵּאָמֵר there

תֵּאָמֵר

תֵּאָמְרִי [1]

That's quite enough. Don't you agree ?

But there's הֵאָמֵר

And הֵאָמְרוּ

Compensating while they order you.

Visible נ in the Nifal is quite fickle—oh so fickle—it only preforms in the affix and participle.

Fickle Nif`al

---

1. Erratum: יֵאָמְרִי should be תֵּאָמְרִי Unfortunately, the barbershop boys disbanded before the error could be corrected.

MUSIC CREDITS

CD Aleph Bet

Alef Bet: Hebrew version from the ALEF BET. Music and lyrics by Debbie Friedman. © 1981 Deborah Lynn Friedman (ASCAP). Sounds Write Productions, Inc. (ASCAP).

Oti me (Sign of DDO + Suffix): "Knowing Me, Knowing You," by ABBA. © Copyright 1976 for the world by Universal/Union Songs AB, Stockholm, Sweden. All rights reserved. Courtesy of EMI Music Publishing.

So Is It Eesh (The Noun H): "America" © 1980, Stonebridge Music. All rights administered by Sony/ATV music publishing, 8 Music Square West, Nashville, TN 37203. All rights reserved. Used by permission.

If It's a Man (Third Heh Affix): "Escape (The Piña Colada Song)," used by express permission of The Holmes Line of Music, Inc.

CD Shab'chi

"Shamah Vatismach Tsion" (Psalm 97:8): Music used with permission by Linda Hirschhorn.

"Hodu": Music used with permission by Stephen Richards.

"Dodi Li" (Song of Songs 2:16 and 3:6): Music used with permission by Steven Sher.

"Al Tashlicheni": Music used with permission by Velvel Pasternak.

Adonai Ro'i (Psalm 23), "On Bended Knee": Music by Robert Gay © 1989 Integrity Music.

"Or Zaruah" (Psalm 97:11): Music used with permission by Jeff Klepper © 1975.

"Mi Mizrach Shemesh" (Psalm 113:3–9): Music used with permission by Saul Zim.

"Hodu L'Adonai" (Psalm 136): Music used with permission by Sam Asher.

INDEX